Lecture Notes in Computer Science 1330

Edited by G. Goos, J. Hartmanis and J. van Leeuwen

Advisory Board: W. Brauer   D. Gries   J. Stoer

Springer
Berlin
Heidelberg
New York
Barcelona
Budapest
Hong Kong
London
Milan
Paris
Santa Clara
Singapore
Tokyo

Gert Smolka (Ed.)

Principles and Practice
of Constraint Programming
– CP 97

Third International Conference, CP 97
Linz, Austria, October 29 – November 1, 1997
Proceedings

 Springer

Series Editors

Gerhard Goos, Karlsruhe University, Germany

Juris Hartmanis, Cornell University, NY, USA

Jan van Leeuwen, Utrecht University, The Netherlands

Volume Editor

Gert Smolka
Programming Systems Lab, Universität des Saarlandes, Geb. 45
Postfach 15 11 50, D-66041 Saarbrücken, Germany
E-mail: smolka@ps.uni-sb.de

Cataloging-in-Publication data applied for

Die Deutsche Bibliothek - CIP-Einheitsaufnahme

Principles and practice of constraint programming : third international
conference ; proceedings / CP '97, Linz, Austria, October 29 - November 1,
1997. Gert Smolka (ed.). - Berlin ; Heidelberg ; New York ; Barcelona ;
Budapest ; Hong Kong ; London ; Milan ; Paris ; Santa Clara ; Singapore ; Tokyo
: Springer, 1997.
  (Lecture notes in computer science ; Vol. 1330)
  ISBN 3-540-63753-2

CR Subject Classification (1991): D.1, D.3.2-3, I.2.3-4, F.3.2, F.4.1, I.2.8,
H.3.3

ISSN 0302-9743
ISBN 3-540-63753-2 Springer-Verlag Berlin Heidelberg New York

Typesetting: Camera-ready by author
SPIN 10645640   06/3142 – 5 4 3 2 1 0   Printed on acid-free paper

Foreword

This volume contains the proceedings of CP97, the Third International Conference on Principles and Practice of Constraint Programming. It will take place at Schloss Hagenberg near Linz, Austria from October 29 to November 1, 1997. The previous CP conferences took place at Cassis, France (1995) and at Cambridge, MA, USA (1996). They were preceded by a workshop on Orcas Island, WA, USA (1994). The proceedings of these events have been published in the LNCS series of Springer-Verlag as volumes 874, 976, and 1118.

Constraints have emerged as the basis of a representational and computational paradigm that draws from many disciplines and can be brought to bear on many problem domains. The call for papers encouraged submissions from all disciplines concerned with constraints, including artificial intelligence, computational logic, databases, operations research, programming languages, and symbolic computation.

CP97 attracted 132 submissions, the highest number so far. The program committee selected 37 papers for presentation at the conference. The geographical distribution of submitting and accepted authors was as follows: America (30, 12), Asia (14, 2), Australia (2,1), Europe (106, 28). The most active country was France with 34 submitting and 14 accepted authors, followed by the USA (21, 9), the UK (17, 4) and Germany (15, 4). Submission and refereeing were handled smoothly through the Internet.

Besides the 37 accepted papers, this volume contains the abstracts of the 2 invited talks and the 3 tutorials.

A total of 8 constraint-related workshops are associated with the conference. Three of them will take place on the two days preceding the conference, and the others will take place on the last day of the conference.

More information about CP97 can be found in the Web at
http://www.mpi-sb.mpg.de/conferences/CP97/.

Last but not least I would like to thank the authors of all submitted papers, the referees, the sponsors, the members of the program and organizing committees, the conference chair, and the publicity chair for their efforts. Special thanks goes to Tobias Müller, Joachim Walser, and Jörg Würtz who worked with me in Saarbrücken.

Saarbrücken, July 1997   Gert Smolka
                                                   Program Committee Chair

Conference Chair

Bruno Buchberger   RISC

Program Chair

Gert Smolka   DFKI and Universität des Saarlandes

Publicity Chair

Andreas Podelski   Max-Planck-Institut

Program Committee

Franz Baader	RWTH Aachen
Frédéric Benhamou	University of Orléans
Alex Brodsky	George Mason University
Yves Caseau	Bouygues
Hoon Hong	RISC
John Hooker	CMU
Joxan Jaffar	National University of Singapore
Claude Kirchner	INRIA Lorraine and CRIN
Michael Maher	Griffith University
Kim Marriott	Monash University
Dave McAllester	AT&T Research
Ken McAloon	Brooklyn College
Bernhard Nebel	University of Freiburg
Tobias Nipkow	TU München
Martin Odersky	University of South Australia
Catuscia Palamidessi	University of Genova
Andreas Podelski	Max-Planck-Institut
Jean-François Puget	ILOG
Francesca Rossi	University of Pisa
Thomas Schiex	INRA
Bart Selman	AT&T Research
Gert Smolka	DFKI and Universität des Saarlandes
Peter J. Stuckey	University of Melbourne
Edward Tsang	University of Essex
Peter van Beek	University of Alberta
Mark Wallace	ICL/Imperial College

Sponsors

COMPULOG NET	Saarbrücken
ILOG	Paris
PrologIA	Marseille
DFKI	Kaiserslautern and Saarbrücken
MPI	Saarbrücken
RISC	Linz

CP Organizing Committee

Alan Borning	University of Washington
Alain Colmerauer	University of Marseille
Eugene Freuder	University of New Hampshire
Jean-Pierre Jouannaud	University of Paris Sud
Jean-Louis Lassez	New Mexico Tech
Ugo Montanari	University of Pisa
Anil Nerode	Cornell University
Vijay Saraswat	AT&T Research
Pascal Van Hentenryck	Brown University
Ralph Wachter	Office of Naval Research

List of Additional Referees

The Program Committee thanks the many additional referees: F. Ajili, L. Allison, R. Backofen, C. Bessiere, C. Bliek, A. Bockmayr, N. Boland, A. Borning, P. Borovansky, J. E. Borrett, H.-J. Bürckert, A. Bud, O. Caprotti, B. Carlson, C. Castro, W. Charatonik, Charman, D. Clark, E. Contejean, D. Corbett, B. Davey, F. de Boer, G. Delzanno, B. Demoen, Y. Dimopoulos, J. Doerre, E. Domenjoud, D. Duchier, H. El-Sakkout, M. Emele, A. Evgeni, F. Fages, G. Farr, B. N. Freeman-Benson, Furnon, M. Gabbrielli, Gaspin, D. Gerdemann, C. Gervet, R. Giacobazzi, R. Goebel, D. Q. Goldin, A. Gollu, M. Gyssens, M.-S. Hacid, W. Harvey, M. Henz, M. Hermann, W. Hui, E. Hyvönen, K. Jackson, P. Kilby, J. Knoop, L.-P. Ku, B. Kuijpers, A. Kwan, P. Ladkin, W. Landerl, C. Lau, T. L. Lau, M. Leconte, H. W. Leong, O. Lhomme, V. Liatsos, B. Liu, H. Lock, A. Macdonald, J. Maraist, S. Merz, B. Meyer, G. Milne, M. Minimair, P.-E. Moreau, T. Müller, O. Mueller, Narendran, A. Neubacher, J. Niehren, S. Novello, W. Nutt, A. Poetzsch-Heffter, Z. Qian, G. Ramalingam, R. Ramirez, S. Ratschan, J. Régin, J. Renz, E. T. Richards, J. Richts, C. Ringeissen, R. Rodosek, Rogerie, L. Sais, W. Schreiner, C. Schulte, K. U. Schulz, H. Seidl, W. Snyder, W. Stoecher, A. Strohmaier, T. Stützle, V. Tam, C. Tinelli, A. P. Tomás, D. Toman, R. Treinen, C. Tretkoff, Trombettoni, K. C. Tsui, M. Van Caneghem, Van Gucht, J. Van den Bussche, G. Verfaillie, M. Vincent, S. Vorobyov, U. Waldmann, J. P. Walser, T. Walsh, G. Wetzel, H. Wiklicky, T. Wilke, L. Wong, J. Würtz, R. Yap, L. Yinghao, Q. Zhao, J. Zhou.

Contents

Tutorial

Session 3

Session 4

Session 5a

Session 7a

Session 7b

Tutorial

Visual Solver
A Modeling Language
for Constraint Programming

Pascal Van Hentenryck

Brown University, Box 1910, Providence, RI 02912 (USA)
Email: pvh@cs.brown.edu

Abstract

Probably the main contribution of constraint programming is the observation that constraint-solving techniques from various areas can be embedded in programming languages to offer effective tools to tackle a variety of combinatorial search problems. The benefits come from the ease of programming which reduces development time and encourage more experimentation and tuning.

Many constraint programming languages are however "constrained" by the environment they are embedded into or by the natural desire to offer a general-purpose programming language. These host languages are appropriate for some aspects of the task at hand but they may be obstacles to a natural expression of some other components of the application. For instance, constraint logic programming is based a clean semantic framework offering nondeterminism for free but it has little support to stating constraints and heuristics at a high level. A C++ library such as Ilog Solver is an efficient and extensible tool for constraint programming offering the advantage of object orientation but search is less natural and the specificities of C++ may be an obstacle to non-computer scientists.

This state of affairs is hardly new and was experienced before the operations research community, where the use of linear (and nonlinear) programming code used to be a difficult task. The inception of modeling languages such as GAMS and AMPL satisfied the need to abstract irrelevant details of the programming languages and tools. These languages made it possible to state linear programming problems almost as in textbooks and scientific papers.

This talk describes a similar effort for constraint programming and illustrates the approach using VISUAL SOLVER, a modeling language for constraint programming. VISUAL SOLVER makes it possible to state many combinatorial search problems in a form close to a mathematical description of the problem. It goes beyond traditional modeling languages both by supporting traditional constraint programming technology and by letting practitioners specify both the problem statement and the heuristics used to find solutions.

Narrowing a $2n$-Block of Sortings in $\mathcal{O}(n \log n)$

Noëlle Bleuzen Guernalec and Alain Colmerauer[1]

Abstract

Let D be a totally ordered set and n a positive integer. Call $2n$-*block* a Cartesian product of $2n$ closed and possibly empty intervals of D. Let *sort* be the set of all $2n$-tuples of elements of D of the form $(x_1, \ldots, x_n, y_1, \ldots, y_n)$, where $(y_1, \ldots, y_n)$ is the n-tuple obtained by sorting in increasing order the terms of the n-tuple $(x_1, \ldots, x_n)$.

This paper is devoted to the study of an algorithm of complexity $\mathcal{O}(n \log n)$, which, given a $2n$-block P, computes, in the sense of inclusion, the smallest $2n$-block containing the set *sort* $\cap P$.

1 Introduction

A sortedness constraint expresses that an n-tuple $(y_1, \ldots, y_n)$ is equal to the n-tuple obtained by sorting in increasing order the terms of another n-tuple $(x_1, \ldots, x_n)$. We write it as

$$(x_1, \ldots, x_n, y_1, \ldots, y_n) \in sort.$$

W.J. Older, F. Swinkels and M. van Emden introduced this constraint for elegantly stating and solving problems of the job-shop scheduling type [4]. More recently Jianyang Zhou [5, 6] has solved well known difficult job-shop scheduling problems by introducing a sortedness constraint with $3n$ variables: the n added integer variables being used for making explicit a permutation linking the x_is to the y_is.

We are interested in *narrowing* a sortedness constraint, *within intervals*, of the form:

$$\begin{pmatrix} (x_1, \ldots, x_n, y_1, \ldots, y_n) \in sort \; \wedge \\ x_1 \in A_1 \; \wedge \; \cdots \; \wedge \; x_n \in A_n \; \wedge \\ y_1 \in B_1 \; \wedge \; \cdots \; \wedge \; y_n \in B_n \end{pmatrix},$$

where the A_is and B_is are closed intervals of the general domain of x_is and y_is. By "narrowing" we mean: substituting for intervals A_i and B_i the smallest intervals X_i and Y_i, in the sense of inclusion, which do not modify the set of solutions of the constraint. It must be noted that, to decide if the constraint within intervals has at least one solution, it is sufficient to verify, after narrowing, that none of the new intervals is empty.

As BNR-Prolog has taught us, this narrowing of constraint, within intervals, applies to any kind of elementary constraint and allows progress in the solving of a conjunction of constraints by narrowing, one after another, each elementary constraint, within intervals, until the intervals attached to the different variables reach a fixed point [3].

The purpose of this paper is to present and justify an algorithm for narrowing the sortedness constraint, within intervals, in $\mathcal{O}(n \log n)$ elementary operations. It is organized in 10 parts.

---

[1]Laboratoire d'Informatique de Marseille, ESA 6077, CNRS et Universités de Provence et de la Méditerranée

Parts 1 and 2 are devoted to this introduction and to the notations. Parts 3 to 7, which are very technical, establish the necessary results for proving theorem 8. This theorem, which constitutes part 8, gives and justifies the main lines of the proposed algorithm. Part 9 details the algorithm with an example while establishing its complexity. Part 10 suggests perspectives for this work.

2 Notations and statement of the problem

Generally speaking, if $(E, \preceq)$ is an ordered set, composed of a set E and an order relation $\preceq$ over E, we call *interval* of $(E, \preceq)$ any subset of E, possibly empty, which is of the form

$$\{x \in \mathbf{D} \mid a \preceq x \text{ and } x \preceq b\},$$

where a and b are any elements of E. The interval is written $[a, b]$. When the ordered set is $(\mathbf{N}, \leq)$, where $\mathbf{N}$ is the set of natural integers, we write $i..j$ for $[i, j]$. An n-*block* of $(E, \preceq)$ is a subset of E^n of the form $A_1 \times \cdots \times A_n$, where each A_i is an interval of $(E, \preceq)$.

Let $(\mathbf{D}, \preceq)$ be a given ordered set, where $\mathbf{D}$ has at least two elements and where $\preceq$ is a total order relation. We use $\prec$ to denote the relation obtained by removing all pairs of equal elements from $\preceq$. As an example of an ordered set, the set $(\mathbf{R}, \leq)$ of reals or the set $(\mathbf{Z}, \leq)$ of integers as well as the set $(\mathbf{N}, \leq)$ can be taken, with their natural orderings.

Also let n be a given positive integer. We denote by $\mathcal{P}_n$ the set of permutations of $1..n$, that is to say the set of one-to-one mappings from $1..n$ onto $1..n$. If x is an element of $\mathbf{D}^n$ we write $x_1, \ldots, x_n$ the elements of $\mathbf{D}$ such that $x = (x_1, \ldots, x_n)$. If, for each i of $1..(n-1)$, we have $x_i \preceq x_{i+1}$ then x is said to be *increasing* and if, for each i of $1..(n-1)$, we have $x_{i+1} \preceq x_i$ then x is said to be *decreasing*. If x is an element of $\mathbf{D}^n$, then $x\!\uparrow$ denotes the increasing element y of $\mathbf{D}^n$ defined by

$$y_1 = x_1 \text{ and } y_i = max(x_i, y_{i-1}), \text{ for each } i \text{ in } 2..n$$

and $x\!\downarrow$ denotes the increasing element y of $\mathbf{D}^n$ defined by

$$y_n = x_n \text{ and } y_i = min(x_i, y_{i+1}), \text{ for each } i \text{ in } 1..(n-1).$$

If x and y are elements of $\mathbf{D}^m$ and $\mathbf{D}^n$, then $x \cdot y$ denotes the element $(x_1, \ldots, x_m, y_1, \ldots, y_n)$ of $\mathbf{D}^{m+n}$ and if f is a mapping from $1..n$ into $1..n$, then $x \circ f$ denotes the element $(x_{f(1)}, \ldots, x_{f(n)})$ of $\mathbf{D}^n$. According to these notations, the *sort* relation is simply the subset of $\mathbf{D}^{2n}$:

$$sort = \{(x \circ \alpha) \cdot x \mid \alpha \in \mathcal{P}_n \text{ and } x \text{ is an increasing element of } \mathbf{D}^n\}$$

The ordered set $(\mathbf{D}^n, \preceq^n)$ is naturally introduced by defining the partial order relation $\preceq^n$ as: $x \preceq^n y$ if and only if, for each i from $1..n$, we have $x_i \preceq y_i$. The intervals of $(\mathbf{D}^n, \preceq^n)$ will be called n-*intervals*. It must be noticed that the n-interval $[a, b]$ is none other than the n-block $[a_1, b_1] \times \cdots \times [a_n, b_n]$. In $(\mathbf{D}^n, \preceq^n)$ a set $\{x, y\}$ of two elements does not always have a least and a greatest element but always has a greatest lower and a least upper bound, which are such that

$$
\begin{aligned}
inf\{x, y\} &= (min\{x_1, y_1\}, \ldots, min\{x_n, y_n\}), \\
sup\{x, y\} &= (max\{x_1, y_1\}, \ldots, max\{x_n, y_n\})
\end{aligned}
$$

The problem, which is the object of this paper, can now be formulated as follows:

Problem Given a $2n$-interval P, show that, in the sense of inclusion, the least $2n$-interval Q which contains $sort \cap P$ always exist and give an efficient algorithm to compute Q.

To express the computation of Q we need a final notation. Given a subset r of $\mathbf{D}^n$ and integers i, j such that $1 \le i \le j \le n$ we define $proj_i^j(r)$ to be the set,

$$proj_i^j(r) = \{y \in \mathbf{D}^{(j+1)-i} \mid \text{there exists } x \in r \text{ with } y = (x_i, \ldots, x_j)\}$$

Throughout this paper we need to manipulate mappings f from subsets of $\mathbf{N}$ into subsets of $\mathbf{N}$ and, more generally, correspondences in $\mathbf{N}$. By *correspondence* in $\mathbf{N}$ we mean a triplet of the form (I, s, J), where I and J are subsets of $\mathbf{N}$ and s is a subset of $I \times J$ representing any set of arrows from elements of I to elements of J. The correspondence is said to be *finite* if I and J are finite and the correspondence (I', s', J') is said to be a *restriction* of the correspondence (I, s, J) if $I' \subseteq I$ and $J' \subseteq J$ and $s' = s \cap (I' \times J')$. We say that a correspondence in $\mathbf{N}$ is of *type* $(\downarrow\!\!\diagdown)$ if it is of the form

$$(\{i, i'\}, \{(i, j), (i, j'), (i', j)\}, \{j, j'\}), \text{ with } i < i' \text{ and } j < j'$$

and is of type $(\diagup\!\diagdown)$ if it is of the form

$$(\{i\}, \{(i, j), (i, j'')\}, \{j, j', j''\}), \text{ with } j < j' \text{ and } j' < j''.$$

With respect to mappings f from a set I into a set J, we adopt the usual conventions. We call *graph* of f and we write $graph(f)$ the set of ordered pairs (i, j) such that $i \in I$ and $j = f(i)$. If I' is a subset of I, we write $f(I')$ for $\{f(i) \mid i \in I'\}$. If g is a mapping from J into K then $g \circ f$ denotes the mapping $i \mapsto g(f(i))$ from I into K. If f is a one-to-one mapping from I onto J then f^{-1} denotes the one-to-one mapping $f(i) \mapsto i$ from J onto I.

If I and J are subsets of $\mathbf{N}$ and if f and g are mappings from I into J, we write $f \overset{i,j}{=} g$ to signify that i and j are elements of I, that $f(i) = g(j)$, that $f(j) = g(i)$ and that $f(k) = g(k)$ for all elements k of $I - \{i, j\}$. We write $f \ll g$ to signify that there exist integers i, j such that $f \overset{i,j}{=} g$ and $i < j$ and $g(i) < g(j)$. We terminate this part by a very useful property of the $\ll$ relation.

Property 1 If I and J are finite, there exists no infinite sequence of mappings from I to J which is of the form $f_1, f_2, f_3, \ldots$, with $f_{i-1} \ll f_i$ for each $i > 1$.

Proof. Let i be an integer with $i > 1$. Let $|f_i| = \sum_{k \in I} k \times f_i(k)$ and let $\{p, q\}$ be the set of the two integers such that $f_{i-1} \overset{p,q}{=} f_i$ and $p < q$. We have $|f_i| - |f_{i-1}| = (q - p) \times (f_i(q) - f_i(p))$ and thus $|f_i| - |f_{i-1}| > 0$. The sequence $|f_1|, |f_2|, |f_3|, \ldots$ being strictly increasing, the sequence $f_1, f_2, f_3, \ldots$ is entirely composed of distinct terms and is thus finite, since also the set of possible terms is finite.

3 Preliminary results

Before confronting the heart of the problem, here are some preliminary results which are easy to understand.

Property 2 If a, a', d, d' are elements of $\mathbf{D}^n$, the following equality holds:

$$sort \cap [a \cdot d, a' \cdot d'] = sort \cap [a \cdot (d\!\uparrow), a' \cdot (d'\!\downarrow)].$$

Lemma 1 Let a, a', e, e' be elements of $\mathbf{D}^n$ with e and e' increasing. If there exists a permutation α of $1..n$ such that the set $[a, a'] \cap [e \circ \alpha, e' \circ \alpha)]$ is not empty then the set $sort \cap [a \cdot e, a' \cdot e']$ is not empty.

Proof. Let α be a permutation such that the set $E = [a, a'] \cap [e \circ \alpha, e' \circ \alpha)]$ is not empty and let x be an element of E. If (j, k) is an ordered pair of indices, taken in $1..n$, such that $j < k$ and $x_k \prec x_j$ then, since e and e' are increasing, the n-tuple obtained by exchanging x_j and x_k in x still belongs to E. By a sequence of such exchanges it is then possible to put terms of the n-tuple x in increasing order and thus to obtain an element of the set $sort \cap [a \cdot e, a' \cdot e']$. Thus this set is not empty.

Theorem 1 Let $[a \cdot e, a' \cdot e']$ be a $2n$-interval, with a, a', e and e' being elements of $\mathbf{D}^n$ and e and e' increasing. For each element i of $1..n$, let
$$I_i = \{j \in 1..n \,|\, [a_i, a_i'] \cap [e_j, e_j']\}.$$
(1) The set I_i is an interval of $(\mathbf{N}, \leq)$.
(2) If i and j are elements of $1..n$ such that the sets I_i and I_j are not empty then the following implication holds: $a_i' \preceq a_j' \implies \max I_i \leq \max I_j$.
(3) When $[e, e']$ is not empty, the set I_i can be computed as follows: Let α, α' be two permutations of $1..2n$ such that the sequences $x = (a \cdot e') \circ \alpha$ and $x' = (e \cdot a') \circ \alpha'$ are increasing and, for all pairs (k, l) of elements of $1..2n$, satisfy the implication: $x_k = x_l, \alpha(k) < \alpha(l) \implies k < l$, and the implication: $x_k' = x_l', \alpha'(k) < \alpha'(l) \implies k < l$. Let, for each i in $1..n$,
$$E_i = \{j \in 1..2n \,|\, \alpha^{-1}(i) < j \text{ and } n < \alpha(j)\},$$
$$E_i' = \{j \in 1..2n \,|\, j < \alpha'^{-1}(i+n) \text{ and } \alpha'(j) \leq n\}.$$
Then
$$I_i = \begin{cases} \emptyset, & \text{if } E_i = \emptyset \text{ or } E_i' = \emptyset, \\ (\alpha(\min E_i) - n) .. (\alpha'(\max E_i')), & \text{otherwise.} \end{cases}$$

Proof. The proof, which we do not detail, is based on the fact that, if $[a_i, a_i']$ and $[d_j, d_j']$ are non empty intervals, then $[a_i, a_i'] \cap [d_j, d_j']$ is not empty if and only if we have together $a_i \preceq d_j'$ and $d_j \preceq a_i'$ and that, in this case, $[a_i, a_i'] \cap [d_j, d_j'] = [\max \{a_i, d_j\}, \min \{a_i', d_j'\}]$.

To prove point (3), we use the fact that $x_k = a_{\alpha(k)}$ or $x_k = e_{\alpha(k)-n}'$, depending on whether $\alpha(k) \leq n$ or $n < \alpha(k) \leq n$, and the fact that $x_k' = e_{\alpha'(k)}'$ or $x_k' = a_{\alpha'(k)-n}'$, depending on whether $\alpha'(k) \leq n$ or $n < \alpha'(k) \leq n$.

4 The relation *graphmin*

We now introduce a subset of $\mathbf{N}^2$ which plays an important role in what is to follow.

Definition 1 Let (I, s, J) be a finite correspondence in $\mathbf{N}$. We denote by $graphmin(I, s, J)$ the subset of s defined by
$$graphmin(I, s, J) = \begin{cases} \emptyset, \text{ if } \mu(I, s, J) = \emptyset, \\ \\ \{(i, j)\} \cup graphmin(I', s \cap (I' \times J'), J'), \\ \text{if } \mu(I, s, J) = \{(i, j)\} \text{ and } I' = I - \{i\} \text{ and } J' = J - \{j\}. \end{cases}$$

with

$$\mu(I,s,J) = \begin{cases} \emptyset, \text{ if } I = \emptyset, \\ \emptyset, \text{ if } I \neq \emptyset \text{ and } \{j \in J \,|\, (\min I, j) \in s\} = \emptyset, \\ (\min(I), \min\{j \in J \,|\, (\min I, j) \in s\}), \text{ in the other cases.} \end{cases}$$

We notice that $graphmin(I, s, J)$ is the graph of an injective mapping from a subset of I into J. The remainder of this part is devoted to establishing a theorem about $graphmin(I, s, J)$.

Lemma 2 Let (I, s, J) be a finite correspondence in $\mathbf{N}$ with no restriction of type $(\downarrow\!\!\times\!\!\downarrow)$ and let F be the set of one-to-one mappings from I onto J, with graphs included in s. If F is not empty and if f is an element of F, for which there exists no element g of F with $f \ll g$, then $graph(f) = graphmin(I, s, J)$.

Proof. Let f be an element of F for which there exists no element g of F with $f \ll g$ and let m be the number of elements of I. If $m = 1$ then $graph(f)$ and $graphmin(I, s, J)$ are equal to $\{\min(I), \min(J)\}$ and thus equal. Let us form the hypothesis that the equality $graph(f) = graphmin(I, s, J)$ holds for $m \geq 1$ and let us show that the equality holds for $m+1$. If the set I has $m+1$ elements then it is not empty and, since $(\min(I), f(\min(I))) \in s$, the set $\{j \in J \,|\, (\min I, j) \in s\}$ is not empty. So there exists an ordered pair (i,j) such that $\mu(I, s, J) = \{(i,j)\}$, with $i = \min(I)$, and such that by letting $I' = I - \{i\}$, $J' = J - \{j\}$ and $s' = s \cap (I' \times J')$, we have

$$graphmin(I, s, J) = \{(i,j)\} \cup graphmin(I', s', J'). \tag{1}$$

Let us show that $j = f(i)$. If it is not the case, there exists $j' < j$ with $(i,j') \in s$. Since f is a one-to-one mapping from I onto J, let $i' = f^{-1}(j)$. Since $i = \min(I)$ we have $i < i'$. Since $i < i'$ and $j' < j$ and $\{(i,j),(i,j'),(i',j')\} \subseteq s$ and no restriction of s is of type $(\downarrow\!\!\times\!\!\downarrow)$, we conclude that $(i',j) \in s$. Thus, by letting $g \overset{i,i'}{=} f$, we have $f \ll g$ and $g \in F$, which contradicts the way f has been chosen.

Now let f' be the mapping into J such that $graph(f') = graph(f) - \{(i, f(i))\}$ and let F' by the set of one-to-one mappings from I' onto J', with graphs included in s. The mapping f' belongs to F' and, since there exists no element g of F such that $f \ll g$, there exists no element g' of F' such that $f' \ll g'$. No restriction of the correspondence (I, s, J) being of type $(\downarrow\!\!\times\!\!\downarrow)$, no restriction of the correspondence (I', s', J') is of type $(\downarrow\!\!\times\!\!\downarrow)$. By induction hypothesis, we have thus $graph(f') = graphmin(I', s', J')$, that is to say $graphmin(I', s', J') = graph(f) - \{(i,j)\}$. With equality (1), we conclude that $graphmin(I, s, J) = graph(f)$.

Theorem 2 (Property of graphmin) *Let (I, s, J) be a finite correspondence in $\mathbf{N}$ with no restriction of type $(\downarrow\!\!\times\!\!\downarrow)$ and let F be the set of one-to-one mappings from I onto J, with graphs included in s. If F is not empty then the mapping into J, the graph of which is $graphmin(I, s, J)$, belongs to F and is the only element f of F for which there exists no element g of F such that $f \ll g$.*

Proof. Let F' be the set of elements f' of F for which there exists no element g of F with $f' \ll g$. If F is not empty, according to property 1, it is possible to construct a finite and not extendable sequence $e_0, e_1, \ldots, e_m$ of elements of F such that $e_{i-1} \ll e_i$, for all i in $1..m$, and thus e_m belongs to F'. The set F' being not empty, according to lemma 2, the graphs of all its elements are equal to $graphmin(I, s, J)$.

5 Stable and shiftable subsets of indices

Throughout this part we suppose that s is a subset of $(1..n)^2$ such that no restriction of the correspondence $(1..n, s, 1..n)$ is of type $(\downarrow\!\!\!\nearrow)$ or of type $(\nearrow\!\!\!\searrow)$ and such that $graphmin\,(1..n, s, 1..n)$ is the graph of an element γ of $\mathcal{P}_n$.

A non-empty subset J of $1..n$ is s-*stable* if all the sets of the form $f^{-1}(J)$, with $f \in \mathcal{P}_n$ and $graph\,(f) \subseteq s$, are equal. The set J, as also, the strictly increasing sequence $(k_1, \ldots, k_m)$ of its elements are s-*shiftable* if, for each i of $1..(m-1)$, we have $(\gamma^{-1}(k_i), k_{i+1}) \in s$.

We present now, under the form of a theorem, an algorithm for partitioning $1..n$ in s-stable and s-shiftable subsets. The juxtaposition of finite sequences of integers is written with a dot, the empty sequence is written ε and the set of the terms of a sequence x is written $set\,(x)$.

Theorem 3 (Partition in stable and shiftable subsets) *If we apply as many times as possible one of the transformations which follow to the 4-tuple $(1, \varepsilon, \emptyset, (1, \ldots, n))$, we obtain deterministically a final 4-tuple of the form $(1, \varepsilon, E', \varepsilon)$, where E' is a set which we write $decomp\,(s)$. The elements of $decomp\,(s)$ are s-stable and s-shiftable subsets of $1..n$ and form a partition of $1..n$.*

1. $(1, x, E, y \cdot z) \longrightarrow (2, x \cdot y, E, z)$,
    if x, y, z are sequences of integers such that xy is non-empty and is the longest possible s-shiftable sequence,

2a. $(2, y, E, \varepsilon) \longrightarrow (1, \varepsilon, E \cup \{set\,(y)\}, \varepsilon)$,
    if y is a non-empty sequence of integers,

2b. $(2, x \cdot y, E, z \cdot z') \longrightarrow (1, x, E \cup \{set\,(y)\}, z \cdot z')$,
    if x, y, z, z' are sequences of integers such that z is of length 1, $x \cdot z$ is a s-shiftable sequence and y is the shortest possible non-empty sequence.

Proof. The sequence of transformations apply on a current 4-tuple of the form (e, u, E, v) which has the six following properties:

$P1$: $u \cdot v$ is a strictly increasing sequence of elements of $1..n$,
$P2$: E is a set of non-empty and disjoint subsets of $1..n$,
$P3$: $set\,(u \cdot v)$ and $\bigcup_{e \in E} e$ are disjoint subsets and their union is equal to $1..n$,
$P4$: if $e = 2$ then u is non-empty and is the longest s-shiftable prefix of $u \cdot v$,
$P5$: if $e = 1$ and $v = \varepsilon$ then $u = \varepsilon$,
$P6$: if $e = 1$ and $v = v' \cdot v''$, with v' of length 1, then $u \cdot v'$ is s-shiftable.

The properties $P1, P2, P3$ hold for the initial 4-tuple and are preserved after each transformation. The property $P4$ holds because of the form of transformation 1. The properties $P5, P6$ hold because of the form of the initial 4-tuple, the form of transformations 2a and 2b and the property $P4$.

Given the fact that transformation 1 requires that $e = 1$, that transformation 2a requires that $e = 2$ and $v = \varepsilon$ and that transformation 2b requires that $e = 2$ and $v \neq \varepsilon$, the transformations are performed deterministically.

In a sequence of transformations, the transformation 1 alternates with the transformation 2a or 2b. After applying the transformation 1, the length of the sequence v strictly decreases because of property $P6$, while after applying the transformation 2a or 2b, it remains unchanged. The sequence of possible transformations is thus finite and leads to a final 4-tuple (e', u', E', e'). If e' is equal to 2 then, according to $P4$, one of the transformations 2a or 2b is applicable. Thus $e' = 1$. If v' is not equal to ε then, according to $P6$, the transformation 1 is applicable. Thus $v' = \varepsilon$ and, according to $P5$, we have $u' = \varepsilon$. The final 4-tuple is thus indeed of the form $(1, \varepsilon, E', \varepsilon)$.

From the form of the final 4-tuple and from properties $P2, P3$ we conclude that the elements of E' constitute a partition of $1..n$. Given property $P4$ and the form of the transformations 2a and 2b, each element of E' is s-shiftable.

It remains only to be proven that each element of E' is s-stable. This property holds for the set E of the initial 4-tuple. Let us suppose that the property holds for the set E of the current 4-tuple (e, u, E, v) and let us show that it holds for the new set E of the 4-tuple obtained after applying a transformation. If we apply transformation number 1, the set E is not changed and thus the property still holds. If we apply transformation number 2a or 2b then, by referring to the definition of the transformations, it is sufficient to show that the $set(y)$ is s-stable. Given property $P3$, the fact that the union of two s-stable subsets is s-stables and the fact that the complement in $1..n$ of a s-stable subset is s-stable, we conclude that $set(u \cdot v)$ is s-stable. If we apply transformation number 2a, we have $y = u \cdot v$ and thus y is s-stable. If we apply transformation number 2b, let us suppose that y is not s-stable and let us show that we are led to a contradiction. There exists thus an element f of $\mathcal{P}_n$ such that $graph(f) \subseteq s$ and $f^{-1}(set(y)) \neq \gamma^{-1}(set(y))$ and thus there exists $i \in 1..n$ such that

$$\gamma(i) \in set(y) \text{ and } f(i) \notin set(y).$$

Since $set(u \cdot v)$ is s-stable, $set(x \cdot y \cdot z \cdot z')$ is s-stable and thus we have $f(i) \in set(x)$ or $f(i) \in set(z \cdot z')$. Let us examine each of these two cases. The unique term of z is written $\bar{z}$ and we take into account, according to property $P1$, that the sequence $x \cdot y \cdot z \cdot z'$ is strictly increasing.

1. $f(i) \in set(x)$. The set $set(x)$ being thus not empty, let $i' = \gamma^{-1}(max(set(x))$. Since $x \cdot z$ is s-shiftable, we have $(i', \bar{z}) \in s$. We have finally

$$\{(i, f(i)), (i', \gamma(i')), (i, \gamma(i)), (i', \bar{z})\} \subseteq s \text{ with } f(i) \leq \gamma(i') < \gamma(i) < \bar{z} \qquad (2)$$

   and, since no restriction of $(1..n, s, 1..n)$ is of type ($\diagup\diagdown$),

$$\{(i, \gamma(i')), (i', \gamma(i))\} \subseteq s. \qquad (3)$$

   It is not possible that $i < i'$, since in that case from (3) and from (2) we conclude that the element of $\mathcal{P}_n$ defined by $g \overset{i,i'}{=} \gamma$ is such that $\gamma \ll g$ and $graph(g) \subseteq s$, which according to theorem 2 is impossible. It is not possible that $i' = i$, since $\gamma(i')$ and $\gamma(i)$ are elements of disjoint sets, $set(x)$ and $set(y)$, and γ and f are elements of $\mathcal{P}_n$. It is not possible that $i' < i$, since in that case, given the fact that no restriction of $(1..n, s, 1..n)$ is of type ($\diagdown\diagup$), from (3) and (2) we conclude that $(i, \bar{z}) \in s$ and then $(\gamma(i), \bar{z})$ is s-shiftable, which contradicts the fact that y is the shortest possible sequence such that $x \cdot z$ is s-shiftable.

2. $f(i) \in set(z \cdot z')$. We have $\{(i, \gamma(i)), (i, f(i))\} \subseteq s$ and, according to $P1$, $\gamma(i) < \bar{z} \leq f(i)$. Since no restriction of $(1..n, s, 1..n)$ is of type ($\diagup\diagdown$) we conclude that $(i, \bar{z}) \in s$ and therefore that $(\gamma(i), \bar{z})$ is s-shiftable, which contradicts the fact that y is the shortest possible sequence such that $x \cdot z$ is s-shiftable. This ends the proof.

This theorem allows us to introduce the mapping $mapmin(s)$ and to establish as corollary its essential property.

Definition 2 (mapmin) We denote by $mapmin(s)$ the mapping from $1..n$ into $1..n$: $i \mapsto min(\{j \in K_i \mid (i, j) \in s\}$, where K_i is the class of $\gamma(i)$ in $decomp(s)$.

Corollary 1 (Property of mapmin) By letting $\varphi = mapmin(s)$, for each i of $1..n$, we have $\varphi(i) = min\{f(i) \mid f \in \mathcal{P}_n \text{ and } graph(f) \subseteq s\}$.

Proof. Let i be any integer of $1..n$ and let K_i be the class of $\gamma(i)$ in $decomp\,(s)$. We know that K_i is a s-stable and s-shiftable subset of $1..n$ and, by definition, $\varphi(i) = min\,(\{j \in K_i \mid (i,j) \in s\}$.

Let us show that there exists $f \in \mathcal{P}_n$, with $graph\,(f) \subseteq s$, such that $\varphi(i) = f(i)$. Let $(k_1, \ldots, k_m)$ be the strictly ordered sequence of the elements of K_i, let $(j_1, \ldots, j_m)$ be the m-tuple $(\gamma^{-1}(k_1), \ldots, \gamma^{-1}(k_m))$ and let p and q be the elements of $1..m$ such that $k_p = \varphi(i)$ and $k_q = \gamma(i)$. Let f be the element of $\mathcal{P}_n$ whose graph is $(graph\,(\gamma) - \{(j_p, k_p), \ldots, (j_q, k_q)\}) \cup \{(j_q, k_p), (j_p, k_{p+1}), \ldots, (j_{q-1}, k_q)\}$. By construction, we have, on the one hand, $\varphi(i) = f(i)$ and, on the other hand, since $\{k_1, \ldots, k_m\}$ is s-shiftable, $graph\,(f) \subseteq s$.

Let g be an element of $\mathcal{P}_n$, with $graph\,(g) \subseteq s$. Let us show that $\varphi(i) \leq g(i)$. Since $\gamma(i) \in K_i$ and since K_i is s-stable, we have $g(i) \in K_i$. Since also $graph\,(g) \subseteq s$, we have $g(i) \in (\{j \in K_i \mid (i,j) \in s\}$ and thus $\varphi(i) \leq g(i)$.

6 Solving half of the problem

Throughout this part we suppose that r is a set of the form

$$r = sort \cap [b \cdot e, b' \cdot e']$$

where b, b', e, e' are elements of $\mathbf{D}^n$ such that b', e and e' are increasing. We let

$$s = \{(i,j) \in (1..n)^2 \mid [b_i, b'_i] \cap [e_j, e'_j] \neq \emptyset\}$$

and γ be the mapping into $1..n$, such that

$$graph\,(\gamma) = graphmin\,(1..n, s, 1..n).$$

Under these conditions and making use of theorems 1 and 2, we obtain without difficulty the lemmas which follow.

Lemma 3 No restriction of the correspondence $(1..n, s, 1..n)$ is of type $(\downarrow\!\!\nwarrow)$ or of type $(\nearrow\!\!\searrow)$.

Lemma 4 If f and g are elements of $\mathcal{P}_n$, with graphs included in s and such that $f \ll g$, and if z is an element of $\mathbf{D}^n$, the following implication holds: $z \preceq^n inf(b' \circ f, e') \Longrightarrow z \preceq^n inf(b' \circ g, e')$.

Lemma 5 if $\gamma \in \mathcal{P}_n$ then $inf(b' \circ \gamma^{-1}, e')$ is an increasing element of $\mathbf{D}^n$.

We can now establish the two results of this part.

Theorem 4 The following equivalence holds: $r \neq \emptyset \iff \gamma \in \mathcal{P}_n$.

Proof. Let us suppose that r is not empty. Let us show that γ is a permutation of $1..n$. There exists thus $\alpha \in \mathcal{P}_n$ and $x \in \mathbf{D}^n$ such that x is increasing, $(x \circ \alpha) \in [b, b']$ and $x \in [e, e']$. Thus $(x \circ \alpha) \in [b, b'] \cap [e \circ \alpha, e' \circ \alpha]$ and, for all i in $1..n$, we have $[b_i, b'_i] \cap [e_{\alpha(i)}, e'_{\alpha(i)}] \neq \emptyset$. It follows that $graph\,(\alpha) \subseteq s$. According to property 1, it is possible to construct a finite non-extendable sequence $f_0, f_1, \ldots, f_m$ of elements f_i of $\mathcal{P}_n$ such that $f_0 = \alpha$ and $f_{i-1} \ll f_i$ and $graph\,(f_i) \subseteq s$, for each i in $1..m$. According to lemma 3 and theorem 2, we have $graph\,(f_m) = graphmin\,(1..n, s, 1..n)$ and thus γ is a permutation of $1..n$.

If γ is a permutation of $1..n$, for each i of $1..n$, we have $[b_i, b'_i] \cap [e_{\gamma(i)}, e'_{\gamma(i)}] \neq \emptyset$, that is to say $[b, b'] \cap [e \circ \gamma, e' \circ \gamma] \neq \emptyset$ and so. according to lemma 1, the set r is not empty.

Theorem 5 Suppose $\gamma \in \mathcal{P}_n$ and let $\varphi = mapmin(s)$. The greatest element $max\,(proj_{n+1}^{2n}(r))$ exists and is equal to $inf(b' \circ \gamma^{-1}, e')$ and, for each i in $1..n$, the least element $min\,(proj_i^i(r))$ exists and is equal to $max(b_i, e_{\varphi(i)})$.

Proof. Let $y = inf(b' \circ \gamma^{-1}, e')$ and $x_i = max(b_i, e_{\varphi(i)})$, for a given i in $1..n$.

Let us show that $y \in proj_{n+1}^{2n}(r)$. By definition of γ, for each i in $1..n$, we have $[b_i, b_i'] \cap [e_{\gamma(i)}, e_{\gamma(i)}'] \neq \emptyset$, thus $[b \circ \gamma^{-1}, b' \circ \gamma^{-1}] \cap [e, e'] \neq \emptyset$ and $y \in [b \circ \gamma^{-1}, b' \circ \gamma^{-1}] \cap [e, e']$. Since then $y \circ \gamma \in [b, b']$, $y \in [e, e']$ and, according to lemma 5, y is increasing, we conclude that $y \in proj_{n+1}^{2n}(r)$.

Let us suppose that $z \in proj_{n+1}^{2n}(r)$ and let us show that $z \preceq^n y$. The element z is thus increasing, $z \in [e, e']$ and there exists $\alpha \in \mathcal{P}_n$ such that $z \circ \alpha \in [b, b']$. Thus $z \in [b \circ \alpha^{-1}, b' \circ \alpha^{-1}] \cap [e, e']$ and $z \preceq^n inf(e', b' \circ \alpha^{-1})$ and $graph(\alpha) \subseteq s$. According to property 1, it is possible to construct a finite non-extendable sequence $f_0, f_1, \ldots, f_m$ of elements f_i of $\mathcal{P}_n$ such that $f_0 = \alpha^{-1}$ and $f_{i-1} \ll f_i$ and $graph(f_i) \subseteq s$, for each i in $1..m$. According to lemma 3 and theorem 2, we have $graph(f_m) = graphmin(1..n, s, 1..n) = graph(\gamma)$ and so, according to lemma 4, we have $z \preceq^n y$. Taking into account what we have proved in the preceding paragraph, $max(proj_{n+1}^{2n}(r))$ exists and is indeed equal to y.

Let us show that $x_i \in proj_i^j(r)$. According to corollary 1, there exists $f \in \mathcal{P}_n$ with $graph(f) \subseteq s$ and $\varphi(i) = f(i)$. It follows that $[b, b'] \cap [e \circ f, e' \circ f] \neq \emptyset$ and thus, by letting $w = sup(b, e \circ f)$ we have $w \in [b, b']$ and $[w, w] \cap [e \circ f, e' \circ f] \neq \emptyset$. According to lemma 1, we have $sort \cap [w \cdot e, w \cdot e'] \neq \emptyset$ and, given the fact that $w \in [b, b']$, we have $w_i \in proj_i^j(r)$. But $w_i = max(b_i, e_{f(i)})$ and $f(i) = \varphi(i)$. Thus $w_i = x_i$ and $x_i \in proj_i^j(r)$.

Let us suppose that $z \in proj_i^j(r)$ and let us show that $x_i \preceq z$. There exists thus $\alpha \in \mathcal{P}_n$ such that $[b, b'] \cap [e \circ \alpha, e' \circ \alpha] \neq \emptyset$ and $max(b_i, e_{\alpha(i)}) \preceq z$. Therefore $graph(\alpha) \subseteq s$. By corollary 1, $\varphi(i) \leq \alpha(i)$, thus $e_{\varphi(i)} \preceq e_{\alpha(i)}$, $max(b_i, e_{\varphi(i)}) \preceq max(b_i, e_{\beta(i)})$ and $y_i \preceq z$. Taking into account what we have proved in the preceding paragraph, $min(proj_i^j(r))$ exists and is indeed equal to x_i, and this for each i in $1..n$.

7 Solving the other half of the problem

In this part, we determine the "first half" of the sequence of least upper bounds and the "second half" of the sequence of greatest lower bounds of the studied $2n$-interval. For this we establish results which are dual to those precedently used for determining the two "other halves" of these sequences.

We suppose that r is a set of the form

$$r = sort \cap [c \cdot e, c' \cdot e']$$

where c, c', e, e' are elements of $\mathbf{D}^n$ such that b, e and e' are increasing. We let

$$s' = \{(i, j) \in (1..n)^2 \mid [c_{(n+1)-i}, c'_{(n+1)-i}] \cap [e_{(n+1)-j}, e'_{(n+1)-j}] \neq \emptyset\}$$

and γ', γ'' be the mappings into $1..n$, defined by

$$graph(\gamma') = graphmin(1..n, s', 1..n),$$
$$graph(\gamma'') = \{(i, j) \in (1..n)^2 \mid ((n+1)-i, (n+1)-j) \in graph(\gamma'')\}.$$

If $\gamma' \in \mathcal{P}_n$, we also let φ', φ'' be the mappings into $1..n$, defined by

$$\varphi' = mapmin(s'),$$
$$graph(\varphi'') = \{(i, j) \in (1..n)^2 \mid ((n+1)-i, (n+1)-j) \in graph(\varphi')\}.$$

Let us consider the ordered set $(\mathbf{D}, \preceq^+)$, where the order is defined by:

$$a \preceq^+ b \iff b \preceq a.$$

To each mathematical being ν defined implicitly with the relation $\preceq$, we associate the mathematical being ν^+ obtained by replacing $\preceq$ by the relation $\preceq^+$. Thus we have $[a,b]^+ = [b,a]$, $\inf^+(E) = \sup(E)$, $\min^+(E) = \max(E)$, etc. We have the equalities and the equivalence:

$$s' = \{(i,j) \in (1..n) \mid [\tilde{c}'_i, \tilde{c}_i]^+ \cap [\tilde{e}'_j, \tilde{e}_j]^+\} \tag{4}$$

$$x \cdot y \in r \iff \tilde{x} \cdot \tilde{y} \in sort^+ \cap [\tilde{c}' \cdot \tilde{e}', \tilde{c} \cdot \tilde{e}]^+ \tag{5}$$

$$proj^i_i(r) = proj^{(n+1)-i}_{(n+1)-i}(sort^+ \cap [\tilde{c}' \cdot \tilde{e}', \tilde{c} \cdot \tilde{e}]^+) \tag{6}$$

$$proj^{2n}_{n+1}(r) = \{y \in \mathbf{D}^n \mid \tilde{y} \in proj^{2n}_{n+1}(sort^+ \cap [\tilde{c}' \cdot \tilde{e}', \tilde{c} \cdot \tilde{e}]^+)\} \tag{7}$$

where x, y are elements of $\mathbf{D}^n$ and $\tilde{z}$ denotes $(z_n, \ldots, z_1)$, if z is $(z_1, \ldots, z_n)$.

Theorem 6 (Dual of theorem 4) The following equivalence holds: $r \neq \emptyset \iff \gamma' \in \mathcal{P}_n$.

Proof. Using, first equivalence (5), then equality (4) and theorem 4 applied to $(\mathbf{D}, \preceq^+)$, we get the equivalences: $r \neq \emptyset \iff sort^+ \cap [\tilde{c}' \cdot \tilde{e}', \tilde{c} \cdot \tilde{e}]^+ \neq \emptyset \iff \gamma' \in \mathcal{P}_n$.

Theorem 7 (Dual of theorem 5) If $\gamma' \in \mathcal{P}_n$ then the least element $\min(proj^{2n}_{n+1}(r))$ exists and is equal to $\sup(co\,\gamma''^{-1}, e)$ and, for each i in $1..n$, the greatest element $\max(proj^i_i(r))$ exists and is equal to $\min(c'_i, e'_{\varphi''(i)})$.

Proof. Let us show the first point of the theorem. We have the sequence of implications: $\gamma' \in \mathcal{P}_n \implies$(since equality (4) and theorem 5 applied to $(\mathbf{D}, \preceq^+)$) $\max^+(proj^{2n}_{n+1}(sort^+ \cap [\tilde{c}' \cdot \tilde{e}', \tilde{c} \cdot \tilde{e}]^+))$ exists and is equal to $\inf^+(\tilde{c} \circ \gamma'^{-1}, \tilde{e}) \implies$(since equivalence (7)) $\max^+(proj^{2n}_{n+1}(r))$ exists and is equal to the element $y \in \mathbf{D}$ such that $\tilde{y} = \inf^+(\tilde{c} \circ \gamma'^{-1}, \tilde{e}) \implies \min(proj^{2n}_{n+1}(r))$ exists and is equal to $\sup(co\,\gamma''^{-1}, e)$.

Let us show the second point of the theorem. Let i be an integer of $1..n$. We have the sequence of implications: $\gamma' \in \mathcal{P}_n \implies$(since equality (4) and theorem 5 applied to $(\mathbf{D}, \preceq^+)$) $\min^+(proj^{(n+1)-i}_{(n+1)-i}(sort^+ \cap [\tilde{c}' \cdot \tilde{e}', \tilde{c} \cdot \tilde{e}]^+))$ exists and is equal to $\max^+(\tilde{c}'_{(n+1)-i}, \tilde{e}'_{\varphi'((n+1)-i)}) \implies$(since equivalence (6)) $\min^+(proj^i_i(r))$ exists and is equal to $\max^+(\tilde{c}'_{(n+1)-i}, \tilde{e}'_{\varphi'((n+1)-i)}) \implies \max(proj^i_i(r))$ exists and is equal to $\min(c'_i, e'_{\varphi''(i)})$.

8 Solving the totality of the problem

In this part, we suppose that r is a subset of $\mathbf{D}^{2n}$ of the form

$$r = sort \cap [a \cdot d, a' \cdot d'],$$

where a, a', d, d' are any elements of $\mathbf{D}^n$. We let

$$(b, b') = (a \circ \pi, a' \circ \pi), \quad (c, c') = (a \circ \pi', a' \circ \pi'), \quad (e, e') = (d\uparrow, d'\downarrow),$$

where π, π' are permutations of $1..n$ computed in order to render b', c increasing. We introduce the subsets of $(1..n)^2$,

$$s = \{(i,j) \in (1..n)^2 \mid [b_i, b'_i] \cap [e_j, e'_j] \neq \emptyset\},$$
$$s' = \{(i,j) \in (1..n)^2 \mid [c_{(n+1)-i}, c'_{(n+1)-i}] \cap [e_{(n+1)-j}, e'_{(n+1)-j}] \neq \emptyset\}$$

and the mappings $\gamma, \gamma', \gamma''$ into $1..n$, defined by

$$graph(\gamma) = graphmin(1..n, s, 1..n),$$
$$graph(\gamma') = graphmin(1..n, s', 1..n),$$
$$graph(\gamma'') = \{(i,j) \in (1..n)^2 \mid ((n+1)-i, (n+1)-j) \in graph(\gamma')\}.$$

If γ and γ' are permutations of $1..n$, we also introduce the mappings φ, φ', φ'' from $1..n$ into $1..n$ defined by

$$\varphi = mapmin(s),$$
$$\varphi' = mapmin(s'),$$
$$graph(\varphi'') = \{(i,j) \in (1..n)^2 \mid ((n+1)-i, (n+1)-j) \in graph(\varphi')\}.$$

Theorem 8 (Basis of the sort narrowing algorithm) *We have the three following results:*
(1) The three properties $r \neq \emptyset$, $\gamma \in \mathcal{P}_n$, $\gamma' \in \mathcal{P}_n$ are equivalent and,
(2) if they hold, letting $f = \varphi \circ \pi^{-1}$, $f'' = \varphi'' \circ \pi'^{-1}$ and i being any integer of $1..n$, we have the equalities

$$min(proj_i^i(r)) = max(a_i, e_{f(i)}), \qquad min(proj_{n+1}^{2n}(r)) = sup(co\gamma''^{-1}, e),$$
$$max(proj_i^i(r)) = min(a_i', e_{f''(i)}'), \qquad max(proj_{n+1}^{2n}(r)) = inf(b' \circ \gamma^{-1}, e'),$$

the left-hand sides of these equalities always existing, and
(3) the $2n$-interval $[q, q']$, with

$$q = min(proj_1^1(r)) \cdot - - - \cdot min(proj_n^n(r)) \cdot min(proj_{n+1}^{2n}(r)),$$
$$q' = max(proj_1^1(r)) \cdot - - - \cdot max(proj_n^n(r)) \cdot max(proj_{n+1}^{2n}(r))$$

is, for inclusion, the smallest $2n$-interval which contains r.

Proof. Let us show the first result. We have the sequence of equivalences: $r \neq \emptyset$ $\iff$ there exist x and y in $\mathbf{D}^n$ with $x \cdot y \in sort \cap [a \cdot d, a' \cdot d']$ $\iff$ (since property 2) there exist x and y in $\mathbf{D}^n$ with $x \cdot y \in sort \cap [a \cdot e, a' \cdot e']$ $\iff$ there exist x and y in $\mathbf{D}^n$ with $(x \circ \pi) \cdot y \in sort \cap [(a \circ \pi) \cdot e, (a' \circ \pi) \cdot e']$ $\iff$ there exist x and y in $\mathbf{D}^n$ with $x \cdot y \in sort \cap [b \cdot e, b' \cdot e']$ $\iff$ (since theorem 4) $\gamma \in \mathcal{P}_n$. Symmetrically, using theorem 4 we show that $r \neq \emptyset \iff \gamma' \in \mathcal{P}_n$.

Let us show the beginning of the second result. We have the sequence of implications: $\gamma \in \mathcal{P}_n$ $\implies$ (since theorem 5) $min(proj_i^i(sort \cap [b \cdot e, b' \cdot e']))$ exists and is equal to $max(b_i, e_{\varphi(i)})$ $\implies$ $min(proj_i^i(sort \cap [(a \circ \pi) \cdot e, (a' \circ \pi) \cdot e']))$ exists and is equal to $max(a_{\pi(i)}, e_{f(\pi(i))})$ $\implies$ $min(proj_i^i(sort \cap [a \cdot e, a' \cdot e']))$ exists and is equal to $max(a_i, e_{f(i)})$ $\implies$ (since property 2) $min(proj_i^i(r))$ exists and is equal to $max(a_i, e_{f(i)})$. Symmetrically, using theorem 7 we show the implication: $\gamma' \in \mathcal{P}_n \implies max(proj_i^i(r))$ exists and is equal to $min(a_i, e_{f'(i)})$

Let us show the remainder of the second result. We have the sequence of implications: $\gamma \in \mathcal{P}_n \implies$ (since theorem 5) $max(proj_{n+1}^{2n}(sort \cap [be, b' \cdot e']))$ exists and is equal to $inf(b' \circ \gamma^{-1}, e') \implies max(proj_{n+1}^{2n}(sort \cap [a \cdot e, a' \cdot e']))$ exists and is equal to $inf(b' \circ \gamma^{-1}, e') \implies$ (since property 2) $max(proj_{n+1}^{2n}(r))$ exists and is equal to $inf(b' \circ \gamma^{-1}, e')$. Symmetrically, using theorem 7 we show the implication: $\gamma' \in \mathcal{P}_n \implies min(proj_{n+1}^{2n}(r))$ exists and is equal to $sup(co\gamma''^{-1}, e)$.

Let us show the third result. Let us first show that if $z \in r$ then $z \in [q, q']$. If $z \in r$ then according to the general definition of $proj$, we have $z_i \in proj_i^i(r)$ and $(z_{n+1}, \ldots, z_n) \in proj_{n+1}^{2n}(r)$. Since we have just shown that, for each i in $1..n$, the least and greatest elements of each of these sets exist, we have $z \in [q, q']$. Let $[p, p']$ be a $2n$-interval such that $r \subseteq [p, p']$. It only remains to prove that $[q, q'] \subseteq [p, p']$. We have $q \in [p, p']$ and $q' \in [p, p']$ and thus $[q, q'] \subseteq [p, p']$.

9 Details and complexity of the algorithm

Theorem 8 gives the bases of an algorithm for computing, in the sense of inclusion, the least $2n$-interval Q containing a subset of $\mathbf{D}^n$ of the form $sort \cap P$, where P

is a given $2n$-interval. We will illustrate this algorithm in an example and, at the same time, estimate its general complexity with respect to n. This complexity will be counted as a number of comparisons, adressings and transfers of elements of **D** or $1..(2n)$. We will execute the algorithm in six steps. For each step we will show that we execute $\mathcal{O}(n)$ or $\mathcal{O}(n \log n)$ elementary operations, which leads to a total complexity of $\mathcal{O}(n \log n)$ elementary operations.

As ordered set we take $(\mathbf{R}, \leq)$ and as initial $2n$-interval we take $P = [a \cdot d, a' \cdot d']$ with

$$
\begin{aligned}
(a, a') &= ((0, 6, 10, 4, 4), (13, 10, 11, 16, 6)), \\
(d, d') &= ((1, 5, 6, 11, 10), (3, 10, 9, 17, 15)).
\end{aligned}
$$

Computing the basic elements

In $\mathcal{O}(n)$ operations, we compute

$$(e, e') = (d{\uparrow}, d'{\downarrow}) = ((1, 5, 6, 11, 11), (3, 9, 9, 15, 15))$$

and, with the help of two sortings, we obtain in $\mathcal{O}(n \log n)$ operations,

$$
\begin{aligned}
(b, b') &= (a \circ \pi, a' \circ \pi) &&= ((4, 6, 10, 0, 4), (6, 10, 11, 13, 16)), \\
(c, c') &= (a \circ \pi', a' \circ \pi') &&= ((0, 4, 4, 6, 10), (13, 16, 6, 10, 11)), \\[4pt]
graph(\pi) &= \{(1, 5), (2, 2), (3, 3), (4, 1), (5, 4)\}, \\
graph(\pi') &= \{(1, 1), (2, 4), (3, 5), (4, 2), (5, 3)\}.
\end{aligned}
$$

Computing s and s'

We are now interested in computing a compact representation of

$$
\begin{aligned}
s &= \{(i, j) \in (1..n)^2 \mid [b_i, b'_i] \cap [e_j, e'_j] \neq \emptyset\}, \\
s' &= \{(i, j) \in (1..n)^2 \mid [c_{(n+1)-i}, c'_{(n+1)-i}] \cap [e_{(n+1)-j}, e'_{(n+1)-j}] \neq \emptyset\}.
\end{aligned}
$$

We first handle s by using theorem 1. We sort, on the one hand, the mixture of the least elements a_i and the greatest elements e'_i and, on the other hand, the mixture of the least elements e_i and the greatest elements a'_i:

$$
\begin{aligned}
b \cdot e' &= (4, 6, 10, 0, 4, 3, 9, 9, 15, 15), \\
e \cdot b' &= (1, 5, 6, 11, 11, 6, 10, 11, 13, 16).
\end{aligned}
$$

While maintaining the original order as much as possible, we get in $\mathcal{O}(n \log n)$ operations,

$$
\begin{aligned}
(b \cdot e') \circ \alpha &= (0, 3, 4, 4, 6, 9, 9, 10, 15, 15), \\
(e \cdot b') \circ \alpha' &= (1, 5, 6, 6, 10, 11, 11, 11, 13, 16),
\end{aligned}
$$

with

$$
\begin{aligned}
(\alpha(1), \ldots, \alpha(10)) &= (4, 1+5, 1, 5, 2, 2+5, 3+5, 3, 4+5, 5+5), \\
(\alpha'(1), \ldots, \alpha'(10)) &= (1, 2, 3, 1+5, 2+5, 4, 5, 3+5, 4+5, 5+5).
\end{aligned}
$$

By scanning the $\alpha(i)$s in increasing order of the is and the $\alpha'(i)$s in decreasing order of the is, we extract in $\mathcal{O}(n)$ operations the information

$$ s = \{(i, j) \in (1..n)^2 \mid j \in I_i\}, \qquad (I_1, \ldots, I_5) = (2..3, \ 2..3, \ 4..5, \ 1..5, \ 2..5). $$

To compute s', we use the fact that

$$ s' = \{(i, j) \in (1..n)^2 \mid (\pi^{-1}(\pi'((n+1)-i)), (n+1)-j) \in s\} $$

and we obtain in $\mathcal{O}(n)$ operations

$$s' = \{(i,j) \in (1..n)^2 \mid j \in I_i'\}, \qquad (I_1', \ldots, I_5') = (1..2,\ 3..4,\ 3..4,\ 1..4,\ 1..5).$$

Computing the two graphmin sets

We now compute

$$\begin{aligned} graph(\gamma) &= graphmin(1..n, s, 1..n) &= \{(1,2),(2,3),(3,4),(4,1),(5,5)\}, \\ graph(\gamma') &= graphmin(1..n, s', 1..n) &= \{(1,1),(2,3),(3,4),(4,2),(5,5)\}. \end{aligned}$$

According to definition 1, the set of ordered pairs which composes $graphmin(1..n, s, 1..n)$ is of the form $\{(1,k_1), \ldots, (m,k_m)\}$ and the k_is are computed in increasing order of the is. If we consider the compact representation of s, each k_i is obtained by choosing the least element of the set $I_i - \{k_1, \ldots, k_{i-1}\}$. At first glance, the computation of γ needs $\mathcal{O}(n^2)$ operations.

To achieve a computation of γ in $\mathcal{O}(n \log n)$ operations, we construct a balanced binary tree of $2n-1$ nodes with n final nodes. Each node is labeled by an element of $1..n$. The final nodes are labeled from left to right by $1, \ldots, n$. The non-final nodes are labeled by the same integer as their right daughters. The computation of each k_i is performed in increasing order of the is and consists in:

(1) Covering a branch which leads from the initial node to a final node labeled l_i, while moving to the right daughter of each non-final node, if I_i is empty or $min\, I_i$ is strictly greater then the label of this daughter, and to its left daughter, otherwise. If l_i is an element of I_i then $k_i = l_i$, otherwise all computations are stopped and we know that r is empty.

(2) Suppressing the reached final node.

(3) Covering the branch in reverse direction and, for each non-final node met, suppressing the node, if it becomes useless, or update its label, if the node is still useful.

The tree being composed of $2n-1$ nodes, its construction will use $\mathcal{O}(n)$ operations. The tree being balanced, its longest branches are composed of $\lceil \log_2 n \rceil$ nodes and thus the computation of one k_i is performed in $\mathcal{O}(\log n)$ operations. The computation of $mapmin(1..n, s, 1..n)$, that is to say of γ, is indeed performed in $\mathcal{O}(n \log n)$. For the same reason, the computation of γ' is performed in $\mathcal{O}(n \log n)$ operations.

In $\mathcal{O}(n)$ operations we also compute,

$$\begin{aligned} graph(\gamma'') &= \{(i,j) \in (1..n)^2 \mid ((n+1)-i, (n+1)-j) \in graph(\gamma')\} \\ &= \{(1,1),(2,4),(3,2),(4,3),(5,5)\}. \end{aligned}$$

Partitioning $1..n$ in stable and shiftable subsets

According to theorem 3, we compute the partitions of $1..n$,

$$decomp(s) = \{\{2,3\},\{1,4,5\}\} \quad \text{and} \quad decomp(s') = \{\{1,2,3,4\},\{5\}\}$$

by the sequences of rewritings

$$\begin{aligned} &(1,\varepsilon,\emptyset,(1,2,3,4,5)) \longrightarrow \\ &(2,(1,2,3),\emptyset,(4,5)) \longrightarrow \\ &(1,(1),\{\{2,3\}\},(4,5)) \longrightarrow \\ &(2,(1,4,5),\{\{2,3\}\},\varepsilon) \longrightarrow \\ &(1,\varepsilon,\{\{2,3\},\{1,4,5\}\},\varepsilon) \end{aligned} \qquad \text{and} \qquad \begin{aligned} &(1,\varepsilon,\emptyset,(1,2,3,4,5)) \longrightarrow \\ &(2,(1,2,3,4),\emptyset,(5)) \longrightarrow \\ &(1,\varepsilon,\{\{1,2,3,4\}\},(5)) \longrightarrow \\ &(2,(5),\{\{1,2,3,4\}\},\varepsilon) \longrightarrow \\ &(1,\varepsilon,\{\{1,2,3,4\},\{5\}\},\varepsilon) \end{aligned}$$

In these rewritings, each integer of $1..n$ which initially occurs in position 4 of the 4-tuple, moves first to position 2, then to position 3. The cost of each of these moves, being essentially the cost of checking whether a sequence of two integers is or is not s-shiftable, is a constant a number of operations, not depending on n. Thus the total cost is $\mathcal{O}(n)$ operations.

Computing the mapmin mappings

For each i from $1..n$ we consider the sets

$$\begin{array}{rcl} K_i & = & \text{the class of } \gamma(i) \text{ in } decomp(s), \\ K_i' & = & \text{the class of } \gamma'(i) \text{ in } decomp(s'). \end{array}$$

In $\mathcal{O}(n)$ operations we obtain

$$\begin{array}{rcl} (K_1,\ldots,K_5) & = & (\{2,3\},\{2,3\}),\{1,4,5\},\{1,4,5\},\{1,4,5\}), \\ (K_1',\ldots,K_5') & = & (\{1,2,3,4\},\{1,2,3,4\},\{1,2,3,4\},\{1,2,3,4\},\{5\}). \end{array}$$

If we go back to the compact representation of s and to definition 2, the set $\{(1,k_1),\ldots,(n,k_n)\}$ of ordered pairs which composes $graph(mapmin(s))$ is obtained by choosing k_i as the least element of the set $I_i \cap K_i$. Given the fact that I_1 is an interval and that K_i is already ordered, the computation of one k_i can be performed by a dichotomic search in $\mathcal{O}(log\,n)$ operations. Thus we obtain, in $\mathcal{O}(n \log n)$ operations

$$\begin{array}{rcl} graph(\varphi) & = & graph(mapmin(s)) & = & \{(1,2),(2,2),(3,4),(4,1),(5,4))\}, \\ graph(\varphi') & = & graph(mapmin(s')) & = & \{(1,1),(2,3),(3,3),(4,1),(5,5))\}. \end{array}$$

and, in $\mathcal{O}(n)$ operations

$$\begin{array}{rcl} graph(\varphi'') & = & \{(i,j) \in (1..n)^2 \,|\, ((n+1)-i,(n+1)-j) \in graph(\varphi')\} \\ & = & \{(1,1),(2,5),(3,3),(4,3),(5,5)\}. \end{array}$$

Final computations

All the remaining computations are performed in $\mathcal{O}(n)$ operations:

$$\begin{array}{rcl} graph(f) & = & graph(\varphi \circ \pi^{-1}) & = & \{(1,1),(2,2),(3,4),(4,4),(5,2)\}, \\ graph(f'') & = & graph(\varphi'' \circ \pi'^{-1}) & = & \{(1,1),(2,3),(3,5),(4,5),(5,3)\}, \end{array}$$

$$\begin{array}{ll} e \circ f = (1,5,11,11,5), & e' \circ f'' = (3,9,15,15,9), \\ c \circ \gamma''^{-1} = (0,4,6,4,10), & b' \circ \gamma^{-1} = (13,6,10,11,16). \end{array}$$

We finally get $Q = [q,q']$ with

$$\begin{array}{rcl} q & = & (1,6,11,11,5) \cdot (1,5,6,11,11), \\ q' & = & (3,9,11,15,6) \cdot (3,6,9,11,15). \end{array}$$

10 Conclusion and prospects

To conclude we would like to indicate three directions in which developments could be added to the work presented here.

The first development is to extend our results by replacing the closed intervals of $\mathbf{D}$ by convex subsets of $\mathbf{D}$ and this in the spirit of what has been done in [1] for the ordered set $(\mathbf{R}, \leq)$.

The second development concerns the link between the sortedness constraint and the "all different" constraint, written $(x_1, \ldots, x_n) \in dif$, which states that the x_is are integers, all different. It must be noted that, if $\mathbf{D}$ is the set of integers which lie between 1 and n, we have

$$
\begin{pmatrix} (x_1, \ldots, x_n) \in dif \ \wedge \\ x_1 \in A_1 \ \wedge \ \cdots \ \wedge \ x_n \in A_n \end{pmatrix} \equiv \begin{pmatrix} \exists y_1 \ldots \exists y_n \\ (x_1, \ldots, x_n, y_1, \ldots, y_n) \in sort \ \wedge \\ x_1 \in A_1 \ \wedge \ \cdots \ \wedge \ x_n \in A_n \ \wedge \\ y_1 \in \{1\} \ \wedge \ \cdots \ \wedge \ y_n \in \{n\} \end{pmatrix},
$$

which allows the narrowing of this particular constraint in $\mathcal{O}(n \log n)$. The move to the general case would provide an alternative of complexity $\mathcal{O}(n \log n)$ to the algorithms described in [2, 6]. These algorithms, based on the subset representatives theorem of Philip Hall, have a complexity of $\mathcal{O}(n^2)$.

The third development is in the study of a narrowing algorithm for the strict sorting constraint within intervals, where $(x_1, \ldots, x_n, y_1, \ldots, y_n) \in strictsort$ expresses that the x_is are all different and that $(y_1, \ldots, y_n)$ is obtained by sorting the x_is in increasing order. It must be noticed that this last development includes the previous mentioned one.

References

[1] Aillaud C., *Résolution de contraintes par analyse de parties convexes de* R, Thèse de doctorat, Laboratoire d'Informatique de Marseille, Université de la Méditeranée, July 1997.

[2] Leconte M., A Bounds-based Reduction Scheme for Constraints of Difference. Constraint-96, Second International Workshop on Constraint-based Reasoning, Key West, Florida, 19 May 1996.

[3] Older W.J. and A. Vellino, Extending Prolog with Constraint Arithmetic on Real Intervals, *Proceeding of the Canadian Conference on Electrical and Computer Engineering*, 1990.

[4] Older W.J., F. Swinkels and M. van Emden, Getting to the Real Problem: Experience with BNR-Prolog in OR, in *Proceedings of the Third International Conference on the Practical Applications of Prolog*, (PAP'95 at Paris), Alinmead Software Ltd, ISBN 0 9 525554 0 9, April 1995.

[5] Zhou J., A constraint program for solving the job-shop problem, *Principles and Practice of Constraint programming*, (Proc. of CP'96, Cambridge, USA), edited by Eugene C. Freuder, Lecture Notes in Computer Science, Springer Verlag, pp 510-524, August 1996.

[6] Zhou J., *Computing Smallest Cartesian Products of Intervals: Application to the Job-shop Scheduling Problem*, Thèse de doctorat, Laboratoire d'Informatique de Marseille, Université de la Méditeranée, March 1997.

Solving Various Weighted Matching Problems with Constraints

Yves   Caseau
Bouygues - Direction Scientifique
1 avenue Eugène Freyssinet
78061 St Quentin en Yvelines cedex
caseau@dmi.ens.fr

François   Laburthe
Ecole Normale Supérieure
D.M.I.
45, rue d'Ulm, 75005 PARIS
laburthe@dmi.ens.fr

Abstract

This paper studies the resolution of (augmented) weighted matching problems within a constraint programming framework. The first contribution of the paper is a set of branch-and-bound techniques that improves substantially the performance of algorithms based on constraint propagation and the second contribution is the introduction of weighted matching as a global constraint (*MinWeightAllDifferent*), that can be propagated using specialized incremental algorithms from Operations Research. We first compare programming techniques that use constraint propagation with specialized algorithms from Operations Research, such as the Busaker and Gowen flow algorithm or the Hungarian method. Although CLP is shown not to be competitive with specialized polynomial algorithms for "pure" matching problems, the situation is different as soon as the problems are modified with additional constraints. Using the previously mentioned set of techniques, a simpler branch-and-bound algorithm based on constraint propagation can outperform a complex specialized algorithm. These techniques have been applied with success to the Traveling Salesman Problems [CL 97], which can be seen as an augmented matching problem. We also show that an incremental version of the Hungarian method can be used to propagate a weighted matching *MinWeightAllDifferent* constraint. This is an extension to the weighted case of the work of Régin [Ré 94], which we show to bring significant improvements on a timetabling example.

1. Introduction

Constraint Logic Programming (CLP) and more generally Constraint-based Programming (CP), has become an interesting approach for solving combinatorial optimization problems [VH 89]. For instance, on problems such as jobshop scheduling it has shown to be as efficient as more traditional approaches based on Operations Research (OR) [CL 94] while delivering more flexibility (i.e. it is easy to adapt the algorithm to a slightly customized problem with additional constraints). Our goal is to investigate the advantages and drawbacks of constraint programming compared to classical combinatorial optimization on the maximum weight matching problem in a bipartite graph and see how these techniques may be combined.

Bipartite matching is interesting and important for three reasons. First, it is a well-understood problem, for which many polynomial algorithms ranging from simple to really elaborate (e.g., [GT 89]) are available. Therefore, the performance of the constraint satisfaction algorithm can be assessed against a rigorous gauge. Second, many real-life problems are either matching or "extended" matching with one or a few additional constraints. It is, therefore, a perfect domain to see where the boundary between flexibility and efficiency should lay. Moreover, many such matching problems are optimization problems with weights, and it may be more indicated to use weighted matching algorithms than to use generic optimization methods with non-weighted techniques. Third, matching is often a part of more complex problems and the efficient propagation of matching constraints is a basic building block of a modern constraint satisfaction system. By looking carefully into matching algorithms, we derive ideas that will be of use to designers of constraint solvers.

The paper is organized as follows. Section 2 describes a "naive" approach to matching and a few improvements that can be implemented easily. We then move on to more complex heuristics and cutting rules and show how they can be used to handle larger problems. Section 3 compares the previous results with two well-known algorithms, the Hungarian (weighted) method and the Busaker & Gowen flow algorithm. We show that the constraint satisfaction approach does not really compare with these specialized algorithms when the problem is to find an optimal matching. On the other hand, it is a plausible approach for finding a set of "very good" solutions. This leads to Section 4, where we look at two extended matching problems: in the first case, we allow the substitution of a new cost matrix for a few (k) edges (machine-task allocation problem with renewal of k machines); in the second case, we study the resolution of two simultaneous matching problem (e.g., in a machine-task allocation problem, maximize production within a bounded energy consumption). For these two variations of the problem, the original algorithms are adapted and compared. Last, we apply in Section 5 the various techniques that were presented in this paper to a time-tabling problem. We show that we can use weighted matching as a global constraint, which captures hard and soft constraints at the same time, enabling a more efficient resolution.

2. Constraint based programming

Formally, the matching problem can be described as follows : Let G=(V,E) be a bipartite graph, the vertex set V can be parted in two shores $V = V_1 \cup V_2$ such that all edges link V_1 to V_2. A *matching* is a set of edges $M \subseteq E$ such that no two of them are adjacent. A *perfect* matching is a matching covering all vertices. We consider the case when $|V_1| = |V_2| = n$ for which a perfect matching corresponds to an assignment between V_1 and V_2 (such matchings frequently arise in production planning, for the assignment of jobs to machines or tasks to technicians). Moreover, we consider the case of a weighted graph and define the weight of a matching as the sum of the weights of its edges. The purpose is then to find, when it exists, a perfect matching of maximal weight (or of minimal weight if all weight w_{ij} are replaced by $A - w_{ij}$), for some large constant A).

2.1. Naive CLP

A natural way to see this problem as a constraint program is to think of the vertices in V_1 as variables and to those in V_2 as values. A vertex in V_1 is linked to the set of values in V_2 which form its domain. A matching corresponds to an assignment for the variables such that different variables are always assigned different values. The problem consists in finding an assignment of maximal weight. This constraint

(*AllDifferent*) [Ré94] is offered as a built-in in most CLP languages. Propagation is often performed by arc-consistency [Ma77], [MM 88]. when a value is assigned to a variable, it is taken out of the domains of the other variables. When a contradiction occurs (because a domain becomes empty), the system backtracks to the previous variable assigned and tries the next possible assignment. For optimization, the algorithm is a classical branch and bound scheme : a variable is selected and all possible values are recursively tried. Once a solution M of weight W has been found, the constraint *weight > W* is added to the system to help pruning subtrees of the search space using simple upper bounds for *weight*.

At any time during the search, two upper approximations of the maximal matching are maintained : the sum σ^+ for all variables of their best possible assignment (for each variable v, we define the value *best(v)* as the maximal value *weight(v,x)* for all possible values x) and reciprocally the sum σ^- for all values of their best possible inverted assignment.

$$\sigma^+ = \sum_{v \in V_1} best(v), \ \sigma^- = \sum_{x \in V_2} best(x),$$

Instead of computing these sums explicitly for each node in the search tree, they are maintained incrementally. Each time a value x is removed from the domain of a variable v, if *weight(x,v)=best(x)* then *best(x)* is re-computed and the difference between the old and the new value is subtracted from σ^+. Similar updates are performed on *best(v)* and σ^- if *weight(x,v)=best(v)*. Whenever one of the bounds σ^+ or σ^- becomes strictly smaller than the goal, one can predict that the upcoming solutions will have a smaller weight than the best one found so far, so this branch of the tree can be cut off.

This propagation algorithm is widespread among the implementations of the *Alldifferent* constraint. In a CLP system, the selection of the node on which to branch is usually done with the *first-fail* principle : one selects a variable with the smallest domain. Assignments are usually tried in decreasing order of weight to drive the search towards matchings with heavy weights (*best first* principle, *greedy* heuristic).

As shown in table 1, this naive algorithm solves problems up to 2×20 nodes within seconds but requires unreasonable amounts of time for larger problems. Although it may not be the case for all implementations of the alldifferent constraint, taking both σ^+ and σ^- as upper bounds is important. The program which just considers σ^+ as upper bound is 10 times slower on 2×10 instances and cannot solve 2×20 problems within reasonable times. This fact gives us a hint of the progress that a symmetrical view of the problem can bring to a constraint approach.

The next two sections (2.2 and 2.3) describe improvements that can be made to the propagation scheme and the heuristics (first fail, best first) in order to improve performance.[1] All the experiments reported in this paper have been done with the CLAIRE programming language[2].

---

[1] For programmers using a blackbox constraint system with no access to the propagation and search engine (as many CLP systems), these changes could only be encoded within the solver: this allows to state the problem with the single command *Alldifferent*, but the changes can only be written by an expert of the constraint system. For programmers using an open constraint system with access to the solver and the propagation engine, the program is a little longer but any user can program these changes.

[2] available at http://www.dmi.ens.fr/~laburthe/claire.html

2.2. Adding symmetry and regret

Many improvements can be made on this algorithm to make it scale up for larger problems. The first idea suggested by the importance of the symmetrical upper bounds is to have a fully symmetrical description of the problem. The model that considers vertices of V_1 as variables and vertices of V_2 as values is an arbitrary breech to the symmetry of the problem (although perfectly valid). A way around this is to add the redundant model where V_2 is seen as the set of variables and V_1 as the set of values. Branching both on vertices from V_1 and V_2 implies some overhead (an inverse of the domain relation must be maintained), but it avoids missing evident decisions (for instance, when a value is in only one domain, it needs to be assigned to that variable). Hence, the matching is done from both sides at the same time. This is very similar to the use of symmetric redundant models for the n-queens problem [Jo 95], as would be expected since the n-queens is a customized matching problem (without weights).

Moreover, the first-fail heuristic for the selection of the vertex on which to branch is not a panacea : The notion of regret gives a more accurate description of the crucial vertices. The regret is usually defined as the difference between the optimal choice and the second best. In our case, if v is a vertex from V_1 and x is a value such that $best(v)=weight(v,x)$, we define $regret(x)$ as the difference between $best(v)$ and the maximum of $weight(v,x')$ for all values $x' \neq x$. Focusing on regret is justified by the fact that problem solutions do not change if a constant is added to all edges incident to one vertex (thus, only relative values matter, as opposed to absolute ones).

The regret is actually the change that will be made to the upper bound if the best (heaviest) assignment for this vertex is discarded. Selecting the vertex with the largest regret as a branching point is an entropic choice in the sense that we try to maximize the impact of this decision. As described in [CL 94], entropic heuristics are a powerful tool for proofs of optimality since they limit the size of the tree by forcing much propagation to happen at each node. To avoid a real slow down of the algorithm at each node, the regret and the best assignment for each node are memorized and updated incrementally.

Another idea would be to somehow re-break the symmetry. At any time, two upper bounds for the matching, σ^+ and σ^- are available. As soon as one of them becomes less than the goal, the branch can be cut. Selecting vertices in V_1 with large regret decreases σ^+ faster than σ^- and conversely. In cases when one of the bounds is clearly better than the other, it could seem worthwhile to encourage this dissymmetry in the choice of the branching node. We implemented this by giving a bonus (or penalty, depending of the situation) during the selection of the branching vertex, proportional to $\sigma^+ - \sigma^-$ to the vertices in V_1. This heuristic is denoted as "balance" in table 1.

The table below illustrates the effect of these techniques on randomly generated instances for 2×20 and 2×30 graphs, each vertex being typically connected to 5 to 8 edges, with weight a random number between 1 and 100. The entries of the table show the number of backtracks (b.) in the search process (1kb.=1000b.) and the running times (on a Pentium Pro 200) for finding an optimal solution and giving the proof of optimality. The naive approach (arc consistency and first fail) behaves poorly, the addition of regret and symmetry brings a gain of a factor 10. The idea of the balance does not really pay off.

	2 × 20	2 × 20	2 × 20	2 × 30	2 × 30	2 × 40	2 × 40
N : Naive Propagation	60 kb. 2 s.	25 kb. 1.2 s.	52 kb. 1.8 s.	600 kb. 23 s.	12 Mb 500 s.	> 10 Mb.	> 10 Mb.
R : N + regret	12 kb.. 0.9 s.	5 kb. 0.6 s.	9 kb. 0.9 s.	330 kb. 13 s.	198 kb. 8 s.	8.1M b. 510 s.	> 10 Mb.
Basic : R + symmetry	800 b. 0.1 s.	3.5 kb. 0.1 s.	800 b. 0.1 s.	27 kb. 1.2 s.	225 kb. 9.5 s.	870 kb. 42 s.	2.7 Mb. 130 s.
B' : Basic + balance	900 b. 0.1 s.	3.5 kb. 0.7 s.	900 b. 0.2 s.	43 kb. 2.5 s.	252 kb. 10 s.	1.1 Mb. 51 s.	2 Mb. 117 s.

Table 1 : Simple constraint programs

2.3   Finer tuning of the algorithm

One of the aspects of the algorithm that can be sharpened is propagation. In addition to upper bound evaluation and domain reduction due to edge selection, we can also do some domain reduction because of the upper bound. As a matter of fact, we can dynamically remove all illegal edges. An edge uv is illegal as soon as $(best(u) - weight(u,v))$ is greater than the available slack $(goal - \sigma^+)$ (or if $best(v)-weight(uv) > goal - \sigma^-$), where $goal$ is the objective weight ($goal$ is subsequently decreased to $weight(M) - 1$ each time an admissible solution M is found). We call this technique *dynamic cut* and report its behavior in table 2. The interest of dynamic cut is two-folds. On the one hand we detect some failures a little earlier (a rather small benefit). On the other hand, we maintain smaller and more relevant domains, which may improve the efficiency of the first-fail principle. Removing meaningless values produces more rapidly the domains with very small cardinals (upto 3) that first-fail tells us to examine. If we want to re-introduce some of the first-fail behavior into our choice heuristic based on regret, we can use a simple trick (used in [CGL93]): select the vertex that will minimize the lexicographic pair

$(min(card(domain(v)),par), -regret(v))$

where par is a fixed parameter. The effect is to select vertices by largest regret while there are still domains with cardinal more than par and to select them by first fail when all domains are smaller than par. This strategy yields some improvements, but only for small values of par (3).

The search tree, as described now has many branches per node. Actually, it may be a waste of time to wonder what edge should be selected for a vertex, once we know that it will not be the best one, since these edges may well look alike and be numerous. The search tree can be constructed differently with a single alternative at each node : either the best edge is the selected one, or it is not. The tree becomes narrower (binary), maybe deeper, but in practice, it prevents the algorithm from wasting time in irrelevant choices. This new branching scheme is reported in table 2 as *binary branching*.

The other tuning that can be done concerns the upper bound that is used for cutting branches of the search tree. Our formula that sums all best choices (σ^+) is a gross estimation of the best assignment. Indeed, if $v \in V_1$ is the favorite choice of p vertices in V_2, we know that we will have to take into account the regret for at least $p-1$ of them (because they cannot all be matched to their common favorite vertex). Therefore, it is possible to tighten the bound by subtracting from σ^+ a conservative estimate of the regrets that will occur (this is an application of the *lookahead* principle because we try to forecast the evolution of the bounds). For each vertex $v \in V_1$, we consider the previous set of vertices x from V_2 such that $weight(v,x) = best(x)$. To this set of p vertices, we associate the sum of all regrets but the highest one, that we call $look(v)$. σ^+ can be replaced by

$$\sigma^+ + \sum\nolimits_{v \in V_1} look(v)$$

This strategy which estimates the difference between the simple bound and the actual choice is called *lookahead* in table 2. Note that the estimation σ^+ corresponds to a relaxation of the matching problem. This could suggest to use Lagrangean relaxation by affecting weights to nodes. In fact, this *lookahead* strategy uses similar ideas by affecting weights to nodes that are related to several others ones in the preference graph (these nodes which prevent the solution of the relaxed problem to be a matching). Moreover, the Hungarian method which associates weights to nodes can also be seen as related to Lagrangean relaxation.

	2×30	2×30	2×40	2×40
basic	27 kb. 1.2 s.	225 kb. 9.5 s.	870 kb. 42 s.	2.7 Mb. 130 s.
dynamic cuts	24 kb. 1.5 s.	105 kb. 8 s.	1,5 Mb. 41 s.	2.2 Mb. 131 s.
binary branching	18 kb. 1.2 s.	95 kb. 6.5 s.	650 kb. 45 s.	2 Mb. 110 s.
lookahead	4,5 kb. 1.2 s.	11 kb. 6 s.	45 kb. 10 s.	98 kb. 21 s.

Table 2 : finer techniques

A few remarks can be made from these results. First, the lookahead heuristic works well, although its benefits (obvious from the numbers of backtracks) only pay off when the size of the problem is large enough. On the other hand, both the dynamic cut and binary branching schemes produce unstable results and it is difficult to measure any significant improvement.

These techniques (propagation, branching, bounding, heuristics) have been successfully applied to the Traveling Salesman Problem (TSP) which can be represented as a weighted matching problems (trying to match each node with its direct successor in the cycle) coupled with a subtour elimination constraint. As described in [CL97], these improvements enable constraint programs to solve 30-city tours instead of 15-city tours (more complex techniques are also given for larger problems).

3. Traditional algorithmic approaches

Matchings have been widely studied by the Operations Research community for years ([CoL 86], [Ge 94]). The two methods presented here do not pretend to be the best ones available today. We made a compromise by limiting ourselves to algorithms which were simple enough to be understood and implemented in a reasonable amount of time, not out of proportion with the implementation times of constraint-based programs :

• *The algorithm of Busaker and Gowen* (described in [GM 79], [VL 90]) embeds the matching problem into a flow problem by adding a source linked to all vertices in V_1 and a sink linked to all vertices in V_2. In this case, the capacities on all edges are set to 1. It is an adaptation of the well-known Ford&Fulkerson maximum flow algorithm to the case of a network with weighted edges. It starts with a null flow and augments it by saturating it along augmenting paths until no augmenting path can be found, meaning that the flow is maximal. This polynomial algorithm runs in $O(MN^2)$, where M is the number of edges and N the number of nodes. However, unlike the Ford&Fulkerson it is not incremental in the sense that it cannot complete any partial flow into a minimal cost maximal flow (it requires the partial flow to be of maximal stream for its cost).

• *The Hungarian method* is an algorithm of the class of primal-dual algorithms often associated to problems stated as linear programs [PS 82]. The primal program consists in finding a maximal matching of minimal weight. The dual program consists in finding positive weights π_u associated to vertices u such that for all edges uv, $\pi_u + \pi_v \leq weight_{uv}$ and such that the sum of the π_u is maximal. The algorithm constructs incrementally the weights π_u, starting with all π_u equal to 0, and constructing the graph G_π formed by the edges uv verifying $\pi_u + \pi_v = weight_{uv}$. The algorithm alternatively works in the dual model (updating the π_u in order to add new edges to the graph G_π) and the primal model (finding augmenting paths in G_π). In the end, the matching in G_π is a minimal weight maximal matching in G. This polynomial algorithm runs in $O(N^3)$. Its major interest compared to the flow algorithm is its incrementality. When one wants to remove an edge uv from the graph and recompute the optimal solution, one just sets $weight_{uv}$ to a large positive constant and remove uv from G_π. It takes then only one iteration to complete the optimal matching.

3.1. Comparison with CLP

For finding an optimal solution to a pure matching program, CP is not competitive with these OR techniques. CP solves reasonably well problems with up to 2×40 or 2×50 nodes, whereas the Hungarian method scales up to problems well over 2×100 nodes (on our 2×40 examples, solved in 70 or 80 000 backtracks and approximately 200 s. by our best constraint programs, the flow algorithm takes 1 s. and the Hungarian method takes 0,3 s.). However, if one no longer considers the problem of finding one optimal solution, but all optimal solutions (or rather all solutions within a given distance of the optimum), then CLP becomes a plausible competitor. Table 3 reports this experiment: four programs are compared:

• The first one is just a straightforward adaptation of our previous constraint program *basic*. Instead of stopping at the first solution, we explore the whole tree.

• The second is a similar branch and bound exploration where the flow algorithm is used to evaluate the optimal matching at each node instead of using an upper bound estimate. The flow algorithm is actually only triggered when one of the edges of the current "optimal" matching is removed from this dynamic graph.

• The third program is similar with a different branching scheme. For each edge of the original optimal solution we explore two branches : either the edge is part of the matching or it is removed from the dynamic graph.

• The fourth program is a branch and bound algorithm similar to the third one, except that the Hungarian method is used instead of the flow algorithm. We here take advantage of the incrementality of the Hungarian method (its ability to recompute the optimal matching in a single iteration when an edge is discarded at a node of the search tree).

For this exploration, the bottleneck is the amount of computation performed at each node of the search tree. The incremental Hungarian method is the best algorithm since it explores very small search trees (all explored branches lead to an admissible solution), however, the constraint algorithm is a fair competitor because it performs much less work per node.

	2×20			2×30			
	1% 4 sol.	2% 9 sol.	5% 127 sol.	0 % 1 sol.	0,5%. 3 sol.	1% 8 sol.	2,5% 56 sol.
Basic	1249 b. 0.1 s.	1832 b. 0.2 s.	8000 b. 0.4 s.	14 kb. 0.7 s.	24 kb. 1.1 s.	38 kb. 2s.	140kb. 10 s.
Flow algorithm	137 b. 9 s.	224 b. 13 s.	2000 b. 100 s.	100 b. 26 s.	172 b. 37 s.	215 b. 48 s.	1,5kb. 200 s.
Flow algorithm with new branching	57 b. 5 s.	136 b. 10 s.	1570 b. 110 s.	34 b. 13 s.	80 b. 22 s.	195 b. 51 s.	1 kb. 160 s.
Hungarian matching	21 b. 0.1 s.	58 b. 0.1 s.	1155 b. 0.7 s.	0 b. 0.2 s.	17 b. 0.3 s.	46 b. 0.4 s.	916 b. 3 s.

Table 3 : finding all solutions

Hence for the problem of finding all near-optimal perfect matchings, the constraint program behaves better than our basic Operations Research program (the adaptation of the flow algorithm) and not as well as our smarter O.R. program (incremental Hungarian method). The big advantage of the constraint program is it simplicity: it is indeed much easier to implement than both of the O.R. algorithms (naive and smart). It seems therefore to be good candidate for real-life matching problems involving a few additional constraints (and which thus require more exploration of the space of solutions than the pure problem).

4. Complex matching

In this section, we address the case of two real-life variations of the matching problem. Ad-hoc algorithms could also probably be specially designed for these variations of the problem. However, from a methodological point of view, we decided to consider only adaptations of the original solutions that could be implemented in a reasonable amount of times (since the constraints programs are adapted in a matter of minutes).

4.1 Replacing k machines

Suppose that in a plant, the manager has the funds to replace k machines among the n, by newer ones. We want to find an optimal assignment (maximum weight = bringing maximal production) of tasks to machines, given that newer machines are more efficient than older ones. This means that the matching problem is extended with the additional choice of those k vertices in V_1 for which we prefer to use a different weight matrix (say *weight'* instead of *weight*). For the sake of comparison, we implemented three solutions for this problem, one using constraint propagation and two O.R. solutions, a basic adaptation of the flow algorithm and a smart adaptation of the Hungarian method:

• The first one is a straightforward adaptation of our constraint-based program *basic*. The principle is to postpone the choice of the k "new" vertices as much as possible, but to take them into account with a modified upper bound estimate. Instead of taking the sum of the best choices for all nodes, we add to this sum σ^+ (resp. σ^-) the sum of the k heaviest edges in the "difference graph" (defined by the gain in the production function between new and old machines, i.e. considering $weight'(uv)$ - $weight(uv)$ as the weight of the edge uv). Like the bounds σ^+ and σ^-, this estimate can be maintained incrementally.

• The second program is based on the flow algorithm. It goes through a search tree where the nodes at depth i correspond to the choice of the ith machine to replace. All branches are explored. Whenever a decision of replacement is made, the production function is updated (i.e., the second weight function is used for the ith machine). At each node, the upper bound (computed for pruning) is the sum of the optimal solution for a matching in the original graph (where i of the k decisions have been made) and of the optimal solution for a matching of cardinal $k\text{-}i$ in the difference graph.

• The third program is based on the Hungarian method. The algorithm goes through the same search tree as the program looking for all near optimal solutions (cf section 3.3) : at each node a vertex v from V_1 (resp. V_2) is selected and each branch matches one of the vertices x of V_2 (resp. V_1) to v by removing all edges vx' for $x' \neq x$. The first branch explored corresponds to the current assignment of v in the solution given by the Hungarian method. The upper bound is the sum of the best possible matching (given by the Hungarian method) with an estimate of a sub-matching of size k in the "difference graph" (same estimate as for the constraint algorithm)

| | 2 × 20 | | | 2 × 30 | | | 2 × 40 | | |
	$k = 1$	$k = 2$	$k = 3$	$k = 1$	$k = 2$	$k = 3$	$k = 1$	$k = 2$	$k = 3$
Constraints	266b	433b	735b	19kb	27kb	26kb	3,3Mb	2 Mb	4,4Mb
	0,1s.	0.1s.	0.1s.	2.1 s.	3 s.	9.9 s.	800 s.	400 s.	700 s.
Flow	5 s.	30 s.	200 s.	16 s.	70 s.	400 s.	50 s.	400 s.	1150 s.
Hungarian Matching	20b.	22b.	31b.	30b.	30b.	34b.	40b.	71b.	107b.
	0.1 s.	0.1 s.	0.1 s.	0.2 s.	0.2 s.	0.3 s.	0.4 s.	0.7 s.	1 s.

Table 4 : replacing k machines

Figure 4 shows these three strategies on a few problems. The constraint-based approach performs better than the approach based on the flow algorithm but not as well as the algorithm using the Hungarian method. The constraint approach is much faster than this smart O.R. algorithm for n=10, a little faster for n=20, somewhat slower for n=30 and much slower for n=40 (which is anyway the upper limit for the constraint-based approaches on pure matching problems). Its main advantage is its simplicity (it took a few simple lines of code to modify the upper bound in the original constraint algorithm) compared to both O.R. algorithms. This makes the constraint approach a good solution for small and mid-sized problems (even for values of k up to 10), while the solution based on the incremental Hungarian method is well adapted to large problems.

4.2. Bi-matching

This second problem addresses the case of the combination of two matching problems (with two distinct weight matrices), where one problem is used for satisfiability and the other one for optimization (in a task-to-machine assignment, this amounts to maximizing production while keeping the energy consumption below a certain level). The difficulty varies according to the role played by the passive matching problem : if the value chosen for the maximal energy consumption is low or high, the energy matching is dominating the problem or is marginal. On the other hand, intermediate values make the problem much harder, because the shape of the solution space is equally affected by both matching problems. This implies that the distribution of feasible solutions in the search tree is no longer concentrated in one or a few areas, but is more dispersed. From a linear programming perspective, a bi-matching problem is made of three components: the matching constraints (shared by the two matching problems), the energy consumption constraint and the cost function that represent the optimization on production. A classical approach in such a situation is to use Lagrangean relaxation to push the energy constraint into the cost function.

Here again, we implemented several solutions that find the maximal production for a matching which consumption is less than a given constant E :

• The first one is also a straightforward adaptation of our basic constraint program. The search is guided by the optimization on the production. The consumption constraint is only used for pruning: Two lower bounds of the consumption γ^+ and γ^- are estimated by the sum of the edges of least consumption for each vertex set. Moreover, instead of considering the regret for the production function, we consider the sum of the regrets for both the production and the energy function. Therefore, this program is obtained by a simple replication of a few lines from the original *basic* program, where energy is substituted to production.

• The second algorithm is a branch and bound algorithm using twice the (incremental) Hungarian method. Two Hungarian matchings are constructed: one of maximal production and one of minimal consumption. Branching is based on the Hungarian matching of maximal solutions. Both these matchings are used to prune: a branch can be cut off when the minimal consumption is strictly greater than E or when the maximal production is less than the best one found so far.

• The third one and fourth are based on Lagrangean relaxation with Busaker's flow algorithm and the Hungarian method. The general principle of this method is to put some constraints in the objective function with a certain coefficient, and to vary the value of this coefficient [Re 93], assuming that the relaxed problem (i.e., without the constraint that was pushed into the cost function) is simpler to solve. Here, If we "push" the energy constraint into the cost function, we obtain a simple matching problem that we solve with the flow algorithm. The objective function becomes the total weight of the matching with the following weight function on the edges:

$$weight_\lambda (u,v) = production(u,v) + \lambda (E - energy(u,v))$$

Let us call f(λ) the value of the maximum matching for $weight_\lambda$. By construction, f(λ) (for $\lambda \geq 0$) is an upper bound for the original problem since the energy consumption has to be smaller than E. Now, if we compute the value F which is the minimal value for f(λ) when λ varies ($\lambda \geq 0$), F is also an upper bound (that can be found through a dichotomic search). This provides us with an upper bound of high quality, and also, while varying the value of λ, a possible lower bound (if one of the λ yields an admissible energy). These bounds are computed at each node of the search tree, and branching is made on the edges of the matching of the optimal flow, as was indicated in the third approach in the previous section. The third program is a straightforward implementation of the Lagrangean relaxation with the flow algorithm, the fourth one is an implementation of the Lagrangean relaxation with the Hungarian method, that tries to be as incremental as possible (trying to keep part of the dual solution for similar values of λ)

E	2×20				2×30			
	800	600	550	400	1300	1100	900	700
2 IHM (inc. Hung. Match.)	102b 0.3 s.	2.4kb 7 s.	2.6kb 7.1 s.	276b 0.9 s.	3.2 kb 12 s.	140kb 500 s.	204kb 900 s	14kb. 60 s.
Lagragean Relaxation with the flow algorithm	20b. 21 s.	31b. 32 s.	102b. 101 s.	22b. 20 s.	107b. 242 s.	31b. 72 s.	197b. 420 s.	87b. 167 s.
Lagragean Relaxation with the Hung. Match.	14b. 5.1 s.	64b. 16 s.	80b. 18 s.	28b. 7 s.	86b. 50 s.	28b. 12 s.	180b. 70 s.	296b. 69 s.
Constraints (Basic)	1kb. 0.4 s.	28kb. 1.2 s.	30kb. 1.3 s.	2kb. 0.1 s.	204kb 13 s.	1,5Mb 80 s.	8 Mb 410 s.	900kb 43 s.

Table 5 : bi-matching

Table 5 compares all four algorithms on two problems where the cost and weight functions are randomly generated with values ranging from 1 to 100. There is a balance between optimization on the cost and feasibility on energy : they both can cut the search tree. If E is small (close to the value of a minimal energy consumption matching), the energy is responsible for all the pruning and the program behaves like a simple matching one. Symmetrically, if E is large, the problem is almost unconstrained and looks like a simple maximal production matching program. The hardest situation is when energy and cost are both responsible for pruning the search tree. This situation corresponds to $E \cong 550$ and $E \cong 900$ in our examples. Lagrangean relaxation pays off for large problems, when no criterion dominates the other. However, it seems that for real life problems a criterion most often dominates the other. From this point of view, the constraint approach is much more efficient.

Here again, the constraint program performs better than the simple O.R. algorithm (with the two incremental Hungarian matchings). But it also performs better (except for the balanced situation for n=30) than the complex LR program. In fact, the Hungarian method is only mildly incremental for the Lagrangean relaxation scheme. The dual solution cannot be easily repaired after a change of weight function.

5. Application

In the previous section we have shown the strengths of the constraint-propagation approach compared with more specialized algorithms. We shall now see that these techniques should be combined and not opposed. We consider a time-tabling problem which consists of filling a weekly schedule with a set of lessons (of duration 1 to 4 hours). Each lesson is given a set of possible start times and a set of preferred start times. The schedule is made of 10 half-days of 4 hours and lessons should not be interrupted. This section illustrates how weighted matching techniques can be applied to such a problem and provide significant improvement. We notice that if all lessons were of duration 1, this problem would indeed be a matching problem. This suggests a straightforward relaxation where we consider lessons to be interruptible. Second, preferences can be encoded using weights so that the minimum weight matching corresponds to the assignment using as many preferred start times as possible.

In the rest of the paper, we consider m lessons l_1 ... l_m, and a schedule with n time slots of length 1 hour (n = 10 x 4). For each lesson, we are given two lists of time slots (integers between 1 and n) that represent respectively the set of possible and preferred start times. The goal is to find a start time for each lesson so that

- no two lessons overlap. This is the usual disjunctive scheduling constraint: for all pairs of lessons l,l' either $start(l') \geq start(l) + duration(l)$ or $start(l) \geq start(l') + duration(l')$

- each lesson fits into a half day. So within a half day (says the ith half-day, covering the time units $\{4i+1, 4i+2, 4i+3, 4i+4\}$), lessons of duration 4 can only start at the first unit $(4i+1)$, lessons of size 3 can only start at units $4i+1$ and $4i+2$, etc.

- the number of defaults, defined by the number of lessons which are assigned a start time outside the set of preferred times, is minimal

This problem is very dependent on the range of input data. The problem can be seen as the combination of a satisfiability problem (filling the schedule) and an optimization problem (an assignment problem). When the lessons are large, if there are enough of them, the problem may look like a bin-packing, where the preference optimization is almost irrelevant. On the other hand, with smaller lessons, the packing is much easier and the optimization problem dominates. Similarly, the difficulty of the preferences (i.e., the tightness of the preference sets) will augment the importance of the optimization component of the problem. We have picked three problems that are representative of different situations: Problem 1 uses rather short lessons (such as in a high-school schedule) with complex preferences (the optimum is 6 defaults). Problem 2 is similar (from a lesson size point of view) but has simpler preferences (the optimum is 1). The last problem uses larger lessons to explore how the algorithm would react to a problem where satisfiability is an issue.

In order to exploit the matching relaxation, we decompose each lesson of duration k into k units of 1 hour. The total number U of units is, therefore, the sum of the durations of the lessons. The matching that we need to build associates its start time (a time slot) to each unit. For a unit u associated to a lesson l, and a time slot i, we give a weight to each edge (u,i) as follows:

$w(u,i) = +\infty$ if u cannot happen at i because it would imply an illegal start time for the lesson l,

$w(u,i) = 1000$ if u can happen at i but this implies a start time outside the preferred set,

$w(u,i) = 1000 - 12 / k$ if u happens at i when the lesson l starts at one of its preferred time.

We can now define $MinWeightAllDifferent(\{start(u_1), ..., start(u_U)\}, w)$ as the minimum weight matching for this graph. Recall that this value can be computed efficiently with the Hungarian matching, and that it can also be maintained incrementally throughout the search procedure (section 3. described how to recompute this value when a few edges have been removed in the graph). Since the lesson l has k units, it is straightforward to check that an optimal solution of our time-tabling problem will correspond to a minimum weight matching. For each schedule with D defaults, the value of the matching is *1000 * U - 12 * D*. Thus, if we search for a solution with less than D defaults, we can use the redundant constraint :

$$MinWeightAlldifferent(\{start(u_1), ... , u_U\}, w) \leq 1000 * U - 12 *D \qquad (1)$$

To solve the three problems, we have used a branch-and-bound algorithm that minimizes the number of defaults. Branching is done on the starting time of a lesson, trying all preferred values first. The lesson on which to branch is picked using the first-fail heuristics. Each start time decision is propagated as follows:

- We discard values from other lessons that could cause an overlap with the lesson that has been assigned.
- The start time of the units composing the lessons are set accordingly.
- When the number of default reaches the upper bound, all edges that are not preferred are removed.
- We use a redundant constraint to detect when it becomes impossible to place large lessons. For each value d of duration that is strictly larger than half of a half-day (for example 3 hours), we compute the set of lessons *lessons(d)* with this duration and the union of all possible half days for these lessons *possible(d)*. we then check that *possible(d) $\geq$ lessons(d)*. Finally, we check that *possible({4,3,2}) $\geq$ lessons(4) + lessons(3) + lessons(2) / 2*.

	Problem 1 (24 lessons 39h)	Problem 2 (26 lessons 40h)	Problem 3 (14 lessons 39h)
1. simple propagation	189 kb. 1541 s.	286 kb. 1040 s.	43 kb. 246 s.
2. matching cut	31 kb. 177 s.	269 kb. 1008 s.	27 kb. 160 s.
3. Regin's filter	31 kb. 197 s.	269 kb. 1243 s.	27 kb. 160 s.
4. weighted matching cut	3511 b. 29 s.	234 b. 2.6 s.	17 kb. 120 s.
5. 4 + global consistency	1206 b. 30 s.	184 b. 2.9 s.	5943 b. 106 s.
6. 4 + « shaving »	382 b. 96 s.	183 b. 11 s.	5888 b. 314 s.

Table 6 : Applying various weighted matching techniques to a time-tabling problem

Table 6 gives the result obtained with the following approaches :

1. The first method only performs constraint propagation.
2. The second method checks that the underlying matching problems (for the units) is still feasible (i.e., there exists a perfect matching).
3. The third method removes all edges that do not belong to at least one perfect matching using Régin's algorithm [Ré94].
4. The fourth method uses our new global constraint *MinWeightAllDifferent* (1) which is propagated as explained earlier using the incremental Hungarian method.
5. The fifth method uses a look-ahead consistency check trying for each un-assigned lesson l to discard all preferred (respectively non-preferred) edges. « Trying » here means to detect if the removal of the values would create a contradiction through the propagation of the constraints. If a contradiction is detected, we deduce that the lesson l must start at a preferred (resp. non-preferred) time.
6. The sixth method applies a global consistency technique which consists of trying each possible start time and removing those who produce a contradiction. This is similar to the shaving technique that is used for jobshop scheduling [CL96].

A few conclusions can be drawn from these experiments.

- First, our global constraint *MinWeightAllDifferent* brings a serious improvement over standard propagation (local consistency). For problem 2, the number of backtracks is divided by a factor of 1000. Moreover, the overhead for keeping the value of the minimal weight matching up to date with the incremental Hungarian method is very reasonable, compared to the cost of simple matching propagation and bounding for defaults. Indeed, with the addition of the *MinWeightAllDifferent* the average time per backtrack over the three instances goes from 4,1 ms. to 7,3 ms. Therefore, the gain in search tree sizes turns into a real speedup.

- Second, the propagation of the unweighted matching constraint (the difference constraint), which can be done very efficiently with the filtering algorithm proposed in [Ré 94], has a marginal impact on the resolution of the problem compared to the propagation of the weighted matching constraint.

- Third, it seems a good idea to check global consistency by performing a limited breadth-first exploration of the search tree (limited to depth one). This seems to work better for branching decisions based on satisfaction of lessons (method 5) rather than for actual assignments of time slots to lessons (method 6). This is due to the fact that the complexity of method 5 is smaller than that of method 6. Moreover, these global consistency techniques work best for time-tables with large blocks (lessons with duration 3 and 4), rather than on problems with small lessons, where the matching relaxation is more accurate.

6. Conclusion

A first conclusion might be that constraint propagation is not a competitive technique for pure weighted matching problems. Specialized algorithms are simple enough and should be used appropriately. On the other hand, constraint propagation is a more plausible approach to augmented matching problems. Depending on the complexity of additional constraints and the size of the problem, the performances obtained (easily) with a CP approach range from reasonable to excellent, compared to more specialized approaches. In the few cases where this is not good enough, the best approach is to incorporate some of the weighted matching techniques into a constraint based branch and bound search.

The first contribution of this paper is a set of generic techniques that improve the performance of constraint-based branch-and-bound algorithms for such problems, namely a binary branching scheme based on regret, the use of the implicit symmetry and the look-ahead bounding functions. These techniques may be applied to any augmented matching problem and were actually applied with success to the Traveling Salesman Problem [CL97].

Our second contribution is to show that indeed a weighted matching can be considered as a global constraint (*MinWeightAlldifferent*), since we know how to propagate it efficiently using the incremental version of the Hungarian algorithm. This is a very useful global constraint, as we have shown with our time-tabling example. A constraint solver that offers this feature will be able to solve problems with hard and soft constraints at the same time, taking advantage of the weights, whereas a system that relies on simple matching only will implement soft constraints as a second layer, in a much less efficient way. We must also notice that this feature allows us to combine the best of both worlds for the two augmented problems that we studied in Part 4: we keep the simplicity and flexibility of the constraint-based approach, while ensuring the robustness of the underlying matching algorithm.

Acknowledgments

We would like to thank an anonymous referee for his helpful comments and suggestions on an earlier version of this paper.

References

[CGL93] Y. Caseau, P.-Y. Guillo, E. Levenez. *A Deductive and Object-Oriented Approach to a Complex Scheduling Problem.* Proc. of DOOD'93, Phoenix, 1993.

[CL94] Y. Caseau, F. Laburthe. *Improved CLP Scheduling with Tasks Intervals.* Proc. of the 11th International Conference on Logic Programming, P. Van Hentenryck ed., The MIT Press, 1994.

[CL96] Y. Caseau, F. Laburthe. *Cumulative Scheduling with Task Intervals.* Proc. of the Joint International Conference and Symposium on Logic Programming, M. Maher ed., The MIT Press, 1996.

[CL97] Y. Caseau, F. Laburthe. *Solving small TSPs with Constraints.* Proc. of the 14th International Conference on Logic Programming, L. Naish ed., The MIT Press, 1997.

[CoL86] T. Cormen, C. Leiserson, R. Rivest. *Introduction to Algorithms.* The MIT Press, 1986

[Ge 94] B. Gerards. *Matching.* in Handbook in Operations Research and Management Science (Networks) eds. M.O. Ball *et al,* 1994.

[GM 79] M. Gondran, M. Minoux. *Graphes and Algorithmes.* Eyrolles, 1979 (french) and J. Wiley, 1984

[GT 89] H.N. Gabow, R.E. Tarjan. *Faster Scaling algorithms for network problems.* SIAM Journal of Computing, **18**, 1979

[Jou 95] J. Jourdan. *Concurrence et coopération de modèles multiples.* Ph. D. Thesis, Paris VII University , 1995

[Ma 77] A.K. Mackworth. *Consistency in networks of relations.* Artificial Intelligence, **8**, 1977.

[MM 88] R. Mohr, G. Massini. *Running efficiently arc consistency, syntactic and structural pattern recognition.* Springer Verlag, 1988

[PS82] C. Papadimitrou, K. Steiglitz. *Combinatorial Optimization.* Prentice Hall, 1991

[Ré 94] J.C. Régin. *A Filtering Algorithm for Constraints of Difference in CSPs* Proc. of AAAI, 1994.

[Re 93] C. Reeves. *Modern Heuristic techniques for combinatorial problems.* Halsted Press, 1993.

[VH 89] P. Van Hentenryck. *Constraint satisfaction in Logic Programming.* The MIT Press, 1989

[VL 90] J. van Leuwen. *Graph Algorithms.* in Handbook of Theoretical Computer Science, Elsevier Science Publishers, 1990.

A Filtering Algorithm
for Global Sequencing Constraints

Jean-Charles RÉGIN and Jean-François PUGET

ILOG S.A.
9, rue de Verdun, BP 85
94253 Gentilly Cedex, FRANCE
e-mail : regin@ilog.fr

Abstract. Sequencing constraints have proved very useful in many real-life problems such as rostering or car sequencing problems. They are used to express constraints such as: every sequence of 7 days of work must contain at least 2 days off. More precisely, a global sequencing constraint (gsc) C is specified in terms of an ordered set of variables $X(C) = \{x_1, ..., x_p\}$ which take their values in $D(C) = \{v_1, ..., v_d\}$, some integers q, min and max and a given subset V of $D(C)$. On one hand, a gsc constrains the number of variables in $X(C)$ instantiated to a value $v_i \in D(C)$ be in an interval $[l_i, u_i]$. On the other hand, a gsc constrains for each sequence S_i of q consecutive variables of $X(C)$, that at least min and at most max variables of S_i are instantiated to a value of V. In this paper, we propose an automatic reformulation of a gsc in terms of global cardinality constraints. This is equivalent to defining a powerful filtering algorithm for a gsc which deals with a part of the globality of the constraint. We illustrate the power of our approach on a set of difficult car sequencing problems.

1 Introduction

1.1 Constraint Network and filtering algorithm

A constraint network (CN) consists of a set of variables, each of them associated with a domain of possible values, and a set of constraints which link up the variables and define the set of combination of values that are allowed. The search for an instantiation of all variables that satisfy all the constraints is called a Constraint Satisfaction Problem (CSP), and such an instantiation is called a solution of a CSP.

A lot of problems can be easily coded in term of CSP. For instance, CSP has already been used to solve problem of scene analysis, placement, resource allocation, crew scheduling, time tabling, scheduling, frequency allocation, car sequencing ... A recent paper of Simonis [Sim96] presents a survey on industrial studies and applications developed over the last ten years.

Unfortunately, CSP is an NP-Complete problem. Thus, many works have been carried out in order to try to reduce the time needed to solve a CSP. Some of the proposed methods modify the original CSP for a new CSP that has the same set of solutions, but which is easier to solve. The modifications are done by filtering algorithms, that remove values of variables that cannot belong to any solution of the current CSP. So, if the cost of such an algorithm is less than the time required by the backtrack algorithm to discover many times the same inconsistency, then the resolution will be speeded up.

The most widely used filtering algorithm is based on arc consistency[Mac77]. Some efficient algorithms achieving arc consistency for binary or n-ary constraints have been developed for twenty years. However, by taking into account the semantics of the constraints, more efficient filtering algorithm especially dedicated to each kind of constraint can be devised. For instance, [VDT92] have presented AC-5 a general framework to exploit efficiently some knowledge about binary constraints.

Moreover, the use of the semantics is often the only way to avoid memory consumption problems when dealing with non binary constraints. In fact, this approach prevents you from explicitly represent all the combinations of values allowed by the constraint. Last, specific filtering algorithms make it possible to use Operations Research techniques or graph theory. This is the case for the diff-n and cumulative constraints of CHIP [BC94], for ILOG Scheduler based on the edge-finder algorithm [Nui94], or for the IlcAllDiff and IlcDistribute constraints of ILOG Solver [Rég94, Rég96].

In this paper we are interested in global sequencing constraints and we propose such a filtering algorithm for them.

A global sequencing constraint (gsc) C is specified in terms of a ordered set of variables $X(C) = \{x_1, ..., x_p\}$ which take their values in $D(C) = \{v_1, ..., v_d\}$, some integers q, min and max and a given subset V of $D(C)$. On one hand, a gsc constrains the number of variable in $X(C)$ instantiated to a value $v_i \in D(C)$ be in an interval $[l_i, u_i]$. On the other hand, a gsc constrains for each sequence S_i of q consecutive variables of $X(C)$, that at least min and at most max variables of S_i are instantiated to a value of V

These constraints arise in many real-life problems such as car sequencing and rostering problems where a lot of min/max constraints have to be verified for each period of q consecutive time units. In a rostering problem, one has to chose a type of work for each day, satisfying various constraints. Sequencing constraints are useful for expressing regulations such as:

– each sequence of 7 days must contain at least 2 days off.

– A worker cannot work more than 3 night shifts every 8 days.

1.2 The car sequencing problem

Car sequencing problems arise on assembly lines in factories in the automotive industry.

There, an assembly line makes it possible to build many different types of cars, where the types correspond to a basic model with added options. In that context, one type of vehicle can be seen as a particular configuration of options.

Without loss of generality, we can assume that it is possible to put multiple options on the same vehicle while it is on the line. In that way, virtually any configuration (taken as an isolated case) could be produced on the assembly line. In contrast, for practical reasons (such as the amount of time needed to do so), a given option really cannot be installed on every vehicle on the line. This constraint is defined by what we call the "capacity" of an option. The capacity of an option is usually represented as a ratio p/q where for any sequence of q cars on the line, at most p of them will have that option.

The problem in car sequencing then consists of determining in which order corresponding cars should be assembled, while keeping in mind that we must build a certain number of cars per configuration.

For instance, consider the following version of the problem [DSV88]:

- 10 cars to build;

- 5 options available for installation;

- 6 configurations required.

The following chart indicates which options belong to which configuration: • indicates that configuration j requires option i; a blank means configuration j does not require option i. The chart also shows the capacity of each option as well as the number of cars to build for each configuration.

option	capacity	configurations					
		0	1	2	3	4	5
0	1/2	•				•	•
1	2/3			•	•		•
2	1/3	•			•		
3	2/5	•	•		•		
4	1/5		•				
number of cars		1	1	2	2	2	2

For example, the chart indicates that option 1 can be put on at most two cars for any sequence of three cars. Option 1 is required by configurations 2, 3, and 5. We define the demand for an option to be the sum of the demand for the configurations requiring that option. For instance, the demand for option 1 is equal to 6.

With gsc we can easily formulate this problem by:

- Creating a variable for each car that should be assembled on the line. The domain of these variables are the set of possible configurations. The variable array represents the sequence of the cars on the assembly line and is denoted by X.

- Creating for each option j with a capacity p_j/q_j a gsc defined on X that constrains on one hand, the number of times a configuration is assigned to a variable in X to be equal to its demand. On the other hand, this gsc constrains for each sequence of q_j consecutive variables of X that at least 0 and at most p_j variables of the sequence are instantiated to a configuration which requires the option j.

Some systems provide an efficient way to define constraints similar to gsc, see [BC94] for instance. However, an easy way to define a global constraint does not necessarily mean that the system handles efficiently the constraint as a global constraint. For instance, consider the model consisting of ([Smi96]):

- adding a variable o_{ij} with domain $\{0, 1\}$ for each variable x_i of X.

- adding a constraint between x_i and o_{ij} such that $o_{ij} = 1$ iff x_i is instantiated to a configuration that requires option j.

- adding several constraints in order to ensure that the capacity constraint of the option is satisfied. That is if the capacity is p_j/q_j and for each sequence $x_{i_1}, ..., x_{i_{q_j}}$ of q_j consecutive variables, a constraint ensuring that the sum of the variables $o_{i_1 j}, ..., o_{i_{q_j} j}$ is at most p_j.

These constraints are equivalent to the set of gsc, i.e. they accept the same set of solutions. However the filtering is less powerful as each filtering is done independently from the others. Thus, in practice, a lot of inconsistencies are detected by these systems only when a lot of variables are instantiated.

A possible solution to this problem is to add *implied constraints*. An implied constraint for a given CSP is a constraint that can be deduced from the other constraints of the CSP, but which introduces a filtering algorithm that can reveal inconsistencies which are not discovered by the combination of the filtering algorithms of the other constraints. So the introduction of implied constraints can lead to a reduction of the number of backtracks needed to find one solution or to prove that there is none.

The introduction of implied constraints is quite important for the resolution. For instance, it is said in [DSV88]: "[the introduction of implied constraints] will improve drastically the efficiency of the basic program by detecting failures as soon as possible".

In this paper, we propose to reformulate the CSP using the powerful global cardinality constraint [Rég96], in order to obtain more powerful filtering algorithm.

First, we give some preliminaries and we formally define the global sequencing constraints. After, we propose a filtering algorithm for them. Then, for the car sequencing we introduce new variable and value orderings. At last, we present a few experiments and we conclude.

2   Preliminaries

A finite *constraint network* $\mathcal{P}$ is defined as a set of n *variables* $X = \{x_1, ..., x_n\}$, a set of current finite *domains* $\mathcal{D} = \{D(x_1), ..., D(x_n)\}$ where $D(x_i)$ is the set of possible *values* for variable x_i, and a set $\mathcal{C}$ of *constraints* between variables.

Then, a constraint C on the ordered set of variables $X(C) = (x_{i_1}, ..., x_{i_k})$ is a subset of the Cartesian product $D(x_{i_1}) \times ... \times D(x_{i_k})$ that specifies the allowed combinations of values for the variables $x_{i_1} \times ... \times x_{i_k}$. An element of $D(x_{i_1}) \times ... \times D(x_{i_k})$ is called a tuple of $X(C)$. $T(C)$ denotes the set of tuples of $D(x_{i_1}) \times ... \times D(x_{i_k})$ that are allowed by C.

Let $\mathcal{P} = (X, \mathcal{D}, \mathcal{C})$ be a constraint network, $C \in \mathcal{C}$ be a constraint:
- C is *consistent* iff $T(C) \neq \varnothing$.
- (x, v) is *consistent with* C iff $x \notin X(C)$ or $\exists t \in T(C)$ such that v appears in t at the same position as x in $X(C)$; otherwise (x, v) is *inconsistent* with C.
- C is *arc consistent* iff $\forall x_i \in X(C), \forall v \in D(x_i), v$ is consistent with C

For convenience, we will denote by:
- $D(C)$ the union of domains of variables of $X(C)$;
- $\#(v, t)$ the number of occurrences of the value v in the tuple t;
- $\#(v, Y)$ the number of times the value v can be assigned to a variable of Y;
- $\#(v, t, S)$ the number of times the value v is assigned to a variable of S in the tuple t.

In the following we will use global cardinality constraints [Rég96]. A *global cardinality constraints* (gcc) is defined by the minimal and the maximal number of occurrences of each value of $D(C)$ in each tuple of the constraints. The minimal and the maximal number of occurrences of each value can be different from the others.

Definition 1 *A global cardinality constraint is a constraint C in which each value $v_i \in D(C)$ is associated with two positive integers l_i and u_i and*
$$T(C) = \{ t \text{ such that } t \text{ is a tuple of } X(C)$$
$$\text{and } \forall v_i \in D(C) : l_i \leq \#(v_i, t) \leq u_i\}$$
It is noted $gcc(X(C), l, u)$, where $l = \{l_i\}$ and $u = \{u_i\}$.

A global sequencing constraint is a gcc for which for each sequence S_i of q consecutive variables of X, the number of variables of S_i instantiated to any value $v_i \in V \subseteq D(C)$ must be in an interval $[min, max]$.

Definition 2 *A global sequencing constraint is a constraint C associated with three positive integers min, max, q and a subset of values $V \subseteq D(C)$ in which each value $v_i \in D(C)$ is associated with two positive integers l_i and u_i and*
$$T(C) = \{ t \text{ such that } t \text{ is a tuple of } X(C)$$
$$\text{and } \forall v_i \in D(C) : l_i \leq \#(v_i, t) \leq u_i$$
$$\text{and for each sequence } S \text{ of } q \text{ consecutive}$$
$$\text{variables: } min \leq \sum_{v_i \in V} \#(v_i, t, S) \leq max\}$$
It is noted $gsc(X(C), V, min, max, q, l, u)$, where $l = \{l_i\}$ and $u = \{u_i\}$.

3   Filtering algorithm

From the previous definitions, one can see that global sequencing constraints are close to global cardinality constraints, because they are more general but also because for each sequence of consecutive variable we can define a particular gcc. Our approach is to reformulate the gsc in terms of a set of gcc using a transformation of the constraint network.

This reformulation is in fact equivalent to producing a specialized filtering algorithm for the gsc. This filtering algorithm is the combination of the filtering algorithms of the resulting reformulated problem.

For the sake of clarity, we explain the transformation using a single gsc $gsc(X(C), V, min, max, q, l, u)$.

Definition 3 *Let S be a sequence of consecutive variables of $X(C)$ such that $|S| \leq q$. An **abstract value** of S, denoted by $e(S)$, is a value that does not belong to $D(C)$. An **abstract variable** of a variable x of S w.r.t $e(S)$ is a variable y with a domain equal to $V \cup \{e(S)\}$ such that*

$$y = x \quad xor \quad y = e(S)$$

$Y(e(S), S)$ denotes the set of the abstract variables of the variables of S w.r.t. $e(S)$.

The constraint "$x = y$ xor $y = e(S)$" is equivalent to the constraint "if $x \in V$ then $x = y$ else $y = e(S)$".

In other words, either x and y are instantiated to the same value belonging to V, or x is instantiated to a value not in V and y is instantiated to $e(S)$. We can then prove the following property.

Property 1 *Let $gsc(X(C), V, min, max, q, l, u)$ be a gsc and S be a sequence of consecutive variables of $X(C)$ s.t. $|S| \leq q$ then*

$$|S| - max \leq \#(e(S), Y(e(S), S)) \leq q - min$$

proof:

Suppose that all the variables of S are instantiated. By construction, the number $\#(e(S), Y(e(S), S))$ is exactly the number of variables x_i in S that are instantiated to a value not belonging to V. Thus, the number of variables x_i in S that are instantiated to a value of V is: $\#(V, X) = |S| - \#(e(S), Y(e(S), S))$.

Assume $|S| = q$.
From the definition of the gsc, we know that $\#(V, X)$ must be in the interval $[min, max]$, i.e. $min \leq |S| - \#(e(S), Y(e(S), S)) \leq max$. After rewriting we obtain $q - max \leq \#(e(S), Y(e(S), S)) \leq q - min$.

Assume now $|S| < q$.
Let R be any sequence of $q - |S|$ consecutive variables such that $S \cup R$

forms a sequence of q consecutive variables and $e(S) = e(R)$. We just proved $min \leq |S| + |R| - \#(e(S), Y(e(S), S) \cup Y(e(R), R)) \leq max$. This equation is equivalent to $|S| + |R| - \#(e(R), Y(e(R), R)) - max \leq \#(e(S), Y(e(S), S)) \leq |S| + |R| - \#(e(R), Y(e(R), R)) - min$. By definition $0 \leq \#(e(R), Y(e(R), R)) \leq |R|$, thus $|S| - max \leq \#(e(S), Y(e(S), S)) \leq |S| + |R| - min$, which is equivalent to $|S| - max \leq \#(e(S), Y(e(S), S)) \leq q - min$. ⊙

Now, let us see how to express the gsc as a whole by a set of global cardinality constraints. This can be done easily by splitting $X(C)$ into a partition of sequences $\mathcal{P} = \{S_1, ..., S_p\}$ and by choosing the abstract values associated with each sequence pairwise distinct. In this case, each $e(S_i)$ can only be assigned to variables of $Y(e(S_i), S_i)$. Then we can define a gcc on the variables $\cup_{S_i \in \mathcal{S}} Y(e(S_i), S_i)$ in which the values v_k of V are constrained by l_k and u_k, and the abstract values $e(S_i)$ are constrained by $|S_i| - max$ and $q - min$.

More formally we have:

Definition 4 *Consider*
- $\mathcal{P} = \{S_1, ..., S_p\}$ *a partition of $X(C)$ into sequences of at most q consecutive variables,*
- $E(\mathcal{P}) = \{e(S_i) \text{ s.t. } S_i \in \mathcal{P} \text{ and } S_i \neq S_j \Rightarrow e(S_i) \neq e(S_j)\}$ *a set of pairwise distinct abstract values,*
- $Y(E(\mathcal{P}), \mathcal{P}) = \bigcup_{S_i \in \mathcal{P}} Y(e(S_i), S_i)$

The global sequential cardinality constraint $gscc(\mathcal{P}, V, E(\mathcal{P}), q, min, max, l, u)$ is the global cardinality constraint $gcc(Y(E(\mathcal{P}), \mathcal{P}), l, u)$, where $l = \{l_i\} \cup \{|S_i| - max\}$ and $u = \{u_i\} \cup \{q - min\}$.

This transformation is interesting if the abstract values are really constrained, that is if $|S_i|$ is close to q. Since no condition have been made on the partition $\mathcal{P}$, such a result can be easily obtained. For instance, if $|X(C)| = q.p + r$ with, p and $r < q$ two positive integers, we can define $\mathcal{P} = \{S_1, S_2, ..., S_{p+1}\}$ by grouping into S_1 the variables with index from 1 to r of $X(C)$ and then by grouping into S_i, $1 < i \leq p + 1$, the variables with index from $r + 1 + q(i - 1)$ to $r + qi$.

With such a definition of $\mathcal{P}$ the gscc will take globally into account all the sequences belonging to $Y(E(\mathcal{P}), \mathcal{P})$. So, we will have a powerful filtering algorithm for this group of sequence constraints, because we can achieve the arc consistency for the gscc. However, we do not take into account all the possibles sequences of length q.

In order to obtain this result we propose to define a set of q partitions into sequences, such that any sequence of q consecutive variables of $X(C)$ belongs to exactly one partition, and then to define the gscc for each partition.

Each partition is defined in a way similar to the way we have just presented $(n = |X(C)|)$:
The first partition $\mathcal{P}_1$ is defined by the sequence S_{11} that contains only the first variable of $X(C)$ and by the sequences S_{1i}, $1 < i \leq \lfloor 1 + (n-1)/q \rfloor$, that contain the variables from $1 + (i - 1)q$ to iq of $X(C)$, and eventually by the sequence that contains the variables of $X(C)$ not contained in the previous sequences. The

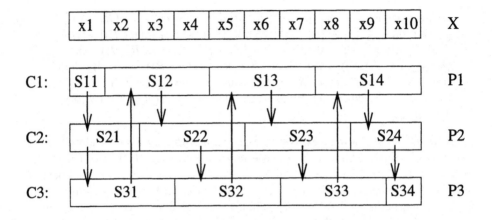

a ———➤ b   means b is the successor of a

Fig. 1. Construction of Q for option 2.

second partition $\mathcal{P}_2$ is defined by the sequence S_{21} that contains the first and the second variables of $X(C)$ and by the sequences S_{2i}, $1 < i \leq \lfloor 2 + (n-1)/q \rfloor$, that contain the variables from $2 + (i-1)q$ to $1 + iq$ of $X(C)$, and eventually by the sequence that contains the variables of $X(C)$ not contained in the previous sequences. The other sequences are defined similarly.

Definition 5 *Given a sequence of variables $X(C) = \{x_k\}$, $k = 1..n$, and an integer q, the **sequence of order q, i, j** of $X(C)$, denoted by $Seq(X(C), q, i, j)$, is the sequence of variables of $X(C)$ with index ranging from $max(1, i+1+q(j-2))$ to $min(n, i + q(j-1))$, where $i = 1..q$, $j \geq 1$ and $i+1+q(j-2) \leq n-q+1$. For a given value of i, the partition of $X(C)$ defined by the sequences $Seq(X(C), q, i, j)$, $j \geq 1$ and $i + 1 + q(j-2) \leq n-q+1$ is denoted by $Partition(X(C), q, i)$.*

Figure 1 represent all such sequences for $n = 10$ and $q = 3$.

We then define a gscc for each partition, using the abstract variables corresponding to each sequence in the partitions.

Definition 6 *Let C be gsc defined on $X(C)$ and associated with V, min, max, l, u and q. With the notation introduced in definition 4 and 5 we define for each value i from 1 to q:*

- *$\mathcal{P}_i = Partition(X(C), q, i)$;*
- *$E_i = E(\mathcal{P}_i)$ such that $i \neq j \Rightarrow E_i \cap E_j = \varnothing$ (all the abstract values are pairwise different);*
- *$Y_i = Y(E(\mathcal{P}_i), \mathcal{P}_i)$;*
- *K_i is the set of constraints needed to define the abstract variables Y_i of $X(C)$ (see definition 3);*

- $C_i = gscc(\mathcal{P}_i, V, E_i, q, min, max, l, u)$

The constraint network

$$Q = (X(C) \cup (\bigcup_{i=1..q} Y_i), D(C) \cup (\bigcup_{i=1..q} E_i), \bigcup_{i=1..q} C_i \cup \bigcup_{i=1..q} K_i)$$

is called the basic constraint network associated with a gsc.

We have the following proposition:

Proposition 1 *Let* $C = gsc(X(C), V, min, max, q, l, u)$ *be a gsc defined on* $X(C)$, $\Pi = (X(C), D(C), \{C\})$ *be a constraint network and* Q *the basic constraint network associated with* C *then,* Π *is satisfiable iff* Q *is satisfiable.*

proof:

We show first that each solution of Π can be extended into a solution of Q. Consider a variable x_k of $X(C)$ instantiated to a value v in a given solution of Π. For each abstract variable y_{ki} of x_k, if $v \in V$, we instantiate y_{ki} with the abstract value from which y_{ki} has been defined, else (if $v \notin V$), we instantiate y_{ki} with v. These assignments satisfy the constraints in Q.

Conversely, consider a solution of Q. Consider x_k of $X(C)$. If one abstract variable y_{ki} of x_k is such that $y_{ki} = v$ and v is not an abstract value, then because of the constraints between x_k and each of the y_{ki}, all the $y_{ki} = v$, and $x = v$. In the remaining case, we have that for all i, y_{ki} is instantiated to an abstract value and $x = v_k$ s.t. $v_k \notin V$. Then the assignments for the x_k satisfy the gsc.$\odot$

So, a gsc can be filtered by applying the arc consistency to the basic constraint network associated with it. However, we can still improve our model. In fact, we have shown that a gsc can be represented by a set of gscc. But the communication between these gscc is poor, because we do not take into account the fact that several gscc are defined for one gsc. We can add some other constraints that link the different abstract values.

Definition 7 *Let* S *be any sequence, we will denote by* $\#e(S)$ *the variable equal to* $\#(e(S), Y(e(S), S))$. *We also say that the successor of a sequence of abstract variables* $Y(e(S), S)$ *with* $S = Seq(X(C), q, i, j)$ *is the sequence of abstract variables* $Y(e(R), R)$ *with* $R = Seq(X(C), q, i+1, j)$ *if* $i < q$, *and that the successor of* $Y(e(S), S)$ *with* $S = Seq(X(C), q, q, j)$ *is* $Y(e(R), R)$ *with* $R = Seq(X(C), q, 1, j+1)$.

Intuitively, the successor of a sequence is in fact the same sequence translated by one variable (cf. figure 1).

For convenience, we will respectively denote by $first(O)$ and $last(O)$ the first and the last variable of any ordered set O.

Proposition 2 *Let Q be the basic constraint network associated with a gsc, F be a sequence* $Y(e(S), S)$, *L be its successor, then:*

- *if* $|F| = |L| + 1$ *then*
  - $first(F) = e(F) \Leftrightarrow \#e(F) = \#e(L) + 1$
  - $first(F) \neq e(F) \Leftrightarrow \#e(F) = \#e(L)$

- *if* $|F| = |L|$ *then*
  - $first(F) = e(F)$ *and* $last(L) \neq e(L) \Leftrightarrow \#e(F) = \#e(L) + 1$
  - $((first(F) = e(F)$ *and* $last(L) = e(L))$
    or $(first(F) \neq e(F)$ *and* $last(L) \neq e(L))) \Leftrightarrow \#e(F) = \#e(L)$
  - $first(F) \neq e(F)$ *and* $last(L) = e(L) \Leftrightarrow \#e(F) = \#e(L) - 1$

- *if* $|F| = |L| - 1$ *then*
  - $last(L) = e(L) \Leftrightarrow \#e(F) = \#e(L) - 1$
  - $last(L) \neq e(L) \Leftrightarrow \#e(F) = \#e(L)$

sketch of proof:

Let F_X and L_X be the sequences of variables of $X(C)$ respectively from which F and L have been created (if $F = Y(e(S), S)$ then $F_X = S$ for instance). Then $\#e(F) = |\{x \in F_X s.t. D(x) \cap V = \varnothing\}|$ and $\#e(L) = |\{x \in L_X s.t. D(x) \cap V = \varnothing\}|$. Consider, for instance, the case $|F| = |L| + 1$. We have $F_X = \{first(F_X)\} \cup L_X$. Suppose $first(F) = e(F)$ then $D(first(F_X)) \cap V = \varnothing$ so $\#e(F) = 1 + |\{x \in (F_X - \{first(F_X)\}) s.t. D(x) \cap V = \varnothing\}| = 1 + |\{x \in L_X s.t. D(x) \cap V = \varnothing\}| = 1 + \#e(L)$. By a similar reasoning we can prove the other cases. $\odot$

Definition 8 *Let C be a gcc and Q be the basic network associated with C. The constraint network* $\mathcal{R}$ *equal to Q in which the constraints in the proposition 2 have been added is called the **enhanced constraint network** associated with C.*

Finally we have the property:

Proposition 3 *Let* $C = gsc(X(C), V, min, max, q, l, u)$ *be a gsc, and* $\mathcal{R}$ *the enhanced constraint network associated with C then,* $\mathcal{R}$ *is satisfiable iff Q is satisfiable.*

The proof of this proposition follows directly from the fact that the constraints in proposition 2 are implied by the gsc.

4 Experiments for the car sequencing problem

Our experiments are done using Ilog Solver, a commercial constraint programming library that supports the definition of new constraint types.

As filtering is incomplete, i.e. it removes some inconsistent values but not every inconsistent values, the backtracking algorithm must still be used. We use a variant of the backtracking algorithm, known as MAC, where filtering is applied at each node in the search tree [PL95]. Although filtering prunes drastically the tree search, the order in which the tree is explored is very important. A poor ordering will lead to poor performance. Some very general variable orderings are quite satisfactory for random problems, such as the first-fail principle (select first the variable with the smallest domain).

For the car sequencing problem, value ordering prove to be quite important. In a previous work, Smith noted [Smi96]: "[The] variables should be assigned consecutively; leaving gaps in the sequence to be assigned later, will cause severe difficulties. Hence, any kind of dynamic variable ordering, which will leave such gaps, will increase the search."

However, her words must not be considered out of their context. In fact, Smith also noted: "there is an interaction between the implied constraints chosen, and the variable ordering: they cannot be chosen independently.". As the transformation we have proposed add implied gcc in a systematical manner, we may not suffer from the same limit. Hence, we may be able to chose different value orderings, hoping for more efficiency.

For the variable ordering we can observe that the variables at the extremities are less constrained than the variables in the middle of the global sequence. Hence, our variable ordering consists in chosing the variable closest to the middle of the sequence.

Less attention has been paid to value ordering. However, our experiments show that without careful value ordering, the difficult problems cannot be solved in a reasonable amount of time.

After some analysis of the problem, it is clear that the most difficult constraints are tied to options. However, in a standard MAC algorithm, the basic decision is to assign a value to a variable, i.e. assign a *configuration* to a car. This is not directly tied to the difficult constraints. For instance, suppose that option 1 is required by configurations 1, 2, and 3. Suppose furthermore that we assign configuration 1 to a given car, and that there will be no solution with this assignment, because of the capacity associated with option 1. Then the algorithm will backtrack, and try another value, say configuration 2. Then for the same reason (capacity of option 1) this will lead to a failure. In other words we may have a trashing behavior. This was observed experimentally on randomly generated problems taken from [Smi96].

Following this analysis, we tried a new type of value ordering: try to assign first the options for which the demand is closer to the capacity. We define the slack of an option with capacity p_j/q_j required to be scheduled k_j times, as follows:

$$n - q_j(k_j/p_j)$$

This is a good measure of the usage of the option. If the slack is negative, then the capacity constraint of the option cannot be satisfied. If the slack is large, then the capacity constraint is easy to satisfy.

Our enumeration algorithm is a combination of these two orderings that departs from the standard backtracking algorithm. Instead of selecting a variable, and then a value for it, we will proceed following a progressive reduction of the domains of the variables. Indeed, we select first the option with the smallest slack, and then we try to assign it to the variables. Assigning an option o to a variable x amounts to removing the configurations that do not use o from the domain of x. Hence this is in general a domain reduction, not an assignment per se.

More precisely, the option o_j with the smallest slack is selected. Assume this option is required k_j times. Then we try to assign this option to k variables. This requires a tree search, where the variables closest to the middle of the global sequence are tried first. After each assignment, the filtering of all constraints are applied, as in MAC. If we succeed to assign o k times, the algorithm is recursively called with a new option. If not, then there is a backtrack to the previous level of the algorithm.

Our algorithm is still a backtracking algorithm were filtering of constraints are applied at each node. The definition of nodes is different from the standard backtrack algorithm, where branches correspond to the assignment of a value to a variable. In our case, a branch corresponds to the assignment of an option to a variable, i.e. a domain reduction for that variable. Moreover a given variable can appear at different levels in the tree, as its domain can be reduceed several times. Consider for instance that configuration c_1, that requires option o_1 and o_2 is assigned to x in a given solution. Then x may appear two times in the branches leading to that solution, a first one when o_2 is assigned to it, and a second time when o_1 is assigned to x.

This algorithm thus tries to consider first the most constrained choices. Experimentally, the algorithm was able to solve some difficult instances of [Smi96] with a very small number of backtracks. Moreover, it appears that our filtering algorithm subsumes all the implied constraints proposed in [Smi96] and in [DSV88].

4.1 Results

Our approach has been applied to data given by a major car manufacturer. Unfortunately, these data cannot be disclosed. Therefore, we present one classical instance from [DSV88] (instance 0) and some random instances which have been found hard to solve (instances 1 to 4). These instances are reproduced under the permission of Barbara Smith. On the one hand, instances 0 and 3 are given as an example in the Ilog Solver 4.0 User's manual. Hence, any user of Solver 4.0 will be able to reproduce our experiments. On the other hand, we hope that these instances will be considered as a benchmark in the future.

For all instances, 100 cars have to be built, and 5 installation options are available. The capacities of the options are the same for all the instances, that is : 1/2 for option 0, 2/3 for option 1, 1/3 for option 2, 2/5 for option 3, and 1/5 for option 4. Each line of a tabular represents an option. The line number i represents the option number i. The last line represents the number of cars that must have the invoked configuration.

instance #0:

configurations																	
0	1	2	3	4	5	6	7	8	9	10	11	12	13	14	15	16	17
•	•	•		•	•	•	•					•					
•	•	•	•	•					•	•	•			•			
		•	•				•		•	•	•						•
	•		•			•			•			•				•	
•							•				•				•		
5	3	7	1	10	2	11	5	4	6	12	1	1	5	9	5	12	1

instance #1:

configurations																					
0	1	2	3	4	5	6	7	8	9	10	11	12	13	14	15	16	17	18	19	20	21
•	•	•					•		•	•		•	•			•	•	•	•	•	
	•	•	•			•	•			•		•			•		•	•			•
	•		•				•	•	•	•	•	•								•	•
•				•			•	•	•					•	•				•		•
		•										•		•		•	•	•		•	•
6	10	2	2	8	15	1	5	2	3	2	1	8	3	10	4	4	2	4	6	1	1

instance #2:

configurations																					
0	1	2	3	4	5	6	7	8	9	10	11	12	13	14	15	16	17	18	19	20	21
•			•					•	•	•	•	•		•		•	•		•	•	
		•			•		•	•	•		•	•		•		•			•	•	•
				•		•	•						•		•		•		•		•
	•		•		•	•			•	•		•				•	•		•		•
								•			•		•		•	•		•		•	
13	8	7	1	12	5	5	6	3	12	8	2	2	1	4	4	1	2	1	1	1	1

instance #3:

configurations																								
0	1	2	3	4	5	6	7	8	9	10	11	12	13	14	15	16	17	18	19	20	21	22	23	24
•	•		•		•			•	•					•	•	•	•	•	•	•				
	•	•		•		•			•	•			•	•		•	•	•			•	•	•	
		•	•		•		•		•	•	•			•				•					•	
•		•			•	•		•	•					•			•			•	•	•		
		•								•			•	•		•			•	•	•	•	•	•
7	11	1	3	15	2	8	5	3	4	5	2	6	2	2	4	3	5	2	4	1	1	1	1	2

instance #4:

configurations																						
0	1	2	3	4	5	6	7	8	9	10	11	12	13	14	15	16	17	18	19	20	21	22
					•	•			•	•		•	•	•	•	•	•				•	
		•		•	•	•		•	•			•			•	•			•		•	•
			•	•		•	•				•	•	•			•			•			•
•			•	•	•					•	•	•	•				•				•	
•	•					•	•											•		•	•	•
2	2	5	4	4	1	3	4	19	7	10	1	5	2	6	4	8	1	4	2	4	1	1

The time we give are expressed in second and mesured with Solver 4.0 with Windows NT 4.0 on a Pentium Pro 200Mhz machine. The options order column represents the order that has been chosen to select the next variable and the next value to assign. For example, for instance 0, we first consider the variables that can be instantiated to a configuration that requires option 0. If such a variable is found then this variable is instantiated to a configuration which requires option 0. If no such variables exist then we consider the variables that can be instantiated to a configuration that requires option 3 and we repeat the process

If we consider only the basic constraint network associated with each gsc, the performances of our approach dramaticly decrease. The orders we proposed are also important. After a lot of experiments we present them because we think they are the most robust. Moreover, it seems that we can prove the insatisfiability of hard instances only with the kind of order we propose. Such results are difficult to obtain for car sequencing problem and are quite important for rostering problems.

instance	options order	time	number of fails	solution
0	0 1 4 2 3	2.3	0	yes
1	0 3 4 2 1	1.9	0	yes
2	0 2 3 1 4	422	9355	no solution
3	0 4 1 2 3	3.5	41	no solution
4	?	?	?	?

Note that instance #4 remains an open problem.

5   Conclusion

In this paper we have presented a filtering algorithm for global sequencing constraints. This algorithm is powerful because it deals with a part of generality of the constraints and because it exploits the pruning performance of global cardinality constraints. Moreover, for the car sequencing problem, we have proposed new variable and value orderings. The principle of these orderings should easily be used for other problems. The experiments we made for car sequencing problem shows that our method can solve almost all the tested problem with few backtracks and proves that certain difficult instances have no solution with a small number of backtracks.

6 Acknowledgments

We would like to thank very much Barbara Smith for helpful discussions and for some hard instances of the car sequencing problem that she friendly gave us. Also, we would like to thank the reviewer Ω for useful comments on a draft of this paper.

References

[BC94]   N. Beldiceanu and E. Contejean. Introducing global constraints in chip. *Journal of Mathematical and Computer Modelling*, 20(12):97–123, 1994.

[DSV88]   M. Dincbas, H. Simonis, and P. Van Hentenryck. Solving the car-sequencing problem in constraint logic programming. In *ECAI'88, proceedings of the European Conference on Artificial Intelligence*, pages 290–295, 1988.

[Mac77]   A.K. Mackworth. Consistency in networks of relations. *Artificial Intelligence*, 8:99–118, 1977.

[Nui94]   W.P. Nuijten. *Time and Resource Constrained Scheduling: A Constraint Satisfaction Approach*. PhD thesis, Eindhoven University of Technology, 1994.

[PL95]   J-F. Puget and M. Leconte. Beyong the glass box: Constraints as objects. In John Lloyd, editor, *Logic Programming, Proceedings of the 1995 International Symposium*, pages 513–527. The MIT Press, Portland, Oregon, 1995.

[Rég94]   J-C. Régin. A filtering algorithm for constraints of difference in CSPs. In *AAAI-94, proceedings of the Twelth National Conference on Artificial Intelligence*, pages 362–367, Seattle, Washington, 1994.

[Rég96]   J-C. Régin. Generalized arc consistency for global cardinality constraint. In *AAAI-96, proceedings of the Thirteenth National Conference on Artificial Intelligence*, pages 209–215, Portland, Oregon, 1996.

[Sim96]   H. Simonis. Problem classification scheme for finite domain constraint solving. In *CP96, Workshop on Constraint Programming Applications: An Inventory and Taxonomy*, pages 1–26, Cambridge, MA, USA, 1996.

[Smi96]   B.M. Smith. Succeed-first or fail-first: A case study in variable and value ordering. In *proceedings ILOG Solver and ILOG Scheduler Second International Users' Conference*, Paris, France, 1996.

[VDT92]   P. Van Hentenryck, Y. Deville, and C.M. Teng. A generic arc-consistency algorithm and its specializations. *Artificial Intelligence*, 57:291–321, 1992.

Semantics and Expressive Power
of a Timed Concurrent Constraint Language

Frank de Boer[1], M . Gabbrielli[2] and M.C. Meo[3]

[1] Universiteit Utrecht, The Netherlands
frankb@cs.ruu.nl
[2] Università di Pisa, Italy
gabbri@di.unipi.it
[3] Università di L'Aquila, Italy
meo@univaq.it

Abstract. We consider a timed extension of concurrent constraint programming, called *tccp*. For this language we define a denotational model which is fully abstract wrt the standard notion of observables (input-output pairs). We also define a fully abstract semantics for a sublanguage of *tccp*, called *ccpx*, which essentially is standard concurrent constraint programming (*ccp*), provided that we interpret the parallel operator in terms of "maximal parallelism" rather than of interleaving. Finally we compare the expressive power of these languages. We show that *tccp* is strictly more expressive than *ccpx* which, in its turn, is strictly more expressive than *ccp*.

1 Introduction

Many "real-life" computer applications which maintain some ongoing interaction with external physical processes involve time-critical aspects. Such applications, so called real-time systems, thus require appropriate languages which allow for the specification of such timing constraints as that a signal is required within a bounded time interval. Several concurrent imperative languages based on synchronous communication have been specifically designed for modeling real-time systems [1, 8, 9, 11]. These languages are based on the *perfect synchrony* hypothesis: A program reacts to the input signals by producing *instantly* the required output.

Recently several declarative languages based on constraints have been proposed for modeling real-time applications. Timing primitives can be defined in Oz [20] and real-time extensions of the asynchronous concurrent language *ccp* have been introduced in [17, 18, 2]. In particular, these languages resulting from ccp extensions are built around the hypothesis of *bounded asynchrony* [17]: Computation takes a bounded period of time rather than being instantaneous and the whole system evolves in cycles corresponding to time units. However, while in [17] a time unit is identified with the time needed for a (deterministic) *ccp* process to terminate a computation and the passing of time is explicitly modeled by a temporal next operator, in [2] we introduced directly a timed interpretation of the usual programming constructs of *ccp* by fixing the time needed for the execution of the basic actions of *ccp* as one time unit and interpreting action prefixing as the next operator. An explicit timing primitive was also introduced in order to allow for the specification of the previously mentioned timing constraints, so called time-outs. The resulting language, called *tccp*, provides a natural timed extension of *ccp*. In particular, differently from the language in [17], it does not require explicit transfer of information across time boundaries, allows for non-determinism and has a simple semantics for the hiding operator.

In this paper we first define a denotational model for *tccp*, based on sequences of pair of constraints, which is fully abstract wrt the input/output notion of observables. Intuitively, each pair $\langle c_i, d_i \rangle$ represents a computation step performed by the agent A which, at time i, assuming c_i as input constraint produces the constraint d_i. This model is similar to existing ones for imperative languages [5] and ccp [3]. However, the presence of a timed interpretation for the language constructs introduces new issues when considering the problem of full abstraction. In fact, the parallel operator in *tccp* is interpreted in terms of "maximal parallelism", i.e. at each moment every enabled agent of the system is activated. This interpretation is natural when considering a language for real-time applications and it is different from the one of standard ccp, where parallelism is interpreted in terms of interleaving. This fact, together with the presence of an explicit timing primitive, forbids us to use the results and techniques which already exist for ccp [3]. Indeed, in order to obtain full abstraction, we also need some further assumptions on the constraint system.

We then consider full abstraction for the language *ccpx*, obtained from *tccp* by dropping the explicit timing primitive. Also in this case we cannot apply the usual ccp results and we need further assumptions on the constraint system. This is worth noticing, since *ccpx* is essentially standard *ccp*, provided that $\|$ is interpreted in terms of maximal parallelism rather than of interleaving.

In the second part of the paper we compare the expressive power of the languages *tccp*, *ccpx* an *ccp*. Intuitively, a (programming) language $\mathcal{L}$ is more expressive than a language $\mathcal{L}'$ if each program written in $\mathcal{L}'$ can be translated into an $\mathcal{L}$ program in such a way that the intended observable behavior of the original program is preserved. This notion has been formalized under the name of *embedding* as follows [15]. Consider two languages $\mathcal{L}$ and $\mathcal{L}'$ and let $\mathcal{P}_\mathcal{L}$ and $\mathcal{P}_{\mathcal{L}'}$ denote the set of the programs which can be written in $\mathcal{L}$ and in $\mathcal{L}'$, respectively. Assume that the meaning of programs is given by two functions (observables) $\mathcal{O} : \mathcal{P}_\mathcal{L} \to Obs$ and $\mathcal{O}' : \mathcal{P}_{\mathcal{L}'} \to Obs'$ which associate to each program the set of its observable properties (thus Obs and Obs' are assumed being some suitable powersets). Then we say that $\mathcal{L}$ is more expressive than $\mathcal{L}'$, or equivalently that $\mathcal{L}'$ can be embedded into $\mathcal{L}$, if there exist a mapping $\mathcal{C} : \mathcal{P}_{\mathcal{L}'} \to \mathcal{P}_\mathcal{L}$ (compiler) and a mapping $\mathcal{D} : Obs \to Obs'$ (decoder) such that, for each program P' in $\mathcal{P}_{\mathcal{L}'}$, the following equality holds

$$\mathcal{D}(\mathcal{O}(\mathcal{C}(P'))) = \mathcal{O}'(P').$$

Clearly, as discussed in [15, 4], in order order to use the notion of embedding as a tool for language comparison some further restrictions should be imposed on the decoder, on the compiler and on the notion of observables. Otherwise previous equation would satisfied by any Turing complete language, provided that we choose a powerful enough $\mathcal{O}$ for the target language. Usually these conditions indicate how easy is the translation process and how reasonable is the decoder (for example, often $\mathcal{C}$ is required to be compositional wrt the operators of the language). Since we are mainly interested in separation results which express the non embeddability of a language into another, we will consider rather weak assumptions on $\mathcal{C}$ and $\mathcal{D}$ (they are weaker than those used in [4]).

The technique that we use for separating different languages is a simplification of that one used in [4] and essentially consists in exhibiting a property of the operational semantics which holds for the target language $\mathcal{L}$ and not for the source one $\mathcal{L}'$. We show that *tccp* cannot be embedded in *ccpx* and in *ccp* when considering a very general class of observables which covers all the properties derivable from finite computations. Differently from the case of [4], we do not have to consider termination modes in this case. Termination modes are used to establish our second separation result which shows that *ccpx* cannot be embedded into *ccp*.

2 The *tccp* language

In this section we introduce the *tccp* language defined in [2] and provide its operational semantics via a transition system.

As any other language of the *ccp* family, *tccp* is defined parametrically wrt to a given *constraint system*. The notion of constraint system has been formalized in [16] following Scott's treatment of information systems and using some ideas from cylindric algebras. We refer to [16] for the deatils of such a formalization. Here we recall that a constraint system $C = \langle \mathcal{C}, \leq, \sqcup, true, false, Var, \exists_x, d_{xy} \rangle$ is a a a complete algebraic lattice (where $\sqcup$ is the lub operation, *true* and *false* are the least and the greatest elements, respectively) augmented with functions $\exists_x : \mathcal{C} \rightarrow \mathcal{C}$ for each variable $x \in Var$[4] and where $\mathcal{C}$ contains elements d_{xy} (so called diagonal elements) for each pair of variables $x, y \in Var$. The functions $\exists_x$ and the diagonal elements are defined by the following axioms

(i) $c \vdash \exists_x(c)$,
(ii) if $c \vdash d$ then $\exists_x(c) \vdash \exists_x(d)$,
(iii) $\exists_x(c \sqcup \exists_x(d)) = \exists_x(c) \sqcup \exists_x(d)$,
(iv) $\exists_x(\exists_y(c)) = \exists_y(\exists_x(c))$.
(v) $true \vdash d_{xx}$,
(vi) if $z \neq x, y$ then $d_{xy} = \exists_z(d_{xz} \sqcup d_{zy})$,
(vii) if $x \neq y$ then $d_{xy} \sqcup \exists_x(c \sqcup d_{xy}) \vdash c$.

which give them the flavour of existential quantification and of equalities, respectively. Indeed, $\exists_x$ is used to model the hiding operator of the language while diagonal elements allow to model the parameter passing mechanism. In the sequel we will identify a system C with its underlying set of constraints $\mathcal{C}$ and we will denote $\exists_x(c)$ by $\exists_x c$.

The basic idea underlying *ccp* is that computation progresses via monotonic accumulation of information in a global store. Information is produced by the concurrent and asynchronous activity of several agents which can add (*tell*) a constraint to the store. Dually, agents can also check (*ask*) whether a constraint is entailed by the store, thus allowing synchronization among different agents. Parallel composition in *ccp* is modeled by the interleaving of the basic actions of its components.

When querying the store for some information which is not present (yet) a *ccp* agent will simply suspend until the required information has arrived. In real-time applications however often one cannot wait indefinitely for an event. Consider for example the case of a bank teller machine. Once a card is accepted, the machine asks the authorization of the bank to release the requested money. If the authorization does not arrive within a reasonable amount of time, then the card should be given back to the customer. A real-time language should then allow us to specify that, in case a given time bound is exceeded (i.e. a *time-out* occurs), the wait is interrupted and an alternative action is taken. Moreover in some cases it is also necessary to abort an active process A and to start a process B when a specific event occurs (this is usually called *preemption* of A). For example, according to a typical pattern, A is the process controlling the normal activity of some physical device, the event indicates some abnormal situation and B is the exception handler.

In order to be able to specify these timing constraints in *ccp*, in [2] the *tccp* language was designed by introducing a discrete global clock and assuming that *ask* and *tell* actions take one time-unit. Computation evolves in steps of one time-unit, so called clock-cycles, and action prefixing is considered the syntactic marker which distinguishes a time instant from the next one. Furthermore it is assumed that parallel processes are executed on different processors, which implies that at each moment every enabled agent of the system is activated. This assumption gives rise to what is called *maximal parallelism*. The time in

---

[4] We assume that there exists a denumerable set of variables *Var* with typical elements $x, y \ldots$

between two successive moments of the global clock intuitively corresponds to the response time of the underlying constraint system. Thus essentially in this model all parallel agents are synchronized by the response time of the underlying constraint system. On the basis of the above assumptions a timing construct of the form **now** c **then** A **else** B was introduced which can be interpreted as follows: If the constraint c is entailed by the store at the current time t then the above agent behaves as A at time t, otherwise it behaves as B at time t. As shown in [2, 17] this basic construct allows one to derive such timing mechanisms as time-out and preemption. Thus we have the following syntax for *tccp*:

Definition 1 *tccp* **Language.** Assuming a given cylindric constraint system C the syntax of *tccp agents* is given by the following grammar:

$$A ::= \textbf{stop} \mid \text{tell}(c) \rightarrow A \mid \sum_{i=1}^{n} \text{ask}(c_i) \rightarrow A_i \mid \textbf{now } c \textbf{ then } A \textbf{ else } B \mid A \parallel B \mid \exists x A \mid p(x)$$

where the c, c_i are supposed to be *finite constraints* (i.e. algebraic elements) in C. A *tccp program* P is then an object of the form $D.A$, where D is a set of procedure declarations of the form $p(x) : -A$ and A is an agent. Moreover we will denote by *ccpx* the language obtained by dropping the *now then else* construct in the previous definition.

Action prefixing is denoted by $\rightarrow$, non-determinism is introduced via the guarded choice construct $\sum_{i=1}^{n} \text{ask}(c_i) \rightarrow A_i$, parallel composition is denoted by $\parallel$, and a notion of locality is introduced by the agent $\exists x A$ which behaves like A with x considered local to A, thus hiding the information on x provided by the external environment. We will often use $+$ to denote $\sum_{i=1}^{2}$. We assume that the declarations do no contain multiple declarations of the same procedure variable and do not contain free procedure variables (that is all the procedure variables occurring in the agent A, with $p(x) : -A \in D$ are defined in D). Moreover in the sequel when referring to an agent A a set of declarations D is always implicitly assumed.

The operational model of *tccp* can be formally described by a transition system $T = (Conf, \longrightarrow)$ where we assume that each transition step takes exactly one time-unit. Configurations (in) *Conf* are pairs consisting of an agent and a constraint in C representing the common *store*. The transition relation $\longrightarrow \subseteq Conf \times Conf$ is the least relation satisfying the rules R1-R11 in Table 1 and characterizes the (temporal) evolution of the system. So, $\langle A, c \rangle \longrightarrow \langle B, d \rangle$ means that if at time t we have the agent A and the store c then at time $t + 1$ we have the agent B and the store d.

It is worth noting that, according to Rules R7 and R8, the parallel composition operator is modeled in terms of *maximal parallelism*: The agent $A \parallel B$ executes in one time-unit all the initial enabled actions of A and B. Thus, for example, the agent $A :$ $(ask(c) \rightarrow stop) \parallel (tell(c) \rightarrow stop)$ evaluated in the store c will (successfully) terminate in one time-unit, while the same agent in the empty store will take two time-units to terminate. To describe locality in rule R9 the syntax has been extended by an agent $\exists^d x A$ where d is a local store of A containing information on x which is hidden in the external store. Initially the local store is empty, i.e. $\exists x A = \exists^{true} x A$.

Using the transition system we can define the following (standard) notion of observables which considers the input/output of terminating computations, including the deadlocked ones. Here and in the sequel $\longrightarrow^*$ denotes the reflexive and transitive closure of the relation $\longrightarrow$.

Definition 2. Let A be an agent. We define $\mathcal{O}_{io}(A) = \{\langle c, d \rangle \mid \langle A, c \rangle \longrightarrow^* \langle B, d \rangle \nrightarrow \}$.

$$\mathbf{R1} \quad \langle \mathbf{tell}(c) \to A, c \rangle \longrightarrow \langle A, c \sqcup d \rangle$$

$$\mathbf{R2} \quad \langle \textstyle\sum_{i=1}^{n} \mathbf{ask}(c_i) \to A_i, d \rangle \longrightarrow \langle A_j, d \rangle \qquad j \in [1, n] \text{ and } d \vdash c_j$$

$$\mathbf{R3} \quad \frac{\langle A, d \rangle \longrightarrow \langle A', d' \rangle}{\langle \mathbf{now}\ c\ \mathbf{then}\ A\ \mathbf{else}\ B, d \rangle \longrightarrow \langle A', d' \rangle} \quad d \vdash c$$

$$\mathbf{R4} \quad \frac{\langle A, d \rangle \not\longrightarrow}{\langle \mathbf{now}\ c\ \mathbf{then}\ A\ \mathbf{else}\ B, d \rangle \longrightarrow \langle A, d \rangle} \quad d \vdash c$$

$$\mathbf{R5} \quad \frac{\langle B, d \rangle \longrightarrow \langle B', d' \rangle}{\langle \mathbf{now}\ c\ \mathbf{then}\ A\ \mathbf{else}\ B, d \rangle \longrightarrow \langle B', d' \rangle} \quad d \not\vdash c$$

$$\mathbf{R6} \quad \frac{\langle B, d \rangle \not\longrightarrow}{\langle \mathbf{now}\ c\ \mathbf{then}\ A\ \mathbf{else}\ B, d \rangle \longrightarrow \langle B, d \rangle} \quad d \not\vdash c$$

$$\mathbf{R7} \quad \frac{\langle A, c \rangle \longrightarrow \langle A', c' \rangle \quad \langle B, c \rangle \longrightarrow \langle B', d' \rangle}{\langle A \parallel B, c \rangle \longrightarrow \langle A' \parallel B', c' \sqcup d' \rangle}$$

$$\mathbf{R8} \quad \frac{\langle A, c \rangle \longrightarrow \langle A', c' \rangle \quad \langle B, c \rangle \not\longrightarrow}{\substack{\langle A \parallel B, c \rangle \longrightarrow \langle A' \parallel B, c' \rangle \\ \langle B \parallel A, c \rangle \longrightarrow \langle B \parallel A', c' \rangle}}$$

$$\mathbf{R9} \quad \frac{\langle A, d \sqcup \exists_x c \rangle \longrightarrow \langle B, d' \rangle}{\langle \exists^d x A, c \rangle \longrightarrow \langle \exists^{d'} x B, c \sqcup \exists_x d' \rangle}$$

$$\mathbf{R10} \quad \langle p(y), c \rangle \longrightarrow \langle \exists^{d_{xy}} x A, c \rangle \qquad p(x) :: A \in D,\ x \neq y$$

$$\mathbf{R11} \quad \langle p(x), c \rangle \longrightarrow \langle A, c \rangle \qquad p(x) :: A \in D$$

Table 1. The transition system for *tccp*.

3 The denotational model

The operational semantics which associates to an agent A its observables $\mathcal{O}_{io}(A)$ is not compositional. A compositional characterization of the operational semantics can be obtained by using sequences of pairs of finite constraints, so called *timed reactive sequences*, to represent *tccp* computations.

Here we describe a denotational model which associates to an agent a set of sequences, thus differing from the one given in [2] which used functions from sequences to sequences as denotations. The model in [2] is fully abstract when observing traces obtained by the partial results of computations. Unfortunately, on the contrary of what was stated in [2], such a result cannot be extended directly to the case of the input/output observables.

In our setting, a timed reactive sequence has the form $\langle c_1, d_1 \rangle \cdots \langle c_n, d_n \rangle \langle d, d \rangle$ and represents a computation of a *tccp* agent. Intuitively, a pair of constraints $\langle c_i, d_i \rangle$ represents a computation step performed by the agent A which, at time i, transforms the global store from c_i to d_i. The last pair indicate that we have reached a "resting point", i.e. that given the input d the agent does not produce any further information. Since in

---

D0 $[stop] = \{\langle c_1, c_1 \rangle \langle c_2, c_2 \rangle \cdots \langle c_n, c_n \rangle \in S \mid n \geq 1\}$

D1 $[tell(c) \to A] = \{\langle d, d \sqcup c \rangle \cdot s \in S \mid s \in [A]\}$

D2 $[\sum_{i=1}^{n} ask(c_i) \to A_i] = \{s \cdot s' \in S \mid s = \langle d_1, d_1 \rangle \cdots \langle d_m, d_m \rangle$
$\quad\quad d_j \nvdash c_i \text{ for each } j \in [1, m\text{-}1], i \in [1, n],$
$\quad\quad d_m \vdash c_h \text{ and } s' \in [A_h] \text{ for an } h \in [1, n]\}$

$\quad \cup$

$\quad\quad \{s \in S \mid s = \langle d_1, d_1 \rangle \cdots \langle d_m, d_m \rangle$
$\quad\quad d_j \nvdash c_i \text{ for each } j \in [1, m], i \in [1, n]\}$

D3 $[\textbf{now } c \textbf{ then } A \textbf{ else } B] = \{s \in S \mid s = \langle c', d \rangle \cdot s' \text{ and either}$
$\quad\quad c' \vdash c \text{ and } s \in [A] \text{ or } c' \nvdash c \text{ and } s \in [B]\}$

D4 $[A \parallel B] = [A] \; \bar{\parallel} \; [B]$

D5 $[\exists x A] = \{s \in S \mid \text{there exists } s' \in [A] \text{ such that}$
$\quad\quad \exists_x s = \exists_x s', s' \text{ is x-connected and } s \text{ is x-invariant}\}$

D6 $[p(y)] = [\exists x (tell(d_{xy}) \to p(x))]$ $\quad\quad\quad\quad p(x) : -A \in D, \; x \neq y$

D7 $[p(x)] = [tell(true) \to A]$ $\quad\quad\quad\quad\quad\quad p(x) : -A \in D$

Table 2. Denotational semantics of *tccp*

tccp computations the store evolves monotonically, it is natural to assume that reactive sequences are monotonically increasing. So in the following we will assume that each timed reactive sequence $\langle c_1, d_1 \rangle \cdots \langle c_{n-1}, d_{n-1} \rangle \langle c_n, c_n \rangle$ satisfies the following condition: $d_i \vdash c_i$ and $c_j \vdash d_{j-1}$. for any $i \in [1, n-1]$ and $j \in [2, n]$.

Since the constraints arising from computation steps are finite, we also assume that a reactive sequence contains only finite constraints[5]. The set of all reactive sequences will be denoted by S and its typical elements by $s, s_1 \ldots$.

The denotational model is defined by the equations in Table 2 by using a standard least fixpoint construction based on the cpo $(\wp(S), \subseteq)$. Given two sequences s and s', we denote by $s \cdot s'$ the sequence resulting from the concatenation of s and s'.

Definition 3 Denotational semantics. The denotational semantics $[\,] : Agents \to S$ is the least function, wrt the ordering induced by $\subseteq$, which satisfies the equations in Table 2.

Before giving the correctness and full abstraction results let us briefly discuss the equations and the related notations. The agent **Stop** cannot perform any computation step, so the result of a computation for **Stop** with input constraint c is always c. Therefore,

---

[5] Note that here we implicitly assume that if c is a finite element then also $\exists_x c$ is finite. This is however a natural assumption, since the agent $\exists_x tell(c)$ produces the same result as $tell(\exists_x c)$. So if the first agent is allowed by the syntax (being c finite) also the second one should be allowed.

the denotation of **Stop** consists of all the finite sequences of "stuttering steps" of the form $\langle c_1, c_1\rangle \cdots \langle c_n, c_n\rangle$, which contain only the information provided by the input constraints c_i's. Equation **D1** shows that the effect of a *tell(c)* action is the addition of c to the current store. The addition of a pair to the sequence s' representing a computation of A corresponds to the assumption that the evaluation of *tell(c)* in the agent $\mathbf{tell}(c) \rightarrow A$ takes one time unit. Equation **D2** shows that a computation of $\sum_i \mathbf{ask}(c_i) \rightarrow A_i$ has an initial period of waiting for (a constraint stronger than) one of the constraints c_i. During this waiting period only the environment is active by producing the constraints d_i while the process itself generates the stuttering steps $\langle d_i, d_i\rangle$. Also in this case the addition of a pair $\langle d_i, d_i\rangle$ corresponds to the assumption that the evaluation of an ask action takes one time-unit. Here however we can add several pairs since the external environment can take several time-units to produce the required constraint. When the contribution of the environment is strong enough to entail a c_h, then the agent A_h is evaluated thus producing a sequence s'. The resulting sequence is then obtained by adding s' to the initial waiting period. According to equation **D3**, a sequence s in the denotation of **now** c **then** A **else** B corresponds to a computation of A, if the initial store (c') entails c, to a computation for B otherwise. To describe denotationally the parallel composition we use the (commutative) partial operator $\bar{\|} \in \mathcal{S} \times \mathcal{S} \rightarrow \mathcal{S}$ defined as follows:

$$\langle c_1, d_1\rangle \cdots \langle c_n, d_n\rangle \cdot \langle d, d\rangle \bar{\|} \langle c_1, e_1\rangle \cdots \langle c_n, e_n\rangle \cdot \langle d, d\rangle = \langle c_1, d_1 \sqcup e_1\rangle \cdots \langle c_n, d_n \sqcup e_n\rangle \cdot \langle d, d\rangle.$$

Note that we require that the two arguments of the parallel operator agree at each point of time with respect to the contribution of the environment (the c_i's) and that they have the same length (in all other cases the parallel composition is assumed being undefined). The operator $\|$ used in equation **D4** is the obvious extension of the above defined operator to set of sequences. In equation **D5**, in order to define the denotation of $\exists x A$, given a sequence s' representing a computation for A we first check that s' is x-connected, i.e. that no information on x is present in the input constraints of s' which has not been already accumulated by the computation of the agent A itself. This reflects the fact that, when considering the computation for $\exists x A$, the information on x produced by the external environment is hided. Formally, given a sequence $s' = \langle c_1, d_1\rangle \cdots \langle c_n, c_n\rangle$, we say that s' is x-connected if (i) $\exists_x c_1 = c_1$ (that is, the input constraint of s' does not contain information on x) and (ii) $\exists_x c_i \sqcup d_{i-1} = c_i$ for each $i \in [2, n]$.

Then we construct the resulting sequence s by assuming that its computation steps do not provide more information on x. This reflects the fact that the information produced by A on x is hided to the external environment and is formalized by assuming that s is x-invariant, i.e. that for all computation steps $\langle c, d\rangle$ of s, $d = \exists_x d \sqcup c$ holds.

Finally we consider the contribution of the external environment up to the information on x, i.e. we require that $\exists_x s = \exists_x s'$ where $\exists_x s$ denotes the sequence resulting from the pointwise application of $\exists_x$ to the constraints appearing in the sequence s. Recursion is modeled, as usual, by a least fixpoint construction. In rule **D6** the diagonal element d_{xy} performs the parameter passing, while in rule **D7** we have a simple body replacement, since the formal and actual parameter coincide. The correctness of this semantic model is expressed by the following.

Theorem 4 Correctness. *For any agent A we have*

$$\mathcal{O}_{io}(A) = \{\langle c, d\rangle \mid \text{ there exists } \langle c, d_1\rangle\langle c_2, d_2\rangle \cdots \langle c_n, d\rangle\langle d, d\rangle \in [\![A]\!]$$
$$\text{such that } c_i = d_{i-1} \text{ for each } i \in [2, n]\}.$$

Note that a sequence of the form $\langle c, d_1 \rangle \langle d_1, d_2 \rangle \cdots \langle d_{n-1}, d \rangle \langle d, d \rangle$, called a connected sequence, represents a computation for an agent where c is the input constraint and, at each time instant, the assumed contributions of the environment have been already produced by the agent itself. The last pair $\langle d, d \rangle$ ensures us that the computation has reached a "resting point", where no further information can be produced.

3.1 Full abstraction for *tccp*

The previous model however introduces unnecessary distinctions, since it distinguishes *tccp* agents whose observables (as defined by $\mathcal{O}_{io}$) are the same under any possible context. This is shown by the following example. Here and in the following a context $C[\ ]$ is simply an agent with a 'hole'. The agent $C[A]$ then represents the result of replacing the hole in $C[\ ]$ by A.

Example 1. Consider the *tccp* agents

$$A : ask(true) \to C \quad \text{and} \quad B : ask(true) \to C$$
$$+$$
$$ask(true) \to D$$

where C and D are the agents

$$C : tell(c) \to (ask(d) \to stop \quad \text{and} \quad D : tell(true) \to (ask(d) \to stop$$
$$+ \qquad\qquad\qquad\qquad\qquad\qquad +$$
$$ask(true) \to loop) \qquad\qquad\qquad ask(true) \to loop)$$

with $d \geq c$, $c \neq d$ and where *loop* is defined by the declaration $loop : - ask(true) \to loop$. We have $[\![A]\!] \neq [\![B]\!]$, since $\langle true, true \rangle \langle true, true \rangle \langle d, d \rangle \in [\![A]\!] \setminus [\![B]\!]$. However the agents A and B cannot be distinguished by any *tccp* context. In fact, since A "contains" B, clearly $\mathcal{O}_{io}(C[B]) \subseteq \mathcal{O}_{io}(C[A])$ for any context $C[\ ]$. Moreover, *because of maximal parallelism*, also the other inclusion holds. Intuitively, if the agent D produces a result in the context $C'[\ ]$, the constraint d required by the $ask(d)$ guard must be provided by the external environment $C'[\ ]$ at the same time in which the $tell(true)$ is performed (otherwise the rule of maximal parallelism forces the computation to enter the loop branch). Since $c \leq d$, clearly if we replace $tell(true)$ by $tell(c)$ we cannot observe any difference. So also the agent C can be successfully evaluated in $C'[\ ]$ and it produces the same result as D.

Note that, in the above example, the presence of $+$ and of the "loop" agent in the definition of C and D is essential. In fact it is easy to see that if either the branch $ask(true) \to loop$ is missing or *loop* is replaced by a terminating agent then A and B could be distinguished by simply considering either the empty context or a context of the form $[\ ] \parallel ask(true) \to (ask(c) \to tell(ok) + ask(true) \to tell(nok))$. It is also worth noticing that A and B as defined above could be distinguished when considering *ccp* rather than *tccp*, since in *ccp* parallelism is interpreted in terms of interleaving.

In order to identify agents like the previous ones and to obtain full abstraction wrt $\mathcal{O}_{io}$ we need to define a suitable abstraction on denotations. Following the standard practice, we define such an abstraction by introducing an operation which "saturates" the denotation of an agent by adding all those sequences which do not give raise to new observables under any context. However, differently from the standard ccp setting we need two further assumptions.

We require that the constraint systems is a finitary domain, i.e. that for each finite (algebraic) element $c_0 \in C$ the set $\{d_0 \mid d_0 \leq c_0 \text{ and } d_0 \text{ is finite }\}$ is finite. Note that this assumption, which is satisfied by many constraint systems, implies that if c_0 is finite then $\exists_x c_0$ is finite, as required before. Moreover, we assume that the constraint system is weakly relative pseudo-complemented. Weak relative pseudo-complement has been defined in [7] for (semi-) lattices by relaxing the standard notion of relative pseudo-complement. In our setting, a constraint system C is weakly relative pseudo-complemented if for each pair c, d of constraints in C such that $c \leq d$, there exists a (unique) constraint $d \setminus c$ (called the weak relative pseudo-complement of c wrt d) such that

1. $c \sqcup (d \setminus c) = d$ and
2. if $c \sqcup d' = d$ for some d' then $(d \setminus c) \leq d'$.

Assuming that the constraint system satisfies previous properties we can simply define the saturation condition as follows.

Definition 5 Saturation. Let s, s' be reactive sequences. Then we define $s \preceq s'$ (s is less connected than s') iff for some sequences s_1 and s_2 we have $s = s_1 \cdot \langle a, b \rangle \langle c, d \rangle \cdot s_2$, $s' = s_1 \cdot \langle a, b' \rangle \langle c, d \rangle \cdot s_2$ and $(c \setminus b') \leq (c \setminus b)$ holds. Moreover we define the (equivalence) relation $\simeq$ as follows: $s \simeq s'$ iff the sequence s and s' differ only in the number of repetitions of the last element. Given a set of reactive sequences S, we denote by $\alpha(S)$ the least set S' such that the following hold:

(i) $S \subseteq S'$,
(ii) if $s' \in S'$ and either $s \preceq s'$ or $s \simeq s'$, then $s \in S$.

So, given a set of sequences S, the saturation α is defined pointwise on S and adds all those sequences which differ from those already in S either in the number of "stuttering" steps at the end, or in the fact that they are "less connected". Intuitively, the fact that s is less connected than s' means that the gaps existing between what is produced (d_i) and what is assumed at the next time instant (c_{i+1}) are bigger in s than in s'. In other words, when composing sequences via the $\|$ operator, s needs more "tell" contributions than s' in order to obtain a connected sequence. For this reason, the less connected sequences can be added safely to the semantics without affecting its correctness.

The semantics $\alpha(\llbracket A \rrbracket)$ identifies the agents A and B of previous example, since $\langle true, true \rangle \langle true, c \rangle \langle d, d \rangle \in \llbracket B \rrbracket$ from which we can derive that $\langle true, true \rangle \langle true, true \rangle \langle d, d \rangle \in \alpha(\llbracket B \rrbracket)$. It can be easily verified that the semantics $\alpha(\llbracket A \rrbracket)$ resulting from previous saturation is still correct (α does not introduce any connected sequence) and compositional. Moreover, we have the following result.

Theorem 6 Full abstraction. *Assume that the constraint system is weakly relative pseudo-complemented. Then, for any pair of tccp agents A and B, $\alpha(\llbracket A \rrbracket) = \alpha(\llbracket B \rrbracket)$ iff $\mathcal{O}_{io}(C[A]) = \mathcal{O}_{io}(C[B])$ for each context $C[\cdot]$.*

The proof of the above theorem is omitted for space reasons. However it is worth noting that it is quite different from the full abstraction proof of ccp [3]. In fact in that case the proof is based on the construction of a distinguishin context which recognize a sequence s by simply "mirroring" it, i.e. by asking what s tells and telling what s asks. Since ccp has an interleaving model for $\|$, when composing (in parallel) s and its "mirror image" we can simply alternate their actions and therefore produce an observable result. Here, because of maximal parallelism, in order to construct a distinguishing context we need to assume that the constraint system is weakly relative pseudo-complemented: The idea is simply that if $\langle c_i, d_i \rangle \langle c_{i+1}, d_{i+1} \rangle$ appears in the sequence s then the "mirror sequence" now contains $\langle c_i, c_{i+1} \setminus d_i \rangle \langle c_{i+1}, true \rangle \ldots$, i.e. the mirror sequence filles the gaps which are present in the sequence s.

It is worth noting that assuming only that the constraint system is a complete lattice (without any further requirement) and assuming that the correctness result has the form of Theorem 4, full abstraction cannot be obtained by using a saturation condition which is defined pointwise on set of sequences obtained from the semantics $[\![\,]\!]$. This is the content of the following.

Proposition 7. *Let* C *be the constraint system* $\langle \{\, true, d_1, d_2, d_3, false \,\}, \leq, \sqcup, true, false \rangle$ *where* d_1, d_2 *and* d_3 *are not comparable. Then there exists no* $\alpha : \wp(S) \to \wp(S)$ *such that the following hold:*

1. *$\alpha(S) = \bigcup_{s \in S} \alpha'(s)$ for some function α',*
2. *$\alpha([\![\,]\!])$ is fully abstract,*
3. *if $\langle c_1, d_1 \rangle \ldots \langle c_n, d_n \rangle$ is a connected sequence in $\alpha([\![A]\!])$ then $\langle c_1, d_n \rangle \in \mathcal{O}_{io}(A)$.*

3.2 Full abstraction for *ccp* with maximal parallelism

In this section we consider the full abstraction problem for the language *ccpx* obtained from *tccp* by dropping the *now then else* statement. Being *ccpx* a sublanguage of *tccp* clearly the semantics $\alpha([\![A]\!])$ is still correct when considering *ccpx*. However, it is easy to see that it is not anymore fully asbtract. In fact we now then need a stronger saturation (i.e. one which identifies more) than the previous one. We assume now that the constraint system is relatively pseudo-complemented, i.e. that for each pair c, d of constraints in C such that $c \leq d$, there exists a (unique) constraint $d \setminus c$[6] (called the relative pseudo-complement of c wrt d) such that

1. $c \sqcup (d \setminus c) \geq d$ and
2. if $c \sqcup d' \geq d$ for some d' then $(d \setminus c) \leq d'$.

Note that if a lattice is relatively pseudo-complemented then it is also weakly relatively pseudo-complemented, while in general the converse does not need to hold [7]. The saturation on sets of sequences is now defined as follows.

Definition 8. *Let* s *and* s' *be reactive sequences. We define* $s \preceq' s'$ *(s is less connected than s') iff for some sequences s_1 and s_2 we have $s = s_1 \cdot \langle a, b \rangle \langle c, d \rangle \cdot s_2$, $s' = s_1 \cdot \langle a, b' \rangle \langle c', d \rangle \cdot s_2$, $c' \vdash c$ and $(c' \setminus b') \leq (c \setminus b)$ holds. Given a set of reactive sequences S, we denote by $\beta(S)$ the least set S' such that the following hold:*

(i) $S \subseteq S'$,
(ii) *if $s' \in S'$ and either $s \preceq' s'$ or $s \simeq s'$, then $s \in S'$ ($\simeq$ is defined as in Definition 5).*

The semantics given by $\beta([\![A]\!])$ is still correct (also in this case the abstraction β does not introduce new connected sequences) and compositional (this is proved by using the additional conditions used in the definition of β). Moreover, we have the following.

Theorem 9 Full abstraction. *Assume that C is relatively pseudo-complemented. Then, for any pair of tccp agents A and B, $\beta([\![A]\!]) = \beta([\![B]\!])$ iff $\mathcal{O}_{io}(C[A]) = \mathcal{O}_{io}(C[B])$ for each context $C[\cdot]$.*

---

[6] For the sake of simplicity we use here the same notation used for weak relative pseudo-complement.

4 Comparing *tccp* and *ccp* with maximal parallelism

Clearly *ccpx* can be embedded into *tccp*, being the former a sublanguage of the latter. As for the other direction, intuitively the presence of the *now then else* construct should augment the expressivity of the language, since it allows to check also for the absence of information. We provide now a formal justification for this intuition by showing that *tccp* cannot be embedded into *ccpx*. As a corollary, we obtain also that *tccp* cannot be embedded into standard *ccp*.

In this section we will consider the following general abstract notion of observables $\mathcal{O}_\alpha$ which essentially distinguishes finite computations from infinite ones. Since our separation results are given wrt $\mathcal{O}_\alpha$, they hold for any notion of observables which can be obtained as instance of $\mathcal{O}_\alpha$.

Definition 10. Let A be a generic (either *tccp* or *ccpx*) agent. We define

$$\mathcal{O}_\alpha(A) = \{\theta \mid \text{ there exists } c \in C \text{ s.t. } \langle A, c \rangle \longrightarrow^* \langle B, d \rangle \not\longrightarrow \text{ and } \theta = \alpha(\langle A, c \rangle \cdots \langle B, d \rangle) \}$$

where α is any total (abstraction) function from the set of sequences of configurations to a suitable set (the domain of observables).

Note that any observable property which can be extracted from finite computations (e.g. input/output pairs, traces etc.) can be obtained as an instance of $\mathcal{O}_\alpha$, by suitably defining α. In the following we denote by $\mathcal{A}_t$ and by $\mathcal{A}_x$ the *ccp* and *ccpx* agents, respectively, and we will assume that the observables $\mathcal{O}_t : \mathcal{A}_t \to Obs_t$ and $\mathcal{O}_x : \mathcal{A}_x \to Obs_x$ are both instances of $\mathcal{O}_\alpha$ (so, as resulting from previous definition, both Obs_t and Obs_x are some suitable powersets).

When translating programs, in general it is quite natural to require that the decoder (of the results) cannot extract any information from an empty set and, conversely, that it cannot cancel all the information contained in a set. Therefore we will require that

(i) $\forall O \in Obs_x$, $\mathcal{D}(O) = \emptyset$ iff $O = \emptyset$.

This assumption is weaker than those made in [4], where it was assumed that the decoder is defined pointwise on the set of observable properties and that it preserves the (success, failure or deadlock) termination modes.

As for the compilation process, in general it is also natural to require modular compilation of parallel agents, i.e. to require compositionality of $\mathcal{C}$ wrt the $\|$ operator. In our case, having the source and the target language the same $\|$ operator, it is natural to preserve it during the translation. So, as in [4], we assume that

(ii) $\mathcal{C}(A \parallel B) = \mathcal{C}(A) \parallel \mathcal{C}(B)$.

In order to separate *tccp* and *ccpx* we exhibit now a semantic property of the abstract observables which holds for the target language (*ccpx*) and not for the source one (*tccp*).

As for *ccpx*, it is easy to verify that if there exists a terminating computation for the agent $A \parallel B$ then there exist finite computations for both the agents A and B. Thus we have the following.

Proposition 11. *Let A be a ccpx agent. If $\mathcal{O}_\alpha(A) = \emptyset$ then $\mathcal{O}_\alpha(A \parallel B) = \emptyset$ for any other ccpx agent B.*

On the other hand previous result does not hold for *tccp*. In fact, the presence of the *now the else* statement enforces a non-monotonic behavior in the sense that adding more information to the store can inhibit some computations, because the corresponding *else* branches are discarded. Consider for example the agents

$$A : tell(c) \text{ and } B : now \ c \ then \ loop \ else \ tell(true) \rightarrow (ask(c) \rightarrow stop$$
$$+$$
$$ask(true) \rightarrow loop)$$

It is easy to see that $\mathcal{O}_\alpha(B) = \emptyset$ while $\mathcal{O}_\alpha(A \parallel B) \neq \emptyset$. Thus, using Proposition 11 and the conditions (i) and (ii) we obtain the following result.

Theorem 12. *When considering any notion of observables which is an instance of $\mathcal{O}_\alpha$, the language tccp cannot be embedded into ccpx.*

Since Proposition 11 holds also when considering standard *ccp* agents we have the following.

Corollary 13. *When considering as observables instances of $\mathcal{O}_\alpha$, the language tccp cannot be embedded into ccp.*

5 Comparing maximal parallelism and interleaving

As previously mentioned, standard *ccp* is obtained by *ccpx* by simply replacing the previous (maximal) parallel operator $\parallel$ for the operator $\parallel_i$ which is interpreted in terms of interleaving[7]. Despite this similarity, we will show that *ccpx* is strictly more expressive than standard *ccp*.

The operational semantics of standard *ccp* can be defined in terms of the transition system T' obtained from the one given in Table 1 by replacing rules **R7** and **R8** for the rule **Ri** in Table 5. Since in the following it will be clear from the context which transition system is being used, to simplify the notation we will denote by $\rightarrow$ also the relation defined by T'.

$$\textbf{Ri} \quad \frac{\langle A, c \rangle \longrightarrow \langle A', d \rangle}{\begin{array}{l} \langle A \parallel_i B, c \rangle \longrightarrow \langle A' \parallel_i B, d \rangle \\ \langle B \parallel_i A, c \rangle \longrightarrow \langle B \parallel_i A', d \rangle \end{array}}$$

Table 3. The transition rule for $\parallel_i$.

In order to show that *ccp* can be embedded into *ccpx* we define inductively a translation T_a from *ccp* agents to *ccpx* agents as follows:

$$\begin{array}{ll}
T_a(tell(c)) = tell(c) & T_a(\Sigma_{i=1}^n ask(c_i) \rightarrow A_i) = p_{\Sigma_{i=1}^n ask(c_i) \rightarrow A_i} \\
T_a(A \parallel_i B) = T_a(A) \parallel T_a(B) & T_a(\exists x A) = \exists x \ T_a(A) \\
T_a(p(x)) = p(x) &
\end{array}$$

---

[7] There remains a minor difference in the syntax of *tell* agents, which however is not relevant.

where, given a $ccpx$ agent $A \equiv \Sigma_{i=1}^{n} ask(c_i) \rightarrow A_i$, the agent p_A is defined as follows:

$$p_A :- (\Sigma_{i=1}^{n} ask(c_i) \rightarrow T_a(A_i)) + ask(true) \rightarrow p_A$$

The translation of a set of declarations D into $ccpx$, denoted by $T_d(D)$, is obtained in the obvious way by applying the T_a to all the agents appearing in D and by augmenting D with the declarations of the agents p_A introduced by T_a. This translation clearly allows us to simulate the interleaving execution model of standard ccp by using maximal parallelism, since the branch $ask(true) \rightarrow p_A$ in the definition of p_A allows one to postpone the evaluation of the agent A also when considering maximal parallelism.

Proposition 14. *Let A be a ccp agent. There exists a derivation $\langle A, c \rangle \longrightarrow^* \langle B, d \rangle \not\longrightarrow$ for a given set of declarations D iff there exists a derivation $\langle T_a(A), c \rangle \longrightarrow^* \langle T_a(B), d \rangle \not\longrightarrow$ for the set of declarations $T_d(D)$.*

As a consequence of previous proposition, the standard notion of observables (i/o pairs and resting points) are preserved by the translation. So ccp can be embedded into $ccpx$.

We show now that $ccpx$ cannot be embedded into (standard) ccp. Differently from the case of previous section, here we have to consider a more refined notion of (abstract) observables $\mathcal{O}'_\alpha$ which takes into account also the termination modes and the input constraints. So we consider the following definition

$$\mathcal{O}'_\alpha(A) = \{ \langle \theta, ss \rangle \mid \langle A, true \rangle \longrightarrow^* \langle Stop, d \rangle \text{ and } \theta = \alpha(\langle A, true \rangle \cdots \langle Stop, d \rangle) \}$$
$$\cup$$
$$\{ \langle \theta, dd \rangle \mid \langle A, true \rangle \longrightarrow^* \langle B, d \rangle \not\longrightarrow \text{ with } B \neq Stop \text{ and } \theta = \alpha(\langle A, true \rangle \cdots \langle B, d \rangle) \}$$

where $Stop$ represents any agent which contains only $stop$, $\|$ ($\|_i$) and $+$ and where α is defined as before[8]. Thus, in the remaining of this section, we assume that the observables $\mathcal{O}_x$ for $ccpx$ and $\mathcal{O}_c$ for standard ccp are instances of $\mathcal{O}'_\alpha$. Analogously to the previous case, here $\mathcal{O}_c$ is the function $\mathcal{O}_c : \mathcal{A}_c \rightarrow Obs_c$, where $\mathcal{A}_c$ denote ccp agents.

As before, we require that the decoder $\mathcal{D}$ cannot transform an empty set of results into a non-empty one and vice versa. However, here we have to take into account also the termination mode. So we assume that

(i-a) $\forall O \in Obs_c$, there exists θ such that $\langle \theta, ss \rangle \in \mathcal{D}(O)$ iff there exists σ such that $\langle \sigma, ss \rangle \in O$.

As for the compiler, now we require also the compositionality wrt the choice operator. This requirement is rather natural, since both the source and the target language use the same choice construct. So we assume that:

(ii-a) $\mathcal{C}(A \parallel B) = \mathcal{C}(A) \parallel_i \mathcal{C}(B)$ and
(iii-a) $\mathcal{C}(\Sigma_{i=1}^{n} ask(i) \rightarrow A_i) = \Sigma_{i=1}^{n} \mathcal{C}(ask(i) \rightarrow A_i)$.

To obtain the separation result we use the property of ccp computations formalized by the following proposition.

Proposition 15. *Let A and B be ccp agents. If $\langle \theta, ss \rangle \in \mathcal{O}_c(A \parallel_i B)$ then $\langle \theta, ss \rangle \in \mathcal{O}_c((A' + A) \parallel_i B)$, for any ccp agent A'.*

---

[8] Here we assume implicitly that $\longrightarrow$ is the relation defined by the appropriate transition system for the language ($ccpx$ or ccp) considered.

Previous property does not hold for *ccpx*. In fact, even though $A \parallel B$ has a successful derivation, it can happen that (the guard in) A is enabled by the constraints by B. In this case, due to maximal parallelism, the computation for $(A + A') \parallel B$ can be forced to choose A' and therefore to enter a "wrong" (i.e. non-terminating) branch. For example, this is the case when considering the agents $A : ask(c) \to tell(c)$, $A' : ask(true) \to loop$ and $B : tell(c)$. Therefore we have the following.

Theorem 16. *When considering as observables instances of $\mathcal{O}'_\alpha$, the language ccpx cannot be embedded into ccp.*

6 Conclusions

We have defined a fully abstract semantics for the timed concurrent constraint language *tccp* and for *ccp* with maximal parallelism (*ccpx*). Due to the presence of maximal parallelism, these semantics and the proofs of full abstraction are rather different from the one for standard *ccp*, in particular we need a different kind of distinguishing context. Fully abstract semantics for timed ccp languages are given also in [17, 18]. However the languages considered in these papers are different from *tccp*, in particular they do not assume maximal parallelism. For this reason the results in [17, 18] are substantially different from ours. A denotational model for *tccp* was defined in [2], however it is fully abstract only when observing the "traces" obtained from the intermediate results of computations.

The fully abstract semantics of *tccp* and *ccpx* are more "concrete" than the one for *ccp*, i.e. they need less identifications. This reflects the fact that tccp and ccpx are more expressive than *ccp*. More precisely, we have shown that, under some reasonable assumptions for the notion of "embedding", *tccp* cannot be embedded in *ccpx* which, in turn, cannot be embedded into *ccp*. In other words, these three languages have a strictly decreasing expressive power. The reason for this ordering is intuitively clear in the case of *tccp*, since the presence of the *now then else* statement enforce a kind of non-monotonic behaviour which allows to check for absence of information. For example, assuming a finite set of function symbols, this allows to check whether a variable is not instantiated, similarly to the $Var(x)$ builtin of Prolog. As for the second comparison, the fact that *ccpx* is more expressive than *ccp* is due to the presence of maximal parallelism which, in a sense, augments the control on the (global) choice. In fact, in presence of maximal parallelism one can force the computation to discard some (non enabled) branches which could became enabled later on (because of the information produced by parallel agents), while this is not possible when considering an interleaving model. In other words, the languages *ccpx* and *tccp* are sensitive to delays in adding constraints to the store, whereas this is not the case for *ccp*.

We are currently investigating the extension of these results to consider also confluent ccp languages [6, 13] and infinite computations. Preliminary results show that also in this case *tccp* is more expressive than *ccp* which, in turn, is more expressive than confluent *ccp*. In this case the separation results are even more significant, since they can be used to show that fair merge [14] can be expressed in *tccp* and not in *ccp*, while angelic merge [14] can be expressed in *ccp* and not in confluent (in the sense of [6]) *ccp*.

References

1. G. Berry and G. Gonthier. The ESTEREL programming language:Design, semantics and implementation. *Science of Computer Programming*, 19(2):87-152, 1992.

2. F.S. de Boer and M. Gabbrielli. Modeling Real-time in Concurrent Constraint Programming. In J. Lloyd editor, *Proc. Int'l Logic Programming Symposium*, ILPS'95. The MIT Press, 1995.

3. F.S. de Boer and C. Palamidessi. A Fully Abstract Model for Concurrent Constraint Programming. In S. Abramsky and T.S.E. Maibaum, editors, *Proc. of TAPSOFT/CAAP, LNCS 493*, pages 296–319. Springer-Verlag, 1991.

4. F.S. de Boer and C. Palamidessi. Embedding as a tool for language comparison. *Information and Computation*, 108(1):128-157, 1991.

5. S. Brookes. *A fully abstract semantics of a shared variable parallel language.* In Proc. of LICS, 1993.

6. M. Falaschi, M. Gabbrielli, K. Marriott and C. Palamidessi. Confluence and concurrent constraint programming. In *Proc. AMAST 95, LNCS 936*, pages 531–545. Springer-Verlag, Berlin, 1995.

7. R. Giacobazzi, C. Palamidessi and F. Ranzato. Weak Relative Pseudo-Complements of Closure Operators, em Algebra Universalis, 36(3): 405-412, 1996.

8. N. Halbwachs, P. Caspi, and D. Pilaud. The synchronous programming language LUSTRE. In *Special issue on Another Look at Real-time Systems*, Proceedings of the IEEE, 1991.

9. D. Harel. Statecharts: A Visual Formalism for Complex Systems. *Science of Computer Programming* 8, pages 231-274, 1987.

10. L. Henkin, J.D. Monk, and A. Tarski. *Cylindric Algebras (Part I).* North-Holland, 1971.

11. P. Let Guernic, M. Let Borgue, T. Gauthier, and C. Let Marie. Programming real time applications with SIGNAL. In *Special issue on Another Look at Real-time Systems*, Proceedings of the IEEE, 1991.

12. J. Jaffar and M. J. Maher. *Constraint logic programming: A survey.* Journal of Logic Programming, 19/20, pp. 503–581, 1994.

13. K. Marriott and M. Oderski. A Confluent calculus for concurrent constraint programming with guarded choice. In *Proc. CP'95 Conf. on Principles and Practice of Constraint Programming*, 1995.

14. P. Panangaden and V. Shanbhogue. The expressive power of Indeterminate Dataflow Primitives. *Information and Computation 98(1)*, 99–131, 1992.

15. E. Y. Shapiro. The family of concurrent logic programming languages. *ACM Computing Surveys*, 21(3):412-510, 1989.

16. V.A. Saraswat and M. Rinard. Concurrent constraint programming. In *Proc. of seventeenth ACM Symposium on Principles of Programming Languages*, pages 232–245. ACM, New York, 1990.

17. V.A. Saraswat, R. Jagadeesan, and V. Gupta Foundations of Timed Concurrent Constraint Programming. In S. Abramsky editor, *Proc. of the Ninth Annual IEEE Symposium on Logic in Computer Science*, pages 71–80. IEEE Computer Press, July 1994.

18. V.A. Saraswat, R. Jagadeesan, and V. Gupta Default Timed Concurrent Constraint Programming. In *Proc. of POPL 95*, 1995.

19. V.A. Saraswat, M. Rinard, and P. Panangaden. Semantic Foundation of Concurrent Constraint Programming. In Proc. Eighteenth Annual ACM Symp. on Principles of Programming Languages, ACM, pages 333-353, 1991.

20. Gert Smolka. The Oz Programming Model. In Jan van Leeuwe editor, *Computer Science Today*, vol. 1000 of LNCS. Springer-Verlag, 1995.

Solving Classes of Set Constraints
with Tree Automata

P. Devienne, JM. Talbot and S. Tison *
{devienne,talbot,tison}@lifl.fr

Laboratoire d'Informatique Fondamentale de Lille
CNRS - URA 369
Université des Sciences et Technologies de Lille

Abstract. Set constraints is a suitable formalism for static analysis of programs. However, it is known that the complexity of set constraint problems in the most general cases is very high (NEXPTIME-completeness of the satisfiability test). Lots of works are involved in finding more tractable subclasses.

In this paper, we investigate two classes of set constraints shown to be useful for program analysis: the first one is an extension of definite set constraints including the main feature of quantified set expressions. We will show that the satisfiability problem for this class is *EXPTIME-complete*.

The second one concerns constraints of the form $X \subseteq exp$, where *exp* is built with function symbols, the intersection and union connectives and projection operators.

The dual aspects of those two classes allows to find a common approach for solving both of them. This approach uses as basic tool tree automata, which are suitable both for computation and representing the solution of those solving problems. It leads also to simple algorithms and an easy characterization of complexity.

1   Introduction

Set constraints allow to express relations between sets of (ground) terms. They can be defined as inclusion or non-inclusion between expressions built over variables, function symbols and set operators. The set operators that are encountered in most works are intersection, union, complementation and projection. The main problems that have been addressed concerning set constraints are the classical ones of the constraint paradigm, that is, satisfiability [AW92] [GTT93][MNP97], entailment [CP97a] [MN97] and solving [AM91] [Hei92b]. They have been shown very useful for program analysis [Hei92b][Hei94][MNP97]. Satisfiability problem for the largest class of set constraints (where all the set operations cited above can occur) has been proved to be NEXPTIME-complete [CP94] and the complexity remains the same if projection is omitted [Ste94]

---

* This work was supported in part by the HCM project CONSOLE (CHRXCT940495)

[BGW92] [Tom94]. This leads to a wide interest for more tractable subclasses, defined according to the different considered set operations and/or other syntactic restrictions.

In this paper, we extend the class of definite set constraints [Hei92a] by allowing a "membership expression" operator in the left hand-side of inclusion. This operator is a limited form of the quantified set expressions introduced in [Hei92b]. It looks like $\{x \mid f(x,x) \in Y \wedge g(x,y) \in Z\}$. Such an expression would be interpreted as the set $\{a\}$ if for instance $Y = \{f(a,a), f(b,c), f(c,b), f(d,d)\}$ and $Z = \{f(a,b), g(a,b)\}$. We propose an algorithm for testing satisfiability of a system of such set constraints and prove that this problem is *EXPTIME*-complete. Podelski and Charatonik proposed in [CP97b] a method *à la* Heintze for approximating non-failure semantics of logic programs. This analysis amounts to computing the greatest solution (over sets of finite or infinite trees) of a class of set constraints, symmetric of the one used by Heintze [Hei92a], that is of the form $X \subseteq exp$, where exp is built over function symbols, intersection, union and projection. Their method, dealing with sets of finite or infinite trees, combines syntactic transformations of the constraints with tree automata for testing emptiness of variables and representing the greatest solution.

We propose in this paper an elegant and homogeneous framework for solving definite set constraints with "membership expression" operator and the second class (over finite trees). This framework is based on tree automata providing a tool both for computation and representation of the solution of the constraints. The solving algorithms are described as relations (defined as inference rules) over tree automata. This leads to a very simple and uniform approach, in which the dual aspects of those two classes are revealed. Roughly speaking, for set constraints with intersection, we start with an "empty" automaton (*i.e.* each variable is interpreted as the empty set) and we modify this automaton (by adding terms into the interpretation of the variables) according to the constraints. For the second class, we start from the "universe" automaton (*i.e.* each variable is interpreted as the set of all terms) and we remove terms from the interpretation of the variables according to the constraints.

After giving a few definitions and properties about set constraints in the next section, we present our basic tool, that is tree automata in section 3. Section 4 is devoted to an algorithm for deciding satisfiability of definite set constraints with "membership expression" operator. Finally, section 5 deals with an algorithm for computing the greatest solution (over finite trees) for the class of set constraints introduced in [CP97b].

2 Preliminaries

We assume given a finite set of function symbols Σ and $\mathcal{V}$ a countable set of (set) variables (denoted $X, Y, Z, X_1, X_2, ..$). *TERM*(Σ) is the set of ground terms built over Σ.

Inclusion set constraints are defined as inclusion ($sexp_1 \subseteq sexp_2$) between set expressions, built over Σ, $\mathcal{V}$, boolean connectives $\{\cup, \cap\}$ and projection symbols f_i^{-1} (with $f \in \Sigma$ and $1 \leq i \leq arity(f)$).

$$sexp ::= X \mid f(sexp_1, .., sexp_n) \mid sexp \cup sexp' \mid sexp \cap sexp' \mid f_i^{-1}(sexp)$$

We extend this "classical" definition with an other operator, called "membership expression" operator, which is a limited form of the quantified operator introduced in [Hei92b]. Given V, a set of first-order variable ranged over by x,y,z,.. , this extended class is described by adding

$$sexp ::= \{x \mid s_1 \in sexp_1 \wedge ... \wedge s_l \in sexp_l\} \subseteq X$$

where the s_i's belong to $TERM(\Sigma \cup V)$ and where (first-order) variables different from x occuring in the s_i's are implicitly existentialy quantified.

As usual, a set (or system) of set constraints will be viewed as the conjunction of those ones.

An interpretation $\mathcal{I}$ is a valuation which maps set variables onto sets of ground terms and can be extended on set expressions in the following way:

- $\mathcal{I}(f(t_1, .., t_n)) = \{f(s_1, .., s_n) | s_1 \in \mathcal{I}(t_1), .., s_n \in \mathcal{I}(t_n)\}$.
- $f_i^{-1}(t) = \{s_i \mid \exists s_1, .., s_{i-1}, s_{i+1}, .., s_n, \ f(s_1, .., s_n) \in \mathcal{I}(t)\}$
- $\cap$ and $\cup$ are interpreted in a canonical way.
- $s \in \mathcal{I}(\{x \mid s_1 \in se_1 \wedge ... \wedge s_l \in se_l\})$ iff there exists σ, a substitution from $Var(s_1) \cup ... \cup Var(s_n) \setminus \{x\}$ onto $TERM(\Sigma)$, such that $\forall i \in \{1, .., l\}, \ (\sigma \circ [x/s])(s_i) \in \mathcal{I}(se_i)\}$.

$\mathcal{I}$ is a model (or a solution) of $sexp_1 \subseteq sexp_2$ iff $\mathcal{I}(sexp_1) \subseteq \mathcal{I}(sexp_2)$. $\mathcal{I}$ is a model of a system of set constraints SC if it is a model of each constraint of SC. SC is said to be satisfiable if it has a model. $SOL(SC)$ denotes the set of models of SC.

A partial order is defined on interpretations for a set of variables $\mathcal{V}'$ as: $\mathcal{I} \preceq \mathcal{I}'$ iff $\forall X \in \mathcal{V}', \mathcal{I}(X) \subseteq \mathcal{I}'(X)$.

SC has a least (resp. a greatest) solution $\mathcal{I}_{min}$ (resp. $\mathcal{I}_{max}$) iff $\forall \mathcal{I} \in SOL(SC)$, $\mathcal{I}_{min} \preceq \mathcal{I}$ (resp. $\mathcal{I} \preceq \mathcal{I}_{max}$). One should notice that for all X,

- $t \in \mathcal{I}_{min}(X) \Leftrightarrow \forall \mathcal{I} \in SOL(SC), t \in \mathcal{I}(X)$
- $t \in \mathcal{I}_{max}(X) \Leftrightarrow \exists \mathcal{I} \in SOL(SC), t \in \mathcal{I}(X)$

3 Tree Automata

The basic tool for the two classes we consider is tree automata, more precisely an extension of ascending tree automata [GS84].

Definition 1. An n-ranked tree automaton (TA) $\mathcal{A}$ is a tuple $(\Sigma, \mathcal{Q}, \mathcal{F}, \mathcal{S})$ where Σ is a set of function symbols, $\mathcal{Q}$ is a finite set of states, $\mathcal{F} = (F_1, .., F_n)$, is a tuple of sets of final states $(F_i \subseteq Q)$ and S is a set of transition rules of the form:

$$f(q_1, .., q_m) \to q$$

where $f \in \Sigma$ is a m-ary symbol and $\{q, q_1, .., q_m\} \subseteq Q$ [1]

In fact, we consider only a restricted subclass of such automata, that is the class of deterministic and complete TA (denoted TA_{dc}).

Definition 2. A TA is said to be

- **deterministic** iff $\forall r_i, r_j \in S$, s.t. $i \neq j$, r_i and r_j don't have the same left hand-side.
- **complete** iff $\forall f \in \Sigma$, $\forall q_1, .., q_m \in Q$, $\exists q \in Q$ s.t. $f(q_1, .., q_m) \to q \in S$

A deterministic and complete tree automata runs over $TERM(\Sigma)$. This run is formally defined using a function run_A from $TERM(\Sigma \cup Q)$ (*i.e.* the set of terms built over Σ and Q where states are viewed as constants) onto Q s.t.

Definition 3. For all $t \in TERM(\Sigma \cup Q)$, $run_A(t) = q$ iff $t \to_A^* q$

where $\to_A^*$ is the transitive closure of the *move* function $\to_A$ defined from $TERM(\Sigma \cup Q)$ onto itself as $t \to_A t'$ iff $t = T[l]$, $t' = T[r]$ and $l \to r \in S$.

The language recognized by a n-ranked TA_{dc} A is a tuple $(L_1, .., L_n)$ where L_i is a set of ground terms defined by $\forall t \in TERM(\Sigma)$, $t \in L_i$ iff $run_A(t) \in F_i$.

A basic property for automaton states is *reachability*.

Definition 4. A state q is said to be reachable in a TA A iff there exists a term t in $TERM(\Sigma)$ s.t. $run_A(t) = q$. *Reachable(A)* will denote the set of reachable states in a TA A

This definition implies, in particular, that if $q \in F_i$ and q is reachable, then L_i is non-empty.

4 Definite Set Constraints with "Membership Expression" Operator

In this section, we present a method using tree automata for deciding satisfiability for a class of set constraints, defined as an extension of definite set constraints by allowing "membership expression" operator in the left hand-side of inclusion. Hence, those constraints will be of the form $sexp_1 \subseteq sexp_2$, where $sexp_1$ is built with function symbols, intersection and union connectives, projection and "membership expression" operators and $sexp_2$ is built with intersection connectives and function symbols.

---

[1] This definition of transition rule includes the case where f is a constant symbol: $a \to q$.

One should notice that this class contains (syntactically) both definite set constraints [Hei92a] and (positive) set constraints with intersection [CP97a].

Without loss of generality, we may assume that those constraints are in "shallow" form:

$$f(X_1, .., X_m) \subseteq X$$
$$\{x \mid s_1 \in X_1 \wedge ... \wedge s_l \in X_l\} \subseteq Z$$
$$X \subseteq f(X_1, .., X_m)$$

This transformation can be achevied with a polynomial time and space algorithm, by adding "fresh" variables and by noticing that $X \subseteq Y \cap Z \Leftrightarrow X \subseteq Y \wedge X \subseteq Z$, $X \cup Y \subseteq Z \Leftrightarrow X \subseteq Z \wedge Y \subseteq Z$, $X \cap Y \subseteq Z \Leftrightarrow \{z \mid z \in X \wedge z \in Y\} \subseteq Z$ and $f_i^{-1}(X) \subseteq Y \Leftrightarrow \{x \mid f(y_1, .., y_{i-1}, x, y_{i+1}, .., y_m) \in X\} \subseteq Y$.

4.1   Algorithm

Let $\mathcal{SC}$ be a system of set constraints and $\{X_1, ..., X_n\}$ be the set of (set) variables occurring in $\mathcal{SC}$. We will consider the set of TA_{dc} $\mathcal{A} = (\Sigma, \mathcal{Q}, \mathcal{F}, \mathcal{S})$ s.t. Σ is the signature of $\mathcal{SC}$, $\mathcal{Q} = \{0, 1\}^n$ (the vectors of size n of boolean values) and $\mathcal{F} = (F_1, .., F_n)$ where F_i is the set of states having 1 on the ith component.
In other words, for a ground term t, if the state equal to $run_A(t)$ has 1 on its ith component, then t belongs to X_i in any solution.

We present our algorithm as a system of inference rules $\mathcal{R}$. Starting from the "empty" automaton, $\mathcal{R}$ computes either a tree automaton representing the least solution of a system of set constraints if it is satisfiable or $\bot$ otherwise. Since $\Sigma, \mathcal{Q}$ and $\mathcal{F}$ are fixed, no difference is made between an automaton and its set of transition rules.

Notations:

- for $q, q' \in \mathcal{Q}$, $switch\_on(q, i) = q'$ iff $\forall j$, $q' \in F_j \Leftrightarrow (q \in F_j \vee i = j)$ [2]
- S_0 denotes the automaton having the right hand-sides of its rules set to $\{0\}^n$
- $Subst(E, F)$ will denote the set of substitutions having E for domain and ranging over the set F.
- lhs stands for any left hand-side of transition rules.

Let $\mathcal{R}$ be the following system of inference rules:

- (Compose)

$$\frac{S \cup \{f(q_1, .., q_m) \to q\}}{S \cup \{f(q_1, .., q_m) \to switch\_on(q, i)\}} \quad \text{if} \begin{cases} f(X_{i_1}, .., X_{i_m}) \subseteq X_i \in \mathcal{SC} \\ \forall k, \ q_k \in F_{i_k} \end{cases}$$

---

[2] q' is equal to q except (possibly) on position i which is set to 1 in q'.

- (Clash)

$$\frac{S \cup \{f(q_1,..,q_m) \to q\}}{\bot} \quad \text{if} \begin{cases} X_i \subseteq g(X_{i_1},..,X_{i_l}) \in \mathcal{SC} \\ f \neq g, \ q \in F_i \\ \{q_1,..,q_m\} \subseteq \text{Reachable}(S) \end{cases}$$

- (Project)

$$\frac{S \cup \{lhs \to q\}}{S \cup \{lhs \to switch\_on(q, i_k)\}} \quad \text{if} \begin{cases} X_i \subseteq g(X_{i_1},..,X_{i_{m'}}) \in \mathcal{SC} \\ \exists \ g(q_{i_1},..,q_{i_{m'}}) \to q' \in S \ \text{s.t.} \\ q' \in F_i, \ q = q_{i_k} \\ \{q_{i_1},..,q_{i_{m'}}\} \backslash \{q_{i_k}\} \subseteq \text{Reachable}(S) \end{cases}$$

- (Member)

$$\frac{S \cup \{lhs \to q\}}{S \cup \{lhs \to switch\_on(q, i)\}} \quad \text{if} \begin{cases} \{x \mid \bigwedge_l s_l \in X_{i_l}\} \subseteq X_i \in \mathcal{SC} \\ \exists \sigma' \in \text{Subst}(\bigcup_l \text{Var}(s_l) \backslash \{x\}, \text{Reachable}(S)) \\ \text{s.t.} \forall l, \text{runs}_S((\sigma' \circ [x/q](s_l))) \in F_{i_l} \end{cases}$$

Informally, the first rule means that for any solution $\mathcal{I}$, if for all k, $t_k \in \mathcal{I}(X_{i_k})$, then according to the considered constraint $f(t_1,..,t_k) \in \mathcal{I}(X_i)$. (Clash) means that there exists a ground term $f(t_1,..,t_m)$ in $\mathcal{I}(X_i)$ for any interpretation $\mathcal{I}$; therefore, according to the constraint, the system has no solution. For the (Project) rule, if a term $g(t_1,..,t_{m'})$ belongs to $\mathcal{I}(X_i)$, then according to the constraint, for any solution and any k, $t_k \in \mathcal{I}(X_{i_k})$. The last rule means that if for a term t, the "existential" variables can be instanciated with ground terms (which is implies by the reachability condition over states) in such a way that the so-instanciated s_l belongs to $\mathcal{I}(X_{i_l})$, then $t \in \mathcal{I}(X_i)$ for any solution $\mathcal{I}$.

$\mathcal{R}$ defines a relation $\to_{\mathcal{R}}$ on $TA_{dc} \cup \{\bot\}$. Our algorithm computes a final automaton S_f s.t. $S_0 \to_{\mathcal{R}}^* S_f$ and $\forall S$, if $S_f \to_{\mathcal{R}} S$, then $S = S_f$ (i.e. S_f is a fix-point of $\to_{\mathcal{R}}$).

4.2 Termination

Let us consider a partial order $\preceq_Q$ on Q defined as: $q \preceq_Q q'$ iff $q \in F_i \Rightarrow q' \in F_i$. This order is used to define a partial ordering relation $\preceq_A$ on TA_{dc} as: $A \preceq_A A'$ iff for any left hand-side lhs, $lhs \to q \in A$ and $lhs \to q \in A'$ implies that $q \preceq_Q q'$.
We extend $\preceq_A$ onto $TA_{dc} \cup \{\bot\}$ by laying down: $\forall A \in TA_{dc}, \ A \preceq_A \bot$.
It is easy to see that $S \to_{\mathcal{R}} S'$ implies that $S \preceq_A S'$. Since TA_{dc} is finite, this allows us to conclude for termination of our algorithm.

4.3 Correctness

In this section, we deal with soundness and completeness of our method. Starting with the former, we prove first an important lemma.

Lemma 5. *For an automaton S, let the properties (a) and (b) defined by:*

(a) $\forall f(q_1,..,q_m) \to q \in S,\ \forall t_1,..,t_m \in TERM(\Sigma),$

$$\forall \mathcal{I} \in SOL(SC),\ \bigwedge_{1 \le k \le m}\ \bigwedge_{\{j|q_k \in F_j\}} t_k \in \mathcal{I}(X_j) \Rightarrow \bigwedge_{\{j|q \in F_j\}} f(t_1,..,t_m) \in \mathcal{I}(X_j)$$

(b) $\forall t \in TERM(\Sigma \cup V),\ \forall \sigma \in Subst(Var(t), \mathcal{Q}),\ \forall \alpha \in Subst(Var(t), TERM(\Sigma)),$

$$\forall \mathcal{I} \in SOL(SC),$$

$$\bigwedge_{\{y|y \in Var(t)\}}\ \bigwedge_{\{j|\sigma(y) \in F_j\}} \alpha(y) \in \mathcal{I}(X_j) \Rightarrow \bigwedge_{\{j|run_S(\sigma(t)) \in F_j\}} \alpha(t) \in \mathcal{I}(X_j)$$

If (a) and (b) hold for S, $S \to_{\mathcal{R}} S'$ and $S' \ne \bot$, then (a) and (b) hold for S'.

Proof.
For Part (a): the property (a) remains true for unchanged rules. Let
$f(q_1,..,q_m) \to q \in S$ be the rule modified into $f(q_1,..,q_m) \to switch\_on(q,i)$ in
S. Since (a) holds for S, it is sufficient to check for the modified rule that:

$$\bigwedge_{1 \le k \le m}\ \bigwedge_{\{j|q_k \in F_j\}} t_k \in \mathcal{I}(X_j) \Rightarrow f(t_1,..,t_m) \in \mathcal{I}(X_i)$$

So, according to the rule applied for $\to_{\mathcal{R}}$:

- for (Compose): by the conditions of the rule, $\forall k$, $q_k \in F_{i_k}$. So, it can
  be deduced that $f(t_1,..,t_m) \in f(\mathcal{I}(X_{i_1}),..,\mathcal{I}(X_{i_m}))$. Since $\mathcal{I}$ is a solution,
  $f(t_1,..,t_m) \in \mathcal{I}(X_i)$.
- for (Project): since $\mathcal{I}$ is a solution, $\forall h$, $g(s_1,..,s_{m'}) \in \mathcal{I}(X_j) \Rightarrow s_h \in \mathcal{I}(X_{i_h})$
  Let us consider the term $t = g(z_1,..,z_{h-1}, f(y_1,..,y_m), z_{h+1},..,z_{m'})$, the sub-
  stitutions σ' and σ'' s.t. $\sigma'(z_j) = q_{i_j}$ and $\sigma''(y_j) = q_j$, and $\sigma = \sigma' \circ \sigma''$. Since
  $\forall j \in \{1,..,h-1,h+1,..,m'\}$, q_{i_j} is a reachable state in S, there exists
  $s_j \in TERM(\Sigma)$ s.t. $run_S(s_j) = q_{i_j}$. Let α' be a substitution s.t. $\alpha'(z_j) = s_j$.
  Let $\forall j$, $\alpha''(y_j) = t_j$. One should notice that $run_S(\sigma(t)) = q'$ according to
  the hypothesis of (Project). So, since (b) holds for S, for any solution $\mathcal{I}$,

$$\bigwedge_{1 \le o \le m} \bigwedge_{\{p|q_o \in F_p\}} t_o \in \mathcal{I}(X_p) \wedge \bigwedge_{1 \le o \le m' \wedge o \ne h} \bigwedge_{\{p|q_{i_o} \in F_p\}} s_o \in \mathcal{I}(X_p)$$
$$\Rightarrow$$
$$\bigwedge_{\{p|q' \in F_p\}} g(s_1,..,f(t_1,..,t_m),..,s_{m'}) \in \mathcal{I}(X_p)$$

Moreover, since $\forall j \in \{1,..,h-1,h+1,..,m'\}, run_S(s_j) = q_{i_j}$ and since (b)
holds in S, $\bigwedge_{1 \le o \le m' \wedge o \ne h} \bigwedge_{\{p|q_{i_o} \in F_p\}} s_o \in \mathcal{I}(X_p)$ holds.
Using the facts that $q' \in F_i$ and that $\mathcal{I}$ is a solution, (a) holds in this case.

- for (Member): since $\mathcal{I}$ is a solution, $\forall \alpha \in Subst(\bigcup_l Var(s_l), TERM(\Sigma))$,
  $\bigwedge_l \in \mathcal{I}(X_{i_l}) \Rightarrow \alpha(x) \in \mathcal{I}(X_i)$.

For Part (b): we are going to prove that there exists a suitable substitution α, *i.e.* such that $\alpha(x) = f(t_1, .., t_m)$ and

$$\forall l, \bigwedge_{1 \le k \le m} \bigwedge_{\{j | q_k \in F_j\}} t_k \in \mathcal{I}(X_j) \Rightarrow \alpha(s_l) \in \mathcal{I}(X_{i_l})$$

Let $\sigma = [x/q] \circ \sigma'$, where σ' is the substitution used for $\rightarrow_{\mathcal{R}}$. The reachability condition (defined in the inference rule) implies that there exists a substitution α' from $\bigcup_l Var(s_l) \setminus \{x\}$ onto $TERM(\Sigma)$ s.t. $run_S(\alpha'(y)) = \sigma'(y)$. Let $\alpha = [x/f(t_1, .., t_m)] \circ \alpha'$.

By noticing that $run_S(\sigma(s_l)) \in F_{i_l}$ (by the condition of the inference rule) and by appling part (b) (which holds for S), we must prove that:

$$\forall l, \forall y \in Var(s_l), \bigwedge_{1 \le k \le m} \bigwedge_{\{j | q_k \in F_j\}} t_k \in \mathcal{I}(X_j) \Rightarrow \bigwedge_{\{j | \sigma(y) \in F_j\}} \alpha(y) \in \mathcal{I}(X_j)$$

This is obviously true for $y \ne x$, by applying part (b) since $\alpha(y)$ is ground and $\sigma(y) = run_S(\sigma(y))$ and for $y = x$ since (a) holds for S.

We are going to prove that if (a) holds for S, then (b) does so: by induction on the structure of t:

- if t is a constant symbol or a variable, then it is straightforward that the property (a) implies (b).
- if $t = f(s_1, .., s_m)$. One should notice that $\alpha(t) = f(\alpha(s_1), .., \alpha(s_m))$. By the induction assumption, (b) holds for s_k for any k. Let $run_S(\sigma(s_k)) = q_k$, so $\bigwedge_{\{y | y \in Var(t)\}} \bigwedge_{\{j | \sigma(y) \in F_j\}} \alpha(y) \in \mathcal{I}(X_j) \Rightarrow \bigwedge_{\{j | q_k \in F_j\}} \alpha(s_k) \in \mathcal{I}(X_j)$.
  Let $q = run_S(\sigma(t)) = run_S(f(\sigma(s_1), .., \sigma(s_m)))$; since (a) holds for $f(q_1, .., q_m) \rightarrow q \in S$, (b) holds in this case.

Then, soundness can easily be deduced from lemma 5.

Theorem 6 (Soundness). *Let S_f be a final computed automaton,*

- *If $S_f \ne \perp$, then for any solution $\mathcal{I}$, $\forall t \in TERM(\Sigma)$,*

$$\forall i, \ run_{S_f}(t) \in F_i \Rightarrow t \in \mathcal{I}(X_i)$$

- *If $S_f = \perp$, then SC is not satisfiable.*

Proof. For the first case: it is easy to see that in lemma 5, (a) and so (b) hold for S_0; therefore, by lemma 5, both of them hold for S_f. Thus, this case is the particular case of the property (b) for S_f for ground terms ($TERM(\Sigma)$).

For the second case: let us consider an automaton S_e s.t. $S_e \ne \perp$ and $S_e \rightarrow_{\mathcal{R}} S_f = \perp$. For the considered rule $f(q_1, .., q_m) \rightarrow q$, since $\{q_1, .., q_m\}$ are reachable, there exists $\{t_1, .., t_m\} \subseteq TERM(\Sigma)$ s.t. $\forall k, run_{S_e}(t_k) = q_k$. So, by using the transition rule, there exists a term $t = f(t_1, .., t_m)$ s.t. $run_{S_e}(t) = q$. Since $q \in F_i$, lemma 5 implies for S_e that $f(t_1, .., t_m) \in \mathcal{I}(X_i)$, for any solution $\mathcal{I}$. According to the constraint, there can not be such a solution.

Let $\mathcal{S}_f$ be the computed automata as a fix-point of $\rightarrow_\mathcal{R}$. If $\mathcal{S}_f \neq \bot$, we are going to prove that the language recognized by $\mathcal{S}_f$ is a solution.

Theorem 7 (Completeness). *Let $(L_1, .., L_n)$ be the language recognized by $\mathcal{S}_f$, let $\mathcal{I}_f$ be an interpretation s.t. $\forall X_i, \mathcal{I}_f(X_i) = L_i, \mathcal{I}_f$ is a solution of SC*

Proof. According to the different kinds of set constraints:

- For $f(X_{i_1}, .., X_{i_m}) \subseteq X_i$: let $\{t_1, .., t_m\} \subseteq TERM(\Sigma)$ s.t. $t_k \in \mathcal{I}_f(X_{i_k})$, by definition $run_{\mathcal{S}_f}(t_k) \in F_{i_k}$. Since $\mathcal{S}_f$ is a fix-point, $run_{\mathcal{S}_f}(f(t_1, .., t_m)) \in F_i$. Therefore $f(t_1, .., t_m) \in \mathcal{I}_f(X_i)$.
- For $X_i \subseteq g(X_{i_1}, .., X_{i_{m'}})$: let $t \in TERM(\Sigma)$ s.t. $t \in \mathcal{I}_f(X_i)$. If $t = f(t_1, .., t_m)$ and $f \neq g$, by definition $run_{\mathcal{S}_f}(t) \in F_i$. Thus, (Clash) would be applied, that is impossible since $\mathcal{S}_f \neq \bot$. So, $t = g(t_1, .., t_{m'})$. This implies that there exists a rule $g(q_{i_1}, .., q_{i_{m'}}) \rightarrow q'$ s.t. $run_{\mathcal{S}_f}(g(t_1, .., t_{m'})) = q' \in F_i$, by definition of L_i, and $\forall k, run_{\mathcal{S}_f}(t_k) = q_{i_k}$. So, for any k, t_k is of the form $f(s_1, .., s_m)$, which implies that there exists a transition rule $f(q_1, .., q_m) \rightarrow q_{i_k}$. Since the rule (Project) has been applied in this case (since $\mathcal{S}_f$ is a fix-point), $run_{\mathcal{S}_f}(t_k) \in F_{i_k}$; thus, $t_k \in \mathcal{I}_f(X_{i_k})$.
- For $\{x \mid s_1 \in X_{i_1} \wedge ... \wedge s_l \in X_{i_l}\} \subseteq X_i$: let t be a ground term in $\mathcal{I}_f(\{x \mid s_1 \in X_{i_1} \wedge ... \wedge s_l \in X_{i_l}\})$. By definition of an interpretation, there exists $\alpha' \in Subst(\cup_k Var(s_k) \backslash \{x\}, TERM(\Sigma))$ such that $\forall k, (\alpha' \circ [x/t])(s_k) \in \mathcal{I}_f(X_{i_k})$. Hence, by definition of $\mathcal{I}_f, \forall k, run_{\mathcal{S}_f}((\alpha' \circ [x/t])(s_k)) \in F_{i_k}$. By defining $\sigma'(y) = run_{\mathcal{S}_f}(\alpha'(y))$ and since $\mathcal{S}_f$ is a fix-point, $run_{\mathcal{S}_f}(t) \in F_i$ and thus, $t \in \mathcal{I}_f(X_i)$.

One can deduce from this that our algorithm computes a unique $\mathcal{S}_f$, which represents exactly the least solution of SC if SC is satisfiable or is equal to $\bot$ if SC is not satisfiable.

4.4 Complexity

The problem of deciding the satisfiability of a system of such set constraints has an easy lower bound, since this class contains the class of set constraints with intersection [CP97a] for which satisfiability test is *EXPTIME-complete* [3].

Proposition 8. *Deciding whether a system of definite set constraints with "membership expression" operator is satisfiable is EXPTIME-hard.*

We are now going to prove that our algorithm is in *EXPTIME*. For this, we consider a particular strategy for the application of inference rules. An iteration consists in applying for each set constraint of the system the inference rules on each transition rule successively . This ensures that for one iteration one state at least has been "switched". This iteration is repeated until a fix point is reached.

---

[3] for a problem of size n, $EXPTIME(n) = \bigcup_k DTIME(2^{n^k})$

Let v (resp. n) be the number of variables (resp. of set constraints) occurring in the input system and s the maximal size of a membership expression. Let f be the number of function symbols of Σ and a the maximal arity.

There are exactly 2^v states and at most $2^{v\,a}f$ rules in an automaton. We denote T the size of an automaton, that is at most $2^{v\,a}f\,(a+1)\,v$. We assume that testing if a state is final for F_i or "switching" a state can be achieved in a constant time. The reachability of a state can be tested in a linear time w.r.t. T.

For an application of a rule of $\rightarrow_{\mathcal{R}}$, it costs in time $O(a)$ for (Compose) and $O(a\,T)$ for (Clash). For (Project), the reachability test of states in the left hand-side of the rule selected rule costs at most $O(a\,T)$ and finding an other suitable rule $O(2^{v\,a}f\,a\,T)$. For (Member), there are at most $2^{v\,s}$ possibilities for choosing reachable states and for a choice, it costs $o(s)$ for testing membership.

Therefore, an iteration can be achieved in at most $O(c\,2^{2\,v\,s}v\,s\,n)$ (where c is a constant depending on the signature). Since the number of iteration is at most equal to the number of bits to "switch" on (that is $v.f2^{v.a}$), the solution is computed in at most $O(c'\,2^{3\,v\,s}v^2\,s\,n)$ (where c' is a constant depending on the signature).

Proposition 9. *Deciding whether a system of definite set constraints with "membership expression" operator is satisfiable is EXPTIME-complete.*

Proof. straigthforward, by proposition 8 and the polynomial transformation algorithm for "shallow" form.

5 Greatest Model

In this section, we deal with a class of set constraints introduced by Podelski and Charatonik in [CP97b] for non-failure analysis of logic programs. They can be viewed as the counterpart of those one used by Heintze [Hei92a] for program analysis, since the left hand-side of a constraint is a variable and the right hand-side consists in functional compositions, projections, unions and intersections.

As for definite set constraints with "membership expression" operator, we are going to consider a "shallow" form [4]:

$$X \subseteq f(X_1, .., X_m)$$
$$X \subseteq Y \cup Z$$
$$X \subseteq f_i^{-1}(Y)$$

It is easy to see that those constraints are always satisfiable [5]. Our algorithm aims to compute the greatest solution of a system of this class.

---

[4] Intersections can be cancelled since $X \subseteq Y \cap Z \Leftrightarrow X \subseteq Y \wedge X \subseteq Z$.

[5] The interpretation $\mathcal{I}_\varnothing$, defined as $\forall X$, $\mathcal{I}_\varnothing(X) = \varnothing$ is an obvious solution.

5.1 Algorithm

The encoding of this problem is exactly the same as for definite set constraints with "membership expression" operator. Starting with the "universe" automaton, our algorithm (presented as a system of inference rules) computes a tree automaton representation of the greatest solution of a system of set constraints.

Notations:

- $switch\_off(q, i) = q'$ iff $\forall j$, $q' \notin F_j \Leftrightarrow q \notin F_j \vee i = j$, that is q' is equal to q except (possibly) on the ith component which is set to 0 in q'.
- S_1 will denote the automaton having the right hand-sides of its rules set to $\{1\}^n$.

Let $\mathcal{R}$ the following system of inference rules

- (Compose)

$$\frac{S \cup \{f(q_1, .., q_m) \to q\}}{S \cup \{f(q_1, .., q_m) \to switch\_off(q, i)\}} \quad \text{if} \quad \begin{cases} X_i \subseteq g(X_{i_1}, .., X_{i_l}) \in SC \text{ and} \\ \text{either } g \neq f \\ \text{or } g = f \text{ and } \exists k, q_k \notin F_{i_k} \end{cases}$$

- (Union)

$$\frac{S \cup \{f(q_1, .., q_m) \to q\}}{S \cup \{f(q_1, .., q_m) \to switch\_off(q, i)\}} \quad \text{if} \quad \begin{cases} X_i \subseteq X_{i_1} \cup X_{i_2} \in SC \text{ and} \\ q \notin F_{i_1}, q \notin F_{i_2} \end{cases}$$

- (Project)

$$\frac{S \cup \{f(q_1, .., q_m) \to q\}}{S \cup \{f(q_1, .., q_m) \to switch\_off(q, i)\}} \quad \text{if} \quad \begin{cases} X_i \subseteq g_j^{-1}(X_k) \in SC \\ \{q_1, .., q_m\} \subseteq Reachable(S) \\ \forall g(q_{i_1}, .., q_{i_l}) \to q' \in S \\ q_{i_j} = q \wedge \forall p, q_{i_p} \in Reachable(S) \\ \Rightarrow \\ q' \notin F_k \end{cases}$$

Intuitively, the first rule means that, according to the constraint, no term $f(t_1, .., t_m)$ can belong to $\mathcal{I}(X_i)$ for any solution $\mathcal{I}$ and for a term $g(t_1, .., t_l)$ s.t. $t_k \notin \mathcal{I}(X_{i_k})$, $g(t_1, .., t_l) \notin \mathcal{I}(X_i)$. For (Union), if for any solution $\mathcal{I}$, $t \notin \mathcal{I}(X_{i_1})$ and $t \notin \mathcal{I}(X_{i_2})$, then $t \notin \mathcal{I}(X_i)$. (Project) means that if, for a term t_j, for any solution $\mathcal{I}$ and for any term $g(t_1, .., t_l)$, $g(t_1, .., t_l) \notin \mathcal{I}(X_k)$, then $t_j \notin \mathcal{I}(X_i)$.

Starting from S_1, our algorithm computes S_f a fix-point of $\to_{\mathcal{R}}$ that is $S_1 \to_{\mathcal{R}}^* S_f$ and $S_f \to_{\mathcal{R}} S$ implies $S = S_f$.

5.2 Termination

We can define a partial ordering relation $\preceq_{\mathcal{Q}}^{\downarrow}$ on states as $q' \preceq_{\mathcal{Q}}^{\downarrow} q$ iff $q' \notin F_j \Rightarrow q \notin F_j$. It can be extended as a partial ordering $\preceq_{\mathcal{A}}^{\downarrow}$ on TA_{dc} (like $\preceq_{\mathcal{A}}$ for $\preceq_{\mathcal{Q}}$). The termination comes from the facts that $S \to_{\mathcal{R}} S'$ implies that $S \preceq_{\mathcal{A}}^{\downarrow} S'$ and that the set TA_{dc} is finite.

5.3 Correctness

We start with soundness. For this, we are going to prove that our algorithm computes a solution.

Let $(L_1, .., L_n)$ be the language recognized by $\mathcal{S}_f$ and $\mathcal{I}_f$ be the interpretation defined by $\forall X_i, \mathcal{I}_f(X_i) = L_i$.

Theorem 10. *$\mathcal{I}_f$ is a solution of SC.*

Proof. Let us assume that $\mathcal{I}_f$ is not a solution. Therefore, there exists a violated constraint in SC. According to the different kind of constraints:

- $X_i \subseteq f(X_{i_1}, .., X_{i_m})$: there exist a term t such that $t \in \mathcal{I}_f(X_i)$ and $t \notin \mathcal{I}_f(f(X_{i_1}, .., X_{i_m}))$. By definition, it should be noticed that $run_{\mathcal{S}_f}(t) \in F_i$. If $t = g(t_1, .., t_l)$, there exists in $\mathcal{S}_f$ a rule $g(q_1, .., q_l) \to q$ s.t. $q \in F_i$. This is impossible since $\mathcal{S}_f$ is a fix-point. If $t = f(t_1, .., t_m)$, it implies that there exists a k s.t. $t_k \notin \mathcal{I}_f(X_{i_k})$, that is $run_{\mathcal{S}_f}(t_k) \notin F_{i_k}$. So, there exists a rule $f(q_1, .., q_l) \to q$ in SC, s.t. $run_{\mathcal{S}_f}(t) = q \in F_i$ and $q_k \notin F_{i_k}$, which is impossible.
- $X_i \subseteq X_{i_1} \cup X_{i_2}$: there exist a term t s.t. $t \in \mathcal{I}_f(X_i)$, $t \notin \mathcal{I}_f(X_{i_1})$ and $t \notin \mathcal{I}_f(X_{i_2})$ So, by definition, $run_{\mathcal{S}_f}(t)$ belongs to F_i, but neither to F_{i_1} nor to F_{i_2}. Impossible since $\mathcal{S}_f$ is a fix-point.
- $X_i \subseteq g_j^{-1}(X_k)$: there exists a term t s.t. $t \in \mathcal{I}_f(X_i)$ and $t \notin \mathcal{I}_f(g_j^{-1}(X_k))$. So, for any term $g(t_1, .., t_l)$ s.t. $t_j = t$, $g(t_1, .., t_l) \notin \mathcal{I}_f(X_k)$. So, for any $g(q_{i_1}, .., q_{i_l}) \to q'$ s.t. $q_{i_1}, .., q_{i_l}$ are reachable, $q' \notin F_k$. Since $run_{\mathcal{S}_f}(t) \in F_i$, this would imply that $\mathcal{S}_f$ is not a fix-point.

We deal now with completeness by starting with proving a basic lemma which states an invariant property of $\to_{\mathcal{R}}$.

Lemma 11. *For an automaton S, let the properties (a) and (b) defined by:*

(a) $\forall f(q_1, .., q_m) \to q \in S, \forall t_1, .., t_m \in TERM(\Sigma),$

$$\forall \mathcal{I} \in SOL(SC), \bigwedge_{1 \leq o \leq m} \bigwedge_{\{p \mid q_o \notin F_p\}} t_o \notin \mathcal{I}(X_p) \Rightarrow \bigwedge_{\{p \mid q \notin F_p\}} f(t_1, .., t_m) \notin \mathcal{I}(X_p)$$

(b) $\forall t \in TERM(\Sigma \cup V), \forall \sigma \in Subst(Var(t), \mathcal{Q}), \forall \alpha \in Subst(Var(t), TERM(\Sigma))$

$$\forall \mathcal{I} \in SOL(SC),$$

$$\bigwedge_{\{y \mid y \in Var(t)\}} \bigwedge_{\{p \mid \sigma(y) \notin F_p\}} \alpha(y) \notin \mathcal{I}(X_p) \Rightarrow \bigwedge_{\{p \mid run_S(\sigma(t)) \notin F_p\}} \alpha(t) \notin \mathcal{I}(X_p)$$

If (a) and (b) hold for S and $S \to_{\mathcal{R}} S'$, then (a) and (b) hold for S'

Proof. For (a): as in lemma 5 and for the same reasons, it is sufficient to prove for a switch to 0 on i on the modified rule that:

$$\bigwedge_{1 \le o \le m} \bigwedge_{\{p | q_o \notin F_p\}} t_o \notin \mathcal{I}(X_p) \Rightarrow f(t_1, .., t_m) \notin \mathcal{I}(X_i) \text{ holds for } S'$$

So, according to the rule applied for $\rightarrow_{\mathcal{R}}$:

- For (Compose): if $g \ne f$, so for any terms $t_1, .., t_m$ in $TERM(\Sigma)$, $f(t_1, .., t_m) \notin \mathcal{I}(g(X_{i_1}, .., X_{i_m}))$, therefore $f(t_1, .., t_m) \notin \mathcal{I}(X_i)$. If $f = g$, the conditions of (a) and the inference rule implies that $\exists k, \forall t_k, t_k \notin \mathcal{I}(X_{i_k})$. Thus, $f(t_1, .., t_m) \notin \mathcal{I}(f(X_{i_1}, .., X_{i_m}))$. Since $\mathcal{I}$ is a solution, $f(t_1, .., t_m) \notin \mathcal{I}(X_i)$.
- For (Union): since (a) holds for unchanged parts of S in S', $q \notin F_{i_1}, q \notin F_{i_2}$ implies that $f(t_1, ..t_m) \notin \mathcal{I}(X_{i_1})$ and $f(t_1, ..t_m) \notin \mathcal{I}(X_{i_2})$. Since $\mathcal{I}$ is a solution, (a) holds.
- For (Project): let us consider a term $t = g(z_1, .., z_{j-1}, f(y_1, .., y_m), z_{j+1}, .., z_l)$. For any substitution ranging on ground terms α' ($\alpha'(z_o) = s_o$), let σ' ranging over (reachable) states s.t. $\sigma'(z_o) = q_{i_o} = run_S(s_o)$. Let σ'' (resp. α'') be a substitution s.t. $\forall o, \sigma''(y_o) = q_o$ (resp. $\alpha''(y_o) = t_o$). Finally, let $\sigma = \sigma' \circ \sigma''$ and $\alpha = \alpha' \circ \alpha''$.
  (b) holds in S (in particular for t, α and σ). Moreover, (b) implies for the s_o that:

$$\bigwedge_{(1 \le o \le l \wedge o \ne f)} \bigwedge_{\{p | q_{i_o}\} \notin F_p} s_o \notin \mathcal{I}(X_p)$$

Finally, since the conditions of the (Project) rule implies that $run_S(\sigma(t)) \notin F_k$, it can be deduced from these that:

$$\bigwedge_{1 \le o \le m} \bigwedge_{\{p | q_o \notin F_p\}} t_o \notin \mathcal{I}(X_p) \Rightarrow g(s_1, .., s_{j-1}, f(t_1, .., t_m), s_{j+1}, .., s_l) \notin \mathcal{I}(X_k)$$

As $\mathcal{I}$ is a solution, the condition implies that $f(t_1, .., t_m) \notin \mathcal{I}(X_i)$.

For (b): for any S, by induction on the structure of t. The proof goes in a similar way to lemma 5 (b).

Theorem 12 (Completeness). $\forall t \in TERM(\Sigma)$,

$$(\exists \mathcal{I} \in SOL(SC) \ t \in \mathcal{I}(X_i)) \Rightarrow run_{S_f}(t) \in F_i$$

Proof. Since (b) obviously holds for S_1, by lemma 11, it holds for S_f. This implies for ground terms that $\forall \mathcal{I} \in SOL(SC)$, $\bigwedge_{\{p | run_{S_f}(t) \notin F_p\}} t \notin \mathcal{I}(X_p)$.
So, $run_{S_f}(t) \notin F_i \Rightarrow \forall \mathcal{I} \in SOL(SC), t \notin \mathcal{I}(X_i)$.

This implies that S_f is unique and represents the greatest solution of the system of set constraints.

5.4 Complexity

We apply for those set constraints the same strategy as for definite set constraints with "membership expression" operator.

Let f (resp. a) be the number of functions symbols (resp. the maximal arity) in Σ. n (resp. v) will denote the number of constraints (resp. of variables) in $\mathcal{SC}$. The number of states and transition rules, and the size of an automaton (T) are the same as for the previous class. Therefore, the maximal number of iterations remains the same.

For a rule and a set constraint: (Union) can be achieved in constant time $O(c)$. (Compose) costs in time at most $O(a)$ and (Project) $O(2^{a\,v}a\,T)$

So, globally this exponential-time algorithm costs at most $O(2^{4v\,a}n\,f^3\,a^2)$.

6 Conclusion

We have proposed in this paper a common approach based on tree automata for two different problems concerning set constraints. Tree automata are shown to be suitable both for computing and representing the solution of those twos: the first one was a satisfiability test for an extension of definite set constraints with "membership expression" operator and the second one computing the greatest solution for a class of set constraints, which can be viewed as the symmetric of those used for set-based analysis [Hei92a]. This approach leads to an easy characterization of complexity of those problems.

It is known that definite set constraints and (positive) set constraints with intersection have the same expressiveness in the sense of sets of solutions. However, adding the "membership expression" operator strictly increases the expressivity. In a practical point of view, a representation of states with "undefined" components (*i.e.* meaning either 1 or 0) and considering at a step only rules involving reachable states should give an efficient implementation. We also aim to extend our approach to infinite trees as done in [CP97b]. This could be achieved by considering the automata in a descending way and modifying the condition of reachability. As mentioned in [CP97a], set constraints with union (that is inclusion between expressions built over function symbols and the union operator) is not dual to set constraints with intersection. It seems that our method cannot easily address this class of constraints. Therefore, the complexity of the satisfiability problem for set constraints with union remains open.

Acknowledgements
The authors thank anonymous referees for their helpful comments and suggestions.

References

[AM91]   A. Aiken and B. Murphy. Implementing Regular Trees. In *Proceedings of the 5th ACM Conference on Functional Programming and Computer Architecture*, LNCS 523, pages 427–447, aug 1991.

[AW92]   A. Aiken and E.L. Wimmers. Solving Systems of Set Constraints. In *Proceedings of the 7th IEEE Symposium on Logic in Computer Science*, pages 329–340, 1992.

[BGW92] L. Bachmair, H. Ganzinger, and U. Waldmann. Set Constraints are the Monadic Class. Technical Report MPI-I-92-240, Max-Planck-Institut für Informatik, dec 1992.

[CP94]   W. Charatonik and L. Pacholski. Set Constraints with Projections are in NEXPTIME. In *Proceedings of the 35th Symposium on Foundations of Computer Science*, pages 642–653, 1994.

[CP97a] W. Charatonik and A. Podelski. Set Constraints with Intersection. In *Proceedings of the 12th IEEE Symposium on Logic in Computer Science*, 1997.

[CP97b] W. Charatonik and A. Podelski. Solving Set Constraints for Greatest Models. Technical Report MPI-I-2-004, Max-Planck-Institut für Informatik, 1997.

[GS84]   F. Gécseg and M. Steinby. *Tree Automata*. Akadémiai Kiadó, Budapest, 1984.

[GTT93] R. Gilleron, S. Tison, and M. Tommasi. Solving systems of set constraints with negated subset relationships. In *Proceedings of the 34th Symp. on Foundations of Computer Science*, pages 372–380, 1993.

[Hei92a] N. Heintze. Practical Aspects of Set Based Analysis. In *Proceedings of theJoint International Conference and Symposium on Logic Programming*. MIT-Press, nov 1992.

[Hei92b] N. Heintze. *Set Based Program Analysis*. PhD thesis, Carnegie Mellon University, sep 1992.

[Hei94] N. Heintze. Set-based Analysis of ML Programs. In *Lisp and Functional Programming*, pages 306–317. ACM, 1994.

[MN97]   M. Müller and J. Niehren. Entailment of Set Constraints is not Feasible. Technical report, Universität des Saarlandes, Programming Systems Lab, 1997. Available at http://www.ps.uni-sb.de/ mmueller/papers/conp.ps.Z.

[MNP97] M. Müller, J. Niehren, and A. Podelski. Inclusion Constraints over Non-Empty Sets of Trees. In *Proceedings of 7th International Joint Conference CAAP/FASE - (TAPSOFT'97)*, LNCS 1214, pages 345–356, apr 1997.

[Ste94] K. Stefansson. Systems of Set Constraints with Negative Constraints are NEXPTIME-Complete. In *Proceedings of the 9th IEEE Symposium on Logic in Computer Science*, 1994.

[Tom94] M. Tommasi. *Automates et Contraintes Ensemblistes*. PhD thesis, Université des Sciences et Technologies de Lille, 1994.

The Logic of Search Algorithms: Theory and Applications*

Ian P. Gent[1] and Judith L. Underwood[2]

[1] APES Research Group, Department of Computer Science,
University of Strathclyde, Glasgow G1 1XH, United Kingdom. ipg@cs.strath.ac.uk
[2] BeAUTy Research Group, Department of Computing Science,
University of Glasgow, Glasgow G12 8QQ, United Kingdom. jlu@dcs.gla.ac.uk

Abstract. Many search algorithms have been introduced without correctness proofs, or proved only with respect to an informal semantics of the algorithm. We address this problem by taking advantage of the correspondence between programs and proofs. We give a single proof of the correctness of a very general search algorithm, for which we provide Scheme code. It is straightforward to implement service functions to implement algorithms such as Davis-Putnam for satisfiability or forward checking (FC) for constraint satisfaction, and to incorporate conflict-directed backjumping (CBJ) and heuristics for variable and value ordering. By separating the search algorithm from problem features, our work should enable the much speedier implementation of sophisticated search methods such as FC-CBJ in new domains, and we illustrate this by sketching an implementation for the Hamiltonian Circuit problem.

1 Introduction

The constraint satisfaction community has an excellent record of introducing intelligent search procedures for binary constraint satisfaction problems. However, the record is less impressive in formally proving such algorithms correct, and in encouraging the application of the same search methods to other NP-complete problems. These two failings represent problems for the community both theoretically, in the absence of formal correctness proofs, and practically, in that the most appropriate search techniques may be reinvented in several problem classes, or simply not used at all outside the CSP community.

In this paper we show that both the theoretical and practical problems can be addressed by separating out the search algorithm from the details of the problem domain. We give a correctness proof of a very general search algorithm using techniques from theoretical computer science, and give Scheme code implementing this algorithm. Then we sketch implementations of a number of search algorithms in a variety of NP-complete problem domains simply by providing

---

* Judith Underwood is supported by EPSRC award GR/L/15685. We thank members of APES, particularly Patrick Prosser and Toby Walsh for their code. We especially thank Mr Denis Magnus for his invaluable contributions to our research.

service functions to our code. To get the full benefit of, say, conflict-directed backjumping (CBJ), domain-specialist need not implement it, nor even understand all the nuances of the technique. If suitably extended, our sketches could form the basis of full correctness proofs of algorithms which have not yet been proved correct, for example MAC-CBJ (maintaining arc-consistency with CBJ.)

2   The Logic of Programs

We consider problems which may be described by a finite set of variables, each of which may take a finite number of values, and a decidable predicate P on an assignment of values to these variables. In this section, we prove a theorem which essentially states that for any problem instance, either there is or is not an assignment which satisfies P. In classical logic, this theorem is trivial. However, we treat the theorem *constructively*: in order to show that this theorem is true in a constructive logic, we must have a decision procedure which, given a problem instance, produces a satisfying assignment if one exists. The proof we give here is designed in such a way that it constitutes a correctness proof of a large family of backtracking search algorithms. The connection between the proof and the algorithms it proves correct is best described by constructive type theory. Type theories are widely used in the theorem proving and formal methods communities [4, 14, 9]; we outline here the main ideas and how they will be used in this setting.

In general, a type theory is an expressive logical language together with rules describing properties of types and terms of each type. Types can be interpreted as formulas; this idea is known as the *Curry-Howard correspondence* [12]. For example, $A \to B$ is the type of functions from A to B, but it also expresses the logical implication that if we know $A \to B$ and A, we know B. More precisely, if we have a *proof* of $A \to B$ and a *proof* of A then we can produce a proof of B. A proof of $A \to B$ is simply any function f from A to B; similarly, a proof of A is an element a of A, and the resulting proof of B is produced by applying f to a. Thus, proofs are programs and programs are proofs.

Given a reasonably expressive language of formulas, we may specify the desired behaviour of a function by stating a theorem; a proof of that theorem then corresponds to a function which is guaranteed to have that behaviour. For example, the theorem $\forall x : N. \exists y : N. (y^2 \leq x) \wedge (x < (y+1)^2)$ asserts that for any natural number x, there exists a natural number y which is the integer part of the square root of x. A constructive proof of this theorem would correspond a function which actually computes the integer square root.

Type theoretic proofs generally carry more information than ordinary programs do since, in addition to producing data, they must provide proofs of properties of the data. Also, not all mathematical proofs can be expressed in a way which corresponds to a program; we work in a constructive type theory which restricts the proof techniques to those which do generate programs.

This approach has many advantages. It is easier to check a proof automatically than to check code, since the proof contains logical information which is not necessarily used in the computation. This means that code extracted from a proof is guaranteed correct, given the correctness of the proof development and program execution environments. Another significant advantage is in modularity. The proof is, in general, more abstract than the code. For example, the proof may say "choose the next variable to set". Computationally, this is a requirement that a function p-choose-var[3] exists and satisfies certain requirements, namely, that it actually returns a variable from the set of unused variables. The proof requires the existence of such a function but does not specify how it is to be implemented. Thus, a new function may be supplied which implements some variable ordering heuristic, and as long as it satisfies the requirements generated by the proof, the program using this new function is still guaranteed correct.

To avoid having to present a complex type theory, we present the proof in ordinary mathematical language. The Scheme program corresponding to this proof is given in full in the Appendix. This correspondence is informal – although we have formalized the core of the proof in Lego [14, 18] and extracted a type theoretic program, we have not produced our code by translating that program to Scheme by some verified method. However, the code we present closely follows the structure of the proof, and in theory could be shown to behave in the same way as the extracted program. To reinforce the connection, in the presentation of the proof we will frequently refer to the corresponding sections of the program.

The remainder of this section is devoted to a proof of the following theorem:

Theorem 1. *Given a finite set of variables, Varset, a finite set of values Valset, and a predicate P on assignments of variables to values, then*

$$(\exists A : Assign(Varset, Valset) . P(A)) \lor (\forall A : Assign(Varset, Valset) . \neg P(A))$$

The notation $A : Assign(Varset, Valset)$ means A is in the type of assignments of values in *Valset* to variables in *Varset*. If an assignment A is only defined on a subset *Vars* of *Varset*, this is denoted by $A : Assign(Vars, Valset)$. Thus, if $A : Assign(Vars, Valset)$, a value has been assigned to every variable in *Vars*. On the types *Varset* and *Valset*, and on the type of assignments, we assume we have the strict ($\subset$) and non-strict ($\subseteq$) subset/subassignment orderings.

We prove Theorem 1 as a corollary to a more general theorem about partial assignments, in which we have introduced conflict sets explicitly. Constructive logic has a *semantics of evidence*: to prove $\forall A : Assign(Varset, Valset) . \neg P(A)$, we must show, for any A, some kind of evidence that the assumption $P(A)$ leads to a contradiction. This is given in the form of a conflict set, which is a set CS of variables in the current assignment A and a guarantee that if A' satisfying $P(A')$ exists, the value of some $v \in CS$ in A' is different from its value in A. This ensures that no extension of A satisfies P. The conflict set is only one way of expressing this, and the idea of the proof will succeed for any kind of structure from which we can conclude $\neg(\exists A'.A \subseteq A' \land P(A'))$. We will later use our logical description of conflict sets to justify backjumping and forward checking.

---

[3] Typographically, names in teletype font are also the names of functions in the Scheme code in the Appendix, or of service functions required to be implemented in a given domain for the Scheme code to work.

Theorem 2. *Given a finite set of variables, Varset, a finite set of values Valset, and a predicate P on full assignments of values to variables, then*

$$\forall Vars \subseteq Varset.$$
$$\forall A : Assign(Vars, Valset) .$$
$$\exists A' : Assign(Varset, Valset) . A \subseteq A' \land P(A')$$
$$\lor$$
$$\exists CS \subseteq Vars. \forall A' : Assign(Varset, Valset) .$$
$$P(A') \to \exists v_0 \in CS. Val\_of(v_0, A') \neq Val\_of(v_0, A)$$

Theorem 1 follows from Theorem 2 by taking *Vars* to be empty, and noting that this requires CS to be empty and thus $P(A)$ leads to a contradiction.

The proof of Theorem 2 will be by induction. The proof is designed so that its computational meaning is a function which performs backtracking search. A proof by induction over a well-founded partial order corresponds to a function defined by well-founded recursion; thus the function can be defined recursively but evaluation is guaranteed to terminate because each recursive call must be applied to arguments which are smaller in the partial order. Such a recursive call corresponds to use of the inductive hypothesis in the proof. Type theoretic languages usually make this explicit by using a special operator for defining functions inductively. To make the code more readable, we use ordinary recursive calls but emphasize that the recursion must terminate.

There are actually two inductions involved in the proof of the theorem. The first is on the size of the set of variables yet to be assigned values. Given a variable to set, the second induction is on the size of the set of values of that variable which have not been tested. This leads to two functions, **test** and **enumerate-domain**. The function **test** takes a given partial assignment and tries to extend it by setting a new variable, while **enumerate-domain** takes a partial assignment and a new variable and tries the possible values for that variable.

We describe in some detail the core of the proof and show how it corresponds to a backtracking search procedure. We then discuss various extensions and generalizations, including propagation and backjumping. These extensions fit naturally into the framework arising from the proof.

We use some abbreviations. If $A : Assign(Vars, Valset)$, let $Result(A)$ be

$$(\exists A' : Assign(Varset, Valset) . A \subseteq A' \land P(A'))$$
$$\lor (\exists CS \subseteq Vars. \forall A' : Assign(Varset, Valset) .$$
$$P(A') \to \exists v_0 \in CS. Val\_of(v_0, A') \neq Val\_of(v_0, A))$$

Result(A) denotes both the formula above and the type of the result of applying the search procedure to the partial assignment A – it returns either a full assignment extending A and satisfying P, or it returns a conflict set. We also abbreviate $\exists v_0 \in CS. Val\_of(v_0, A') \neq Val\_of(v_0, A))$ to *Conflict(CS, A', A)* in order to have a concise notation for the fact that CS describes why the assignment A cannot be extended to a satisfying assignment A'.

Proof of theorem. The proof of the theorem corresponds to the function **test**. Given a partial assignment A, **test** applied to A returns a element of *Result(A)* .

The proof is by induction on the size of the set of unassigned variables, *Varset* − *Vars*. The base case is when this set is empty. Then the assignment A assigns a value to every variable. We assume that we have a lemma **check-full** which, given a full assignment A, proves *Result(A)* . Computationally, the lemma **check-full** is a function which takes a full assignment A as an argument and returns either A (since A is the only assignment extending A) along with evidence that $P(A)$ is true or returns a conflict set CS, along with a proof that CS really is a conflict set. If the proofs are irrelevant to remaining computation, they need not be returned as objects, but there still remains an obligation on the function **check-full** that if it returns an assignment then P holds for that assignment, and if it returns a conflict set then the set has the specified property. Note that if P does not hold for a full assignment A, then *Varset* is a valid conflict set.

For the inductive case of this first induction, we assume we have a nonempty set of unset variables, *Varsleft*. We have the following as an inductive hypothesis:

$$IH1 : \forall s \subset Varsleft.\forall A' : Assign(Varset - s, Valset) .Result(A')$$

and we must prove $\forall A : Assign(Varset - Varsleft, Valset) .Result(A)$. In other words, given an assignment $A : Assign(Varset - Varsleft, Valset)$ we need to construct either an assignment extending A or a conflict set for A.

Computationally, the inductive hypothesis is a function from assignments A' to *Result(A')* , where $A' : Assign(Varset - s, Valset)$ and s is a subset of *Varsleft*. Given $A : Assign(Varset - Varsleft, Valset)$, we can apply this function to any assignment extending A. Since a call to the inductive hypothesis corresponds to a recursive call, in the code we simply call the function **test** recursively.

We construct *Result(A)* by trying the possible extensions of A. We choose a variable in *Varsleft*. Computationally, this is the application of the function **p-choose-var**. We now prove the result for A by using the following lemma:

Lemma 3. *Given $A : Assign(Varset - Varsleft, Valset)$ and $v \in Varsleft$,*

$$\forall Vals \subseteq Valset$$
$$\exists A' : Assign(Varset, Valset) .A \subseteq A' \wedge P(A') \wedge Val\_of(v, A') \in Vals$$
$$\vee \exists CS \subseteq Varset - Varsleft.\forall A' : Assign(Varset, Valset) .$$
$$Val\_of(v, A') \in Vals \rightarrow P(A') \rightarrow Conflict(CS, A`, A)$$

This lemma is represented computationally by the function **enumerate-domain**. The lemma is proved by induction on the size of the set *Vals*. Given the lemma, we can prove *Result(A)* by applying the lemma with *Vals* = *Valset*.

The base case of the induction is when *Vals* is empty. There is no full assignment extending A which gives v a value in $\emptyset$, so we must have a conflict set CS. The property which CS must satisfy is trivial, since $Val\_of(v, A') \in Vals$ will always be false, so the empty set is acceptable for CS.

In the inductive case, we have a second inductive hypothesis:

$IH2(vs_0) : \forall vs \subset Vals.$
    $\exists A' : Assign(Varset, Valset) \ .A \subseteq A' \wedge P(A') \wedge Val\_of\,(v, A') \in vs$
  $\vee\ \exists CS \subseteq Varset - Varsleft.\forall A' : Assign(Varset, Valset)\ .$
      $Val\_of\,(v, A') \in vs \rightarrow P(A') \rightarrow Conflict(CS, A', A)$

We then wish to prove

    $\exists A' : Assign(Varset, Valset)\ .A \subseteq A' \wedge P(A') \wedge Val\_of\,(v, A') \in Vals$
  $\vee\ \exists CS \subseteq Varset - Varsleft.\forall A' : Assign(Varset, Valset)\ .$
      $Val\_of\,(v, A') \in Vals \rightarrow P(A') \rightarrow Conflict(CS, A', A)$

Here, *Vals* represents the set of values which have yet to be tried as values of the variable v. Thus, to apply the second inductive hypothesis (corresponding to a recursive call to **enumerate-domain**), we must reduce this set. So choose a value n in *Vals*. Computationally, this is the function **p-val**. Let $A_{v=n}$ be the assignment A extended with v equal to n.

We could immediately apply the first inductive hypothesis, which computationally is a recursive call to **test**. This corresponds to simple backtracking search. However, we wish to allow for early detection and pruning of impossible partial assignments. Thus, we assume we have a function **check** which, when applied to $A_{v=n}$, returns one of two things. If $A_{v=n}$ is consistent, **check** returns some kind of success token. If $A_{v=n}$ is already inconsistent, **check** returns a conflict set CS for $A_{v=n}$: a subset of $Varset - Varsleft$ such that

$$\forall A' : Assign(Varset, Valset)\ .P(A') \rightarrow Conflict(CS, A', A_{v=n})$$

If **check** does not return a conflict set for the partial assignment, we must try partial assignments extending $A_{v=n}$. Since $A \subset A_{v=n}$, we apply the first inductive hypothesis, calling **test** recursively. The result of applying **test** is of type $Result(A_{v=n})$; that is, either an assignment A' extending $A_{v=n}$ such that $P(A')$, or a conflict set for $A_{v=n}$, as described above. If we have a solution, we are done.

If not, then we have a conflict set (call it $CS1$) for $A_{v=n}$, either derived from **check** or from the recursive call to **test**. Now we remove n from *Vals* and apply the second inductive hypothesis (via a recursive call to **enumerate-domain**) with the set $Vals - \{n\}$. If the result is an $A' : Assign(Varset, Valset)$ such that $A \subseteq A'$ and $P(A')$, then we are done. Otherwise, we have a second conflict set $CS2 \subseteq Varset - Varsleft$ satisfying

$$\forall A' : Assign(Varset, Valset)\ .(Val\_of\,(v, A') \in Vals - \{n\}) \rightarrow$$
$$P(A') \rightarrow Conflict(CS, A', A)$$

Now let $CS = CS1 \cup CS2$. Then $CS \subseteq Varset - Varsleft$, and it is easy to check that CS satisfies

$$\forall A' : Assign(Varset, Valset)\ .(Val\_of\,(v, A') \in Vals) \rightarrow$$
$$P(A') \rightarrow Conflict(CS, A', A)$$

This finishes the inductive case of the lemma, and thus the whole proof.

Modifications to the proof

As presented, this proof corresponds to a fairly simple backtracking search procedure. It has the potential for pruning (via the **check** function), variable ordering heuristics (via **p-choose-var**) and value ordering heuristics (via **p-val**). These functions will, in general, be problem-specific, so the proof cannot describe them in detail. However, the proof does describe minimum requirements for these functions which ensure correctness of the resulting code.

The proof can be extended to describe techniques like conflict-directed backjumping and propagation. The latter requires very little modification to the proof. Note that the only properties we have assumed about assignments are that we can order them (by prefix or subset) so we can say $A' \subseteq A$, and that we can look up the value of a variable v in an assignment A using $Val\_of(v, A)$. The actual type of an assignment may be much more complicated – it may, for instance, include information about eliminated values of future variables. Such information can be computed by the **check** function, and returned to the main function by having **check** take an assignment structure A and return a (possibly modified) assignment structure A'. The proof only requires that the values of the variables in $Vars$ be the same in A and A'.

To introduce the information which may have been computed in this way, we add a step at the beginning of the second induction. Instead of beginning with the whole set of values $Valset$, we assume we have a lemma which, given a partial assignment A and a variable v returns a set $Vals$ of values to be tried together with conflict set CS satisfying[4]

$$\forall A' : Assign(Varset, Valset) . (Val\_of(v, A') \in Valset - Vals) \to$$
$$P(A') \to Conflict(CS, A', A)$$

We cannot eliminate values for no reason; we must still be able to produce the evidence, in the form of a conflict set, that these values are impossible.

If a technique such as forward checking reduces the domain of a variable to a singleton set, the value can be committed to. This is often called 'propagation', and can be the key to the success of search algorithms. For example in Davis-Putnam (DP), this is 'unit propagation'. In CSP's, propagation happens implicitly if forward checking is used with the FF (smallest domain first) heuristic. Our proof allows for propagation without change, because **p-choose-var** is at liberty to pick a variable with domain size 1 if it exists, as long as **p-var-cs** returns an appropriate conflict set. Our code, however, contains a special function **propagate** which is called if commitment is possible: **propagate** is simply a special case of **enumerate-domain** when the domain is known to be of size 1. We have included it for pedagogical purposes to clarify the distinction between propagation and heuristic choice. The extension of our proof for this changed situation would be straightforward.

The extension of the proof to include backjumping is somewhat more subtle. In the code below, we implement backjumping using the Scheme opera-

---

[4] In our code the conflict set is returned by **p-var-cs** and the remaining values enumerated by **p-domain-rest**.

tor `call/cc`, or `call-with-current-continuation`. When (`call/cc` (`lambda`
(`k`) ...)) is evaluated, `k` becomes bound to the current continuation; in other
words, `k` represents the rest of the computation, apart from that remaining in
the body of the `call/cc`. When `k` is applied to an argument, the computation
returns immediately to the context which existed when `k` was created, and the
argument passed to `k` is used in the place of the `call/cc` (`lambda` (`k`) ...)
term. Thus, `call/cc` is essentially a functional goto; it allows control to jump
immediately to another part of the program.

In this program, we use `call/cc` to create continuations which represent
points to which the search might backjump. Backjumping occurs when a conflict set is found which eliminates more of the search tree than its local situation
requires. A continuation is created whenever a variable is set to create a partial assignment. Should we discover, deep in the search tree, that this partial
assignment is inconsistent, we return immediately to this point by applying the
continuation to the evidence of inconsistency, in the form of a conflict set.

To get this computational behaviour from the proof, we use the fact that
`call/cc` can be given the type $((\alpha \to \bot) \to \alpha) \to \alpha$ for any type α [11, 17, 16,
23]. This corresponds to a form a proof by contradiction; if, from the assumption
that α is false, we can prove α, then we have a contradiction so α must be true.
This form of reasoning is not strictly constructive, but in this case we still have a
computational meaning for it. Although a constructive formal system like Lego
does not permit classical reasoning, we can add it by adding an assumption to
the theorem that `call/cc` has type $((\alpha \to \bot) \to \alpha) \to \alpha$. In the proof of the
theorem, we add an extra assumption of the form $\forall A_0 \subset A.\neg Result(A_0)$. These
assumptions are satisfied by the creation of continuations with `call/cc`. When
we produce a more general conflict set than is required and wish to backjump,
we use the appropriate continuation[5] to return immediately to the right stage
in the computation. Logically, this step is an unnecessarily roundabout proof of
$Result(A)$. If the conflict set CS is really a valid result for some previous partial
assignment A_0, then we use the assumption $\neg Result(A_0)$ to get a contradiction
and hence to conclude anything, and in particular $Result(A)$. However, when
the continuation corresponding to the assumption $\neg Result(A_0)$ is applied, the
computation returns to the point where A_0 is being tried by `enumerate-domain`,
the conflict set CS is now treated as a conflict set for A_0, and computation
continues from that point.

This logical treatment of the control ensures that backjumping is sound; we
can only backjump when we have evidence that there is no solution in the part
of the search tree we are pruning. The proof corresponding to a backjumping
algorithm is more complex than the proof corresponding to a simple backtracking algorithm; since the program is more complex as well this should not be
surprising. It is perhaps surprising that the modifications necessary are not even
more complex. Apart from the assumptions mentioned above, we only add a

---

[5] I.e. the continuation associated with the most recently assigned variable in the conflict set. In our code we assume this is returned by `cs-deepest`. We have not proved
correct this and a number of other functions implementing abstract data types.

function/lemma **backjump** which takes a conflict set and applies the continuation corresponding to the deepest conflict, and a data structure which stores the continuations as they are created.

3 Applications: Existing and New Algorithms

It is clear that the above results can be applied to many problem domains. However, the generality of our approach extends not only to search for different problems, but to different search algorithms. Provided code is supplied for the auxiliary functions which meets the obligations needed for our proof, a correct search algorithm will result. However, different search methods can be implemented, depending on exactly how the obligations are met. For example, **check** can perform more or less complicated calculations at each stage. Different amounts of checking will result in different amounts of pruning and propagation. Similar comments apply to other auxiliary functions, allowing for example for variable and value ordering heuristics.

To illustrate how a variety of algorithms can be developed, we give sketches of how to implement algorithms for SAT, CSP, and the Hamiltonian Circuit (HC) problem. While the sketches are not proofs, they could be expanded to give full proofs of the correctness of the relevant algorithms: in some cases this remains important future work. Because of our framework, full proofs could be given just by proving the relevant auxiliary functions correctly implemented. Such proofs should not in general be difficult, yet the result would be correctness proofs of algorithms never formally proved correct (DP with CBJ for SAT or MAC-CBJ for the CSP) or never even previously described (FC-CBJ for HC.)

In describing implementations, we have not focussed on efficiency issues. Reasonably efficient implementations can be based on the following sketches, because our Scheme code allows the auxiliary function to manipulate and update a problem data structure. This enables implementations to cache computations in this data structure to maintain, for example, a data structure for the heuristic values of unassigned variables, rather than recomputing these after every instantiation.

Application: Satisfiability

We consider SAT problems in clausal form. A literal is a negated (negative) or unnegated (positive) variable. A clause is a disjunction of literals, and the whole problem a conjunction of the clauses in the problem. Variables take the value true or false. An assignment satisfies the problem if every clause contains a literal satisfied by the assignment, a positive literal being satisfied by the value true and a negative literal by the value false.

The standard algorithm for SAT is the Davis-Putnam (DP) algorithm [6, 5] though we describe it here (as is often done) without pure literal deletion. However we do present it with both a variable- and a value- ordering heuristic.

DP: Variables are, as would be expected, the variables in the problem. If all clauses have been satisfied by a partial assignment we can stop searching (p-domain-end?)[6] and the problem has been solved (so **check-full** need do

---

[6] To ease reference to our code we mention in passing relevant Scheme functions when describing our implementations.

nothing.) A partial assignment is unsatisfiable if it makes every literal false in some clause: in this situation a valid conflict set is every variable in the partial assignment (check). One reasonable variable-ordering heuristic is to consider only the clauses not yet satisfied and with fewest unassigned literals, and then pick the first variable occurring in the first such clause in the problem (p-choose-var). A value-ordering heuristic is to first give the variable the value true or false according to whether it was in a positive or negative literal (p-val). We can commit (p-commit?) if there is a unit clause under the current partial assignment, i.e. any clause with exactly one unassigned literal. The variable to set (p-commit-var) is the remaining variable to the value it has in the unit clause (p-commit-val). In this situation, the conflict set in evidence of the commitment is again all variables in the partial assignment (p-commit-var-cs).

We implemented the auxiliary functions as described above in Scheme, and tested our code against special-purpose DP code with the same heuristics written independently in Common Lisp.[7] We tested 20 random 3-SAT problems (described for example in [1]) with from 100 to 500 clauses in steps of 1 clause. In each of these 8020 tests both implementations found identical solutions in identical numbers of nodes searched. Such experiments provide confidence that we have implemented the service functions correctly.

DP-CBJ: To implement conflict-directed backjumping in our framework is now easy. We need only change the way conflict sets are returned. When we find an unsatisfied clause, a valid conflict set is just the set of variables occurring in that clause (check). When we find a unit clause, a valid conflict set is just the set of assigned variables occurring in the clause (p-var-cs).

The algorithm DP-CBJ has been reported by Bayardo and Schrag [1]. They have shown that it can outperform the best implementations of DP without CBJ and compete with the best local search methods for SAT [2]. However we are not aware of a formal correctness proof of the algorithm: extending our sketch above into one should be straightforward.

Application: Binary Constraint Satisfaction

Conflict-directed backjumping was first described in the context of binary CSPs [19] so it is natural to apply our framework to that domain. A problem consists of a number of variables each of which can take a value from a finite domain. Each constraint acts on two variables, and rules out a subset of the possible pairs of values from the two domains. An assignment of variables to values is a solution if there are no conflicts with any of the constraints.

CBJ: If all variables have been set we can stop searching (p-domain-end?), and the problem has been solved if all constraints are satisfied (check-full). A partial assignment is unsatisfiable if the pair of values of the current variable and any other variable is ruled out by some constraint: in this situation a valid conflict set is the current variable and the other variable in the conflict (check). Following Prosser [19] we return the conflict with the shallowest variable in the search tree,

---

[7] We thank Toby Walsh for supplying this code. Our code runs considerably slower than Walsh's through using lists for all data structures.

if there is more than one conflict. We pick the smallest unassigned variable in the lexicographic order (p-choose-var). Similarly a trivial value-ordering heuristic is to return each value in the variable's domain in lexicographic order (p-val), and we consider all values so do not need a conflict set for any ruled out values (p-var-cs). We perform no forward checking (p-commit? always returns false.)

We implemented the auxiliary functions as described above in Scheme, and tested our code against special-purpose CBJ code written independently, also in Scheme.[8] When run on problem generated randomly in a standard way (see for example [21]) with 10 variables, 10 values, 23 constraints, and constraint tightness varying from 0.01 to 0.99 in steps of 0.1, the two implementations produced identical results in the solutions found, number of nodes searched, number of checks performed and conflicts found, on 100 problems at each point.

As well as backjumping techniques such as CBJ, propagation techniques such as forward checking are often used, and indeed it would not be difficult to implement FC-CBJ in our framework. A more sophisticated propagation technique is 'maintaining arc consistency' (MAC) [22]. MAC has been combined with CBJ to yield MAC-CBJ [20] and this algorithm has been extensively studied empirically [10]. However we are not aware of a correctness proof of MAC-CBJ. It is therefore particularly interesting to sketch how MAC-CBJ can be implemented in our framework, and therefore how a proof of its correctness might be given.

Forward checking removes values from the domains of future variables which are inconsistent with the assigned value of the current variable. MAC is based on the following observation. If some given value in the domain of one variable conflicts with every value in the current domain of a second variable, we can remove the given value from the domain of the first variable: the given value is said to be 'unsupported' by the second variable.

The key to FC and MAC is the removal of values from variables' domains. Our framework requires evidence in the form of a conflict set for any such removal. But, especially in the case of MAC, construction and maintenance of such conflict sets requires considerable care. Fortunately, this care can be exercised by our search code, leaving only the initial construction of conflict sets to special purpose code. To do this, it is convenient to introduce additional variables representing the removal of a given value from a given variable's domain: such variables can be true or false.[9] When the auxiliary functions detect a value removal, they can report this to the search algorithm by committing the value of an additional variable to true, together with a conflict set representing the reason why the value false is impossible. Later, when the relevant natural variable is chosen, p-var-cs can return the reduced domain together with a conflict set consisting of the additional variables representing all the value removals. This idea makes it comparatively straightforward to implement MAC-CBJ.

MAC-CBJ: If all natural variables have been set (p-domain-end?) we can

---

[8] We thank Patrick Prosser for supplying the independent code. The two implementations are of comparable speed. Our code happens to run slightly faster than Prosser's.

[9] The apparent increase in the number of variables is not a representational problem, as we can name them via some convention, for example (removal var8 red).

stop searching, and the problem has been solved if all constraints are satisfied (check-full). A partial assignment is unsatisfiable if the domain of some unassigned variable is empty, given the value removals made so far. In this situation a valid conflict set is simply the set of additional variables representing the value removals for the variable with empty domain (check), since to find a solution we must restore at least one value to the domain, i.e. change one of the additional variables from true to false. A well-known variable-ordering heuristic is to pick the variable with smallest domain, i.e. least unremoved values (p-choose-var) and we continue to consider remaining values in lexicographic order (p-val). The conflict set for removed values is simply the set of additional variables representing any value removals (p-var-cs). We can make a commitment if some value of an unassigned variable conflicts with the chosen value of the current natural variable (p-commit?), committing the relevant additional variable representing the removal (p-commit-var) which we set to true (p-commit-val), the conflict being with the current natural variable (p-var-cs). We can also make a commitment whenever a given value of a variable is unsupported by a second variable (p-commit?). We can commit to removing the given value of the first variable (p-commit-var, p-commit-val). The removal depends on the current domain of the second variable. Thus a valid conflict set is the set of additional variables representing all value removals so far from the domain of the second variable (p-commit-var-cs). An additional point is that we must look for value removals as a preprocessing step, to establish arc consistency. The first value removal has an empty conflict set: in other words, if this additional variable is ever backjumped to, the problem is insoluble.

Application: Hamiltonian Circuit

The Hamiltonian Circuit problem is to visit all nodes in a graph exactly once and returning the starting point, while only traversing edges that appear in the graph. The problem is NP-complete and a phase transition in solubility has been observed [3, 7]. Algorithms analogous to forward checking have been given, for example by Martello [15], but we are not aware of CBJ having been described for this problem. In our framework it is more natural to implement CBJ rather than chronological backtracking. We consider the problem for directed graphs. We sketch an implementation of the analog of FC-CBJ for this problem.

To apply our technique to this problem, we need to specify the variables and values and describe when and how conflict sets are produced for partial assignments. Variables are nodes in the graph, and possible values for each node n are the nodes accessible by out-arcs from n. When n_1 is assigned n_2, n_2 can be removed from the domains of all future variables; the conflict set which justifies this removal is $\{n_1\}$. Thus we have forward checking for Hamiltonian circuits. A commitment can be made if there is a node with only one out-arc (or only one in-arc) remaining (p-commit-var, p-commit-val). The conflict set justifying this is the set of variables which caused any other out-arcs (or in-arcs) to be removed (p-commit-var-cs). Similarly, when choosing a node heuristically (p-choose-var), we must construct the conflict set of variables which caused any out-arcs from this node to be removed (p-var-cs).

There are three cases in which a partial assignment is inconsistent, and a conflict set is produced by check: there is a node with no in-arcs remaining, there is a node with no out-arcs remaining, or there is a cycle which is not a circuit. If some node n has no in-arcs, a conflict set is the set of nodes in the original graph which had out-arcs to n, since all of these nodes must have been assigned other values. If some node n has no out-arcs, a conflict set is the set of nodes in the original graph which had out-arcs to nodes to which n also had an out-arc. Finally, if there is a cycle which is not a circuit, the conflict set is the set of nodes in that cycle.

For efficiency in an implementation, when an arc from n_1 to n_2 is added to the circuit, the nodes n_1 and n_2 can be collapsed, and the irrelevant arcs deleted, following the description given for example by Martello. However, this is invisible to the search functions – the interface can be written so that test and enumerate-domain see only values in the original problem.

4   Related Work

Following Prosser's introduction of conflict-directed backjumping (CBJ) [19], Ginsberg [8] and Kondrak & van Beek [13] have given proofs of the correctness of CBJ and also related the numbers of nodes searched by different algorithms. The significant advance of our work is in its underlying basis in formal semantics and in its generality. Ginsberg gave proofs of pseudo-code written in English, and Kondrak & van Beek of Prosser's Pascal-like pseudo-code: thus neither proof applies to code for which formal semantics exists. Our results are very general because they apply to a wide variety of search algorithms, and a wide variety of problem classes, all obtainable from the Scheme code we have presented by implementing suitable service functions.

5   Conclusions

We have shown the way that correct implementations of important search algorithms can be achieved in great generality. We have shown this by sketching implementations within our framework of algorithms for diverse problems such as constraint satisfaction, satisfiability, and Hamiltonian circuit. Sophisticated algorithms such as conflict-directed backjumping (CBJ) for each can be implemented without detailed knowledge of the working of the backjumping process.

The importance of our work lies in its generality and its ability to deliver correctness proofs of algorithms. In the future, we hope to use this to extend our sketches to full correctness proofs, most especially for important algorithms that have not to our knowledge been formally proved correct, for example MAC-CBJ for the constraint satisfaction problem and Davis-Putnam with CBJ for satisfiability. While our framework already implicitly allows for techniques such as forward checking, we also hope to expand our general proof and code to incorporate these explicitly, and therefore to further ease the speedy development of good search algorithms in new domains.

90

References

1. R.J. Bayardo and R.C. Schrag. Using CSP look-back techniques to solve exceptionally hard SAT instances. In *CP-96*, pages 46–60. Springer, 1996.
2. R.J. Bayardo and R.C. Schrag. Using CSP look-back techniques to solve real-world SAT instances. In *Proceedings, AAAI-97*, 1997.
3. P. Cheeseman, B. Kanefsky, and W.M. Taylor. Where the really hard problems are. In *Proceedings of the 12th IJCAI*, pages 331–337, 1991.
4. R. Constable et al. *Implementing Mathematics with The Nuprl Development System*. Prentice-Hall, New Jersey, 1986.
5. M. Davis, G. Logemann, and D. Loveland. A machine program for theorem-proving. *Comms. ACM*, 5:394–397, 1962.
6. M. Davis and H. Putnam. A computing procedure for quantification theory. *J. Association for Computing Machinery*, 7:201–215, 1960.
7. J. Frank and C. Martel. Phase transitions in random graphs. In *Proceedings, Workshop on Studying and Solving Really Hard Problems, CP-95*, 1995.
8. M.L. Ginsberg. Dynamic backtracking. *Journal of AI Research*, 1:25–46, 1993.
9. J. Y. Girard, P. Taylor, and Y. Lafont. *Proofs and Types*. Cambridge Tracts in Computer Science, Vol. 7. Cambridge University Press, 1989.
10. S.A. Grant and B.M. Smith. The phase transition behaviour of maintaining arc consistency. In *Proceedings of ECAI-96*, pages 175–179, 1996.
11. T. Griffin. A formulas-as-types notion of control. In *Proc. of the Seventeeth Annual Symp. on Principles of Programming Languages*, pages 47–58, 1990.
12. W. Howard. The formulae-as-types notion of construction. In J. P. Seldin and J. R. Hindley, editors, *To H. B. Curry: Essays on Combinatory Logic, Lambda Calculus, and Formalism*, pages 479–490. Academic Press, 1980.
13. G. Kondrak and P. van Beek. A theoretical evaluation of selected backtracking algorithms. *Artificial Intelligence*, 89:365–387, 1997.
14. Zhaohui Luo. *Computation and Reasoning: A Type Theory for Computer Science*. Oxford University Press, 1994.
15. S. Martello. An enumerative algorithm for finding Hamiltonian circuits in a directed graph. *ACM Transactions on Mathematical Software*, 9:131–138, 1983.
16. C. Murthy. *Extracting Constructive Content from Classical Proofs*. PhD thesis, Cornell University, Dept. of Computer Science, 1990. (TR 89-1151).
17. C. Murthy. An evaluation semantics for classical proofs. In *Proceedings of the Fifth Annual Symposium on Logic in Computer Science*, 1991.
18. R. Pollack. *The Theory of Lego*. PhD thesis, University of Edinburgh, 1995. Available as report ECS-LFCS-95-323.
19. P. Prosser. Hybrid algorithms for the constraint satisfaction problem. *Computational Intelligence*, 9:268–299, 1993.
20. P. Prosser. Maintaining arc-consistency with conflict-directed backjumping. Res. rep. 95-177, Dept. of Computer Science, University of Strathclyde, UK, 1995.
21. P. Prosser. An empirical study of phase transitions in binary constraint satisfaction problems. *Artificial Intelligence*, 81:127–154, 1996.
22. D. Sabin and E.C. Freuder. Contradicting conventional wisdom in constraint satisfaction. In *Proceedings of ECAI-94*, pages 125–129, 1994.
23. J. Underwood. *Aspects of the Computational Content of Proofs*. PhD thesis, Cornell University, 1994.

Appendix: Scheme Code

```scheme
;;; Written by Judith Underwood and Ian Gent, 1997
;;; This code may be copied and used freely, with due credit, but we provide no warranties or guarantees of any kind.

(define (search check check-full)
  (let ((res (call-with-current-continuation
               (lambda (terminate)
                 (test (make-data) (make-problem) 0 check check-full terminate)))))
    res))

(define (test data problem depth check check-full terminate)
  (cond ((p-end? problem)
         (check-full data problem))
        ((p-commit? problem)
         (let* ((new-problem (p-commit-var problem))
                (var (p-var new-problem))
                (result (propagate
                          data
                          (make-result-fail (p-commit-var-cs data new-problem))
                          var new-problem (+ 1 depth)
                          check check-full terminate)))
           (if (result-succeed? result)
               (solved data result terminate)
               result)))
        (t
         (let* ((new-problem (p-choose-var problem))
                (var (p-var new-problem))
                (result (enumerate-domain
                          data
                          (make-result-fail (p-var-cs data new-problem))
                          var new-problem (+ 1 depth)
                          check check-full terminate))  )
           (if (result-succeed? result)
               (solved data result terminate)
               result)))))

(define (propagate data result-so-far var problem depth check check-full terminate)
  (let* ((new-problem (p-domain-commit problem))
         (assign (make-assign var (p-commit-val new-problem)))
         (this-result
           (call-with-current-continuation
             (lambda (k)
               (let* ((new-data (data-add (make-datum assign k depth result-so-far) data))
                      (checkres (check new-data problem))
                      (result (if (result-succeed? checkres)
                                  (test new-data new-problem depth check check-full terminate)
                                  checkres)))
                 (if (result-succeed? result)
                     (solved new-data result terminate)
                     result))))))
    (backjump data
              (result-cleanup (result-merge result-so-far this-result) depth)
              terminate)))

(define (enumerate-domain data result-so-far var problem depth check check-full terminate)
  (if (p-domain-end? problem)
      (backjump data (result-cleanup result-so-far depth) terminate)
      (let* ((new-problem (p-domain-choose problem))
             (assign (make-assign var (p-val new-problem)))
             (this-result
               (call-with-current-continuation
                 (lambda (k)
                   (let* ((new-data (data-add
                                      (make-datum assign k depth result-so-far)
                                      data))
                          (checkres (check new-data problem))
                          (result (if (result-succeed? checkres)
                                      (test new-data new-problem depth check check-full terminate)
                                      checkres)))
                     (if (result-succeed? result)
                         (solved new-data result terminate)
                         result))))))
        (enumerate-domain data
                          (result-merge result-so-far this-result)
                          var
                          (p-domain-rest problem)
                          depth
                          check check-full terminate))))

(define (backjump data result terminate)
  (if (null? (result-cs result))
      (terminate result)
      (let ((back (data-depth data (cs-deepest (result-cs result)))))
        ((datum-continuation back)
         (result-cleanup result (datum-depth back))))))

(define (solved data result terminate)
  (terminate (make-result-success (data-solution data))))
```

Verification of Parallel Systems
Using Constraint Programming*

Stephan Melzer

Institut für Informatik
Technische Universität München, Germany
e-mail: melzers@informatik.tu-muenchen.de

Abstract. Liveness properties of parallel systems usually specify that in every execution certain states are eventually reached. Therefore, violation of such a property can only be detected in infinite executions. In this paper we introduce a semi-decision method that is based on structural Petri net analysis and makes use of the constraint programming paradigm. By a semi-decision method we understand a procedure which may answer 'yes', so that in this case the parallel system satisfies the property, or 'don't know'. We give an implementation of our method in terms of the constraint programming tool 2lp. An application of our approach to a snapshot algorithm demonstrates how constraint programming can beat classical exact methods such as model checking.
KEYWORDS: Verification, Petri nets, constraint programming, finite-state systems.

1 Introduction

In the field of verification the automatic verification of finite-state parallel systems has become a very interesting and important aspect of computer science. The crucial point of the verification task is to develop techniques that do not suffer from the state explosion problem. This problem comprehends the fact that the number of states of a parallel system can grow exponentially in the number of components. Accordingly, every technique that enumerates explicitly all states of a system cannot be applied to practical-sized systems.

Many research has been carried out to tackle the state explosion problem:

- Encode the state space in a more compact representation [21, 14] without an explicit enumeration.
- Use some kind of equivalence that allows to consider only one representative of each class [15, 26].
- Make usage of symbolic computations and represent the whole state space symbolically [9, 7].

All these approaches are designed to capture the state space exactly. If an upper (resp. lower) approximation of the state space is considered, then *only*

* This work has been supported by the Sonderforschungsbereich 342 Teilprojekt A3.

a semi-verification method that involves false-positive (resp. false-negative) results can be obtained, but the verification performance is improved, because the approximation techniques are less complex than exact ones.

In this field some linear algebraic techniques like abstract interpretation [16, 11], structural Petri net analysis [22, 24] and other [10] are already developed. Most of them allow the verification of so-called *safety* properties. These properties are invariant over all states of the system, e.g. deadlock-freedom and absence of critical states. In order to decide whether a system violates a safety property only finite executions have to be considered. On the contrary, *liveness* properties specify properties about infinite behaviour, e.g starvation-freedom. These properties guarantee that in every execution certain states are eventually reached. Therefore, violation of such a property can only be detected for infinite executions. We are using Petri nets [24] to model our parallel systems, but there would be no problem in recasting them for communicating automata [10] or for CCS [23] processes of the form $(P_1 \mid \ldots \mid P_n)\backslash L$, where the P_i are regular.

Thus, our aim is to present an upper approximation of the set of infinite executions and using constraint programming to decide satisfiability of certain liveness properties w.r.t. the parallel system under consideration allowing false-positive results.

More precisely, we take a parallel system π and translate it into the semantical domain of a special class of Petri nets [24], then we derive a set of constraints C_π such that their solutions describe a superset of infinite executions of the system π. Finally, we add[2] some constraints $C_{\neg\phi}$ expressing the negation of a desired property ϕ such that infeasibility of $C_\pi \wedge C_{\neg\phi}$ implies satisfiability of ϕ w.r.t. π.

Practical experiences showed that the constraints C_π are too weak to express the behaviour of π, i.e., the gap between the exact set of infinite executions and its upper approximation C_π often contains solutions that are at the same time also solutions of $C_{\neg\phi}$. The existence of such false-positive solutions makes the application of this approach in practice fruitless.

In order to tackle this problem we derive some disjunctive constraints C_δ from the system that are no model for most of the above-mentioned false-positive solutions. Thus, we have to check the infeasibility of $C_\pi \wedge C_\delta \wedge C_{\neg\phi}$ which can be done by a constrain&generate-strategy using the 2lp [20].

Since we are focusing in this contribution on basic ideas and the usage of the constraint programming paradigm for an improved special case, we refer to [12] where we described a systematic way to obtain C_δ and $C_{\neg\phi}$ for general liveness properties. On the contrary, the general approach does not support a constrain&generate-strategy, but makes use of a generate&test-strategy. The general approach is mainly inspired by the automata-theoretic approach of Wolper and Vardi [28, 27].

It may be criticized that our test is involved in solving an NP-complete problem, namely the infeasibility test of $C_\pi \wedge C_\delta \wedge C_{\neg\phi}$, which may require exponential time. Complexity results show that almost all interesting verification problems about finite-state systems are PSPACE-complete. Polynomial tests for

---

[2] We denote the conjunction of constraints by the logical operator '$\wedge$'.

such problems are bound to have very poor quality, as confirmed by our experiments. NP-complete tests lie between the poor quality polynomial tests and the PSPACE-complete exact methods.

The paper is organized in the following way: In section 2 we give a short introduction to the basics of Petri net theory which are needed for understanding the paper. Section 3 introduces the notation for modelling parallel systems. We give an example to show how to use this notation. In section 4 we show how to obtain the constraints C_π and to express some liveness properties $C_{\neg\phi}$. In section 5 we introduce the disjunctive constraints C_δ that improve significantly the straightforward approach derived in section 4. Section 6 contains an exemplary implementation of the feasibility test of $C_\pi \wedge C_\delta \wedge C_{\neg\phi}$ in terms of the constraint programming tool 2lp and applies it to a more complex example – a snapshot algorithm. Finally, section 7 concludes and gives an outlook on further work.

2   Some Basic Concepts of Petri Nets

A triple (P, T, F) is a *net* if P and T are disjoint sets and F is a subset of $(P \times T) \cup (T \times P)$. The elements of P are called *places* (symbolized by circles) and the elements of T *transitions* (symbolized by rectangles). We identify F with its characteristic function on the set $(P \times T) \cup (T \times P)$. The *preset* of $x \in P \cup T$, denoted by $^\bullet x$, is the set $\{y \in P \cup T \mid F(y, x) = 1\}$. The *postset* of $x \in P \cup T$, denoted by $x^\bullet$, is the set $\{y \in P \cup T \mid F(x, y) = 1\}$. The pre- and postset of a subset of $P \cup T$ are the union of the pre- and post-sets of its elements. A transition t has a *side-condition* to place p if and only if $p \in {}^\bullet t \cap t^\bullet$.

A *marking* M of a net (P, T, F) is a mapping[3] $M : P \to \{0, 1\}$. A four-tuple $N = (P, T, F, M_0)$ is a *Petri net* if (P, T, F) is a net and M_0 is a marking of (P, T, F) (called the *initial marking* of N). A marking M *enables* a transition t if $\forall p \in P\colon F(p, t) \leq M(p)$. If t is enabled at M, then it can *occur*, and its occurrence leads to a new marking M' (denoted $M \xrightarrow{t} M'$), defined by $M'(p) = M(p) - F(p, t) + F(t, p)$ for every place p. A sequence of transitions $\sigma = t_1 t_2 \ldots t_n$ is an *occurrence sequence* if there exist markings $M_1, M_2, \ldots, M_n$ such that $M_0 \xrightarrow{t_1} M_1 \xrightarrow{t_2} \ldots M_{n-1} \xrightarrow{t_n} M_n$. M_n is the marking reached by the occurrence of σ, also denoted by $M_0 \xrightarrow{\sigma} M_n$. An infinite sequence of transitions $\sigma = t_1 t_2 \ldots$ is an infinite occurrence sequence if there exist markings $M_1, M_2, \ldots$ such that $M_0 \xrightarrow{t_1} M_1 \xrightarrow{t_2} M_2 \ldots$.

3   The Programming Notation B(PN)²

There exists a huge number of parallel programming notations to encode parallel systems, e.g. Esterel [1], Lustre [17], CCS [23], CSP [18], Promela [19], and B(PN)² [5] and just as many parallel programming languages, e.g. occam, Ada, Modula-3. In order to apply formal methods to practical problems, we need a

---

[3] In general, we can consider every finite subset of $\mathbb{N}$ instead of $\{0, 1\}$.

programming notation which is as simple as possible and as much as flexible. Due to the fact that many of the above-mentioned notations are specialized on certain hardware topologies (shared memory-, message based-topology) or equipped by a burden of concepts which are irrelevant for the verification task, we choose $B(PN)^2$ as modelling language due to its good compromise on flexibility and simplicity. It supports both topologies whereas message buffers are modelled via FIFO buffers with a capacity ranking from zero (handshake) up to infinity (unbounded capacity). It is a block-structured programming notation which features procedures, a nested parallel construct, guarded commands and non-determinism, but it does not support priorities and structural data.

Behind $B(PN)^2$ an abundant theory [4] has been glued together that allows a compositional translation of a program π into a Petri net N_π. Properties of π can be translated into properties over elements of N_π. This enables the usage of the Petri net theory for the verification of desired properties of π.

Now, we present the syntax of $B(PN)^2$ and show how to encode Peterson's mutual exclusion algorithm [25] in $B(PN)^2$.

Syntax of $B(PN)^2$. In Figure 1 the formal syntax of $B(PN)^2$ is given. Key words are printed in `teletype` while identifiers are printed in *italic*. In order

```
program  ::= block
block    ::= begin scope end
scope    ::= com | var varlist : type; scope
varlist  ::= var-name | varlist, varlist
type     ::= set | set init const | chan cap of set    (cap ∈ IN ∪ {ω})
com      ::= 〈 expr 〉 | com‖com | com;com | do alt-set od
alt-set  ::= com;exit | com;repeat | alt-set [] alt-set
expr     ::= 'v | v' | v | c! | c? | const | expr op expr | op expr | (expr)
             const ∈ IN, op ∈ {+, −, *, /, ∧, ∨, ¬, <, >, =}
```

Fig. 1. Syntax of $B(PN)^2$.

to become more familiar with this programming notation we stress upon some features of $B(PN)^2$ [2]:

- *Atomic actions.* The expressions given in between angular brackets denote atomic actions. In the translation into a Petri net, every such action is associated with one, or a set of alternative, single transitions. The expression of an atomic action is a predicate over pre- and postvalues of variables touched by the action. For instance, an atomic action expressing the assignment $x := y$ would be written as $\langle x' = {}'y \wedge y' = {}'y \rangle$, whereas ${}'v$ (resp. v') denotes the prevalue (resp. postvalue) of v. Any value change which makes the predicate true enables the action. For convenience, we use the unprimed version of a variable to denote its pre- and postvalue in a single term, e.g., $\langle x' = {}'y \wedge y' = {}'y \rangle$ can also be written as $\langle x' = y \rangle$.

- *Unification of shared memory and channel communication.* To describe channel communication in predicative style, $B(PN)^2$ features c? and c! as primitives denoting the value last read on channel c and the value last output to channel c, respectively. They are analogous to the pre- and postvalues of variables.
- *Unification of choices and loops.* $B(PN)^2$ contains a single **do-od** clause both for choices and for loops. The symbol [] separates alternatives, which can be ended either by the keyword **exit** (indicating the exit from the loop) or by the keyword **repeat** (indicating a repetition of the loop).

Peterson's Mutual Exclusion Algorithm. In Figure 2 we show how to encode Peterson's mutual exclusion algorithm [25] in $B(PN)^2$. The a's and b's on the righthand side are used to identify the atomic actions. The first **do-od** construct encodes process p_1 with its actions $a_1, \ldots, a_4$ while the second process is built from the actions $b_1, \ldots, b_4$. The critical section of p_1 (resp. p_2) lies between action a_3 and a_4 (resp. b_3 and b_4). The mutual exclusion property specifies that both processes never enter simultaneously their critical sections. This is a so-called *safety* property. Moreover, we want to guarantee that every process that

```
begin
    var in1, in2 : {false, true} init false;
    var hold : {1,2} init 1;

    do
        ( in1' = true );                       a₁
        ( hold' = 1 );                         a₂
        ( in2=false ∨ hold=2 );                a₃
        ( in1' = false ); repeat               a₄
    od
||
    do
        ( in2' = true );                       b₁
        ( hold' = 2 );                         b₂
        ( in1=false ∨ hold=1 );                b₃
        ( in2' = false ); repeat               b₄
    od
end
```

Fig. 2. Peterson's mutual exclusion algorithm.

wants to enter its critical section (occurrence of action a_1, resp. b_1) does eventually reach its critical section (occurrence of action a_3, resp. b_3). This property is typically called *starvation-freedom*.

In Figure 3 the associated Petri net is depicted. We use the action names with indices to indicate the corresponding transitions, e.g, action a_3 is translated into two transitions a_{3_1} and a_{3_2}. Transition a_{3_1} represents the first clause (in2=false) of action a_3, while transition a_{3_2} stands for the second clause (hold=2). Similar, action a_2 is translated into two transitions a_{2_1} and a_{2_2}. Hereby, a_{2_1} considers the case that hold has the value 1 before action a_2 occurs and transition a_{2_2} considers the case where hold has value 2.

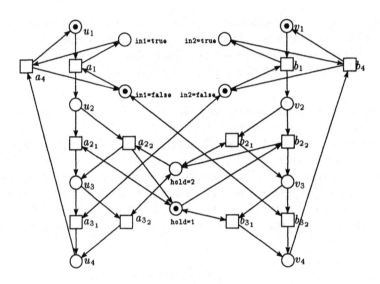

Fig. 3. The associated Petri net.

4 Certain Liveness Properties and a Verification Method

In this section we show how to obtain a set of constraints C_π that describes a linear upper approximation of the set of infinite occurrence sequences.

The fact that we restrict ourselves to finite-state systems is reflected in the definition of a *marking* of a Petri net, i.e., a function with domain $\{0, 1\}$. Therefore, every infinite occurrence sequence σ can only contain finitely many different markings. This implies the existence of a subsequence σ' of σ that reproduces a marking M, i.e., $\sigma = \sigma_1 \sigma' \sigma_2$ and $M \xrightarrow{\sigma'} M$. The existence of a reproduced marking M and a subsequence σ' allows the following observation:

For each place p the number of tokens added by (the firing of) the input transitions of p is equal to the number of tokens removed by the output transitions. If we denote by $\#(\sigma', t)$ the number of times that transition t occurs in subsequence σ', every reproducing sequence σ' satisfies the linear constraint $c_\pi(p)$ defined as:

$$c_\pi(p) : \sum_{t \in {}^\bullet p} \#(\sigma', t) = \sum_{t \in p^\bullet} \#(\sigma', t). \tag{1}$$

Let us abstract from a concrete subsequence and substitute $\#(\sigma, t)$ by a semi-positive variable $X(t)$. Now, we integrate the previous conclusion into the next definition.

Definition 1. Constraints C_π. Given a net $N_\pi = (P_\pi, T_\pi, F_\pi)$, we define the set of constraints C_π in the following way:

$$C_\pi = \bigwedge_{p \in P_\pi} c_\pi(p).$$

Given a subsequence $M \xrightarrow{\sigma} M$, C_π has at least one solution, namely $X := (\#(\sigma, t_1), \#(\sigma, t_2), \ldots, \#(\sigma, t_n))$. Thus, a necessary condition for the existence of an infinite occurrence sequence in N_π is the feasibility of C_π.

More precisely, every suffix σ' of an infinite occurrence sequence σ that contains only the transitions occurring infinitely often has a corresponding solution X of C_π. The reader who is familiar with Petri net theory will recognize X as a so called semipositive T-invariant [24].

We wish to verify that every infinite occurrence sequence satisfies a desirable property, or, equivalently, that there does not exist any infinite occurrence sequence satisfying the negation of this desirable property. The negation of the property can often be expressed by means of *constraints* on the variables X of C_π. Here are two examples:

- Progress.

  Suppose that in a program π exist some refresh actions which have to be executed from time to time. If $t_1, \ldots, t_m$ are the transitions of N_π corresponding to the refresh actions, then the sequences σ that violate the progress property are those satisfying

  $$X(t_1) + X(t_2) + \ldots + X(t_m) = 0.$$

- Fairness.

  Sometimes we want to specify progress of some actions in relation to the progress of some other actions. E.g., if process p_1 executes infinitely often its actions then process p_2 should also execute its actions. If $t_1, \ldots t_{n_1}$ are the transitions belonging to process p_1 and resp. $t'_1, \ldots t'_{n_2}$ to p_2, then all unfair sequences satisfy

  $$X(t_1) + \ldots + X(t_{n_1}) > 0 \quad \wedge \quad X(t'_1) + \ldots + X(t'_{n_2}) = 0.$$

Many liveness properties can be described in terms of constraints over the number of times transitions occurring periodically. We will now show how to express starvation-freedom of Peterson's algorithm in such a way.

In Peterson's algorithm every process that wants to enter its critical section will eventually become critical. Therefore, a starving execution would be that process p_1 enters infinitely often its critical section while process p_2 waits infinitely often to become critical after setting its variable in2 to true. On the one hand, the fact that *process p_1 becomes infinitely often critical under the assumption that p_2 wants but never gets critical* can be expressed by $X(a_{3_2}) > 0$. Transition a_{3_2} corresponds to action a_3, more precisely to the case hold = 2. On the other hand, the fact that *p_2 never becomes critical* can be easily specified by $X(b_{3_1}) + X(b_{3_2}) = 0$, because both transitions are associated to action b_3 that signals the entrance into the critical section of process p_2. Thus, such a starving sequence satisfies[4]

$$X(a_{3_2}) > 0 \quad \wedge \quad X(b_{3_1}) + X(b_{3_2}) = 0.$$

For the sequel we denote the previous property by ξ and the previous constraint by $\mathcal{C}_{\neg\xi}$.

A naive approach would take the constraints $\mathcal{C}_P$ for Peterson's algorithm P and the constraints $\mathcal{C}_{\neg\xi}$ and show that there exists no common solution. The justification for this approach is that every infinite occurrence sequence σ of N_P implies the existence of a solution of $\mathcal{C}_P$ corresponding to the transitions occurring infinitely often. If there exists no solution of $\mathcal{C}_P$ and $\mathcal{C}_{\neg\xi}$ then no reproducing subsequence exists that violates ξ, thereby no infinite occurrence sequence violates ξ.

The reason why this approach has to fail lies in the structure of the constraints $\mathcal{C}_\pi$ itself. All transitions t that are in the pre- and postset of a place p have no term $X(t)$ appearing in constraint $c_\pi(p)$ that would express its connectivity to place p, because they cancel each other out. Such places play the role of a side-condition for the occurrence of a transition. For example, action a_3 tests whether in2=false or hold=2 are satisfied. The associated transition a_{3_1} (resp. a_{3_2}) has a side-condition to the place representing in2=false (resp. hold=2), i.e., ${}^\bullet a_{3_1} \cap a_{3_1}^\bullet$ contains place in2=false and ${}^\bullet a_{3_2} \cap a_{3_2}^\bullet$ contains hold=2. Therefore, for both places neither $X(a_{3_1})$ nor $X(a_{3_2})$ appears in their equation[5] c_P. To be complete we now give all constraints $\mathcal{C}_P$ for Peterson's algorithm:

$$c_P(u_1) : X(a_4) = X(a_1)$$
$$c_P(u_2) : X(a_1) = X(a_{2_1}) + X(a_{2_2})$$
$$c_P(u_3) : X(a_{2_1}) + X(a_{2_2}) = X(a_{3_1}) + X(a_{3_2})$$
$$c_P(u_4) : X(a_{3_1}) + X(a_{3_2}) = X(a_4)$$
$$c_P(v_1) : X(b_4) = X(b_1)$$
$$c_P(v_2) : X(b_1) = X(b_{2_1}) + X(b_{2_2})$$
$$c_P(v_3) : X(b_{2_1}) + X(b_{2_2}) = X(b_{3_1}) + X(b_{3_2})$$
$$c_P(v_4) : X(b_{3_1}) + X(b_{3_2}) = X(b_4)$$
$$c_P(\text{in1} = \text{false}) : X(a_4) = X(a_1)$$
$$c_P(\text{in1} = \text{true}) : X(a_1) = X(b_4)$$
$$c_P(\text{in2} = \text{false}) : X(b_4) = X(b_1)$$
$$c_P(\text{in2} = \text{true}) : X(b_1) = X(b_4)$$
$$c_P(\text{hold} = 1) : X(b_{2_2}) = X(a_{2_2})$$
$$c_P(\text{hold} = 2) : X(a_{2_2}) = X(b_{2_2}).$$

---

[4] In general, we also have to consider the opposite case, but in the sequel we omit it for simplicity.

[5] E.g., $c_P(\text{in2} = \text{false}) : X(b_4) + X(a_{3_1}) = X(b_1) + X(a_{3_1}) \Leftrightarrow X(b_4) = X(b_1)$.

It is easy to see that these constraints do not contain any side-conditions. Therefore, it is not surprising that $C_P \wedge C_{\neg \xi}$ has solutions that do not correspond to any infinite occurrence sequence, because side-conditions are essential for the correctness of Peterson's algorithm. The vectors X' with $X'(t) > 0$ for $t \in \{a_1, a_{2_1}, a_{3_2}, a_4\}$ and $X'(t) = 0$ else, solve both constraints C_P and $C_{\neg \xi}$. Because transition a_{2_1} tests whether hold=1 is satisfied and transition a_{3_2} tests whether hold=2 is satisfied and X' does not contain any transition that changes the value of variable hold from 1 to 2, no infinite occurrence sequence exists that corresponds to such solutions X'. This kind of argumentation has already been introduced and applied in an ad-hoc and manual proof method [13]. But in [13] this argument is used after the calculation of all solutions of $C_\pi \wedge C_{\neg \phi}$. That procedure is already implemented as automatical test [12] and corresponds to a generate&test-strategy. In the next section we introduce an approach that covers these side-conditions and makes use of a constrain&generate-strategy.

5 The Improvement

In the previous section we have seen that side-conditions are the main drawback of the usage of C_π. These side-conditions appear in Petri nets at places that correspond to values of variables. If an action in a $B(PN)^2$ program tests the value of a variable, then the associated transitions have a side-condition to each place corresponding to the tested value.

Given a variable ν with domain D_ν of a $B(PN)^2$ program π and let $N_\pi = (P_\pi, T_\pi, F_\pi)$ be the corresponding net, we use the set $T_{i,j}^\nu \subseteq T_\pi$ to denote the transitions that change the value[6] of variable ν from i to j. E.g., $T_{t,f}^{in1} = \{a_4\}$ and $T_{1,1}^{hold} = \{a_{2_1}, b_{3_2}\}$. Using this definition we are able to describe the fact that a binary variable that is tested infinitely often on its two different values has to change its value infinitely often. More precisely, for every infinite occurrence sequence σ and for every binary variable ν with domain $D_\nu = \{\nu_1, \nu_2\}$ the disjunctive constraint $c_\delta(\nu)$:

$$\left(\sum_{t \in T_{\nu_1,\nu_1}^\nu} \#(\sigma,t) > 0 \wedge \sum_{t \in T_{\nu_2,\nu_2}^\nu} \#(\sigma,t) > 0 \right) \Rightarrow \left(\sum_{t \in T_{\nu_1,\nu_2}^\nu} \#(\sigma,t) > 0 \wedge \sum_{t \in T_{\nu_2,\nu_1}^\nu} \#(\sigma,t) > 0 \right)$$

has to be satisfied. In our example we obtain for variable hold the following disjunctive constraint:

$$c_\delta(\text{hold}) : \quad \underbrace{\#(\sigma,a_{2_1}) + \#(\sigma,b_{3_2}) > 0}_{T_{1,1}^{hold}} \wedge \underbrace{\#(\sigma,a_{3_2}) + \#(\sigma,b_{2_1}) > 0}_{T_{2,2}^{hold}}$$

$$\Rightarrow \underbrace{\#(\sigma,b_{2_2}) > 0}_{T_{1,2}^{hold}} \wedge \underbrace{\#(\sigma,a_{2_2}) > 0}_{T_{2,1}^{hold}}$$

---

[6] In the sequel, we abbreviate true by t and false by f.

If we substitute $\#(\sigma, t)$ by $X(t)$ in $c_\delta(\mathbf{hold})$, then $\mathcal{C}_P \wedge \mathcal{C}_{\neg \xi} \wedge c_\delta(\mathbf{hold})$ has no solution, which implies that all infinite occurrence sequences of Peterson's algorithm are starvation-free.

For a binary variable ν of a $B(PN)^2$ program the constraint $c_\delta(\nu)$ is just a single disjunctive constraint, but for variables with a domain containing more than two elements, we have to consider a family of disjunctive constraints. The next definition faces this aspect:

Definition 2. Family $c_\delta(\nu)$ for $|D_\nu| > 2$. Given a variable ν of a $B(PN)^2$ program π and let $N_\pi = (P_\pi, T_\pi, F_\pi)$ be the associated net, the family of constraints $c_\delta(\nu)$ is defined in the following way:

$$c_\delta(\nu) : \bigcup_{\substack{D_1 \uplus D_2 \uplus D_3 = D_\nu \\ D_1, D_2 \neq \emptyset}} \left(\left(\bigwedge_{\eta=1}^{2} \bigwedge_{i \in D_\eta} \sum_{\substack{t \in T_{i,j}^\nu \cup T_{j,i}^\nu \\ j \in D_\eta}} X(t) > 0 \right) \wedge \bigwedge_{\substack{i \in D_3 \\ j \in D_\nu}} \sum_{t \in T_{i,j}^\nu \cup T_{j,i}^\nu} X(t) = 0 \right.$$

$$\left. \Rightarrow \sum_{\substack{t \in T_{i,j}^\nu \\ i \in D_1, j \in D_2}} X(t) > 0 \wedge \sum_{\substack{t \in T_{i,j}^\nu \\ j \in D_1, i \in D_2}} X(t) > 0 \right)$$

The intuition of the previous definition is that if variable ν has infinitely often the values of subset D_1 and has also infinitely often values of subset D_2 and does not have infinitely often values of subset D_3, then transitions have to occur infinitely often that exchange values of D_1 and D_2.

In order to give an impression how definition 2 works and how the family c_δ looks like, we apply it to a variable μ with $D_\mu = \{1, 2, 3\}$. The family $c_\delta(\mu)$ contains six different disjunctive constraints:

$$c_\delta(\mu) : \quad \{ \qquad \underbrace{c_\delta^{(1)}(\mu)}_{D_1=\{3\},D_2=\{2\},D_3=\{1\}} \qquad , \qquad \underbrace{c_\delta^{(2)}(\mu)}_{D_1=\{3\},D_2=\{1\},D_3=\{2\}} \qquad , \qquad \underbrace{c_\delta^{(3)}(\mu)}_{D_1=\{1\},D_2=\{2\},D_3=\{3\}}$$

$$\underbrace{c_\delta^{(4)}(\mu)}_{D_1=\{1,2\},D_2=\{3\},D_3=\emptyset} \quad , \quad \underbrace{c_\delta^{(5)}(\mu)}_{D_1=\{1,3\},D_2=\{2\},D_3=\emptyset} \quad , \quad \underbrace{c_\delta^{(6)}(\mu)}_{D_1=\{2,3\},D_2=\{1\},D_3=\emptyset} \quad \}$$

We exemplarily pick out $c_\delta^{(3)}$ and $c_\delta^{(4)}$:

$$c_\delta^{(3)} : \left(\sum_{t \in T_{1,1}^\mu} X(t) > 0 \wedge \sum_{t \in T_{2,2}^\mu} X(t) > 0 \wedge \sum_{\substack{t \in T_{1,3}^\mu \cup T_{3,1}^\mu \cup \\ T_{3,3}^\mu \cup T_{2,3}^\mu \cup T_{3,2}^\mu}} X(t) > 0 \right) \Rightarrow$$

$$\left(\sum_{t \in T_{1,2}^\mu} X(t) > 0 \wedge \sum_{t \in T_{2,1}^\mu} X(t) > 0 \right)$$

$$c_\delta^{(4)} : \left(\sum_{t \in T_{1,1}^\mu \cup T_{1,2}^\mu} X(t) > 0 \wedge \sum_{t \in T_{2,2}^\mu \cup T_{2,1}^\mu} X(t) > 0 \wedge \sum_{t \in T_{3,3}^\mu} X(t) > 0 \right) \Rightarrow$$

$$\left(\sum_{t \in T_{1,3}^{\mu} \cup T_{2,3}^{\mu}} X(t) > 0 \quad \wedge \quad \sum_{t \in T_{3,1}^{\mu} \cup T_{3,2}^{\mu}} X(t) > 0 \right)$$

Complexity Remark. The number of disjunctive constraints of a family $c_\delta(\nu)$ grows exponentially in the size of D_ν. This fact is not surprising because a result of [12] shows that the problem to decide whether a given Petri net has a solution X for $C_\pi \wedge C_\delta$ is NP-complete. Therefore, a restriction to problem-specific constraints or a selection done by the user might be needed in more complex cases. E.g., in Peterson's algorithm the constraints $c_\delta(\text{in1}) \wedge c_\delta(\text{in2})$ are redundant for proving starvation-freedom.

Actually, the mutual exclusion property of Peterson's algorithm can also be proven by an approach introduced in [22] featuring an implementation in terms of constraint programming.

6 An Implementation in 2lp

We are using 2lp [20] as underlying constraint programming framework, because on the one hand 2lp is closer to linear programming as to logic programming which fits better to our specification and on the other hand it offers an easy prototyping by C-like programming notation. We implemented a constraint generator that translates a program π into a 2lp-program $C_\pi \wedge C_\delta$ such that the answer *No feasible solution exists* corresponds to the satisfiability of the property under consideration w.r.t. π. If there exists a solution then we cannot decide whether it is a counterexample or *just* a false-positive solution. In order to give an impression of the translation into a 2lp program, we present a fragment of the corresponding program for Peterson's algorithm and $C_{\neg\xi}$:

\\ The constraints C_P
X(a_4) == X(a_1);
X(a_1) == X(a_{2_1}) + X(a_{2_2});
X(a_{2_1}) + X(a_{2_2}) == X(a_{3_1}) + X(a_{3_2});
X(a_{3_1}) + X(a_{3_2}) == X(a_4);
X(b_4) == X(b_1);
X(b_1) == X(b_{2_1}) + X(b_{2_2});
X(b_{2_1}) + X(b_{2_2}) == X(b_{3_1}) + X(b_{3_2});
X(b_{3_1}) + X(b_{3_2}) == X(b_4);
X(a_4) == X(a_1);
X(a_1) == X(b_4);
X(b_4) == X(b_1);
\\ to be continued on rhs.

X(b_1) == X(b_4);
X(b_{2_2}) == X(a_{2_2});
X(a_{2_2}) == X(b_{2_2});
\\ The constraints $C_{\neg\xi}$
X(a_{3_2}) >= 1.0;
X(b_{3_1}) + X(b_{3_2}) == 0.0;
\\ The constraint $c_\delta(hold)$
either X(a_{2_1}) + X(b_{3_2}) == 0.0;
or X(a_{3_2}) + X(b_{2_1}) == 0.0;
or X(b_{2_2}) + X(a_{2_2}) >= 1.0;
printf ("May exist a counterexample.");

Similar to Peterson's algorithm, we are able to verify starvation-freedom for other mutual exclusion algorithms, like Dekker's or Dijkstra's solution [25]. For the latter algorithms starvation-freedom is only satisfied under a fairness assumption. Therefore, we express the fairness assumption also as a set of constraints and add it to $C_\pi \wedge C_{\neg\xi} \wedge C_\delta$.

Now we want to show how our method works for a more complex example – a snapshot algorithm.

A snapshot algorithm. In a distributed system each process only knows its own *local* state. However, under certain circumstances one process must be able to check the local state of all other processes – not absolutely at the same time, but each at a future point in time. This *global* state is called snapshot and makes information about *stable properties* available , e.g. termination of single processes or deadlock of the whole system.

It is possible to generate this snapshot with *or* without a monitor process [6]. We implement a simplified version with a monitor process presented in [3].

Specification. Suppose a given distributed system with N processes and one single monitor process M. Every process can synchronously communicate with its neighbour processes and with the monitor process. The task of the snapshot algorithm is to enable any process at any time to initiate a snapshot that is generated in the monitor process M. After the generation of a single snapshot all processes receive it, and then they are reinitialized.

Implementation. In [3] a method is presented to extend a given CSP-program [18] by means of certain code fragments that enable repeated snapshots. Due to lack of space we omit the explanation of the extension and refer to [6, 3] for a detailed description. However, we applied this extension to a ring architecture with four processes. The following $B(PN)^2$-program describes the implementation of four processes connected via a ring:

```
begin
var c₀, c₁, c₂, c₃ : chan 0 of {data, signal};
var info, restart : chan 0 of {id₀, id₁, id₂, id₃};

proc process (const id : {id₀, id₁, id₂, id₃}, ref in : chan 0 of {data, signal},
    ref out : chan 0 of {data, signal})
begin
var active, sent : {true, false} init false;
    do
       ⟨ active = false ⟩; ⟨ active' = true ⟩; ⟨ info! = id ⟩; repeat
    []
       ⟨ in? = signal ⟩;
       do
          ⟨ active = true ⟩; exit;
       []
          ⟨ active = false ⟩; ⟨ active' = true ⟩; ⟨ info! = id ⟩; exit;
       od; repeat
    []
       ⟨ active = true ∧ out! = signal ∧ sent = false ⟩; ⟨ sent' = true ⟩; repeat
    []
       ⟨ restart? = id ⟩; ⟨ active' = false ⟩; ⟨ sent' = false ⟩; repeat
    od
end;
```

proc monitor (**const** id_0 : $\{id_0, id_1, id_2, id_3\}$, **const** id_1 : $\{id_0, id_1, id_2, id_3\}$,
    const id_2 : $\{id_0, id_1, id_2, id_3\}$, **const** id_3 : $\{id_0, id_1, id_2, id_3\}$)
begin
var rec_0, rec_1, rec_2, rec_3, $snapshot\_generated$: $\{$**true**, **false**$\}$ **init false**;
   do
      $\langle$ $info?$ $= id\_0 \wedge$ rec$\_0$' $=$ **true** $\rangle$; **repeat**
    $[]$
      $\langle$ $info?$ $= id\_1 \wedge$ rec$\_1$' $=$ **true** $\rangle$; **repeat**
    $[]$
      $\langle$ $info?$ $= id\_2 \wedge$ rec$\_2$' $=$ **true** $\rangle$; **repeat**
    $[]$
      $\langle$ $info?$ $= id\_3 \wedge$ rec$\_3$' $=$ **true** $\rangle$; **repeat**
    $[]$
      $\langle$ $rec\_0 =$ **true** $\wedge$ $rec\_1 =$ **true** $\wedge$ $rec\_2 =$ **true** $\wedge$ $rec\_3 =$ **true** $\rangle$;
      $\langle$ $snapshot\_generated$' $=$ **true** $\rangle$;
      $\langle$ $restart!$ $= id\_0 \wedge$ rec$\_0$' $=$ **false** $\rangle$; $\langle$ $restart!$ $= id\_1 \wedge$ rec$\_1$' $=$ **false** $\rangle$;
      $\langle$ $restart!$ $= id\_2 \wedge$ rec$\_2$' $=$ **false** $\rangle$; $\langle$ $restart!$ $= id\_3 \wedge$ rec$\_3$' $=$ **false** $\rangle$;
      $\langle$ $snapshot\_generated$' $=$ **false** $\rangle$; **repeat**
   od
end;

process (id_0, c_0, c_1) $\|$ process (id_1, c_1, c_2) $\|$ process (id_2, c_2, c_3) $\|$
process (id_3, c_3, c_0) $\|$ monitor (id_0, id_1, id_2, id_3)
end

Verification and results. One fundamental property of the snapshot algorithm is that a snapshot is generated infinitely often. Suppose that the transitions T_{snap} correspond to the action $\langle$ $snapshot\_generated$' $=$ **true** $\rangle$ of the monitor process, the solutions of C_π violating this property satisfy $\sum_{t \in T_{snap}} X(t) = 0$.

We generated C_π and C_δ for the local variables $sent$, $mode$ in 90 seconds[7] and checked infeasibility of $C_\pi \wedge C_\delta \wedge C_{\neg \phi}$ in 6 seconds. Net N_π consists of 146 places and 150 transitions. We should remark at this point that without our improved constraints C_δ the method would fail, because the constraints $C_\pi \wedge C_{\neg \phi}$ have 55 different[8] false-positive solutions. All these solutions are excluded by C_δ. In comparison, the general method of our approach [12] that uses a generate&test- instead of a constrain&generate-strategy, takes 436 seconds to verify the property. We also verified Bouge's snapshot algorithm for five (resp. six, seven) processes in 30 (resp. 371, 3360) seconds.

---

[7] This time was very large, but this is due to the fact that the implementation of the compiler from B(PN)^2 into Petri nets has not been optimized yet.

[8] Given a solution, the set of variables that have non-zero values, corresponds to a set of transitions. 'Different' is related to the latter sets.

A comparison to exact methods shows the advantage of our semi-decision approach. The SPIN tool [19] aborts even for four processes after a few minutes due to a memory overflow (128 MBytes are exceeded). And it could not be verified by the stubborn set method either. We tried to compute the stubborn reduced reachability graph for four processes using Starke's INA tool, but had to abort the process after 20 hours, when 206000 reduced states had been generated. Another example cannot be shown here due to lack of space, but we want to mention that we also verified Chang and Robert's leader election algorithm [8].

7 Conclusion

We have presented a semi-decision test for the satisfiability of certain liveness properties w.r.t. parallel systems. We showed how to improve the approach by considering disjunctive constraints and implemented the test in the constraint programming tool 2lp. We have shown that there exist real algorithms for which our test allows to verify a property that cannot be proven using exact methods. We finish our contribution with a comment on the implementation in 2lp: Linear programming plays an important role in net theory, but it is often too restrictive. Constraint programming tools like 2lp open a wide range of new possibilities in the application of structural objects like invariants, siphons and traps to verification problems. For our future work we plan to combine structural net theory with constraint programming, yielding more expressive and efficient verification methods.

Acknowledgements. The author thanks Javier Esparza and Robert Riemann for their critical comments on an earlier version of this paper.

References

1. G. Berry and G. Gonthier. The Esterel synchronous programming language: Design, semantics, implementation. *Science of Computer Progr.*, 19(2):87–152, 1992.
2. E. Best. Partial order verification with PEP. In D. Peled, G. Holzmann, and V. Pratt, editors, *Proc, POMIV'96, Partial Order Methods in Verification.* American Mathematical Society, August 1996.
3. E. Best. *Sematics of Sequential and Parallel Programs.* Prentice Hall, 1996.
4. E. Best, R. Devillers, and J. G. Hall. The Box Calculus: A New Causal Algebra with Multi-Label Communication. In *Advances in Petri Nets 92*, volume 609 of *LNCS*, 21 – 69, 1992.
5. E. Best and R. P. Hopkins. B(PN)^2 – a Basic Petri Net Programming Notation. In *Procs. of PARLE '93*, volume 694 of *LNCS*, 379 – 390, 1993.
6. L. Bouge. Repeated Synchronous Snapshots and their Implementation in CSP. In *Procs. of 12th ICALP*, volume 194 of *LNCS*, 63 – 70, 1981.
7. R. E. Bryant. Graph-based algorithm for boolean function manipulation. *IEEE Transactions on Computers*, C-35(8):677 – 691, August 1986.
8. E. Chang and R. Roberts. An Improved Algorithm for Decentralised Extrema-finding in Circular Distributed Systems. *Communications of the ACM*, 22(5):281–283, 1979.

9. E. M. Clarke, E. A. Emerson, and A. P. Sistla. Automatic verification of finite-state concurrent systems using temporal logic specifications, testing and verification. *ACM Transactions on Progr. Languages and Systems*, 8(2):244 – 263, 1986.

10. J. C. Corbett. *Automated Formal Analysis Methods for Concurrent and Real-Time Software*. PhD thesis, University of Massachusetts at Amherst, 1992.

11. P. Cousot and N.Halbwachs. Automatic discovery of linear restraints among variables of a program. In *5th ACM Symposium on Principles of Progr. Languages*.

12. J. Esparza and S. Melzer. Model-Checking LTL using Constraint Programming. Sonderforschungsbericht 342/07/97 A, Technische Universität München, 1997 (also via WWW: http://www.informatik.tu-muenchen.de/~melzers).

13. J. Esparza and G. Bruns. Trapping Mutual Exclusion in the Box Calculus. *Theoretical Computer Science*, 153:95 – 128, 1996.

14. J. Esparza, S. Römer, and W. Vogler. An Improvement of McMillan's Unfolding Algorithm. In *Procs. of TACAS '96*, volume 1055 of *LNCS*, 87 – 106, 1996.

15. P. Godefroid. *Partial-Order Methods for Verification of Concurrent Systems*, volume 1032 of *LNCS*, 1996.

16. N. Halbwachs. About synchronous programming and abstract interpretation. In *Procs. of SAS '94*, volume 864 of *LNCS*, 179–192, 1994.

17. N. Halbwachs, P. Caspi, P. Raymond, and D. Pilaud. The synchronous dataflow programming language LUSTRE. *Proc. of the IEEE*, 79(9):1305–1320, 1991.

18. C. A. R. Hoare. Communicating sequential processes. *Communications of the ACM*, 21(8):666 – 677, 1978.

19. G. J. Holzmann. *Basic Spin Manual*. AT&T Bell Laboratories, Murray Hill.

20. K. McAloon and C. Tretkoff. *Optimization and Computational Logic*. John Wiley & Sons, 1996.

21. K. L. McMillan. Using unfoldings to avoid the state explosion problem in the verification of asynchronous circuits. In *4th Workshop on Computer Aided Verification*, pages 164 – 174, 1992.

22. S. Melzer and J. Esparza. Checking system properties via integer programming. In *Procs. of ESOP '96*, volume 1058 of *LNCS*, 250 – 264, 1996.

23. R. Milner. *Communication and Concurrency*. Prentice-Hall, 1989.

24. T. Murata. Petri nets: Properties, analysis and application. *Procs. of the IEEE*, 77(4):541–580, 1989.

25. M. Raynal. *Algorithms for Mutual Exclusion*. North Oxford Academic, 1986.

26. A. Valmari. A Stubborn Attack on State Explosion. *Formal Methods in System Design*, 1:297 – 322, 1992.

27. M. Y. Vardi. An automata-theoretic approach to linear temporal logic. In *Logics for Concurrency*, volume 1043 of *LNCS*, 238 – 266, 1995.

28. M. Y. Vardi and P. Wolper. An automata-theoretic approach to atomatic program verification. In *Procs. of the 1st Symposium on Logics in Computer Science*, pages 322 – 331, 1986.

Random Constraint Satisfaction:
A More Accurate Picture

Dimitris Achlioptas,[1]* Lefteris M. Kirousis,[2]** Evangelos Kranakis,[3]***
Danny Krizanc,[3]† Michael S.O. Molloy,[1]‡ and Yannis C. Stamatiou[2]§

[1] Department of Computer Science, University of Toronto, Toronto, ON M5S 3G4,
Canada
[2] Department of Computer Engineering and Informatics, University of Patras, Rio,
26500 Patras, Greece
[3] School of Computer Science, Carleton University, Ottawa, ON K1S 5B6, Canada

Abstract. Recently there has been a great amount of interest in Random Constraint Satisfaction Problems, both from an experimental and a theoretical point of view. Rather intriguingly, experimental results with various models for generating random CSP instances suggest a "threshold-like" behavior and some theoretical work has been done in analyzing these models when the number of variables becomes large (asymptotic). In this paper we prove that the models commonly used for generating random CSP instances *do not* have an asymptotic threshold. In particular, we prove that as the number of variables becomes large, *almost all* instances they generate are trivially overconstrained. We then present a new model for random CSP and, in the spirit of random k-SAT, we derive lower and upper bounds for its parameters so that instances are "almost surely" underconstrained and overconstrained, respectively. Finally, for the case of one of the popular models in Artificial Intelligence we derive sharper estimates for the probability of being overconstrained, as a function of the number of variables.

1 Introduction

A *constraint network* comprises n variables, with their respective domains, and a set of *constraint relations* each binding a subset of the variables (for a complete definition see Section 2). Given a constraint network, the *Constraint Satisfaction Problem* (CSP) is that of determining the n-tuples of value assignments that are

---

* Supported by a Natural Sciences and Engineering Research Council (NSERC) of Canada PGS B Scholarship. E-mail: optas@cs.toronto.edu
** Partially supported by the EU ESPRIT Long-term Research Project ALCOM-IT (Project Nr. 20244). E-mail: kirousis@ceid.upatras.gr
*** Supported in part by an NSERC grant. E-mail: kranakis@scs.carleton.ca
† Supported in part by an NSERC grant. E-mail: krizanc@scs.carleton.ca
‡ Supported in part by an NSERC grant. E-mail: molloy@cs.toronto.edu
§ Partially supported by the EU ESPRIT Long-term Research Project ALCOM-IT (Project Nr. 20244). E-mail: stamatiu@fryni.ceid.upatras.gr

compatible with all the constraints. CSP is a fundamental problem in Artificial Intelligence, with applications ranging from scene labeling to scheduling and knowledge representation [10, 22, 28].

In recent years, there has been a growing interest in the study of the relation between the parameters that define an instance of CSP (i.e., number of variables, domain size, tightness of constraints etc.) and: (i) the likelihood that the instance has a solution, (ii) the difficulty with which such a solution may be discovered. An extensive account of relevant results, both experimental and theoretical, can be found in [3]. One of the most commonly used practices for conducting experiments with CSP is to generate a large set of random instances, all with the same defining parameters, and then for each instance in the set to use heuristics for deciding if a solution exists (in general, CSP is NP-complete). The proportion of instances that have a solution is used as an indication of the "likelihood", while the average time taken, per instance, captures a notion of "hardness" for such instances.

Research in this direction originated from research on random instances not of general CSP, but of specific problems like SAT and colorability (see [8]). Especially, for random instances of SAT, Mitchell et al. [24] pointed out that some distributions that are commonly used in such experiments are uninteresting since they generate formulas that are almost always very easy to satisfy. On the other hand, they reported that the distribution where each formula has precisely k literals per clause, i.e., where it is an instance of k-SAT, can generate some very hard formulas for $k \geq 3$. In particular, they reported that for $k = 3$ the following remarkable behavior is observed in experiments: let r denote the ratio of clauses to variables. For $r < 4$ almost all formulas are satisfiable and a satisfying truth assignment is easy to find. For $r > 4.5$ almost all formulas are unsatisfiable. Finally, a "50%-point" seems to appear around 4.2, the same point where the computational complexity of finding a satisfying truth assignment is maximized. Further experimental results as well the connection of this threshold behavior to transition phenomena in physics are described in [20].

The experimental results have motivated a theoretical interest in understanding the behavior of random k-SAT formulas, as the number of variables becomes asymptotic. In the following we give a brief summary of the strongest known results. We will say that a sequence of events $\mathcal{E}_n$ occurs "almost surely" if $\Pr[\mathcal{E}_n]$ tends to one as n tends to infinity. For $k = 2$, a sharp threshold was proved in [9, 16]: A random instance of 2-SAT is almost surely satisfiable if $r < 1$ and almost surely unsatisfiable if $r > 1$. For $k = 3$, there has been a series of results [6, 7, 5, 13, 19, 15, 21, 11] narrowing the area for which we do not have almost surely (un)satisfiability. The best bounds currently known come from [15] where it was proven that a random instance of 3-SAT is almost surely satisfiable if $r < 3.003$, and [21] where it was proven that a random instance of 3-SAT is almost surely unsatisfiable if $r > 4.598$. For general k, the best known lower bound for r is $\Theta(2^k/k)$ [7, 9, 15] while 2^k is an easy upper bound and was improved by a constant factor in [21] by extending the techniques used for 3-SAT. Very recently, Friedgut [14] made great progress towards establishing the *existence* of a threshold for k-SAT for all values of k, although he does not determine its asymptotic location.

For general CSP, there is accumulating *experimental* evidence that there exists a *critical region* for the defining parameters of a random instance. That is, determining the existence of a solution tends to be hard for randomly generated instances with defining parameters in this region. On the other hand, random instances with defining parameters outside this region, seem to either almost certainly have a solution or to almost certainly not and, furthermore, finding a solution when one exists tends to be easy. Moreover, the "hard" region seems to narrow as the number of variables increases. This has led to the belief that a threshold phenomenon underlies random CSP when the number of variables, n, becomes asymptotic [8, 17, 25, 26, 29, 30, 31] in a spirit similar to random k-SAT. In [26], Smith and Dyer examine a well-established model for generating random CSP with binary constraints. Using the first moment method they derive a condition on the defining parameters subject to which the probability that a random instance has a solution tends to zero as n tends to infinity. Thus they show that a random CSP with defining parameters in the region defined by this condition almost surely does not have a solution. They also study the variance of the number of solutions as a function of the defining parameters.

In this paper we show that if the fraction of permissible pairs of value assignments in each constraint is a constant (as, e.g., it is assumed in [26]), then as the number of variables increases, the probability that a random CSP has a solution tends to zero. This implies that a threshold phenomenon *cannot* underlie random instances of CSP generated using the current models, including those examined in [26], since asymptotically *almost all* instances generated, will not have a solution. The threshold-like picture given by experimental results is misleading, since the problems with defining parameters in what is currently perceived as the underconstrained region (because a solution can be found fast) are in fact overconstrained for large n (obviously, larger than the values used in experiments). Roughly speaking, the reason for this deficiency of the standard model of random general CSP is the fact that the forbidden pairs of values for two constrained variables are chosen at random and each with a constant probability, so that there is a constant positive probability that a bound variable cannot be set to any of its values, for local reasons only. This constant positive probability of a local inconsistency can then be made, asymptotically with n, arbitrarily close to 1. Let us point out, however, that this phenomenon does not appear in specific CSPs (like SAT or colorability), where there is some structure, or even no randomness at all, in the forbidden pairs of values for two constrained variables. Thus, a new parameterization (model) is necessary for random general CSP before any asymptotic analysis can be performed.

We make a first step in this direction by proposing a simple new model and analyzing it. That is, we show how to almost surely find a solution for a random CSP if its defining parameters lie within an area of the parameter space of the new model (underconstrained problems) and we also provide a counting argument showing that no solution exists for random CSP with defining parameters in another area of the parameter space (overconstrained problems). The analysis for the underconstrained region exploits a connection to random graphs while the counting argument is based on a technique introduced by Kirousis, Kranakis and Krizanc in [21]. Finally, we analyze the popular model (Model B) examined in [26], and derive a sharper upper bound for the probability of having a solution than the one provided by the first moment method [26]. Since, as we show, this model is in fact unsuitable for asymptotic analysis, our bound is a function of the defining parameters *and* n and we hope that it might prove useful in setting up experiments.

2 Definitions and notation

A *constraint network* consists of a set of variables $X_1, \ldots, X_n$ with respective domains $D_1, \ldots, D_n$, and a set of constraints $\mathcal{C}$. For $2 \leq k \leq n$ a constraint $R_{i_1, i_2, \ldots, i_k} \in \mathcal{C}$ is a subset of $D_{i_1} \times D_{i_2} \cdots D_{i_k}$, where the $i_1, i_2, \ldots, i_k$ are distinct. We say that $R_{i_1, i_2, \ldots, i_k}$ is of arity k and that it bounds the variables $X_{i_1}, \ldots, X_{i_k}$. For a given constraint network, the *Constraint Satisfaction Problem* (CSP), asks for all the n-tuples $(d_1, \ldots, d_n)$ of values such that $d_i \in D_i$, $i = 1, \ldots, n$, and for every $R_{i_1, i_2, \ldots, i_k} \in \mathcal{C}$, $(d_{i_1}, d_{i_2}, \ldots, d_{i_k}) \notin R_{i_1, i_2, \ldots, i_k}$. Such an n-tuple is called a *solution* of the CSP. The decision version of the CSP is determining if a solution exists.

For an instance Π of CSP with n variables, its *constraint hypergraph* G^Π (or just G when no confusion may arise) has n vertices $v_1, v_2, \ldots, v_n$, which correspond to the variables of Π and it contains a hyperedge $\{v_{i_1}, v_{i_2}, \ldots, v_{i_k}\}$ iff there exists a constraint of arity k that bounds the variables $X_{i_1}, X_{i_2}, \ldots, X_{i_k}$. We will use a convenient graph-theoretic representation of a CSP instance Π, defined as follows: The *incompatibility hypergraph* of Π, C^Π (or just C, when no confusion may arise) is an n-partite hypergraph. The ith part of C^Π corresponds to variable X_i of Π and it has exactly $|D_i|$ vertices, one for each value in D_i. In C^Π there exists a hyperedge $\{v_{i_1}, v_{i_2}, \ldots, v_{i_k}\}$, iff the corresponding values $d_{i_1} \in D_{i_1}$, $d_{i_2} \in D_{i_2}$, $\ldots$, $d_{i_k} \in D_{i_k}$ are in (not allowed by) some constraint that bounds the corresponding variables. Hence, the decision version of CSP is equivalent to asking if there exists a set of vertices in C containing exactly one vertex from each part while not "containing" any hyperedge, i.e., whether there exists an independent set with one vertex from each part.

In order to keep the exposition that follows more intuitive and less technical, we will detail our arguments only for CSP with constraints of arity 2. The generalization to CSP with constraints of arity $k > 2$ is straightforward.

2.1 Currently used models for random CSP

In generating random CSP instances it is common practice to make the simplifying assumption that all the variable domains contain the same number of values $D \geq 2$. Hence, fixing n and D, the generation of a random CSP is usually done in two steps. First, the constraint graph G is constructed as a random graph and then for each edge (constraint) in G a set of edges (incompatible pairs of values) is inserted in C. A general framework for doing this is presented in [25, 26]. More precisely,

Step 1. *Either each one of the $\binom{n}{2}$ edges is selected to be in G independently with probability p_1, or we uniformly select a random set of edges of size $p_1\binom{n}{2}$.*

Step 2. *Either for every edge of G each one of the D^2 edges in C is selected with probability p_2, or for every edge of G we uniformly select a random set of edges in C of size p_2D^2.*

The parameter p_1 determines how many constraints exist in a CSP instance and it is called *constraint density*, whereas p_2 determines how restrictive the constraints are and it is called *constraint tightness*. The parameter $p_2 \in (0, 1)$ is taken to be a constant independent of any other model parameters. Since, p_2 is a constant, p_1 is varied so that there are $\Theta(n)$ incompatible pairs of values in total. It is not hard to see that unless the total number of incompatible pairs of values is $\Theta(n)$ the resulting instances are underconstrained or overconstrained. Combining the options for the two steps, we get four slightly different models for generating random CSP which have received various names in the past literature. In particular, in the terminology used in [26], if both 1 and Step 2 are done using the first option (the $G_{n,p}$ fashion, in random graphs terminology) then we get Model A, while if they are both done using the second option (the $G_{n,m}$ fashion, in random graphs terminology), we get Model B. Our criticism in the next section pertains to all four models.

3 Shortcomings of currently used models

Let Π be a random CSP with D or more incompatible pairs in each constraint (suppose that we use the second option for Step 2). We will prove below that, as the number of variables grows, Π almost surely has no solution. Before presenting the proof, we note that according to the parameterization there are p_2D^2 incompatible pairs in each constraint so our condition is equivalent to $p_2 \geq 1/D$. Hence, our result implies that the currently used models are asymptotically uninteresting except, perhaps, for a small region of their parameter space (when $p_2 < 1/D$). We discuss this point further in section 3.1.

For every constraint R the probability, p_f, that some vertex (value) v in the domain of one of the two variables bound by R, is adjacent to (incompatible with) all the values in the domain of the other variable depends only on D. Moreover, since there are at least D edges in each constraint, this probability is a strictly positive constant (since D is a constant). We call such a value v *flawed*. It is clear that a solution of Π cannot contain flawed values (since at least one constraint would be violated). Hence, if all the values in the domain of some variable are flawed, Π has no solution. For a variable bound by D or more constraints there is a strictly positive probability that all the values in its domain are flawed. Since in a random graph on n vertices (the constraint graph of an instance Π) with $\Theta(n)$ edges (constraints) there are, asymptotically, unboundedly many $(\Omega(n))$ vertices with degree a given constant, the probability that at least one variable will contain only flawed values gets, asymptotically, arbitrarily close to one. Therefore, almost surely a random instance of CSP generated according to the currently used models is overconstrained. We make this argument formal below.

Consider the constraint graph G (of an instance Π). Recall, that the degree of a vertex in G is the number of constraints by which the corresponding variable is bound. Since the total number of edges (constraints) in G is $\Theta(n)$, using methods from Chapter 8 of [2], it is not hard to verify that the degree of each vertex (variable) is, asymptotically, a Poisson distributed random variable with mean a constant, for both options for Step 1. This implies that for any constant d there almost surely exist $\Omega(n)$ vertices that have degree exactly d. Consider the following procedure: Initialize S to contain all vertices of G that have degree exactly D. While S is not empty, pick a variable (vertex) v from S and (i) examine whether all values in its domain are flawed, (ii) remove from S the vertex v and all vertices adjacent to it in G.

Since initially $S = \Omega(n)$ and in each step we remove no more than $D + 1$ variables from S, the above procedure will be repeated $\Omega(n)$ times. Moreover, each time we examine a variable v the outcome is independent of all previous information "exposed" by the procedure, since none of the constraints that bind v was examined in previous steps (otherwise, v would have already been removed from S). Finally, the probability that all values in the domain of v are flawed is no less than the probability that each one of the D constraints binding v makes a distinct value in its domain flawed. This last probability is, clearly, p_f^D i.e., it depends only on D. Hence, the examination steps of the above procedure form a sequence of Bernoulli trials of length $\Omega(n)$ where the probability of success in each trial is lower bounded by a positive constant (i.e., independent of n). Thus, as n tends to infinity the probability that there exists a variable with all the values in its domain flawed, tends to one.

Finally, if we use the first option for step 2 and take p_2 so that the expected number of incompatible pairs is D or more, then each constraint has a constant probability of having at least D incompatible pairs and the same arguments, as above, can be applied.

3.1 A new model for random CSP

We would like to emphasize that "fixing" the old models by conditioning on each value having degree less than D in C^Π, will probably not lead to any interesting new models. This is because the old models generate many other *local* flaws similar to the one in the previous section. For example, we could have a pair of variables where neither is impossible to set by itself but where every setting of one makes it impossible to set the other (again for some local reasons as for the previous problem).

Regarding the fact that the specific flaw we point out does not appear for $p_2 < 1/D$ our feeling is that $1/D$ is probably not a "critical" value for p_2 and that in fact the models may remain problematic for $p_2 < 1/D$. What would be, perhaps, more important and certainly more practically relevant, is shifting from constraints that contain an entirely random subset of $p_2 D^2$ forbidden pairs to constraints were this subset has some structure. For example, assume that $p_2 = 1/D$ and that in each constraint between two variables v, w the i-th vertex (value) in the domain of v is incompatible with the j-th vertex in the domain of w iff $i = j$. Then, a random instance of this CSP encodes the problem of coloring a random graph with $p_1 n$ edges using D colors. This is an extremely interesting problem asymptotically, with numerous papers written on the subject (for an introduction see [2, 4]).

We feel that suggesting and analyzing interesting models that lack trivial local inconsistencies is a very worthwhile goal. In what follows, we put forward a new model that is simple to state and analyze, as is the case with currently used models, which does not suffer from trivial local inconsistencies. In this model, for a random CSP instance Π, it will be more intuitive to describe directly how to generate C^Π (as opposed to the two-step procedure described in Subsection 2.1).

Definition 3 (Model E). C^Π is as a random n-partite graph with D nodes in each part constructed by uniformly, independently and with repetitions selecting $m = p\binom{n}{2} D^2$ edges out of the $\binom{n}{2} D^2$ possible ones.

Model E, similarly to the currently used models, will only be interesting when the total number of constraints, m, is $\Theta(n)$. In this case, the expected number of repeated edges is insignificant ($O(1)$) and allowing repetitions in the definition simplifies the analysis of the model. Observe that if in each part of the n-partite graph described above we compress all D vertices into a single vertex, without eliminating any multiple occurrences of edges, we obtain a multigraph on n vertices with m edges. We denote this multigraph by G_m^Π (one can think of G_m^Π as the "constraint" multigraph). Since for instances generated according to model E the m edges of the n-partite graph are selected uniformly, independently and with repetitions, it is easy to see that the same is true for the m edges of G_m^Π and hence G_m^Π is a random multigraph (in the $G_{n,m}$ model). The following two facts will be very useful:

Fact 4. *If for an instance Π of CSP, every connected component of G_m^Π has at most one cycle then Π has at least one solution.*

Fact 4 is well known for $D = 2$ (see [9], where a proof is given in terms of 2-SAT) and having $D > 2$ only makes things easier for that proof. Moreover,

Fact 5. *If a random multigraph G is formed by selecting uniformly, independently and with repetitions $\frac{n}{2}$ edges then, almost surely, all the components of G will contain at most one cycle.*

Fact 5 is the analog of Theorem 5e in [12] when edges are selected with repetitions. By facts 4,5 we get

Theorem 6. *If for a random instance Π generated using Model E, C^Π has fewer than $\frac{n}{2}$ edges then Π almost surely has a solution.*

We feel that substantially stronger bounds can be derived by a more sophisticated analysis of this model and we leave this as future work.

4 Bounding the overconstrained region

4.1 The first moment method

Let Π be a random CSP with n variables, generated in any of the ways defined so far. By $\mathcal{A}_n$ we denote the set of all value assignments for Π, and by $\mathcal{S}_n$ we denote the random set of solutions of Π. We are interested in establishing a condition subject to which the probability that Π has a solution decreases exponentially with n. Such a condition is readily provided by the *first moment* method (for excellent expositions see [2] and [27]). That is, by first noting that

$$E[|\mathcal{S}_n|] = \sum_{\Pi} \left(\Pr[\Pi] \cdot |\mathcal{S}_n(\Pi)| \right) \tag{1}$$

and then noting that

$$\Pr[\Pi \text{ has a solution}] = \sum_{\Pi} \left(\Pr[\Pi] \cdot I_\Pi \right), \tag{2}$$

where for an instantiation of the random variable Π the indicator variable I_Π is defined as

$$I_\Pi = \begin{cases} 1 \text{ if } \Pi \text{ has a solution,} \\ 0 \text{ otherwise.} \end{cases}$$

Hence, from (1) and (2) we get

$$\Pr[\Pi \text{ has a solution}] \leq E[|\mathcal{S}_n|]. \tag{3}$$

Calculating $E[|\mathcal{S}_n|]$ is much easier than calculating $\Pr[\Pi \text{ has a solution}]$. As an illustration we apply the first moment method to the model we suggest, with $m = rn$. There are D^n possible value assignments and each one of the $\binom{n}{2} D^2$ possible incompatible pairs has a probability of $1/D^2$ to appear in a random value assignment. Since, we have m constraints,

$$\Pr[\Pi \text{ has a solution}] \leq E[|\mathcal{S}_n|] = D^n \left(1 - \frac{1}{D^2} \right)^m = \left(D \left(1 - \frac{1}{D^2} \right)^r \right)^n. \tag{4}$$

Hence, if $r > \ln(1/D)/\ln(1 - 1/D^2) \approx D^2 \ln D$ then $D(1 - \frac{1}{D^2})^r < 1$ and the probability that Π has a solution drops exponentially with n, asymptotically tending to zero.

4.2 The method of local maxima

The price paid for the simplicity of the first moment method is that instances with a very large number of solutions, although they may occur with very small probability, contribute substantially to $E[|\mathcal{S}_n|]$. Hence, by substituting $|\mathcal{S}_n(\Pi)|$ for I_Π we might be giving away "a lot". The technique introduced in [21], when applied to CSP, amounts to "compressing" $\mathcal{S}_n$ by requiring value assignments not only to be solutions of Π but to also satisfy a certain "local maximality" condition. The underlying intuition is that for a random solution of Pi, if we choose a variable at random and change its value, the probability we will end up with a non-solution is rather small. Consequently, solutions (when they exist) tend to appear in large "clusters" and instead of counting all solutions in a cluster we need only count a representative one (locally maximum). We feel that this clustering is not specific to the model we put forward and that it is closely related to the notion of *influence* introduced in [18]. Hence, the technique could potentially apply to other models for random CSP. This technique has already been applied to random SAT [21] and random graph coloring [1], in each case giving the best bounds currently known.

Definition 7. For each variable in Π fix an arbitrary ordering of the values in its domain. The set $\mathcal{S}_n^{\sharp}$ is defined as the random set of value assignments A such that

1. A is a solution of Π (written $A \models \Pi$), and
2. any value assignment obtained from A by changing the value of exactly one variable to some greater value, is not a solution of Π.

For a value assignment A, $A(X, v)$ will denote the value assignment obtained by changing the value assigned to variable X by A to a value v that is greater than the value assigned by A. The number of possible such changes for a value assignment A will be denoted by $sf(A)$.

Lemma 8. $\Pr[\Pi \text{ has a solution}] \leq E[|\mathcal{S}_n^{\sharp}|]$.

Proof. It is enough to observe that if Π has a solution then $\mathcal{S}_n^{\sharp}$ is not empty. The rest of the proof is identical to the proof of equation (3). □

Since $\mathcal{S}_n$ can be written as the sum of D^n indicator variables, one for each possible value assignment A and nonzero iff A is a solution of Π, we obtain the following lemma by conditioning on $A \in \mathcal{S}_n$:

Lemma 9. $E[|\mathcal{S}_n^{\sharp}|] = \Pr[A \in \mathcal{S}_n]\sum_{A\in\mathcal{A}_n} \Pr[A \in \mathcal{S}_n^{\sharp} \mid A \in \mathcal{S}_n]$.

5 The method of local maxima for Model E

In this section we apply the method of local maxima to random CSP instances generated using Model E, according to which we select uniformly a set of $m = rn$ incompatibility edges.

Theorem 10. *For a randomly generated binary CSP instance Π, let $\zeta = 1 - e^{-\frac{2r}{D^2-1}}$. If $(1 - \frac{1}{D^2})^r \frac{1-\zeta^D}{1-\zeta} < 1$ then $\Pr[\Pi$ has a solution] tends to 0 as n tends to infinity.*

Proof. As we argued earlier, $\Pr[A \in \mathcal{S}_n] = (1 - \frac{1}{D^2})^m$. We will compute an upper bound to $\Pr[A \in \mathcal{S}_n^{\sharp} \mid A \in \mathcal{S}_n]$. Fix a value assignment $A \in \mathcal{S}_n$. Since $A \in \mathcal{S}_n$, every pair of values of A is *not* adjacent (incompatible) in C. Consequently, conditioning on $A \in \mathcal{S}_n$ implies that the set of possible edges has cardinality $D^2 \binom{n}{2} - \binom{n}{2} = (D^2 - 1)\binom{n}{2}$. Now consider changing the value of variable X to a new value v greater than the value of X in A. The event $A(X, v) \notin \mathcal{S}_n$ occurs iff among the m edges in C, there is an edge connecting v with some other value in $A(X, v)$. Hence,

$$\Pr[A(X, v) \notin \mathcal{S}_n] = 1 - \left(1 - \frac{\binom{n-1}{2-1}}{(D^2 - 1)\binom{n}{2}}\right)^m$$

$$= 1 - \left(1 - \frac{2}{(D^2 - 1)n}\right)^{rn}$$

$$= 1 - e^{-\frac{2r}{D^2-1}} + o(1).$$

The events $A(X_i, v_j) \notin \mathcal{S}_n$, for each X_i, v_j are not independent. On the other hand, as we saw above, the set of edges associated with each such event is disjoint with all other such sets. Intuitively, any such event $A(X_i, v_j) \not\models \Pi$ "exposes" only edges that can be of no harm to any other such event. Moreover, it exposes that at least one of the m edges was "used" to cause $A(X_i, v_j) \not\models \Pi$. Hence, the events $A(X_i, v_j) \not\models \Pi$ are in fact negatively correlated. Formally, this fact follows from the main Theorem in [23]. This implies,

$$\Pr[A \in \mathcal{S}_n^{\sharp} \mid A \in \mathcal{S}_n] \le \left(1 - \left(1 - \frac{2}{n(D^2 - 1)}\right)^{rn}\right)^{sf(A)}$$

$$= \left(1 - e^{-\frac{2r}{D^2-1}} + o(1)\right)^{sf(A)}.$$

If for each value assignment A we let k_i denote the number of variables assigned the i-th smallest value in their domain then, by Lemmas 8 and 9, we get:

$\Pr[\Pi$ has a solution]

$$\le \left(1 - \frac{1}{D^2}\right)^m \sum_{A \in \mathcal{A}_n} \Pr[A \in \mathcal{S}_n^{\sharp} \mid A \in \mathcal{S}_n]$$

$$\le \left(1 - \frac{1}{D^2}\right)^m \sum_{k_1, k_2, \ldots, k_D} \binom{n}{k_1, k_2, \ldots, k_D} \prod_{j=1}^{D} \left(1 - e^{-\frac{2r}{D^2-1}} + o(1)\right)^{(D-j)k_j}$$

$$= \left(\left(1 - \frac{1}{D^2}\right)^r \sum_{j=0}^{D-1} (1 - e^{-\frac{2r}{D^2-1}})^j + o(1)\right)^n$$

$$= \left(\left(1 - \frac{1}{D^2} \right)^r \frac{1 - \zeta^D}{1 - \zeta} + o(1) \right)^n , \text{ where } \zeta = 1 - e^{-\frac{2r}{D^2 - 1}}$$

□

Note, that the condition given by the theorem is more relaxed than the condition $\left(1 - \frac{1}{D^2} \right)^r D < 1$, derived earlier by the first moment method, since $\frac{1 - \zeta^D}{1 - \zeta} = \sum_{j=0}^{D-1} (1 - e^{-\frac{2r}{D^2 - 1}})^j < D$. For example, when $D = 3$ the first moment method gives $r < 9.32$ while Theorem 10 gives $r < 8.21$.

When the arity of the constraints is $k > 2$, the following can be proved by extending in a straightforward manner the arguments given above:

Theorem 11. *For a randomly generated k-ary CSP instance Π according to Model E, if $(1 - \frac{1}{D^k})^r \frac{1 - \zeta^D}{1 - \zeta} < 1$, where $\zeta = 1 - e^{-\frac{kr}{D^k - 1}}$, then $\Pr[\Pi$ has a solution] tends to 0 as n tends to infinity.*

6 The method of local maxima for model B

We will now use the method of local maxima in order to derive better estimations for the probability of a random CSP instance having a solution for a popular model in Artificial Intelligence, called Model B in [25, 26]. As we showed in section 3, this model suffers from the shortcoming that when n tends to infinity the probability that a randomly generated instance has a solution tends to zero. However, when n is fixed and relatively small, it is unlikely that there will arise a variable with all the values in its domain flawed for many interesting values of the defining parameters (we know this from experiments!). We illustrate this with the following example:

Consider, for the sake of simplicity in the calculations of the example and only for this paragraph, the model where each constraint edge is selected independently with probability p_1 and for each selected constraint edge, each incompatibility edge is selected in the same way with probability p_2 (Model A, in [25, 26]) and suppose we have n_0 variables. Let v be a fixed value in the domain of a fixed variable X. Each constraint that bounds X makes v flawed with probability p_2^D. Hence, if X is bound by c constraints, the probability that v is flawed is $1 - (1 - p_2^D)^c$ and the probability that all the values in the domain of X are flawed is $(1 - (1 - p_2^D)^c)^D$. Even if we are very generous and take $c = n_0$ for $n_0 = 200, D = 10, p_2 = 1/2$ the expected number of variables that have all the values in their domain flawed is less than 10^{-5} and, hence, so is the probability that such a vertex exists. So, the following estimate which improves over the first moment one, might be useful in suggesting fruitful parameter ranges for conducting experiments with Model B.

Recall that for an instance Π, G is generated by first selecting $m_1 = p_1 \binom{n}{2} = cn$ constraints and C is constructed by selecting $m_2 = p_2 D^2$ incompatible pairs (edges in C) for each constraint edge in G. Consider a value assignment A that is a solution of Π and a change of some variable X in A to a value v greater than X's value in A. We count the possible edge occurrences in C that would imply $A(X,v) \not\models \Pi$ and divide them by the total number of edges than can be present under the condition that $A \models \Pi$.

$A(X,v) \not\models \Pi$ iff at least one of the m selected constraints involves X and another variable, and contains an edge connecting v and the value assigned to the variable by A. The number of "bad" edges is $(n-1)\binom{D^2-1}{m_2-1}$, while conditioning on $A \models \Pi$ implies that the set of possible edges has cardinality $\binom{n}{2}\binom{D^2-1}{m_2}$. Therefore, for each of the m_1 selected constraint edges of Π, the probability that $A(X,v)$ is not a solution, given $A \models \Pi$, is:

$$\frac{(n-1)\binom{D^2-1}{m_2-1}}{\binom{n}{2}\binom{D^2-1}{m_2}} = \frac{2m_2}{n(D^2-m_2)}$$

implying

$$\Pr[A(X,v) \not\models \Pi \mid A \in \mathcal{S}_n] = 1 - \left(1 - \frac{2p_2}{n(1-p_2)}\right)^{m_1}.$$

Arguing similarly to the proof of Theorem 10 we can show that the events $A(X_i, v_j) \not\models \Pi$ are negatively correlated for each X_i and v_j, getting

$$\Pr[A \in \mathcal{S}_n^\sharp \mid A \in \mathcal{S}_n] \leq \left(1 - \left(1 - \frac{2p_2}{n(1-p_2)}\right)^{m_1}\right)^{sf(A)}. \tag{5}$$

Again, if for each value assignment A we let k_i denote the number of variables assigned the i-th smallest value in their domain then, by Lemmas 8 and 9 and setting $\zeta = 1 - \left(1 - \frac{2p_2}{n(1-p_2)}\right)^{m_1}$, we get:

$\Pr[\Pi$ has a solution$]$

$$\leq (1-p_2)^{m_1} \sum_{A \in \mathcal{A}_n} \Pr[A \in \mathcal{S}_n^\sharp \mid A \in \mathcal{S}_n]$$

$$\leq (1-p_2)^{m_1} \sum_{k_1,k_2,\ldots,k_D} \binom{n}{k_1,k_2,\ldots,k_D} \prod_{j=1}^{D} \left(1 - \left(1 - \frac{2p_2}{n(1-p_2)}\right)^{m_1}\right)^{(D-j)k_j}$$

$$= (1-p_2)^{m_1} \left(\sum_{j=0}^{D-1} \left(1 - \left(1 - \frac{2p_2}{n(1-p_2)}\right)^{m_1}\right)^{j}\right)^{n}$$

$$= (1-p_2)^{m_1} \left(\frac{1-\zeta^D}{1-\zeta}\right)^{n}.$$

Acknowledgments

We would like to thank David Mitchell for his useful comments.

References

1. D. Achlioptas and M. Molloy, "Almost all graphs with 2.522 n edges are not 3-colorable," *Manuscript,* University of Toronto.
2. N. Alon, J.H. Spencer, and P. Erdös, *The Probabilistic Method,* J. Wiley, New York (1992).
3. D.G. Bobrow and M. Brady, eds., *Special Volume on Frontiers in Problem Solving: Phase Transitions and Complexity,* Guest editors: T. Hogg, B.A. Hubermann, and C.P. Williams, *Artificial Intelligence,* Vol. 81, Numbers 1–2 (1996).
4. B. Bollobás, *Random Graphs,* Academic Press, London (1985).
5. A.Z. Broder, A.M. Frieze, and E. Upfal, "On the satisfiability and maximum satisfiability of random 3-CNF formulas," *Proceedings of the Fourth Annual ACM-SIAM Symposium on Discrete Algorithms* (1993) 322–330.
6. M.-T. Chao and J. Franco, "Probabilistic analysis of two heuristics for the 3-satisfiability problem," *SIAM Journal on Computing,* Vol. 15 (1986) 1106–1118.
7. M.-T. Chao and J. Franco, "Probabilistic analysis of a generalization of the unit-clause literal selection heuristic for the k-satisfiability problem," *Information Science,* Vol. 51 (1990) 289–314.
8. P. Cheeseman, B. Kanefsky and W. Taylor, "Where the really hard problems are," *Proceedings of IJCAI '91* (1991) 331–337.
9. V. Chvátal and B. Reed, "Mick gets some (the odds are on his side)," in *Proceedings of 33rd IEEE Symposium on Foundations of Computer Science* (1992) 620–627.
10. R. Dechter, "Constraint networks," in S. Shapiro (ed.), *Encyclopedia of Artificial Intelligence,* Wiley, New York, 2nd ed. (1992) 276–285.
11. O. Dubois and Y. Boufkhad, *A General Upper Bound for the Satisfiability Threshold of Random r-SAT Formulae,* Preprint, LAFORIA, CNRS-Université Paris 6, 1996.
12. P. Erdös and A. Rényi, "On the evolution of random graphs," *Publ. of the Math. Inst. of the Hung. Acad. Sci.,* Vol. 5 (1960) 17–61.
13. A. El Maftouhi and W. Fernandez de la Vega, "On random 3-SAT", *Combinatorics, Probability and Computing,* Vol. 4 (1995) 189–195.
14. E. Friedgut, "Sharp thresholds for graph properties and the k-sat problem," *Manuscript in preparation.*
15. A. Frieze and S. Suen, "Analysis of two simple heuristics on a random instance of k-SAT," *Journal of Algorithms,* Vol. 20 (1996) 312–355.
16. A. Goerdt, "A threshold for satisfiability," in I.M. Haven and V. Koubek (eds.) *Proceedings of the Symposium on the Mathematical Foundations of Computer Science* (1992) 264–274.
17. T. Hogg, "Refining the phase transition in combinatorial search," in [3], 127–154.
18. J. Kahn, G. Kalai, and N. Linial, "The influence of variables on Boolean functions", *Proceedings of the 29th Annual Symposium on the Foundations of Computer Science* (1988) 68–80.
19. A. Kamath, R. Motwani, K. Palem, and P. Spirakis, "Tail bounds for occupancy and the satisfiability threshold conjecture," *Random Structures and Algorithms,* Vol. 7 (1995) 59–80.
20. S. Kirkpatrick and B. Selman, "Critical behavior in the satisfiability of random Boolean expressions," *Science* 264, pp 1297–1301, 1994.
21. L. M. Kirousis, E. Kranakis, and D. Krizanc, "Approximating the unsatisfiability threshold of random formulas," *Proceedings of the Fourth Annual European Symposium on Algorithms, ESA '96,* (1996) 27–38.

22. A.K. Mackworth, "Constraint satisfaction," in S. Shapiro (ed.) *Encyclopedia of Artificial Intelligence*, Wiley, New York, 2nd ed. (1992) 285–293.
23. C. McDiarmid, "On a correlation inequality of Farr," *Combinatorics, Probability and Computing*, Vol. 1 (1992) 157–160.
24. D. Mitchell, B. Selman, and H. Levesque, *Generating hard satisfiability problems*, Artificial Intelligence, Vol. 81 (1996), 17–29.
25. P. Prosser, "An empirical study of phase transitions in binary constraint satisfaction problems," in [3], 81–109.
26. B.M. Smith and M.E. Dyer, "Locating the phase transition in binary constraint satisfaction problems," in [3], 155–181.
27. J. H. Spencer, *Ten Lectures on the Probabilistic Method*, 2nd edition, SIAM, Philadelphia (1994).
28. D. Waltz, "Understanding line drawings of scenes with shadows," *The Psychology of Computer Vision*, McGraw-Hill, New York (1975) 19–91.
29. C. Williams and T. Hogg, "Using deep structure to locate hard problems," *Proceedings of AAAI-92* (1992) 472–477.
30. C. Williams and T. Hogg, "Extending deep structure," *Proceedings of AAAI-93*, (1993) 152–158.
31. C. Williams and T. Hogg, "Exploiting the deep structure of constraint problems," *Artificial Intelligence*, Vol. 70 (1994) 73–117.

Heavy-Tailed Distributions in Combinatorial Search

Carla P. Gomes[1], Bart Selman[2], and Nuno Crato[3]

[1] Rome Laboratory, Rome Lab, NY 13441-4505, gomes@ai.rl.af.mil
[2] Computer Science Department, Cornell University, Ithaca, NY 14853,
selman@cs.cornell.edu
[3] Dept. of Mathematics, New Jersey Institute of Technology, Newark, NJ 07102,
USA, ncrato@m.njit.edu

Abstract. Combinatorial search methods often exhibit a large variability in performance. We study the cost profiles of combinatorial search procedures. Our study reveals some intriguing properties of such cost profiles. The distributions are often characterized by very long tails or "heavy tails". We will show that these distributions are best characterized by a general class of distributions that have no moments (i.e., an infinite mean, variance, etc.). Such non-standard distributions have recently been observed in areas as diverse as economics, statistical physics, and geophysics. They are closely related to fractal phenomena, whose study was introduced by Mandelbrot. We believe this is the first finding of these distributions in a purely computational setting. We also show how random restarts can effectively eliminate heavy-tailed behavior, thereby dramatically improving the overall performance of a search procedure.

1 Introduction

Combinatorial search methods exhibit a remarkable variability in the time required to solve any particular problem instance. For example, we see significant differences on runs of different heuristics, runs on different problem instances, and, for stochastic methods, runs with different random seeds. The inherent exponential nature of the search process appears to magnify the unpredictability of search procedures. It is not uncommon to observe a combinatorial method "hang" on a given instance, whereas a different heuristic, or even just another stochastic run, solves the instance quickly.

We explore the cost distribution profiles of search methods on a variety of problem instances. Our study reveals some intriguing properties of such cost profiles. The distributions are often characterized by very long tails or "heavy tails". We will show that these distributions are best captured by a general class of distributions that have no moments, *i.e.*, they have infinite mean, variance, etc.

Carla P. Gomes works for Rome Laboratory as a Research Associate. This work was performed while the second author was at AT&T Laboratories, Florham Park, NJ 07932-0971.

Heavy-tailed distributions were first introduced by the Italian-born Swiss economist Vilfredo Pareto in the context of income distribution. They were extensively studied mathematically by Paul Lévy in the period between the world wars. Lévy worked on a class of random variables with heavy tails of this type, which he called *stable* random variables. However, at the time, these distributions were largely considered probabilistic curiosities or pathological cases mainly used in counter-examples.This situation changed dramatically with Mandelbrot's work on fractals. In particular, two seminal papers of Mandelbrot (1960, 1963) were instrumental in establishing the use of stable distributions for modeling real-world phenomena.

Recently, heavy-tailed distributions have been used to model phenomena in areas as diverse as economics, statistical physics, and geophysics. More concretely, they have been applied in stock market analysis, Brownian motion, wheather forecasts, earthquake prediction, and recently, for modeling time delays on the World Wide Web (e.g., Mandelbrot 1983; Samorodnitsky and Taqqu 1994). We believe our work provides the first demonstration of the suitability of heavy-tailed distributions in modeling the computational cost of combinatorial search methods.

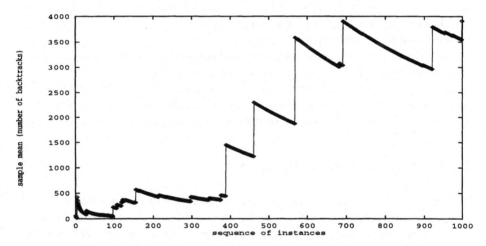

Figure 1a: Erratic behavior of mean cost value.

Various researchers studying the computational nature of search problems have informally observed the erratic behavior of the mean and the variance of the search cost. This phenomenon has led them to use the median cost to characterize search difficulty. The heavy-tailed distributions provide a formal framework explaining the erratic mean and variance behavior. See Figure 1, for a preview of this phenomenon. Figure 1a shows the mean cost calculated over an increasing number of runs, on the same instance, of a backtrack style search procedure (details below). Contrast this behavior with that of the mean

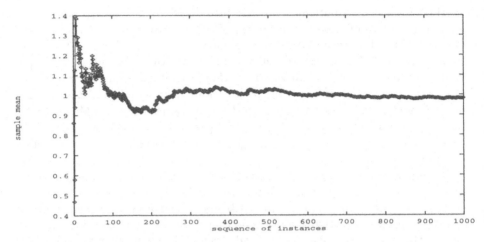

Figure 1b: Mean for a standard distribution (gamma).

of a standard probability distribution (a gamma distribution; no heavy tails) as given in Figure 1b. In Figure 1b, we see that the sample mean converges rapidly to a constant value with increasing sample size. On the other hand, the heavy-tailed distribution in Figure 1a shows a highly erratic behavior of the mean that does not stabilize with increasing sample size.[4]

As a direct practical consequence of the heavy-tailed behavior of cost distributions, we show how randomized *restarts* of search procedures can dramatically reduce the variance in the search behavior. In fact, we will demonstrate that a search strategy with restarts can eliminate heavy-tailed distributions. This may explain the common informal use of restarts on combinatorial search problems.

2 Structured Search Problems

The study of the complexity and performance of search procedures when applied to realistic problems is greatly hampered by the difficulty in gathering realistic data. As an alternative, researchers heavily resort to randomly generated instances or highly structured problems from, *e.g.*, finite algebra. The random instances clearly lack sufficient structure, whereas the finite algebra problems are, in some sense, too regular. In order to bridge this gap, we introduced a new benchmark domain, the *Quasigroup Completion Problem* (Gomes and Selman 1997a).

A quasigroup is an ordered pair $(Q, \cdot)$, where Q is a set and $(\cdot)$ is a binary operation on Q such that the equations $a \cdot x = b$ and $y \cdot a = b$ are uniquely solvable for every pair of elements a, b in Q. The *order* N of the quasigroup is the cardinality of the set Q. The best way to understand the structure of a

---

[4] The median, not shown here, stabilizes rather quickly at the value 1.

quasigroup is to consider the N by N multiplication table as defined by its binary operation. The constraints on a quasigroup are such that its multiplication table defines a *Latin square*. This means that in each row of the table, each element of the set Q occurs exactly once; similarly, in each column, each element occurs exactly once (Denes and Keedwell 1974).

An *incomplete* or *partial latin square* P is a partially filled N by N table such that no symbol occurs twice in a row or a column. The Quasigroup Completion Problem is the problem of determining whether the remaining entries of the table can be filled in such a way that we obtain a complete latin square, that is, a full multiplication table of a quasigroup. We view the pre-assigned values of the latin square as a *perturbation* to the original problem of finding an arbitrary latin square. Another way to look at these pre-assigned values is as a set of additional problem constraints on the basic structure of the quasigroup.

There is a natural formulation of the problem as a Constraint Satisfaction Problem. We have a variable for each of the N^2 entries in the multiplication table of the quasigroup, and we use constraints to capture the requirement of having no repeated values in any row or column. All variables have the same domain, namely the set of elements Q of the quasigroup. Pre-assigned values are captured by fixing the value of some of the variables.

Colbourn (1983) showed the quasigroup completion problem to be NP-complete. In previous work, we identified a clear phase transition phenomenon for the quasigroup completion problem (Gomes and Selman 1997a). See Figures 2 and 3. From the figures, we observe that the costs peak roughly around the same ratio (approximately 42% pre-assignment) for different values of N. (Each data point is generated using 1,000 problem instances. The pre-assigned values were randomly generated.) This phase transition with the corresponding cost profile allows us to tune the difficulty of our problem class by varying the percentage of pre-assigned values.

An interesting application area of latin squares is the design of statistical experiments. The purpose of latin squares is to eliminate the effect of certain systematic dependency among the data (Denes and Keedwell 1974). Another interesting application is in scheduling and timetabling. For example, latin squares are useful in determining intricate schedules involving pairwise meetings among the members of a group (Anderson 1985). The natural perturbation of this problem is the problem of completing a schedule given a set pre-assigned meetings.

The quasigroup domain has also been extensively used in the area of automated theorem proving. In this community, the main interest in this domain has been driven by questions regarding the existence and nonexistence of quasigroups with additional mathematical properties (Fujita et al. 1993; Lam et al. 1989).

3 Computational Cost Profiles

In this section, we consider the variability in search cost due to different search heuristics. As our basic search procedure, we use a complete backtrack-style

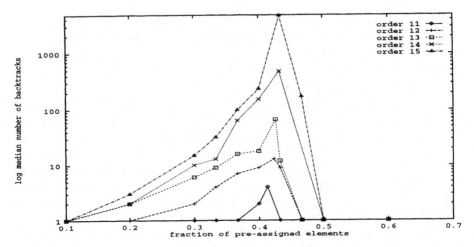

Figure 2: The Complexity of Quasigroup Completion (Log Scale).

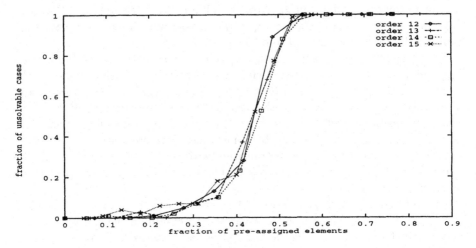

Figure 3: Phase Transition for the Completion Problem.

search method. The performance of such procedures can vary dramatically depending on the way one selects the next variable to branch on (the "variable selection strategy") and in what order the possible values are assigned to a variable (the "value selection strategy").

One of the most effective strategies is the so-called First-Fail heuristic.[5] In the First-Fail heuristic, the next variable to branch on is the one with the smallest remaining domain (*i.e.*, in choosing a value for the variable during the backtrack search, the search procedure has the fewest possible options left to explore —

---

[5] This is really a prerequisit for any reasonable backtrack-style search method. In theorem proving and Boolean satisfiability, the rule is related to the powerful unit-propagation heuristic.

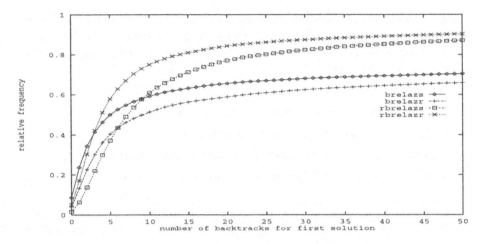

Figure 4: Finding quasigroups of order 20 with 10% pre-assigned values.

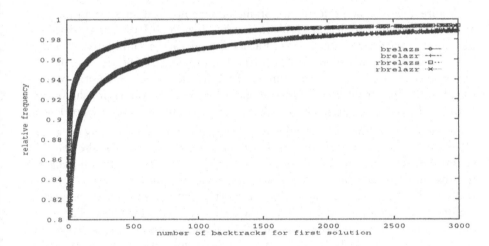

Figure 5: Finding quasigroups of order 10 at the phase transition.

leading to the smallest branching factor). We consider a popular extension of the First-Fail heuristic, called the Brelaz heuristics (Brelaz 1979), which was originally introduced for graph coloring procedures.

The Brelaz heuristic specifies a way for breaking ties in the First-fail rule: If two variables have equally small remaining domains, the Brelaz heuristic proposes to select the variable that shares constraints with the largest number of the remaining unassigned variables. A natural variation on this tie-breaking rule is what we call the "reverse Brelaz" heuristic, in which preference is given to the variable that shares constraints with the *smallest* number of unassigned variables. Any remaining ties after the (reverse) Brelaz rule are resolved randomly. (Note that such tie breaking introduces a stochastic element in our complete search method.) One final issue left to specify in our search procedure is the order in which the values are assigned to a variable. In the standard Brelaz, value assignment is done in lexicographical order (*i.e.*, systematic). In our experiments, we consider four strategies:

- *Brelaz-S* — Brelaz with systematic value selection,
- *Brelaz-R* — Brelaz with random value selection,
- *R-Brelaz-S* — Reverse Brelaz with systematic value selection, and
- *R-berlaz-R* — Reverse Brelaz with random value selection.

We encoded this problem in C++ using ILOG SOLVER, a powerful C++ constraint programming library (Puget 1994). ILOG provides a backtracking mechanism that allows us to keep track of variables and their domains, while maintaining arc-consistency (van Hentenryck *et al.* 1992).

Figure 4 shows the performance profile of our four strategies for an instance of the quasigroup completion problem of order 20 with 10% pre-assigned values, *i.e.*, in the underconstrained area. Each curve gives the cumulative distribution obtained for each strategy by solving the problem 10,000 times. The cost (horizontal axis) is measured in number of backtracks, which is directly proportional to the total runtime of our strategies. For example, the figure shows that R-Brelaz-R, finished roughly 80% of the 10,000 runs in 15 backtracks or less.

First, we note that the (cumulative) distributions have surprising long tails after a steep initial climb. We will return to this issue below. We also see that that R-Brelaz-R dominates the other strategies over almost the full range of the distribution. (Brelaz-S dominates very early on but the difference is not statistically significant.) Figure 5 shows the performance profile on an instance of the quasigroup completion problem in the critically constrained area. The initial climb followed by a long tail is even more dramatic. In this case, R-Brelaz-R and R-Brelaz-S give virtually the same performance, and both dominate the other two strategies.

These profiles suggest that it is difficult to take advantage of combining different heuristics in order to reduce variability. It was our initial intention to build so-called algorithm portfolios to reduce variability (Huberman *et al.* 1997 and Gomes and Selman 1997b). However, with one strategy dominating over the full profile there is no clear payoff in combining different heuristics, at least in this domain. In fact, it may well be the case that on a given problem domain, one can often find a single dominating heuristic. Our study here is not meant to be exhaustive regarding the full spectrum of search heuristics. In particular, we restricted ourselves to variations on the well-known Brelaz search heuristic.

In the next section, we concentrate on a perhaps more striking feature of the cost distributions: the *long tails*. As we will see in our section on "restarts", the heavy tail behavior can be exploited effectively to reduce variability in the search cost.

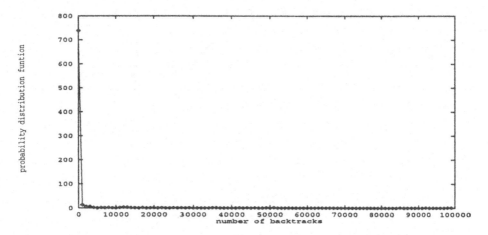

Figure 6a: Probability distribution exhibiting heavy-tailed behavior.

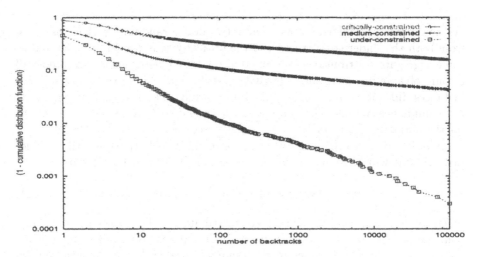

Figure 6b: Log-log plot of heavy-tailed behavior.

4 Heavy-Tailed Distributions

Figure 6a shows the heavy-tailed nature of our cost distributions in a more direct manner. The probability distribution was obtained using R-Brelaz-R on an instance of the quasigroup completion problem of order 20 with 5% preplacement.[6]

---

[6] Work on exceptionally hard problems provides further support for the heavy tailed nature of the distributions (Gent and Walsh 1993; Smith and Grant 1995). However, the heavy tails we observed appear more ubiquitous: We observed heavy-tails in the majority of solvable instances in the under-constrained area and also in the majority of solvable instances in the critically constrained area. For other recent related work on cost distributions, see Frost et al. (1997) and Kwan (1995).

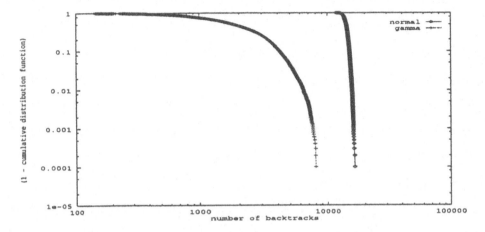

Figure 6c: Log-log plot of standard distributions (no heavy tails).

We considered the distributions of over two dozen randomly picked instances from both the under-constrained and the critically constrained area, as well as some aggregate distributions. We found heavy-tailed distributions for almost all of our solvable instances and aggregate distributions. Some very easy solvable instances did not exhibit heavy tails. Interestingly, the unsolvable instances do not exhibit heavy-tails. The gamma and normal distributions were the best fit for the majority of our unsolvable instances (see also Frost et al. (1997)).

In order to model the long tail behavior of our distributions, we will consider distributions which asymptotically have tails of the Pareto-Lévy form, *viz.*

$$\Pr\{X > x\} \sim C.x^{-\alpha}, \quad x > 0 \tag{1}$$

where $\alpha > 0$ is a constant. These are distributions whose tails have a *hyperbolic decay*. For the case which concerns us it suffices to consider this tail behavior for the positive values of the random variable X. So, in what follows we will assume that the distribution has support on the positive half line, i.e., $\Pr\{0 \leq X < \infty\} = 1$.

Mandelbrot (1983) provides an excellent introduction to these distributions with a discussion of their inherently self-similar or fractal nature. For a complete treatment of stable distributions see either Zolotarev (1986), or the more modern approach of Samorodnitsky and Taqqu (1994). See also de Lima (1997). In what follows, we simply outline the main results we will need to use.

A random variable X is said to have a *stable distribution* if for any $n > 1$ there is a positive number C_n and a real number D_n such that

$$X_1 + X_2 + \cdots + X_n \overset{\mathcal{D}}{=} C_n X + D_n, \tag{2}$$

where $X_1, X_2, \ldots, X_n$ are independent copies of X and $\overset{\mathcal{D}}{=}$ stands for equality in distribution. From this definition, it can be shown that the following is implied

$$C_n = n^{1/\alpha} \tag{3}$$

for some $0 < \alpha \leq 2$ (Samorodnitsky and Taqqu 1994). The constant α is called the *index of stability* of the distribution. Stable distributions with $\alpha < 2$ have heavy tails of the Pareto-Lévy type. The index of stability is the same α which appears in equation (1).

Since the existence or nonexistence of moments is completely determined by the tail behavior, it is simple to check that the index of stability α is the *maximal moment exponent* of the distribution. For $\alpha < 2$, moments of X of order less than α are finite while all higher order moments are infinite, i.e., $\alpha = \sup\{a > 0 : \mathrm{E}|X|^a < \infty\}$. For example, when $\alpha = 1.5$, the distribution only has a finite mean but no finite variance. When $\alpha = 0.6$, the distribution does not have a finite mean nor a finite variance.

While it is relatively easy to define a stable distribution, only in a few particular cases the density of the stable distributions is known in its *closed* form.

It should be noted, however, that distributions with tails of the form (1) are in the *domain of attraction* of stable distributions, *i.e.*, properly normalized sums of variables with tails of the Pareto-Lévy type converge in distribution to an α-stable random variable. This additive character of stable distributions matches the additive nature of the number of nodes searched in subtrees of the backtrack tree. This provides some intuition behind the suitability of the stable distributions for modeling search cost distributions.

In order to check for the existence of heavy tails in our distributions, we proceed in two steps. First, we graphically analyze the tail behavior of the sample distributions. Second, we formally estimate the index of stability.

If a Pareto-Lévy tail is observed, then the rate of decrease of the estimated density is hyperbolic — *i.e.*, slower than the exponential rate. The complement to one of the cumulative distribution also displays a hyperbolic decay

$$1 - F(x) = \Pr\{X > x\} \sim C.x^{-\alpha}. \tag{4}$$

Then, for an heavy-tailed random variable, a log-log plot of the frequency of observed backtracks after x should show an approximate linear decrease at the tail. Moreover, the slope of the observed linear decrease provides an estimate of the index α. In contrast, for a distribution with an exponentially decreasing tail, the log-log plot should show a faster-than-linear decrease of the tail.

Since the described behavior is a property of the tail we should mainly be concerned with the last observations, say the 10% observations that display a higher number of backtracks.

In Figure 6b, we have plotted three empirical cumulative distributions. One based on the probability distribution from Figure 6a (under-constrained), another for a medium constrained (solvable) instance, and a third for a critically constrained (solvable) instance. The linear nature of the tails in this log-log plot directly reveals tails of the Pareto-Lévy type.

For contrast we show in Figure 6c the log-log plots of two standard probability distributions. We see sharp rounded drop-off of both curves — indicating the absence of heavy tails. The distributions are given by the cost profiles on two unsolvable instances of our quasigroup completion problem. One is a rare unsolvable problem in the underconstrained area (best fit: a gamma distribution), the other is an unsolvable instance in the critically constrained region (best fit: normal distribution).

To complement our visual check of Figure 6b, and obtain an estimate of the index of stability (the value of α), we use the method of Hall (1982), which performs a regression on the extreme tails. Let $X_{n1} \leq X_{n2} \leq \ldots \leq X_{nn}$ be the order statistics, i.e., the ordered values of the sample $X_1, X_2 \ldots, X_n$ of the obtained number of backtracks. Set $r < n$ as a truncation value which allows us to consider only the extreme observations. We obtain the estimator

$$\hat{\alpha}_r = \left(r^{-1} \sum_{j=1}^{r} \log X_{n,n-j+1} - \log X_{n,n-r} \right)^{-1} \tag{5}$$

This is a maximum likelihood estimator and Hall (1982) has established its asymptotic normality. Hall has also determined the optimal choice of the truncation parameter r. However, since this parameter is a function of the *unknown* parameters of the distribution, we adhere here to the common practice of using a set of values in the range $\{n/10, \ n/25\}$. This corresponds to severe truncations, which allow us to be more confident in our results.

We examined over two dozen distributions, and found values for α that are consistent with the infinite variance hypothesis ($\alpha < 2$) and, in many cases, they point to the nonexistence of the mean ($\alpha < 1$). The estimates of α for the distributions in Figure 6b were consistent with the hypothesis of infinite variance and infinite mean. The standard deviation in the estimates of the α values were consistently an order of magnitude smaller than the estimates themselves, pointing to highly significant coefficients.

Are heavy-tailed distributions able to explain the strange sample mean discussed in the introduction? In other words, are stable distributions with index of stability of the order of magnitude of those estimated, able to generate data which reproduces the pattern shown in Figure 1a?

By using the method of Chambers, Mallows, and Stuck (1976), we generated random samples from a stable distribution, and calculated the mean as function of the number of samples. The resulting sequence of partial means is portrayed on Figure 7. The comparison between Figures 1a and 7 is striking, as the general wild oscillations are very similar and characteristic of heavy-tailed distributions.

5 Exploiting Heavy-Tailed Behavior

For our heavy-tailed distributions, we see that our procedures are in some sense most effective early on in the search. This suggests that a sequence of short runs instead of a single long run may be a more effective use of our computational

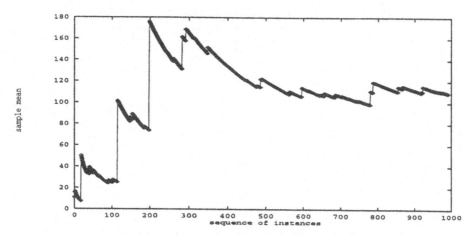

Figure 7: Behavior of mean for example stable distribution.

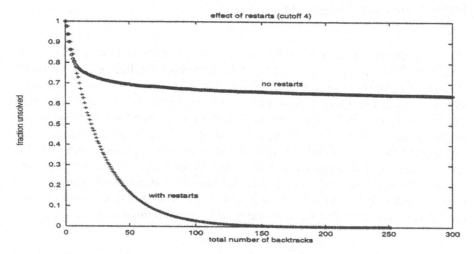

Figure 8a: Using restarts to exploit heavy-tailed behavior.

resources. We explore this idea by considering a fixed limit L on our overall cost ("run time"). From the cumulative cost distribution and L, we can determine what our expected probability of *not* solving the instance is because the search procedure runs out of time. We can also compute this "probability of failure" for a procedure that quickly restarts. Figures 8a and 8b give the results of such an analysis. (For more detailed results on the derivations of the probability distributions for restarts, see Gomes and Selman, Rome Lab Technical Report, 1997. For related work, see Gomes and Selman 1997b.)

The analysis was done for the completion problem of an instance of order 20 with 5% pre-placed. See distribution in Figure 6a. From Figure 8a, we see

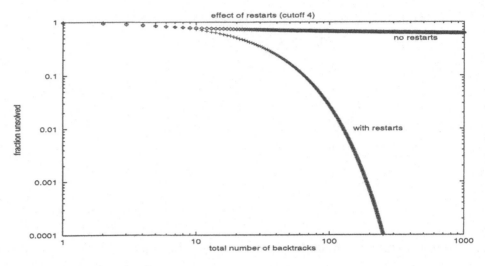

Figure 8b: Log-log plot for restarts.

that without restarts and given a total of 50 backtracks, we have a failure rate of around 70%. Using restarts (every 4 backtracks), this failure rate drops to around 10%. With an overall limit of only 150 backtracks, the restart startegy solves the instance almost always, whereas the original procedure still has a failure rate of around 70%. Such a dramatic improvement due to restarts is typical for heavy tailed distributions — in particular, we get similar results on critically constrained instances. Finally, Figure 8b shows a clear downward curve for the restart strategy. This suggests that the heavy-tailed nature of the cost distribution has disappeared. And, thus, we see that random restarts provide an effective mechanism for dealing with heavy-tailed cost distributions. These results explain the informal popularity of restart strategies in combinatorial search methods.

6   Conclusions and Future Work

We have revealed the special heavy-tailed nature of the cost distribution of combinatorial search procedures. We showed how such distributions can be modeled as stable distributions with heavy Pareto-Lévy type tails. Our analysis explains the empirically observed erratic behavior of the mean and variance of the cost of combinatorial search. And, more generally, the high variability observed between runs of such procedures.

Stable distributions have recently been used to capture a variety of real-world phenomena, such as stock market and wheather patterns. We believe our results are the first indication of the occurrence of such distributions in purely computational processes. We hope that our results will further stimulate research along these lines by employing the special statistical tools available in this area.

We also showed how a "restart" strategy is an effective remedy against the heavy-tailed phenomena. Restarts drastically reduce the probability of failure under limited time resources and reduce the overall variability of the method. Of course, when heavy tails are absent, restarts are much less effective. In our study, we did not encounter heavy tails for unsolvable instances.

Acknowledgments We would like to thank Karen Alguire for developing an exciting tool for experimenting with the quasigroup completion problem. We also would like to thank Nort Fowler for many useful suggestions and discussions, and Neal Glassman for suggesting the domain of combinatorial design as a potential benchmark domain. The first author is a research associate with Rome Laboratory and is funded by the Air Force Office of Scientific Research, under the New World Vistas Initiative (F30602-97-C-0037 and AFOSR NWV project 2304, LIRL 97RL005N25).

References

Anderson, L. (1985). Completing Partial Latin Squares. *Mathematisk Fysiske Meddelelser*, 41, 1985, 23–69.

Brelaz, D. (1979). New methods to color the vertices of a graph. *Comm. of the ACM* (1979) 251–256.

Chambers, John M., Mallows, C.L., and Stuck, B.W. (1976) A method for simulating stable random variables. *Journal of the American Statistical Association* 71, 340–344.

Cheeseman, Peter and Kanefsky, Bob and Taylor, William M. (1991). Where the Really Hard Problems Are. *Proceedings IJCAI-91*, 1991, 163–169.

Colbourn, C. (1983). Embedding Partial Steiner Triple Systems is NP-Complete. *J. Combin. Theory* (A) 35 (1983), 100-105.

Dechter, R. (1991) Constraint networks. *Encyclopedia of Artificial Intelligence* John Wiley, New York (1991) 276-285.

de Lima, Pedro J.F. (1997). On the robustness of nonlinearity tests to moment condition failure. *Journal of Econometrics* **76**, 251–280.

Denes, J. and Keedwell, A. (1974) Latin Squares and their Applications. *Akademiai Kiado, Budapest, and English Universities Press*, London, 1974.

Frost, Daniel , Rish, Irina, and Vila, Lluís (1997) Summarizing CSP hardness with continuous probability distributions. *Proc. AAAI-97*.

Fujita, M., Slaney, J., and Bennett, F. (1993). Automatic Generation of Some Results in Finite Algebra *Proc. IJCAI*, 1993.

Freuder, E. and Mackworth, A. (Eds.). *Constraint-based reasoning*. MIT Press, Cambridge, MA, USA, 1994.

Gent, I. P. and Walsh, T.. (1993). Easy Problems are Sometimes Hard, the DIMACS Challenge on Satisfiability Testing. Piscataway, NJ, Oct. 1993. Full version AIJ (Hogg et al. 1996).

Gent, I. and Walsh, T. (1996) The Satisfiability Constraint Gap. *Artificial Intelligence*, 81, 1996.

Gomes, C.P. and Selman, B. (1997a) Problem Structure in the Presence of Perturbations *Proc. AAAI-97*, Providence, RI, 1997.

Gomes, C.P. and Selman, B. (1997b) Algorithm Portfolio Design: Theory vs. Practice, *Proc. UAI-97*, Providence, RI, 1997.

Hall, Peter (1982) On some simple estimates of an exponent of regular variation. *Journal of the Royal Statistical Society, *B** 44, 37–42.

Huberman, B.A., Lukose, R.M., and Hogg, T. (1997). An economics approach to hard computational problems. *Science*, 265, 51–54.

Hogg, T., Huberman, B.A., and Williams, C.P. (Eds.) (1996). Phase Transitions and Complexity. *Artificial Intelligence*, 81 (Spec. Issue; 1996)

Kirkpatrick, S. and Selman, B. (1994) Critical Behavior in the Satisfiability of Random Boolean Expressions. *Science*, 264 (May 1994) 1297–1301.

Kwan, Alvin C. M. (1995) Validity of normality assumption in CSP research, *PRI-CAI'96: Topics in Artificial Intelligence. Proceedings of the 4th Pacific Rim International Conference on Artificial Intelligence*, 459–465.

Lam, C., Thiel, L., and Swiercz, S. (1989) The Non-existence of Finite Projective Planes of Order 10. *Can. J. Math.*, Vol. XLI, 6, 1989, 1117–1123.

Mandelbrot, Benoit B. (1960) The Pareto-Lévy law and the distribution of income. *International Economic Review* 1, 79–106.

Mandelbrot, Benoit B. (1963) The variation of certain speculative prices. *Journal of Business* **36**, 394–419.

Mandelbrot, B. (1983) *The fractal geometry of nature.* Freeman: New York. 1983.

Mitchell, D., Selman, B., and Levesque, H.J. (1989) Hard and easy distributions of SAT problems. *Proc. AAAI-92*, San Jose, CA (1992) 459–465.

Puget, J.-F. (1994) A C++ Implementation of CLP. *Technical Report 94-01* ILOG S.A., Gentilly, France, (1994).

Russell, S and Norvig P. (1995) *Artificial Intelligence a Modern Approach.* Prentice Hall, Englewood Cliffs, NJ. (1995).

Samorodnitsky, Gennady and Taqqu, Murad S. (1994) *Stable Non-Gaussian Random Processes: Stochastic Models with Infinite Variance*, Chapman and Hall, New York.

Selman, B. and Kirkpatrick, S. (1996) Finite-Size Scaling of the Computational Cost of Systematic Search. *Artificial Intelligence*, Vol. 81, 1996, 273–295.

Smith, B. and Dyer, M. Locating the Phase Transition in Binary Constraint Satisfaction Problems. *Artificial Intelligence*, 81, 1996.

Smith, B. and Grant S.A., Sparse Constraint Graphs and Exceptionally Hard Problems. *IJCAI-95*, 646–651, 1995. Full version in AIJ (Hogg et al. 1996).

van Hentenryck, P. , Deville, Y., and Teng Choh-Man (1992) A generic arc consistency algorithm and its specializations. *Artificial Intelligence*, 57, 1992.

Williams, C.P. and Hogg, T. (1992) Using deep structure to locate hard problems. *Proc. AAAI-92*, San Jose, CA, July 1992, 472–277.

Zhang, W. and Korf, R. A Study of Complexity Transitions on the Asymmetric Travelling Salesman Problem. *Artificial Intelligence*, 81, 1996.

Zolotarev, V.M. (1986) One-dimensional Stable Distributions. Vol. 65 of "Translations of mathematical monographs", American Mathematical Society. Translation from the original 1983 Russian Ed.

Counting, Structure Identification and Maximum Consistency for Binary Constraint Satisfaction Problems

Gabriel Istrate*

Department of Computer Science,
University of Rochester,
Rochester, NY 14627 USA,
istrate@cs.rochester.edu

Abstract. Using a framework inspired by Schaefer's generalized satisfiability model [Sch78], Cohen, Cooper and Jeavons [CCJ94] studied the computational complexity of constraint satisfaction problems in the special case when the set of constraints is closed under permutation of labels and domain restriction, and precisely identified the tractable (and intractable) cases.

Using the same model we characterize the complexity of three related problems:
1. counting the number of solutions.
2. structure identification (Dechter and Pearl [DP92]).
3. approximating the maximum number of satisfiable constraints.

1   Introduction

Determining consistency (satisfiability) of a constraint satisfaction problem is hard (NP-complete) in general [Mac77], even in the case when all constraints are binary. However, "real-world" instances need not be that hard, since they may be subject to several conditions on the nature of their constraints. It is therefore important to precisely characterize the special cases for which deciding consistency is tractable. Inspired by Schaefer's earlier work on the complexity of generalized satisfiability [Sch78], Cohen, Cooper and Jeavons [CCJ94] defined a theoretical framework for this problem and identified the tractable (and intractable) cases, under the additional hypothesis that the set of constraints involved is closed under two operations, domain restriction and label permutation. They proved that consistency can be decided in polynomial time if all constraints belong to a special class of constraints, called *0/1/all constraints*, and is NP-complete in all other cases.

Consistency is, however, not the only problem whose computational complexity is worth investigating. In some instances knowing *the number of solutions* is important (see Dechter and Itai [DI92] for a discussion). Another problem, called

---
* Supported in part by the NSF grant CCR-9701911

structure identification, introduced in Dechter and Pearl [DP92], deals with deciding whether a set of models is the set of *all* models of some constraint network. Finally, in many practical situations having a good *approximation algorithm* is important, as it might help [Kor95] in finding a maximally consistent assignment.

In this paper we study the above-mentioned three problems in the framework from [CCJ94]. As in the case of propositional satisfiability [KS96], structure identification is related (in a very precise manner) to satisfiability: it is tractable precisely when satisfiability is tractable, and it is coNP-complete when satisfiability is NP-complete. For the counting problem, we identify a subclass of the 0/1/all constraints for which counting can be done in polynomial time, and show that counting models is hard (#P-complete) in all other cases. Finally, we show that all cases of the optimization problem are APX-complete, that is, it is unlikely that they have efficient approximation algorithms with arbitrarily good performance.

2 Definitions

2.1 Notions from Computational Complexity Theory

Throughout this paper we will assume reader's familiarity with "standard" computational complexity notions, such as (nondeterministic) Turing machines, classes P, NP, and NP-completeness. In particular the standard tool used for classifying decision problems is the notion of $\leq_m^P$ reduction: decision problem A reduces to decision problem B if there is a polynomial time computable function f that maps instances of A to instances of B such that $\forall x : x \in A \Leftrightarrow f(x) \in B$.

The analogue of the class NP in the context of counting problems is #P, the class of all functions that count the number of accepting paths of a nondeterministic polynomial-time Turing machines. The corresponding notion of completeness is called #P-*completeness* and can be defined as follows: function $f \in$ #P reduces to function $g \in$ #P if there is a polynomial time computable function h (called *parsimonious reduction*) such that, for every x $f(x) = g(h(x))$, i.e. the number of accepting paths of the Turing machine defining f on input x is the same as the number of accepting paths of the Turing machine defining g on input $h(x)$. However, to prove #P-*completeness* we will not reason about Turing machines, but reduce the problem of computing the number of solutions for an instance of a known #P-complete problem A to the problem of counting the number of solutions to the instance of CSP we are concerned with. One particular #P-complete problem, defined and used in [CH96], is

Definition 1. [Positive 2SAT] *(#POS − 2SAT):*

INSTANCE: A $2CNF$ formula Φ, whose clauses contain exactly two positive variables.

QUESTION: How many satisfying assignments does Φ have ?

The following notions (from e.g. [KMSV94]) provide precise definitions for studying the complexity of obtaining approximate solutions for optimization problems.

Definition 2. An *NP optimization problem* (NPO) Π is a 4-tuple $(I, sol, c, goal)$ such that:

1. I is the set of the *instances of Π* and is recognizable in polynomial time.
2. Given an instance x of Π, $sol(x)$ denotes the set of *feasible solutions of x*. These solutions are *short*, that is, there is a polynomial p such that, for any $y \in sol(x)$, $|y| \leq p(|x|)$. Moreover, it is decidable in polynomial time whether $y \in sol(x)$.
3. Given an instance x and a feasible solution y of x, $c(x, y)$ denotes the positive integer *cost of y*. The function c is computable in polynomial time and is also called *objective function*.
4. $goal \in \{max, min\}$.
5. the *optimal value of Π on input x* is

$$OPT_\Pi(x) = goal\{c(x, y) : y \text{ feasible solution for } x\}.$$

Given an NP-optimization problem Π and a function $\alpha : \mathbf{N} \Rightarrow \mathbf{N}$, we say that an algorithm A is *an α-approximation algorithm for Π*, if for every instance x of Π of size n, A produces, in time polynomial in n, a solution y to x of value in the range $[OPT_\Pi(x)/\alpha(n), \alpha(n) \cdot OPT_\Pi(x)]$. We say Π *is α-approximable* if such an algorithm exists. We define APX to be the class of NPO problems which have constant-factor approximation algorithms.

The following definition formalizes the idea of a problem that is hard to approximate within some constant parameter c, by requiring that the existence of such an efficient approximation algorithm would provide an efficient algorithm for SAT (hence P = NP):

Definition 3. For c a positive integer, we say that problem Π *is hard to approximate within factor c* if there is a polynomial time reduction f from SAT to Π that maps instances of SAT having length n into instances of Π having the same length $l(n)$, and, for every two formulas of size n, $\Phi_1 \in SAT$, $\Phi_2 \notin SAT$, $OPT(f(\Phi_1))/OPT(f(\Phi_2)) > c$.

Indeed, if a problem Π that is hard to approximate within factor c has a polynomial time computable procedure A that is a c-approximation algorithm, one can solve SAT in polynomial time as follows (details omitted):

1. First we show that (under these two hypotheses) there is a polynomial time computable function $f(\cdot, \cdot)$ that, having as input a pair of CNF formulas (F, G) returns one of the two formulas that is "more likely" to be satisfiable (formally $f(F, G) \in \{F, G\}$ and $F \in SAT \vee G \in SAT \Rightarrow f(F, G) \in SAT$); such a function is called *a p-selector*.
2. We use a result of Selman [Sel82] that states that a selector function for SAT can be turned into an efficient decision algorithm.

Definition 4. A problem is *APX*-complete if it is in *APX* and hard to approximate within some constant factor.

Problems that are *APX*-complete are unlikely to possess arbitrarily good efficient approximation algorithms.

2.2 Constraint satisfaction problems

This paragraph provides a quick overview of [CCJ94], as well as defining the relevant constraint-related notions.

Definition 5. If $m \geq 2$, a *width-m constraint satisfaction problem*, (CSP), also called *m*-constraint network, consists of a finite set of nodes, N, (identified by the integers $1, 2, \ldots n$). With each pair of nodes, (i,j), we associate (at most) one *constraint* $C_{i,j}$, which is a nonempty subset of $\{0, 1, \ldots m - 1\}^2$. A *model (satisfying assignment) for a CSP* is a labelling $F_1 \ldots F_n$ of the nodes with values from $A_m = \{0, 1, \ldots, m - 1\}$ that satisfies each constraint (that is, for every pair (i, j) of vertices, $(F_i, F_j) \in C_{i,j}$). Whenever S is a set of constraints having the same width, we will use the term *S-constraint network* for networks whose constraints all belong to S.

For every pair (i, j) of vertices in a constraint network, we define *the projection of constraint $C_{i,j}$ onto node i* by $A_i(j) = \{x \in A_m : (\exists y \in A_m), (x, y) \in C_{i,j}\}$. For convenience we will represent the various constraints that appear in this paper as a set of pairs, and identify constraints of different width that coincide as lists of pairs. Whenever we will refer to a constraint, it will mean the constraint of the right width from its equivalence class.

Definition 6. [CSP(S)]: For a finite set of constraints S, the decision problem $CSP(S)$ is specified as follows:

INPUT: An *S*-constraint network Φ.
QUESTION: Is Φ consistent ?

Note that *every S*-constraint network is an instance of the problem $CSP(S)$.

Definition 7. A width-m constraint $C_{i,j}$ between nodes i and j is called *a directed 0/1/all constraint* if

$$\forall x(\exists y, z((x, y) \in C_{i,j} \wedge (x, z) \in C_{i,j} \wedge y \neq z) \Rightarrow \forall w \in A_j(i)((x, w) \in C_{i,j})) \quad (1)$$

In other words, each label $x \in A_m$ is consistent with zero, one or all of the labels in $A_j(i)$.

$C_{i,j}$ will be called *a 0/1/all constraint* if both $C_{i,j}$ and $C_{j,i} = \{(y, x) : (x, y) \in C_{i,j}\}$ are directed 0/1/all constraints.

Example 8. Every width-2 binary constraint is a 0/1/all constraint, since any label "on the left-hand side" is consistent with zero, one or all (i.e. two) labels on the right hand side, and a corresponding statement holds for the right hand side as well.

Example 9. Constraint C_1 in Figure 1 is an example of a constraint that is not 0/1/all, since each label is consistent with exactly two of the three labels on the opposite side.

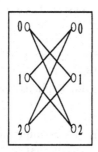

Fig. 1. Constraint C_1.

We will also need three types of constraints defined in [CCJ94]:

Definition 10. A constraint C between nodes i and j is

- *a complete constraint* iff $C = A \times B$, for some sets $A \subseteq A_m$, $B \subseteq A_m$.
- *a permutation constraint* iff there exist two sets $A \subseteq A_m$, $B \subseteq A_m$ such that C coincides with a bijection between A and B.
- *a two-fan constraint* iff there exist $x \in A \subseteq A_m$ and $y \in B \subseteq A_m$ such that $C = (\{x\} \times B) \cup (A \times \{y\})$.

Cohen, Cooper and Jeavons proved that a constraint is 0/1/all iff it is either a complete, permutation, or a two-fan constraint.

We will also employ the following *operations on constraints*:

- *label restriction*: if C is a constraint between nodes i and j, and if $A \subseteq A_m$, $B \subseteq A_m$, define $C|_{A \times B} = \{(p,q) \in C : p \in A, q \in B\}$.
- *label permutation*: If C is a constraint between nodes i and j, and if π, σ are permutations of A_m define $C^{\pi \times \sigma} = \{(\pi(p), \sigma(q)) : (p,q) \in C\}$.

We will call a set S of constraints closed under some operation, if it contains every constraint obtained from constraints in S using that operation.

The following characterization of tractable constraints was proven in [CCJ94]:

Proposition 11. *Let S be any set of constraints closed under label restrictions and permutations. If S contains only 0/1/all constraints then $CSP(S) \in$ P, otherwise $CSP(S)$ is NP-complete.*

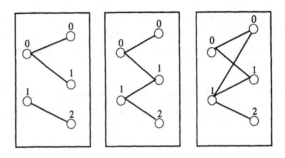

Fig. 2. Constraints C_2, C_3, C_4.

Three special constraints were defined and used to prove Proposition 11. They will subsequently be denoted by C_2, C_3, C_4 and are displayed in Figure 1.

The following concept, while not explicitly introduced in [CCJ94], is useful in explaining the proof:

Definition 12. A set of constraints S *implements constraint* R if there is a constraint network C (using constraints that are obtained from constraints in S via label restrictions and permutations) such that $\forall x_1, x_2 : (x_1, x_2) \in R \iff \exists y_1, \ldots y_n$ such that $(x_1, x_2, y_1, \ldots y_n)$ satisfies C.

It is easily observed that if S is closed under the two label operations defined above and implements R then $CSP(\{R\}) \leq_m^P CSP(S)$. Using this concept, the proof can be explained by the following sequence of steps:

- A polynomial time algorithm is developed for the tractable case of $CSP(S)$.
- If S contains some constraint that is not 0/1/all then (Lemma 6.1 in [CCJ94]) S can implement one of C_2, C_3, C_4.
- Any of C_2, C_3, C_4 implements constraint C_1 (this is a special case of Lemma 6.2 in [CCJ94]).
- graph 3-coloring reduces to $CSP(\{C_1\})$.

3 Results

3.1 Counting the number of models

In this section we study the problem of counting the number of solution of a CSP. This parameter was essential (in an average-case context) in obtaining approximations of the location of the phase transition in binary constraint satisfaction problems [SD96]. The problem we study is formalized as follows:

Definition 13. [Problem #$CSP(S)$]:

INSTANCE: A constraint network C whose constraints belong to set S.
QUESTION: How many satisfying assignments does C have ?

Theorem 14. *Let S be a set of constraints closed under label permutations and restrictions. If all constraints in S are either complete or permutation constraints then #CSP(S) can be solved in polynomial time, otherwise it is #P-complete.*

Proof. The key to proving Theorems 14 and 18 (from the next section) is the following "parsimonious" concept of implementation, essentially from [KS96] :

Definition 15. A set of constraints S *faithfully implements* constraint R if there is a constraint network C in variables $\{x_1, x_2, y_1, \ldots, y_k\}$ (using constraints that are obtained from constraints in S via label restrictions and permutations) and functions $f_1, \ldots f_k$, $f_i : \{0, 1, \ldots, m\}^2 \to \{0, 1, \ldots, m\}$ such that

$$R(x_1, x_2) \equiv (\exists y_1, \ldots, y_k) : C(x_1, x_2, y_1, \ldots, y_k) \wedge (\bigwedge_{i=\overline{1,k}} (y_i \equiv f_i(x_1, x_2))). \quad (2)$$

Let us note that a representation that uses *no* auxiliary variables is faithful, and that faithful representation is transitive.

Cohen, Cooper and Jeavons prove that any constraint R that is not 0/1/all implements one of the constraints C_2, C_3, C_4 which in turn implement every non-null binary constraint on $\{0, 1, 2\}$. The representation of C_2, C_3, C_4 by R is faithful, as it uses no auxiliary variable, and so is the implementation of every constraint using C_2. However, their construction *does not* yield a faithful implementation of every non-null constraint using C_3 or C_4. We still can get around:

Lemma 16. *Constraints C_3 and C_4 faithfully implement C_2 (and consequently every non-null constraint on $\{0, 1, 2\}$).*

Proof. We will show that C_3 faithfully implements C_2 and C_4 faithfully implements C_3, and use the transitivity of faithful implementation.

Let $\tilde{C}_3 = \{(0, 0), (0, 2), (1, 1), (1, 2)\}$. $\tilde{C}_3$ can be obtained from C_3 by permuting labels 1 and 2 "on the right hand side". It is easy to see that $C_2(x, y) \equiv C_3(x, y) \wedge \tilde{C}_3(x, y)$, so C_3 faithfully implements C_2.

Similarly, let $\tilde{C}_4 = \{(0, 0), (0, 2), (1, 0), (1, 1), (1, 2)\}$. $\tilde{C}_4$ can be obtained from C_4 by permuting labels 1 and 2 "on the right hand side", and $C_3(x, y) \equiv C_4(x, y) \wedge \tilde{C}_4(x, y)$.

For the last part of the statement we use the transitivity of faithful representation. □

Let us proceed with the proof of theorem :
Case 1: *S contains only complete/permutation constraints.*
We give a polynomial time algorithm that counts the number of models of an S-constraint network C. First replace each complete constraint in C by two constraints on a single variable, and, without loss of generality also denote by C the resulting constraint network. Denote by $x \equiv y$ the transitive closure of relation "x, y are the arguments of some permutation constraint in C".

It is easy to see that $\equiv$ is an equivalence relation and that, if $x \equiv y$, then any two models (if any) of C that coincide on x coincide on y: construct a graph whose vertices correspond to nodes in C and whose edges correspond to permutation constraints in C. Then equivalence classes of $\equiv$ correspond to connected components in this graph. Setting the value of variable x induces a unique value for all variables that are adjacent to x in the above graph, and this can be "propagated" to y. Models for the restriction of the constraint network to the equivalence class of variable x can be enumerated by making x assume all possible values, "propagating" this assignment to all nodes of the equivalence class, and testing how many of these settings are really models for the restricted network.

Therefore, counting models for C amounts to counting models for the restriction of C to every equivalence class of $\equiv$, a task that can be accomplished via the above-described procedure, and multiplying the results.

Case 2: *S contains a two-fan constraint R that is neither complete, nor a permutation constraint.*

Constraint $C_5(x, y) = \{(0, 1), (1, 0), (1, 1)\}$ can be obtained from R via label permutations and restrictions: if R can be represented as $(\{x\} \times B) \cup (A \times \{y\})$, and if $x_1 \in A, x \neq x_1, y_1 \in B, y \neq y_1$, first use label restrictions "on both sides" to sets $\{x, x_1\}$ and $\{y, y_1\}$, then use label permutations on both sides to obtain C_5. Hence R faithfully implements C_5, therefore there is a parsimonious reduction from $CSP(\{C_5\})$ to $CSP(S)$. But $CSP(\{C_5\})$ is essentially $\#POS - 2SAT$.

Case 3: *S contains a constraint that is not 0/1/all.*

In this case, from the previous lemma it follows that S faithfully implements constraint C_2 which, in turn, implements every non-null constraint on $\{0, 1, 2\}$. Let $C_6 = \{(0, 1), (1, 0), (1, 1), (2, 2)\}$ be one of these constraints. C_5 can be obtained from C_6 by eliminating label 2 "on both sides", hence S faithfully implements constraint C_5 and we reason as in the previous case.

$\square$

3.2 Structure identification

In this paragraph we study the following problem, studied under the name *structure identification* in [DP92], and (in the context of satisfiability problems) under the name *inverse satisfiability* in [KS96]:

Definition 17. [Structure identification/inverse consistency $(INVCSP(S))$]:

INSTANCE: A positive integer m, a family S of constraints over $\{0, 1, \ldots m\}$, and a set of vectors $M \subseteq \{0, 1, \ldots m\}^n$.
QUESTION: Is there an S-constraint network C whose models are precisely the vectors in M?

Structure identification is the task of discovering an useful structure underlying several observations, therefore it is related to learning. A comparison with learning can be found in [DP92].

Theorem 18. *Let S be a set of constraints closed under label permutations and restrictions. If all constraints in S are 0/1/all constraints then $INVCSP(S)$ can be solved in polynomial time, otherwise it is coNP-complete.*

Proof. If $CSP(S) \in$ P then $INVCSP(S) \in$ P. Indeed, given a set of vectors $M \subseteq \{0, 1, \ldots, m\}^n$, first construct the S constraint network Φ that consists of all constraints that are satisfied by every model of M. It is clear that $M \subseteq models(\Phi)$. To see that the equality of the two sets can be decided in polynomial time, consider the tree that has the initial constraint network at the root, its children are the m constraint networks obtained by setting the value of node 1 to $0, 1, \ldots, m$, and so on. Note that if the CSP at the root is a 0/1/all formula, so are the CSP's corresponding to intermediate levels, since the class of 0/1/all constraints is closed under label restrictions. Consider the following recursive procedure:

Procedure 1 CountModels(Φ)

---

if (Φ is consistent) **then**
    $models = 0$;
    {let Φ_i be the formula obtained by setting the node of Φ with smallest index to i}
    for $i = 0$ to m **do**
        $models = models + CountModels(\Phi_i)$;
    end for
    return $models$;
else
    return 0;
end if

It can be shown that the procedure $CountModels$ will compute the number of models of Φ in time proportional to the number of nodes in the tree we described for which the associated formula is satisfiable. This number is $O(|models(\Phi)|)$, so the running time is not necessarily polynomial in $|M|$. However, we can easily modify the procedure to attain the desired running time, if all we want to know is whether $|M| = |models(\Phi)|$: associate an integer c with the last level of the tree. c is initially set to zero and is incremented whenever a new model is found. If, at some moment, c grows beyond $|M|$ the computation is aborted. The number of nodes in the tree that determine recursive calls is $O(n|M|)$ (since only nodes corresponding to the first $|M|$ models of Φ (if that many) and their ancestors are considered). Using Proposition 11, this yields the first part of Theorem 18. For the second part we need the following concept:

Definition 19. A set of vectors $M \subseteq \{0, 1, \ldots, m\}^n$ is *2-consistent* with a vector $m \in \{0, 1, \ldots, m\}^n$, if for every two positions $1 \leq i < j \leq n$, there is a vector $\bar{m} \in M$ that coincides with m on positions i, j. M is *2-closed* if it contains every vector that is 2-consistent with it.

Let $m \geq 1$, and let S_m be the set of all nontrivial binary constraints over $\{0, 1, \ldots, m\}$. We have:

Lemma 20. *A set of vectors $M \subset \{0, 1, \ldots, m\}^n$ is the set of models of some S_m constraint network iff M is 2-closed.*

Proof. The set of models of an S_m constraint network Φ is 2-closed: consider a model t that is 2-consistent with all models of M but fails to satisfy a constraint C of Φ. Let x and y be the variables involved in this constraint. Then the model of M that coincides with t on x and y fails to satisfy C, a contradiction.

If, on the other hand, M is 2-closed, consider the S_m-network Φ that contains all constraints in S_m that are satisfied by every model of M. We claim that the models of Φ are exactly the vectors in M. Indeed, suppose Φ has a model $t \notin M$. Then t is 2-consistent with M, since if the 2-consistency condition were not satisfied for some positions $1 \leq i < j \leq n$, then the constraint $C(x, y) \equiv "(x \neq t_i)$ or $(y \neq t_j)$ " would be satisfied by every model in M, so it would appear in Φ, but is not satisfied by t. Since t is 2-consistent with M and M is 2-closed, it follows that $t \in M$, a contradiction.

$\square$

To prove Theorem 18 we will show that whenever S contains a constraint R that is not 0/1/all, $\overline{CSP(S_2)} \leq_m^P INVCSP(\{R\})$ (where we interpret S_2 as the set of *width-m constraints* that are equivalent to a constraint over $\{0, 1, 2\}$). Since, by the result in [CCJ94], $CSP(S_2)$ is NP-complete, this proves the coNP-hardness of $INVCSP(S)$. Membership in coNP is easy: it can be easily noticed that the unique candidate for an S-formula for M is the formula Φ constructed as in the proof of Lemma 20. Therefore $M \in INVCSP(S)$ is equivalent to "all models of Φ are in M".

Let S be a set of width-m constraints, let R be a constraint in S that is not 0/1/all.

Let Φ be an S_2-constraint network with $n \geq 5$ nodes and c constraints, and $\bar{I}$ be the number of pairs (W, T) with W a set of four nodes of Φ and $T : W \Rightarrow \{0, 1, 2\}$ an assignment to the variables in W that is consistent with every constraint of Φ. Denote $\bar{n} = n \cdot (\bar{I} + 2) + p$, (where p is going to be defined later) and consider the set of vectors $M \subseteq \{0, 1, 2\}^{\bar{n}}$, $M = \{m_{W,T}\}_{W,T}$, where (W, T) span all the pairs described previously.

Model $m_{W,T}$ is defined as follows: we encode each of the n nodes in Φ using $\bar{I} + 2$ positions, and then complete the vector with p additional positions. The encoding corresponding to the node i consists of two parts, a *value pattern* containing the first two digits, and a *padding pattern* that uses the rest of $\bar{I}$ positions. If node i appears in W and is assigned value 0 (1,2) by T define the value pattern of $m_{W,T}$ to be 10 (01,02 respectively). Otherwise define the value pattern to be 00.

To define the padding pattern corresponding to every node i use a fixed enumeration of the $\bar{I}$ pairs (W, T). If node i is not in W, let the padding pattern corresponding to node i be 1^I, else, if t is the index of (W, T) in the enumeration, define the padding pattern to be $0^t 1^{I-t}$. Use $\overline{m_{W,T}}$ to denote the length $n \cdot (\bar{I}+2)$ vector created so far, and let $\overline{M} = \{\overline{m_{W,T}}\}_{W,T}$.

It remains to define p and describe how to complete each $\overline{m_{W,T}}$ with p more digits. Let Φ_1 be the S_2-constraint network consisting of all S_2-constraints that are *satisfied* by all vectors $\overline{m_{W,T}}$. Use R to faithfully implement each such constraint, obtaining the R-network Φ_2, and define p to be the total number of auxiliary nodes used in such implementations. This specifies a bijection between the additional positions in the vectors $m_{W,T}$ and auxiliary nodes in the implementation of constraints in Φ_1.

To complete $\overline{m_{W,T}}$ on the p positions, note that the faithful representation of clauses in Φ_1 (combined with the fact that $\overline{m_{W,T}}$ satisfies all S_2-constraints in Φ_1) requires an unique value for each of the p additional nodes. Complete $\overline{m_{W,T}}$ with all values specified in this way.

The following claim establishes the theorem:

Claim 21. *M is the set of models of an R-constraint network C if and only if Φ is inconsistent.*

Proof. Suppose that M is the set of models of an R-constraint network C and Φ is satisfiable. Let s be a satisfying assignment for Φ. Use the above-mentioned encoding for value and padding patterns to create a length $n \cdot (\bar{I} + 2)$ vector $\bar{s}$ encoding s. Then, by the definition of pairs (W, T) it follows easily that $\bar{s}$ is 4-compatible (hence 2-compatible) with $\overline{M}$, so it satisfies Φ_1. Complete $\bar{s}$ with the p positions specified by the faithful representations, just as in the case of $\overline{m_{W,T}}$.

The newly obtained vector $\hat{s}$ is 2-compatible with M: since every auxiliary node depends on at most two initial nodes, the two compatibility of $\hat{s}$ with M follows form the 4-compatibility of $\bar{s}$ with $\overline{M}$.

But from Lemma 20 it follows that $M = models(C)$ is 2-closed, therefore $\bar{s} = m_{W,T}$ for some pair (W, T). However, this is impossible, since each $m_{W,T}$ has exactly four padding patterns equal to 1^I, while $\bar{s}$ has $n \geq 5$ such patterns.

Suppose now that Φ is inconsistent. Then $\overline{M}$ is 4-closed: since the transition from a sequence of zeros to a sequence of ones in the padding patterns of $\overline{m_{W,T}}$ is unique to each $m_{W,T}$ that contains the corresponding node, any model t that is 4-compatible with $\overline{M}$ coincides in the positions corresponding to a node i with some model $\overline{m_{W,T}}$. If, on the other hand, the node i does not appear in W it is easy to see that $t = \overline{m_{W,T}}$. Therefore $t \in \overline{M}$: if it were not so then t would encode a satisfying assignment for Φ. So $\overline{M}$ is 4-closed (hence 2-closed), therefore $\overline{M} = models(\Phi_1)$, hence M is the set of models of C, the conjunction of R-constraints that faithfully implement constraints in Φ_1.

$\square$

3.3 Maximum consistency

In this section we study the following problem, investigated (under the name PCSP) by Freuder and Wallace [FW92].

Definition 22. [Maximum consistency] ($MAXCSP(S)$):

INSTANCE: An S constraint network Φ.
QUESTION: Find an assignment that maximizes the number of satisfied constraint of Φ.

The next result shows that requiring closure under both label permutations and restrictions makes the classification of $MAXCSP(S)$ somewhat non-interesting, since no cases have arbitrarily good approximation algorithms. It implies that, in order to isolate "easy" cases we have to give up at least one of the two closure operations, and partly motivates the use of *incomplete* algorithms for obtaining approximate solutions, such as *heuristic repair* [FW], or local search [CFG+96].

Theorem 23. *Let S be a closed under label permutations and restrictions. Then $MAXCSP(S)$ is APX-complete.*

Proof. The membership of $MAXCSP(S)$ in APX (for any set of constraints S) is easy: given a constraint network Φ with c constraints in variables $x_1, x_2, \ldots, x_n$, a random assignment will fail to satisfy a fixed clause with probability at most $1 - 1/m^2$. It follows that a random assignment will satisfy at least c/m^2 clauses of Φ. Finding such an assignment can be easily performed using the method of conditional probabilities, just as in the case of $MAX2SAT$ (see [MR95]). It remains to prove APX-completeness. We will show that for every set S with the desired properties, there is a restriction of $MAXCSP(S)$ that captures an APX-complete problem (the fact that this is enough to prove APX completeness follows from the definition of this concept).

Case 1: *All constraints in S are complete.*

Consider the constraint $C_7 = \{(1,0)\}$. C_7 can be obtained from constraints in S via label permutations and restrictions, by restricting labels to singleton sets "on both sides", and then using label permutations to obtain the desired constraint, so it is in S. But $MAXCSP(\{C_7\})$ can be seen as *the satisfiability problem $MAXSAT(\{C_7\})$* which is seen to be APX-complete using Theorem 2.2 in [KSW96].

Case 2: *S contains some permutation constraint R that is not complete.*

Consider $C_8 = \{(0,1),(1,0)\}$. C_8 can easily be obtained from a permutation constraint using label restrictions and permutations. But $MAXCSP(\{C_8\})$ is essentially $MAXCUT$, which is known to be APX-complete.

Case 3: *S contains some two-fan constraint R that is not complete.*

Then the following constraints can be obtained from R by label permutations and restrictions: $C_9 = \{(0,1),(1,0),(1,1)\}, C_{10} = \{(0,0),(1,0),(1,1)\}, C_{11} = \{(0,0),(0,1),(1,1)\}, C_{12} = \{(0,0),(0,1),(1,0)\}$. But the problem $MAX2SAT$ is essentially equivalent to $MAXCSP(\{C_9, C_{10}, C_{11}, C_{12}\})$.

Case 4: *S contains some constraint that is not 0/1/all.*

In this case S contains one of C_2, C_3, C_4. It is easy to see that C_8 can be obtained from any of them by "eliminating label 2 on the right hand side" and then using label permutations, hence $MAXCSP(S)$ captures once more $MAXCUT$.

$\square$

Note 24. Our proofs remain valid in the case of *weighted* constraints, if all the weights are nonnegative. Indeed, membership in APX (for every problem $MAXCSP(S)$) was essentially proven in [Lau96], while APX-hardness follows since the unweighted problems are subcases of weighted ones.

4 Conclusions

We have studied the complexity of three operations that are relevant for constraint programming using the framework from [CCJ94] and isolated maximal tractable classes for them. An obvious open problem is to extend this work to the general case. In particular, Theorem 23 shows that to obtain a relevant classification we need to consider a more general case. It would be interesting to see what versions of $MAXCSP(S)$ are hard/easy to approximate when S is only closed to label permutations (but not to label restrictions). We believe that the following result is true:

Definition 25. A width-m complete constraint is *essentially unary* if at least one of the sets A, B from the definition of completeness is equal to $\{0, 1, \ldots, m\}$.

Conjecture 26. *Let S be a set of constraints that is closed under label permutations. If S contains only essentially unary constraints then $MAXCSP(S)$ can be solved in polynomial time, otherwise it is APX-complete.*

Acknowledgment

We thank Mitsunori Ogihara for many useful comments.

References

[CCJ94] M. Cooper, D. Cohen, and P. Jeavons. Characterizing tractable constraints. *Artificial Intelligence*, 65:347–361, 1994.
[CFG+96] D. Clark, J. Frank, I. Gent, E. MacIntyre, N. Tomov, and T. Walsh. Local search and the number of solutions. In E. Freuder, editor, *Principles and Practice of Constraint Programming-CP'96*, number 1118 in Lecture Notes in Computer Science, pages 323–337. Springer Verlag, 1996.
[CH96] N. Creignou and M. Hermann. Complexity of generalized counting problems. *Information and Computation*, 125(1):1–12, 1996.
[DI92] R. Dechter and A. Itai. Finding all solutions if you can find one. In *Workshop on Tractable Reasoning, AAAI'92*, pages 35–39, 1992.
[DP92] R. Dechter and J. Pearl. Structure identification in relational data. *Artificial Intelligence*, 58:237–270, 1992.

[FW]   E. Freuder and R. Wallace. Heuristic methods for over-constrained con-
          straint satisfaction problems. In *CP'95 Workshop on Over-Constrained
          Systems*.

[FW92]   E. Freuder and R. Wallace. Partial constraint satisfaction. *Artificial Intel-
          ligence*, 58(1–3):21–70, 1992.

[KMSV94] S. Khanna, R. Motwani, M. Sudan, and U. Vazirani. On syntactic versus
          computational views of approximability. In *Proceedings of the 34th IEEE
          Symposium on Foundations of Computer Science*, pages 819–830. IEEE
          Computer Society, 1994.

[Kor95]   R. Korf. From approximate to optimal solutions: A case study of number
          partitioning. In *Proceedings of the 14th IJCAI*, pages 266–272, 1995.

[KS96]   D. Kavvadias and M. Sideri. The inverse satisfiability problem. In *Pro-
          ceeding of the Second Annual International Computing and Combinatorics
          Conference*, pages 250–259, 1996.

[KSW96]   S. Khanna, M. Sudan, and D. Williamson. A complete classification of the
          approximability of maximization problems derived from boolean constraint
          satisfaction. Technical Report TR96-062, Electronic Colloquium on Com-
          putational Complexity, http://www.eccc.uni-trier.de/eccc/, 1996.

[Lau96]   H. Lau. A new approach for weighted constraint satisfaction: theoretical
          and computational results. In E. Freuder, editor, *Principles and Practice
          of Constraint Programming-CP'96*, number 1118 in Lecture Notes in Com-
          puter Science, pages 323–337. Springer Verlag, 1996.

[Mac77]   A. Mackworth. Consistency in network of relations. *Artificial Intelligence*,
          8:99–118, 1977.

[MR95]   R. Motwani and P. Raghavan. *Randomized Algorithms*. Cambridge Univer-
          sity Press, 1995.

[Sch78]   T. J. Schaefer. The complexity of satisfiability problems. In *Proceedings of
          the 13th ACM Symposium on Theory of Computing*, pages 216–226, 1978.

[SD96]   B. Smith and M. Dyer. Locating the phase transition in binary constraint
          satisfaction problems. *Artificial Intelligence Journal*, 81(1–2):155–181, 1996.

[Sel82]   A. Selman. Analogues of semirecursive sets and effective reducibilities to
          the study of NP complexity. *Information and Control*, 52:36–51, 1982.

Statistical Analysis of Backtracking on Inconsistent CSPs *

Irina Rish and **Daniel Frost**

Department of Information and Computer Science
University of California, Irvine, CA 92697-3425
{irinar,frost}@ics.uci.edu

Abstract. We analyze the distribution of computational effort required by backtracking algorithms on unsatisfiable CSPs, using analogies with reliability models, where lifetime of a specimen before failure corresponds to the runtime of backtracking on unsatisfiable CSPs. We extend the results of [7] by showing empirically that the lognormal distribution is a good approximation of the backtracking effort on unsolvable CSPs not only at the 50% satisfiable point, but in a relatively wide region. We also show how the *law of proportionate effect* [9] commonly used to derive the lognormal distribution can be applied to modeling the number of nodes expanded in a search tree. Moreover, for certain intervals of C/N, where N is the number of variables, and C is the number of constraints, the parameters of the corresponding lognormal distribution can be approximated by the *linear lognormal model* [11] where mean log(deadends) is linear in C/N, and variance of log(deadends) is close to constant. The linear lognormal model allows us to extrapolate the results from a relatively easy overconstrained region to the hard critically constrained region and, in particular, to use more efficient strategies for testing backtracking algorithms.

> All models are wrong, but some are useful.
> *George E.P. Box*

1 Introduction

Empirical evidence presented in [7] demonstrates that the distribution of effort required to solve CSPs randomly generated at the 50% satisfiable point, when using a backtracking algorithm, can be approximated by two standard families of continuous probability distribution functions. Solvable problems can be approximated by the Weibull distribution and unsolvable problems by the lognormal distribution. Both distribution are widely used in reliability theory for modeling the lifetime of a product. An analogy between a product's lifetime and an algorithm's runtime suggests reliability models may be applicable to the statistical analysis of algorithms.

---

* This work was partially supported by NSF grant IRI-9157636, Air Force Office of Scientific Research grant AFOSR 900136, Rockwell Micro grant 22147, and UC Micro grant 96-012.

In this paper we focus on unsatisfiable problems, extending the results of [7] to a wider range of parameters (not just the 50% point) and studying how the parameters of the distribution depend on the parameters of a problem generator. We show empirical results for the Davis-Putnam Procedure augmented with the heuristic proposed in [1] on random 3SAT problems, and for the algorithm BJ+DVO [6] on random binary CSPs.

Our results on a variety of CSP problems and different backtracking algorithms suggest that the lognormal distribution captures some inherent properties of backtracking search on unsatisfiable CSPs. The lognormal distribution can be derived from the *law of proportionate effect* [2] which is used to model certain natural processes, such as failure of a material due to the growing size of fatigue cracks.

We observed at certain regions of C/N ratio, including a relatively wide region around the transition point, that the performance of backtracking fits the *linear lognormal model* [11]. This model allows us to compute the parameters of the lognormal distribution in a relatively easy overconstrained region (say, for C/N around 6 for 3SAT) and extrapolate the results to the transition region.

Clearly, studies of artificial random problems are limited since they do not reflect real applications. However, random problems are useful for systematic analysis of algorithms. Also, some real applications can be studied statistically and may accommodate a similar analysis to the one we propose here. One example is scheduling problems (e.g., airline scheduling) which has to take into account daily changes within the same system. Another example is the performance analysis of inference in a knowledge base on a variety of queries.

In the next section, we describe the random problem generators and the algorithms we experimented with. Section 3 gives some statistical background. The law of proportionate effect and its applicability to backtracking search are discussed in section 4. Section 5 presents empirical study and the models we propose. In section 6, we give a summary of our results, discuss their practical importance, and outline some directions for further research.

2 Problems and Algorithms

The binary CSP experiments reported in this paper were run on a model of uniform random binary constraint satisfaction problems that takes four parameters: N, D, T and C. The problem instances are binary CSPs with N variables, each having a domain of size D. The parameter T (tightness) specifies the probability that a value pair in a constraint is disallowed. The parameter C specifies the probability of a binary constraint existing between two variables.

We also experimented with random 3SAT problems which can be viewed as a type of CSP with ternary constraints and $D = 2$. The random 3SAT problem generator was implemented as proposed in [10] for $k = 3$. It takes as an input the number of variables N, the number of literals per clause, k, and the number of clauses C, and generates each clause by choosing k variables randomly and flipping the sign of each literal with probability $p = 0.5$.

For binary CSPs, we present results using algorithm BJ+DVO [6], which combines backjumping, forward checking style domain filtering, and a dynamic variable ordering scheme. On 3SAT, we experimented with another backtracking algorithm, the Davis-Putnam Procedure (DPP) [4] augmented with the heuristics proposed in [1]. We measure the hardness of a problem by counting the total number of deadends, including "internal" (non-leaf) deadends. On unsatisfiable problems, this number just coincides with the number of nodes explored in the search tree.

3 Statistical Background

The *two-parameter lognormal distribution* is based on the well-known normal or Gaussian distribution. If the logarithm of a random variable is normally distributed, then the random variable itself shows a lognormal distribution. The density function, with *scale* parameter μ and *shape* parameter σ, is

$$f(t) = \begin{cases} \frac{1}{\sqrt{2\pi}\sigma t} \exp\left(\frac{-(\log t - \mu)^2}{2\sigma^2}\right), & t > 0 \\ 0, & t \le 0 \end{cases}$$

and the cumulative lognormal distribution function is

$$F(t) = \Phi\left(\frac{\log t - \mu}{\sigma}\right),$$

where $\Phi(\cdot)$ is the standard normal cumulative distribution function. The mean value of the lognormal distribution is $E = exp(\mu + \sigma^2/2)$. Simple formulas for the median and mode are given by $exp(\mu)$ and $exp(\mu - \sigma^2)$, respectively. Note that for a lognormally distributed variable t, log median equals mean $log(t)$.

Given a population sample $x_1, ..., x_n$ and a parameterized probability distribution family, there are several methods for estimating the parameters that best match the data. We used *maximum likelihood estimators (MLE)*[3]: $\mu =$ mean log(deadends), $\sigma =$ square root of the variance of log(deadends) (correcting a misstatement in [7], the MLE for the lognormal distribution is completely satisfactory).

4 The Proportionate Effect Model

One of the oldest and most widely used methods for deriving the lognormal distribution is the *law of proportionate effect* [2]. This law states that if the growth rate of a variable at each step in a process is in random proportion to its size at that step, then the size of the variable at time n will be approximately lognormally distributed. In other words, if the value of a random variable at time i is X_i, and the relationship

$$X_i = X_{i-1} \times b_i$$

holds, where $(b_1, b_2, \ldots, b_n)$ are positive independent random variables, then the distribution of X_i is, for large enough i, lognormally distributed. The law of proportionate effect follows from the central limit theorem, since

$$log(X_n) = \sum_i^n log(b_i)$$

and the sum of independent random variables $log(b_i)$ converges to the normal distribution.

In the context of constraint satisfaction problems, we will now show that the number of nodes on level i of the search tree explored by backtracking is distributed lognormally when i is sufficiently large. We restrict our attention to the simple backtracking algorithm with a fixed variable ordering $(Y_1, \ldots, Y_N)$ and to the inconsistent random binary CSPs with the parameters $\langle N, D, T, C \rangle$ (inconsistency implies that the entire search tree needs to be explored).

Let X_i be the number of nodes on search tree level $i, 1 \le i \le N$. The branching factor b_i at each level is defined as X_i/X_{i-1} for $2 \le i \le N$, and $b_1 = D$. For $i > 1$, b_i is randomly distributed in $[0, D]$ and specifies how many values of variable Y_{i-1} are consistent with the previous assignment. The probability of a value k for Y_{i-1} being consistent with the assignment to $Y_1, \ldots, Y_{i-2}$ is

$$p_i = (1 - CT)^{i-2},$$

where C is the probability of a constraint between Y_{i-1} and a previous variable. T is the probability of a value pair to be prohibited by that constraint. Then the branching factor b_i is distributed binomially with parameter p_i. On each level i, b_i is independent of previous b's. Note that b_i are non-negative (positive for all levels except the deepest level in the tree reached by backtracking) and can be greater than or less than 1 (since b_i can be zero, the low of proportionate effect is not entirely applicable for some deep levels of the search tree). Then

$$X_i = b_1 \times b_2 \times \ldots \times b_i,$$

is lognormally distributed by the law of proportionate effect.

This derivation applies to the distribution of nodes on each particular level i, where i is large enough. It still remains to be shown how this analysis relates to the distribution of the total number of nodes explored in a tree. In a complete search tree, the total number of nodes $\sum_{i=0}^{N} D^i = (D^{N+1} - 1)/(D-1) \approx D^N \frac{D}{D-1}$ is proportional to the number of nodes at the deepest level, D^N. A similar relation may be possible to derive for a backtracking search tree.

Satisfiable CSPs do not fit this scheme since the tree traversal is interrupted when solution is found. As mentioned above, empirical results also point to substantial difference in behavior of satisfiable and unsatisfiable problems.

5 Empirical Results

We experimented with the DPP and BJ+DVO algorithms described above, running 10,000 experiments per each combination of parameters (in the underconstrained region we had to ran up to 100,000 experiments in order to find a satisfactory amount of unsatisfiable problems). For each instance we recorded whether a solution was found and the number of deadends (including internal deadends, as mentioned above).

Experiments on 3SAT with 100, 125, 175 and 200 variables and $C/N \in [3, 10]$, and on binary CSPs with 75, 100 and 150 variables and various values of D, T and C, demonstrate a good fit of the lognormal distribution to the empirical data for unsolvable problems. Figure 1 shows histograms (vertical bars) and continuous lognormal distributions (curved lines) for selected experiments, using the algorithms DPP on 3SAT with $N = 175$ and several values of C/N (on the left) and BJ+DVO on binary CSPs with $N = 100$, $D = 8$, $T = 0.5$ and several values of C (on the right). The x-axis unit is deadends. Vertical dotted lines indicate median of data, while $\wedge$ indicates mean. The data has been grouped in 100 intervals of equal length summarized by each vertical bar. Data greater than the maximum number of nodes indicated on the x-axis has been truncated from the charts. The y-axis shows the fraction of the sample that is expected (for the distribution functions) or was found to occur (for the experimental data) within each range. The "count" means the number of instances for each set of parameters. We can see that the lognormal distribution with MLE parameters captures the wide variety of shapes in the empirical distributions.

We examined several distributions, such as the normal, lognormal, gamma, Weibull, and inverse Gaussian distributions, which all have an exponential tail and which all have similar curves in certain parameter ranges. When σ is small (e.g. less than 0.5) the lognormal distribution looks quite similar to the normal distribution. Also, for small σ, the gamma distribution can sometimes provide a slightly better fit (see Figure 2(a)). When the data is strongly skewed, e.g. $\sigma > 1$, the lognormal distribution typically models the data better than the gamma (see Figure 2 (b)).

Assuming the lognormal distribution of the unsatisfiable problems, we would like to know how the parameters μ and σ depend on the parameters of the problem and on heuristic employed by the specific backtracking algorithm.

Figure 3(a) shows how μ and σ depend on the C/N ratio for unsatisfiable 3SAT problems. Similar data but for both satisfiable and unsatisfiable binary CSPs are shown in Figure 4(b).

It is striking that on 3SAT problems σ is practically constant on a wide range of C/N for different N (a closer look at σ reveals a very slow growth in the transition region). The growth of σ in transition region is more pronounced in binary CSPs (Figure 4(b)).

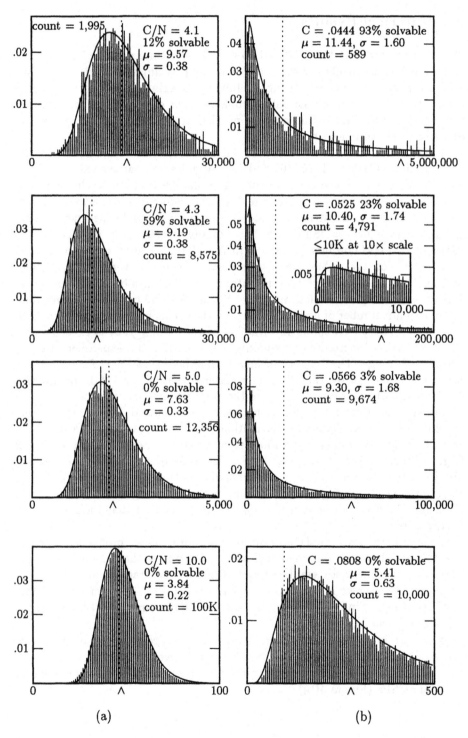

Fig. 1. Lognormal fit to empirical distributions for DPP on 3SAT (a) and BJ+DVO on binary CSPs (b).

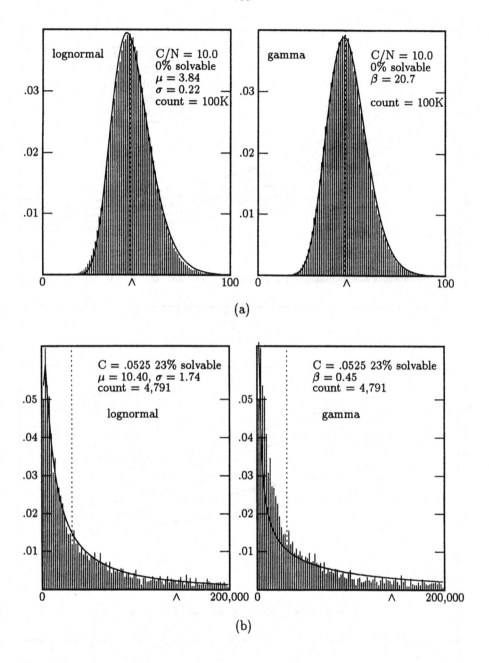

Fig. 2. Comparison of lognormal and gamma distribution functions on two samples of data from Figure 1. β is the shape parameter of the gamma distribution. Typically, the gamma distribution is as good a fit or better than lognormal when the shape is fairly symmetrical (which happens for small σ, such as $\sigma = 0.22$ in the first row). But the lognormal provides a substantially better fit for skewed and long-tailed distributions of data with larger σ, as in the second row ($\sigma = 1.74$).

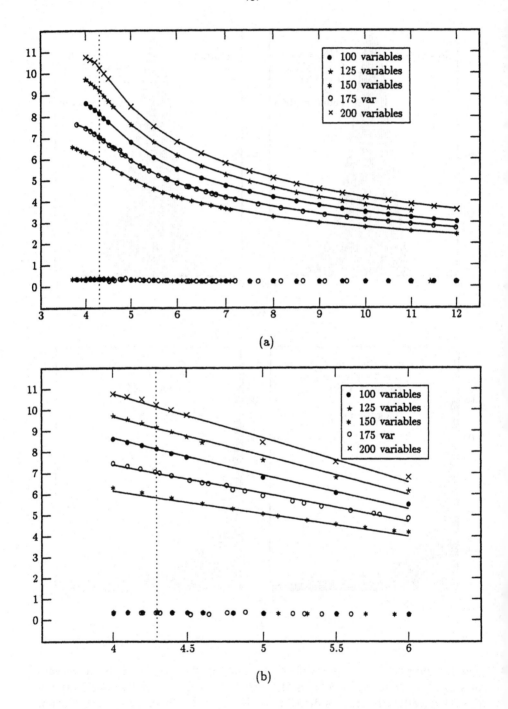

Fig. 3. Parameters μ and σ as functions of C/N in a wide region (a) and near the transition (b)

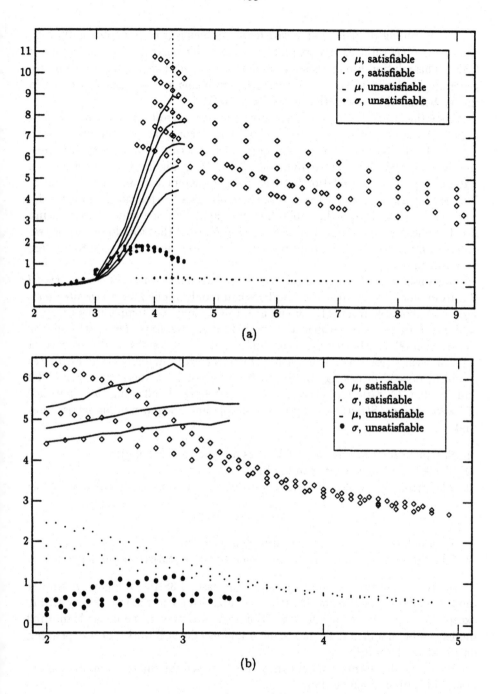

Fig. 4. Parameters μ and σ as functions of C/N for both satisfiable and unsat-isfiable 3SAT problems with N=100, 125, 150, 175 and 200 (a) and for binary CSPs with D=3, T=2/9, and N=75, 100, and 150(b). Steeper lines correspond to larger values of N.

The mean log(deadends) of unsatisfiable problems grows monotonically with decreasing C/N ratio, except sometimes in the underconstrained region of binary CSPs. This relationship implies that underconstrained inconsistent problems are generally harder to solve than inconsistent problems at the transition point (a theory behind this observation is discussed in [12]).

Since the transition region is usually of major interest, we introduce a simplified model that suits that particular region. For example, for 3SAT with $C/N < 6$, the parameter μ (mean log(deadends)) can be approximated sufficiently accurately by a linear function of C/N (see Figure 3(b) and Table 1). Table 1 displays the correlation between the parameters μ, σ, and the C/N ratio. We see that μ is practically linear in C/N in all cases (correlation is almost -1). The last two columns in the table show the negative slope which is decreasing (i.e. the lines become steeper) with increasing N. Note that the slope for σ is two orders of magnitude smaller than the slope for μ, so that σ can be approximated by a constant.

Our observations can be described by the so-called *linear-lognormal model* [11] from reliability studies. The model is commonly applied for *accelerated testing*. In an example from [11], an engineer selects four test temperatures for the equipment to be tested which are referred to as the *stress levels* (the higher the stress level the shorter the mean lifetime of a unit tested), and runs several tests on each stress level. Then, using the linear-lognormal model, he estimates μ and σ, instead of testing equipment for all possible temperatures. For CSPs and 3SAT, C/N ratio plays the role of the "stress level" affecting the "lifetime" of backtracking. Strictly speaking, the simple linear-lognormal model assumes that

1. Specimen life t at any stress level has a lognormal distribution.
2. The standard deviation σ of log life is constant.
3. The mean log life at a (possibly transformed by some $f(x)$) stress level x is

$$\mu(x) = \gamma_0 + \gamma_1 x.$$

Parameters σ, γ_0, and γ_1 are estimated from data.
4. The random variations in the specimen lives are statistically independent.

All these assumptions are satisfied in the case of 3SAT problems. A similar model can be applied to the backtracking algorithms on random binary CSPs, except that σ grows within the transition region. However, the linear-lognormal model can be modified to fit increasing σ and usually still works for σ depending on the stress level [11].

The linear lognormal model can be used as well for the overconstrained region, but with a different slope.

In figure 4, we plotted μ and σ computed for both satisfiable problems and unsatisfiable problems on 3SAT (Figure 4(a)) and on binary CSPs (Figure 4(b)). Although the satisfiable problems do not fit the lognormal distribution, μ and σ still provide useful information on the complexity of backtracking (recall that μ = mean log(deadends) and σ = standard deviation log(deadends)). We see

Table 1. Dependence between μ, σ and C/N for unsatisfiable 3SAT problems: correlation and slope are given for each parameter as a function of C/N.

N	Correlation		Slope	
	μ	σ	μ	σ
100	-0.9949	-0.9716	-1.0735	0.0410
125	-0.9957	-0.5873	-1.3550	0.0438
150	-0.9963	-0.8734	-1.6130	0.0468
175	-0.9956	-0.9632	-1.8504	0.0613
200	-0.9957	-0.9159	-2.0925	0.0741

that there is no peak at the transition point in mean log(deadends) for either satisfiable or unsatisfiable problems considered separately. The most difficult unsatisfiable problems appear in satisfiable region, and the most difficult satisfiable ones appear in unsatisfiable region. The complexity peaks for satisfiable and unsatisfiable problems seem to occur on the opposite sides of the narrow transition region located within $C/N \in [2,4]$ rather than at the transition point (see Figure 4).

6 Conclusions and Future Work

In this paper, we focus on unsatisfiable CSP problems, supporting the claim made in [7] that the lognormal distribution approximates well the computational effort required by backtracking-based algorithms on unsatisfiable CSP instances from the 50% satisfiable region. In addition, 1. we extend this claim to the non-crossover regions; 2. we show a connection between the performance of backtracking and the law of proportionate effect used to derive the lognormal distribution; 3. we show the applicability of the linear-lognormal model in a relatively wide area around the transition point; 4. we propose using accelerated testing techniques developed in reliability studies for design of experiments with backtracking algorithms.

When testing an algorithm on variety of problems (or comparing several algorithms with each other), we would like to know what is the optimal way to spend a fixed amount of resources to get a good estimate of the algorithms' performance. The theory of accelerating testing [11] provides us with *optimal test plans* which minimize the effort of conducting experiments while maximizing the accuracy of the estimates of the model's parameters, given the linear-lognormal model described above. The approach is to select the stress levels (C/N ratios) and to split the number of samples (experiments) among those in such a way that an optimal test will be obtained.

The results presented in this paper suggest the following strategy for estimating parameters μ and σ for an algorithm and distribution of problems: test a sufficiently large set of relatively easy unsatisfiable problems in the overconstrained region, estimate distribution parameters from these samples, derive the coefficients of the linear lognormal model from those data, and extrapolate the results to the critical region. Empirical evaluation of accelerated testing strategies for 3SAT and binary CSPs is an area for future research.

There are also many theoretical issues to be investigated: what is the appropriate non-linear model for μ as a function of C/N for fixed N? how does it change with increasing N? how does σ depend on C/N? how to select an optimal test plan, i.e. the set of C/N points and the number of experiments per point for a nonlinear model?

An important direction for further research is obtaining useful statistical models, both empirically and theoretically, for satisfiable problems, and combining them with the models of unsatisfiable problems.

Another interesting direction is to investigate the applicability of our results to real-life problems, and to different types of backtracking algorithms, including optimization techniques such as branch-and-bound.

Acknowledgments

We would like to thank Rina Dechter, Eddie Schwalb, and anonymous reviewers whose valuable comments helped to improve the paper.

References

1. J. M. Crawford and L. D. Auton. Experimental results on the crossover point in satisfiability problems. In *Proceedings of the Eleventh National Conference on Artificial Intelligence*, pages 21–27, 1993.
2. E. L. Crow and K. Shimizu. *Lognormal distributions: theory and applications*. Marcel Dekker, Inc., New York, 1988.
3. R. B. D'Agostino and M. A. Stephens. *Goodness-Of-Fit Techniques*. Marcel Dekker, Inc., New York, 1986.
4. M. Davis, G. Logemann, and D. Loveland. A Machine Program for Theorem Proving. *Communications of the ACM*, 5:394–397, 1962.
5. R. Dechter and I. Rish. Directional resolution: The davis-putnam procedure, revisited. In *Proceedings of KR-94*, pages 134–145, 1994.
6. D. Frost and R. Dechter. In search of the best constraint satisfaction search. In *Proceedings of the Twelfth National Conference on Artificial Intelligence*, 1994.
7. D. Frost, I. Rish, and L. Vila. Summarizing csp hardness with continuous probability distributions. In *Proceedings of the Fourteenth National Conference on Artificial Intelligence*, page (to appear), 1997.
8. R. M. Haralick and G. L. Elliott. Increasing Tree Search Efficiency for Constraint Satisfaction Problems. *Artificial Intelligence*, 14:263–313, 1980.
9. N. R. Mann, R. E. Schafer, and N.D.Singpurwalla. *Methods for Statistical Analysis of Reliability and Life Data*. John Wiley & Sons, New York, 1974.
10. D. Mitchell, B. Selman, and H. Levesque. Hard and Easy Distributions of SAT Problems. In *Proceedings of the Tenth National Conference on Artificial Intelligence*, pages 459–465, 1992.

11. W. Nelson. *Accelerated Testing: Statistical Models, Test Plans, and Data Analyses.* John Wiley & Sons, New York, 1990.
12. P. van Beek and R. Dechter. Constraint tightness and looseness versus global consistency. *Journal of ACM*, page to appear, 1997.

Using Constraint Propagation for Complex Scheduling Problems: Managing Size, Complex Resources and Travel

Yves Caseau

Bouygues, Direction Scientifique, France
caseau@dmi.ens.fr

1. Introduction

The goal of this tutorial is to study the application of constraint propagation to complex scheduling problems. There have already been many good tutorials in previous conferences on jobshop scheduling, so this tutorial is focused on more "difficult" problems, because of their size and the presence of additional constraints, such as travel between the different tasks that have to be scheduled. This tutorial is mostly targeted towards practitioners and should provide the attendees with practical techniques and insights for solving complex problems. However, the tutorial will also include a detailed analysis of a few state-of-the-art algorithms and should thus be also of interest to anyone with theoretical interests in scheduling and routing. To ensure that the tutorial is self-contained, we will start with a summary of the traditional constraint propagation (and branching) techniques that are used for jobshop scheduling. We will then examine how these techniques scale up for larger problems (those that we currently know how to solve to optimality).

The second part of the tutorial deals with complex resources and cumulative scheduling. We will first look at extended propagation techniques that apply to the cumulative case and introduce a few techniques from Operations Research. We will then focus on different branching techniques and explain why chronological branching is the most used method in commercial scheduling tools. We will introduce limited discrepancy search (LDS) as a way to tackle larger problems. LDS has proven in the past few years to be a very promising technique to extend the range of application of constraint programming to larger problems.

The last part of the tutorial deals with the handling of travel in scheduling. We introduce various examples that involve the travel of one or many resources, or that involve set-up that depends on previous history and act as a distance between tasks. We show how to combine constraint propagation techniques from different scheduling and routing models. We also show that for large problems or problems with multiple traveling resources it is necessary to use techniques from Operations Research such as local optimization. We end the tutorial with the presentation of a hybrid algorithm for scheduling/routing problems that uses LDS and constraint propagation mixed with local moves. This algorithm provides state-of-the-art results on standard VRPTW benchmarks.

2. Job-shop Scheduling

The tutorial starts with a brief survey of constraint propagation techniques for jobshop scheduling. We study:

- classical CP model and PERT propagation

- task intervals and redundant constraints (and various implementations of the edge-finder algorithm)

- different branching schemes that use the edge-finding principle introduced by Carlier&Pinson. The combination of the proper branching and propagation techniques is necessary to be competitive with other approaches from Operations Research.

- a global consistency technique called « shaving ». Shaving consists of trying the extreme values of a domain and propagating to see if a contradiction occurs, in which case the extreme value can be removed. When applied recursively, shaving produces the currently best known results for solving jobshop problems to optimality.

These techniques make constraint programming a competitive technique for solving "medium-sized" problems to optimality. We show how the shuffle method (a meta-level local search based on CP search) extends the applicability of the previous approach. Instead of running the search a large number of times with increasingly tight bounds for the makespan, shuffle consists of keeping a fragment of the previous solution as a seed to build a new one. In practice, the efficient edge-finding mechanisms enable to complete such partial solutions into a full ones with very limited search. When a fragment does not work, we use another one. This is a heuristic method (performing iterative improvement), but it is significantly faster than the usual approach and is well suited for large problems, since we get closer to the optimal solution (optimality cannot be guaranteed).

We then propose different heuristics that may be used to address even larger problems (many thousand tasks). For such problems, we use a limited look-ahead mechanism : in order to choose among the branches of a choice point, we go into all of them, propagate, and assess *a posteriori* the relevance of the branch. When only the best branch is kept, this mechanism yields an informed greedy heuristic; when a limited amount of backtracking is kept (using LDS), this yields a more robust algorithm. The key is to build a good heuristic using constraint propagation as a decision-making guide.

3. Cumulative Scheduling

The second part of the tutorial deals with complex resources that can process more than one task at a time. We use a cumulative model, where each task can consume a certain level of the resource (between two fixed bounds) and the amount of time necessary to perform the task is defined by a product:

$$consumption \times time = constant \quad (\text{"area" of the task}).$$

We will also briefly study the case when the consumption may vary over time (between the two fixed bounds) which is called the semi-preemptive case. We first study the key resolution techniques:

- extended constraint propagation using task intervals. The task interval paradigm can be easily extended to the cumulative case.

- resource consumption histograms. We introduce the "fixed part consumption" from Operations Research and show how it is used to provide stronger propagation.

- chronological branching scheme. We present a chronological branching scheme with intelligent backtracking and dominance rules inspired by the pioneering work by Demeulemeester.

These techniques may be used to solve medium-sized problems to optimality with competitive performance and robustness (measured with standard benchmarks from Operations Research). For larger problems, we need to simplify the search algorithm towards a more heuristic approach. We present a Limited Discrepancy Search approach that gives interesting results. This approach uses a heuristic to evaluate a better ordering of the branches for each decision. We decide to explore more than one branch only when the degree of confidence for this ordering is too small. Moreover, the total number of choice points is bounded in order to provide a guaranteed limit on the execution time.

4. Scheduling and Travel

In this last part of the tutorial, we try to take the travel that occurs between tasks into account. This may be due to a robot moving pieces in a shop, or because the resources themselves need to travel from one task's location to another. It is also common to find set-up times between the tasks (e.g., for changing tools) that depend on the pair *(current task, previous task)*. It is easy to realize that these variable setups may be considered as a distance between tasks.

We first focus on the travel associated with one resource and we show how constraint models for scheduling and traveling salesman problems can be merged. This leads to various extensions of the TSPTW (traveling salesman problem with time windows). TSPTW is a difficult problem, for which constraint programming is one of the currently best known resolution techniques. We show how, depending on the balance between scheduling and travel constraints, various propagation techniques can be used, from the addition of simple lower bounds for the travel time to the task interval model, to the use of a model based on sequences of tasks. For the latter case, we describe a set of propagation algorithms ranging from simple subtour elimination, to strong connection checking and to the computation of a minimal weight spanning tree as a lower bound. This approach has many applications, such as the scheduling of take-offs for airplanes (which exhibits a variable "setup" depending on airplane pairs).

We then turn to the many-resource case, which is a kind of a routing problem. We explain why it is important to use techniques from Operations Research, such as local optimization, to solve such problems. Therefore, constraint propagation for such hybrid problems becomes one of the many techniques that one uses in a hybrid program. This is explained with a LDS algorithm for scheduling/routing problems that heavily relies on a combination of constraint propagation and local moves.

Understanding and Improving the MAC Algorithm

Daniel Sabin and Eugene C. Freuder

Department of Computer Science,
University of New Hampshire,
Durham, NH, 03824-2604,
USA

Abstract. Constraint satisfaction problems have wide application in artificial intelligence. They involve finding values for problem variables where the values must be consistent in that they satisfy restrictions on which combinations of values are allowed. Recent research on finite domain constraint satisfaction problems suggest that Maintaining Arc Consistency (MAC) is the most efficient general CSP algorithm for solving large and hard problems. In the first part of this paper we explain why maintaining full, as opposed to limited, arc consistency during search can greatly reduce the search effort. Based on this explanation, in the second part of the paper we show how to modify MAC in order to make it even more efficient. Experimental results prove that the gain in efficiency can be quite important.

1 Introduction

Constraint satisfaction problems (*CSPs*) involve finding values for problem variables subject to constraints that are restrictions on which combinations of values are allowed. They have many applications in artificial intelligence, ranging from design to diagnosis, natural language understanding to machine vision.

The complete description of a CSP is given by specifying the set of variables, the set of potential values for each variable, called its domain, and the set of constraints. The basic solution method is backtrack search. A solution is an assignment of one value to each variable such that all the constraints are simultaneously satisfied.

In order to improve efficiency, very often search is interleaved with consistency inference (constraint propagation) which is used to prune values during search. The basic pruning technique involves establishing or restoring some form of *arc consistency*, pruning values that become inconsistent after making search choices. Recent research on finite domain CSPs suggests that *Maintaining Arc Consistency (MAC)* (Sabin & Freuder 1994) is the most efficient general CSP algorithm (Grant & Smith 1995) (Bessiere & Regin 1996). Using implementations based on AC-7 or AC-Inference (Bessiere, Freuder, & Regin 1995) (Regin 1995), which have a very good space and worst case running time complexity, and a new dynamic variable ordering heuristic (Bessiere & Regin 1996), MAC can solve problems which are both large and hard.

The enhanced look ahead allows MAC to make a much more informed choice in selecting the next variable and/or value, thus avoiding costly backtracks later on during search. However, additional search savings will be offset by the additional costs if proper care is not taken during the implementation. There are two sources of overhead in implementing MAC:

- the cost of restoring arc consistency after a decision has been made during search (either to instantiate a variable or to delete a value)
- the cost of restoring the problem in the previous state in case the current instantiation leads to failure.

Specifically, most of the effort is spent in deleting inconsistent values, during the propagation phase, and adding them back to the domains, after backtracking. This paper proposes two ways in which we can lower these costs:

- *Instantiate less.* In the context of maintaining full arc consistency, the search algorithm can focus on instantiating only a subset of the original set of variables, yielding a partial solution which can be extended, in a backtrack free manner, to a complete solution. Depending on the problem's density, the size of this subset, and thus the effort to find a solution, can be quite small.
- *Propagate less.* Instead of maintaining the constraint network in an arc consistent state, we propose to maintain an equivalent state, less expensive to achieve because it requires less propagation, which is:
  - only partially arc consistent, but
  - guaranteed to extend to a fully arc consistency state.

The rest of the paper is organized as follows. Section 2 presents examples and observations that motivate the main ideas behind the two improvements mentioned above. Section 3 discusses related work. Section 4 describes more formally the methods we propose for improving MAC. The last section presents experimental evidence that proves that the gain in efficiency can be quite large.

2 Example

(Grant & Smith 1995) presents a major study of the performance of MAC[1] over a large range of problem sizes and topologies. The results demonstrate that the size of the search trees is much smaller for MAC than for FC and that MAC produces backtrack-free searches over a considerably larger number of problems across the entire range of density/tightness values commonly used to characterize random problem space.

If we expected MAC to do better than FC, due to its enhanced look-ahead capabilities, our own experiments showed an unexpected result: that on problems with low and medium constraint densities (up to 0.5 – 0.6) a static variable

---

[1] The authors describe a "weak" form of MAC; we believe that the results would have been even stronger if the experiments had been done with the MAC we describe in Figure 4.

ordering heuristic, instantiating variables in decreasing order of their degree in the constraint graph, is in general more effective in the context of MAC than the popular dynamic variable ordering based on minimal domain size. In the majority of cases the gain in efficiency was due to a lower number of backtracks, very large regions of the search space being backtrack-free.

Trying to understand how can a static variable ordering be better than a dynamic one is what lead us to the ideas we will present next on a couple of examples. We restrict our attention here to *binary* CSPs, where the constraints involve two variables. One way of representing a binary CSP is in the form of a constraint graph. Nodes in the graph are the CSP variables and the constraints form the arcs.

Let us now consider the example represented by the constraint graph in Figure 1a, and see what happens during the search for a solution. For the sake of simplicity, assume that all constraints are *not-equal* and all domains are equal to the set $\{r, g, b\}$.

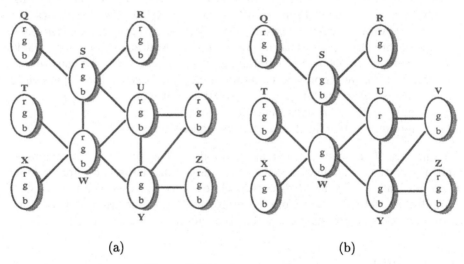

(a)   (b)

Figure 1. Sample constraint net

We are ready now to explain what we mean by *instantiate less*. Suppose that MAC will choose for some obscure (for now) reason, U as the first variable to be instantiated. After selecting value r, the algorithm will eliminate all the other values in the domain of U and will propagate the effects of these removals, restoring arc consistency, as shown in Figure 1b.

At this point the reader can verify that no matter which variable is next instantiated, and no matter which value is selected for the instantiation, MAC will find a complete solution without having to backtrack. Furthermore, we claim that if we had been interested only in finding out whether the problem is satisfiable or not, the algorithm could have stopped after having successfully instantiated variable U and have returned an affirmative answer. Why? Take a look at Figure 2a, which presents the state of the problem after instantiating variable U.

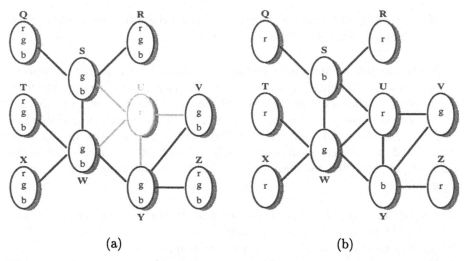

Figure 2. The constraint net after instantiating variable U (a) and a complete solution (b)

Intuitively, since r is the only value left in the domain of U and it supports (is consistent with) all the values remaining in the domains of neighbor variables, it will itself always have a support as long as these domains are not empty. U thus becomes irrelevant for the search process trying to extend this partial solution, and we can temporarily "eliminate" from further consideration both U and all constraints involving it.

If we ignore the grayed part of the constraint net, the constraint graph becomes a tree. This, plus the fact that every value in the domain of any variable is supported by at least one value at each neighbor (the network is arc consistent), implies that the problem is globally consistent and makes it possible to find a complete solution in a backtrack-free manner, for example the one in Figure 2b. In fact, for this reason, MAC is able to find all the solutions involving $U = r$ without having to backtrack. But what makes U so special ? If we look again to the graph in Figure 2a, we see that

- all the cycles in the graph have one node in common, the one corresponding to variable U, and
- by eliminating this node and all the edges connected to it we obtain an acyclic graph.

A set of nodes which "cut" all the cycles in a graph is called *cycle cutset*. In our case, the set $C = \{ U \}$ represents a minimal cycle cutset for the graph in Figure 2a. It is obvious that the graph obtained from the original one by eliminating the nodes in any cycle cutset and the related edges is acyclic.

The observations made on the graph in our example are directly supported by research on discrete domain CSPs (Dechter & Pearl 1988) (Freuder 1982), and are similar to the results presented in (Hyvonen 1992) in the form of the following two theorems:

(1) An acyclic constraint net is globally consistent iff it is arc consistent.

(2) If the variables of any cutset of a constraint net S are singleton-valued, then S is globally consistent iff it is arc consistent.

If after all the variables in some cutset are instantiated the net is arc consistent, we can "eliminate" these variables and their related constraints from the problem, as shown above. This cuts the loops and makes the constraint net acyclic. In this case, according to Theorem (1), local consistency is equivalent to global consistency. In addition, regardless of the order in which variables are instantiated, a complete solution can be found without any backtracking. We can now present a first modified version of MAC, in the form of the following algorithm:

1. Enforce arc consistency on the constraint network. If the domain of any variable becomes empty, return failure
2. Identify a cycle-cutset C of the constraint graph
3. Instantiate all variables in C while maintaining full arc consistency in the entire constraint network. If this is not possible, return failure
4. Use any algorithm to extend the partial solution obtained in step 3 to a complete solution, in a backtrack-free manner.

So far we showed that, in order to guarantee the existence of a complete solution in the context of maintaining arc consistency, it is sufficient to obtain a partial solution, by successfully instantiating only a subset of the variables, namely the cycle-cutset of the constraint graph. A simple heuristics to find a cycle-cutset is to order the variables in decreasing order of their degree, which explains why this static ordering worked so well with MAC.

Let us see if we can do better by *propagating less*. As we indicated earlier, after each modification MAC tries to restore the network to an arc consistent state. We claim that it is sufficient to bring the network to a partially arc consistent state only. More exactly, we need to maintain arc consistency just in part of the constraint graph, involving only some of the variables and constraints of the original CSP.

Figure 3 presents the constraint graph of our example, in which variables not involved in any cycle have been grayed. Once arc consistency is established, these variables become irrelevant for the search process. If the problem is inconsistent, none of this variables can be the source of the inconsistency. If there is a partial solution instantiating any of the normal variables in Figure 3, we are guaranteed to be able to extend it to a complete solution in a backtrack-free manner. Therefore, they can be disconnected from the constraint network, until we decide whether it is possible to instantiate successfully the variable which are left. During search the algorithm will propagate any change, and restore consistency accordingly, only in a (potentially small) part of the network. This partially arc consistent state is equivalent with the fully arc consistent state in the sense that both lead to exactly the same set of complete solutions.

A related idea was described in (Rossi 1995). The author presents a more general method, which removes redundant hidden variables from a CSP, based on the level of local consistency of the problem. Although developed independently and motivated by different goals, if we use only arc consistency the two methods eliminate similar sets of variables. There is a difference though: being dynamic, our method eliminates a superset of the set of redundant hidden variables eliminated by the methods presented in (Rossi 1995).

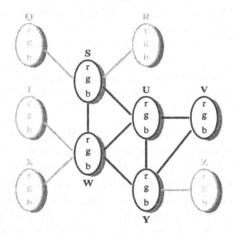

Figure 3. The constraint net after eliminating the variables in $\mathcal{T}$

Once all the variables which are still part of the network are instantiated, it is enough to reconnect the variables previously disconnected and to enforce arc consistency (or directed arc consistency) in order to obtain global consistency and to extend the partial solution to a complete solution in a backtrack-free manner.

The two ideas, *instantiate less* and *propagate less*, can now be combined under the name of *MACE (MAC Extended)*, which instantiates only a subset of the CSP variables while maintaining only a partially arc consistent state of the constraint network. The gain in efficiency is twofold. Instantiating a smaller number of variables aims at reducing the number of backtracks (and, accordingly, the number of constraint-checks, nodes visited, values deleted, etc.). Since the variables disconnected are not part of any cycle-cutset, and hence, will not be instantiated in the first phase of the algorithm, the limited propagation implied by the second idea does not influence at all the number of backtracks or nodes visited, but reduces the number of constraint checks and values deleted.

3   Related Work

The idea of using the cycle-cutset of a constraint graph to improve the efficiency of CSP algorithms was used in (Dechter & Pearl 1988) as part of the *cycle-cutset method (CC)* for improving backtracking on discrete domain CSPs. (Hyvonen 1992) uses it for *interval CSPs*. A related idea is used in (Solotorevsky, Gudes, & Meisels 1996) for solving *distributed CSPs*.

Dechter and Pearl's cycle-cutset method can be described by the following scheme.

1. Partition the variables into two sets: a cycle-cutset of the constraint graph, C, and $\mathcal{T}$, the complement of C
2. Find a(nother) solution to the problem with variables in C only, by solving it independently. If no solution can be found, return failure
3. Remove from the domain of variables in $\mathcal{T}$ all values incompatible with the values assigned to variables in C and achieve directed arc consistency at variables in $\mathcal{T}$. If the domain of any variable becomes empty, restore all variables in $\mathcal{T}$ to their original state and repeat step 2
4. Use a backtrack-free search for extending the partial solution found in step 2 to a complete solution.

The major problem with the cycle-cutset method is its potential for thrashing. One type of thrashing is illustrated by the following example. Suppose the variables in C are instantiated in the order $X, Y, \ldots$ Suppose further that there is no value for some variable Z in $\mathcal{T}$ which is consistent, according to constraint C_{XZ}, with value a for X. Whenever the solution to the cutset instantiates X to a, step 2 will fail. Since this can happen quite often, the cycle-cutset method can be very inefficient. We can eliminate this type of thrashing if we make the constraint network arc consistent before search starts, in a preprocessing phase.

A different type of thrashing, which cannot be eliminated by simply preprocessing the constraint network, is the following. Suppose that after making the network arc consistent initially, the domain of variable Z contains two values, c and d. Furthermore, value a for X supports value c on C_{XZ}, but does not support d. On the other hand, value b for Y supports d and not c on C_{YZ}. The cycle-cutset method will discover the inconsistency only while trying to instantiate Z, and this failure will be repeated for each solution of the cutset problem instantiating X to a and Y to b.

Our approach maintains arc consistency during the search (in fact, it maintains an equivalent state, as explained above). This eliminates both sources of thrashing and leads to substantial improvements over the cycle-cutset method.

4 Implementation

The goal of our paper is to compare the performance of three algorithms: MAC, the cycle-cutset method (CC), and the new algorithm we propose, MACE.

Figure 4 presents a high level description of the basic MAC algorithm.

It is worth stressing the differences between MAC and another algorithm that restores arc consistency arc consistency, called *Really Full Lookahead (RFL)* (Nadel 1988). Once the constraint network is made arc consistent initially (line 1), MAC restores arc consistency after each instantiation, or forward move, (lines 12–14), as RFL does, and, in addition:

- whenever an instantiation fails, MAC removes the refuted value from the domain and restores arc consistency (lines 6–7 and 19–20);

```
    MAC ( in: Var ; out: Sol ) return boolean
1       consistent ← INITIALIZE( )
2       while consistent do
3           (X, val_x) ← SELECT( Var, 0 )
4           if SOLVE( (X, val_x), Var \ {X}, Sol, 1 ) then
5               return true
6           D_x ← D_x \ {val_x}
7           consistent ← D_x ≠ ∅ and PROPAGATE( Var \ {X}, 1 )
        □
8       return false
    □
    SOLVE( in: (X, val_x), Var, Sol, level ; out: Sol ) return boolean
9       Sol ← Sol ∪ {(X, val_x)}
10      if level = N then
11          return true
12      for each a ∈ D_x, a ≠ val_x do
13          D_x ← D_x \ {a}
14      consistent ← PROPAGATE( Var, level )
15      while consistent do
16          (Y, val_y) ← SELECT( Var, level )
17          if SOLVE( (Y, val_y), Var \ {Y}, Sol, level+1 )
18              return true
19          D_y ← D_y \ {val_y}
20          consistent ← D_y ≠ ∅ and PROPAGATE( Var \ {Y}, level )
        □
21      Sol ← Sol \ {(X, val_x)}
22      RESTORE( level )
23      return false
    □
```

Fig. 4. Generic MAC Algorithm – Top Level Procedures

– after each modification of the network, both after instantiation and refutation, MAC chooses a (possible new) variable, as well as a new value (lines 3 and 16).

For our experiments we implemented a slightly improved version of MAC, called MAC-7ps (Regin 1995). According to the results presented in (Bessiere, Freuder, & Regin 1995), (Bessiere & Regin 1996) and (Regin 1995), MAC-7ps is the best general-purpose CSP algorithm to date. It is an AC-7 based implementation of the basic MAC, with one notable improvement: special treatment of singleton variables. The idea is roughly the following. After restoring arc consistency, singleton variables can be disconnected temporarily from the network. The goal is to avoid studying the constraints connecting other variables to the singletons. A detailed description of the implementation can be found in (Regin 1995).

MACE and CC need an algorithm to find a cycle-cutset. There is no known polynomial algorithm for finding the minimum cycle-cutset. There are several heuristics which yield a good cycle-cutset at a reasonable cost. The simplest sorts first the variables in decreasing order of their degree. Then, starting with the variable with the highest degree, as long as the graph still has cycles, add the variable to the cycle-cutset and remove it, together with all the edges involving it, from the graph. Assuming that lexical ordering is used to break ties, this method yields for our example the cycle-cutset presented in Figure 5a. Variables are added to the cutset in the order W, S and U. The worst case run time complexity for this heuristic is $O(ne)$.

A smaller cutset can be obtained if, before adding a variable to the cutset, we check whether it is part of any cycle or not. For example, after removing W from the graph, S is not involved in a cycle anymore, and, with the new algorithm, we find the cycle cutset in Figure 5b. The worst case time complexity for this heuristics is $O(ne)$. Additional work leads to an even smaller cutset. The cutset shown in Figure 2a is obtained by a third heuristic, which determines dynamically the number of cycles in which each variable is involved and adds to the cutset at each step the variable participating in the most cycles. The worst case time complexity of this heuristic is $O(n^2e)$.

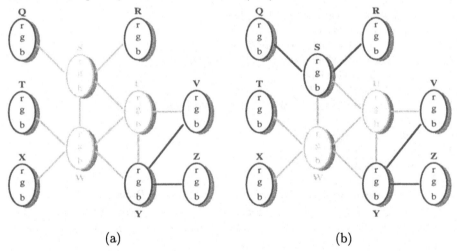

(a)   (b)

Figure 5. Different cycle-cutsets for the example in Figure 1

We used the same algorithm to find a cycle cutset in implementing both CC and MACE. We performed the tests using both the second and the third heuristic presented above. Based on our results, the third heuristic yields slightly smaller cutsets which translate sometimes into small gains in efficiency, but no major improvement. In the case of large problems probably the second heuristic is the best choice, because of its lower cost. Due to the space restriction, we report in this paper only the results obtained using the third heuristic.

The implementation of CC is straightforward. Since there is no requirement on the algorithm to solve the cutset subproblem, to keep the comparison with MACE as fair as possible, we used MAC-7ps as our choice.

To implement MACE, we modified the algorithm in Figure 4 as follows.

• After enforcing arc consistency, procedure INITIALIZE (line 1) partitions the set of variables into two sets, one of which is the cycle-cutset C. Disconnect from the constraint network all variables which are not involved in any cycle and add them to the set of disconnected variables, initially empty, $\mathcal{U}$.

- Restrict procedure SELECT (lines 3 and 16) to choose only from among variables in $\mathcal{C}$.

- Whenever a variable becomes a singleton disconnect it from the network and add it to $\mathcal{U}$. If this makes other variables "cycle-free", disconnect them and add them to $\mathcal{U}$ as well. Continue this process until no more variables can be disconnected.

- Once all variables in $\mathcal{C}$ have been successfully instantiated, reconnect all variables in $\mathcal{U}$ and eliminate from their domains all values incompatible with the values assigned to variables in the cutset. Enforce directed arc consistency with respect to some width-1 order on the problem containing only variables in the complement of $\mathcal{C}$ and conduct a backtrack-free search for a complete solution.

5 Experiments

We tested our approach on random binary CSPs described by the usual four parameters: number of variables, domain size, constraint density and constraint tightness. We generate only connected constraint graphs (connected components of unconnected components can be solved independently). Therefore the number of edges for a graph with n vertices is at least $n - 1$ (for a tree, density=0) and at most $n(n - 1)/2$ (for a complete graph, density=1). Constraint density is the fraction of the possible constraints beyond the minimum $n - 1$, that the problem has. Thus, for a problem with constraint density D and n variables, the exact number of constraints that the problem has is $\lfloor n - 1 + D(n - 1)(n - 2)/2 \rfloor$.

Constraint tightness is defined as the fraction of all possible pairs of values from the domains of two variables, that are not allowed by the constraint. So, for a domain size of d and a constraint tightness of t, the exact number of pairs allowed by the constraint is $\lfloor (1 - t)d^2 \rfloor$.

The tests we conducted addressed the problem of finding a single solution to a CSP (or determining that no solution exists). We ran three sets of experiments on hard random problems problems, situated on the ridge of difficulty in the density/tightness space.

For the first two sets we generated problems with 20 variables and domain size of 20. The density of the constraint graph varies between 0.05 and 0.95, with a step of 0.05, while the tightness varies between $T_{crit} - 0.08$ and $T_{crit} + 0.08$, with a step of 0.01. For each pair of values (density, tightness) we generated 10 instances of random problems, which gives us roughly a total of 3,200 problems per set.

The problems in the third set have 40 variables and domain size of 20. We expected the problems in this set to be much harder than the ones in the previous sets. Therefore the constraint density varies only between 0.05 and 0.30. The tightness varies between $T_{crit} - 0.08$ and $T_{crit} + 0.08$, with a step of 0.01. We generated again 10 instances of random problems for each (density, tightness) pair, which gives us almost 1,000 problems for this set.

We present the results of the experiments using two types of plots. One type represents, on the same graph, the performance of two algorithms in terms of constraint checks, as a function of tightness. Due to space restrictions, the results from different sets of problems, with different densities, are ploted on the same graph (e.g. Figure 6).

The second type of plots represents the ratio between the performance of two algorithms as a function of tightness, in the form of a set of points. Again, results from different sets of problems, with different densities, are ploted on the same graph. Each point on the graph represents the average over the 10 problems generated for the corresponding (density, tightness) pair (e.g. Figure 8).

It is very important what measure is used to judge the performance of algorithms. The usual measure in the literature is the number of constraint checks performed by an algorithm during the search for a solution. Whenever establishing that a value a for a variable X is consistent with a value b for a variable Y, a single consistency check is counted. Constraint checks are environment independent, but are highly dependent on the efficiency of the implementation. In our case, since we use more or less the same implementation for all the algorithms, we choose this measure as being representative for the search effort.

We ran experiments comparing the performance of three algorithms: the cycle-cutset method, MAC-7ps and MACE. All algorithms used the dynamic variable ordering heuristic proposed in (Bessiere & Regin 1996), choosing variables in increasing order of the ratio between domain size and degree.

The first set of experiments compares the performance of the cycle-cutset method and MACE on the first set of test problems. Figure 6 shows the relative average performance of the algorithms in terms of constraint checks.

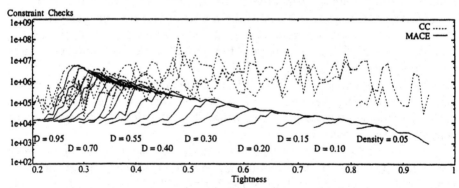

Figure 6. Comparison between the cycle-cutset method and MACE

As we can see, MACE outperforms substantially the cycle-cutset method on problems with densities up to 0.90–0.95, when they have approximately the same performance. The size of the cycle-cutset varies almost liniarly with the density, from 3 for density 0.05 to almost 18 for density 0.95. For problems in the high density area the cutset is almost the entire set of variables (this are 20-variable

178

problems) and therefore the behavior of the two algorithms is almost identical.

As suggested in Section 3, we added an arc consistency preprocessing phase to CC and ran this combination on the same problem sets. The results are presented in Figure 7. As we can see, the preprocessing improves the performance of CC only in the very sparse region, by discovering the arc inconsistent problems. On the rest of the problems the preprocessing had practically no effect.

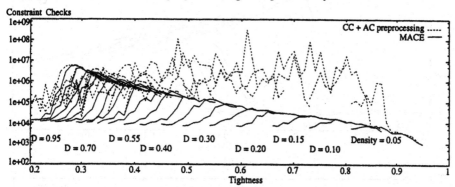

Figure 7. Comparison between the cycle-cutset method with arc-consistency pre-processing and MACE

The same results are presented from a different perspective in Figure 8, which shows the ratio between the constraint checks performed by the cycle-cutset method and MACE. The advantage of MACE is very clear.

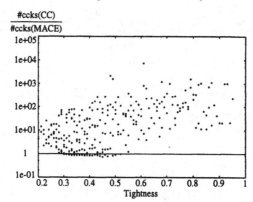

Figure 8. Performance ratio between the cycle-cutset and MACE

The second set of experiments compares the performance of MAC-7ps and MACE. Figure 9 shows the relative average performance of the two algorithms in terms of constraint checks on the second set of problems, with 20 variables. As we can also see from the plot in Figure 10, which shows the ratio between the number of constraint checks for MAC-7ps and MACE on the same set of problems, MACE performs better than MAC-7ps. For problems with high densities (0.9 – 0.95) although MACE still dominates, MAC-7ps wins a few times. Again, the explanation consists in the size of the cycle-cutset, which increases with the density. In this particular area the sets of variables instantiated by the two algorithms become almost the same. Therefore, both algorithms exhibit similar behaviors, MACE being still slightly better than MAC-7ps on average.

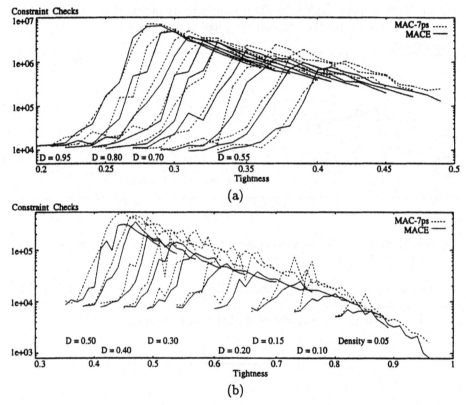

Figure 9. Comparison between MAC-7ps and MACE on problems with 20 variables

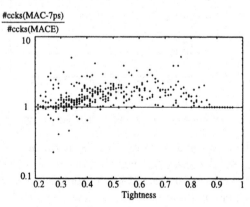

Figure 10. Performance ratio between MAC-7ps and MACE on problems with 20 variables

The last set of experiments studies the scalability of our approach as problem size increases. We therefore compared the performance of MAC-7ps and MACE on problems with 40 variables, using the third set of random problems. Figure 11 shows again the relative average performance of the two algorithms in terms of constraint checks, while Figure 12 presents the same data, but in the form of the ratio between the number of constraint checks for MAC-7ps and MACE. Both plots show again that MACE outperforms MAC-7ps significantly. The data also suggests that MACE scales well, the relative gain in efficiency increasing as the problems become larger.

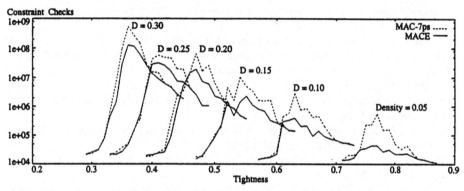

Figure 11. Comparison between MAC-7ps and MACE on problems with 40 variables

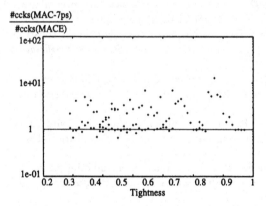

Figure 12. Performance ratio between MAC-7ps and MACE on problems with 40 variables

6 Conclusion

We have analyzed the advantages of maintaining full arc consistency during search. Our analysis led to an improved version of MAC, called MACE. In extensive experiments MACE consistently outperformed MAC.

Acknowledgment

This material is based on work supported by the National Science Foundation under Grant No. IRI-9504316.

References

1. Bessiere, C., and Regin, J.-C. 1996. Mac and combined heuristics: Two reasons to forsake fc (and cbj?) on hard problems. In *Second International Conference on Principles and Practice of Constraint Programming - CP96*, number 1118 in Lecture Notes in Computer Science, 61–75.
2. Bessiere, C.; Freuder, E. C.; and Regin, J.-C. 1995. Using inference to reduce arc consistency computation. In *Proceedings of the Fourteenth International Joint Conference on Artificial Intelligence*, volume I, 592–598.
3. Dechter, R., and Pearl, J. 1987. The cycle-cutset method for improving search performance in ai applications. In *Proceedings of the 3rd IEEE Conference on AI Applications*, 224–230.
4. Dechter, R., and Pearl, J. 1988. Network-based heuristics for constraint satisfaction problems. *Artificial Intelligence* 34(1):1–38.
5. Freuder, E. C. 1982. A sufficient condition for backtrack-free search. *Journal of the ACM* 29(1):24–32.
6. Grant, S. A., and Smith, B. M. 1995. The phase transition behaviour of maintaining arc consistency. Technical Report 95.25, University of Leeds, School of Computer Studies.
7. Hyvonen, E. 1992. Constraint reasoning based on interval arithmetic: the tolerance propagation approach. *Artificial Intelligence* 58(1–3):71–112.
8. Nadel, B. 1988. Tree search and arc-consistency in constraint satisfaction algorithms. In Kanal, L., and Kumar, V., eds., *Search in Artificial Intelligence*. Springer-Verlag. 287–342.
9. Regin, J.-C. 1995. *Developpement d'outils algorithmiques pour l'Intelligence Artificielle. Application a la chimie organique*. Ph.D. Dissertation, Universite Montpellier II.
10. Rossi, F. 1995. Redundant Hidden Variables in Finite domain Constraint Problems. In *Constraint Processing*, number 923 in Lecture Notes in Computer Science, 205–233.
11. Sabin, D., and Freuder, E. C. 1994. Contradicting conventional wisdom in constraint satisfaction. In *Proceedings of the 11th European Conference on Artificial Intelligence*.
12. Solotorevsky, G.; Gudes, E.; and Meisels, A. 1996. Modeling and solving distributed constraint satisfaction problems (dcsps). In *Second International Conference on Principles and Practice of Constraint Programming - CP96*, number 1118 in Lecture Notes in Computer Science, 561–562.

Modelling Exceptionally Hard Constraint Satisfaction Problems

Barbara M. Smith and Stuart A. Grant

School of Computer Studies
University of Leeds
Leeds LS2 9JT, U.K.

Abstract. Randomly-generated binary constraint satisfaction problems go through a phase transition as the constraint tightness varies. Loose constraints give an 'easy-soluble' region, where problems have many solutions and are almost always easy to solve. However, in this region, systematic search algorithms may occasionally encounter problems which are extremely expensive to solve. It has been suggested that in these cases, the first few instantiations made by the algorithm create an insoluble subproblem; an exhaustive search of the subproblem to prove its insolubility accounts for the high cost. We propose a model for the occurrence of such subproblems when using the backtracking algorithm. We calculate the probability of their occurrence and estimate their cost. From this, we derive the theoretical cost distribution when the constraint graph is complete and show that it matches the observed cost distribution in this region. We suggest that a similar model would also account for the exceptionally hard problems that have been observed using more sophisticated algorithms.

1 Introduction

For many types of problem where a large population of problem instances can be examined, there is a phase transition as a problem parameter is varied, as shown by Cheeseman, Kanefsky and Taylor [3]. The phase transition is from a region where almost all problems have many solutions, and are easy to solve, to a region where almost all problems have no solution, and are easy to prove insoluble. Around the phase transition, problems are on average hard to solve, or prove insoluble.

Although the *median* cost of solving problems has a well-defined peak in the region of the phase transition, this is often not where the hardest individual instances occur. Given a large sample of problems, individual problems which are extremely hard to solve may occur in the region where most problems are very easy to solve. This phenomenon was first observed by Hogg and Williams in graph colouring problems [7] and by Gent and Walsh in satisfiability problems [4].

In this paper we consider exceptionally hard instances occurring in populations of randomly-generated binary constraint satisfaction problems (CSPs). A

CSP consists of a set of variables each with a finite set of possible values (its domain), and a set of constraints which must be satisfied. A binary constraint affects a pair of variables, and can be expressed as a set of pairs of values, each pair representing a possible assignment of values to variables which is not allowed by the constraint. We have previously reported exceptionally hard CSPs using the forward checking algorithm [10], and we again use 'ehp' as an abbreviation for 'exceptionally hard problem'.

Previous writers (e.g. Selman and Kirkpatrick [9]), including ourselves, have suggested that these rare instances are not inherently difficult; for instance, simply changing the variable ordering is enough to make such a problem, in an ensemble of randomly-generated instances, no more difficult than the average. However, unless we understand how such instances arise, it is unclear whether all randomly-generated problems have the potentiality to be exceptionally hard, or whether it requires some unknown feature of the problem. As well as this, our main motivation in this paper is to explain the peak found in the highest percentiles in the easy-soluble region, which is discussed in section 2 and appears in Figure 1.

Our intention is to show how exceptionally hard problems can arise and to estimate the cost of solving them, thus deriving a cost distribution. Hogg and Williams [7] also investigated the tail of the cost distribution in the easy-soluble region, based on an assumption of a power-law cost distribution and fitting this to the observed distribution. Here, we will estimate the costs of solving each problem directly from our model.

In order to model the occurrence of exceptionally hard problems, we have chosen a simple algorithm, the basic backtracking algorithm (BT). The algorithm attempts to build up a consistent solution to the CSP by considering each variable in turn, and trying to assign a value to it which is consistent with the existing assignments. If this cannot be done, the algorithm backtracks to the previous variable, and tries a different value for it, proceeding in this fashion until either a complete solution is found or every possible assignment has been tried without success, in which case the problem has no solution. This algorithm is extremely inefficient in comparison with other more widely used CSP search algorithms, such as those which look ahead as each variable is instantiated to see the effect of the instantiation on future variables (e.g. forward checking [6]), or those which attempt to identify, and backtrack to, the true culprit for a failure instead of backtracking chronologically (e.g. conflict-directed backjumping [8]). We choose BT here because its behaviour is sufficiently simple to make analysis tractable. An understanding of how ehps arise in this case will give insights into how more sophisticated algorithms reduce the incidence of ehps compared with BT, but still suffer from them.

2 The Experimental Problems

Our experiments use randomly-generated binary constraint satisfaction problems using four parameters $\langle n, m, p_1, p_2 \rangle$, where n is the number of variables, m is the number of values in each variable's domain, p_1 is the probability that any pair of variables have a constraint between them and p_2 is the probability that the constraint does not allow a particular pair of values.

In previous experimental studies we have defined p_1 and p_2 to be proportions rather than probabilities, in order to reduce the variability within an ensemble of problems. Here, we define them as probabilities so that each pair of forbidden values is generated independently: this makes the analysis more tractable. The change makes no significant difference to our experimental results.

A phase transition is seen when n, m and p_1 are held constant and p_2 is varied, in steps of say 0.01. A set of instances generated in this way is denoted by the tuple $\langle n, m, p_1 \rangle$. A large sample of instances is generated at each value of p_2 and the cost of solving each problem is measured. We use the number of nodes visited as the cost measure: the number of consistency checks is more commonly used as a measure of cost, but the number of nodes visited is an easier measure to model. We plot the median cost, which will show the phase transition, and the higher percentiles, which will reveal any problems which are unusually expensive to solve.

Figure 1 shows the cost percentiles for a sample of $\langle 10, 10, 1.0 \rangle$ problems solved using this algorithm. As previous studies have found, with a variety of

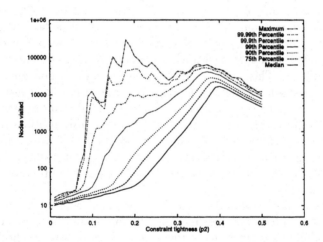

Fig. 1. Search costs for $\langle 10, 10, 1.0 \rangle$ problems using BT - 10,000 problems for each value of p_2

different algorithms, in the region where almost all problems can be solved very quickly, we see a small proportion of problems which are orders of magnitude more expensive to solve.

Hogg and Williams [7] found that the highest percentiles of search cost, for graph colouring problems, show a double peak: one peak over the phase transition and another higher peak in the easy-soluble region. This double peak can be seen in Figure 1. We have found that for larger problems (i.e. larger n), the peak in the easy region is more pronounced. However, whereas exceptionally hard satisfiability or graph colouring problems in the easy region are often unsatisfiable, exceptionally hard CSPs are exclusively soluble problems. In Figure 1, for instance, there are no insoluble problems when $p_2 < 0.34$. Since in this paper we are principally concerned with explaining the causes of exceptionally hard CSPs, we confine ourselves to soluble ehps.

3   When do ehps occur?

Figure 1 shows the median cost beginning to increase more steeply when $p_2 = 0.2$. For smaller values of p_2, at least 50% of problems can be solved without ever backtracking to a previous variable. For instance, when $p_2 = 0.1$, 99% of the problems represented in Figure 1 are solved without backtracking, but in solving the most expensive of the 10,000 problems, the algorithm visits more than 10,000 nodes. Hence, ehps occur in a region of the parameter space where almost all problems can be solved very quickly.

We have examined in detail the behaviour of several CSP algorithms when they encounter exceptionally hard problems. A typical example of an ehp is the most expensive $\langle 10, 10, 1.0 \rangle$ problem when $p_2 = 0.15$, from Figure 1. BT visits over 100,000 nodes in solving this problem, whereas at least 90% of problems with the same parameter values require fewer than 50 nodes. In solving this problem, the algorithm frequently finds partial solutions with 7 of the 10 variables instantiated, and then backtracks, after considering all possible values for the 8th variable, v_8. This is due to the fact that v_8 has no values that are consistent with the first 2 instantiations made. Eventually, the second instantiation is changed, from $v_2=1$ to $v_2=2$, and a solution is found almost immediately, without further backtracking. It is clear that the first two instantiations made ($v_1=1$ and $v_2=1$) create a subproblem which has no solutions; BT cannot discover this fact, however, except by considering all possible consistent instantiations of variables v_3 to v_7, and finding in each case that the partial solution formed cannot be extended to v_8.

We have seen very similar behaviour in ehps when using the forward checking algorithm with fail-first variable ordering [10]: for instance, one problem, from a population of $\langle 50, 10, 0.1 \rangle$ problems, took 376 million consistency checks to solve, when nearly all problems with the same parameter values could be solved by the algorithm in fewer than 10,000 consistency checks. The first few choices made by the algorithm created an insoluble subproblem, but the algorithm could not prove that the subproblem had no solution except by an exhaustive search. Similarly, Gent and Walsh [4] describe a satisfiability problem which required more than 350 million branches to solve: the first choice made by the algorithm led to a very difficult unsatisfiable problem, which required almost all the search effort, whereas the alternative choice led immediately to a solution. Based on the same idea, Bayardo and Schrag [2] show how to create exceptionally hard satisfiability problems by embedding an insoluble subproblem within a larger problem: in this case, the overall problem is unsatisfiable. In 3-colouring problems, Baker [1] similarly points out that a backtracking algorithm can find an algorithm exceptionally hard if the graph is disconnected and the algorithm attempts to assign colours last to a component which has no solutions. He claims that similar behaviour can also occur in soluble problems, but presents experimental evidence to show that in 3-colouring problems, most exceptionally hard instances in the underconstrained region are insoluble.

Whenever we have observed a CSP algorithm in the process of trying to solve a problem which it finds exceptionally hard, the algorithm frequently finds a partial solution with nearly all the variables instantiated, but then fails. After a great deal of searching in the deeper levels of the tree, the algorithm eventually backtracks to a particular variable high in the tree, tries a different value for that variable and then finds a solution without further backtracking. In order to model such an occurrence and estimate the cost of solving the problem, we need to describe precisely what is happening in these cases.

Our hypothesis, based on observation of many instances, is that BT finds a problem in the soluble region exceptionally hard if the first few instantiations made (say the first j) are together inconsistent with all the values of one of the future variables (say variable k), which in the variable ordering will be one of the last to be instantiated. (In the $\langle 10, 10, 1.0 \rangle$ problem described in detail earlier, $j = 2$ and $k = 8$.) Thus the first j instantiations create an insoluble subproblem, which has to be searched completely to prove insolubility. Eventually the algorithm backtracks to the variable j, and tries an alternative instantiation for it. Because ehps occur in the region where almost all searches are backtrack-free, the new instantiation of variable j leads to a solution without further backtracking. Further, the variables between variable j and variable k can be expected to have at least one value which is consistent with all previous assignments. So the algorithm frequently finds partial solutions of length $k - 1$, but encounters a failure on considering variable k and has to backtrack.

We now state precisely conditions for an occurrence of this kind. We call such a problem a (j, k) instance, i.e. the first j instantiations conflict with all values of the variable k, where $k > j$. In the next section we derive the probability of such an instance occurring.

A (j, k) instance occurs when:

- every value of variable k is inconsistent with the first j assignments, *and*
- at least one value of variable k is consistent with the first $j - 1$ assignments[1], *and*
- for every variable 2 to $k - 1$ at least one value is consistent with all previous assignments, *and*
- after the algorithm backtracks to variable j and a new value, consistent with all previous assignments, is assigned to it, variables $j + 1$ to n have at least one value which is consistent with all previous assignments.

Not all instances defined in this way are very expensive to solve: if $k = j + 1$, exploring the m values of variable k and discovering that they are all inconsistent

---

[1] ..otherwise this would be a $(j - 1, k)$ instance as well.

with the previous j assignments adds only m nodes to the cost of a backtrack-free search. However, because backtracking only occurs at level k, the cost of exploring the insoluble subproblem is exponential in $k - j$, so that when j is small and k is large, searches are extremely time-consuming.

Conversely, this description may exclude some exceptionally hard instances. In particular, the requirement that the search should be entirely backtrack-free apart from the search of the insoluble subproblem is very stringent. However, if we dropped the requirement that all variables other than k should have at least one value consistent with all previous assignments, the description would include problems occurring in the phase transition and insoluble region which are no harder than the average: in those regions, it will frequently happen that the first j assignments are inconsistent with all values of a future variable k, but the algorithm may never create a partial solution of length k because other failures occur earlier. Moreover, the genuine ehps in the easy-soluble region which are ruled out by this requirement will not be the most expensive ones: any failure causing the algorithm to backtrack before it reaches variable k reduces the cost.

4 Probability of a (j,k) Instance

From now on, to simplify the analysis, we assume that $p_1 = 1$, i.e. there is a constraint between every pair of variables. Writing $q_2 = 1 - p_2$, the probability that at least one value of variable l is consistent with all previous assignments is then $1 - (1 - q_2^{l-1})^m$. Since all constraints are generated independently, the probability that a problem can be solved without backtracking, i.e. the probability that every variable has at least one value which is consistent with the previous instantiations, is $\prod_{l=2}^{n}(1 - (1 - q_2^{l-1})^m)$.

Similarly, the probability of a (j, k) instance can be calculated by multiplying the probabilities of the component events.
$\Pr\{(j, k)$ instance$\} =$
$\Pr\{$variable k has no value which is consistent with the first j assignments$\}$
$\times \Pr\{$variable k has at least one value which is consistent with the first $j - 1$ assignments$\}$
$\times \Pr\{$at least one value of variables 2 to $k - 1$ is consistent with the previous assignments$\}$
$\times \Pr\{$there is at least one other value of variable j which is consistent with the previous assignments, and when it is assigned, at least one value of variables $j + 1$ to n will be consistent with the previous assignments$\}$

$= \Pr\{$variable k has no value which is consistent with the first j assignments, but not all values are inconsistent with the first $j - 1$ assignments$\}$
$\times \Pr\{$each of variables 1 to $j - 1$ and variables $j + 1$ to $k - 1$ has at least one value which is consistent with the previous assignments$\}$
$\times \Pr\{$variable j has at least two values which are consistent with the previous assignments$\}$

$\times$ Pr{each of variables $j+1$ to n has at least one value which will be consistent with the previous assignments when the alternative value is assigned to variable j}

$$= \left[(1 - q_2^j)^m - (1 - q_2^{j-1})^m\right]$$
$$\times \prod_{r=2, r \neq j}^{k-1} (1 - (1 - q_2^{r-1})^m)$$
$$\times \left[1 - (1 - q_2^{j-1})^{m-1}(1 + (m-1)q_2^{j-1})\right]$$
$$\times \prod_{s=j+1}^{n} (1 - (1 - q_2^{s-1})^m)$$

Note that variable j must have at least two values which are consistent with the previous assignments, because one leads to the insoluble subproblem, and another gives the eventual solution.

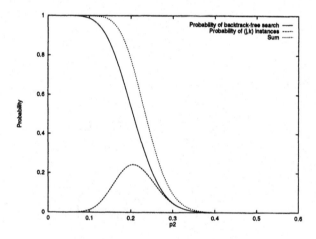

Fig. 2. Probability of backtrack-free search and total probability of (j, k) instances for $\langle 10, 10, 1.0 \rangle$ problems

Given a population $\langle n, m, 1.0 \rangle$ and a range of values of p_2, we can compute the probability of a (j, k) instance, for all possible pairs of values (j, k) with $j < k$, and sum these to find the total probability of this type of instance at each value of p_2. Figure 2 shows the result for $\langle 10, 10, 1.0 \rangle$ problems, together with the probability of backtrack-free search, and their sum (showing what proportion of problems are now accounted for). It can be seen that there is a region where instances of the kind just described account for almost all cases where search is not backtrack-free.

Figure 2 also shows that (j, k) instances are not always rare: when p_2 is around 0.2, they account for about 25% of all instances. Many of these, however, only involve backtracking to the previous variable (i.e. $j = k - 1$), and so are not very expensive. Since (j, k) instances combine backtrack-free search with exploration of the insoluble subproblem, they disappear as p_2 increases, just as backtrack-free search does.

5 Expected Number of Nodes Visited

Having defined a (j, k) instance, we now estimate the number of nodes visited in solving such an instance.

We first estimate the number of nodes visited if a problem can be solved without backtracking. In that case, there are i nodes at level l in the tree if the ith value of variable l is the first that is consistent with all the previous assignments.

The conditional probability that the ith value of variable l is the first to succeed, given that at least one does, is:

$$\frac{(1 - q_2^{l-1})^{i-1} q_2^{l-1}}{1 - (1 - q_2^{l-1})^m}$$

So, the expected number of nodes visited

$$= 1 + \sum_{l=2}^{n} \sum_{i=1}^{m} i \frac{(1 - q_2^{l-1})^{i-1} q_2^{l-1}}{1 - (1 - q_2^{l-1})^m}$$

$$= 1 + \sum_{l=2}^{n} \left(\frac{1}{q_2^{l-1}} - \frac{m q_2^{m(l-1)}}{1 - q_2^{m(l-1)}} \right)$$

The cost of solving a (j, k) instance is the cost of the backtrack-free part of the search, plus the cost of exploring the insoluble subproblem created by the first j assignments.

At any level of the tree between j and k, say level l, for any partial solution which is formed with $l-1$ variables, we shall have to consider all m values of variable l. Some of these will be inconsistent with one of the previous assignments, but by hypothesis, at least one will be consistent with them all, and so will be a parent of nodes at level $l + 1$. Finally, at level k, all m values are inconsistent with the previous assignments and the algorithm backtracks.

Let N_l be the expected number of values at level l which are consistent with all previous assignments.

Then the expected number of nodes visited in exploring the subproblem is $m + m N_{j+1} + m N_{j+1} N_{j+2} + ... + m N_{j+1} N_{j+2}...N_{k-1}$, where:

$$N_l = \sum_{i=1}^{m} i \text{ Pr}\{\text{exactly } i \text{ values of variable } l \text{ are consistent with the previous}$$

$$\text{assignments } | \text{ at least one is}\}$$

$$= \sum_{i=1}^{m} i \frac{\binom{m}{i}(q_2^{l-1})^i(1-q_2^{l-1})^{m-i}}{(1-(1-q_2^{l-1})^m)}$$

$$= \frac{mq_2^{l-1}}{(1-(1-q_2^{l-1})^m)}$$

Hence for any (j,k) instance, we can now calculate its probability and the expected number of nodes required by the backtracking algorithm to solve it.

6   Estimating the Higher Percentiles

We first make the simplifying assumption that if the probability of backtrack-free search is greater than p, then the $100p^{th}$ percentile of nodes visited is the expected number of nodes visited for backtrack free search.

We further assume that in the region where most problem can be solved without backtracking, (j,k) instances are the most expensive problems to solve. In this region, the cost of problems which are neither (j,k) instances nor can be solved without backtracking is assumed to lie between the two categories that have been accounted for. This seems to be a safe assumption as long as the proportion of problems not covered by our model is small.

We already have an estimate of the cost of solving each (j,k) instance, and sort the (j,k) instances in ascending order of estimated cost.

Suppose that some particular instance has probability p_{jk} and estimated cost c_{jk}, and that the total probability of all instances with higher estimated cost than this one is p_{jk}^+, and the next higher cost is c_{jk}^+. Then we estimate that $100(1 - p_{jk}^+ - p_{jk})\%$ of problems have cost less than c_{jk}, and $100p_{jk}^+\%$ of problems have cost c_{jk}^+ or more. So if $(1 - p_{jk}^+ - p_{jk}) < p < 1 - p_{jk}^+$, the $100p^{th}$ percentile can be estimated by linear interpolation between c_{jk} and c_{jk}^+. This gives estimates of the higher cost percentiles.

Figure 3 shows the results for $\langle 10, 10, 1.0 \rangle$ problems. For these parameters, the phase transition occurs at about $p_2 = 0.4$. As confirmed by Figure 1, the probability that a problem is solved without backtracking falls below 0.5 when $p_2 > 0.2$, and so our model does not give an estimate of the median cost beyond this point.

The vertical line in Figure 3 marks the point at which the proportion of problems which are either (j,k) instances or can be solved without backtracking falls to 98%. As p_2 increases further, this proportion decreases rapidly. To the left of the vertical line, we have accounted for nearly all problems, and there is a good fit with the observed percentiles shown in Figure 1 at the higher cost

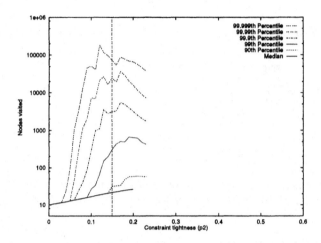

Fig. 3. Estimated percentiles for $\langle 10, 10, 1.0 \rangle$ problems

levels. It is clearly an over-simplification to assume, as we have done, that at any value of p_2 all backtrack-free searches have the same cost; however, there is a good match between the observed and calculated values of p_2 at which the higher percentiles begin to increase sharply.

To the right of the line ($p_2 > 0.15$), Figure 1 shows that the influence of the phase transition becomes increasingly apparent: backtracking, at all levels of the search tree, becomes increasingly frequent in most searches. Our model becomes less and less applicable, and when $p_2 = 0.3$, say, Figure 2 shows that it accounts for only about 10% of problems. However, there continues to be a reasonably close match between the highest estimated and observed percentiles for some way beyond the line, and we have included these higher values of p_2 to show that the (j, k) instances are becoming less expensive to solve as p_2 increases. This explains the dip in the highest percentiles between the easy region and the phase transition region, giving the double peak observed by Hogg and Williams [7].

The lack of smoothness in the higher percentiles in Figure 3 appears to be an effect of all the averaging that has been done within each (j, k) instance in forming the estimates: the percentiles tend to track a particular (j, k) instance for several successive values of p_2, with the estimated cost decreasing as the increasing constraint tightness causes increased pruning in the insoluble sub-problem. At the same time, the probability of the more expensive instances (i.e. with larger $j - k$) increases, so that eventually a given percentile will start to follow a different instance, with a sudden jump in the cost marking the change.

7 Comparison with Other Algorithms

We have shown that the ehps encountered by BT when the constraint graph is complete can be explained by (j, k) instances. Although our analysis currently only applies when $p_1 = 1$, the definition of (j, k) instances would clearly still apply if $p_1 < 1$. Indeed, they might occur more easily if the constraints are sparse: for instance, it could then happen that variable k is only constrained by the first j variables, making a failure more likely. Experimental evidence shows that with more sophisticated algorithms, ehps are more common when the constraint graph is sparse [10]. In the following discussion we therefore assume that the incidence of ehps with BT can also be accounted for by (j, k) instances when $p_1 < 1$.

A (j, k) instance is only a hard problem for the BT algorithm, and even then only for a particular variable and value ordering. For instance, if the values of the first j variables were considered in a different order, different assignments would be made, and the insoluble subproblem would not be created; the problem could then almost certainly be solved without backtracking, just as almost all similar problems can be. Conversely, given a poor variable and value ordering, virtually any problem generated with the right parameters could become a (j, k) instance. For instance, the particular case discussed in section 3 had $j=2$ and $k=8$. Any problem can be an instance of precisely this kind provided that there are values which can be assigned to two of the variables such that between them these assignments conflict with all the values of a third variable. If the first two variables become v_1 and v_2 respectively, and the values causing the conflict are placed first in their domains, and the third variable becomes v_8, we again have an ehp. The observed instance occurred when $p_2 = 0.15$, and although, given a random variable and value ordering, it is unusual with this constraint tightness for the specific assignments $v_1 = 1, v_2 = 1$ to conflict with all values of v_8 (hence the rarity of ehps), it is much more likely that such an instance could be *constructed* by reordering the variables and values.

Exceptionally hard satisfiability problems created by random reordering of the variables have been observed experimentally, by Selman and Kirkpatrick [9]. They ran the Davis-Putnam procedure many times on the same satisfiable expression from the easy-satisfiable region, each time randomly relabelling the variables. The cost distribution, including a small proportion of very high costs, was very similar to that obtained by running DP on many similar randomly-generated satisfiable expressions.

Even if a different random variable or value ordering can convert a particular (j, k) instance into a backtrack-free instance for BT (and v.v.), the algorithm will still encounter (j, k) instances at the same rate. Their incidence can only be reduced by changing the algorithm. Other CSP algorithms may find (j, k) instances easy to solve, but still encounter difficulties themselves.

An algorithm which looks ahead at the effects of each instantiation on future variables would find (j, k) instances easy. The forward checking algorithm (FC) explicitly forms the subproblem consisting of the future variables and the remaining values in their domains which are consistent with the past assignments. In a (j, k) instance, the subproblem formed after the first j assignments would

193

have no values remaining for variable k; FC would detect this, an alternative value would immediately be tried for variable j, and a solution would be found without backtracking.

Similarly, an intelligent backtracking algorithm, such as conflict-directed back-jumping (CBJ), would not be fooled by a (j, k) instance: on reaching variable k for the first time, it would detect that the cause of the failure is variable j and jump back to that variable. Since by hypothesis a solution can then be found without further backtracking, the (j, k) instance would cause the algorithm to backtrack only once.

However, it is known from experimental studies that forward checking does suffer from ehps. In [10], we described something similar to a (j, k) instance. The first j instantiations create an insoluble subproblem; the algorithm repeatedly discovers the infeasibility when it reaches variable k, but can only prove insolubility by an exhaustive search. Clearly, the infeasibility is not simply due to a domain wipeout, which FC would be able to detect immediately, but to some more complex cause; we suggested that in these cases the subproblem contains an arc inconsistency. For instance, it may be that as a result of the first j instantiations, all remaining values of v_k conflict with all remaining values of v_l, where $l > k$. However, Figure 2 shows that when ehps due to (j, k) instances first arise, almost all problems are accounted for by our existing model. Hence, more complex infeasibilities could only occur at higher values of p_2. This is in line with our experiments comparing BT and FC on the same set of problems: FC showed signs of exceptional behaviour in the easy region, but at larger values of p_2, closer to the phase transition.

We found that the combination of FC and CBJ encountered far fewer ehps than FC by itself, but they did still occur. We suggested that this happens when either the proof of arc inconsistency in the subproblem is complex or a higher level of inconsistency is involved: CBJ cannot then jump out of the subproblem. Even so, Baker [1] suggests, based on experiments with graph colouring problems, that a sufficiently intelligent backtracker will avoid ehps altogether.

Hence, in random binary CSPs, there are a number of available strategies for avoiding the insoluble subproblems occurring in ehps: looking ahead to detect the insolubility, as FC does; jumping back out of the subproblem, as CBJ does; or simply restarting the search with a different variable ordering.

However, most real problems have non-binary constraints, and often have global constraints, i.e. involving all the variables. In such a case, these strategies may not work so well. We can imagine something analogous to a (j, k) instance occurring: as a result of the first j instantiations, there is no partial solution with more than $k - 1$ variables which satisfies the constraints, although partial solutions with $k - 1$ variables can be found. If such a situation arises, we should have an insoluble subproblem potentially requiring an exhaustive search to prove insoluble, just as we have seen with the BT algorithm and random binary CSPs.

The strategies which succeed with binary constraints will generally not handle non-binary constraints well, especially those involving most or all of the variables: FC and other lookahead techniques are based on binary constraints and cannot use a constraint to prune the domains of future variables until all but one of the variables involved have been instantiated. An intelligent backtracker will not be able to identify variable j as the true culprit when more recently instantiated variables are also involved in the constraint. Furthermore, in solving real problems, a good variable ordering heuristic is often crucial to success, so that it is not possible to restart with a random re-ordering. This suggests that ehps may be harder to avoid, and possibly more common, in real problems with non-binary constraints.

Experience reported by Gent and Walsh [5] with the travelling salesman decision problem (whether there is a tour of length l or less), can be explained in this way. If l is increased from the minimum possible length, the problem can sometimes become much more difficult to solve, rather than easier as would be expected, and as usually happens. Their explanation of these instances is that an early bad decision can mean that there is no acceptable tour of the remaining cities, but the constraint on the tour length is not violated until nearly all the cities have been considered, resulting in a very time-consuming search. This example confirms that ehps can occur in real problems.

8 Conclusions

We have proposed a model for the occurrence of exceptionally hard binary constraint satisfaction problems in the easy region, based on the creation of an insoluble subproblem following the first few instantiations made by the algorithm. We have used this model to estimate the cost distribution for the simple backtracking algorithm in the region where ehps occur, for the case $p_1 = 1$: the distribution matches that observed in practice. The (j, k) instances are rare cases of exponential cost in a region where most problems can be solved without backtracking and the cost therefore scales quadratically with n.

Our model confirms that exceptionally hard problems in the easy-soluble region are not inherently difficult; they are therefore quite different from the problems occurring in the phase transition, rather than phase transition problems that have somehow strayed into the easy region (although it may possibly be appropriate to view the insoluble ehps that have been found in graph colouring and satisfiability testing in that light).

We have shown that the calculated highest cost percentiles in the easy-soluble region given by our model begin to decrease at the highest values of p_2 to which our model applies, just before the average cost begins to increase towards the phase transition. This gives the second peak in the phase transition, observed by Hogg and Williams.

It is easy to see how to avoid the ehps encountered by BT in solving ensembles of random binary CSPs: a change in the way the algorithm is applied, or a better algorithm, will almost certainly solve the problem very quickly. However, instances analogous to (j, k) instances can occur with more sophisticated algorithms, if much more rarely. We have also suggested that the equivalent of (j, k) instances can occur in non-binary CSPs and may be harder to avoid. More experimental work on this needs to be done. In future, we will also extend our analysis to $p_1 < 1$, and if possible to other algorithms such as FC.

Acknowledgements. The authors are members of the APES group[2] and thank other members of the group for helpful comments on their work. We should also like to thank Martin Dyer for his advice on calculating probabilities. Stuart Grant is partly supported by a studentship from British Telecom plc.

References

1. A. B. Baker. Intelligent Backtracking on the Hardest Constraint Problems. Technical report, CIRL, University of Oregon, Feb. 1995.
2. R. J. Bayardo and R. Schrag. Using CSP Look-Back Techniques to Solve Exceptionally Hard SAT Instances. In *Proceedings CP96*, pages 46–60, 1996.
3. P. Cheeseman, B. Kanefsky, and W. Taylor. Where the *Really* Hard Problems are. In *Proceedings IJCAI-91*, volume 1, pages 331–337, 1991.
4. I. P. Gent and T. Walsh. Easy Problems are Sometimes Hard. *Artificial Intelligence*, 70:335–345, 1994.
5. I. P. Gent and T. Walsh. Phase Transitions from Real Computational Problems. In *Proceedings of the 8th International Symposium on Artificial Intelligence*, pages 356–364, Oct. 1995.
6. R. Haralick and G. Elliott. Increasing tree search efficiency for constraint satisfaction problems. *Artificial Intelligence*, 14:263–313, 1980.
7. T. Hogg and C. P. Williams. The Hardest Constraint Problems: A Double Phase Transition. *Artificial Intelligence*, 69:359–377, 1994.
8. P. Prosser. Hybrid Algorithms for the Constraint Satisfaction Problem. *Computational Intelligence*, 9(3):268–299, 1993.
9. B. Selman and S. Kirkpatrick. Critical behaviour in the computational cost of satisfiability testing. *Artificial Intelligence*, 81:273–295, 1996.
10. B. M. Smith and S. A. Grant. Sparse Constraint Graphs and Exceptionally Hard Problems. In *Proceedings IJCAI95*, volume 1, pages 646–651, 1995.

---

[2] http://www.cs.strath.ac.uk/Contrib/ipg/apes.html

Tabu Search for Maximal Constraint Satisfaction Problems

Philippe Galinier and Jin-Kao Hao

LGI2P
EMA-EERIE
Parc Scientifique Georges Besse
F-30000 Nîmes
France
email: {galinier, hao}@eerie.fr

Abstract. This paper presents a Tabu Search (TS) algorithm for solving maximal constraint satisfaction problems. The algorithm was tested on a wide range of random instances (up to 500 variables and 30 values). Comparisons were carried out with a min-conflicts+random-walk (MCRW) algorithm. Empirical evidence shows that the TS algorithm finds results which are better than that of the MCRW algorithm.the TS algorithm is 3 to 5 times faster than the MCRW algorithm to find solutions of the same quality.

Keywords: Tabu search, constraint solving, combinatorial optimization.

1   Introduction

A finite Constraint Network (CN) is composed of a finite set X of variables, a set D of finite domains and a set C of constraints over subsets of X. A constraint is a subset of the Cartesian product of the domains of the variables involved that specifies which combinations of values are compatible. A CN is said to be binary if all the constraints have 2 variables. Given a CN, the Constraint Satisfaction Problem (CSP) consists in finding one or more complete assignments of values to the variables that satisfy all the constraints [13] while the Maximal Constraint Satisfaction Problem (MCSP) is an optimization problem consisting in looking for an assignment that satisfies the maximal number of constraints [4]. Known to be NP-complete (NP-hard) in general, both MCSP and CSP are of great importance in practice. In fact, many applications related to allocation, assignment, scheduling and so on can be modeled as a CSP or a MCSP.

Methods for solving CSP include many *complete* algorithms based on backtracking and filtering techniques [19] and *incomplete* ones based on repair heuristics such as Min-conflicts [14]. Similarly, methods for solving MCSP include *exact* algorithms based on branch-and-bound techniques [4, 12, 20] and *approximation* ones based on the above mentioned repair heuristics [21].

The main advantage of an *exact* (*complete* for CSP) method is its guarantee of optimality (completeness for CSP). The main drawback of such a method remains the time necessary to compute large scale instances. On the contrary, repair techniques constitute an interesting alternative to deal with instances of very large size although neither optimality nor completeness is guaranteed.

Repair methods belong in fact to a more general class of methods called Local Search (LS). Local search, which is based on the notion of neighborhood, constitutes a powerful approach for tackling hard optimization problems [16, 10]. Starting with an initial configuration, a typical local search method replaces iteratively the current configuration or solution by one of its neighbors until some stop criteria are satisfied; for example, a fixed number of iterations is reached or a sufficiently good solution is found. Well-known examples of LS methods include various hill-climbers, simulated annealing (SA) [11] and Tabu search (TS) [5].

TS is generally considered to be one of the most promising methods in combinatorial optimization and already shows its power for solving many hard problems including the maximal satisfiability [6] and graph-coloring problem [8, 3]. In this study, we are interested in applying TS to solve MCSP and try to answer the following question: is TS a competitive method for this problem ?

This paper presents a TS algorithm for solving MCSP. In order to evaluate the effectiveness of the TS algorithm, extensive experiments are carried out on a wide range of random instances (up to 500 variables and 30 values). Experimental results were compared with a min-conflicts algorithm combined with random walk (MCRW), which is considered to one of the most successful method for MCSP [21].

The paper is organized as follows: after a brief review of repair methods (Section 2), we present Tabu Search and its adaptation to MCSP (Section 3). Then we define the context and method of the experimentation, followed by comparative results between TS and MCRW (Section 4). We conclude the paper with some conclusions and indications about our ongoing work (Section 5).

2 Repair Methods for MCSP

An instance of an optimization problem (S, f) is defined by a set S (search space) of configurations and a cost function $f: S \rightarrow R$ (R being the set of real numbers). Solving such an instance consists in finding a configuration $s \in S$ that has the minimal (or maximal) value of the cost function f.

Given a CN $< X, D, C >$ representing respectively the set of distinct variables, value domains, and constraints, MCSP is the optimization (minimization) problem defined by:

- The set of configurations S is the set of all the complete assignments s defined by $s = \{< V_i, v_i > \mid V_i \in X$ and $v_i \in D_i\}$. Clearly the cardinality of the search space S is equal to the product of the sizes of the domains, i.e. $\prod_{i=1}^{n} |D_i|$.
- The cost $f(s)$ of a configuration s is the number of constraints violated by s.

A typical repair method for MCSP begins with an inconsistent complete assignment, often generated randomly, and then repairs iteratively the current solution. To carry out a repair, a two step process is usually used: first choose a *variable* and then choose a new value for the chosen variable. Many heuristics are possible for both choices leading thus to different repair methods [7]. One example for choosing a value for a given variable is the Min-Conflicts (MC) heuristic [14].

- **Min-Conflicts Heuristic**: For a given conflicting variable[1], pick a value which minimizes the number of violated constraints (break ties randomly); if no such value exists, pick randomly one value that does not increase the number of violated constraints (the current value of the variable is picked only if all the other values increase the number of violated constraints).

A MC-based repair algorithm may consist simply in iterating the MC heuristic. The solving power of such a MC algorithm is limited because it cannot go beyond a local optimum. However, its performance can be largely improved when some noise strategies are introduced in MC. This is exemplified by MCRW which is a MC algorithm combined with the *random-walk* strategy [17]: for a given conflicting variable, pick randomly a value with probability p, apply the MC heuristic with probability $1 - p$. More precisely, a MCRW algorithm can be defined as in Figure 1.

MCRW algorithm

begin
  generate a random configuration s
  $nb\_iter := 0$
  $nb\_moves := 0$
  while $f(s) > 0$ **and** $nb\_moves < max\_moves$ **do**
    if *probability p verified* **then**
      choose randomly a variable V in conflict
      choose randomly a value v' for V
    else
      choose randomly a variable V in conflict
      choose a value v' that minimises the number of conflicts for V
      (the current value is chosen only if all the other values increase the number of violated constraints)
    if v' *is different from the current value of* V **then**
      assign v' to V
      $nb\_moves := nb\_moves + 1$
    $nb\_iter := nb\_iter + 1$
  output(s);
end

Figure 1: The MCRW algorithm

---

[1] A variable is said conflicting if it is involved in some unsatisfied constraints.

This algorithm is controlled by the random probability p, it should be clear that the value for this parameter has a big influence on the performance of the algorithm. The tuning of this parameter is explained in Section 4.3.

An iteration leading to a new configuration different from the current one is called a *move*. Note that for MCRW, many iterations do not lead to a move (see Section 4.1). An optimization is introduced as follows. If an iteration fails to lead to a move for a conflicting variable V, V will not be uselessly considered for the next iterations until a move is effectively carried out.

There are other strategies to help MC to escape from local optima, we can mention for instance Breakout [15] and EFLOP [22].

Recently, some empirical studies have been reported which compare the above mentioned repair methods for solving constraint problems [7, 21]. Experimental evidence shows that MCRW is among the most powerful methods of the repair family. Consequently, MCRW is used in this paper as our reference to evaluate the performance of the TS algorithm.

3 Tabu Search for MCSP

3.1 Tabu Search

This section gives a very brief review of Tabu Search (TS), emphasizing the most important features which have been implemented in our TS algorithm for MCSP. Instructive presentations of TS are given in [5], including many pointers to other applications.

Like any LS method, TS needs three basic components: a *configuration structure*, a *neighborhood function* defined on the configuration structure, and a *neighborhood examination mechanism*. The first component defines the search space S of the application, the second one associates with each point of the search space a subset of S while the third one prescribes the way of going from one configuration to another. A typical TS procedure begins with an initial configuration in the search space S and then proceeds iteratively to visit a series of locally best configurations following the neighborhood. At each iteration, a *best* neighbor $s' \in N(s)$ is sought to replace the current configuration s even if s' does not improve the current configuration in terms of the value of the cost function.

This iterative process may suffer from cycling and get trapped in local optima. To avoid the problem, TS introduces the notion of *Tabu lists*, one of the most important components of the method.

A tabu list is a special short term memory that maintains a selective history H, composed of previously encountered solutions or more generally pertinent attributes of such solutions. A simple TS strategy based on this short term memory H consists in preventing solutions of H from being reconsidered for fonext k iterations (k, called tabu tenure, is problem dependent). Now, at each iteration, TS searches for a best neighbor from this dynamically modified neighborhood $N(H,s)$, instead of from $N(s)$ itself. Such a strategy prevents Tabu from being trapped in short term cycling and allows the search process to go beyond local optima.

Tabu restrictions may be overridden under certain conditions, called *aspiration criteria*. Aspiration criteria define rules that govern whether a solution may be included in $N(H,s)$ if the solution is classified tabu. One widely used aspiration criterion consists of removing a tabu classification from a move when the move leads to a solution better than that obtained so far. Aspiration constitutes an important element of flexibility in TS.

TS uses an aggressive search strategy to exploit its neighborhood. Therefore, it is crucial to have special data structures which allow a fast updating of move evaluations, and reduce the effort of finding best moves. Without this kind of technique, the efficiency of TS may be compromised.

There are other interesting and important techniques available such as intensification and diversification. In this paper, we show that a TS algorithm based on the above mentioned elements may be very efficient and robust for MCSP.

3.2   A TS Algorithm for MCSP

Definition of the neighborhood

We choose for the TS algorithm the following neighborhood function N : $S \rightarrow 2^S$: for each configuration s in S, $s' \in N(s)$ if and only if s and s' are different at the value of a *single conflicting* variable. In other words, a neighbor of a configuration s can be obtained by changing the current value of a conflicting variable in s. Note that the size of this neighborhood $|N(s)|$ varies during the search according to the number of conflicting variables in s.

Tabu list and definition of attributes

A move for MCSP corresponds to changing the value v of a conflicting variable V to another value v', and therefore can be characterized by a couple (attribute) $< variable, value >$. Consequently, when the solution s moves to $s' \in N(s)$ by replacing the current value v of V with a new one v', the $< V, v >$ is classified tabu for the next k iterations. In other words, the value v is not allowed to be re-assigned to V during this period. Like the random probability p for the MCRW algorithm, the tabu tenure k has a big influence on the performance of the TS algorithm. The tuning of this parameter is explained in Section 4.3.

In order to implement the tabu list, we use a $|X|*|D|$ matrix T. Each element of T corresponds to a possible move for the current configuration. When a move is done, the corresponding element of the matrix is set to the current number of iterations plus the tabu tenure k. In this way, it is very easy to know if a move is tabu or not by simply comparing the current number of iterations with that memorized in T.

Aspiration function

The aspiration criterion consists of removing a tabu classification from a move when the move leads to a solution better than the best obtained so far.

Solution evaluation and neighborhood examination

For MCSP, it is possible to develop special data structures to find quickly a best neighbor among the given neighborhood. The main idea, inspired by a technique proposed in [3], is based on a two dimensional table $|X|*|D|$ γ: if v is the current value of V, then $\gamma[V, v]$ indicates the the current number of conflicts for V; for each v' different from v, $\gamma[V, v']$ indicates the the number of conflicts for V if v' is assigned to V. Each time a move is executed, only the affected elements of the table are updated accordingly. In this way, the cost for each move is constantly available and a best move can be found quickly.

This technique is also used by our MCRW algorithm to find quickly a best move among the values of a given (conflicting) variable. In particular, with this data structure, iterations which do not lead to a move will have a negligible cost.

We give in Figure 2 the TS algorithm integrating the above elements.

Tabu algorithm

begin
  generate a random configuration s
  $nb\_iter := 0$
  initialize randomly the tabu list
  while $f(s) > 0$ **and** $nb\_iter < max\_iter$ **do**
    choose a move $< V, v' >$ with the best performance among the non-tabu moves
    and the moves satisfying the aspiration criteria
    introduce $< V, v >$ in the tabu list, where v is the current value of V
    remove the oldest move from the tabu list
    assign v' to V
    $nb\_iter := nb\_iter + 1$
  output(s);
end

Figure 2: The Tabu Search algorithm

Each iteration of TS consists in examining all the values of all the conflicting variables in the current solution s and then carrying out a best move. Unlike MCRW, each iteration modifies a variable and the number of moves carried out by the algorithm is exactly the same as the number of iterations.

4 Experimentation and Results

In this section, we present comparative results between TS and MCRW over several classes of MCSP instances.

4.1 Comparison Criteria

In this study, we choose two criteria to compare TS and MCRW. The first one is the quality of solution measured by the best cost value, *i.e.* the *number of violated constraints*, that a method can find. The second criterion is the computing effort needed by an algorithm to find its best solutions or solutions of a given quality. This second criterion is measured by the *number of moves* and the *running time*.

Note that the number of moves instead of iterations is used in the second criterion. The reason for this choice is the following. For TS, each move coincides with an iteration. But for MCRW, the number of moves is in general much lower than the number of iterations, because an iteration of MCRW does not lead to a move if the current value of the chosen variable is picked. In our implementation, the data structure shared by TS and MCRW has the property that an iteration which does not lead to a move is much less costly than an iteration leading to a move. Therefore, counting iterations instead of moves, will put MCRW at a disadvantage, especially if the iterations which do not lead to a move are frequent. As we explain later, this is indeed the case for MCRW.

4.2 MCSP Instances

Let us note that a *satisfaction* problem (such as CSP and SAT) is very different from an *optimization* problem (such as MCSP and MAX-SAT). There exist some interesting results such as the phase transition phenomenon which seperates under-constrained problems and over-constrained ones [1, 9, 18, 2]. Under-constrained problems tend to have many solutions. Therefore, it is usually easy to find a satisfiable assignment which is also an optimal solution for the optimization problem. Over-constrained problems tend to be easy to be proven unsatisfiable. This means only that they are easy from the point of view of satisfiability, but nothing is known about the difficulty of finding a minimal cost solution from the point of view of optimization.

In summary, for the satisfaction problem, hard instances tend to be around the phase transition. However, for the optimization problem, it is not possible to determine whether a given instance is difficult to solve or not except for under-constrained instances.

In our expriments, we choose a classical and simple binary MCSP model and evaluate the algorithms with instances coming from sufficiently diversified classes.

More precisely, the MCSP model used depends on 4 parameters: the number n of variables, the size d of domains (all domains have the same size), the density *p1* and the tightness *p2* of constraints. A quadruple (n, d, p_1, p_2) defines a particular class. An instance of a given class is built by choosing randomly $p_1.n.(n-1)/2$ constraints among the $n.(n-1)/2$ different pairs of variables and, for each constraint, $p_2.d^2$ forbidden tuples among the d^2 possible tuples. Different instances of a same class can be generated using different random seeds.

Classes used in this work are taken from the following sizes: small (n/d = 50/10), medium (n/d = 100/15), large (n/d = 250/25) and very large (n/d =

300/30, 500/30). For each size, we choose one or several values for the couple
($p1,p2$) in such a way that the instances of the class are not easily satisfiable
and have a cost value smaller than 30.

4.3 Parameter tuning for TS and MCRW

The performance of TS and MCRW is greatly influenced by some parameters:
the size of tabu list tl and the random walk probability p. We use the following
procedure to determine the appropriate values for these parameters for each
class of instances. First, a preliminary study determined the following ranges of
parameter values: $10 \leq tl \leq 35$ and $0.02 \leq p \leq 0.1$. Then, different discrete
values between these ranges were further tested as follows. For TS (respectively
MCRW) each of the values {10, 15, 20, 25, 30, 35, 40, 45} ({0.02, 0.03, 0.04,
0.05, 0.07, 0.1, 0.2, 0.3, 0.4} for MCRW) was used to run 50 times on the class
(10 instances, 5 runs per instance, each run being limited to 50,000 moves) and
the best value identified for the class.

4.4 Results

Problem	Tabu				MCRW					Tabu-MCRW	
	tl	cost value f			p	%	cost value f			min	avg
		min	avg	max			min	avg	max		
50.10.10.60.0	15	4	4	4	0.05	42	4	4	4	0	0
50.10.10.70.0	15	14	14	14	0.05	35	14	14	14	0	0
50.10.30.30.0	15	5	5.08	6	0.05	38	5	5.5	6	0	-0.42
50.10.30.35.0	15	15	15	15	0.05	33	15	15.18	16	0	-0.18
50.10.50.20.0	15	8	8	8	0.05	36	8	8.26	9	0	-0.26
100.15.10.40.0	15	0	1.2	2	0.03	35	1	2.33	4	-1	-1.13
100.15.10.45.0	25	8	9.72	12	0.03	30	8	11.02	13	0	-1.3
100.15.10.50.0	30	20	21.62	24	0.03	26	20	23.18	27	0	-1.55
100.15.30.15.0	10	0	0	0	0.03	27	0	0.06	1	0	-0.06
100.15.30.20.0	20	19	20.78	23	0.03	25	19	22.3	25	0	-1.51
250.25.03.55.0	40	6	8.42	12	0.02	28	6	12.36	15	0	-3.93
250.25.07.30.0	30	7	11.68	14	0.03	34	10	14.66	19	-3	-2.97
250.25.10.21.0	25	3	4.88	7	0.03	33	3	6.9	10	0	-2.02
250.25.10.22.0	30	8	10.86	14	0.03	34	10	14.17	19	-2	-3.31
250.25.10.23.0	35	15	19.18	22	0.02	32	19	22.96	27	-4	-3.77
300.30.03.50.0	45	5	10.1	15	0.03	28	8	14.9	22	-3	-4.79
300.30.05.35.0	35	9	13.96	17	0.02	28	14	18	23	-5	-4.04
300.30.07.25.0	25	1	3.48	6	0.02	32	4	7.04	11	-3	-3.56
500.30.04.25.0	30	0	1.56	3	0.02	36	3	5.97	13	-3	-4.41

Table 1. Comparative results of TS and MCRW, maximum moves = 100,000

Table 1 gives a summary of the results of TS and MCRW for the instances
we have tested in terms of quality of the solutions. To obtain these results,
both algorithms were run 50 times on each instance, each run being given a
maximum of 100,000 moves. The parameter of each algorithm (the size of tabu
list tl and the random-walk probability p) is fixed according to the best value
found during the parametric study. For each algorithm, we give the minimum,
average and maximum value of the cost function. For MCRW, we also give the

average percentage of iterations that lead effectively to moves (column %). The last two columns indicate the difference between the cost function of Tabu and MCRW, in minimum and average.

From the data of Table 1, the following observations may be made. For small instances, both methods obtain the same minimum for the cost function. For medium and large instances, TS obtains better results for 4 out of 10 instances (a smaller cost value, -1 to -4). For the 4 very large instances, TS obtains much better results (-3 to -5). If we look at the average cost of the two algorithms, we see that TS obtains better results than MCRW for 17 out of 19 instances and the same results for the 2 others (seemingly easy ones). Finally, note that less than half (25-42%) of MCRW iterations lead to moves (column %).

Table 2 gives more details about the performance of TS and MCRW. This table shows different values of the cost function together with the number of successful runs, the minimal, average and maximal number of moves (for the successful runs). The last column gives the ratio between the average number of moves between MCRW and TS, and hence indicates how much TS is faster than MCRW (in terms of number of moves). For instance, the first line means that both algorithms reach the cost $f=15$ at each of 50 runs, but TS needs on average a number of moves 3.49 times smaller than MCRW. Note that although only one instance is showed here, other instances have very similar behaviors.

Problem	f	Tabu				MCRW				MCRW/Tabu
		succ.	#moves			succ.	#moves			#moves
			min	avg	max		min	avg	max	avg
300.30.07.25.0	15	50	1656	4299.7	7850	50	6013	15022.2	33009	3.49
	14	50	1918	4864.6	9731	50	6324	17051.6	39896	3.5
	13	50	2010	5622.5	11330	50	6367	21506.4	40769	3.82
	12	50	2018	6755.7	15415	50	8694	25244.7	68226	3.73
	11	50	3326	8545	24332	50	8701	33708.5	75467	3.94
	10	50	4513	10039.8	25924	49	9399	41296.3	96774	-
	9	50	4738	12156.1	26545	45	9438	46655.4	99023	-
	8	50	6293	15773.7	39941	37	17335	53922.2	98593	-
	7	50	6306	22562.5	59051	34	20969	63521.8	95867	-
	6	50	10722	31382.2	70505	20	29033	69506.3	99111	-
	5	49	12764	43022.3	93673	9	51662	70315.4	88173	-
	4	40	18585	52437.2	99010	4	76503	85380	96824	-
	3	26	20799	64812.5	96686	0	-	-	-	-
	2	10	57146	79492.5	97850	0	-	-	-	-
	1	1	94525	94525	94525	0	-	-	-	-
	0	0	-	-	-	0	-	-	-	-

Table 2. More detailed comparative results of TS and MCRW, maximum moves = 100,000 for TS and MCRW

In order to see if MCRW can catch up with TS if MCRW is given more moves, a second experiment was performed with MCRW on 2 medium and 2 large instances. In this experiment, the number of moves is extended from 100,000 to 500,000. Table 3 shows the results of this experiment for 300.30.07.25.0 as in Table 2.

From Table 2, we may make the following remarks about this instance. The minimum cost value that an algorithm can reach at each run is 6 for TS and 11 for MCRW. The minimum cost value reached (at least once) is 1 for TS and 4 for MCRW. For the values that both methods could reach at each run ($f \geq 11$), TS is on average about 3 to 4 times faster than MCRW (in terms of number of moves). For the values between 10 and 4, TS has always a higher number of successful runs than MCRW.

Recall that for MCRW, only iterations leading to a real move are counted. Since such iterations leading to a move represent only 25-50% according to the instance (see Table 1), MCRW requires a number of *iterations* 10 to 15 times higher than that of TS.

Data similar to those of Table 2 are available for all the other instances. From the data, we observe very similar behavior. TS is on average 3 to 5 times faster (in terms of number of moves) than MCRW to reach a given cost value and this factor remains stable across all instances and for different cost values of a given instance.

Problem	f	Tabu				MCRW				MCRW/Tabu
		succ.	#moves			succ.	#moves			#moves
			min	avg	max		min	avg	max	avg
300.30.07.25.0	11	50	3326	8545	24332	50	11739	28242	77551	3.3
	10	50	4513	10039.8	25924	50	11789	39613.3	104638	3.94
	9	50	4738	12156.1	26545	50	15019	48761	107704	4.01
	8	50	6293	15773.7	39941	50	15027	63067.7	132980	3.99
	7	50	6306	22562.5	59051	50	15308	86265.8	227572	3.82
	6	50	10722	31382.2	70505	50	16239	133856	355128	4.26
	5	49	12764	43022.3	93673	47	33298	178486	415849	-
	4	40	18585	52437.2	99010	35	85267	236837	461983	-
	3	26	20799	64812.5	96686	25	106969	304038	493080	-
	2	10	57146	79492.5	97850	12	132130	339752	484847	-
	1	1	94525	94525	94525	1	425855	425855	425855	-
	0	0	-	-	-	0	-	-	-	-

Table 3. More detailed comparative results of TS and MCRW, maximum moves = 100,000 for TS, 500,000 for MCRW

From Table 3, we observe that MCRW (with a maximum of 500,000 moves) obtains solutions comparable to those of TS (with a maximum of 100,000 iterations) in terms of quality. In terms of moves required by MCRW and TS, the ratio remains the same as before, *i.e.* around 3.5 to 4.

Other experiments have been carried out where the two algorithms were run 5 times each with a much larger number of moves (2,000,000) on these instances. Similar results have been observed.

Recall that there are two big differences between the TS and MCRW algorithms. The first one is that TS uses a tabu list while MCRW performs random walks. The second one is that the two algorithms examine the neighborhood according to two different strategies: TS looks at all the conflicting variables while MCRW looks only at a single variable. In other words, MCRW examines much fewer neighbor solutions than TS does at each iteration. Therefore, one may ask if this second factor is responsible for the difference of performance between these two algorithms. In order to see if this is the case, we tested a third algorithm which examines at each iteration all the conflicting variables like in TS.

This new algorithm, that we called Steepest Descent Random Walk (SDRW), proceeds as follows. At each iteration, it performs a random walk with probability p, and a "Steepest Descent" with probability $1 - p$, i.e., it seeks a best possible move among those which do not increase the cost function.

The SDRW algorithm was tested on the five instances of size $n = 100$ in the same conditions as for TS and MCRW. Results are presented in Table 4.

Problem	Tabu					SDRW			Tabu-SDRW	
	tl	cost value f			p	$\%$	cost value f			min	avg
		min	avg	max			min	avg	max		
100.15.10.40.0	15	0	1.2	2	0.45	90	1	4.1	7	1	-2.9
100.15.10.45.0	25	8	9.72	12	0.45	90	10	14.24	18	2	-4.52
100.15.10.50.0	30	20	21.62	24	0.45	89	22	26.95	30	2	-5.33
100.15.30.15.0	10	0	0	0	0.35	73	0	0.6	2	0	-0.6
100.15.30.20.0	20	19	20.78	23	0.40	80	21	26.22	29	2	-5.44

Table 4. Comparative results of TS and SDRW, maximum moves = 100,000

From Table 4, we observe that the results of SDRW are much worse than those of TS. If we compare these results with those of MCRW (Table 1), it is easy to see that SDRW gives even worse results than MCRW does. These results show that the high performance of the TS algorithm is effectively due to the tabu memory.

Table 5 gives information about the running time on a Sun SPARCstation 5 (32 RAM, 75MHz) of the TS and MCRW algorithms[2]. The second and third two columns (*time*) indicate the average running time in seconds of TS and MCRW for carrying out 100,000 *moves*.

Problem	Tabu time	MCRW time	Problem	Tabu time	MCRW time
50.10.10.60.0	64	61	250.25.03.55.0	190	196
50.10.10.70.0	80	70	250.25.07.30.0	200	178
50.10.30.30.0	73	72	250.25.10.21.0	183	190
50.10.30.35.0	89	81	250.25.10.22.0	206	183
50.10.50.20.0	90	86	250.25.10.23.0	226	193
100.15.10.40.0	84	96	300.30.03.50.0	231	226
100.15.10.45.0	111	111	300.30.05.35.0	234	239
100.15.10.50.0	154	127	300.30.07.25.0	205	215
100.15.30.15.0	124	121	500.30.04.25.0	255	279
100.15.30.20.0	142	142			

Table 5. Running times of TS and MCRW for 100,000 moves

From Table 5, we observe that the running time for TS is only about 15% more important than MCRW (more for small size instances, less for large size instances) even if TS searches more larger neighborhood at each iteration. Taking into account Tables 4 and 1, we see that TS is much more efficient than MCRW.

---

[2] Both TS and MCRW are implemented in C++.

5   Conclusion

In this paper, we presented a basic TS algorithm for solving the maximal constraint satisfaction problem. This algorithm was tested and compared on random instances of various sizes (ranging from n/d = 50/10 to n/d = 500/30). Empirical evidence shows that the TS algorithm always finds solutions of better quality, i.e. solutions having smaller number of violated constraints.

Moreover, the TS algorithm is about 3 to 5 times faster than the MCRW algorithm to find solutions of the same quality, in terms of number of moves but also of running time.

This study shows clearly that the TS algorithm is very competitive compared with one of the best repair methods. More generally, Tabu Search has other important features such as intensification and diversification which may improve further the performance of the algorithm. Therefore, TS should be considered to be very promising for solving the MCSP.

Several points are worthy of further studies. First, we do not know if the results of this study would remain valid on instances of other classes or models of MCSP. Moreover, it will be interesting to compare Tabu Search with the most efficient complete algorithms for solving satisfiable instances of CSP.

Acknowledgments

We would like to thank the referees of this paper for their useful comments.

References

1. P. Cheeseman, B. Kanefsky and W.M. Taylor, "Where the really hard problems are", Proc. of the 12th IJCAI'90, pp163-169, 1991.
2. D.A. Clark, J. Frank, I.P. Gent, E. MacIntyre, N. Tomov, T. Walsh, "Local search and the number of solutions", Proc. of CP97, pp119-133, 1996.
3. C. Fleurent and J.A. Ferland, "Genetic and hybrid algorithms for graph coloring", to appear in G. Laporte, I. H. Osman, and P. L. Hammer (Eds.), Special Issue Annals of Operations Research, "Metaheuristics in Combinatorial Optimization".
4. E.C. Freuder and R.J. Wallace, "Partial constraint satisfaction", Artificial Intelligence, Vol.58(1-3) pp21-70, 1992.
5. F. Glover and M. Laguna, "Tabu Search", in C. R. Reeves (Ed.), Modern heuristics for combinatorial problems, Blackwell Scientific Publishing, Oxford, GB, 1993.
6. J.K. Hao and R. Dorne, "Empirical studies of heuristic local search for constraint solving", Proc. of CP-96, LNCS 1118, pp194-208, Cambridge, MA, USA, 1996.
7. P. Hensen and B. Jaumard, "Algorithms for the maximum satisfiability problem", Computing Vol.44, pp279-303, 1990.
8. A. Hertz and D. de Werra, "Using Tabu search techniques for graph coloring". Computing Vol.39, pp345-351, 1987.
9. T. Hogg, B.A. Huberman and C.P. Williams, Artificial Intelligence, Special Issue on the Phase Transition and Complexity. Vol 82, 1996.
10. D.S. Johnson, C.H. Papadimitriou and M. Yannakakis, "How easy is local search?" Journal of Computer and System Sciences, Vol.37(1), pp79-100, Aug. 1988.

11. S. Kirkpatrick, C.D. Gelatt Jr. and M.P. Vecchi, "Optimization by simulated annealing",Science No.220, pp671-680, 1983.
12. J. Larrosa and P. Meseguer, "Optimization-based heuristics for maximal constraint satisfaction", Proc. of CP-95, pp190-194, Cassis, France, 1995.
13. A.K. Mackworth, "Constraint satisfaction", in S.C. Shapiro (Ed.) Encyclopedia on Artificial Intelligence, John Wiley & Sons, NY, 1987.
14. S. Minton, M.D. Johnston and P. Laird, "Minimizing conflicts: a heuristic repair method for constraint satisfaction and scheduling problems", Artificial Intelligence, Vol.58(1-3), pp161-206, 1992.
15. P. Morris, "The Breakout method for escaping from local minima", Proc. of AAAI-93, pp40-45, 1993.
16. C.H. Papadimitriou and K. Steiglitz, "Combinatorial optimization - algorithms and complexity", Prentice Hall, 1982.
17. B. Selman and H.Kautz, "Domain-independent extensions to GSAT: solving large structured satisfiability problems", Proc. of IJCAI-93, Chambery, France, 1993.
18. B.M. Smith, "Phase transition and the mushy region in constraint satisfaction problems", Proc. of ECAI94, pp100-104, 1994.
19. E. Tsang, "Foundations of constraint satisfaction", Academic Press, 1993.
20. R.J. Wallace, "Enhancements of branch and bound methods for the maximal constraint satisfaction problem", Proc. of AAAI-96, pp188-196, Portland, Oregon, USA, 1996.
21. R.J. Wallace, "Analysis of heuristics methods for partial constraint satisfaction problems", Proc. of CP-96, LNCS 1118, pp308-322, Cambridge, MA, USA, 1996.
22. N. Yugami, Y. Ohta and H. Hara, "Improving repair-based constraint satisfaction methods by value propagation", Proc. of AAAI-94, pp344-349, Seattle, WA, 1994.

Reconfigurable Architectures:
A New Vision for Optimization Problems

Y. Hamadi, D. Merceron
{hamadi, merceron}@lirmm.fr

LIRMM UMR 5506 CNRS-UMII, 161 Rue Ada 34392 Montpellier Cedex 5

Abstract. GSAT is a greedy local search procedure. It searches for satisfiable instantiations of formulas under conjunctive normal form. Intrinsically incomplete, this algorithm has shown its ability to deal with formulas of large size that are not yet accessible to exhaustive methods. Many problems such as planning, scheduling, vision can efficiently be solved by using the GSAT algorithm. In this study, we give an implementation of GSAT on Field Programmable Gate Arrays (FPGAs) in order to speed-up the resolution of SAT problems. By this implementation, our aim is to solve large SAT problems and to enable real-time resolution for current size problems. The FPGA technology [12] allows users to adapt a generic logic chip to different tasks. In the framework of SAT problems we show how to quickly adapt our chips to efficiently solve satisfiability problems.

1 Introduction

The local search procedure called GSAT was introduced in [11]. Devised to find satisfiable instantiations of propositional logic formulas, this algorithm has shown its abilities to solve large scale problems for which the so-called complete methods (that are based on the exhaustive examination of the search space) seem unfit.

Our purpose is to offer an adaptation of this algorithm to the reconfigurable architectures by proposing an original implementation based on FPGAs.

Therefore, we follow two main goals. The first one is to change the scale of the accessible optimization problems by offering a hardware implementation, efficient and scalable. The second one is to allow the processing of real-time applications (i.e. : mobile robot vision) by taking advantage of hardware speed-up.

The interest of this work is based on the different application fields of the GSAT procedure which is useful in satisfaction problem solving (SAT) and more generally in optimization problems (MAX-SAT). These include several AI problems and more particularly planning, scheduling and artificial vision.

As the prime work combining satisfiability problems and reconfigurable hardware we can refer to [13]. The hardware power was also used for optimization problems in [1], where a specific digital circuit running a massively parallel algorithm for arc consistency is realized. Hence, using hardware with major tasks in AI is nowadays of great interest. Since it becomes obvious that it is more efficient to adapt hardware to a given problem than to implement this problem on a constrained architecture [8], we show here how to adapt and solve optimization tasks on reprogrammable digital chips.

In this paper, the authors describe the GSAT procedure, and an introductive section on FPGAs allows to approach the different elements of our implementation on a reconfigurable board. Each of the physical compounds of this implementation is then explained and detailed. Thereafter, we present two extensions of the GSAT procedure in order to cope with structured problems. For each of those extensions, we explain how to improve our physical implementation in order to get the same heuristics as in the software implementation of GSAT. Finally, we discuss the performances of our physical implantation relatively to an optimized software GSAT algorithm on several hard instances.

2 The GSAT procedure

Introduced in 1992, GSAT is one of the reparative local search methods. Starting with the postulate that a total instantiation of the variables from the problem to solve brings more information than a partial assignment [6], this procedure starts with an arbitrary instantiation of the problem variables and offers to reach the highest satisfaction degree by a succession of small transformations (repairs).

The procedure (see algorithm 1) uses a CNF[1] logic formula coding the problem to solve. Hence, repairs are only changes of a propositional variable which value is flipped[2].

In order to control the process convergence, a *score* is associated to each variable instantiation (it is represented by the number of satisfied clauses). We search which variable flip would give the best *score* increase by temporarily flipping successively each variable and counting the number of satisfiable clauses. In concrete terms, each repairs is realized by flipping the variable that brought the best *score*.

One of the main features of GSAT is to break the possible *score* equalities by a random choice between variables. This kind of undeterminism allows the procedure to escape from local optima.

The end of the algorithm is controlled by two end-user parameters:

- Max-tries: This parameter represents the maximum number of resolution attempts. It depends on the amount of time that the user accepts to devote to the search.
- Max-flips: It codes the maximum number of repairs (flips) in each attempt. Generally, this parameter is fixed to a small multiple of the number of variables in the formula.

---

[1] A CNF is a conjunction of clauses, a clause is a disjunction of literals, a literal is a propositional variable or it negation.

[2] Flipping a variable is a changing value operation, since the domain of a logical variable is {0,1}, a variable with a value of 0 is set to 1 and *vice versa*.

Algorithm 1: The GSAT algorithm.

GSAT(A,$Max - tries$,$Max - flips$)

A : is a CNF formula

$Max - tries$, $Max - flips$: Integer

begin

    for *(i = 1 to Max − tries)* **do**

        $V \leftarrow$ *an instanciation of the variables*

        for *(j = 1 to Max − flips)* **do**

            if *A satisfiable by V* **then return** *V*

            $p \leftarrow$ *the variable whose the flip yield the*

            most important raise in the number

            of satisfied clauses

            $V \leftarrow V$ with p *flipped*

    return *the best instantiation found.*

end

Definition 1: A *try* is an execution of the external loop of the procedure. It corresponds to a resolution attempts with a starting configuration.

Definition 2: A *flip* is an execution of the internal loop of the procedure. It corresponds to the search of the variable to flip, the variable that gives the best *score* increase.

If no solution is found for the given problem, the instantiation with the best *score* is used as the result.

An incremental implementation of the algorithm provides a pretty good time complexity. The algorithm begins by calculating the *score* of each variable. Then, for each step, the *score* of the flipped variable is reconsidered. We examine the set of clauses where appears this variable. By the way, we recalculate every variable's *score* of the same clauses. For typical problems in the literature, such as hard random 3-SAT, the ratio: #clause/#variables is around 4.3 [10]. Hence the complexity of a flip becomes O(3*4.3) for a hard random 3-SAT.

For a hardware implementation, such a fine technique is useless and expensive in space. In the further sections, we will demonstrate how to provide an efficient parallel processing of the given clauses on reconfigurable hardware.

3 Reconfigurable Hardware

We will present here basic concepts for the reconfigurable hardware, the aim of which is to build a specific design in order to take advantage of the hardware technology. It is obvious that a problem solved by a specific chip will be solved faster than with a generalist processor. Field Programmable Gate Arrays (FPGA) can fit a problem solving even during the runtime.

3.1 A Programmable Chip: FPGA

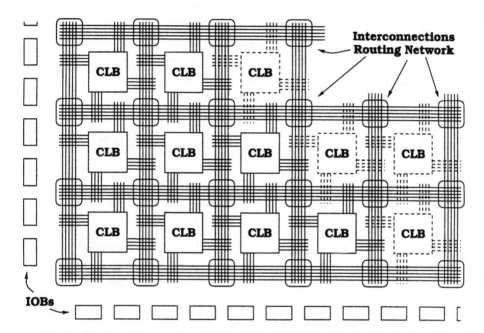

Fig. 1. Partial view of a FPGA.

We hereby introduce Field Programmable Gate Arrays (FPGA) with static RAM based on Look-up tables (LUT in which the logic formulas are implemented). The purpose of reconfigurable architectures is to be able to modify interconnections between the different parts of the system, but above all to adapt the operating part in which are implemented the logic rules. A FPGA allows to work at the logic gate level (AND, OR, NOT, etc...).

We will explicit FPGAs from the Xilinx family[12]. For the user, the global architecture of Xilinx FPGAs is composed of three sorts of elements (see figure 1):

- CLB : Configurable Logic Bloc (see figure 2).
  A CLB is composed of 2 Look-Up Tables of 2^4 bits each. A LUT allows to implement every binary function with 4 input variables. Those 2 LUTs may be inter-connected in order to implement 1 LUT with 5 input variables. Furthermore, each CLB has two flip-flops[3], allowing to memorize logical signals (1 bit each).
- IOBs : Input Output Blocs. This allows the communication between the FPGA and the rest of the board (its neighborhood).

---

[3] A flip-flop is a memory that stores a bit until the next clock step. This allows to synchronize different parts of a design on the clock steps.

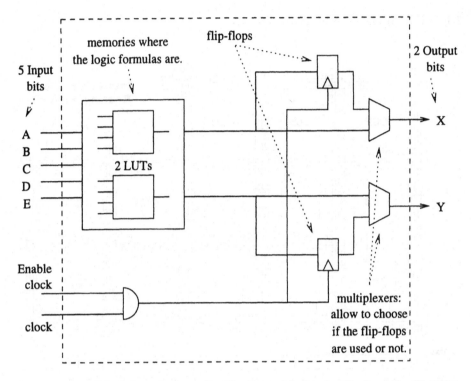

Fig. 2. A simplified description of a Configurable Logic Block of the Xc3090: Here are figured Look-Up tables where the logic formulas are defined, Flip-flops that allow to store bits until the next clock step and multiplexers that allow to choose if flip-flops are used or not.

– Routing Network : local directional connections and global connections.

The FPGAs are identifiable by the number of CLB that they own. For instance, a Xc3090, has 320 CLBs, while a Xc4062 has 2304 CLBs. In order to increase the number of used CLBs, it is also possible to couple several FPGAs on a same board.

3.2 Dynamic reconfiguration

Dynamic reconfiguration of FPGAs increases the density and/or the speed of the design. It is useful to quickly adapt the design of the FPGA to the program running. This reconfiguration is generally made according to the data we want to process. Thus, the reconfigurable hardware fits the problem to solve and is all the more efficient.

Dynamic reconfiguration can be executed in three different ways:

- Alternate between several designs already compiled [3]. Once the compilation achieved, to alternate from several designs takes only a few milli-seconds.
- Modify directly the CLB logic equations with informations only known at run time. We modify directly the bitstream file and reload it on the FPGA. This is one of the fastest way to adapt the hardware to the problem to solve.
- Generate the design at the runtime from a Xilinx NetList File (the low level language of Xilinx FPGAs) with information only known at runtime. This kind of reconfiguration allows to increase the density of the design.

4 Improving GSAT behavior on FPGAs

We want to speed-up the GSAT algorithm by implementing the most costly parts of the algorithm on reconfigurable Hardware. An external software manages the control of the streams and the initialization of each try. First of all GSAT is an algorithm that can be completely implemented on FPGAs, thanks to the simplicity of the elements that compose it. In the following sections, we present the general implementation of GSAT on FPGA, and then, we describe how easy is the dynamic encoding of each part of this implementation on FPGAs.

4.1 General implementation

We present here the method used to achieve a variable flip on the reconfigurable board.

1. Initialization of the vector of variables: The vector of variables is initialized with a random value given by an external software. Each variable bit is going to be flipped serially, and will be restore the step after. This part of the algorithm costs n clock ticks where n is the number of variables in the GSAT problem.
2. Checking the clauses: At each clock step a variable is flipped in (1). With the instantiation of the variables given from (1), we check all the clauses in parallel. Thus, the time spent to check the clauses for a given variable vector is independent from the number of clauses. This part of the algorithm costs 1 clock tick.
3. We count the number of satisfied clauses given by the step (2) in a m bits adder, where m is the number of clauses. This part of the algorithm costs 1 clock step, which means that each clauses are processed in parallel. As opposed to the software implementation of GSAT, we do not count the difference between satisfied clauses of the last flip and the new one. We enumerate all the clauses that are satisfied. Then, at the starting point of a flip (before the first variable of the vector is flipped), the best flip stored must be 0 in (4). As we check all the clauses, it becomes easier to count the number of satisfied clauses.

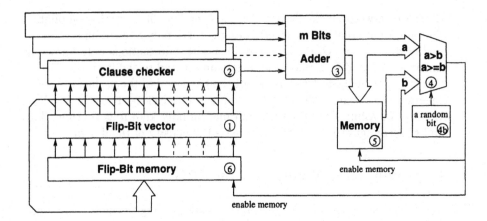

Fig. 3. The general implementation of GSAT on FPGA.

4. The number of satisfied clauses is compared to the maximum satisfied clause number (the *score*) previously given in (5). The comparison is *greater than* or *greater or equal* according to a bit given by a random bit generator (4b). As shown in section 2, this allows to escape from a local optimum. The *score* is 0 before the first variable flip. This part of the algorithm costs 1 clock step.

5. If the number of satisfied clauses is greater than (or *greater or equal*, according to the random bit given by the bit (4b)) the maximum satisfied clause number previously given, we enable the storage of the Adder result in the memory (5).

6. If the number of satisfied clauses is greater than (or *greater or equal*, according to the random bit given by the bit (4b)) the maximum satisfied clause number previously given, we store in (6) the variables vector that gave the new maximum satisfied clause number.

7. At the end of the flips (once every variable has been flipped) we use the vector stored in (6) as the initial vector in (1).

In our implementation, the complexity of a definitive flip is n clock step, while in the software implementation this complexity is $O(12.9)$ for a hard random 3-SAT. To achieve a variable-flip, the constant time complexity of the software implementation seems more efficient. But, this algorithm needs to update several heavy data structures for each variable flip. In section 6, we will see how the hardware with its n elementary operations, is much faster than any optimized software version.

4.2 Flip-bit vector

The Flip-bit vector is the vector of all the variables of the SAT problem to solve. This vector is originally set to a random value by an external software. Each of the variables are serially flipped (becomes '1' if was '0' and becomes '0' if was '1').

In the FPGA implementation, each Flip-bit is a variable that flips its value when it receives the order to do so, sends the order to its right neighbor, and gets back its original value.

A specific initial bit value is set in a Flip-bit by setting this value on the *BitIn* input and by enabling this input (*Enable*=1). The Flip-bit then receives the order to flip by the input *Order*, and sends the order to its right neighbor by the output *SendOrder*. The Flip-bit outputs its value on the pin *Bit* (See figure 4)

Here is a Flip-bit behavior:

1. At the first step, each bit must send the bit that is initially set ($Bit = BitIn$ AND *Enable*). A bit memorizes its value when it is allowed to (Enable=1).
2. If a bit receives an order to flip (*Order*=1), then Bit must inverse itself ($Bit = \overline{Bit}$ AND *Order*).
3. If a bit has just been flipped (when it sends an order to the next bit to inverse), then it must come back to its original value ($Bit = \overline{Bit}$ AND *SendOrder*).
4. In every other cases, the bit must send its original value ($Bit = Bit$ AND $\overline{Enable}$ AND $\overline{Order}$ AND $\overline{SendOrder}$).

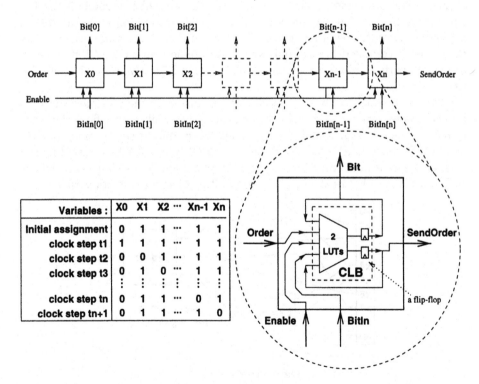

Fig. 4. A Flip-bit vector with a zoom on a flip-bit: An instance of the flip processing is given. After the initial assignment, at each clock step, a variable is flipped and retrieves its value the clock step after.

Then, the output *Bit* for a Flip-bit is defined by:

$Bit = ((BitIn \text{ AND } Enable) \text{ OR } (\overline{\overline{Bit}} \text{ AND } Order) \text{ OR } (\overline{\overline{Bit}} \text{ AND } SendOrder)$
OR $(Bit \text{ AND } \overline{Enable} \text{ AND } \overline{Order} \text{ AND } \overline{SendOrder})$.

When a Flip-bit receives the order to flip, it send the same order to its right neighbor the clock step after. Then the output *SendOrder* of Flip-bit is defined by:

$SendOrder = Order$

If the clock is running at 60 MHz, a clock step takes 16,7 ns. Thus, for 50 variables, a flip cost 50x16,7 = 833,33 ns.

4.3 Clause checkers

This part defines the clause checkers. A clause checker is a unit that takes as input the necessary variables to solve a clause.

All the clauses are treated in parallel, which means at the same time. Therefore, it takes the same time to process one, two or m clauses.

Two kinds of implementations are possible to improve the efficiency of the clause checkers.

The first one is to build a clause with every variables (solving by the way every n-CNF problems), and, at runtime, to choose which variable is used in which clause. Therefore, at runtime, a clause must consider only the variables it needs and consider the others neutral. This solution is interesting because once the design is compiled, we can quickly instantiate on it every n-SAT problem of m clauses with at most n variables. This solution is costly in number of CLB used.

The second one is to build a specific design with only the necessary variables for each clause (see figure 5). This takes longer to compile a specific design than to build a generic design and modify its bitstream during the runtime, but the number of needed CLB is smaller. It only cost 1 CLB for a 3-SAT clause. Figure 5 gives an example of a 3-SAT instantiation. In this example the clauses are defined as follow $C1 = (x1 \vee \overline{x4} \vee \overline{x7})$, $C2 = (x2 \vee \overline{x3} \vee x6)$ and $C3 = (\overline{x4} \vee x5 \vee x8)$

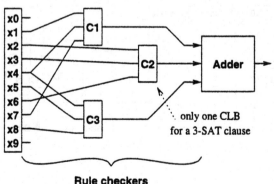

Rule checkers

Fig. 5. An instance of 3-SAT clause checkers .

The equations of each 3-SAT clause is defined in one Look-Up Table.

4.4 Adders

Each of the CLBs we use have only 2 output bits. Therefore we must build k bit Adders from only 2 or 3 bit Adders (respectively called Half-Adder and Full-Adder), where $k = log_2(m)$, and m is the number of clauses. Adders can be dynamically programmed on FPGA, thanks to the Dadda method. Luidgi Dadda gave in 1965 a methodology allowing a minimal building of a m bits Adders with Half and Full-Adders [2].

As shown in [5], Adders are easy to implement dynamically on FPGAs with the Dadda method.

4.5 Memories

It is obvious to make a k bits memory within a FPGA. At the output of each CLB, 2 flip-flops allow to memorize 2 bits until the next clock step. In order to store a bit as long as necessary, one can disable the clock signal on the CLBs used as memories by the input "enable clock" (see figure 2)

4.6 Comparators

In one CLB, we can implement a comparator with only 4 Inputs. This means that we can compare 2 data of 2 bits. We must compare bits of the same weight and pipeline those comparators outputs in order to build a k bits comparator.

As said in section 2, the undeterminism of GSAT in case of *score* equalities, seems to be essential for the algorithm to achieves good results. In our design, in order to keep this feature, we generate on the FPGA a random bit, that control the action of the comparator. The latter, acts like a *greater than* or like a *greater or equal* according to this random bit result. In case of *score* equality of two variables, the random choice of the comparators allows the random choice between these variables. An implemented random bit on a FPGA costs seven CLBs.

5 Heuristics

Several heuristics have been implemented within GSAT in order to efficiently solve structured problems [9]. Some of them like the Random Walk strategy modify the standard scheme of GSAT in the choice of the flipped variable. These particular behavior will be difficult to implement in our hardware. Nevertheless, we present here an adaptation of two heuristics for our hardware implementation. These heuristics tries to take benefits from the previous failures *i.e.* the previous tries. Since in our system, the initialization of each try is provided by an external software, the adaptation of these improvements is made straight away.

5.1 Clause weight heuristic

This technic results from the observation that for some problems, several resolution attempts reach the same unsatisfied final set of clauses. So, each clause has not the same weight on the resolution, some clauses will be much harder to solve. The resolution process must offer more importance to these "hard" clauses.

A way to deal with this kind of problems is to associate a weight to each clause, in order to modify its influence on the global *score*. Thanks to this weight heuristic, the participation of a satisfied "hard" clause is more important. Furthermore, the weight can be automatically found as shown in the following method :

1. Initialize each clause weight to '1'.
2. At the end of each tries, add '1' to each unsatisfied clause weight.

In our FPGA implementation, this method can be applied by modifying the weight of each clause in the adder inputs (see section 4.4). This modification is easy to add since the beginning of each tries is managed by an external software.

5.2 Averaging in previous near solutions

After each attempt, GSAT restarts with a random initial problem variables. However a try that does not give total satisfaction, generally leads to a large number of satisfied clauses. This heuristic offers to reuse parts of the best assignments issued from the two previous tries. Therefore, the starting variables vector for the ith attempt is computed from the bitwise[4] of the two best reached state during the attempts $i - 2th$ and $i - 1th$ (a particular behavior is accomplished for the two first tries).

Once more, this heuristic is used at the initialization step of each try, and may be implemented in the external software that controls the streams at each try.

6 Discussion

The following table illustrates the results given in [9]. It presents the processing of six hard 3-SAT problems (#clause/#variables=4.3). These results are compared with the expected times for our hardware implementation assuming the same state transitions for each problem ($p1$ to $p6$).

Several observations can be done. First of all, the falling-down of the ratio $flip/s$ for the software version. This does not cast doubt over our analysis on the constant time complexity of the optimized software version, but means that the time complexity for a single flip depends of the problem size. Results show that the bigger the problem size is, the more the process needs *tries*. This leads to the definition of several initial instantiations which are time consuming. We must also take into account technological factors, particularly more frequent *cache/central* memory access for large problems.

---

[4] Identical bits representing identical variables are reused, the other ones are randomly choosen.

In our realization the ratio ($flip/s$) is only dependent of the variable number, the clause checking being parallelized. The last column gives the speed-up ratio provided by our method. We can observe that the speed-up is over tens times the optimized software version. Let us remark that our announced times do not take in account the starting instantiation time for each new *try*. An external software manages the control and the initialization of each try on the reconfigurable board. The time needed to update the board (DecPerle1) is around 100ms, since we reuse precompiled bitstreams.

formulas			*optimized – software*				*60MHz hardware*		*SpeedUp*
pb	vars	clauses	$mflips$	tries	time	flips/s	time	flips/s	
p1	50	215	250	6.4	0.4s	4000	1.3ms	12.10^5	300
p2	100	430	500	42.5	6s	3542	35.4ms	60.10^4	169
p3	140	602	700	52.6	14s	2630	85.5ms	42.10^4	163
p4	150	645	1500	100.5	45s	3350	0.3s	40.10^4	120
p5	300	1275	6000	231.8	12mn	1932	6.95s	20.10^4	103
p6	500	2150	10000	995.8	1.6h	1729	83s	12.10^4	70

Reported hardware time are assumed for a 60MHz hardware. The FPGA technology is still growing in both size and speed directions. This looks promising for any reconfigurable application and particularly for ours, allowing the fast processing of larger optimization tasks.

7 Conclusion and future work

The GSAT procedure has obtained very good results in the total satisfaction problems (SAT) and in partial satisfaction problems (MAX-SAT).

This efficiency has aroused our interest for GSAT. Our purpose was, here, to offer an implementation of this algorithm on reconfigurable architectures. This work was guided by two aims. The first one allows the algorithm to go beyond the size limit of the affordable problems. The second one is a real-time processing of classical size problems.

The flexibility of the FPGA technology allowed us to reach these two goals. The adaptation of a hardware for the processing of a given problem is possible thanks to this technology.

Out of the speed-up due to the low level chip, the main interest of our realization emerges from the parallelization of the whole problem clauses satisfiability control. This parallelization gives to our architecture the good feature of scalability in the clauses number. For instance, using FPGAs running at 60MHz, we can process 60.10^6 configurations per second.

The different parts of our implementation have been detailed. The software part is in charge of the generation of initial variables assignments. These initial assignments can easily be improved by the application of particular heuristics. We have shown how to include some GSAT heuristics in our FPGA implementation.

This work finds its motivation in the expected speed-up of large optimization problems solving. Their processing generally needs a distributed search (see [4]), or as shown here, an efficient use of reconfigurable hardware. Other areas of applications are human/machine interactive applications where the real time aspect is a major feature. In the reported experiments, the response time announced in the software version for large problems ($p5$, $p6$) does not fit the time scale of human actions defined by A. Newell in [7]. He defined the human cognitive band (10^{-1} to 10 seconds) which is the time that a human spends to achieve cognitive tasks. A system that would interact with a human agent should fit these specifictions. We expect to explore this real time interactive aspect in order to solve some AI problems in a human/machine collaboration.

Acknowledgment. The authors wish to thank Christian Bessière and Joël Quinqueton for their useful advices.

References

1. P. R. Cooper and M. J. Swain. Arc consistency: parallelism and domain dependence. *Artificial Intelligence*, 58:207–235, 1992.
2. Luidgi Dadda. *Some schemes for parallel multipliers*, volume 19. Alta Frequenza, 1965.
3. James G. Eldredge and Brad L. Hutchings. Rrann: the run time reconfiguration artificial neural network. *In Proc of Custom Integrated Circuits Conference*, pages 77–80, 1994.
4. Y. Hamadi, C. Bessiere, and J. Quinqueton. Gsat distribution. In *Proceedings of the Second International Conference on Multiagent Systems*, page 437, 1996.
5. E. Lemoine and D. Merceron. Run time reconfiguration of FPGA for scanning genomic databases. In D. A. Buell and K. L. Pocek, editors, *Proceedings of IEEE Workshop on FPGAs for Custom Computing Machines*, pages 90–98, Napa, CA, April 1995.
6. S. Minton, M.D. Johnson, A.B. Philips, and P. Laird. Minimizing conflicts: a heuristic repair method for constraint satisfaction problems and scheduling problems. *Artificial Intelligence*, pages 161–205, 1992.
7. A. Newell. Unified theory of cognition. Harvard University Press, 1994.
8. M. Schaffner. Computers formed by the problems rather than problems deformed by the computer. *COMCON Digest*, pages 259–264, 1972.
9. B. Selman and H. Kautz. Domain-independant extensions to gsat : Solving large structured satisfiability problems. In *International Joint Conference on Artificial Intelligence*, pages 290–295, 1993.
10. B. Selman, H. Levesque, and D. Mitchell. Hard and easy distributions of sat problems. In *Proceedings, Tenth National Conference on Artificial Intelligence*, San Jose, CA.
11. B. Selman, H. Levesque, and D. Mitchell. A new method for solving hard satisfiability problems. In *Proceedings, Tenth National Conference on Artificial Intelligence, San Jose, CA*, pages 440–446, 1992.
12. Xilinx Inc. *The Programmable Gate Array Data Book*. Product Briefs, xilinx san jose edition, 1991.
13. M. Yokoo, T. Suyama, and H. Sawada. Solving satisfiability problems using field programmable gate arrays: First results. In *Second International Conference on Principles and Practice of Constraint Programming*, pages 497–509, 1996.

Distributed Partial Constraint Satisfaction Problem

Katsutoshi Hirayama[1] and Makoto Yokoo[2]

[1] Kobe University of Mercantile Marine
5-1-1 Fukae-minami-machi, Higashinada-ku, Kobe 658, JAPAN
E-mail: hirayama@ti.kshosen.ac.jp
[2] NTT Communication Science Laboratories
2-2 Hikaridai, Seika-cho, Soraku-gun, Kyoto 619-02, JAPAN
E-mail: yokoo@cslab.kecl.ntt.co.jp

Abstract. Many problems in multi-agent systems can be described as *distributed Constraint Satisfaction Problems* (distributed CSPs), where the goal is to find a set of assignments to variables that satisfies all constraints among agents. However, when real problems are formalized as distributed CSPs, they are often over-constrained and have no solution that satisfies all constraints. This paper provides the *Distributed Partial Constraint Satisfaction Problem* (DPCSP) as a new framework for dealing with over-constrained situations. We also present new algorithms for solving *Distributed Maximal Constraint Satisfaction Problems* (DM-CSPs), which belong to an important class of DPCSP. The algorithms are called the *Synchronous Branch and Bound* (SBB) and the *Iterative Distributed Breakout* (IDB). Both algorithms were tested on hard classes of over-constrained random binary distributed CSPs. The results can be summarized as SBB is preferable when we are mainly concerned with the optimality of a solution, while IDB is preferable when we want to get a nearly optimal solution quickly.

1 Introduction

Many problems in AI can be formalized as *Constraint Satisfaction Problems* (CSPs), and many researchers have investigated the problems and their algorithms for many years. However, as AI has begun to encounter more realistic problems in the real world, we have found that certain kind of problems in the real world cannot be handled in the conventional CSP framework, and several studies have been made in order to extend the traditional CSP framework.

In [14], Yokoo *et al.* presented a *distributed Constraint Satisfaction Problem* (distributed CSP) as the general framework for dealing with problems in multi-agent systems. A distributed CSP can be considered a CSP in which variables and constraints are distributed among multiple agents and the agents are required to satisfy all constraints by communicating with each other. Many problems in multi-agent systems, such as distributed interpretation problems[9], distributed resource allocation problems[3], distributed scheduling problems[11], and multi-agent truth maintenance systems[7], can be formalized as distributed CSPs.

On the other hand, when a problem designer tries to describe a real problem as a CSP, the resulting CSP is often over-constrained and has no solutions. For such an over-constrained CSP, almost all conventional CSP algorithms just produce a result that says there is no solution. If we are interested in solutions for practical use, the designer has to go back to the design phase and to find another design so that the CSP is not over-constrained. Freuder extended the CSP framework and provided a *Partial Constraint Satisfaction Problem* (PCSP), which is one of the approaches to over-constrained CSPs[4]. In a PCSP, we are required to find consistent assignments to an allowable relaxed problem.

Although a distributed CSP and a PCSP extend the traditional CSP framework in different directions, they are not mutually exclusive. It is not only possible to combine these extensions, but also beneficial because the problems in multi-agent systems can also be over-constrained. This paper provides a formal framework for over-constrained distributed CSPs, the *Distributed Partial Constraint Satisfaction Problem* (DPCSP), and presents two algorithms for solving *Distributed Maximal Constraint Satisfaction Problems* (DMCSPs), which belong to an important class of DPCSP. These algorithms are called the *Synchronous Branch and Bound* (SBB) and the *Iterative Distributed Breakout* (IDB).

This paper is organized as follows. Section 2 and Section 3 introduce the definition of a distributed CSP and a PCSP, respectively, and Section 4 defines a DPCSP and a DMCSP. Algorithms for solving DMCSPs are presented in Section 5, and Section 6 presents an experimental evaluation on randomly generated over-constrained distributed CSPs. Conclusions are given in Section 7.

2 Distributed Constraint Satisfaction Problem

A CSP consists of a pair (V, C), where V is a set of variables, each with a finite and discrete domain, and C is a set of constraints. The domain of a variable is a set of values, each of which can be assigned to the variable. Each constraint is defined over some subset of variables and limits the allowed combinations of variable values in the subset. Solving a CSP involves finding one set of assignments to variables that satisfies all constraints. In some cases, the goal is to find all sets of such assignments.

A distributed CSP can be considered a CSP in which variables and constraints are distributed among multiple agents. To put it formally,

- there exists a set of agents, $1, 2, \ldots, m$;
- for each variable x_j, an agent i is defined such that x_j belongs to i. We mean x_j belongs to i by $belongs(x_j, i)$;
- a constraint C_l is known by an agent i. The predicate $known(C_l, i)$ is used to express that.

We assume, in general, that an agent knows only those constraints relevant to the variables that belong to it. Note that some constraints known by an agent may include other agents' variables, not just its own variables. We refer to such a constraint as an *inter-agent constraint*. A distributed CSP is solved when the following conditions are satisfied for all agents. For each agent i,

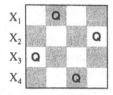

Fig. 1. Example of CSPs (4-queens problem)

- a variable x_j has a value d_j as its assignment for $\forall x_j$ belongs(x_j, i);
- a constraint C_l is true under the above assignments for $\forall C_l$ known(C_l, i).

Fig. 1 illustrates a 4-queens problem, which is a typical CSP. When we view this as a problem where each of four agents tries to determine each queen's position independently, this problem can be described as a distributed CSP.

The algorithms for distributed CSPs must find a solution as quickly as possible. An agent in a distributed CSP has only limited knowledge of the entire problem, and thus important things for the algorithms include how agents communicate with each other and what information is transferred.

3 Partial Constraint Satisfaction Problem

A PCSP is formally described as the following three components[4]:

$$\langle (P, U), (PS, \leq), (M, (N, S)) \rangle,$$

where P is a CSP, U is a set of 'universes', i.e., a set of potential values for each variable in P, $(PS, \leq)$ is a problem space with PS a set of CSPs and $\leq$ a partial order over PS, M is a distance function over the problem space, and (N, S) are necessary and sufficient bounds on the distance between P and some solvable member of PS. We leave the details of each component to [4] due to space limitations. A *solution* of a PCSP is a solvable problem P' from the problem space and its solution, where the distance between P and P' is less than N. Any solution will suffice if the distance between P and P' is not more than S, and all search can terminate when such a solution is found. An *optimal solution* to a PCSP is defined as a solution with a minimal distance between P and P', and the minimal distance is called an *optimal distance*.

4 Distributed Partial Constraint Satisfaction Problem

4.1 Motivation

It is likely that various application problems in multi-agent systems are over-constrained.

In a distributed interpretation problem[9], each agent is assigned a task to interpret a part of sensor data, produce possible interpretations, and help build a globally consistent interpretation through communicating possible interpretations among all of the agents. If an agent makes incorrect interpretations because of errors in the process—for example, noise on the sensor data—, there may be a situation where no globally consistent interpretation exists.

Multi-stage negotiation[3] is a kind of distributed resource allocation problem. Each agent in this problem has a goal (variable) and possible plans to achieve the goal (domain of the variable), and there can be resource conflicts between plan executions by different agents (constraints). The goal of this problem is to find a combination of plans that achieve the goals of all agents at a certain time. It is likely that all the goals cannot be achieved without violating some constraints if not enough resources are available.

While the ordinary distributed CSP framework does require satisfaction of all constraints among agents, it does not give any indication of how we should handle over-constrained distributed CSPs. Thus it makes sense to extend the distributed CSP framework to enable handling of over-constrained distributed CSPs. In [13], Yokoo proposed a method for over-constrained distributed CSPs by introducing *constraint hierarchy*[1] and relaxing the less important constraints if there exists no solution. This method can be applied to problems where constraints are hierarchically structured. However, we recognize that constraints are not always hierarchically structured, and this method is thus unsatisfactory for covering all problems. This research provides a new framework, called the DPCSP, for handling over-constrained distributed CSPs.

4.2 Definition

A DPCSP is formalized as:

- a set of agents, $1, 2, \ldots, m$;
- a PCSP for each agent i, $\langle (P_i, U_i), (PS_i, \leq), (M_i, (N_i, S_i)) \rangle$;
- a global distance function, G,

where P_i is agent i's original CSP that consists of variables belonging to i and constraints that are known by i, U_i is a set of 'universes', i.e., a set of potential values for each variable in P_i, $(PS_i, \leq)$ is a problem space for agent i with PS_i a set of CSPs and $\leq$ a partial order over PS_i, M_i is i's distance function over the problem space, and (N_i, S_i) are i's necessary and sufficient bounds on the distance between P_i and some solvable member of PS_i. The purpose of agent i is to find a solvable CSP, P_i', from the problem space PS_i and its solution, where the distance between P_i and P_i' is less than N_i. Any solution will suffice for agent i if the distance between P_i and P_i' is not more than S_i.

A DPCSP is solved when each of the agents, say i, finds a solvable CSP from the problem space and its solution, such that the distance d_i between the solvable CSP and the original CSP is less than N_i. We refer to such solvable CSPs and their solutions as a *solution* to the DPCSP. Any solution to a DPCSP will suffice if every solution to an individual PCSP suffices. For each solution to a DPCSP, we define a global distance function $G(d_1, d_2, \ldots, d_m)$, which returns the distance of the solution. Using this function, an *optimal solution* is defined as the solution with a minimum distance, and we call the minimum distance an *optimal distance*.

In this paper, we specify the above setting for a DPCSP as follows:

- for each agent i, CSPs in PS_i are produced by removing possible combinations of constraints from P_i;
- the distance between P_i and P_i' (a solvable CSP in PS_i) is measured as the number of constraints removed from P_i;
- a global distance function, $G(d_1, d_2, \ldots, d_m)$, is specified by $\max_i d_i$.

We call this class of DPCSP *Distributed Maximal Constraint Satisfaction Problems* (DMCSPs). The goal of agent i for a DMCSP is to find a solvable CSP and its solution with the number of removed constraints less than N_i. To put it another way, the goal is to find assignments to the variables in P_i with the number of violated constraints in P_i less than N_i.

A DMCSP is solved when each agent, say i, finds assignments with the number of violated constraints less than N_i. We refer to the set of assignments as a *solution* to the DMCSP. Among solutions to the DMCSP, it is the *optimal solution* that minimizes $\max_i d_i$, where d_i is the number of violated constraints on P_i. We call such minimal value of $\max_i d_i$ an *optimal distance* for the DM-CSP. An optimal solution to a DMCSP ensures that we cannot find a solution to the DMCSP, where each agent has assignments with the number of violated constraints less than the optimal distance.

A DMCSP seems to be a reasonable and important class of DPCSP, but we could define other classes of DPCSP. Those classes may include the one that consists of the same definition as a DMCSP except for G, for example, using $\sum_{i=1}^{m} d_i$ instead of $\max_i d_i$ for G. This class is designed to get an optimal solution with the total number of violated constraints over agents minimized. However, it allows an optimal solution in which the number of violated constraints is globally minimized while the violated constraints are concentrated on specific agents. We suppose that might not be a preferable feature for multi-agents systems in terms of equality among agents.

4.3 Example

Fig. 2 shows a distributed 2-coloring problem to illustrate a DMCSP. A node represents a variable and an agent that has the variable. An edge represents a constraint, which means the two connected nodes must be painted in different colors (black or white). An agent knows only the constraints that are relevant to its variable. For example, agent 1 knows only $\{a, c, d\}$. The original CSP for agent 1 (i.e., P_1) consists of a variable: $\{1\}$ with a domain of $\{black, white\}$ and constraints: $\{a, c, d\}$. The current distance of agent 1 is one because it just violates the constraint d, and for other agents: one for agent 2, agent 5 and agent

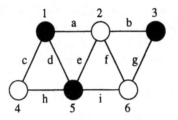

Fig. 2. Distributed 2-coloring problem

6, and zero for agent 3 and agent 4. Suppose $\forall i N_i = 2$, the DMCSP is already solved since the current distances for all agents are less than N_i. The DMCSP with $\forall i N_i = 1$, however, is not solved in this figure because the distances for agent 1, agent 2, agent 5, and agent 6 are not less than N_i. Note that there is no set of assignments that makes the maximal number of constraint violations over agents less than one, and thus the set of assignments in Fig. 2 is the optimal solution to the DMCSP where the optimal distance is one.

5 Algorithms for Distributed Maximal Constraint Satisfaction Problems

In this paper, we develop algorithms that find the optimal solution of a DMCSP.

The simplest algorithms for DMCSPs belong to the class called *centralized algorithms*. One of the centralized algorithms follows this procedure: agents run some leader election algorithm to elect one leader; send all distributed PCSPs to the leader; the leader solves those gathered PCSPs using some maximal constraint satisfaction algorithm[5], while others are idle. If we were interested only in efficiency and not in other aspects, the centralized algorithms might outperform other algorithms because they can make better use of the global knowledge of the entire problem. However, we believe such algorithms are not suitable for a distributed environment from a privacy and security standpoint (who on earth wants to expose an individual's schedule or private information to others?). We therefore develop algorithms on the assumption that each agent's knowledge of the entire problem should remain limited throughout the execution of the algorithms. The algorithms we present in this paper are the *Synchronous Branch and Bound* (SBB) and the *Iterative Distributed Breakout* (IDB).

5.1 Assumption

First of all, we assume the following conditions on communication among agents. These assumptions are quite reasonable for asynchronous communication systems.

- One agent sends messages to the others directly if it knows their addresses. At first an agent knows only the addresses of *neighbors*, a set of agents which share the same inter-agent constraints.
- Although the delay in delivering a message is finite, an upper bound is unknown.
- Between any two agents, messages are received in the order in which they were sent.

Next we introduce the following restrictions on problems. These are just for simplicity, and we can easily generalize our method for larger contexts.

- Each agent has exactly one variable.
- All constraints are binary, i.e., defined over two variables.

5.2 Synchronous Branch and Bound

The Synchronous Branch and Bound (SBB) is a simple algorithm that simulates the branch and bound method for Max-CSPs[5] in a distributed environment. In SBB, variable/agent and value ordering are fixed in advance, and a *path*, partial assignments for all variables, is exchanged among agents to be extended to a complete path. This extension process runs sequentially. To be concrete:

- the first agent in the ordering initiates the algorithm by sending a path that contains only its first value to the second agent;
- when receiving a path from the previous agent in the agent ordering, an agent evaluates the path and the first value of its domain in value ordering, and then sends the path plus the value as a new path to the next agent if its evaluation value is less than the current upper bound, or continues to try next values if the evaluation value is not less than the bound. If values are exhausted, it backtracks to the previous agent by returning the path;
- when receiving a path from the next agent in the agent ordering, an agent changes its assignment to the next value in its value ordering, reevaluates the new path, and sends it to the next if its evaluation value is less than the bound, or if not, continues to try next values. Another backtrack takes place if values are exhausted.

An element of a path actually consists of a variable, a value for the variable, and the number of constraint violations caused by the value. We measure the evaluation value of a path as the maximal number of constraint violations over the variables on the path, and the upper bound as the minimum evaluation value over those of complete paths found so far. Details of SBB are shown in Fig. 3.

Since SBB just simulates the branch and bound method in a distributed environment, it appears obvious that SBB is correct. Soundness is guaranteed since SBB terminates *iff* finding a complete path whose evaluation value is not more than a uniform initial value of S_i or finding no such complete path exists. With sequential control over agents and fixed variable/value orderings, SBB enables agents to do an exhaustive search in distributed search spaces. This

```
procedure initiate
    d_i ← first value in domain;
    send (token, [[x_i, d_i, 0]], n_i) to the next agent;

when i received (token, current_path, ub) from the previous agent do
    previous_path ← current_path;
    n_i ← ub;
    next ← get_next(domain);
    send_token; end do;

when i received (token, current_path, ub) from the next agent do
    [x_i, d_i, nv_i] ← the element related to x_i in current_path;
    n_i ← ub;
    next ← get_next(domain minus all elements up to d_i)
    send_token; end do;

procedure send_token
    if next ≠ 'exhausted' then
        if i = the last agent then
            next_to_next ← next;
            while next_to_next ≠ 'exhausted' do
                best_path ← new_path;
                n_i ← max nv_j in best_path;
                when n_i ≤ s_i do
                    terminate the algorithm; end do;
                next_to_next ← get_next(domain minus all elements up to next_to_next);
            end do;
            send (token, previous_path, n_i) to the previous agent;
        else
            send (token, new_path, n_i) to the next agent; end if;
    else
        if i = the first agent then
            terminate the algorithm;
        else
            send (token, previous_path, n_i) to the previous agent; end if; end if;

procedure get_next(domain)
    if domain = nil then
        return 'exhausted';
    else
        d_i ← first value in domain;
        new_path ← nil;
        counter ← 0;
        if check(previous_path) then
            return d_i;
        else
            return get_next(domain minus d_i); end if; end if;

procedure check(path)
    if path = nil then
        append [x_i, d_i, counter] to new_path;
        return true;
    else
        [x_j, d_j, nv_j] ← first element in path;
        if [x_i, d_i] and [x_j, d_j] are not consistent then
            counter ← counter + 1;
            if counter ≥ n_i or nv_j + 1 ≥ n_i then
                return false
            else
                append [x_i, d_i, nv_j + 1] to new_path;
                return check(path minus first element); end if;
        else
            append [x_i, d_i, nv_j] to new_path;
            return check(path minus first element); end if; end if;
```

Fig. 3. Synchronous branch and bound. Variable(agent) and value ordering are given in advance, and both n_i and s_i for $\forall i$ have uniform values as their initial values. The initial value of s_i should be zero when searching for an optimal solution. The procedure should be initiated only by the first agent in the ordering.

ensures that SBB is complete, i.e., it eventually finds a sufficient solution or finds that there exists no such solution and terminates.

On the other hand, SBB does not allow agents to assign or change their variable values in parallel, and thus SBB cannot take advantage of parallelism.

5.3 Iterative Distributed Breakout

Outline We developed the *distributed breakout*[15] for solving distributed CSPs. This method is characterized by hill-climbing in parallel while excluding neighbors' simultaneous action[6] and the *breakout* method[10] as a strategy for escaping from *quasi-local-minima*. In the distributed breakout, each agent first initializes its assignment arbitrarily, sends its assignment to neighbors with *ok?* messages, and then repeats the following:

- when knowing the current assignments of neighbors by receiving *ok?* messages, an agent evaluates its current assignment by counting the number of violated constraints and also measures the possible improvement of an evaluation value (called *improve*) if the agent changed the assignment to another. The value of *improve* is sent to neighbors with *improve* messages;
- when knowing the current *improves* of neighbors by receiving *improve* messages, an agent compares each of them with its own *improve*, and transfers the right to change an assignment by skipping its next change if the neighbor's *improve* is greater than its own *improve* or does not transfer this right if it's smaller. Ties are broken by comparing agent identifiers. Only the winners for the right to change actually change their assignments, and then all agents send the current assignments to neighbors with *ok?* messages.

This repeated process sometimes leads to a solution to a distributed CSP. However, it often gets stuck when some agent falls into a quasi-local-minimum, where it has at least one constraint violation and has no way to reduce the number of constraint violations. The distributed breakout provides an efficient way to escape from such a quasi-local-minimum. It just increases weights of violated constraints at a quasi-local-minimum and changes an assignment by evaluating the assignment as a weighted sum of violated constraints.

While each agent in the distributed breakout synchronizes its assignment change among neighbors, the overall assignment changes run in parallel. The method is thus especially efficient for critical problem instances with solutions. Another advantage is that it incorporates a procedure to detect whether the algorithm finds a global solution, in contrast with previous distributed constraint satisfaction algorithms that need to invoke the *snapshot* algorithm[2] for detection. On the other hand, one major drawback is that the distributed breakout is not complete, i.e., it may fail to find a solution even if one exists and also cannot determine that no solution exists.

The Iterative Distributed Breakout (IDB) is a method for DMCSPs in which a variant of the distributed breakout is repetitively applied to a DMCSP. The operation of IDB is: set a uniform constant value *ub* to each agent's necessary bound N_i and run the distributed breakout; if the distances of all agents become less than N_i, the agent that detects this fact sets its N_i to $ub - 1$ and propagates its value to make N_i for all agents $ub - 1$. This process is continued until some agent detects that a solution to a DMCSP with $\forall i \ N_i = S_i + 1$ is found.

Detail IDB is very similar to the distributed breakout. It does, however, introduce some extension for handling necessary bounds on distance. The bounds are exchanged by *ok?* and *improve* messages, both of which are also used in the distributed breakout. This paper focuses on the part that handles the necessary bounds and leaves details about the other parts, which are the same as in the distributed breakout, to [15].

- Before starting IDB, an agent assigns a uniform value to its necessary bound. We currently give each agent a predetermined value.
- When receiving *ok?* messages from all neighbors, an agent i counts the number of violated constraints and then sets zero as the evaluation value of its current assignment if the number is less than N_i or, if not, the agent proceeds as in the distributed breakout. IDB thus permits an agent to have an assignment with the number of violated constraints less than N_i.
- For the distributed breakout, it is guaranteed that each agent is satisfied when some agent's *termination_counter* exceeds *diameter* (a diameter of graph). It is also guaranteed for IDB that each agent finds a solution to its individual PCSP with N_i when some agent's *termination_counter* exceeds *diameter*. The agent that finds this fact decreases its N_i by one and sends the new value with *ok?* and *improve* messages.
- When receiving the new value for necessary bounds, an agent knows that it's time for the transition of necessary bounds and sets a variable *broadcast* to true. That forces *termination_counter* to remain at zero.

The details of IDB are shown in Fig. 4.

We can prove inductively that the termination detection of each iteration of IDB is correct by the following fact: some agent i with $N_i = ub$ increases its *termination_counter* from d to $d + 1$ *iff* each of i's neighbors has ub as the value of its necessary bound, has an assignment with the number of violated constraints less than ub, and has a *termination_counter* value of d or more. IDB terminates *iff* detecting the iteration with $N_i = S_i + 1$ terminates. This is when each agent's distance becomes no more than S_i. That indicates that IDB is sound.

While SBB is sequential in terms of value assignments, IDB enables parallel value assignments. However, IDB is not complete, i.e., it may fail to get an optimal solution to a DMCSP; besides, it cannot decide whether a solution is optimal or not even if it actually gets an optimal solution.

6 Evaluation

This section presents an experimental evaluation of SBB and IDB.

procedure initiate
    current_value ← the value randomly chosen from *domain*;
    send (ok?, x_i, *current_value*, n_i) to neighbors;
    goto wait_ok? mode;

wait_ok? mode
when *i* received (ok?, x_j, d_j, *ub*) **do**
    counter ← *counter* + 1; add (x_j, d_j) to *agent_view*;
    when *ub* ≠ n_i **do**
      n_i ← min(n_i, *ub*); *broadcast* ← *true*; **end do**;
    if *counter* = *number_of_neighbors* **then**
      when n_i ≤ s_i and *broadcast* = *false* **do**
        terminate the algorithm; **end do**;
      send_improve;
      counter ← 0; *broadcast* ← *false*;
      goto wait_improve mode;
    else
      goto wait_ok? mode; **end if; end do**;

procedure send_improve
    if # of currently violated constraints < n_i, **then**
      current_eval ← 0;
    else
      current_eval ← evaluation value of *current_value*; **end if**;
    my_improve ← possible maximal improvement;
    new_value ← the value which gives the maximal improvement;
    if *current_eval* = 0 and *broadcast* = *false* **then**
      consistent ← *true*;
    else
      consistent ← *false*; *my_termination_counter* ← 0; **end if**;
    if *my_improve* > 0 **then**
      can_move ← *true*; *quasi_local_minimum* ← *false*;
    else
      can_move ← *false*; *quasi_local_minimum* ← *true*; **end if**;
    send (improve, x_i, *my_improve*, *current_eval*, *my_termination_counter*, n_i) to neighbors;

wait_improve mode
when *i* received (improve, x_j, *improve*, *eval*, *termination_counter*, *ub*) **do**
    counter ← *counter* + 1;
    my_termination_counter ← min(*termination_counter*, *my_termination_counter*);
    when *ub* ≠ n_i **do**
      n_i ← min(n_i, *ub*); *broadcast* ← *true*; **end do**;
    when *improve* > *my_improve* **do**
      can_move ← *false*; *quasi_local_minimum* ← *false*; **end do**;
    when *improve* = *my_improve* and x_j precedes x_i **do**
      can_move ← *false*; **end do**;
    when *eval* > 0 **do**
      consistent ← *false*; **end do**;
    if *counter* = *number_of_neighbors* **then**
      when n_i ≤ s_i and *broadcast* = *false* **do**
        terminate the algorithm; **end do**;
      send_ok; *counter* ← 0; *broadcast* ← *false*; clear *agent_view*;
      goto wait_ok? mode;
    else
      goto wait_improve mode; **end if; end do**;

procedure send_ok
    when *consistent* = *true* and *broadcast* = *false* **do**
      increment *my_termination_counter*;
      when *my_termination_counter* = *diameter* **do**
        n_i ← n_i - 1; *my_termination_counter* ← 0; **end do; end do**;
    when *quasi_local_minimum* = *true* **do**
      increase the weights of violated constraints; **end do**;
    when *can_move* = *true* **do**
      current_value ← *new_value*; **end do**;

Fig. 4. Iterative distributed breakout. Both n_i and s_i for $\forall i$ have uniform values as their initial values. The initial value of s_i should be zero when searching for an optimal solution. The procedure should be initialized by each agent before receiving any message.

problem class	median cycle	mean optimal distance
$\langle 10, 10, 18/45, 0.8 \rangle$	3500	1.0
$\langle 10, 10, 18/45, 0.9 \rangle$	18262	2.0
$\langle 10, 10, 27/45, 0.8 \rangle$	46247	2.4
$\langle 10, 10, 27/45, 0.9 \rangle$	499841	3.4
$\langle 10, 10, 36/45, 0.8 \rangle$	336416	3.6
$\langle 10, 10, 36/45, 0.9 \rangle$	1985700	5.0
$\langle 10, 10, 45/45, 0.8 \rangle$	3435984	4.9
$\langle 10, 10, 45/45, 0.9 \rangle$	21834077	6.0

Table 1. Median cycles for the Synchronous Branch and Bound for finding an optimal solution.

We tested both methods on *random binary distributed CSPs*, which are described as $\langle n, m, p_1, p_2 \rangle$. One problem instance was generated by distributing variables and constraints of an instance of *random binary CSPs* with those 4 parameters. We distributed them such that each agent has exactly one variable and constraints relevant to the variable. The parameters of random binary CSPs are: n is the number of variables; m is the number of values for each variable; p_1 is the proportion of variable pairs that are constrained; and p_2 is the proportion of prohibited value pairs between two constrained variables. When generating an instance of random binary CSPs with $\langle n, m, p_1, p_2 \rangle$, we randomly selected $n(n-1)p_1/2$ pairs of variables, and for each variable pair we set up a constraint such that randomly selected $m^2 p_2$ pairs of values are prohibited.

In the experiments, we chose classes of random binary CSPs with $n = m = 10$, p_1 taking values from $\{18/45, 27/45, 36/45, 45/45\}$, and p_2 from $\{0.8, 0.9\}$. These classes of problems are known to be relatively hard ones for Max-CSPs[8]. Accordingly, we believe that they are suitable for the problems used to evaluate the methods.

Both SBB and IDB are implemented on a discrete event simulator that simulates concurrent activities of multiple agents. On the simulator, there exists a virtual agent called *manager*, which maintains a simulated clock and delivers messages among agents. One cycle of computation consists of: the manager gathers all messages issued by agents, increments one time unit (called *cycle*), and sends the messages to corresponding agents; agents then do their local computation and send messages. We evaluate the cost of algorithms in terms of cycles.

6.1 Cost of Finding an Optimal Solution

Since it is guaranteed that SBB finds an optimal solution, we can measure SBB's cost of finding an optimal solution as cycles to be consumed until SBB finds it. In the experiments, we applied SBB to each of 25 instances randomly generated for each class of problem. Note that we used *conjunctive width heuristics*(width/domain-size)[12] for variable ordering and lexical order

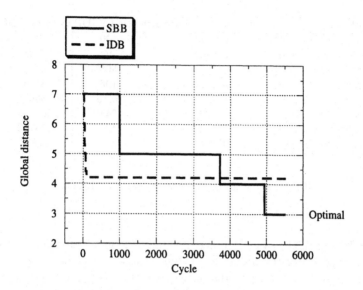

Fig. 5. Anytime curve for an instance of $\langle 10, 10, 27/45, 0.9 \rangle$

for value ordering. Also note that the initial value of $\forall i N_i$ was set to the value of the maximum degree of a constraint graph minus one, and that of $\forall i S_i$ was zero. Table 1 illustrates the median cycle for finding an optimal solution and the mean optimal distance over 25 instances for each class. The cost of finding an optimal solution by SBB clearly seems to be very high.

On the other hand, IDB may fail to get an optimal solution, as stated above, and thus we cannot measure the cost in terms of cycles. However, we conducted an experiment to determine how often IDB fails to get an optimal solution. In this experiment, we ran 10 trials of IDB with randomly chosen initial assignments for each of 25 instances for the class of $n = m = 10, p_1 = 27/45, p_2 = 0.8$ (250 trials in total). Note that the initial values of $\forall i N_i$ and $\forall i S_i$ for IDB are the same as those for SBB. As a result, IDB obtained optimal solutions in 30 trials within the cycle at which SBB found the optimal solutions.

6.2 Anytime Curves

Next we compared IDB with SBB in terms of *anytime curves*. An anytime curve illustrates how the global distance (maximum number of constraint violations over agents) of the best solution found so far is improved as time proceeds. We show an anytime curve for each algorithm on the x-y plane with the x axis being the number of cycles passed by and the y axis being the global distance of the best solution found so far.

The thick line in Fig. 5 shows an anytime curve using SBB for an instance of a class of $n = m = 10, p_1 = 27/45, p_2 = 0.9$. For this instance, SBB finds an optimal solution with the minimum cycles. The dotted line shows an anytime

problem class	nearly-optimal (optimal)	cycle for IDB	cycle for SBB
$\langle 10, 10, 18/45, 0.8 \rangle$	2.2 (1)	100	417
$\langle 10, 10, 18/45, 0.9 \rangle$	3.6 (2)	46	585
$\langle 10, 10, 27/45, 0.8 \rangle$	3.6 (2)	508	2052
$\langle 10, 10, 27/45, 0.9 \rangle$	4.2 (3)	196	3716
$\langle 10, 10, 36/45, 0.8 \rangle$	4.6 (3)	3416	6360
$\langle 10, 10, 36/45, 0.9 \rangle$	6.0 (4)	344	200145
$\langle 10, 10, 45/45, 0.8 \rangle$	5.8 (4)	438	258753
$\langle 10, 10, 45/45, 0.9 \rangle$	7.3 (6)	90	45696

Table 2. Cycles to find nearly-optimal solutions

curve for IDB with the same instance. For IDB, the global distance at a certain cycle is averaged over the results of 10 trials with the same instance.

As shown in Fig. 5, while the curve of SBB eventually converges to the optimal distance, it declines relatively slowly. IDB, on the other hand, has a rapid drop at the beginning, and after that keeps steady at a *nearly optimal distance*. That is not peculiar to this instance but can be seen in other instances of this class or other classes. We conducted the same experiment with other classes and measured the number of cycles IDB consumes to reach a nearly optimal distance. We also measured the number of cycles SBB consumes to outperform the nearly optimal distance. Table 2 shows for each class the measured number of cycles for the nearly optimal distance with the real optimal distance in parentheses. We can see that IDB reaches the nearly optimal distance much sooner than does SBB for all classes.

7 Conclusions

We have presented the distributed partial constraint satisfaction problem as a new framework for dealing with over-constrained distributed CSPs. Since many problems in multi-agent systems can be described as distributed CSPs that are possibly over-constrained, we expect a DPCSP to have great potential in various applications.

We have also presented the synchronous branch and bound and the iterative distributed breakout for solving distributed maximal constraint satisfaction problems, which belong to a very important class of DPCSP. Our experimental results on random binary distributed CSPs show that SBB is preferable when we are concerned with the optimality of a solution, while IDB is preferable when we want to get a nearly optimal solution quickly. Our future work will include developing more efficient algorithms for DMCSPs and applying this framework to more realistic problems.

References

1. A. Borning, B. Freeman-Benson and M. Wilson. Constraint Hierarchies. In *Lisp and Symbolic Computation*, Vol. 5, pp. 223–270, 1992.
2. K. Chandy and L. Lamport. Distributed Snapshots: Determining Global States of Distributed Systems. *ACM Transaction on Computer Systems*, Vol. 3, No. 1, pp. 63–75, 1985.
3. S. E. Conry, K. Kuwabara, V. R. Lesser and R. A. Meyer. Multistage Negotiation for Distributed Constraint Satisfaction. *IEEE Transactions on Systems, Man and Cybernetics*, Vol. 21, No. 6, pp. 1462–1477, 1991.
4. E. C. Freuder. Partial Constraint Satisfaction. In *Proceedings of the Eleventh International Joint Conference on Artificial Intelligence*, pp. 278–283, 1989.
5. E. C. Freuder and R. J. Wallace. Partial Constraint Satisfaction. *Artificial Intelligence*, Vol. 58, No. 1–3, pp. 21–70, 1992.
6. K. Hirayama and J. Toyoda. Forming Coalitions for Breaking Deadlocks. In *Proceedings of First International Conference on Multi-Agent Systems*, pp. 155–162, 1995.
7. M. N. Huhns and D. M. Bridgeland. Multiagent Truth Maintenance. *IEEE Transactions on Systems, Man and Cybernetics*, Vol. 21, No. 6, pp. 1437–1445, 1991.
8. J. Larrosa and P. Meseguer. Phase Transition in MAX-CSP. In *Proceedings of the Twelfth European Conference on Artificial Intelligence*, pp. 190–194, 1996.
9. V. R. Lesser and D. D. Corkill. The Distributed Vehicle Monitoring Testbed: A Tool for Investigating Distributed Problem Solving Networks. *AI Magazine*, Vol. 4, No. 3, pp. 15–33, 1983.
10. P. Morris. The Breakout Method for Escaping from Local Minima. In *Proceedings of the Eleventh National Conference on Artificial Intelligence*, pp. 40–45, 1993.
11. K. P. Sycara, S. Roth, N. Sadeh and M. Fox. Distributed Constrained Heuristic Search. *IEEE Transactions on Systems, Man and Cybernetics*, Vol. 21, No. 6, pp. 1446–1461, 1991.
12. R. J. Wallace and E. C. Freuder. Conjunctive Width Heuristics for Maximal Constraint Satisfaction. In *Proceedings of the Eleventh National Conference on Artificial Intelligence*, pp. 762–768, 1993.
13. M. Yokoo. Constraint Relaxation in Distributed Constraint Satisfaction Problem. In *5th International Conference on Tools with Artificial Intelligence*, pp. 56–63, 1993.
14. M. Yokoo, E. H. Durfee, T. Ishida and K. Kuwabara. Distributed Constraint Satisfaction for Formalizing Distributed Problem Solving. In *Proceedings of the Twelfth IEEE International Conference on Distributed Computing Systems*, pp. 614–621, 1992.
15. M. Yokoo and K. Hirayama. Distributed Breakout Algorithm for Solving Distributed Constraint Satisfaction Problems. In *Proceedings of Second International Conference on Multi-Agent Systems*, pp. 401–408, 1996.

LOCALIZER
A Modeling Language for Local Search

Laurent Michel and Pascal Van Hentenryck

Brown University, Box 1910, Providence, RI 02912 (USA)
Email: {ldm,pvh}@cs.brown.edu

Abstract. Local search is a traditional technique to solve combinatorial search problems which has raised much interest in recent years. The design and implementation of local search algorithms is not an easy task in general and may require considerable experimentation and programming effort. However, contrary to global search, little support is available to assist the design and implementation of local search algorithms. This paper is an attempt to support the implementation of local search. It presents the preliminary design of LOCALIZER, a modeling language which makes it possible to express local search algorithms in a notation close to their informal descriptions in scientific papers. Experimental results on our first implementation show the feasibility of the approach.

1 Introduction

Most combinatorial search problems are solved through global or local search. In global search, a problem is divided into subproblems until the subproblems are simple enough to be solved directly. In local search (LS), an initial configuration is generated and the algorithm moves from the current configuration to a neighborhood configuration until a solution (decision problems) or a good solution (optimization problems) has been found or the resources available are exhausted. The two approaches have complementary strengths, weaknesses, and application areas. The design of global search algorithms is now supported by a variety of tools, ranging from modeling languages such as AMPL [1] and NUMERICA [10] to constraint programming languages such CHIP, ILOG SOLVER, CLP($\Re$), PROLOG-IV, and OZ to name only a few. In contrast, little attention has been devoted to the support of local search (LS), despite the increasing interest in these algorithms in recent years. (Note however there are various efforts to integrate local search in CLP languages, e.g., [9]). The design of LS algorithms is not an easy task however. The same problem can be modeled in many different ways (see for instance [3]), making the design process an inherently experimental enterprise. In addition, efficient implementations of LS algorithms often require maintaining complex data structures incrementally, which is a tedious and error-prone activity.

This paper reports on an attempt to support the design and implementation of LS algorithms. It presents the design of LOCALIZER, a modeling language which makes it possible to describe LS algorithms in a notation close

to the informal presentations of these procedures in scientific papers. LOCAL-
IZER statements are organized around the traditional concepts of LS algorithms
(e.g., neighborhoods, acceptance criteria, and restarting states), they support
the essence of many LS algorithms (e.g., local improvement [6], simulated annealing [4], tabu search [2], and GSAT [8]), and they can be tailored to the
application at hand to exploit its underlying structure. The main technical tool
in LOCALIZER is the concept of *invariant* which relieves users from the need
of maintaining complex data structures incrementally and makes it simpler to
define neighborhoods concisely. As a consequence, LOCALIZER may significantly
simplify the implementation of LS algorithms and supports the design process
by easing and encouraging the experimental work. The practicability of LOCAL-
IZER is demonstrated by some experimental results showing that it compares
well with special-purpose implementations of some LS algorithms.

The main contribution of the paper is to show that local search algorithms can
be supported by very high-level modeling languages which shorten their development time substantially while preserving most of the efficiency of special-purpose
implementations. The paper is a proof of concept: the design of LOCALIZER presented in this paper should not be viewed as a final specification but as a first
step towards supporting local search algorithms. There are several extensions
that are being contemplated, including the support for genetic algorithms (e.g.,
maintaining multiple configurations) and the integration of consistency techniques (e.g., arc-consistency).

The rest of this paper aims at giving readers an informal description of some
of the features of LOCALIZER since space limitations do not allow to cover the full
language in detail. Section 2 is a brief tour of LOCALIZER statements. Sections
3 and 4 illustrate LOCALIZER on two problems: satisfiability (decision problem)
and graph coloring (optimization problem). Section 5 contains the experimental
results and Section 6 concludes the paper.

2   A Brief Tour of LOCALIZER

To understand statements in LOCALIZER, it is best to consider first the underlying computational model. Figure 1 depicts the computational model of LOCAL-
IZER for decision problems. The model captures the essence of most local search
algorithms. The algorithm performs a number of local searches (up to *MaxTries*
and while a global condition is satisfied). Each local search consists of a number
of iterations (up to *MaxIterations* and while a local condition is satisfied). For
each iteration, the algorithm first tests if the state is satisfiable, in which case
a solution has been found. Otherwise, it selects a candidate move in the neighborhood and moves to this new state if this is acceptable. If no solution is found
after *MaxIterations*, the algorithm restarts a new iteration in the state *restart-
State(s)*. The computation model for optimization problems is similar, except
that line 5 needs to update the best solution so far if necessary, e.g. in the case
of a minimization,

```
procedure LOCALIZER
begin
1   s := startState();
2   for i := 1 to MaxTries while Gcondition do
3       for j := 1 to MaxIterations while Lcondition do
4           if satisfiable(s) then
5               return s;
6           select n in neighborhood(s);
7           if acceptable(n) then
8               s := n;
9       s := restartState(s);
    end
```

Fig. 1. The Computation Model of Localizer

```
5           if value(s) < f* then
5.1             f* := value(s);
5.2             best := s;
```

The optimization algorithm of course should initialize f^* properly and return the best solution found at the end of the computation.

```
⟨ Model ⟩ ::= [⟨DataType⟩]
              ⟨Data⟩
              ⟨Variable⟩
              [ ⟨Invariant⟩]
              ⟨Operator⟩
              ⟨Satisfaction⟩
              [ ⟨Objective Function⟩]
              ⟨Neighborhood⟩
              ⟨Start⟩
              [ ⟨Restart⟩]
              [ ⟨Parameter⟩]
              [ ⟨Global Condition⟩]
              [ ⟨Local Condition⟩]
              [ ⟨Init⟩]
```

Fig. 2. The Structure of LOCALIZER Statements

The purpose of a LOCALIZER statement is to specify, for the problem at hand, the instance data, the state, and the generic parts of the computation model (e.g., the neighborhood and the acceptance criterion). A LOCALIZER statement consists of a number of sections as depicted in Figure 2. The instance data is defined by sections **DataType, Data,** and **Init,** using traditional data structures from programming languages. The state is defined as the values of the variables. The neighborhood is defined in the **neighborhood** section, using objects from previous sections. The acceptance criterion is part of the definition of the neighborhood. The initial state is defined in section **Start.** The restarting states are defined in section **Restart,** the parameters (e.g. *MaxIterations*) are given in the **Parameter** section, and the global and local conditions are given in Sections **Global Condition** and **Local Condition.** As mentioned previously, the most original aspects of LOCALIZER are in the specifications of the neighborhood and the acceptance criterion. Of course, some of the notations are reminiscent of languages such as AMPL and Claire at the syntactical level but the underlying concepts are fundamentally different.

Neighborhood The neighborhood in LOCALIZER is defined through basic instructions of the form

> **select [random | best]**
> $op(x_1, \ldots, x_n)$
> **where**
> x_1 **in** S_1;
> $\ldots$
> x_n **in** S_n
> **accept when**
> $\langle$ Acceptance $\rangle$

where *op* is an operator or a sequence of instructions using traditional programming language constructs. In its simplest form, assuming that *s* is the current configuration and *Post(s,i)* represents the configuration obtained by executing *i* in *s*, the instruction defines the neighborhood

$$\{Post(s, op(x_1, \ldots, x_n)) \mid x_1 \in S_1 \& \ldots \& x_n \in S_n\}$$

selects one of its elements, and checks if it satifies the acceptance criterion. When the keyword **best** is present, the instruction selects an element optimizing the value of the objective function and tests it against the acceptance criterion. When the keyword **random** is present, the instruction selects an element of the neighborhood in a random way (which is important in many local search algorithms) and tests it agains the acceptance criterion. The sets in the **select** statements are specified using the syntax:

> $\langle$ Select Set $\rangle$ ::= $\langle$ Set Expr $\rangle$ |
> $\langle$ Set Expr $\rangle$ **minimizing** $\langle$ Expr $\rangle$ |
> $\langle$ Set Expr $\rangle$ **maximizing** $\langle$ Expr $\rangle$

For instance, an instruction of the form

```
select best a[i] := !a[i]
where i in 1..n
accept when ...;
```

may be used to specify the flipping strategy of GSAT, while an instruction of the form

```
select q[i] := v
where
    i in Conflicts;
    v in 1..n minimizing
        sizeof({ j in 1..n | q[j] = v or  q[j] = v + i − j or  q[j] = v + j − i});
accept when ...;
```

is an example of min-conflict heuristics of [5]. The GSAT statement simply states to flip the value of the literal a[i] ($1 \leq i \leq n$) which produces the best improvement in the objective function (keyword **best**). The min-conflict heuristics selects a conflicting variable (e.g., a queen being attacked) and chooses a new value which minimizes the number of conflicts for the variable. Note that best improvement can be easily combined with the min-conflict heuristics simply by adding the keyword **best** after **select**.

Select instructions can also be composed to consider various neighborhoods using the **try** instruction:

```
try
    [Probability:] ⟨ Select Statement ⟩;
    ...
    [Probability:] ⟨ Select Statement ⟩;
end
```

In this case, LOCALIZER considers each **select** statement in sequence until one is successful or all have been considered. The **select** statements can be conditional to a probability in which LOCALIZER considers them with the given probability. The **try** instruction is useful, for instance, to implement the random walk/noise strategy, as implemented in GSAT for instance,

```
try
    0.1:
        select a[i] := !a[i]
        where i in OccurInUnsatClause
        accept when ...;
    default:
        select best a[i] := !a[i]
        where i in 1..n
        accept when ...;
end
```

Here, LOCALIZER flips an arbitrary variable in an unsatisfied clause with a probability of 0.1 and applies the standard strategy with a probability of 0.9. Note that the LOCALIZER simply goes to the next iteration if the selected neighborhood is empty, since other neighborhoods may be non-empty.

Invariants The specification of the set expressions $S_1, \ldots, S_n$ in the select instructions is probably the most interesting part of the neighborhood definitions. These sets are defined in terms of invariants, one of the main concepts of LOCALIZER to simplify the implementation of LS algorithms. Informally speaking, an invariant is an expression of the form $v = exp$ and LOCALIZER guarantees that, at any time during the computation, the value of variable v is the value of the expression exp. Typical examples of invariants are

$$
\begin{array}{l}
v = \textbf{sum}(\; i \; \textbf{in} \; S) \; a[i] \\
C = \{ \; i \; \textbf{in} \; S \mid a[i] = 0 \; \} \\
D[\; i \; \textbf{in} \; I \;] = \{ \; j \; \textbf{in} \; S \mid a[j] = i \; \}.
\end{array}
$$

The first invariant specifies that v is the summation of the $a[i]$ $(i \in S)$, the second invariant specifies that C is the set of i such that $a[i] = 0$, and the last invariant specifies that $D[i]$ $(i \in I)$ is the set of all j in S such that $a[j] = i$. More generally, invariants are specified using expressions using standard arithmetic operators, boolean connectives, aggregate operators such as summation, product, maximum, minimum, and sizeof, conditional expressions, explicit sets, sets defined implicitly using expressions, and set union, intersection, and difference.

LOCALIZER uses efficient incremental algorithms to maintain these invariants during the computation, automating one of the tedious and time-consuming tasks of LS algorithms. For instance, whenever a value $a[k]$ is changed, v, C, and $D[j]$ are updated in constant time in our current implementation.[1] As a consequence, invariants make it possible to specify **what** needs to be maintained incrementally without considering **how** to do so.

Acceptance Statements Once an element of the neighborhood has been selected, LOCALIZER determines if it is an appropriate move. The acceptance statement is built using the syntax

$$
\begin{array}{l}
\langle \text{ Acceptance } \rangle ::= \langle \text{ Criterion } \rangle \; [\rightarrow \langle \text{ Statement } \rangle] \\
\langle \text{ Criterion } \rangle ::= \textbf{always} \mid \\
\qquad \textbf{improvement} \mid \\
\qquad \textbf{noDecrease} \mid \\
\qquad \langle \text{ Expr } \rangle \mid \\
\qquad \langle \text{ Criterion } \rangle \; \textbf{and} \; \langle \text{ Criterion } \rangle \mid \\
\qquad \langle \text{ Criterion } \rangle \; \textbf{or} \; \langle \text{ Criterion } \rangle \mid \\
\qquad \textbf{not} \; \langle \text{ Criterion } \rangle
\end{array}
$$

The main part of the acceptance statement is the acceptance criterion. The optional statement is useful to implement some termination condition and it

---

[1] Of course, other constructs cannot be updated in constant time. A complete description of the algorithms cannot be included for space reasons.

is discussed later on. Keyword **always** accepts all moves, **improvement** accepts a move only if it improves the value of the objective function, and **noDecrease** accepts a move only if it does not degrade the value of the objective function. The acceptance criteria can also be expressed using a Boolean expression involving the objects defined by the invariants. All these basic cases can be combined with Boolean connectives. For instance, a local improvement strategy is specified as

```
        select
            ...
        accept when improvement;
```

while a tabu-search strategy is specified using a statement of the form

```
            select
                ...
            where
                o in S
            accept when
                o notin Tabu
```

Acceptance statements can also be combined using an instruction of the form

```
        try
            [ Probability: ] ⟨ Acceptance ⟩;
                ...
            [ Probability: ] ⟨ Acceptance ⟩;
        end
```

which tries each acceptance criterion in sequence until one has succeeded or all have failed. A criterion may be associated with a probability, in which case LOCALIZER considers the statement with the given probability. To specify the probability easily, LOCALIZER also provides, as a keyword **delta**, the variation of the objective function produced by the move. For instance, a typical simulated annealing procedure uses the acceptance criterion

```
            try
                improvement;
                e^{-delta/t}: always;
            end
```

where t is the temperature. This criterion accepts a move if it improves the value of the objective function or, if not, with a probability $e^{-\mathbf{delta}/t}$.

The acceptance statement makes it possible to associate an action with each acceptance criterion, which is useful to express some termination condition. For instance, to implement a strategy which terminates when the objective function has been stable for a number of iterations, one would write:

```
Neighborhood:
    select
    ...
    accept when
        try
            improvement → nbStableIter := 0;
            noDecrease → nbStableIter++;
        end;
Local Condition:
    nbStableIter ≤ maxStableIter;
```

3 Satisfiability

We now illustrate LOCALIZER on a number of applications. Our first application is satisfiability (SAT) and we illustrate how GSAT [8] can be expressed in LOCALIZER. GSAT illustrates many aspects of LOCALIZER as well as several interesting modeling issues.

Problems in GSAT are described in terms of a number of clauses, each clause consisting of a number of literals. As is traditional, a literal is simply an atom (positive atom) or the negation of an atom (negative atom). The goal is to find an asssignment of Boolean values to the atoms such that all clauses are satisfied, a clause being satisfied if one of its positive atoms is true or one of its negative atoms is false. The basic idea of GSAT is to start from a random assignment of Boolean values and to select the atom which, when its value is inverted, produces a state with the largest number of clauses satisfied. Note that GSAT accepts only moves which do not decrease the number of clauses satisfied.

3.1 A Simple Model of GSAT

Figure 3 depicts a simple model of GSAT.

Instance Representation In the model, atoms are represented by integers from 1 to n and a clause is represented by two sets: its set of positive atoms p and its set of negative atoms n. A SAT problem is simply an array of m clauses. The actual instance is described in the Init section which is not shown.

State Definition The state is specified by the truth values of the atoms and is captured in the array a, where $a[i]$ represents the truth value of atom i.

Neighborhood The neighborhood uses two invariants: the number of true literals for clause i, denoted by $nbtl[i]$, and the number of clauses satisfied, denoted by $nbClauseSat$. $nbtl[i]$ is computed by counting the number of positive atoms and the negation of the negative atoms. $nbClauseSat$ is the number of satisfied clauses. LOCALIZER maintains these invariants incrementally: in particular, each time a variable $a[j]$ is changed, the invariants are recomputed in time linearly proportional to the number of occurrences of j. The neighborhood is then defined by specifying that LOCALIZER must flip the value of the atom which produces a state maximizing the number of clauses satisfied, according to the description of GSAT. The acceptance criterion specifies that the new state should not decrease the number of clauses satisfied.

The satisfiability section specifies that the state is a solution when all clauses are satisfied, which can stated simply in terms of the available data items. The objective function simply maximizes the number of clauses satisfied. The initial state consists of a random assignment of the variables.

It is useful at this point to step back and to look at the simplicity of the model. It is difficult in fact to imagine a more compact definition and invariants clearly play an important role in the model simplicity.

```
                Solve
Data Type:
    clause = record
        p : set of integer;
        n : set of integer;
        end;
Data:
    m: integer = ...;
    n: integer = ...;
    cl: array[1..m] of clause = ...;
Variable:
    a: array[1..n] of Boolean;
Invariant:
    nbtl[ i in 1..m ] = sum(i in cl[i].p) a[j] + sum(j in cl[i].n) !a[j];
    nbClauseSat = sum(i in 1..m) (nbtl[i] > 0);
Satisfiable:
    nbClauseSat = m;
Objective Function:
    maximize nbClauseSat;
Neighborhood:
    select best a[i] := !a[i]
    where i in 1..n
    accept when noDecrease;
Start:
    forall(i in 1..n)
        random(a[i]);
```

Fig. 3. A Simple Model of GSAT

3.2 A More Incremental Model of GSAT

As mentioned previously, the same problem can often be expressed in many different ways. In this section, we study a more incremental version of GSAT which is depicted in Figure 4. The interest of the new model for this paper lies in the illustration of several interesting features, which we now describe.

The simple model is incremental in the computation of the invariants but it does not maintain the set of candidates for flipping incrementally: the candidates are obtained by evaluating the number of clauses satisfied in the new state obtained by flipping each variable. The new model is completely incremental and maintains the set of candidates for flipping at any computation step. This new model is significantly faster than the simple model, while remaining easy to design. Note that LOCALIZER cannot in general deduce such optimizations automatically, given the fact that operators may be arbitrarily complex and that some problems are not amenable easily to such optimizations.

The Model The representation is the same as in the simple model. However, the **Data** section contains two additional sets: $po[i]$ represents the set of clauses in which atom i appears positively, while $no[i]$ represents the set of clauses in which atom i appears negatively.

Neighborhood The invariants are more involved in this model and they maintain incrementally the set of candidates which can be selected for a flip. The informal meanings of the new invariants are the following. $g01[i]$ represents the change in satisfied clauses when changing the value of atom i from false to true, assuming that atom i is currently false. Obviously, the flip produces a gain for all unsatisfied clauses where atom i appears positively. It also produces a loss for all clauses where i appears negatively and is the only atom responsible for the satisfaction of the clause. $g10[i]$ represents the change in satisfied clauses when changing the value of atom i from true to false, assuming that atom i is currently true. It is computed in a way similar to $g01$. $gain[i]$ represents the change in satisfied clauses when changing the value of atom i. It is implemented using a conditional expression in terms of $g01[i]$, $g10[i]$, and the current value of atom i. $maxGain$ is simply the maximum of all gains. Finally, $Candidates$ describes the set of candidates for flipping. It is defined as the set of atoms whose gain is positive and maximal. Once the invariants have been described, the neighborhood is defined by flipping one of the candidates. There is no need to specify an optimization qualifier, since this information is already expressed in the invariants. Note that some invariants in this model involve sets, conditional expressions, and aggregation operators which are maintained incrementally. They clearly illustrate the significant support provided by LOCALIZER. Users can focus on describing the data needed for their application, while LOCALIZER takes care of maintaining these data efficiently.

Adding Weights Reference [7] proposes to handle the special structure of some SAT problems by associating weights to the clauses and updating these weights each time a new local search is initiated. We now show how easy it is to integrate

```
                Solve
Data Type:
    clause = record
        p : set of integer;
        n : set of integer;
        end;
Data:
    m: integer = ...;
    n: integer = ...;
    cl: array[1..m] of clause = ...;
    po: array[ i in 1..n] of set of integer = { c in 1..m | i in cl[c].p };
    no: array[ i in 1..n] of set of integer = { c in 1..m | i in cl[c].n };
Variable:
    a: array[1..n] of Boolean;
Invariant:
    nbtl[ i in 1..m ] = sum(i in cl[i].p) a[j] + sum(j in cl[i].n) !a[j];
    g01[ i in 1..n ] = sum(j in po[i]) (a[j] = 0) - sum(j in no[i]) (a[j] = 1);
    g10[ i in 1..n ] = sum(j in no[i]) (a[j] = 0) - sum(j in po[i]) (a[j] = 1);
    gain[ i in 1..n ] = if a[i] then g10[i] else g01[i];
    maxGain = max(i in 1..n) gain[i];
    Candidates = { i in 1..n | gain[i] = maxGain and gain[i] ≥ 0 };
    nbClauseSat = sum(i in 1..m) (nbtl[i] > 0);
Satisfiable:
    nbClauseSat = m;
Neighborhood:
    select a[i] := !a[i]
    where i in Candidates;
    accept when always;
Start:
    forall(i in 1..n)
        random(a[i]);
```

Fig. 4. A More Incremental Model of GSAT

this feature. The changes consist in introducing weight variables $w[i]$ in the state, in modifying the computations of the invariants for $g01$ and for $g10$ by multiplying the appropriate terms by the weights, i.e.,

```
g01[ i in 1..n ] = sum(j in po[i]) w[j]×(a[j] = 0) - sum(j in no[i]) w[j]×(a[j] = 1);
g10[ i in 1..n ] = sum(j in no[i]) w[j]×(a[j] = 0) - sum(j in po[i]) w[j]×(a[j] = 1);
```

and in updating the weights after each local search by adding a restarting section

```
Restart:
    forall(i in 1..m)
        w[i] := w[i] + (a[i] = 0);
```

The rest of the statement remains exactly the same, showing the ease of modification of LOCALIZER statements.

4 Graph Coloring

This section considers the graph coloring problem, i.e., the problem of finding the smallest number of colors to label a graph such two adjacent vertices have a different color. It shows how a simulated annealing algorithm proposed in [3] can be expressed in LOCALIZER. Of particular interest is once again the close similarity between the problem description and the model. Note that graph coloring could be expressed as an instance of SAT as could any NP-Complete problem. However, it is often desirable to specialize the local search to the problem at hand and LOCALIZER makes it possible to exploit the special structure of each problem.

For a graph with n vertices, the algorithm considers n colors which are the integers between 1 and n. Color class C_i is the set of all vertices colored with i and the bad edges of C_i, denoted by B_i, are the edges whose vertices are both colored with i. The main idea of the algorithm is to minimize the objective function $\sum_{i=1}^{n} 2|B_i||C_i| - |C_i|^2$. This function is interesting since its local minima are valid colorings. To minimize the function, the algorithm chooses a vertex and chooses a color whose color class is non-empty or one of the unused colors. It is important to consider only one of the unused colors to avoid a bias towards unused colors. A move is accepted if it improves the value of the objective function or, if not, with a standard probability of simulated annealing algorithms.

The model is depicted in Figure 5 and it closely follows the above description. The state is given by the variables $v[i]$ which represent the colors of vertices and by the temperature t. The invariants describe the set C_i, B_i, and the objective function. The unused color is obtained by taking the smallest unused color. The set of candidate colors are thus all the "used" colors together with the selected unused color. The total number of bad edges is also maintained to decide satisfiability. The neighborhood is then described in a simple way by choosing a vertex and a candidate color. Acceptance obeys the standard simulated annealing criterion (as was already shown in Section 2) and the temperature is updated in the restarting section. Once again, the design of the model is essentially a direct formalization of the informal statement of the algorithm and the distance between the model and the informal statement is small. The main component of the model is the specification of the data structures which can be done declaratively, without specifying the implementation details.

5 Experimental Results

This section describes some preliminary results on the implementation of LO-CALIZER (about 10,000 lines of C++). The goal is not to report the final word on the implementation but rather to suggest that LOCALIZER can be implemented

```
                    Optimize
Data Type:
    edge = record
        s : integer;
        t : integer;
        end;
Data:
    n: integer = ...;
    E: set of edge = ...;
Variable:
    v : array[1..n] of 1..n;
    t : integer;
Invariant:
    C[i in 1..n] = { j in 1..n | v[j] = i };
    Empty = { i in 1..n | size(C[i]) = 0 };
    unused = minof(Empty);
    Candidates = { i in 1..n | size(C[i]) > 0 or i = unused };
    BadEdges = { e in E | v[e.s] = v[e.t] };
    B[i in 1..n] = { e in BadEdges | v[e.s] = i };
    f = sum(i in 1..n) (2×size(C[i])×size(B[i]) - size(C[i])²)
Satisfiable:
    size(BadEdges) = 0;
Objective Function:
    minimize f;
Neighborhood:
    select v[i] := c
    where
        i in 1..n;
        c in Candidates;
    accept when
        try
            improvement;
            e^delta/t : always;
        end;
Start:
    forall(i in 1..n)
        random(v[i]);
Restart:
    T := factor × T;
    forall(i in 1..n)
        random(v[i]);
```

Fig. 5. A Graph Coloring Model

with an efficiency comparable to specific local search algorithms. To demonstrate practicability, we compare LOCALIZER with GSAT, which is generally recognized as a fast and very well implemented system. The experimental results were carried out as specified in [8]. Table 1 gives the number of variables (V), the number of clauses (C), and MaxIterations (I) for each class of benchmarks as well as the CPU times in seconds of LOCALIZER (L), the CPU times in seconds of GSAT (G) as reported in [8], and the ratio L/G. The times of GSAT are given on a SGI Challenge with a 70 MHz MIPS R4400 processor. The times of LOCALIZER were obtained on a SUN SPARC-10 40MHz and scaled by a factor 1.5 to account for the speed difference between the two machines. LOCALIZER times are for the incremental model presented in Section 3. Note that this comparison is not perfect (e.g., the randomization may be different) but it is sufficient for showing that LOCALIZER can be implemented efficiently.

	V	C	I	L	G	R
1	100	430	500	19.54	6.00	3.26
2	120	516	600	40.73	14.00	2.91
3	140	602	700	54.64	14.00	3.90
4	150	645	1500	154.68	45.00	3.44
5	200	860	2000	873.11	168.00	5.20
6	250	1062	2500	823.06	246.00	3.35
7	300	1275	6000	1173.78	720.00	1.63
Av.						3.38

Table 1. Experimental Results

As can be seen, GSAT is 3.38 times faster than LOCALIZER on the benchmarks and the two systems scale in about the same way. The gap between the two systems is about one machine generation (i.e., on modern workstations, LOCALIZER runs as efficiently as GSAT on machines of three years ago), which is really acceptable given the preliminary nature of our (unoptimized) implementation.

6 Conclusion

The main contribution of this paper is to show that local search can be supported by modeling languages to shorten the development time of these algorithms substantially, while preserving the efficiency of special-purpose algorithms. To validate this claim, we presented the preliminary design of the modeling language LOCALIZER. LOCALIZER statements are organized around the traditional concepts of local search and may exploit the special structure of the problem at hand. The main conceptual tool underlying LOCALIZER is the concept of invariant which make it possible to specify complex data structures declaratively.

These data structures are maintained incrementally by LOCALIZER automating one of the most tedious and error-prone parts of local search algorithms. Preliminary experimental results indicate that LOCALIZER can be implemented to run with an efficiency comparable to specific implementations.

Our current research focuses on building a large collection of applications in LOCALIZER to understand the strengths and limitations of the language, to study how frameworks such as Guided Local Search [11] and dynamic k-opt [6] can be supported, and to identify which extensions are needed to turn our initial design into a practical tool. We are also contemplating extensions of the language to support genetic algorithms (e.g., maintaining multiple configurations) and to integrate consistency techniques to enhance the expressivity of invariants. Longer term research will explore how LOCALIZER can be turned into a programming language library to guarantee extensibility and wide applicability for expert users, while preserving the right level of abstraction.

Acknowledgments This paper is dedicated to the memory of Paris C. Kanellakis who kept on gently pressuring us to pursue this topic. Thanks to D. McAllester and B. Selman for many discussions on this research and to the reviewers and Jean-François Puget for their comments. This research was supported in part by the ONR Grant N00014-94-1-1153 and an NSF NYI Award.

References

1. R. Fourer, D. Gay, and B.W. Kernighan. *AMPL: A Modeling Language for Mathematical Programming*. The Scientific Press, San Francisco, CA, 1993.
2. F. Glover. Tabu Search. *Orsa Journal of Computing*, 1:190–206, 1989.
3. D. Johnson, C. Aragon, L. McGeoch, and C. Schevon. Optimization by Simulated Annealing: An Experimental Evaluation; Part II, Graph Coloring and Number Partitioning. *Operations Research*, 39(3):378–406, 1991.
4. S. Kirkpatrick, C. Gelatt, and M. Vecchi. Optimization by Simulated Annealing. *Science*, 220:671–680, 1983.
5. S. Minton, M.D. Johnston, and A.B. Philips. Solving Large-Scale Constraint Satisfaction and Scheduling Problems using a Heuristic Repair Method. In *AAAI-90*, August 1990.
6. C.H. Papadimitriou and K. Steiglitz. *Combinatorial Optimization: Algorithms and Complexity*. Prentice-Hall, Englewood Cliffs, NJ, 1982.
7. B. Selman and H. Kautz. An Empirical Study of Greedy Local Search for Satisfiability Testing. In *AAAI-93*, pages 46–51, 1993.
8. B. Selman, H. Levesque, and D. Mitchell. A New Method for Solving Hard Satisfiability Problems. In *AAAI-92*, pages 440–446, 1992.
9. P. Stuckey and V. Tam. Models for Using Stochastic Constraint Solvers in Constraint Logic Programming. In *PLILP-96*, Aachen, August 1996.
10. P. Van Hentenryck, L. Michel, and Y. Deville. *Numerica: a Modeling Language for Global Optimization*. The MIT Press, Cambridge, Mass., 1997.
11. C. Voudouris and E. Tsang. Partial Constraint Satisfaction Problems and Guided Local Search. In *PACT-96*, London, April 1996.

Operational Semantics and Confluence of Constraint Propagation Rules

Slim Abdennadher

Computer Science Department, University of Munich
Oettingenstr. 67, 80538 München, Germany
Slim.Abdennadher@informatik.uni-muenchen.de

Abstract. Constraint Handling Rules (CHR) allow one to specify and implement both propagation and simplification for user-defined constraints. Since a propagation rule is applicable again and again, we present in this paper for the first time an operational semantics for CHR that avoids the termination problem with propagation rules.
In previous work [AFM96], a sufficient and necessary condition for the confluence of terminating simplification rules was given inspired by results about conditional term rewriting systems. Confluence ensures that the solver will always compute the same result for a given set of constraints independent of which rules are applied. The confluence of propagation rules was an open problem. This paper shows that we can also give a sufficient and a necessary condition for confluence of terminating CHR programs with propagation rules based on the more refined operational semantics.

1 Introduction

Constraint Logic Programming [vH91, JM94] combines the declarativity of logic programming with the efficiency of constraint solving. As it runs, a constraint-based program successively generates pieces of partial information called constraints. The constraint solver has the task to collect, combine, and simplify them and to detect their inconsistency.

Constraint Handling Rules

Constraint handling rules (CHR) [Frü95] are a high-level language for writing constraint solvers. CHR are basically a committed-choice language consisting of guarded rules with multiple heads. There are two kinds of rules: Simplification rules rewrite constraints to simpler constraints while preserving logical equivalence (e.g. $X \leq Y, Y \leq X \Leftrightarrow X = Y$). Propagation rules add new constraints, which are logically redundant but may cause further simplification (e.g. $X \leq Y, Y \leq Z \Rightarrow X \leq Z$). Repeated application of the rules incrementally solves constraints (e.g. $A \leq B, B \leq C, C \leq A$ leads to $A = B$, $B = C$).
A simplification rule can be understood as a conditional term rewriting rule. Since a propagation rule does not rewrite constraints but adds new ones, conditional term rewriting systems cannot directly express them. Even though

every propagation rule (e.g. $X \leq Y, Y \leq Z \Rightarrow X \leq Z$) can be written as a simplification rule (e.g. $X \leq Y, Y \leq Z \Leftrightarrow X \leq Y, Y \leq Z, X \leq Z$), this is of little use, since such a simplification rule is applicable again and again. A propagation rule needs an "applicability condition" to prevent its reapplication. In implementations, termination of propagation rules is achieved by never applying a rule a second time to the same constraints. In this respect the operational semantics presented in [Frü95] is far from the implementation, since this applicability condition is not considered there (and thus a propagation rule can be applied infinitely many times). In this paper we give a new operational semantics that is more faithful to the actual implementations of CHR by avoiding the trivial nontermination of propagation rules.

Confluence

Typically, more than one rule is applicable to a conjunction of constraints. It is obviously desirable that the result of a computation in a solver will always be the same, semantically and syntactically, no matter which of the applicable rules is applied. This important property of any constraint solver is called confluence. In [AFM96] a decidable, sufficient and necessary syntactic condition for confluence of terminating simplification rules was introduced. This condition adopted and extended the terminology and techniques of conditional term rewriting systems [DOS88]. A straightforward translation of the results in this field was not possible, because the CHR formalism gives rise to phenomena not appearing in term rewriting systems. These phenomena include the existence of global knowledge (the built-in constraint store) and local variables (variables which appear only on the right-hand side of a rule).

The idea of the confluence criterion is to test joinability of finitely many minimal pairs of states (i.e. test whether the states result in the same final state). These so-called critical pairs can be derived from rules with overlapping heads (i.e. having at least a common instance of some head constraint). We then have to show that joinability of these minimal pairs is necessary and sufficient for joinability of arbitrary pairs of states, i.e. that critical pairs can be extended to any context in which two rules can be applied with different results.

Propagation rules are not covered by [AFM96]. An operational formulation of the semantics of the propagation rule turned out to be a bigger problem than it seems at a first glance. There are two conditions constraining this formulation: On the one hand we want to avoid trivial nontermination caused by applying the same propagation rule again and again. On the other hand the calculus defining the operational semantics should be monotonic in order to provide a well-defined system for the user and as a necessary condition for reasoning about confluence. Monotonicity means that if a computation can be executed in a context, then the same computation can be executed in any extension of this context (that contains additional information). In [Meu96] several applicability conditions for propagation rules were proposed and analyzed. The two main ideas for an applicability condition were integrating into the states a memory for all propagations rules together with the corresponding constraints that already fired (memory condition) and a test, whether application of a propagation rule really adds new information to the state (redundancy test). But these applicability conditions failed to meet both requirements formulated above. The redundancy test does not avoid trivial nontermination. The memory condition results in a nonmonotonic calculus because the addition of information to the memory can inhibit the application of some propagation rules.

The study of applicability conditions in connection with confluence is necessary as the following example illustrates (the symbol @ separates the rule name from the rule; see Section 2 for details of the syntax of CHR).

Example 1.1. Consider the following CHR program:

r1 @ p $\Rightarrow$ q.
r2 @ r,q $\Leftrightarrow$ true.
r3 @ r,p,q $\Leftrightarrow$ s.
r4 @ s $\Leftrightarrow$ p,q.

Rule r1 is a propagation rule, while rules r2,r3,r4 are simplification rules. Rule r1 states that the constraint p implies q. Operationally, if we find p in the current state, we add the logical consequence q as redundant constraint. Rule r2 means that the conjunction r,q is logically true. Rule r3 says that the conjunction r,p,q can be simplified to s. Rule r4 simplifies the constraint s into the conjunction p,q.

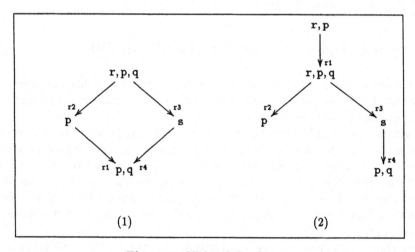

Figure 1. Violated Confluence

The rewriting of r,p,q leads in case (1) (Figure 1) to the same result p,q no matter which rules are applied in which order. In case (2) (Figure 1) the rewriting of r,p,q (which results from the application of r1 to r,p) leads to different results p and p,q since the propagation rule r1 has already been applied to p and thus cannot be reapplied. So confluence is violated.

Contribution of the paper

In this paper we refine the operational semantics presented in [Frü95] including a suitable applicability condition for propagation rules. To avoid the trivial non-termination of such rules our solution is to maintain information about propagation rules that can possibly be applied to a given set of user-defined constraints. This information consists of "tokens", which are a propagation rule and the set of candidate constraints. We integrate into the states a token store, and a propagation rule can only be applied if the token store contains the appropriate token. This token-based control leads to a monotonic operational semantics. In order to take into account the tokens we introduce then a new notion of critical pairs. Finally we give a decidable, sufficient and necessary syntactic condition for confluence of terminating CHR programs with propagation rules.

Organization of the Paper

The next section introduces the syntax of constraint handling rules (CHR) and the refined operational semantics. Section 3 extends the notion of confluence to CHR programs with propagation rules. Finally, we conclude with a summary and directions for future work.

2 Syntax and Operational Semantics of CHR

In this section we give the syntax and a new operational semantics of Constraint Handling Rules. We assume some familiarity with (concurrent) constraint logic programming [JM94, Sar93].

Constraint are considered to be special first-order predicates. We use two disjoint sorts of predicate symbols: *built-in predicates* and *user-defined predicates*. Intuitively, built-in predicates are defined by some constraint theory and handled by an appropriate constraint solver, while user-defined predicates are those defined by a CHR program. We call an atomic formula with a built-in predicate a *built-in constraint* and atomic formula with a user-defined predicate a *user-defined constraint*.

Throughout the paper we expect some constraint theory CT to be given which has the following properties:

- CT is consistent.
- CT does not contain any user-defined predicates.
- CT defines among other built-in predicates equality ("$\doteq$") as syntactic equality using for example Clark's axiomatization.

2.1 Syntax of CHR

Definition 2.1. A CHR *program* is a finite set of rules. There are two basic kinds of rules.[1] A *simplification rule* is of the form

$$Rulename @ H_1, \ldots, H_i \Leftrightarrow G_1, \ldots, G_j \mid B_1, \ldots, B_k.$$

A *propagation rule* is of the form

$$Rulename @ H_1, \ldots, H_i \Rightarrow G_1, \ldots, G_j \mid B_1, \ldots, B_k,$$

where *Rulename* is a unique identifier of a rule, the head $H_1, \ldots, H_i$ is a non-empty conjunction[2] of user-defined constraints, the guard $G_1, \ldots, G_j$ is a conjunction of built-in constraints and the body $B_1, \ldots, B_k$ is a conjunction of built-in and user-defined constraints. Conjunctions of constraints as in the body are called *goals*. If the guard is empty, the symbol $\mid$ is omitted.

2.2 Operational Semantics of CHR

We define the operational semantics of a given CHR program P as a transition system that models the operations of the constraint solver defined by P.

States

Definition 2.2. A *state* is a tuple

$$<Gs, C_U, C_B, \mathcal{T}, \mathcal{V}>.$$

Gs is a conjunction of user-defined and built-in constraints called *goal store*. C_U is a conjunction of user-defined constraints, likewise C_B is a conjunction of built-in constraints. C_U and C_B are called *user-defined and built-in (constraint) store*, respectively. $\mathcal{T}$ is a set of tokens (token store) of the form $R@C$, where C is a conjunction of user-defined constraints and R a rulename. $\mathcal{V}$ is an ordered sequence of variables. An empty goal store or user-defined store is represented by $\top$. The built-in store cannot be empty. In its most simple form it consists only of *true* or *false*.

Intuitively, Gs contains the constraints that remain to be solved, C_B and C_U are the built-in and the user-defined constraints, respectively, accumulated and simplified so far and $\mathcal{T}$ contains information about the propagation rules with the respective constraints which they can be possibly applied on.

---

[1] There is a third hybrid kind of rule called simpagation rule [BFL+94]. Since simpagation rules are abbreviations for simplification rules there is no need to discuss them in this paper.

[2] For conjunction in rules we use the symbol "," instead of "∧".

Definition 2.3. A variable X in a state $<Gs, C_U, C_B, \mathcal{T}, \mathcal{V}>$ is called

- *global*, if X appears in $\mathcal{V}$.
- *local*, if X does not appear in $\mathcal{V}$.
- *strictly local*, if X appears in C_B only.

Definition 2.4. The *logical reading* of a state $<Gs, C_U, C_B, \mathcal{T}, \mathcal{V}>$ is the formula

$$\exists \bar{y} \ Gs \wedge C_U \wedge C_B,$$

where $\bar{y}$ are the local variables of the state. Note that the global variables remain free in the formula.

Token store

A propagation rule needs an applicability condition to avoid trivial nontermination. Our approach stores information about propagation rules which can be possibly applied to a given set of user-defined constraints. Once a propagation rule has been applied to user-defined constraints, the appropriate token is removed (**Propagate**) so that the rule cannot be reapplied again to the same constraints.

The token store of a state contains rulenames together with the corresponding conjunctions of user-defined constraints that unify with the heads of the respective propagation rules. The updating of the token store by introducing user-defined constraints depends on the introduced constraints and the current user-defined store (**Introduce**).

This dependency is manifested in the multiset $T_{(C, C_U)}$ of tokens, which computes the new possibilities for apply propagation rules involving the new constraint C:

Definition 2.5. Let P be a CHR program and C a user-defined constraint.

$$T_{(C, C_U)} := \{R@H' \mid (R \ @ \ H \Rightarrow G \mid B) \in P, H' \text{ is a subconjunction of } C \wedge C_U,$$
$$C \text{ is a conjunct of } H', \text{ and } H' \text{ unifies with } H\}$$

is the *tokenset* of C with respect to C_U.
If C is a conjunction of constraints $C_1, \ldots, C_n$ then

$$T_{(C, C_U)} := T_{(C_1, C_U)} \cup T_{(C_2, C_1 \wedge C_U)} \cup \ldots \cup T_{(C_n, C_1 \wedge \ldots \wedge C_{n-1} \wedge C_U)}$$

Subconjunctions can be defined in the natural way similar to subsets:

Definition 2.6. Let $C = \bigwedge_{i=1}^{n} C_i$ be a conjunction of constraints, π a permutation on $[1, \ldots, n]$, and $m \leq n$, then $\bigwedge_{i=1}^{m} C_{\pi_k}$ is a subconjunction of C.

A Normal Form for States

We will assume that states are in a unique normal form that abstracts away the specifics of the built-in constraint solver: The normal form considers those states equivalent that impose the same built-in constraints and the same token store on the goal and on the user-defined constraint store. We model the normalization with a function that maps equivalent states into a syntactically unique representative state (up to variable renaming and order of conjuncts). The normalization function simplifies the built-in constraint store, projects out strictly local variables, propagates implied equations all over the state and deletes superfluous tokens from the token store. Most constraint solvers naturally support this functionality since they work with normal forms anyway. For the following theorems it is important to make the requirements on the normalization function more precise. The first three points of the definition of the normalization function $\mathcal{N}$ is a formalization of the update operation presented in [AFM96].

Definition 2.7. A function $\mathcal{N} : \mathcal{S} \to \mathcal{S}$, where $\mathcal{S}$ is the set of all states, is a *normalization function*, if it fulfills the following conditions:
Let $\mathcal{N}(<Gs, C_U, C_B, T, \mathcal{V}>) = <Gs', C'_U, C'_B, T', \mathcal{V}>$. We assume that there is a fixed order on all variables appearing in a state such that global variables are ordered as in $\mathcal{V}$ and precede all local variables.

1. *Equality propagation:* Gs', C'_U and $\mathcal{V}'$ derive from Gs, C_U and $\mathcal{V}$ by replacing all variables X, for which $CT \models \forall\, (C_B \to X \dot{=} t)$ holds,[3] by the corresponding term t, except if t is a variable that comes after X in the variable order.
2. *Projection:* The following must hold:
$$CT \models \forall\, ((\exists \bar{x} C_B) \leftrightarrow C'_B),$$
   where $\bar{x}$ are the strictly local variables of $<Gs', C'_U, C_B, T', \mathcal{V}>$.
3. *Uniqueness:* If
$$\mathcal{N}(<Gs_1, C_{U1}, C_{B1}, T_1, \mathcal{V}>) = <Gs'_1, C'_{U1}, C'_{B1}, T'_1, \mathcal{V}> \text{ and}$$
$$\mathcal{N}(<Gs_2, C_{U2}, C_{B2}, T_2, \mathcal{V}>) = <Gs'_2, C'_{U2}, C'_{B2}, T'_2, \mathcal{V}> \text{ and}$$
$$CT \models (\exists \bar{x} C_{B1}) \leftrightarrow (\exists \bar{y} C_{B2})$$
   holds, where $\bar{x}$ and $\bar{y}$, respectively, are the strictly local variables of the two states, then:
$$C'_{B1} = C'_{B2}.$$
4. *Token elimination:* $T' = T \cap T_{(C_U, T)}$

The uniqueness property of $\mathcal{N}$ guarantees that there is exactly one representation for each set of equivalent built-in constraint stores. Therefore we can assume that an inconsistent built-in store is represented by the constraint *false*.

An important property of $\mathcal{N}$ is that it preserves the logical reading of states:

---

[3] $\forall F$ is the universal closure of a formula F.

Lemma 2.8. Let be

$$\mathcal{N}(<Gs, C_U, C_B, T, V>) = <Gs', C'_U, C'_B, T', V>.$$

Then the following equivalence holds

$$CT \models \forall \ (\exists \bar{x}(Gs \wedge C_U \wedge C_B) \leftrightarrow \exists \bar{x}'(Gs' \wedge C'_U \wedge C'_B)),$$

where $\bar{x}$ and $\bar{x}'$ are the local variables in S and S', respectively.

Computation Steps

Given a CHR program P we define the transition relation $\mapsto$ by introducing four kinds of *computation steps*. The aim of the computation is to incrementally reduce arbitrary states to states that contain no goals and, if possible, the simplest form of user-defined constraints.

Notation: Capital letters denote conjunctions of constraints. By equating two constraints, $c(t_1, \ldots, t_n) \doteq c(s_1, \ldots, s_n)$, we mean $t_1 \doteq s_1 \wedge \ldots \wedge t_n \doteq s_n$. By $(p_1 \wedge \ldots \wedge p_n) \doteq (q_1 \wedge \ldots \wedge q_n)$ we mean $p_1 \doteq q_1 \wedge \ldots \wedge p_n \doteq q_n$. Note that conjuncts can be permuted since conjunction is associative and commutative, and that we will identify all states containing the built-in store *false*.

Solve
$$\frac{C \text{ is a built-in constraint}}{<C \wedge Gs, C_U, C_B, T, V> \mapsto \mathcal{N}(<Gs, C_U, C \wedge C_B, T, V>)}$$

Introduce
$$\frac{C \text{ is a user-defined constraint}}{<C \wedge Gs, C_U, C_B, T, V> \mapsto \mathcal{N}(<Gs, C \wedge C_U, C_B, T \cup T_{(C,C_U)}, V>)}$$

Simplify
$$\frac{(H \Leftrightarrow G \mid B) \text{ is a fresh variant of a rule in } P \text{ with the variables } \bar{x}}{CT \models C_B \rightarrow \exists \bar{x}(H \doteq H' \wedge G)}$$
$$\overline{<Gs, H' \wedge C_U, C_B, T, V> \mapsto \mathcal{N}(<Gs \wedge B, C_U, H \doteq H' \wedge C_B, T, V>)}$$

Propagate
$$\frac{(R@H \Rightarrow G \mid B) \text{ is a fresh variant of a rule in } P \text{ with the variables } \bar{x}}{CT \models C_B \rightarrow \exists \bar{x}(H \doteq H' \wedge G)}$$
$$\overline{<Gs, H' \wedge C_U, C_B, \{R@H'\} \cup T, V> \mapsto \mathcal{N}(<Gs \wedge B, H' \wedge C_U, H \doteq H' \wedge C_B, T, V>)}$$

Figure 2. Computation Steps

In the **Solve** computation step, the built-in solver normalizes the resulting state after moving a constraint C from the goal store to the built-in store. **Introduce** transports a user-defined constraint C from the goal store into the user-defined constraint store and adds the tokenset of C with respect to C_U, $T_{(C,C_U)}$ (i.e. information about the propagation rules that can fire after adding a new constraint to the user-defined store), to the token store, and finally normalizes the resulting state. To **Simplify** user-defined constraints H' means to replace them by the body B of a fresh variant[4] of a simplification rule $(H \Leftrightarrow G \mid B)$ from the program, provided H' matches[5] the head H and the resulting guard G is implied by the built-in constraint store, and finally to normalize the resulting state. To **Propagate** user-defined constraints H' means to add B to the goal store Gs and remove the token $R@H$ from the token store if H' matches the head H of a propagation rule $(H \Rightarrow G \mid B)$ in the program and the resulting guard G is implied by the built-in constraint store, and finally to normalize the resulting state.

Lemma 2.9. Normalization has no influence on application of rules, i.e.

$$S \mapsto S' \text{ holds iff } \mathcal{N}(S) \mapsto S'.$$

This claim is shown by analyzing each kind of computation step.

Definition 2.10. $S \mapsto^* S'$ holds iff

$$S = S' \text{ or } S' = \mathcal{N}(S) \text{ or } S \mapsto S_1 \mapsto \ldots \mapsto S_n \mapsto S' \quad (n \geq 0).$$

Definition 2.11. An *initial state* for a goal Gs is of the form:

$$<Gs, \top, \text{true}, \emptyset, \mathcal{V}>,$$

where $\mathcal{V}$ is the sequence of the variables occuring in Gs.
A *final state* is either of the form

$$<Gs, C_U, \text{false}, \mathcal{T}, \mathcal{V}>$$

(such a state is called *failed*) or of the form

$$<\top, C_U, C_B, \mathcal{T}, \mathcal{V}>.$$

with no computation step possible anymore and C_B not *false* (such a state is called *successful*).

Example 2.12. We define a user-defined constraint for less-than-or-equal, $\leq$, that can handle variable arguments:

```
r1 @ X≤X  ⇔  true.
r2 @ X≤Y, Y≤X ⇔ X=Y.
r3 @ X≤Y, Y≤Z ⇒ X≤Z.
r4 @ X≤Y, X≤Y ⇔ X≤Y.
```

---

[4] Two expressions are variants if they can be obtained from each other by a variable renaming. A fresh variant contains only variables that do not occur in the state.

[5] Matching rather than unification is the effect of the existential quantification over the head equalities: $\exists \bar{x}(H \doteq H')$.

The CHR program implements reflexivity (**r1**), antisymmetry (**r2**), transitivity (**r3**) and idempotence (**r4**) in a straightforward way. The reflexivity rule **r1** states that $X \leq X$ is logically true. Hence, whenever we see the constraint $X \leq X$ we can simplify it to **true**. The antisymmetry rule **r2** means that if we find $X \leq Y$ as well as $Y \leq X$ in the current store, we can replace them by the logically equivalent $X = Y$. The transitivity rule **r3** propagates constraints. It states that the conjunction $X \leq Y$, $Y \leq Z$ implies $X \leq Z$. Operationally, we add the logical consequence $X \leq Z$ as a redundant constraint. The idempotence rule **r4** absorbs multiple occurrences of the same constraint.

A computation of the goal $A \leq B \wedge C \leq A \wedge B \leq C$ proceeds as follows (Note that $\mathcal{V} = [A, B, C]^6$):

$$<\underline{A \leq B} \wedge C \leq A \wedge B \leq C, \top, \text{true}, \emptyset, \mathcal{V}>$$

$\mapsto$ (**Introduce**) $\quad <\underline{C \leq A} \wedge B \leq C, A \leq B, \text{true}, \emptyset, \mathcal{V}>$

$\mapsto$ (**Introduce**) $\quad <\underline{B \leq C}, A \leq B \wedge C \leq A, \text{true}, \mathcal{T}_1, \mathcal{V}>$
$$\mathcal{T}_1 = \{\text{r3@} C \leq A \wedge A \leq B\}$$

$\mapsto$ (**Introduce**) $\quad <\top, A \leq B \wedge C \leq A \wedge B \leq C, \text{true}, \mathcal{T}_2, \mathcal{V}>$
$$\mathcal{T}_2 = \mathcal{T}_1 \cup \{\text{r3@} A \leq B \wedge B \leq C, \text{r3@} B \leq C \wedge C \leq A\}$$

$\mapsto$ (**Propagate** with **r3**) $<\underline{C \leq B}, A \leq B \wedge C \leq A \wedge B \leq C, \text{true}, \mathcal{T}_3, \mathcal{V}>$
$$\mathcal{T}_3 = \{\text{r3@} A \leq B \wedge B \leq C, \text{r3@} B \leq C \wedge C \leq A\}$$

$\mapsto$ (**Introduce**) $\quad <\top, A \leq B \wedge C \leq A \wedge B \leq C \wedge \underline{C \leq B}, \text{true}, \mathcal{T}_4, \mathcal{V}>$
$$\mathcal{T}_4 = \mathcal{T}_3 \cup \{\text{r3@} C \leq B \wedge B \leq C, \text{r3@} B \leq C \wedge C \leq B\}$$

$\mapsto$ (**Simplify** with **r2**) $<\underline{B = C}, A \leq B \wedge C \leq A, \text{true}, \mathcal{T}_5, \mathcal{V}>$
$$\mathcal{T}_5 = \{\text{r3@} C \leq A \wedge A \leq B\}$$

$\mapsto$ (**Solve**) $\quad <\top, \underline{A \leq B} \wedge B \leq A, B = C, \mathcal{T}_6, \mathcal{V}>$
$$\mathcal{T}_6 = \{\text{r3@} B \leq A \wedge A \leq B\}$$

$\mapsto$ (**Simplify** with **r2**) $<\underline{A = B}, \top, B = C, \emptyset, \mathcal{V}>$

$\mapsto$ (**Solve**) $\quad <\top, \top, A = B \wedge B = C, \emptyset, \mathcal{V}>$

Note that, since the application of **Simplify** removes constraints from the user-defined store, $\mathcal{N}$ reduces the set of tokens accordingly.

3 Confluence of CHR programs

We adopt and extend the terminology and techniques of conditional term rewriting systems [DOS88]. A straightforward translation of the results in this field was not possible, because the CHR formalism gives rise to phenomena not appearing in term rewriting systems. Similar to contextual rewriting [ZR85], CHR programs are more powerful than the classical conditional rewriting because they use an additional context. On the one hand the entailment test requires knowledge of the current state of the built-in store. On the other hand the application of a propagation rule requires knowledge of the current state of the token store. Confluence guarantees that any computation starting from an arbitrary given initial state results in the same final state. We first define what it means that two computations have the same result.

---

[6] In the following the square brackets [ ] denote a sequence.

Definition 3.1. Two states S_1 and S_2 are called *joinable* if there exist states S_1', S_2' such that $S_1 \mapsto^* S_1'$ and $S_2 \mapsto^* S_2'$ and S_1' and S_2' are variants.

Definition 3.2. A CHR program is called *confluent* if the following holds for all states S, S_1, S_2:

$$\text{If } S \mapsto^* S_1, S \mapsto^* S_2 \text{ then } S_1 \text{ and } S_2 \text{ are joinable.}$$

Definition 3.3. A CHR program is called *locally confluent* if the following holds for all states S, S_1, S_2:

$$\text{If } S \mapsto S_1, S \mapsto S_2 \text{ then } S_1 \text{ and } S_2 \text{ are joinable.}$$

The joinability of all state pairs derived from a common direct ancestor state can not be checked to analyze the local confluence of a given CHR program due to the existence of infinitely such states. However, it is possible to construct a finite number of minimal states where more than one rule is applicable. A direct common ancestor state consists of the heads and guards of the rules. It is obvious that there is only a finite number of such states for a given program. These states can be extended to any context, i.e. to all possible ancestor states by adding constraints and tokens to the components of the state.

We now further restrict to nontrivial direct common ancestor states: Joinability can only be destroyed if one rule inhibits the application of the other rule. The application of a rule may remove constraints from the user-defined store and introduce new constraints. Only the removal of constraints can affect the applicability of another rule, in case the removed constraint is needed by the other rule. To possibly inhibit each other, one rule must be a simplification rule and the two rules must overlap, i.e. have at least one head atom in common in the ancestor state. The pair of states resulting from this overlap is called *critical pair*.

Definition 3.4. Let R be a rule.

$$\text{survive}(R) := \begin{cases} \text{true} & \text{, if } R \text{ is a simplification rule} \\ H_1 \wedge \ldots \wedge H_n, & \text{if } R \text{ is a propagation rule with head } H_1, \ldots, H_n \end{cases}$$

survive(R) computes the conjunction of those constraints from the head of a rule R that will not be deleted from the constraint store by the application of R.

Definition 3.5. Let R be a rule with guard G, body B and head H and let R' be a rule with guard G', body B' and head H'. R and R' are simplification rules or a simplification rule and a propagation one. Let $\{H_i \,|\, 1 \le i \le n\}$ and $\{H_i' \,|\, 1 \le i \le m\}$ be the set of atoms H and H' respectively, then the triple

$$\left(\begin{array}{c} G \wedge G' \wedge H_{i_1} \dot{=} H_{j_1}' \wedge \ldots \wedge H_{i_k} \dot{=} H_{j_k}', \\ (B, \text{survive}(R) \wedge H_{j_{k+1}}' \wedge \ldots \wedge H_{j_m}') =\!\downarrow\!= (B', \text{survive}(R') \wedge H_{i_{k+1}} \wedge \ldots \wedge H_{i_n}), \\ \nu \end{array} \right)$$

is called a *critical pair* of the two rules R and R'. $\{i_1, \ldots, i_n\}$ and $\{j_1, \ldots, j_m\}$ are permutations of $\{1, \ldots, n\}$ and $\{1, \ldots, m\}$, respectively and $1 \leq k \leq \min(n, m)$. $\mathcal{V}$ is the set of variables appearing in $H_1, \ldots, H_n, H'_1, \ldots, H'_m$.

Example 3.6. Consider the program for $\leq$ of Example 2.12. The following critical pair stems from unifying the first atom of the head of the antisymmetry rule (r2) with the first atom of the head of the transitivity rule (r3):

$$(\text{true} \quad , \quad (\text{X} \leq \text{Z}, \text{X} \leq \text{Y} \wedge \text{Y} \leq \text{Z} \wedge \text{Y} \leq \text{X}) = \downarrow = (\text{X=Y}, \text{Y} \leq \text{Z}) \quad , \quad [\text{X}, \text{Y}, \text{Z}])$$

Critical pairs represent minimal pairs of states resulting from an overlap. Since critical pairs are minimal, the token store of the states must also be minimal. Two rules can only be applied to the overlap if the user-defined store contains the appropriate user-defined constraints and the token store contains the appropriate token, in case the applied rule is a propagation rule. After applying the rules to the overlap the user-defined stores of the resulting states contain the remaining user-defined constraints, the goal stores will be extended with the constraints coming from the body of the rules, and the appropriate token is removed from the token stores either by the transition **Propagate** or by the normalization function $\mathcal{N}$, in case the applied rule is a simplification rule (i.e., the removed constraints occur in the appropriate token).

Definition 3.7. A critical pair $(G, (B_1, H_1) = \downarrow = (B_2, H_2), \mathcal{V})$ is called *joinable* if $<B_1, H_1, G, \emptyset, \mathcal{V}>$ and $<B_2, H_2, G, \emptyset, \mathcal{V}>$ are joinable.

The choice of the token stores of the states represented by the critical pair is motivated by the minimality criterion for these states: it covers the case that all propagation rules (except possibly one) have already been applied to the constraints of the user-defined store before the direct ancestor state was reached.

Example 3.8. The critical pair in Example 3.6 is joinable. A computation sequence beginning with $<\text{X} \leq \text{Z}, \text{X} \leq \text{Y} \wedge \text{Y} \leq \text{Z} \wedge \text{Y} \leq \text{X}, \text{true}, \emptyset, \mathcal{V}>$, where $\mathcal{V} = [\text{X}, \text{Y}, \text{Z}]$ proceeds as follows:

$$<\underline{\text{X} \leq \text{Z}}, \text{X} \leq \text{Y} \wedge \text{Y} \leq \text{Z} \wedge \text{Y} \leq \text{X}, \text{true}, \emptyset, \mathcal{V}>$$

$\mapsto$ (**Introduce**) $\quad <\top, \text{X} \leq \text{Z} \wedge \underline{\text{X} \leq \text{Y}} \wedge \text{Y} \leq \text{Z} \wedge \underline{\text{Y} \leq \text{X}}, \text{true}, T, \mathcal{V}>$
$\qquad\qquad\qquad T = \{\text{r3@Y} \leq \text{X} \wedge \text{X} \leq \text{Z}\}$
$\mapsto$ (**Simplify** with r2) $<\underline{\text{X} = \text{Y}}, \text{X} \leq \text{Z} \wedge \text{Y} \leq \text{Z}, \text{true}, \emptyset, \mathcal{V}>$
$\mapsto$ (**Solve**) $\qquad\qquad <\top, \underline{\text{X} \leq \text{Z}} \wedge \underline{\text{X} \leq \text{Z}}, \text{X} = \text{Y}, \emptyset, \mathcal{V}>$
$\mapsto$ (**Simplify** with r4) $<\top, \text{X} \leq \text{Z}, \text{X} = \text{Y}, \emptyset, \mathcal{V}>$

A computation sequence beginning with $<\text{X} = \text{Y}, \text{Y} \leq \text{Z}, \text{true}, \emptyset, \mathcal{V}>$ results in the same final state:

$$<\underline{\text{X} = \text{Y}}, \text{Y} \leq \text{Z}, \text{true}, \emptyset, \mathcal{V}>$$
$\mapsto$ (**Solve**) $<\top, \text{X} \leq \text{Z}, \text{X} = \text{Y}, \emptyset, \mathcal{V}>$

With this new notion of critical pairs we are now in a position to give a sufficient and necessary condition for local confluence. The idea of this criterion is to test joinability of the critical pairs. We then have to show that joinability of these minimal pairs is necessary and sufficient for joinability of arbitrary pairs of states with a common direct ancestor, i.e. that critical pairs can be extended to any context. The proof for the following theorem can be found in [Abd97]. The proof is an extension and simplification of the one presented in [AFM96] taking into account the propagation rules and their tokens.

Theorem 3.9. A CHR program is locally confluent iff all its critical pairs are joinable.

Proof. (Idea) *The if-direction:* Assume that we are in state S where there are two or more possibilities of computation:

$$S \mapsto S_1 \text{ and } S \mapsto S_2.$$

We investigate all pairs of possible computation steps and show that S_1 and S_2 are joinable. There are ten relevant combinations:

1. **Solve + Solve**
2. **Solve + Introduce**
3. **Solve + Simplify**
4. **Solve + Propagate**
5. **Introduce + Introduce**
6. **Introduce + Simplify**
7. **Introduce + Propagate**
8. **Simplify + Simplify**
9. **Simplify + Propagate**
10. **Propagate + Propagate**

According to the assumption that logical consequence is monotonous and that the constraint theory preserves commutativity of the conjunction, 1-7 are easily shown. The cases 8 and 9 are the main part of the proof: Similar to conditional term rewriting systems [DOS88] we distinguish two situations: Disjoint Peaks (i.e., no constraint of the head of the rule unifies with a constraint of the head of the other rule) and Critical Peaks (i.e., at least one constraint of the head of the rule unifies with a constraint of the head of the other rule). The first situation is trivial. For the proof of the second situation the assumption that all critical pairs are joinable is needed. We show that critical pairs can be extended to S_1 and S_2 without losing joinability. Case 10 is also easily shown, since the application of two propagation rules onto a state requires that the token store of this state contains the appropriate tokens and that after application of **Propagate** only one token will be removed.

The only-if-direction: We assume that we have a locally confluent CHR program with a critical pair, which is not joinable. We lead this assumption to a contradiction. We distinguish two different cases: The non-joinable critical pair either stems from two simplification rules or stems from a simplification rule and a propagation rule. We construct a state, on which the application of the rules leads to the states represented by the non-joinable critical pair. Since the program is locally confluent the states must be joinable. This leads to a contradiction.

Definition 3.10. A CHR program is called *terminating*, if there are no infinite computations.

The following corollary is an immediate consequence of Theorem 3.9 and Newman's lemma [New42]:

Corollary 3.11. A terminating CHR program is confluent iff its critical pairs are joinable.

The Corollary 3.11 gives a decidable characterization of confluent terminating CHR programs: Joinability of a given critical pair is decidable for a terminating CHR program (i.e. finite computations) and there are only finitely many critical pairs.

The CHR program presented in Example 1.1 is not confluent. We show now, how our token-based approach can detect the non-confluence.

Example 3.12. We consider one of the critical pairs stemming from the rules r2 and r3 of Example 1.1:

The critical pair $(\mathbf{true}$, $(\mathbf{true},\mathbf{p})=\downarrow=(\mathbf{s},\top)$, $\square)$ is not joinable, because computation sequences beginning with the states $<\mathbf{true},\mathbf{p},\mathbf{true},\emptyset,\emptyset>$ and $<\mathbf{s},\top,\mathbf{true},\emptyset,\emptyset>$ do not result in the same final state:

$$<\underline{\mathbf{true}},\mathbf{p},\mathbf{true},\emptyset,\emptyset>$$
$$\mapsto (\mathbf{Solve}) <\top,\mathbf{p},\mathbf{true},\emptyset,\emptyset>$$

All computation sequences beginning with $<\mathbf{s},\top,\mathbf{true},\emptyset,\emptyset>$ will result in the same state even if they differ in the order of application of computation steps:

	$<\underline{\mathbf{s}},\top,\mathbf{true},\emptyset,\emptyset>$
$\mapsto$ (**Introduce**)	$<\top,\underline{\mathbf{s}},\mathbf{true},\emptyset,\emptyset>$
$\mapsto$ (**Simplify** with r4)	$<\mathbf{p}\wedge\mathbf{q},\top,\mathbf{true},\emptyset,\emptyset>$
$\mapsto$ (**Introduce**)	$<\underline{\mathbf{q}},\mathbf{p},\mathbf{true},\{\mathrm{r1@p}\},\emptyset>$
$\mapsto$ (**Introduce**)	$<\overline{\top},\underline{\mathbf{p}}\wedge\mathbf{q},\mathbf{true},\{\mathrm{r1@p}\},\emptyset>$
$\mapsto$ (**Propagate** with r1)	$<\underline{\mathbf{q}},\mathbf{p}\wedge\mathbf{q},\mathbf{true},\emptyset,\emptyset>$
$\mapsto$ (**Introduce**)	$<\overline{\top},\mathbf{p}\wedge\mathbf{q}\wedge\mathbf{q},\mathbf{true},\emptyset,\emptyset>$

4 Conclusion and Future Work

In this paper, we have presented for the first time a refined operational semantics for Constraint Handling Rules that is more faithful to their actual implementations. This operational semantics avoids the trivial nontermination of the propagation rules. Our approach was to maintain information about propagation rules that can possibly be applied to a given set of user-defined constraints in the form of tokens. A propagation rule can only be applied if the token store contains the appropriate token.

We solved the open problem of a confluence test for CHR programs with propagation rules by extending the notion of critical pairs taking into account the token-based control and giving a decidable, sufficient and necessary condition for confluence through joinability of critical pairs (extending the results of [AFM96]). Interesting directions for future work include

- investigation of so-called completion methods to make a non-confluent CHR program confluent and
- determination of sufficient conditions guaranteeing that the combination of confluent constraint solvers is confluent as well.

Acknowledgements

I would like to thank Thom Frühwirth, Holger Meuss and Norbert Eisinger for useful comments on a preliminary version of this paper.

References

Abd97. S. Abdennadher. Rewriting concepts in the study of confluence of constraint handling rules. Technical report PMS-FB-1997-15, Institute of Computer Science, Ludwig–Maximilians–University Munich, January 1997.

AFM96. S. Abdennadher, T. Frühwirth, and H. Meuss. On confluence of constraint handling rules. In E. Freuder, editor, *Proceedings of the Second International Conference on Principles and Practice of Constraint Programming, CP'96*, LNCS 1118. Springer, August 1996.

BFL+94. P. Brisset, T. Frühwirth, P. Lim, M. Meier, T. Le Provost, J. Schimpf, and M. Wallace. *ECL'PS° 3.4 Extensions User Manual*. ECRC Munich Germany, July 1994.

DOS88. N. Dershowitz, N. Okada, and G. Sivakumar. Confluence of conditional rewrite systems. In J.-P. Jouannaud and S. Kaplan, editors, *Proceedings of the 1st International Workshop on Conditional Term Rewriting Systems*, LNCS 308, pages 31–44, 1988.

Frü95. T. Frühwirth. Constraint handling rules. In A. Podelski, editor, *Constraint Programming: Basics and Trends*, LNCS 910. Springer, 1995.

JM94. J. Jaffar and M. J. Maher. Constraint logic programming: A survey. *Journal of Logic Programming*, 20:503–581, 1994.

Meu96. Holger Meuss. Konfluenz von Constraint-Handling-Rules-Programmen. Master's thesis, Institut für Informatik, Ludwig–Maximilians–Universität München, 1996.

New42. M. H. A. Newman. On theories with a combinatorial definition of equivalence. In *Annals of Math*, volume 43, pages 223–243, 1942.

Sar93. V.A. Saraswat. *Concurrent Constraint Programming*. MIT Press, Cambridge, 1993.

vH91. P. van Hentenryck. Constraint logic programming. *The Knowledge Engineering Review*, 6:151–194, 1991.

ZR85. H. Zhang and J. L. Remy. Contextual rewriting. In Jean-Pierre Jouannaud, editor, *Proceedings of the 1st International Conference on Rewriting Techniques and Applications*, volume 202 of *LNCS*, pages 46–62, Dijon, France, May 1985. Springer.

AC-Unification of Higher-Order Patterns*

Alexandre Boudet and Evelyne Contejean

LRI, CNRS URA 410
Bât. 490, Université Paris-Sud, Centre d'Orsay
91405 Orsay Cedex, France

Abstract. We present a complete algorithm for the unification of higher-order patterns modulo the associative-commutative theory of some constants $+_1, \ldots, +_n$. Given an AC-unification problem over higher-order patterns, the output of the algorithm is a finite set DAG solved forms [9], constrained by some flexible-flexible equations with the same head on both sides. Indeed, in the presence of AC constants, such equations are always solvable, but they have no minimal complete set of unifiers [13]. We prove that the algorithm terminates, is sound, and that any solution of the original unification problem is an instance of one of the computed solutions which satisfies the constraints.

Introduction

Higher-order unification is undecidable [8], yet the unification of higher-order patterns, a subset of the terms of the simply-typed λ-calculus is decidable, and useful in practice [11,12]. The combination of algebraic and functional programming paradigms [10] leads one to investigate higher-order unification modulo equational theories. Unification of higher-order patterns will also be a key to higher-order extensions of membership equational logic described in [5].

The problem we address here is the unification of higher-order patterns modulo the associativity and commutativity of some constant symbols. This was partially achieved by Qian and Wang [13] who used a combination algorithm by Jouannaud and Kirchner [9] for first-order unification algorithms, and an AC1-unification algorithm for solving elementary AC problems. The most surprising result in their paper is that although unification of patterns is unitary in the standard case, in the AC case a single flexible-flexible equation with the same head has no minimal complete set of unifiers. Their algorithm is not complete because AC-unification of pure patterns (*i.e.* involving only one AC constant) is more involved than in the first-order case and one cannot just use an AC or AC1-unification algorithm as a black box in the case of patterns (see the example in Section 3.2). Our main contribution is to present a complete AC-unification algorithm for pure patterns. The paper is organized as follows. The next section briefly recalls some background on patterns and equational theories. Section 2 introduces a *variable abstraction* rule and recalls all but one of

---

* This research was supported in part by the EWG CCL, the HCM Network CONSOLE, and the "GDR de programmation du CNRS".

Nipkow's rules for pattern unification. Section 3 gives an algorithm for unification of pure AC-patterns, and section 4 shows how one gets an AC-unification algorithm by combining the previous steps using some standard techniques for combining first-order unification algorithms.

1 Preliminaries

We assume the reader is familiar with simply-typed lambda-calculus, and equational unification. Some background is available in e.g. [7,9,2] for lambda-calculus and unification in (combinations of) first-order equational theories. We shall use the following notations: $\lambda x_1 \cdots \lambda x_n.s$ will be written $\lambda \overline{x_n}.s$, or even $\lambda \overline{x}.s$ if n is not relevant. If in a same expression $\overline{x}$ appears several times it denotes the same sequence of variables. In addition, we will use the notation $t(u_1, \ldots, u_n)$ or $t(\overline{u_n})$ for $(\cdots (tu_1) \cdots)u_n$. If π is a permutation of $(1, \ldots, n)$, $\overline{x_n}^\pi$ stands for the sequence $x_{\pi(1)}, \ldots, x_{\pi(n)}$. The free (resp. bound) variables of a term t are denoted by $\mathcal{FV}(t)$ (resp. $\mathcal{BV}(t)$). The notation $t[u]_p$ stands for a term t with a subterm u at some position p. Upper-case $X, F, G, L, L_1, \ldots$ denote free variables, lower-case $x, x_1, y, z, \ldots$ bound variables, and $a, b, f, g, \ldots$ constants.

1.1 Patterns

Definition 1. A pattern is a term of the simply-typed λ-calculus in β-normal form in which the arguments of a free variable are η-equivalent to distinct bound variables.

For instance, $\lambda xyz.f(H(x,y), H(x,z))$ and $\lambda x.F(\lambda z.x(z))^1$ are patterns while $\lambda xy.G(x,x,y)$, $\lambda xy.H(x,f(y))$ and $\lambda xy.H(F(x),y)$ are not patterns.

We always assume that the terms are in η-long β-normal form [7,12,13], the β and η rules being respectively oriented as follows:
$(\lambda x.M)N \to_\beta M\{x \mapsto N\}$ (only the free occurrences of x are replaced by N),
$F \to_\eta \lambda \overline{x_n}.F(\overline{x_n})$ if the type of F is $\alpha_1 \to \ldots \to \alpha_n \to \alpha$, and α is a base type.
The η-long β-normal form of a term t is denoted by $t \updownarrow_\beta^\eta$. Pattern unification is decidable, a result by Miller [11], refined by Nipkow [12]:

Theorem 2. *The unifiability of patterns is decidable and if two patterns are unifiable, there is an algorithm computing a unique most general unifier.*

We define now what we mean by "associative-commutative operators".

1.2 Equational theories, E-unification and AC-unification

Let $E = \{l_1 \simeq r_1, \ldots, l_n \simeq r_n\}$ a set of *axioms* such that l_i and r_i are terms of the same type, for $1 \leq i \leq n$. The *equational theory* $=_E$ generated by E is the

---

[1] We will always write such a pattern in the (η-equivalent) form $\lambda x.F(x)$, where the argument of the free variable F is *indeed* a bound variable.

least congruence[2] containing all the instances of the axioms of E. The theory we consider here is the associative-commutative theory of one or more constant operators.

We distinguish some binary constant operators which are associative and commutative (which we denote by $+, +_1, \ldots$), and that we write in infix notation. The other constants are called *free*. Actually, we shall use a flattened representation, and when a term is written in the form $t_1 + \cdots + t_n$, it is implicitly assumed that the top symbol of the t_is is not $+$. For instance, the term $\lambda xyz. + (+(F(x, y), H(y, z)), F(x, y))$ will be written $\lambda xyz.F(x, y) + H(y, z) + F(x, y)$. In addition, we will sometimes write it $\lambda xyz.2F(x, y) + H(y, z)$, with the usual convention that nt stands for $\underbrace{t + \cdots + t}_{n \text{ times}}$, where n is a positive integer.

Definition 3. The associative-commutative (AC) theory of $+$ is the equational theory presented by $AC(+) = \{(x + y) + z \simeq x + (y + z), x + y \simeq y + x\}$. The theory $AC(+_1, \ldots, +_n)$ is the theory presented by $AC(+_1) \cup \cdots \cup AC(+_n)$. In the sequel, we will refer to AC and $=_{AC}$ when $+_1, \ldots, +_n$ are not relevant.

Definition 4 (Unification problems). An *equation* is a pair $< s, t >$ of patterns of the same type, denoted by $s = t$. A unification problem is either $\top$ (the trivial problem), or $\perp$ (the unsolvable problem), or a (disjunction of) conjunction(s) of equations of the form $P \equiv s_1 = t_1 \wedge \cdots \wedge s_n = t_n$. A substitution σ is an *E-unifier* of P if $s_i\sigma$ and $t_i\sigma$ are equivalent modulo $\eta\beta$-equivalence and the theory $=_E$ for $1 \leq i \leq n$, which we write $s_i =_{\beta\eta E} t_i$.

Since we consider only terms in η-long β-normal form, the following result from Tannen will allow us to restrict our attention to $=_E$ instead of $=_{\beta\eta E}$:

Theorem 5 ([6]). *For any terms u and v, $u =_{\beta\eta E} v$ if and only if $u \uparrow_\beta^\eta =_E v \uparrow_\beta^\eta$.*

In the case of AC-theories, we can assume without loss of generality that the AC-operators have types of the form $\alpha \to \alpha \to \alpha$ for some type α. Indeed, if it wasn't so, then $(a+b)+c$ and $a+(b+c)$ would not be of the same type. Further, we assume that α is a base type. Nevertheless, we can still define a "higher-order +". Consider two terms u and v of type $\sigma \to \alpha$ where α is a base type. Then define $u +_{\sigma \to \alpha} v$ as the term $\lambda x.u(x) + v(x)$ of type $\sigma \to \alpha$.

Under the above assumptions, there cannot be an abstraction below an AC-operator, since otherwise either the term would not be in η-long β-normal form, or the AC-operator would not apply to a base type.

2 Purification

In this section we start by giving a *Variable abstraction* rule which is obviously correct and terminating, and allows us to split the original problem into pure subproblems.

---

[2] *i.e.*, compatible *also* with application and abstraction, in our context.

Definition 6. A unification problem P is *pure* in the free theory if it contains no AC symbol. P is *pure* in the AC-theory of $+$ if the only constant occurring in P is the associative-commutative constant $+$.

Definition 7. A subterm u of a term t is an *alien* subterm if it occurs immediately under an AC symbol and its head is not a free variable, or if it occurs immediately under a free constant and its head is an AC symbol.

Applying repeatedly the following rule will yield a problem with no alien subterms.

VA

$\lambda \overline{x}.t[u]_p = \lambda \overline{x} s \quad \rightarrow \quad \lambda \overline{x}.t[H(\overline{y})]_p = \lambda \overline{x}.s \ \wedge \ \lambda \overline{y}.H(\overline{y}) = \lambda \overline{y}.u$

if u is an alien subterm of $t[u]_p$ at position p, and $\overline{y} = \mathcal{FV}(u) \cap \overline{x}$, where H is a new variable.

Clearly, **VA** alone terminates, and we introduce some syntax for the unification problems obtained after applying it as long as possible.

Definition 8. A unification problem in the theory $AC(+_1, \ldots, +_n)$ will be written in the form

$$P \equiv P_F \cup P_0 \cup P_1 \cup \cdots \cup P_n$$

where

- P_0 is pure in the free theory, containing no equations of the form $\lambda \overline{x}.F(x_1, \ldots, x_n) = \lambda \overline{x}.F(x_{\pi(1)}, \ldots, x_{\pi(n)})$ (where π is a permutation of $(1, \ldots, n)$),
- P_F contains all the flexible-flexible equations with the same heads described above.
- P_i is a pure unification problem in the AC theory of $+_i$, the arguments of $+_i$ being of the form $F(\overline{x})$ where F is a free variable.

We will also distinguish some equations that will not be written in η-long β-normal form.

Definition 9. An equation in a unification problem P is *quasi-solved* if it is of the form $F = s$ where F is a free variable and $F \notin \mathcal{FV}(s)$. A quasi-solved equation $F = s$ of a unification problem P is *solved* in P if F has no other free occurrence in P.

We can now present some of the rules of Nipkow's algorithm [12] which are valid in the presence of $=_{AC}$. Only part of the work is done here since two special cases are not treated, namely the flexible-flexible equations with the same free variable on both sides and the equations where the top constant is associative-commutative. We also introduce some new rules which are specific to AC-unification.

Dec-free
$\lambda \overline{x}.a(s_1, \ldots, s_n) = \lambda \overline{x}.a(t_1, \ldots, t_n) \wedge P_{\emptyset} \quad \rightarrow$
$\lambda \overline{x}.s_1 = \lambda \overline{x}.t_1 \wedge \cdots \wedge \lambda \overline{x}.s_n = \lambda \overline{x}.t_n \wedge P_{\emptyset}$
if a is a free constant symbol or a bound variable of $\overline{x}$.

FR-free
$\lambda \overline{x}.F(\overline{y_n}) = \lambda \overline{x}.a(s_1, \ldots, s_m) \wedge P_{\emptyset} \quad \rightarrow$
$\lambda \overline{y_n}.H_1(\overline{y_n}) = \lambda \overline{y_n}.s_1 \wedge \cdots \wedge \lambda \overline{y_n}.H_m(\overline{y_n}) = \lambda \overline{y_n}.s_m$
$\wedge\ P_{\emptyset}\{F \mapsto a(H_1(\overline{y_n}), \ldots, H_m(\overline{y_n}))\}$
$\wedge\ F = \lambda \overline{x}.a(H_1(\overline{y_n}), \ldots, H_m(\overline{y_n}))\}$
If F is a free variable, a a free constant and $F \notin \mathcal{FV}(s_i)$ for $1 \leq i \leq m$, where
$H_1, \ldots, H_m$ are new variables.

FF$\neq$
$\lambda \overline{x}.F(\overline{y_n}) = \lambda \overline{x}.G(\overline{z_m}) \wedge P_{\emptyset} \quad \rightarrow$
$P_{\emptyset}\{F \mapsto \lambda \overline{y_n}.H(\overline{v_p}), G \mapsto \lambda \overline{z_m}.H(\overline{v_p})\}$
$\wedge\ F = \lambda \overline{y_n}.H(\overline{v_p}) \wedge G = \lambda \overline{z_m}.H(\overline{v_p})$
if F and G are different free variables where $\overline{v_p} = \overline{y}_n \cap \overline{z_m}$.

Fail1
$\lambda \overline{x}.a(\overline{s}) = \lambda \overline{x}.b(\overline{t}) \quad \rightarrow$
$\perp$
if a and b are constants or bound variables and $a \neq b$.

Fail2
$\lambda \overline{x}.F(\overline{y}) = \lambda \overline{x}.a(\overline{s}) \quad \rightarrow$
$\perp$
if F is free in $\overline{s}$ or $a \in \overline{x} \setminus \overline{y}$.

Fig. 1. A subset of Nipkow's rules for the unification of higher-order patterns

The rules of figure 1 are a subset of those presented by Nipkow and as such, they terminate. These rules are to be applied to the pure subproblem P_0. Note, however that Nipkow explicitly states that his termination proof relies on the fact that he uses lists, and not multisets (conjunctions in our case). Hence, the conjunction operator must not be considered as associative commutative when applying these rules. It has to be noticed that the rules **FR-free** and **FR$\neq$** make some solved equations appear. These equations will *not* be put in η-long β-normal form, and no rule of figure 1 will apply to them.

Note that the rule **Fail1** is still correct if a or b is an AC constant due to Tannen's theorem and to the fact that AC-theories are collapse-free.

Some cases are missing in figure 1, which is not surprising, since they require a special treatment in the presence of AC constants. A first case we omitted above is the flexible-flexible case with equal heads. It has been noticed by Qian

272

and Wang that although such equations are always solvable, they do not have finite complete sets of AC-unifiers. That is why we will freeze them and just check for the compatibility of such equation with the rest of the problem. The second case that has not been considered yet is the pure AC subproblems.

Another rule is added to those of figure 1 which just ignores the flexible-flexible equations with same heads and *freezes* them by storing them in P_F. This is made necessary by the fact that even if P_0 does not contain such equations at the beginning, some may appear by applying the other rules.

Freeze
$$P_F \wedge (s = t \wedge P_0) \wedge P_1 \wedge \cdots \wedge P_n \;\rightarrow\; (s = t \wedge P_F) \wedge P_0 \wedge P_1 \wedge \cdots \wedge P_n$$
if $s = t$ is a flexible-flexible equation where s and t have the same head variable.

Once the **VA** has been applied as long as possible to the original problem, and the rules of figure 1 plus the rule **Freeze** have been applied as long as possible to the subproblems P_0 and P_F, the problem has the form

$$P_F \wedge P_0 \wedge P_1 \wedge \cdots \wedge P_n$$

where

- P_F contains only flexible-flexible equations with the same free constant on both sides,
- P_0 is in a DAG solved form, from which a most general unifier is trivially obtained by applying a variable elimination rule.
- P_i is a pure problem in the AC-theory of $+_i$.

We extend the usual notion of DAG solved forms so as to take into account the frozen equations.

Definition 10. A problem P is in a *DAG solved form* if it is of the form $P' \wedge P_F$ where

- P' is a conjunction $F_1 = t_1 \wedge \cdots \wedge F_n = t_n$ of quasi-solved equations, containing no cycle as in the premise of the **Cycle** rule of figure 2 (section 4), and where each F_i occurs exactly once as a left-hand side of an equation,
- P_F is a conjunction of frozen equations of the form $\lambda \overline{x}.F(\overline{x}) = \lambda \overline{x}.F(\overline{x}^\pi)$ such that if $F = \lambda \overline{x}.u(\overline{x})$ is in P', then $u(\overline{x}) =_{\eta\beta AC} u(\overline{x}^\pi)$.

What we are left to do is to solve the pure AC subproblems (this is the object of the next section), to recombine the different solved subproblems $P_0, P_1, \ldots, P_n$, and to check the compatibility of the frozen flexible-flexible equations with the rest of the problem. This will be done in section 4.

3 Elementary AC-unification of higher-order patterns

In this section, we show how to handle the two cases that we omitted in the previous section.

3.1 Flexible-flexible equations with the same head variable

Actually, there is not much to do with such equations. Indeed, even though they are always solvable, they do not have finite complete sets of AC-unifiers. This was noticed by Qian and Wang [13] who give the following example:

Example 11 ([13]). Consider the equation $e \equiv \lambda xy.F(x,y) = \lambda xy.F(y,x)$ in the AC-theory of $+$. For $m \geq 0$, the substitution

$$\sigma_m = \{\mathcal{F} \mapsto \lambda xy.G_m(H_1(x,y) + H_1(y,x), \ldots, H_m(x,y) + H_m(y,x))\}$$

is an AC-unifier of e. On the other hand, every solution of e is an instance of some σ_i. In addition σ_{n+1} is strictly more general than σ_n.

Hence, AC-unification of patterns is not only infinitary, but *nullary*, in the sense that some problems do not have *minimal* complete sets of AC-unifiers [14].

As Qian and Wang, we keep these equations as constraints, and we will see in section 4, how to check the compatibility of such constraints with the rest of the solutions.

3.2 Elementary AC-unification: an example

Before giving the algorithm for elementary AC-unification, let us develop an example which will help to follow the remainder of this section. Consider the equation

$$\lambda xyz.2F(x,y,z) + F(y,z,x) = \lambda xyz.2G(x,y,z)$$

A solution σ may introduce a term $t(x,y,z)$ which does not depend on the order of its arguments (*i.e.* $t(x,y,z) = t(y,z,x)$). Such a term is introduced 2α times by $2F(x,y,z)\sigma$ and α times by $F(y,z,x)\sigma$. On the other hand $t(x,y,z)$ must be introduced 2β times by $2G(x,y,z)\sigma$ where (α, β) is a positive solution of the linear Diophantine equation $3n = 2m$. The set of minimal positive solutions of this equation is $\{(2,3)\}$. Let L_1 be a new variable and assume that θ is such that $L_1(x,y,z)\theta = L_1(y,z,x)\theta = L_1(z,x,y)\theta$. Then

$$\{F \mapsto \lambda(x,y,z).2L_1(x,y,z)\theta, G \mapsto \lambda(x,y,z).3L_1(x,y,z)\theta\}$$

is a solution of the original equation.
On the other hand, σ may introduce a term $t(x,y,z)$ which depends on the order of its variables (*i.e.* $t(x,y,z) \neq t(y,z,x))^3$. Assume that $F(x,y,z)\sigma$ intro-

---
[3] This case was not considered in [13], since AC-unification was a black box: this is why the algorithm is not complete

duces α_1 times $t(x, y, z)$, α_2 times $t(y, z, x)$ and α_3 times $t(z, x, y)$. In this case, $G(x, y, z)$ introduces respectively $\beta_1, \beta_2, \beta_3$ times the terms $t(x, y, z)$, $t(y, z, x)$ and $t(z, x, y)$ where $(\alpha_1, \alpha_2, \alpha_3, \beta_1, \beta_2, \beta_3)$ are positive solutions of the system of linear Diophantine equations

$$2n_1 + n_3 = 2m_1$$
$$2n_2 + n_1 = 2m_2$$
$$2n_3 + n_2 = 2m_3$$

Each of the above equations ensures that the respective numbers of occurrences of $t(x, y, z)$, $t(y, z, x)$ and $t(z, x, y)$ introduced by σ in both hands of the equation are the same. The set of minimal positive solutions of this system is $\{(2,0,0,2,1,0),(0,2,0,0,2,1),(0,0,2,1,0,2)\}$ Let us associate the new variables L_2, L_3, L_4 with each of these solutions. A solution of the original problem is

$$\{ F \mapsto \lambda xyz.\ 2L_1(x, y, z)\theta + 2L_2(x, y, z) + 2L_3(y, z, x) + 2L_4(z, x, y),$$
$$G \mapsto \lambda xyz.\ 3L_1(x, y, z)\theta + 2L_2(x, y, z) + L_2(y, z, x) + 2L_3(y, z, x)$$
$$+ L_3(z, x, y) + L_4(x, y, z) + 2L_4(z, x, y)\}$$

provided that $L_1(x, y, z)\theta = L_1(y, z, x)\theta = L_1(z, x, y)\theta$. As in the first-order AC-unification, some of the new variables may be omitted as long as one has a well-formed substitution (i.e. not mapping a variable onto an "empty" term).

3.3 Elementary AC-unification

We show now how to solve a pure equation modulo AC in the general case. The technique naturally extends to the solving of pure problems as in the first-order case, but the notations are already quite involved, and we prefer to restrict our presentation to the case of a single equation. We can assume without loss of generality that the problem has the form:

$$P \equiv \lambda \overline{x}. \sum_{i=1}^{n_1} \sum_{\pi \in \Pi} a_{i,\pi} F_i(\overline{x}^\pi) = \lambda \overline{x}. \sum_{i=n_1+1}^{n_2} \sum_{\pi \in \Pi} a_{i,\pi} F_i(\overline{x}^\pi)$$

where Π is a subgroup of the group of permutations over all the variables of $\overline{x}$. Π is actually the subgroup generated by the permutations occuring in the problem[4]. Note that some of the $a_{i,\pi}$s may be equal to zero.

As in the example, a solution of the problem may introduce a term $t(\overline{x})$, which is invariant under some permutations of its arguments. These permutations are a subgroup Π_0 of Π. Let us denote by $P_{Dioph}^{\Pi_0}$ the following linear Diophantine system in $n_2 \times \mathrm{Card}(\Pi)$ natural unknowns $y_{i,\pi}$:

---

[4] In the example, Π is equal to $\{\pi_0, \pi_1, \pi_2\}$, where $\pi_0 = \{x \mapsto x, y \mapsto y, z \mapsto z\}$, $\pi_1 = \{x \mapsto y, y \mapsto z, z \mapsto x\}$, $\pi_2 = \{x \mapsto z, y \mapsto x, z \mapsto y\}$

$$\bigwedge_{i=1}^{n_2} \bigwedge_{(\pi_1,\pi_2)\,|\,\Pi_0\circ\pi_1=\Pi_0\circ\pi_2} y_{i,\pi_1} = y_{i,\pi_2}$$

$$P_{Dioph}^{\Pi_0} \equiv \qquad\qquad\qquad \bigwedge$$

$$\bigwedge_{\pi'\in\Pi}\sum_{i=1}^{n_1}\sum_{\pi\in\Pi} a_{i,\pi^{-1}\circ\pi'}y_{i,\pi} = \sum_{i=n_1+1}^{n_2}\sum_{\pi\in\Pi} a_{i,\pi^{-1}\circ\pi'}y_{i,\pi}$$

and by P_{Dioph} the disjunction $\bigvee_{\Pi_0}$ subgroup of Π $P_{Dioph}^{\Pi_0}$. $y_{i,\pi}$ is the number of occurrences of a given term $t(\overline{x})$ in $F_i(\overline{x}^\pi)$. The first part of $P_{Dioph}^{\Pi_0}$ states that t is invariant under the permutations of Π_0, and the second part states that the number of $t(\overline{x}^{\pi'})$s is the same on both sides of the equation.

Definition 12. Let $\mathcal{P} = \bigcup_{\Pi_0} \mathcal{P}_{\Pi_0}$ be a subset of minimal solutions of the linear Diophantine system P_{Dioph}, where each $\mathcal{P}_{\Pi_0}$ is a subset of minimal solutions of $P_{Dioph}^{\Pi_0}$. $\mathcal{P}$ is said to be *great enough* if

$$\forall i \in \{1,\dots,n_2\} \sum_{\Pi_0}\sum_{m\in\mathcal{P}_{\Pi_0}}\sum_{\pi\in\Pi/\Pi_0} m(i,\pi) > 0$$

Proposition 13. *Let $\mathcal{P}$ be any subset of the minimal solutions of P_{Dioph}, which is great enough. Then $\sigma_{\mathcal{P}}$ is a solution of P:*

$$\sigma_{\mathcal{P}} = \{F_i \mapsto \lambda\overline{x}.\sum_{\Pi_0}\sum_{m\in\mathcal{P}_{\Pi_0}}\sum_{\pi'\in\Pi/\Pi_0} m(i,\pi')L_m(\overline{x}^{\pi'})\}$$

where $L_m, m \in \mathcal{P}_{\Pi_0}$ is a new variable constrained by $\forall\pi\in\Pi_0\ L_m(\overline{x}^\pi) = L_m(\overline{x})$.

Proof. Since $\mathcal{P}$ is great enough, $\sum_{\Pi_0}\sum_{m\in\mathcal{P}_{\Pi_0}}\sum_{\pi'\in\Pi/\Pi_0} m(i,\pi')L_m(\overline{x}^{\pi'})$ is a non-empty sum for all i, hence $F_i\sigma_{\mathcal{P}}$ is well-defined. Moreover, we have:

$\sum_{i=1}^{n_1}\sum_{\pi\in\Pi} a_{i,\pi}(F_i\sigma_{\mathcal{P}})(\overline{x}^\pi) =$

$\sum_{i=1}^{n_1}\sum_{\pi\in\Pi} a_{i,\pi}\sum_{\Pi_0}\sum_{m\in\mathcal{P}_{\Pi_0}}\sum_{\pi'\in\Pi/\Pi_0} m(i,\pi')L_m(\overline{x}^{\pi'\circ\pi}) =$

$\sum_{\Pi_0}\sum_{m\in\mathcal{P}_{\Pi_0}}\sum_{\pi\in\Pi}\sum_{i=1}^{n_1}\sum_{\pi''\in\Pi/\Pi_0} a_{i,\pi}m(i,\pi^{-1}\circ\pi'')L_m(\overline{x}^{\pi''}) =$

$\sum_{\Pi_0}\sum_{m\in\mathcal{P}_{\Pi_0}}\sum_{\pi''\in\Pi/\Pi_0}(\sum_{\pi\in\Pi}\sum_{i=1}^{n_1} a_{i,\pi}m(i,\pi^{-1}\circ\pi''))L_m(\overline{x}^{\pi''}) =$

$\sum_{\Pi_0}\sum_{m\in\mathcal{P}_{\Pi_0}}\sum_{\pi''\in\Pi/\Pi_0}(\sum_{\pi'''\in\Pi}\sum_{i=1}^{n_1} a_{i,\pi''\circ\pi'''^{-1}}m(i,\pi'''))L_m(\overline{x}^{\pi''}) =$

since m is a solution of $P_{Dioph}^{\Pi_0}$

$\sum_{\Pi_0}\sum_{m\in\mathcal{P}_{\Pi_0}}\sum_{\pi''\in\Pi/\Pi_0}(\sum_{\pi'''\in\Pi}\sum_{i=n_1+1}^{n_2} a_{i,\pi''\circ\pi'''^{-1}}m(i,\pi'''))L_m(\overline{x}^{\pi''}) =$

$\sum_{i=n_1+1}^{n_2}\sum_{\pi\in\Pi} a_{i,\pi}(F_i\sigma_{\mathcal{P}})(\overline{x}^\pi)$

Proposition 14. *$\{\sigma_{\mathcal{P}} \mid \mathcal{P}$ is great enough$\}$ is a complete set of solutions for P.*

Proof. Let σ be a solution of P. Let $\{t_j^\pi\}_{j\in J,\pi\in\Pi}$ be a set of terms which contains all the immediate alien subterms of the $F_i\sigma$, and such that

$$\forall j,k\ (\exists\pi,\pi'\ t_j^\pi = t_k^{\pi'}) \Leftrightarrow (j=k)$$

$F_i\sigma$ may be written as $\lambda\overline{x}.\sum_{j\in J}\sum_{\pi'\in\Pi} \alpha_{i,j,\pi'}t_j(\overline{x}^{\pi'})$ σ is a solution, hence by the theorem of Tannen [6]:

$$\sum_{i=1}^{n_1} \sum_{\pi \in \Pi} a_{i,\pi}(F_i\sigma)(\overline{x}^\pi) =_{AC} \sum_{i=n_1+1}^{n_2} \sum_{\pi \in \Pi} a_{i,\pi}(F_i\sigma)(\overline{x}^\pi)$$

$$\sum_{i=1}^{n_1} \sum_{\pi \in \Pi} a_{i,\pi}(\sum_{j \in J} \sum_{\pi' \in \Pi} \alpha_{i,j,\pi'} t_j(\overline{x}^{\pi' \circ \pi})) =_{AC} \sum_{i=n_1+1}^{n_2} \sum_{\pi \in \Pi} a_{i,\pi}(\sum_{j \in J} \sum_{\pi' \in \Pi} \alpha_{i,j,\pi'} t_j(\overline{x}^{\pi' \circ \pi}))$$

$$\sum_{j \in J} \sum_{i=1}^{n_1} \sum_{\pi \in \Pi} \sum_{\pi' \in \Pi} a_{i,\pi} \alpha_{i,j,\pi'} t_j(\overline{x}^{\pi' \circ \pi}) =_{AC} \sum_{j \in J} \sum_{i=n_1+1}^{n_2} \sum_{\pi \in \Pi} \sum_{\pi' \in \Pi} a_{i,\pi} \alpha_{i,j,\pi'} t_j(\overline{x}^{\pi' \circ \pi})$$

Hence, by hypothesis, for all $j \in J$, we have

$$\sum_{i=1}^{n_1} \sum_{\pi \in \Pi} \sum_{\pi' \in \Pi} a_{i,\pi} \alpha_{i,j,\pi'} t_j(\overline{x}^{\pi' \circ \pi}) =_{AC} \sum_{i=n_1+1}^{n_2} \sum_{\pi \in \Pi} \sum_{\pi' \in \Pi} a_{i,\pi} \alpha_{i,j,\pi'} t_j(\overline{x}^{\pi' \circ \pi})$$

Let Π_j be the subgroup of invariant permutations of t_j i. e.
$\Pi_j = \{\pi \in \Pi \mid \lambda\overline{x}.t_j(\overline{x}) = \lambda\overline{x}.t_j(\overline{x}^\pi)\}$. Hence we have for all $\pi'' \in \Pi$:

$$\sum_{i=1}^{n_1} \sum_{\pi,\pi' \mid \pi' \circ \pi \circ \pi''^{-1} \in \Pi_j} a_{i,\pi} \alpha_{i,j,\pi'} t_j(\overline{x}^{\pi''}) =_{AC} \sum_{i=n_1+1}^{n_2} \sum_{\pi,\pi' \mid \pi' \circ \pi \circ \pi''^{-1} \in \Pi_j} a_{i,\pi} \alpha_{i,j,\pi'} t_j(\overline{x}^{\pi''})$$

$$\sum_{i=1}^{n_1} \sum_{\pi,\pi' \mid \pi' \circ \pi \circ \pi''^{-1} \in \Pi_j} a_{i,\pi} \alpha_{i,j,\pi'} =_N \sum_{i=n_1+1}^{n_2} \sum_{\pi,\pi' \mid \pi' \circ \pi \circ \pi''^{-1} \in \Pi_j} a_{i,\pi} \alpha_{i,j,\pi'}$$

$$\sum_{i=1}^{n_1} \sum_{\pi} a_{i,\pi}(\sum_{\pi' \mid \pi' \circ \pi \circ \pi''^{-1} \in \Pi_j} \alpha_{i,j,\pi'}) =_N \sum_{i=n_1+1}^{n_2} \sum_{\pi} a_{i,\pi}(\sum_{\pi' \mid \pi' \circ \pi \circ \pi''^{-1} \in \Pi_j} \alpha_{i,j,\pi'})$$

$$\sum_{i=1}^{n_1} \sum_{\pi} a_{i,\pi}(\sum_{\pi' \mid \pi' \in \Pi_j \circ \pi'' \circ \pi^{-1}} \alpha_{i,j,\pi'}) =_N \sum_{i=n_1+1}^{n_2} \sum_{\pi} a_{i,\pi}(\sum_{\pi' \mid \pi' \in \Pi_j \circ \pi'' \circ \pi^{-1}} \alpha_{i,j,\pi'})$$

$$\sum_{i=1}^{n_1} \sum_{\pi} a_{i,\pi'''^{-1} \circ \pi''}(\underbrace{\sum_{\pi' \mid \pi' \in \Pi_j \circ \pi'''} \alpha_{i,j,\pi'}}_{\beta_{i,j,\pi'''}}) =_N \sum_{i=n_1+1}^{n_2} \sum_{\pi} a_{i,\pi'''^{-1} \circ \pi''}(\underbrace{\sum_{\pi' \mid \pi' \in \Pi_j \circ \pi'''} \alpha_{i,j,\pi'}}_{\beta_{i,j,\pi'''}})$$

For all j, $(\beta_{i,j,\pi})_{i,\pi}$ satisfies moreover $\Pi_j \circ \pi_1 = \Pi_j \circ \pi_2 \Rightarrow \beta_{i,j,\pi_1} = \beta_{i,j,\pi_2}$.
Hence $\beta_j = (\beta_{i,j,\pi})_{i,\pi}$ is a solution of $P_{Dioph}^{\Pi_j}$, β_j is a linear combination of some minimal solutions of $P_{Dioph}^{\Pi_j}$.

Let $\mathcal{P} = \bigcup_{\Pi_0} \mathcal{P}_{\Pi_0}$ be the subset of minimal solutions of P_{Dioph} used at least by one β_j, hence one can write $\forall j$ $\beta_j = \sum_{m \in \mathcal{P}_{\Pi_j}} c_{j,m} m$, where the $c_{j,m}$ are non-negative. We extend the definition of the $c_{j,m}$s for the ms which are minimal solutions of P_{Dioph} but not of $P_{Dioph}^{\Pi_j}$ by 0. Note that σ can be written as:

$$F_i \sigma = \lambda \overline{x}. \sum_{j \in J} \sum_{\pi' \in \Pi} \alpha_{i,j,\pi'} t_j(\overline{x}^{\pi'})$$
$$= \lambda \overline{x}. \sum_{j \in J} \sum_{\overline{\pi'''} \in \Pi/\Pi_j} \sum_{\pi' \in \Pi_j \circ \pi'''} \alpha_{i,j,\pi'} t_j(\overline{x}^{\pi'})$$
$$= \lambda \overline{x}. \sum_{j \in J} \sum_{\overline{\pi'''} \in \Pi/\Pi_j} (\sum_{\pi' \in \Pi_j \circ \pi'''} \alpha_{i,j,\pi'}) t_j(\overline{x}^{\pi'''})$$
$$= \lambda \overline{x}. \sum_{j \in J} \sum_{\overline{\pi'''} \in \Pi/\Pi_j} \beta_{i,j,\pi'''} t_j(\overline{x}^{\pi'''})$$
$$= \lambda \overline{x}. \sum_{j \in J} \sum_{\overline{\pi'''} \in \Pi/\Pi_j} (\sum_{m \in \mathcal{P}} c_{j,m} m(i, \pi''')) t_j(\overline{x}^{\pi'''})$$
$$= \lambda \overline{x}. \sum_{m \in \mathcal{P}} \sum_{j \in J} \sum_{\overline{\pi'''} \in \Pi/\Pi_j} c_{j,m} m(i, \pi''') t_j(\overline{x}^{\pi'''})$$

Let us define θ as $\forall m \in \mathcal{P}$ $L_m \mapsto \lambda \overline{x}. \sum_{j \in J} c_{j,m} t_j(\overline{x})$. θ is a valid substitution since if $c_{j,m} \neq 0$, the subgroup of invariant permutations of t_j is Π_j, hence $L_m \theta$ satisfies the constraint. It is easy to verify that σ is equal to $\sigma_{\mathcal{P}} \theta$.

We have shown how to solve a pure equation modulo AC, but actually, we solve systems of such equations P_{+_i}, together with the frozen equations in P_F which involve a variable occurring in P_{+_i}. Such frozen equations may be considered as pure equations, without any AC symbols. Obviously Proposition 13 and Proposition 14 are still valid.

4   Recombination

We first present a combination algorithm for combining the solutions of the different solved subproblems. It is closely inspired by our algorithm for (first-order) AC-unification. [1,4,3]. There, the termination proof is based on the notion of *shared variables* which we adapt here. With this modification of the notion of shared variables, our proof can be reused exactly as such since it basically relies upon the fact that solving a pure subproblem will not increase the number of shared variables.

4.1   Combination

In the previous section, we have seen how to turn $P_F \wedge P_i$ into an equivalent problem $P'_F \wedge P'_i$ where P'_i is now solved and P'_F may contain additional frozen flexible-flexible equations. Now, it may happen that solving a subproblem P_i yields some solved equations of the form $F = \lambda \overline{x}.G(\overline{x})$. These equations are by definition solved in P_i, but the free variables F and G may occur in some other subproblem P_j. Replacing F by $\lambda \overline{x}.G(\overline{x})$ in the other subproblems may make some of them unsolved.

Definition 15. Two distinct non-solved free variables are *shared* in P_i if they both occur in P_i and are identifiable outside P_i. Two non-solved free variables F_1 and F_k are *identifiable outside* P_i if there exists a sequence $(F_1, F_2), (F_2, F_3), \ldots, (F_{n-1}, F_k)$ such that for $1 \leq i < k$, both F_i and F_{i+1} have a free occurrence in some problem P_j with $i \neq j$.

The rules of figure 2 mimic those mentioned above for first-order AC-unification. They have to be applied as follows. If P_0 is not solved, then it will be solved by using the rules of figure 1. The pure AC subproblems will be solved using the algorithm for elementary AC unification of patterns of section 3. In both cases, the flexible-flexible equations with the same free variable on both sides are frozen in P_F. Let us stress that the frozen equations in P_F are never used, nor altered at this stage. In particular, the substitutions are *not* applied to P_F.

Solve
$P_i \quad \rightarrow \quad P_i'$
if P_i is not solved, and P_i' is a solved form of P_i.

Variable-Replacement
$F = \lambda \overline{x}.G(\overline{y}) \ \wedge \ P \quad \rightarrow \quad F = \lambda \overline{x}.G(\overline{y}) \ \wedge \ P\{F \mapsto \lambda \overline{x}.G(\overline{y})\}$
if both F and G have a free occurrence in P.

Clash
$F = s \wedge F = t \quad \rightarrow \quad \bot$
if s and t have different constant heads.

Cycle
$F_1 = t_1[F_2] \ \wedge \ F_2 = t_2[F_3] \cdots \ \wedge \ F_n = t_n[F_1] \quad \rightarrow \quad \bot$
if there is a constant on the path between the head and $F_{i+1(mod\ n)}$ in some t_i.

Fig. 2. The combination rules

The following lemmas are the same as in the first-order case, and we omit the proofs which translate naturally in our context.

Lemma 16. Solve *does not increase the number of shared variables in any of the subproblems* $P_0, \ldots, P_n$.

Lemma 17. *If* **Variable-Replacement** *makes a solved subproblem* P_i *unsolved, then it decreases the multiset of the numbers of shared variables in* $P_0, \ldots, P_n$.

The termination proof is then provided by the following measure which compares lexicographically

1. The multiset of the numbers of shared variables in $P_0, \ldots, P_n$,
2. the number of unsolved subproblems in $\{P_0, \ldots, P_n\}$.

Proposition 18. *The rules of figure 2 terminate and yield either the unsolvable problem $\perp$, or a problem*

$$P \equiv P_F \wedge P_0 \wedge \cdots \wedge P_n$$

where

- *P_F contains only flexible-flexible equations with the same head variable on both sides,*
- *P_i is solved for $0 \leq i \leq n$,*
- *each free variable F occurs at most once in $P_0 \wedge \cdots \wedge P_n$ as a left-hand side of an equation,*
- *there is no cycle as in the premise of the rule* **Cycle.**

What the above proposition says is that the problem obtained, if one forgets the frozen part P_F, is a DAG-solved form (see [9]), that is a problem from which a unifier is trivially obtained by applying as long as possible a variable elimination rule. We make a technical (yet cost-less) assumption on the rule **Solve** that will ease the termination proof of the next section. If solving a pure subproblem yields a solved equation $F = \lambda \overline{x}.L(\overline{x})$ and a frozen equation $\lambda \overline{x}.L(\overline{x}) = \lambda \overline{x}.L(\overline{x}^\pi)$, where L is a new variable, then L is replaced by F in the rest of the problem, and the frozen equation is replaced by $\lambda \overline{x}.F(\overline{x}) = \lambda \overline{x}.F(\overline{x}^\pi)$. In other words, we want to avoid to just rename a variable by a variable of a frozen equation.

4.2 Frozen variables

The problem that we have omitted so far is that of the frozen flexible-flexible equations. As we have seen in section 3, such equations have no minimal complete set of unifiers, hence the solution (suggested by Qian and Wang) to keep them as *constraints*. In practice, such equations will never be explicitly solved, but one still needs to test their compatibility with the rest of the problem.

This is achieved by applying the rules of figure 3. By abuse of notations, we write $t(\overline{x})$ and $t(\overline{x}^\pi)$, even if all the variables of $\overline{x}$ do not appear in t so as to be able to apply the permutations. The only rule that may seem to cause non-termination is **Merge**, since **Compatibility** and **Incompatibility** can obviously cause no trouble, and **Propagate** will eventually lead to applying **Compatibility**, **Incompatibility** or **Merge**. But **Merge** may make some previously solved problems unsolved. One has then to apply again as long as possible the rules of figure 2.

Lemma 19. Merge *cannot be applied infinitely many times.*

Compatibility

$$\lambda \overline{x}.F(\overline{x}) = \lambda \overline{x}.F(\overline{x}^\pi) \ \wedge \ F = \lambda \overline{x}.u(\overline{x}) \ \rightarrow \ F = \lambda \overline{x}.u(\overline{x})$$
if $\lambda \overline{x}.u(\overline{x}) =_{\eta\beta AC} \lambda \overline{x}.u(\overline{x}^\pi)$.

Incompatibility

$$\lambda \overline{x}.F(\overline{x}) = \lambda \overline{x}.F(\overline{x}^\pi) \ \wedge \ F = \lambda \overline{x}.u(\overline{x}) \ \rightarrow \ \perp$$
if $\lambda \overline{x}.u(\overline{x})$ is ground and $\lambda \overline{x}.u(\overline{x}) \neq_{\eta\beta AC} \lambda \overline{x}.u(\overline{x}^\pi)$.

Propagate

$$\lambda \overline{x}.F(\overline{x}) = \lambda \overline{x}.F(\overline{x}^\pi) \ \wedge \ F = \lambda \overline{x}.\gamma(t_1(\overline{x}), \ldots, t_n(\overline{x})) \ \rightarrow$$
$$\lambda \overline{x}.t_1(\overline{x}) = \lambda \overline{x}.t_1(\overline{x}^\pi) \ \wedge \ \cdots \ \wedge \ \lambda \overline{x}.t_n(\overline{x}) = \lambda \overline{x}.t_n(\overline{x}^\pi)$$
if γ is not an AC constant.

Merge

$$\lambda \overline{x}.F(\overline{x}) = \lambda \overline{x}.F(\overline{x}^\pi) \ \wedge \ F = \lambda(\overline{x}).t_1(\overline{x}) + \cdots + t_n(\overline{x}) \ \rightarrow$$
$$\lambda(\overline{x}).t_1(\overline{x}) + \cdots + t_n(\overline{x}) = \lambda(\overline{x}).t_1(\overline{x}^\pi) + \cdots + t_n(\overline{x}^\pi)$$
If $+$ is an AC constant.

Fig. 3. The rules for testing the compatibility of the frozen part with the solved subproblems.

Proof (Sketched). If solving P_i makes it possible to apply **Merge** to some other problem P_j, then the solving of P_i must have created a new frozen equation $\lambda \overline{x}.F(\overline{x}) = \lambda \overline{x}.F(\overline{x}^\pi)$, where F appeared free in both P_i and P_j. We call such a variable a *weakly shared variable*. Note also that this occurs only when F has no value with head $+_i$. After applying **Merge**, P_j is to be solved again but this time the value of F will be a term with head $+_j$. Hence, no new frozen equation with variable F will be created by solving P_j. The key of the proof relies on the following lemma.

Lemma 20. *No rule of figures 2 and 3 creates new weakly shared variables.*

Theorem 21. *The following algorithm terminates and computes a DAG solved form for for unification of higher-order patterns modulo AC.*

1. *Apply as long as possible* **VA**,
2. *as long as possible do*
   (a) *apply as long as possible the rules of figure 2*
   (b) *apply the rules of figure 3 until a DAG solved form is obtained, or some pure subproblem is made unsolved by* **Merge**.

5 Conclusion

We have presented a unification algorithm for higher-order patterns modulo AC. This will have applications in functional programming, algebraic-functional programming and hopefully for testing the local confluence of higher-order rewrite systems in the presence of associative-commutative constants. Our result will not extend as such to E-unification of higher-order patterns for an arbitrary theory E, since the algorithm heavily relies on the properties of AC. Yet, it will be interesting to apply similar methods to other well-known theories of interest. We have in mind the usual extensions of AC (like AC1, ACI,...), but also richer theories like Abelian groups or Boolean rings. This will require not only to design an elementary unification algorithm for these theories, but also to adapt the combination method to non-regular or collapsing equational theories.

References

1. Alexandre Boudet. *Unification dans les Mélanges de Théories équationnelles*. Thèse de doctorat, Université Paris-Sud, Orsay, France, February 1990.
2. Alexandre Boudet. Combining unification algorithms. *Journal of Symbolic Computation*, 16:597–626, 1993.
3. Alexandre Boudet. Competing for the AC-unification race. *Journal of Automated Reasoning*, 11:185–212, 1993.
4. Alexandre Boudet, Evelyne Contejean, and Hervé Devie. A new AC-unification algorithm with a new algorithm for solving diophantine equations. In *Proc. 5th IEEE Symp. Logic in Computer Science, Philadelphia*, pages 289–299. IEEE Computer Society Press, June 1990.
5. A. Bouhoula, J.-P. Jouannaud, and J. Meseguer. Specification and proof in membership equational logic. In Michel Bidoit and Max Dauchet, editors, *Theory and Practice of Software Development*, volume 1214 of *Lecture Notes in Computer Science*, Lille, France, April 1997. Springer-Verlag.
6. Val Breazu-Tannen. Combining algebra and higher-order types. In *Proc. 3rd IEEE Symp. Logic in Computer Science, Edinburgh*, July 1988.
7. R. Hindley and J. Seldin. *Introduction to Combinators and λ-calculus*. Cambridge University Press, 1986.
8. Gérard Huet. *Résolution d'équations dans les langages d'ordre $1, 2, \ldots \omega$*. Thèse d'Etat, Univ. Paris 7, 1976.
9. Jean-Pierre Jouannaud and Claude Kirchner. Solving equations in abstract algebras: A rule-based survey of unification. In Jean-Louis Lassez and Gordon Plotkin, editors, *Computational Logic: Essays in Honor of Alan Robinson*. MIT-Press, 1991.
10. Jean-Pierre Jouannaud and Mitsuhiro Okada. Executable higher-order algebraic specification languages. In *Proc. 6th IEEE Symp. Logic in Computer Science, Amsterdam*, pages 350–361, 1991.
11. D. Miller. A logic programming language with lambda-abstraction, function variables, and simple unification. In P. Schroeder-Heister, editor, *Extensions of Logic Programming*. LNCS 475, Springer Verlag, 1991.
12. T. Nipkow. Higher order critical pairs. In *Proc. IEEE Symp. on Logic in Comp. Science*, Amsterdam, 1991.
13. Zhenyu Qian and Kang Wang. Modular AC-Unification of Higher-Order Patterns. In Jean-Pierre Jouannaud, editor, *First International Conference on Constraints in Computational Logics*, volume 845 of *Lecture Notes in Computer Science*, pages 105–120, München, Germany, September 1994. Springer-Verlag.
14. Jörg H. Siekmann. Unification theory. *Journal of Symbolic Computation*, 7(3 & 4), 1989. Special issue on unification, part one.

On the Complexity of Unification and Disunification in Commutative Idempotent Semigroups

Miki Hermann[1] and Phokion G. Kolaitis[2] *

[1] LORIA (CNRS), BP 239, 54506 Vandœuvre-lès-Nancy, France, hermann@loria.fr
[2] Computer Science Department, University of California, Santa Cruz, CA 95064, U.S.A., kolaitis@cse.ucsc.edu

Abstract. We analyze the computational complexity of elementary unification and disunification problems for the equational theory ACI of commutative idempotent semigroups. From earlier work, it was known that the decision problem for elementary ACI-unification is solvable in polynomial time. We show that this problem is inherently sequential by establishing that it is complete for polynomial time (P-complete) via logarithmic-space reductions. We also investigate the decision problem and the counting problem for elementary ACI-matching and observe that the former is solvable in logarithmic space, but the latter is #P-complete. After this, we analyze the computational complexity of the decision problem for elementary ground ACI-disunification. Finally, we study the computational complexity of a restricted version of elementary ACI-matching, which arises naturally as a set-term matching problem in the context of the logic data language LDL. In both cases, we delineate the boundary between polynomial-time solvability and NP-hardness by taking into account two parameters, the number of free constants and the number of disequations or equations.

1   Introduction and Summary of Results

Among all equational theories studied in the context of unification and automated deduction, the equational theory AC of commutative semigroups is undoubtedly the one that has attracted the most attention. There are many applications, however, in which the operators at hand may satisfy other equational axioms in addition to associativity A and commutativity C. For this reason, various extensions of AC have also been examined. A particularly natural and useful such extension is the equational theory ACI of commutative idempotent semigroups, which augments AC with the idempotence axiom I: $(\forall x)(x * x = x)$. ACI provides perhaps the simplest way to consider finite sets of objects that are represented by free constants, without being hampered by the drawbacks of a full Set datatype specification. Moreover, simpler set constraints can be treated by considering unification problems in commutative idempotent semigroups.

---

* Research of this author was partially supported by NSF Grant CCR-9610257.

The computational complexity of general ACI-matching and general ACI-unification (that is, the terms to be unified or matched may contain both free function and free constant symbols) was investigated by Kapur and Narendran [KN86,KN92], who established that these decision problems are NP-complete. In contrast, they also proved that elementary ACI-unification with a finite number of free constants is solvable in polynomial time [KN92]. More recently, Narendran [Nar96] showed that ground elementary ACIU-disunification is NP-hard, where ACIU is the extension of ACI with a unit element.

In this paper, we investigate further the computational complexity of elementary ACI-unification and ACI-disunification with a finite number of free constants. First, we establish that elementary ACI-unification with at least two free constants is a P-hard problem, which means that every decision problem solvable in polynomial time can be reduced to elementary ACI-unification with two free constants via some logarithmic-space reduction. This complements the aforementioned result of Kapur and Narendran [KN92] stating that elementary ACI-unification with a finite number of free constants is solvable in polynomial time. Moreover, it suggests strongly that elementary ACI-unification is inherently sequential and, thus, lacks "fast parallel" algorithms (see [GHR95]). We also investigate the decision problem and the *counting* problem for elementary ACI-matching, where the latter is the problem of finding the number of minimal complete ACI-matchers of a given finite system of equations between terms. In [HK95a], we introduced counting problems in equational matching and embarked on a study of their computational complexity as a way to obtain lower bounds on the performance of algorithms for finding minimal complete sets of matchers. Here, we observe that the decision problem for ACI-matching is solvable in LOGSPACE, but the counting problem for ACI-matching is #P-complete. Since #P-complete problems are considered to be highly intractable (see [Joh90,Pap94]), this shows a dramatic difference in computational complexity between a decision problem in equational matching and its corresponding counting problem. It should be noted that Baader and Büttner [BB88] designed an algorithm for finding a minimal complete set of elementary ACI-unifiers of a *single* equation between two terms. They also computed explicitly the cardinality of this minimal set and pointed out that it can be an "enormous number".

After this, we analyze the computational complexity of the decision problem for elementary ground ACI-disunification. We delineate the boundary between polynomial-time solvability and NP-hardness by taking into account two parameters, the number of free constants and the number of disequations. Specifically, we show that, when the number of disequations is fixed, the decision problem for elementary ground ACI-disunification with any number of free constants is solvable in polynomial time. In contrast, when the number of disequations is unbounded, the decision problem for elementary ground ACI-disunification is NP-hard, as long as at least two free constants are available (the latter result was implicit in Narendran [Nar96]).

Finally, we investigate the computational complexity of a restricted version of elementary ACI-matching, which arises naturally as a set-term matching problem in the context of the logic data language LDL. This problem asks: given a system of elementary ACI-equations, does there exist an ACI-matcher such that every variable is instantiated by a single constant? This restricted ACI-matching problem has been introduced by Shmueli, Tsur, and Zaniolo [STZ92], and also studied by Arni, Greco, and Saccà [AGS96] under the name *bounded set-term matching*. Here, we show that restricted ACI-matching with two free constants and an unbounded number of equations is NP-complete, but restricted ACI-matching with a fixed number of free constants and a fixed number of equations is solvable in polynomial time.

2 Preliminaries

A *signature* $\mathcal{F}$ is a countable set of function and constant symbols. If $\mathcal{X}$ is a countable set of variables, then $\mathcal{T}(\mathcal{F}, \mathcal{X})$ denotes the set of all terms over the signature $\mathcal{F}$ and the variables in $\mathcal{X}$. A *ground term* is a term without variables.

An *identity* over $\mathcal{F}$ is a first-order sentence of the form $(\forall x_1)\ldots(\forall x_n)(l = r)$, where l and r are terms in $\mathcal{T}(\mathcal{F}, \mathcal{X})$ with variables among $x_1,\ldots,x_n$. Every set E of identities can be viewed as the set of *equational axioms* of an *equational theory* Th(E) consisting of all identities over $\mathcal{F}$ that are logically implied by E. By an abuse of terminology, we will often say the "equational theory E", instead of the "equational theory Th(E)". The notation $s =_E t$ denotes that the identity $(\forall x_1)\ldots(\forall x_n)(s = t)$ is a member of Th(E). We write $\mathcal{T}(\mathcal{F}, \mathcal{X})/=_E$ to denote the term algebra modulo the equational theory E. Similarly, $\mathcal{T}(\mathcal{F})/=_E$ denotes the *ground* term algebra modulo E, which is also the initial algebra of E.

An *E-unification* problem is a finite set Γ of equations $s = t$ between terms from $\mathcal{T}(\mathcal{F}, \mathcal{X})$. A *solution* (or a *unifier*) of a unification problem Γ is a substitution ρ such that $s\rho =_E t\rho$ for every equation $s = t$ in Γ, which means that the system of equations in Γ has a solution in the term algebra $\mathcal{T}(\mathcal{F}, \mathcal{X})/=_E$. Since solutions are closed under instantiations of variables by arbitrary terms, this is also equivalent to having a solution in the ground term algebra $\mathcal{T}(\mathcal{F})/=_E$ (and, consequently, equivalent to having a solution in every model of E). An E-matching problem is an E-unification problem Γ such that for every equation $s = t$ in Γ the term t is ground.

An *E-disunification* problem is a finite set Δ of equations $s = t$ and disequations $s' \neq t'$ between terms from $\mathcal{T}(\mathcal{F}, \mathcal{X})$. A *solution* of a disunification problem Δ is a substitution ρ such that $s\rho =_E t\rho$ for every equation $s = t$ in Δ, and $s'\rho \neq_E t'\rho$ for every disequation $s' \neq t'$ in Δ. As before, this means that the system of equations and disequations in Δ has a solution in the term algebra $\mathcal{T}(\mathcal{F}, \mathcal{X})/=_E$. It should be emphasized, however, that this is *not* always equivalent to having a solution in the ground term algebra $\mathcal{T}(\mathcal{F})/=_E$, as solutions to systems of disequations may not be closed under substitutions of variables by ground terms. A *ground solution* of a disunification problem Δ is a solution ρ of Δ in the ground term algebra $\mathcal{T}(\mathcal{F})/=_E$, that is, ρ is both a ground substitution and a solution of Δ. A *ground disunification problem* is a disunification problem in which only ground solutions are sought.

If E is a set of identities, then $sig(E)$ is the set of all function and constant symbols occurring in some member of E. From now on we assume that $\mathcal{F} \setminus sig(E)$ consists of constants symbols *only*. Thus, the only symbols of the signature $\mathcal{F}$ that do not occur in some member of E are *free* constants. In this case, we speak of *elementary E-unification* and *elementary E-disunification*.

In the sequel, we will analyze the computational complexity of elementary unification and disunification problems by taking into account the number of equations, the number of disequations, and the number of free constants. For this reason, we introduce the following notation. If k and m are two positive integers, then $E(k; m)$ is the collection of all elementary E-unification problems Γ with k equations such that $\mathcal{F} \setminus sig(E)$ consists of m free constants. We put

$$E(\omega; m) = \bigcup_{k \geq 1} E(k; m) \quad \text{and} \quad E(\omega; \omega) = \bigcup_{k,m \geq 1} E(k; m).$$

If k is a non-negative integer, and l and m are two positive integers, then $E(k, l; m)$ is the collection of all elementary E-disunification problems Γ with k equations, l disequations and such that $\mathcal{F} \setminus sig(E)$ consists of m free constants. We also put

$$E(k, \omega; m) = \bigcup_{l \geq 1} E(k, l; m) \quad \text{and} \quad E(\omega, l; \omega) = \bigcup_{k,m \geq 1} E(k, l; m),$$

Our main focus will be on the equational theory ACI of commutative idempotent semigroups. For this theory, the signature $\mathcal{F}$ consists of free constants and a binary function symbol $*$ that is assumed to be associative, commutative, and idempotent. Thus, the equational axioms of ACI are the identities

A: $(\forall x)(\forall y)(\forall z)(x*(y*z) = (x*y)*z)$, C: $(\forall x)(\forall y)(x*y = y*x)$, I: $(\forall x)(x*x = x)$

Note that if $\mathcal{F} = \{*, c_1, \ldots, c_m\}$, then the ground term algebra $\mathcal{T}(\mathcal{F})/=_{\text{ACI}}$ is the commutative idempotent semigroup freely generated by $c_1, \ldots, c_m$.

We will also encounter briefly the equational theory ACIU of commutative idempotent monoids. For this theory, the signature $\mathcal{F}$ contains also a constant symbol 1, which is the *unit* element for $*$. Thus, ACIU satisfies also the identity U: $(\forall x)(x*1 = x)$. If $\mathcal{F} = \{*, c_1, \ldots, c_m\}$, then the ground algebra $\mathcal{T}(\mathcal{F})/=_{\text{ACIU}}$ is the commutative idempotent monoid freely generated by $c_1, \ldots, c_m$.

3 Elementary ACI-unification and ACI-matching

Kapur and Narendran [KN92] showed that the decision problem for elementary ACI-unification with a finite number of free constants is solvable in polynomial time, even when the signature $\mathcal{F}$ is part of the input. More precisely, consider the following decision problem.

ELEMENTARY ACI-UNIFICATION: Given a finite set $\{c_1, \ldots, c_m\}$ of free constants and an elementary $\text{ACI}(\omega; m)$-unification problem Γ over the signature $\mathcal{F} = \{*, c_1, \ldots, c_m\}$, does Γ have a solution?

Kapur and Narendran [KN92] showed that ELEMENTARY ACI-UNIFICA-
TION can be reduced in polynomial time to PROPOSITIONAL HORN SATIS-
FIABILITY, that is, to the problem: given a Horn[1] formula, does it have a satis-
fying truth assignment? It is well known that PROPOSITIONAL HORN SAT-
ISFIABILITY is solvable in polynomial time; as a matter of fact, it has a linear-
time algorithm [DG84]). Next, we describe Kapur and Naredran's [KN92] re-
duction of ELEMENTARY ACI-UNIFICATION to PROPOSITIONAL HORN
SATISFIABILITY in some detail, since it will be of interest to us in the sequel.

Assume that we are given a set C of m free constants and an elementary
ACI$(\omega; m)$-unification problem Γ. Let $\mathcal{X}_s$ and $\mathcal{X}_t$ be the sets of variables occurring in s and t respectively. For every given free constant c and every variable
$x \in \mathcal{X}_s \cup \mathcal{X}_t$, we introduce a propositional variable $P_{x,c}$; intuitively, $P_{x,c}$ expresses
the fact that the free constant c does not occur in the value of the solution for
the variable x. For every equation $s = t$ in Γ, we form a set $\Theta(s,t)$ of propositional Horn clauses asserting that a free constant occurs in the left-hand side of
the solved equation if and only if it occurs in the right-hand side of the solved
equation. Formally, the Horn clauses in the set $\Theta(s,t)$ are obtained as follows.

- Let c be a free constant that occurs in s, but does not occur in t. If $\mathcal{X}_t \neq \emptyset$, we
  introduce the Horn clause $(\bigvee_{x \in \mathcal{X}_t} \neg P_{x,c})$. If $\mathcal{X}_t = \emptyset$, we conclude immediately
  that Γ is not ACI-unifiable, since $s = t$ is not ACI-unifiable.
- Let c be a free constant that occurs in t, but does not occur in s. If $\mathcal{X}_s \neq \emptyset$, we
  introduce the Horn clause $(\bigvee_{x \in \mathcal{X}_s} \neg P_{x,c})$. If $\mathcal{X}_s = \emptyset$, we conclude immediately
  that Γ is not ACI-unifiable, since $s = t$ is not ACI-unifiable.
- Let c be a free constant that does not occur in the equation $s = t$. For every
  variable $x \in \mathcal{X}_s$, we introduce the Horn clause $(\bigwedge_{y \in \mathcal{X}_t} P_{y,c} \supset P_{x,c})$ and, for
  every variable $y \in \mathcal{X}_t$, we introduce the Horn clause $(\bigwedge_{x \in \mathcal{X}_s} P_{x,c} \supset P_{y,c})$. If
  $\mathcal{X}_t = \emptyset$, then the first clause is the unit clause $P_{x,c}$. Similarly, if $\mathcal{X}_s = \emptyset$, then
  the second clause is the unit clause $P_{y,c}$.
- Finally, for every variable x occurring in some equation in Γ, we introduce
  the Horn clause $(\bigvee_{c \in C} \neg P_{x,c})$ to ensure that the value of the solution for x
  contains at least one free constant.

Let $\Theta(\Gamma) = \bigcup_{(s=t) \in \Gamma} \Theta(s,t)$. It is now quite straightforward to verify that the
ACI$(\omega; m)$-unification problem Γ has a solution if and only if the set $\Theta(\Gamma)$ of
Horn clauses is satisfiable. Note that $\Theta(\Gamma)$ has size polynomial in m and the size
of Γ; in fact, the size of $\Theta(\Gamma)$ is $O(mkr^2)$, where k is the number of equations
in Γ and r is the maximum size of an equation in Γ. Thus, the decision problem
for elementary ACI-unification is solvable in polynomial time.

Once an algorithmic problem has been shown to be solvable in polynomial
time (and, hence, tractable from the point of view of sequential computation),
it is natural to ask whether it can also be solved "fast in parallel". To formalize
this concept, researchers in computational complexity introduced and studied
in depth the class NC of all decision problems that can be solved in polylog-

---

[1] A *Horn* formula is a conjunction of propositional clauses each of which has at most
one positive literal.

arithmic time using polynomially many processors. It is easy to see that NC contains LOGSPACE and, in turn, is contained in P, where LOGSPACE is the class of problems solvable by a deterministic Turing machine using a logarithmic amount of space in its work tape, and P is the class of problems solvable by a deterministic Turing machine in polynomial time. Although it is widely believed that NC is properly contained in P, the question NC $\stackrel{?}{=}$ P remains one of the outstanding open problems of computational complexity. Starting with the work of Cook [Coo74], researchers identified numerous decision problems that are candidates to manifesting the separation between NC and P. These problems, which are known as P-*complete* problems, are the "hardest" members of P, in the sense that every problem in P can be reduced to them via some logarithmic-space reduction. Establishing that a certain problem is P-complete is viewed as providing strong evidence that this problem is not in NC and, hence, it is inherently sequential. Examples of P-complete problems of relevance to automated deduction include UNIT RESOLUTION [JL76] and SYNTACTIC UNIFICATION [DKM84] (a comprehensive treatment of the theory of P-completeness and a catalogue of P-complete problems can be found in the monograph [GHR95]). Our first result in this paper shows that ELEMENTARY ACI-UNIFICATION yields a new paradigm of a P-complete problem.

Theorem 1. *ACI$(\omega; 2)$-unification is P-complete. In words, the decision problem for elementary ACI-unification with two free constants is P-complete.*

Proof. Plaisted [Pla84] showed that PROPOSITIONAL HORN SATISFIABILITY is a P-complete problem; in fact, he showed that the problem remains P-complete even when restricted to inputs in which each clause has at most three literals. We now present a logarithmic-space reduction of this restricted problem to the decision problem for ACI$(\omega; 2)$-unification.

Let a and b be two free constants. Given a set S of propositional Horn clauses each of which has at most three literals, we generate the following elementary ACI-unification problem $\Gamma(S)$ in the free constants a and b.

1. For every propositional variable X occurring in some clause in S, we introduce a variable $x \in \mathcal{X}$ and the equation $x * a = a * b$.
2. For every unit clause X in S, we introduce the equation $x = b$.
3. For every clause in S of the form $(\neg X \vee \neg Y \vee \neg Z)$, we introduce the equation $x * y * z = a * b$.
4. For every clause of the form $(\neg X \vee \neg Y \vee Z)$, we introduce the equation $x * y * z = x * y$.
5. For every clause of the form $(\neg X \vee Z)$, we introduce the equation $x * z = x$.

We now claim that the set S has a satisfying assignment if and only of the elementary ACI-unification problem $\Gamma(S)$ has a solution. If h is a truth assignment that satisfies every clause in S, then it is easy to see that the substitution

$$x\sigma = \begin{cases} b & \text{if } h(X) = \text{TRUE} \\ a * b & \text{if } h(X) = \text{FALSE} \end{cases}$$

is a solution of the elementary ACI-unification problem $\Gamma(S)$. Conversely, suppose that σ is a solution of $\Gamma(S)$. For every variable x occurring in $\Gamma(S)$, it must be the case that $x\sigma = b$ or $x\sigma = a * b$, since the equations in group (1) above imply that $x\sigma * a =_{\mathrm{ACI}} a * b$. It is now easy to verify that the truth assignment

$$h(X) = \begin{cases} \text{TRUE} & \text{if } x\sigma = b \\ \text{FALSE} & \text{if } x\sigma = a * b \end{cases}$$

satisfies every clause in S. For example, a clause of the form $(\neg X \vee \neg Y \vee Z)$ must be satisfied by h, since, otherwise, it would be the case that $x\sigma = b$, $y\sigma = b$ and $z\sigma = a * b$, which implies that σ is not a solution of the equation $x * y * z = x * y$ associated with this clause.   □

The preceding reduction of PROPOSITIONAL HORN SATISFIABILITY to ELEMENTARY ACI-UNIFICATION made use of two free constants in the signature. It should be noted that the presence of at least two free constants is indispensable in obtaining this P-hardness result. Indeed, the decision problem for ACI(ω; 1)-unification is trivial, as the constant substitution $\lambda x.a$ is a solution of every elementary ACI-unification problem in which a is the only free constant.

Let AC be the equational theory of commutative semigroups. It is well known that at the level of the decision problem elementary AC-matching and elementary AC-unification have the same computational complexity, namely each of these two problems is NP-complete (see [BKN87,KN92]). Moreover, the same holds true for the equational theory ACU of commutative monoids (see [KN92,HK95b]). In contrast to the above, we observe next that the decision problem for elementary ACI-matching is in LOGSPACE and, thus, of lower computational complexity than the decision problem for elementary ACI-unification (unless P collapses to LOGSPACE, which is considered extremely unlikely). We also examine the computational complexity of elementary #ACI-matching, which is the following *counting* problem: given an elementary ACI-matching problem Γ, find the cardinality of the the minimal complete set of ACI-matchers of Γ. Valiant [Val79a,Val79b] developed a complexity theory of counting and enumeration problems by introducing the class #P and identifying problems that are complete for this class under parsimonious[2] reductions. In our earlier papers [HK95a,HK95b], we initiated a systematic investigation of the computational complexity of counting problems in equational matching using concepts and results from the theory of #P-completeness. In particular, we showed that the counting problem for elementary AC-matching, as well as the counting problem for elementary ACU-matching, is #P-complete. It should be noted that a #P-completeness result indicates that the counting problem at hand is highly intractable, in fact it suggests a higher level of intractability than an NP-completeness result for the corresponding decision problem (for more on this point see Johnson [Joh90] and Papadimitriou [Pap94]).

---

[2] A *parsimonious* reduction is a polynomial-time reduction between two counting problems that preserves the number of the solutions of each instance.

Theorem 2. *The decision problem for elementary* ACI-*matching is solvable in logarithmic space, but the counting problem for elementary* ACI-*matching is #P-complete, even when restricted to instances with just two free constants. Thus,*
- ACI$(\omega;\omega)$-*matching is in* LOGSPACE;
- #ACI$(\omega;2)$-*matching is #P-complete.*

Proof. Let Γ be an arbitrary elementary ACI-matching problem, that is, for every equation $s = t$ in Γ, the term t is ground. Let $S(\Gamma)$ be the set of Horn clauses that results from the reduction of elementary ACI-unification to PROPO-SITIONAL HORN SATISFIABILITY, as described in the beginning of this section. An inspection of this reduction reveals that each clause in $S(\Gamma)$ is either a unit clause or a disjunction of negated propositional variables, since the set $\mathcal{X}_t$ of variables of t is empty. This special case of PROPOSITIONAL HORN SATISFIABILITY is solvable in logarithmic space, as one needs only to verify that, for every clause consisting of negated propositional variables, at least one of its propositional variables does not appear as a unit clause.

Next, we focus on elementary #ACI-matching. It is easy to see that this counting problem is in #P (this follows also from more general results in [HK95a]). For the lower bound, we have to show that #ACI$(\omega;2)$-matching is a #P-hard problem. Consider the following counting problem:

#POSITIVE 2SAT: Given a propositional CNF formula φ such that each clause is a disjunction of two propositional variables, find the number of satisfying truth assignments of φ.

Although the underlying decision problem POSITIVE 2SAT is trivial, Valiant showed in [Val79b] that the corresponding counting problem #POSITIVE 2SAT is #P-hard. This is an extreme instance of an interesting phenomenon, first observed by Valiant [Val79a], in which the counting version of an "easy" decision problem may be "hard". We now exhibit a parsimonious reduction of #POS-ITIVE 2SAT to #ACI$(\omega;2)$-matching. Assume that a and b are two free constants. Given a a positive 2SAT propositional formula φ, construct the following ACI$(\omega;2)$-matching problem $\Gamma(\varphi)$:
- for every propositional variable X occurring in φ, introduce a propositional variable x and the equation $x * a = a * b$;
- for every clause $(X \vee Y)$ of φ, introduce the equation $x * y = a * b$.

It is easy to check that there is a one-to-one correspondence between satisfying truth assignments of φ and solutions of $\Gamma(\varphi)$, since for every solution σ of the equation $x * a = a * b$ it must be the case that either $x\sigma = b$ or $x\sigma = a * b$. $\square$

Two remarks are in order now.

1. The preceding Theorem 2 shows that elementary ACI-matching is an algorithmic problem whose decision version is "easy", but its counting version is "hard". Compare this with elementary AC-matching and elementary ACU-matching for which the decision problem is NP-complete [BKN87] and the counting problem is #P-complete [HK95a].

2. In proving that #ACI$(\omega;2)$-matching is a #P-hard problem, the number of equations used varied with the input. In the full paper, we show that

if the number of equations is fixed, then the counting problem for elementary ACI-matching is solvable in polynomial time using a dynamic programming algorithm. More formally, we can show that, for every two positive integers k and m, the counting problem #ACI$(k; m)$ is in the class FP of functions computable in polynomial time. It should also be pointed out that Baader and Büttner [BB88] obtained explicit expressions for the number of most general complete unifiers of elementary ACI-unification problems consisting of a *single* equation.

The proofs of Theorems 1 and 2 can be adapted easily to obtain similar results for elementary ACIU-unification and ACIU-matching. In fact, since a unit element of $*$ is available, a single free constant suffices to obtain the hardness results in each case.

Theorem 3. *The following statements are true for the equational theory* ACIU *of commutative idempotent monoids.*
- ACIU$(\omega; 1)$-*unification is P-complete.*
- ACIU$(\omega; \omega)$-*matching is in* LOGSPACE.
- #ACIU$(\omega; 1)$-*matching is #P-complete.*

4   Ground elementary ACI-disunification

Narendran [Nar96] studied the computational complexity of the equational theory ACIUZ, which is the extension of ACIU with the equational axiom Z: $(\forall x)(x * 0 = 0)$ asserting that $*$ has a *zero* element 0. In particular, he showed that ground elementary ACIUZ-disunification is NP-hard by exhibiting a reduction from 3SAT. An inspection of that proof shows that actually a stronger result is established, namely that ground elementary ACIU-disunification with a single free constant a is NP-complete. Moreover, Narendran [Nar96] commented in a footnote that *"A similar reduction will work also for the* ACI *case. There we have to use two constants, say* a *and* b, *since we do not have the unit* 1.*"* The following result confirms that ground elementary ACI-disunification with two free constants is NP-complete, although the reduction we use is not from 3SAT, but from the problem NOT-ALL-EQUAL 3SAT, which asks: given a 3CNF formula φ, is there a truth assignment such that each clause has at least one true literal and at least one false literal? (see [GJ79, page 259]).

Theorem 4. *For every positive integer* $m \geq 2$, *ground* ACI$(0, \omega; m)$-*disunification is NP-complete. In words, the decision problem for ground elementary* ACI-*disunification with no equations and at least two free constants is NP-complete.*

Proof. Membership in NP is obvious; in fact, even ground ACI$(\omega, \omega; \omega)$-disunification is in NP, as it suffices to guess a ground substitution σ such that $|x\sigma| \leq m$ for every variable x occurring in the given instance, where m is the number of free constants occurring in the instance.

Let C be a set of m free constants, $m \geq 2$, and let a and b two free constants in C. Given a 3CNF formula φ to be tested for NOT-ALL-EQUAL 3SAT, we generate the following ACI$(0, \omega; m)$-disunification problem $\Delta(\varphi)$.

- For every propositional variable X_i occurring in φ, we introduce two variables x_i and y_i, and the following disequations. For every ground term t different than $a * b$ and such that each free constant occurs at most once in t, we introduce the disequation $x_i * y_i \neq t$. For every ground term t' different than a and b, and such that each free constant occurs at most once in t', we introduce the disequations $x_i \neq t'$ and $y_i \neq t'$.

- For every clause of φ of the form $(X_i \vee \neg X_j \vee X_r)$ and for every term t different than $a * b$ and such that each free constant occurs at most once in t, we introduce the disequation $x_i * y_j * x_r \neq t$. In a similar manner, we introduce disequations for clauses of the other possible forms. For example, if a clause is of the form $(\neg X_i \vee \neg X_j \vee X_r)$, then we introduce the disequations $y_i * y_j * x_r \neq t$.

The first group of disequations enforces the following property on every ground substitution σ that is a solution of $\Delta(\varphi)$ in the commutative idempotent semigroup freely generated by the constants in C: for every propositional variable X_i occurring in φ, either $x_i\sigma = a \wedge y_i\sigma = b$ or $x_i\sigma = b \wedge y_i\sigma = a$. In turn, this property implies that for every disequation in the second group at least one variable takes value a and at least one variable takes value b. Thus, there is a truth assignment such that every clause of φ has at least one true and at least one false literal if and only if $\Delta(\varphi)$ has a solution in the commutative idempotent semigroup freely generated by the constants in C. $\qquad\square$

In the above NP-hardness proof, both free constants a and b were used; moreover, the number of disequations that were introduced varied with the size of input. It turns out that if either of these conditions is relaxed, then ground elementary ACI-disunification becomes tractable. First, note that ground elementary ACI-disunification with a single free constant a is trivial, since in this case the ground term algebra $\mathcal{T}(\{*, a\})/=_{\mathrm{ACI}}$ is the singleton $\{a\}$. Next, we will show that ground elementary ACI-disunification with a fixed number of disequations is solvable in polynomial time, even when an arbitrary number of equations is present and an arbitrary number of free constants is available. For this, we need to establish an auxiliary result first.

Lemma 5. *For every positive integer k, there is a polynomial-time algorithm for solving the following decision problem: given a propositional Horn formula θ and k propositional formulas $\psi_1, \ldots, \psi_k$ each in disjunctive normal form, is the formula $\theta \wedge \psi_1 \wedge \cdots \wedge \psi_k$ satisfiable?*

Proof. Let $\theta, \psi_1, \ldots, \psi_k$ be an instance of this problem of size s. Without loss of generality, we may assume that there is a positive integer $n \leq s$ such that each ψ_i consists of exactly n disjuncts. Thus, for every $i \leq k$, $\psi_i \equiv \chi_{i1} \vee \cdots \vee \chi_{in}$, where each χ_{ij} is a conjunction of at most s literals. By distributing conjunctions over disjunctions, we have that

$$\psi_1 \wedge \cdots \wedge \psi_k \equiv \bigvee_{(j_1, \ldots, j_k) \in \{1, \ldots, n\}^k} \chi_{1j_1} \wedge \cdots \wedge \chi_{kj_k}.$$

It follows that the formula $\theta \wedge \psi_1 \wedge \cdots \wedge \psi_k$ is satisfiable if and only if there is a k-tuple $(j_1, \ldots, j_k) \in \{1, \ldots, n\}^k$ such that the formula $\theta \wedge \chi_{1j_1} \wedge \cdots \wedge \chi_{kj_k}$ is satisfiable. Since each of the n^k formulas $\theta \wedge \chi_{1j_1} \wedge \cdots \wedge \chi_{kj_k}$ is a propositional Horn formula, we can apply the polynomial-time algorithm for propositional Horn satisfiability n^k times and, thus, determine in polynomial time whether the formula $\theta \wedge \psi_1 \wedge \cdots \wedge \psi_k$ is satisfiable. □

Theorem 6. *For every positive integer k, ground $\mathrm{ACI}(\omega, k; \omega)$-disunification is in P. In words, ground elementary disunification with k disequations and an arbitrary number of free constants is solvable in polynomial time.*

Proof. Fix a positive integer k. Let Δ be a given $\mathrm{ACI}(\omega, k; \omega)$-disunification problem. Thus, $\Delta = \Gamma \cup \{p_1 \neq q_1, \ldots, p_k \neq q_k\}$, where Γ is an arbitrary elementary ACI-unification problem. Recall Kapur and Narendran's [KN92] reduction of elementary ACI-unification to Propositional Horn Satisfiability, which was described in Section 3. In particular, recall that for every equation $l = r$ this reduction generates a set $\Theta(l, r)$ of Horn clauses. Let θ be the Horn formula $\bigwedge_{(s=t) \in \Gamma} \Theta(s, t)$. For every disequation $p_i \neq q_i$, $1 \leq i \leq k$, consider the set $\Theta(p_i, q_i)$ of Horn clauses generated when the reduction is applied to the equation $p_i = q_i$. For every $i \leq k$, let ϕ_i be the conjunction of all Horn clauses in $\Theta(p_i, q_i)$, and let ψ_i be the formula in disjunctive normal form that is obtained from $\neg \phi_i$ using de Morgan's laws. It is now easy to verify that the $\mathrm{ACI}(\omega, k; \omega)$-disunification problem Δ has a ground solution if and only if the formula $\theta \wedge \psi_1 \wedge \cdots \wedge \psi_k$ is satisfiable. Note that the size of this formula is polynomial in the size of Δ. We can now apply Lemma 5 and obtain the desired polynomial-time algorithm. □

5 Restricted ACI-matching

Set-matching is an important special case of general ACI-matching; its computational complexity has been investigated by Kapur and Narendran [KN86], who showed that this problem is NP-complete. Set-matching, as well as certain variants of it, arise naturally in deductive database systems and in logic-based languages that support complex objects. Shmueli et al. [STZ92] studied set matching problems in the context of LDL, a Horn-clause programming language for deductive database systems. The semantics of LDL require that set-terms consisting of variables and constants be matched in such a way that variables are instantiated only by individual constants. In essence, the problems examined by Shmueli et al. [STZ92] can be formalized as follows: given an elementary ACI-matching problem Γ, is there a a solution ρ of Γ such that, for every variable x occuring in Γ, the value $x\rho$ is equal to one of the constant symbols occurring in Γ? In what follows, we call such problems *restricted* ACI-*matching* problems. Let *restricted* $\mathrm{ACI}(k, m)$-*matching* be the class of restricted ACI-matching problems with k equations and m free constants. The classes *restricted* $\mathrm{ACI}(\omega, m)$-*matching*, *restricted* $\mathrm{ACI}(k, \omega)$-*matching*, and *restricted* $\mathrm{ACI}(\omega, \omega)$-*matching* are defined in an analogous way. Shmueli et al. [STZ92] gave an exponential-time algorithm for restricted $\mathrm{ACI}(\omega, \omega)$-matching. After this, Arni et al. [AGS96] considered *bounded set-term matching*, which, in our terminology, is the same as restricted ACI$(1, \omega)$-matching, that is, restricted ACI-matching with a single equation, but no a priori bound on the number of free constants. An instance of this problem can be written as $XD = C$, where X is a set of variables, C and D are sets of free constants, each set stands for the "product" of its members, and the concatenation XD denotes the union $X \cup D$. Arni et al. [AGS96] pointed out that $XC = D$ has a restricted ACI-matcher if and only if $C \subseteq D$ and $|X| \geq |D \setminus C|$. This gives a simple polynomial-time test for the decision problem for restricted ACI$(1, \omega)$-matching. Moreover, Arni et al. [AGS96] gave an explicit formula for the number of restricted ACI-matchers of a single equation, from which it follows that restricted #ACI$(1, \omega)$-matching is in the class FP of functions computable in polynomial time.

In the sequel, we analyze the computational complexity of restricted ACI-matching by considering once again the interplay between the number of equations and the number of constants. We first observe that a slight modification of the proof of Theorem 4 shows that restricted ACI-matching with no a priori bound on the number of equations is intractable, even if only two free constants are available. This should be contrasted with the low complexity of the decision problem for ACI-matching (cf. Theorem 2).

Theorem 7. *Restricted* ACI$(\omega; 2)$-*matching is a NP-complete problem and restricted* #ACI$(\omega; 2)$-*matching is a #P-complete problem.*

Proof. Since the upper bounds are obvious, we focus on establishing NP-hardness and #P-hardness. For this, we give a parsimonious reduction of NOT-ALL-EQUAL 3SAT to restricted ACI$(\omega, 2)$-matching. For every propositional variable X_i in a given 3CNF formula ϕ, we introduce two variables x_i and y_i, and the equation $x_i * y_i = a * b$, where a and b are free constants. For each clause of ϕ of the form $(X_i \vee \neg X_j \vee X_r)$, we introduce the equation $x_i * y_j * x_r = a * b$. We introduce equations for clauses of the other possible forms in a similar manner. Then ϕ has an assignment that falsifies at least one literal in every clause if and only if the associated system of equations has a restricted ACI-matcher. $\square$

Next, we consider restricted ACI-matching with a fixed number of equations. The main result of this section is that for any two positive integers k and m, the decision problem for restricted ACI(k, m)-matching is solvable in polynomial time. Note that restricted ACI(k, m)-matching can be reduced easily to ground ACI-disunification, but at the expense of introducing an unbounded number of disequations (and so Theorem 6 can not be used). Indeed, for every variable x of a given restricted ACI(k, m)-matching problem with constants $c_1, \ldots, c_m$, we introduce $2^m - m - 1$ new disequations of the form $x \neq c_{i_1} * \cdots * c_{i_r}$, where $2 \leq r \leq m$, and $c_{i_j} \neq c_{i_l}$ for all $j \neq l$; these disequations capture the restriction $x \in \{c_1, \ldots, c_m\}$. It follows that every restricted ACI(k, m)-matching problem with n variables can be reduced to a ground ACI$(k, n(2^m - m - 1); m)$-disunification problem. This approach, however, reduces restricted ACI(k, m)-matching to ground ACI$(k, \omega; m)$-disunification, which is NP-complete (recall Theorem 4). Thus, a different method is needed to establish the tractability of restricted ACI(k, m)-matching.

Fix two positive integers k and m. Let Γ be a restricted ACI(k, m)-matching problem with free constants $c_1, \ldots, c_m$ and variables $x_1, \ldots, x_n$. Each equation of Γ can be written as $XC = D$, where X is a subset of $\{x_1, \ldots, x_n\}$, and C and D are subsets of $\{c_1, \ldots, c_m\}$. For every $i \leq n$, let $C(x_i)$ be the set of all constants that occur in the right-hand side of every equation of Γ in which the variable x_i occurs (that is, $C(x_i)$ is the intersection of the sets D such that x_i occurs in some equation $XC = D$ of Γ). Our polynomial-time algorithm for restricted ACI(k, m)-matching will examine the cardinalities of the sets $C(x_i)$, $1 \leq i \leq n$. Note that if there is a variable x_i such that $C(x_i) = \emptyset$, then Γ has no restricted ACI-matchers. On the other hand, if $C(x_i)$ is a singleton for some variable x_i, then we can eliminate x_i from Γ by replacing it with the unique member of $C(x_i)$. Finally, it may be the case that $|C(x_i)| \geq 2$, for every variable x_i. The next lemma shows that in this case restricted ACI$(k.m)$-matching can be reduced to restricted ACI$(k, m-1)$-matching. In what follows, we will use the notation $XD = c_j C$ to indicate that the right-hand side of this equation is the union $\{c_j\} \cup C$, where $c_j \notin C$.

Lemma 8. *Assume that Γ is a restricted* ACI(k, m)*-matching problem with free constants $c_1, \ldots, c_m$ and variables $x_1, \ldots, x_n$ such that each equation of Γ has a restricted* ACI*-matcher and $|C(x_i)| \geq 2$ for every $i \leq n$. Fix a free constant c_j and assume that $X_1 C_1 = c_j D_1, \ldots, X_r C_r = c_j D_r$ is a list of all equations of Γ in which c_j occurs in the right-hand side, but not in the left-hand side of the equation. Then Γ has a restricted* ACI*-matcher if and only if there is a sequence $z_1, \ldots, z_r$ of (not necessarily distinct) variables with the following properties:*

1. *For every $i \leq r$, the variable z_i occurs in the equation $X_i D_i = c_j D_i$; moreover z_i can occur only in equations in which c_j occurs.*
2. *The system Γ^* obtained from Γ by eliminating all occurrences of the free constant c_j and of the variables $z_1, \ldots, z_r$ has a restricted* ACI*-matcher.*

Proof. If: Take such a sequence $z_1, \ldots, z_r$ of variables and a restricted ACI-matcher ρ^* of Γ^*. Extend $\rho*$ to a substitution ρ on the variables of Γ by assigning c_j as the value of $z_i \rho$, $1 \leq i \leq r$. Then ρ is a restricted ACI-matcher of Γ.

Only If: Suppose that ρ is a restricted ACI-matcher of Γ. Then, for every $i \leq r$, there exists a variable z_i occurring in the equation $X_i C_i = c_j D_i$ and such that $z_i \rho = c_j$. It is clear that z_i can not occur in any equation of Γ in which c_j does not occur. Consider now the system Γ^* obtained from Γ by eliminating all occurrences of the free constant c_j and the variables $z_1, \ldots, z_r$. Define a substitution ρ^* on the variables of Γ^* as follows. If $z\rho \neq c_j$, then $z\rho^* = z\rho$. If $z\rho = c_j$, then put $z\rho^* = c_l$, where c_l is a free constant that is different than c_j and occurs in the right-hand side of every equation of Γ in which z occurs. Note that such a free constant exists, because $|C(z)| \geq 2$. It is now easy to verify that ρ^* is a restricted ACI-matcher of Γ^*. $\square$

Theorem 9. *Let k and m be two positive integers. The decision problem for restricted* ACI(k, m)*-matching is solvable in polynomial time.*

Proof. Let `Propagate-and-Split`(Δ) be the following procedure, where Δ is a system with at most k equations and at most m free constants $c_1, \ldots, c_m$.

1. If only one free constant occurs in Δ, then stop and report that Δ has a restricted ACI-matcher.

2. If one of the equations of Δ does not have a restricted ACI-matcher or if $C(x_i) = \emptyset$ for one of the variables x_i of Δ, then stop and report that Δ does not have a restricted ACI-matcher.

3. Replace every variable x_i such that $|C(x_i)| = 1$ by the unique member of the singleton $C(x_i)$. Let Δ' be the resulting system.

4. Let j be the smallest integer such that the free constant c_j occurs in Δ'. Consider all equations $X_1 C_1 = c_j D_1, \ldots, X_r C_r = c_j D_r$ of Δ' in which c_j occurs in the right-hand side, but not in the left-hand side of the equation. For every sequence $z_1, \ldots, z_l$ of variables such that each z_i occurs in the equation $X_i C_i = c_j D_i$, but does not occur in any equation in which c_j does not occur, generate the system $\Delta'(c_j, z_1, \ldots, z_l)$ obtained from Δ' by eliminating all occurrences of the free constant c_j and the variables $z_1, \ldots, z_l$.

Note that each of the first three steps takes time $O(n)$, where n is the number of variables of Δ. Note also that, after the last step has been completed, at most n^k systems of the form $\Delta'(c_j, z_1, \ldots, z_l)$ are generated; moreover, the number of constants of each such system is one less than the number of constants of Δ.

The above procedure `Propagate-and-Split` gives rise to a polynomial-time algorithm for restricted ACI(k, m)-matching. Let Γ be a restricted ACI$(k.m)$-matching problem. Apply first the procedure to Γ, then to each system generated in the last step, and continue this way until either a restricted ACI-matcher has been found or there are no systems to which the procedure can be applied. Since each application of the last step eliminates a free constant, at most n^{km} systems have to be considered, where n is the number of variables of Γ. Thus, the running time of the algorithm is $O(n^{km+1})$. The correctness of the algorithm follows from the preceding Lemma 8 and the fact that the systems generated by the third step of the procedure satisfy the hypotheses of Lemma 8. $\square$

Note that the running time of the above algorithm for restricted ACI(k, m)-matching depends exponentially on the number m of free constants. It remains an open problem to determine whether restricted ACI(k, ω)-matching can be solved in polynomial time.

6 Concluding Remarks

Combined with the work of Kapur and Narendran [KN92] and Narendran [Nar96], the results presented here provide a fairly complete picture of the computational complexity of elementary ACI-unification and elementary ACI-disunification. Moreover, they shed light on the computational complexity of restricted ACI-matching, a class of constrained set-term matching problems that arose in the development of deductive database systems [STZ92,AGS96].

We conclude by pointing out that in the full version of the paper we venture beyond ACI-unification and ACI-disunification by considering the full first-order theory of free commutative idempotent semigroups with m generators, $m \geq 2$. We analyze the computational complexity of this theory and show it to be PSPACE-complete; moreover, we study the complexity of fragments of this theory obtained by restricting the quantifier alternation or the quantifier-free part of first-order sentences.

References

[AGS96] N. Arni, S. Greco, and D. Saccà. Matching of bounded set terms in the logic language LDL^{++}. *J. Logic Prog.*, 27(1):73–87, 1996.

[BB88] F. Baader and W. Büttner. Unification in commutative idempotent monoids. *Theoretical Comp. Sci.*, 56(3):345–353, 1988.

[BKN87] D. Benanav, D. Kapur, and P. Narendran. Complexity of matching problems. *J. Symb. Comp.*, 3:203–216, 1987.

[Coo74] S.A. Cook. An observation on time-storage trade off. *J. of Comp. and System Sci.*, 9(3):308–316, 1974.

[DG84] W.F. Dowling and J.H. Gallier. Linear-time algorithms for testing the satisfiability of propositional Horn formulae. *J. Logic Prog.*, 1(3):267–284, 1984.

[DKM84] C. Dwork, P.C. Kanellakis, and J.C. Mitchell. On the sequential nature of unification. *J. Logic Prog.*, 1:35–50, 1984.

[GHR95] R. Greenlaw, H.J. Hoover, and W.L. Ruzzo. *Limits to parallel computation: P-completeness theory.* Oxford University Press, New York, 1995.

[GJ79] M.R. Garey and D.S. Johnson. *Computers and intractability: A guide to the theory of NP-completeness.* W.H. Freeman and Co, 1979.

[HK95a] M. Hermann and P.G. Kolaitis. The complexity of counting problems in equational matching. *J. Symb. Comp.*, 20(3):343–362, 1995.

[HK95b] M. Hermann and P.G. Kolaitis. Computational complexity of simultaneous elementary matching problems. In J. Wiedermann and P. Hájek, eds, *Proc. 20th MFCS, Prague (Czech Republic)*, LNCS 969, pp 359–370. Springer, 1995.

[JL76] N.D. Jones and W.T. Laaser. Complete problems for deterministic polynomial time. *Theoretical Comp. Sci.*, 3(1):105–117, 1976.

[Joh90] D.S. Johnson. A catalog of complexity classes. In J. van Leeuwen, ed, *Handbook of Theoretical Computer Science, Volume A*, chapter 2, pp 67–161. North-Holland, Amsterdam, 1990.

[KN86] D. Kapur and P. Narendran. NP-completeness of the set unification and matching problems. In J.H. Siekmann, ed, *Proc. 8th CADE, Oxford (England)*, LNCS 230, pp 489–495. Springer, 1986.

[KN92] D. Kapur and P. Narendran. Complexity of unification problems with associative-commutative operators. *J. of Autom. Reasoning*, 9:261–288, 1992.

[Nar96] P. Narendran. Unification modulo ACI+1+0. *Fundamenta Informaticae*, 25(1):49–57, 1996.

[Pap94] C.H. Papadimitriou. *Computational complexity.* Addison-Wesley, 1994.

[Pla84] D.A. Plaisted. Complete problems in the first-order predicate calculus. *J. of Comp. and System Sci.*, 29(1):8–35, 1984.

[STZ92] O. Shmueli, S. Tsur, and C. Zaniolo. Compilation of set terms in the logic data language (LDL). *J. Logic Prog.*, 12(1 & 2):89–119, 1992.

[Val79a] L.G. Valiant. The complexity of computing the permanent. *Theoretical Comp. Sci.*, 8:189–201, 1979.

[Val79b] L.G. Valiant. The complexity of enumeration and reliability problems. *SIAM J. on Comp.*, 8(3):410–421, 1979.

Ordering Constraints over Feature Trees

Martin Müller[1], Joachim Niehren[1] and Andreas Podelski[2]

[1] Universität des Saarlandes, {mmueller,niehren}@ps.uni-sb.de
[2] Max-Planck-Institut für Informatik, podelski@mpi-sb.mpg.de
Saarbrücken, Germany

Abstract. Feature trees have been used to accommodate records in constraint programming and record like structures in computational linguistics. Feature trees model records, and feature constraints yield extensible and modular record descriptions. We introduce the constraint system $FT_\leq$ of ordering constraints interpreted over feature trees. Under the view that feature trees represent symbolic information, the relation $\leq$ corresponds to the information ordering ("carries less information than"). We present a polynomial algorithm that decides the satisfiability of conjunctions of positive and negative information ordering constraints over feature trees. Our results include algorithms for the satisfiability problem and the entailment problem of $FT_\leq$ in time $O(n^3)$. We also show that $FT_\leq$ has the independence property and are thus able to handle negative conjuncts via entailment. Furthermore, we reduce the satisfiability problem of Dörre's weak-subsumption constraints to the satisfiability problem of $FT_\leq$. This improves the complexity bound for solving weak subsumption constraints from $O(n^5)$ to $O(n^3)$.

Keywords: feature constraints, tree orderings, weak subsumption, satisfiability, entailment, complexity.

1 Introduction

Feature constraints have been used for describing records in constraint programming [2, 24, 23] and record like structures in computational linguistics [13, 12, 20, 18, 19]. Following [3, 5, 4] we consider feature constraints as predicate logic formulae that are interpreted in the structure of feature trees.

A feature tree is a possibly infinite tree with unordered labeled edges and with possibly labeled nodes. Edge labels are functional; i.e., the labels of the edges departing from the same node must be pairwise different. Under the view that feature trees represent symbolic information, the feature tree τ_1 represents less information than the feature tree τ_2 if τ_1 has fewer edges and node labels than τ_2. The relation $\leq$ that we define corresponds to the information ordering in precisely this sense. Algebraically, $\tau_1 \leq \tau_2$ if there is a *homomorphic embed-*

ding from τ_1 to τ_2 (i.e., a mapping from nodes in τ_1 to nodes in τ_2 under which the node labeling is invariant). An example is given in the picture.

We introduce the constraint system $FT_\leq$ of information ordering constraints over feature trees. The system $FT_\leq$ is obtained by adding ordering constraints to the constraint system FT [3]. The syntax of $FT_\leq$ constraints φ is defined by

$$\varphi ::= x \leq x' \mid x[a]x' \mid a(x) \mid \varphi \wedge \varphi'$$

where x and x' are variables and a is a label. The semantics of $FT_\leq$ is given by the interpretation over feature trees where the symbol $\leq$ is interpreted as information ordering on feature trees. The semantics of $x[a]y$ and $a(x)$ are defined as in FT. For instance, both trees depicted above are possible values for x in solutions of the constraint $\text{wine}(x) \wedge x[\text{color}]x' \wedge \text{red}(x')$.

It is clear that $FT_\leq$ is more expressive than FT since the information ordering is antisymmetric (i.e., $(x \leq x' \wedge x' \leq x) \leftrightarrow x = x'$ is valid). As we show in the paper, $FT_\leq$ is strictly more expressive than FT. For instance, no constraint in FT can be equivalent to $x \leq x'$. Also, we do not know of any formula over FT (even with existential quantifiers) equivalent to $\exists x(x_1 \leq x \wedge x_2 \leq x) \wedge \exists x(x_1 \leq x \wedge x_3 \leq x)$; this $FT_\leq$ formula expresses that x_1 is unifiable with both x_2 and x_3 (but does not imply unifiability of x_2 and x_3).

We show that the satisfiability problem of conjunctions of positive and negative $FT_\leq$ constraints $\varphi \wedge \neg \varphi_1 \wedge \ldots \wedge \neg \varphi_n$ is decidable in $O(n^3)$. This result includes a decision procedure for the entailment problem of the form $\varphi' \models \varphi$ since a formula $\varphi' \rightarrow \varphi$ is valid if and only if the formula $\varphi' \wedge \neg \varphi$ is unsatisfiable. To establish our result, we prove that $FT_\leq$ has the fundamental independence property (similar to its relatives RT [6], FT [3], and CFT [24]).

We reduce the satisfiability problem of Dörre's weak-subsumption constraints [7] over feature algebras linearly to the one in $FT_\leq$. Thereby, our algorithm improves on the best known satisfiability test for weak subsumption constraints which uses finite automata techniques and has an $O(n^5)$-complexity bound [7].

Plan of the Paper. Section 2 surveys related work. Section 3 defines $FT_\leq$. Section 4 presents the satisfiability test for $FT_\leq$ constraints. Section 8 contains the completeness proof. Section 5 presents the entailment test for $FT_\leq$ constraints, and proves the independence property of $FT_\leq$. Section 6 defines weak subsumption constraints and reduces their satisfiability problem to the one of $FT_\leq$ constraints. Section 7 shows that $FT_\leq$ is strictly more expressive than FT.

2 Related Work

Ines Constraints. In previous work [17], we have introduced the constraint system INES of inclusion constraints over non-empty sets of trees and a cubic satisfiability test. The satisfiability test for $FT_\leq$ is inspired by and subsumes the one for INES. However, the entailment problems for $FT_\leq$ and INES constraints are different. The entailment problem of INES constraints is coNP-hard [16]. Intuitively, the entailment problem of $FT_\leq$ is less expressive than the one of INES because an $FT_\leq$ constraint φ cannot uniquely describe a single feature tree (in absence of arity constraints); in contrast, INES constraints (which are inclusions between first-order terms with an implicit arity restriction) can uniquely describe a constructor tree as a singleton set. For instance, the INES constraint $x \subseteq a$ describes the singleton $\{a\}$. As a consequence, the entailment proposition $x \subseteq a \wedge a \subseteq y \models x \subseteq y$ holds in INES. No similar entailment phenomenon exists for $FT_\leq$.

Feature Constraints. The constraint system CFT [24] extends FT by arity constraints of the form $x\{f_1,\ldots,f_n\}$, saying that the denotation of x has subtrees exactly at the features f_1 through f_n. CFT subsumes Colmerauer's rational tree constraint system RT [6] but provides finer-grained constraints. The system EF [25] extends CFT by feature constraints $x[y]z$, providing for first-class features. Complete axiomatizations for FT and CFT have been given in [5] and [4], respectively. The satisfiability of EF constraints is shown NP-hard in [25]. The system $FT_\leq(sort)$ extends $FT_\leq$ by allowing a partial order on labels [15].

Subsumption Constraints. Subsumption is an ordering on the domain of feature algebras. Subsumption constraints have been considered in the context of unification-based grammars to model coordination phenomena in natural language [9, 7, 21]. There, one wants to express that two feature structures representing different parts of speech share common properties. For example, the analysis of "programming" and "linguistics" in the phrase

Feature constraints for [$_{NP}$ programming] and [$_{NP}$ linguistics]

should share (but might refine differently) the information common to all noun phrases. Since the satisfiability of subsumption constraints is undecidable [9], Dörre proposed weak subsumption as an decidable approximation of subsumption. As we show, the information ordering over feature trees (as investigated in this paper) coincides with the weak subsumption ordering interpreted over (the algebra of) feature trees.

Independent Constraint Systems. A constraint system has the fundamental *independence property* if negated conjuncts are independent from each other, or: its constraints cannot express disjunctions (we will give a formal definition later). Apart from the mentioned tree constraint systems RT, FT, CFT [6, 1, 24, 3], constraint systems with the independence property include linear equations over the real numbers [14], or infinite boolean algebras with positive constraints [10].

3 Syntax and Semantics of $FT_\leq$

The constraint system $FT_\leq$ is defined by a set of constraints together with an interpretation over feature trees. We assume an infinite set of *variables* ranged over by x,y,z, and an infinite set L of *labels* ranged over by a,b.

Feature Trees. A *path* p is a finite sequence of labels. The *empty path* is denoted by ε and the free-monoid concatenation of paths p and p' as pp'; we have $\varepsilon p = p\varepsilon = p$. Given paths p and q, p' is called a *prefix of* p if $p = p'p''$ for some path p''. A *tree domain* is a non-empty prefix closed set of paths. A *feature tree* τ is a pair (D,L) consisting of a tree domain D and partial labeling function $L : D \rightharpoonup L$. Given a feature tree τ, we write D_τ for its tree domain and L_τ for its labeling function. The set of all feature trees is denoted by $\mathcal{F}$. A feature tree is called *finite* if its tree domain is finite, and *infinite* otherwise.

Syntax. An $FT_\leq$ *constraint* φ is defined by the following abstract syntax.

$$\varphi ::= x \leq y \mid a(x) \mid x[a]y \mid x \sim y \mid \varphi_1 \wedge \varphi_2$$

An $FT_\leq$ constraint is a conjunction of *basic constraints* which are either *inclusion constraints* $x\leq y$, *labeling constraints* $a(x)$, *selection constraints* $x[a]y$, or *compatibility constraints* $x{\sim}y$. Compatibility constraints are needed in our algorithm and can be expressed by first-order formulae over inclusion constraints (see Proposition 1). We identify $FT_\leq$ constraints φ up to associativity and commutativity of conjunction, *i.e.*, we view φ as a multiset of inclusion, labeling, selection, and compatibility constraints. We write φ *in* φ' if all conjuncts in φ are contained in φ'. The *size of a constraint* φ is defined as the number of label and variable occurrences in φ.

Semantics. We next define the structure $\mathcal{F}$ over feature trees in which we interpret $FT_\leq$ constraints. The signature of $\mathcal{F}$ contains the binary relation symbols $\leq$ and $\sim$ and for every label a a unary relation symbol $a()$ and a binary relation symbol $[a]$. In $\mathcal{F}$ these relation symbols are interpreted such:

$$\tau_1 \leq \tau_2 \quad \text{iff} \quad D_{\tau_1} \subseteq D_{\tau_2} \text{ and } L_{\tau_1} \subseteq L_{\tau_2}$$
$$\tau_1[a]\tau_2 \quad \text{iff} \quad D_{\tau_2} = \{p \mid ap \in D_{\tau_1}\} \text{ and } L_{\tau_2} = \{(p,b) \mid (ap,b) \in L_{\tau_1}\}$$
$$a(\tau) \quad \text{iff} \quad (\varepsilon, a) \in L_\tau$$
$$\tau_1{\sim}\tau_2 \quad \text{iff} \quad L_{\tau_1} \cup L_{\tau_2} \text{ is a partial function (on } D_{\tau_1} \cup D_{\tau_2})$$

Let Φ denote first-order formulae built from $FT_\leq$ constraints with the usual first order connectives. We call Φ *satisfiable* (valid) if Φ is satisfiable (valid) in the structure $\mathcal{F}$. We say that Φ *entails* Φ', written $\Phi \models \Phi'$, if $\Phi \to \Phi'$ is valid, and that Φ is *equivalent* to Φ' if $\Phi_1 \leftrightarrow \Phi_2$ is valid. We denote with $V(\Phi)$ the set of variables occurring free in Φ and with $L(\Phi)$ the set of labels occurring in Φ.

Proposition 1. *The formulae $x{\sim}y$ and $\exists z(x\leq z \wedge y\leq z)$ are equivalent in $\mathcal{F}$.*

Proof. Let σ be a variable assignment into $\mathcal{F}$ which also is a solution of the formula $\exists z(x\leq z \wedge y\leq z)$. Since $L_{\sigma(x)} \cup L_{\sigma(y)} \subseteq L_{\sigma(z)}$ and $L_{\sigma(z)}$ is a partial function, $L_{\sigma(x)} \cup L_{\sigma(y)}$ is also a partial function. Hence σ is a solution of $x{\sim}y$. Conversely, if σ is a solution of $x{\sim}y$ then $L_{\sigma(x)} \cup L_{\sigma(y)}$ is a partial function. Thus, the pair $\tau =_{def} (D_{\sigma(x)} \cup D_{\sigma(y)}, L_{\sigma(x)} \cup L_{\sigma(y)})$ is a feature tree and the variable assignment σ' defined by $\sigma'(z) = \tau$ and $\sigma'(x) = \sigma(x)$ for $x \neq z$ is a solution of $x\leq z \wedge y\leq z$. $\qquad\square$

4 Satisfiability Test

We present a set of axioms valid for $FT_\leq$ and then interpret these axioms as an algorithm that solves the satisfiability problem of $FT_\leq$. The axioms and the algorithm are inspired by the ones for INES constraints presented in [17].

Table 1 contains five axiom schemes F1 - F5 that we regard as sets of axioms. The union of these sets of axioms is denoted by F, *i.e.*, F = F1 $\cup \ldots \cup$ F5. For instance, an axiom scheme $x\leq x$ represents the infinite set of axioms obtained by instantiation of the meta variable x. An axiom is either a constraint φ, an implication between constraints $\varphi \to \varphi'$, or an implication $\varphi \to$ *false*.

Proposition 2. *The structure $\mathcal{F}$ is a model of the axioms in F.*

F1	$x \leq x$ and $x \leq y \wedge y \leq z \rightarrow x \leq z$
F2	$x[a]x' \wedge x \leq y \wedge y[a]y' \rightarrow x' \leq y'$
F3	$x \leq y \rightarrow x \sim y$ and $x \leq y \wedge y \sim z \rightarrow x \sim z$ and $x \sim y \rightarrow y \sim x$
F4	$x[a]x' \wedge x \sim y \wedge y[a]y' \rightarrow x' \sim y'$
F5	$a(x) \wedge x \sim y \wedge b(y) \rightarrow false$ for $a \neq b$

Table 1. Satisfiability of $FT_{\leq}$ Constraints.

Proof. By a routine check. For illustration, we prove the statement for the second rule in F3, namely $x \leq y \wedge y \sim y' \rightarrow x \sim y'$. The following implications hold:

$$
\begin{array}{lll}
x \leq y \wedge y \sim y' & \leftrightarrow & x \leq y \wedge \exists z (y \leq z \wedge y' \leq z) \quad \text{Proposition 1} \\
& \rightarrow & \exists z (x \leq z \wedge y \leq z) \quad\quad\quad \text{Transitivity} \\
& \leftrightarrow & x \sim y \quad\quad\quad\quad\quad\quad\quad\quad\; \text{Proposition 1} \qquad \Box
\end{array}
$$

The Algorithm F. The set of axioms F induces a fixed point algorithm F that, given an input constraint φ, iteratively adds logical consequences of $F \cup \{\varphi\}$ to φ. (Observe that actually only constraints of the form $x \leq y$ and $x \sim y$ are derived). More precisely, in every step F inputs a constraint φ and terminates with *false* or outputs a constraint $\varphi \wedge \varphi'$. Termination with *false* takes place if there exists φ'' *in* φ such that $\varphi'' \rightarrow false \in$ F. Output of $\varphi \wedge \varphi'$ is possible if $\varphi' \in$ F or there exists φ'' *in* φ with $\varphi'' \rightarrow \varphi' \in$ F.

Example 1. Inconsistency can be due to incompatible upper bounds. Consider:

$$a(x) \wedge x \leq z \wedge y \leq z \wedge b(y) \rightarrow false \qquad \text{for } a \neq b$$

We may add $x \sim z$ by F3.1, then $z \sim x$ via F3.3, then $y \sim x$ with F3.2, and finally terminate with *false* via F5.

Example 2. We need F4 for deriving the unsatisfiability of the constraint:

$$a(x) \wedge x[a']x \wedge x \leq z \wedge y \leq z \wedge y[a']y' \wedge b(y') \rightarrow false \qquad \text{for } a \neq b$$

Algorithm F may add $x \sim y$ after several steps as shown in Example 1. Then it may proceed with $x \sim y'$ via F4 and terminate with *false* via F5.

Termination. The fixed point algorithm F terminates when reflexivity of inclusion $x \leq x$ (F1.1) is restricted to variables $x \in V(\varphi)$. Given a subset F of F, a constraint φ is called *F-closed* if algorithm F under this restriction and w.r.t. the axioms in F cannot proceed on φ. Note that *false* is not F-closed since it is not a constraint by definition.

Example 3. Our control takes care of termination in presence of cycles like $x[a]x$. For instance, the following constraint is F-closed.

$$x[a]x \wedge x{\leq}y \wedge y[a]y \wedge x{\leq}x \wedge y{\leq}y \wedge x{\sim}x \wedge y{\sim}y \wedge x{\sim}y \wedge y{\sim}x$$

In particular, F2 and F4 do not loop through the cycle $x[a]x$ infinitely often. This example also illustrates why the fixed point algorithm would not be terminating if based in the axiom $x[a]x' \wedge x{\leq}y \rightarrow \exists y'\, (y[a]y' \wedge x'{\leq}y')$.

Proposition 3. *If φ is a constraint with m variables then algorithm F with input φ terminates under the above control in at most $2 \cdot m^2$ steps.* □

Proof. Since F does not introduce new variables, it may add at most m^2 non-disjointness constraints $x{\sim}y$ and m^2 inclusions $x{\leq}y$. □

Proposition 4. *Every F-closed constraint φ is satisfiable over $FT_{\leq}$.*

Proof. See Section 8. □

Theorem 5. *The satisfiability of $FT_{\leq}$ constraints can be decided in time $O(n^3)$ (offline and online, see [11]) where n is the constraint size.*

Proof. Proposition 2 shows that φ is unsatisfiable if F started with φ terminates with *false*. Proposition 4 proves that φ is satisfiable if F started with φ terminates with a constraint. Since F terminates for all input constraints under the above control (Prop. 3) this yields a effective decision procedure. The main idea of the complexity proof is that one needs at most $O(n^2)$ steps (Prop. 3) each of which can be implemented in time $O(n)$. The implementation can be organized incrementally by exploiting that algorithm F leaves the order unspecified in which the axioms are applied. Hence, we obtain that off-line and on-line complexity are the same. The implementation details and the complexity proof are omitted here, since they are similar to those presented in [17]. □

5 Entailment, Independence, Negation

In this section, we give a cubic algorithm testing entailment $\varphi' \models \varphi$ between $FT_{\leq}$ constraints φ' and φ. We then prove the independence property of $FT_{\leq}$. Hence we can solve conjunctions of positive and negative $FT_{\leq}$-constraints $\varphi \wedge \neg\varphi_1 \wedge \ldots \neg\varphi_n$ in time $O(n^3)$. A *basic constraint* μ is a conjunction free constraint φ, *i.e.*, given by the following abstract syntax:

$$\mu ::= x{\leq}y \mid x{\sim}y \mid a(x) \mid x[a]y$$

The entailment $\varphi' \models \varphi$ is equivalent to the fact that the entailment $\varphi \models \mu$ holds for all basic constraints μ *in* φ.

Next we characterize entailment problems $\varphi' \models \mu$ syntactically. We say that a constraint φ *syntactically contains* μ, written $\varphi \vdash \mu$, if one of the following holds:

$$\varphi \vdash a(x) \quad \text{if exists } x' \text{ such that } x' \leq x \wedge a(x') \in \varphi$$
$$\varphi \vdash x \leq y \quad \text{if } x \leq y \text{ in } \varphi \text{ or } x = y$$
$$\varphi \vdash x \sim y \quad \text{if } x \sim y \text{ in } \varphi \text{ or } x = y$$
$$\varphi \vdash x[a]y \quad \text{if exist } x', y' \text{ such that } x'[a]y' \text{ in } \varphi,$$
$$\text{and } \varphi \vdash x \leq x', \varphi \vdash x' \leq x \text{ and } \varphi \vdash y \leq y', \varphi \vdash y' \leq y$$

We say that a first-order formula Φ syntactically contains μ, $\Phi \vdash \mu$, if $\Phi = \varphi \wedge \Phi'$ for some φ and Φ' such that $\varphi \vdash \mu$.

Lemma 6. *Given a F-closed constraint φ, we can compute a representation of φ in linear time that allows to test syntactic containment $\varphi \vdash \mu$ for all μ in time $O(1)$.*

Proof. Simple. □

It is easy to see that syntactic containment is semantically correct, *i.e.*, $\varphi \vdash \mu$ implies $\varphi \models \mu$. For deciding entailment, we have to show that our notion of syntactic containment is semantically complete, *i.e.*, if $\varphi \not\vdash \mu$ then $\varphi \not\models \mu$ (Proposition 13). The idea is to construct a satisfiable extension of φ (its saturation) which syntactically and simultaneously contradicts all μ not syntactically contained by φ (Lemma 12).

Saturation is defined in terms of two operators Γ_1 and Γ_2 on constraints. The operator Γ_2 is such that $\Gamma_2(\varphi)$ contradicts all μ of the form $x \sim y$, $x \leq y$, and $a(x)$ (*i.e.*, no selection constraints) which are not syntactically contained in φ (Lemma 10). The operator Γ_1 serves for contradicting selection constraints. For instance, consider $\varphi \models x[a]y$ where $\varphi = x \leq x \wedge y \leq y$. In this case, $\Gamma_1(\varphi)$ enforces the existence of the feature a in the denotation of x by adding to φ the constraint $x[a]v_{xa}$ for a fresh variable v_{xa}. Now $\Gamma_2(\Gamma_1(\varphi))$ is such that it contradicts either $y \leq v_{xa}$ or $v_{xa} \leq y$. (see Example 4). In this sense, Γ_1 is a "preprocessor" for Γ_2.

Definition 7. Let φ be a constraint, v_1 and v_2 distinct fresh variables, and l_1 and l_2 distinct labels. Furthermore, for every pair of variables $x, y \in V(\varphi)$, and label every label $a \in L(\varphi)$ let l_x and l_{xy} be fresh labels and v_{xa} a fresh variable. We define $\Gamma_1(\varphi)$ and $\Gamma_2(\varphi)$ in dependence of $v_1, v_2, l_x, l_{xy}, v_x$ as follows:

$$\Gamma_1(\varphi) = \varphi \wedge \bigwedge \{x[a]v_{xa} \mid x \in V(\varphi), a \in L(\varphi)\}$$

$$\Gamma_2(\varphi) = \varphi \wedge \bigwedge \{x[l_x]v_x \wedge \neg \exists y'(y[l_x]y') \mid \varphi \not\vdash x \leq y, x, y \in V(\varphi)\} \quad (1)$$
$$\wedge \bigwedge \{x[l_{xy}]v_1 \wedge y[l_{xy}]v_2 \mid \varphi \not\vdash x \sim y, x, y \in V(\varphi)\} \quad (2)$$
$$\wedge \bigwedge \{x \sim v_1 \wedge x \sim v_2 \mid \text{for all labels } a: \varphi \not\vdash a(x), x \in V(\varphi)\} \quad (3)$$

Example 4. Consider the constraint $\varphi_0 = x[a]x \wedge y \leq x$ which is F-closed up to trivial constraints and which does not entail $x[a]y$. In order to contradict $x[a]y$ we compute the F-closure of $\Gamma_1(\varphi_0)$ which is $\Gamma_1'(\varphi_0) = x[a]x \wedge y \leq x \wedge x[a]v_{xa} \wedge y[a]v_{ya} \wedge v_{ya} \leq v_{xa} \wedge v_{xa} \leq x \wedge x \leq v_{xa} \wedge y \leq v_{xa}$ and observe that it does not $v_{xa} \leq y$. By definition of Γ_2, $\Gamma_2(\Gamma_1'(\varphi))$ contradicts $v_{xa} \leq y$. Hence, $\Gamma_2(\Gamma_1'(\varphi))$ also contradicts $x[a]y$.

Lemma 8. *Let φ be an F-closed (and hence satisfiable) constraint. Then $\Gamma_1(\varphi)$ is satisfiable and its F closure $\Gamma_1'(\mu)$ satisfies the following two properties for all basic constraints μ:*

1. *If $\varphi \not\vdash \mu$ and $V(\mu) \subseteq V(\varphi)$, then $\Gamma_1'(\varphi) \not\vdash \mu$.*
2. *If $\varphi \not\vdash x[a]y$ then $\Gamma_1'(\varphi) \not\vdash y \leq v_{xa}$ or $\Gamma_1'(\varphi) \not\vdash v_{xa} \leq y$.*

Proof. The F-closure $\Gamma_1'(\varphi)$ of $\Gamma_1(\varphi)$ has the following form up-to trivial constraints and symmetry of compatibility constraints.

$$\Gamma_1'(\varphi) = \Gamma_1(\varphi) \wedge \bigwedge\{v_{xa} \leq v_{ya} \mid \Phi \vdash x \leq y, a \in L(\varphi)\} \tag{4.1}$$

$$\wedge \bigwedge\{z \leq v_{xa} \mid \text{exists } y : \Phi \vdash z \leq y \wedge y[a]y' \wedge y \leq x, \Phi \not\vdash x[a]\} \tag{4.2}$$

$$\wedge \bigwedge\{v_{xa} \leq z \mid \text{exist } y, y' : \Phi \vdash x \leq y \wedge y[a]y' \wedge y' \leq z, \Phi \not\vdash x[a]\} \tag{4.3}$$

$$\wedge \bigwedge\{v_{xa} \sim z \mid \text{exist } y, y' : \Phi \vdash x \leq y \wedge y[a]y' \wedge y' \sim z, \Phi \not\vdash x[a]\} \tag{4.4}$$

$$\wedge \bigwedge\{v_{xa} \sim z \mid \text{exist } y, y' : \Phi \vdash x \sim y \wedge y[a]y' \wedge y' \leq z, \Phi \not\vdash x[a]\} \tag{4.5}$$

(For instance note that $v_{xa} \leq x' \wedge x' \leq v_{xa}$ in $\Gamma_1'(\varphi)$ if $x[a]x'$ in φ by clauses (4.2, 4.3) and reflexivity). All constraints in $\Gamma_1'(\varphi)$ either belong to $\Gamma_1(\varphi)$ or a derived from it by axioms in F. The F-closedness of $\Gamma_1'(\varphi)$ can be proved by a somewhat tedious case distinction. The same holds for the two additional properties of $\Gamma_1'(\varphi)$ claimed. $\square$

Lemma 9. *If φ is F-closed then $\Gamma_2(\varphi)$ is satisfiable.*

Proof. It is not difficult to show that the constraint part of $\Gamma_2(\varphi)$ is F-closed up to trivial constraints ($x \leq x$ and $x \sim x$) and symmetric compatibility constraints. The critical bit is to check that the negated selection constraints added in clause (1) of $\Gamma_2(\varphi)$ are consistent. Let $\neg \exists y' (y[l_x]y')$ in $\Gamma_2(\varphi)$. We must show that $\Gamma_2(\varphi) \not\models \exists y' (y[l_x]y')$. Assume the converse, $\Gamma_2(\varphi) \models \exists y' (y[l_x]y')$. Then, by Corollary 27 in Section 8, there exist z and z' such that $\Gamma_2'(\varphi) \vdash z \leq y \wedge z[l_x]z'$. By definition of $\Gamma_2(\varphi)$ we know that $z = x$. However, if $\Gamma_2'(\varphi) \vdash x \leq y$ and hence (by definition of Γ_2) $\varphi \vdash x \leq y$ holds, clause (1) does not apply. Thus $\neg \exists y' (y[l_x]y')$ cannot be contained in $\Gamma_2(\varphi)$, in contradiction to our assumption. $\square$

Lemma 10. *Let φ be an $FT_\leq$-constraint and let μ be a basic constraint of the form $x \sim y$, $x \leq y$, or $a(x)$ (i.e., not a selection constraint). Then $\Gamma_2(\varphi) \models \neg \mu$ if and only if $\varphi \not\vdash \mu$.*

Proof. By inspection of the definition of $\Gamma_2(\varphi)$. Clause (1) contradicts entailment of $x \leq y$ by φ by forcing x to have a feature l_x which y must not have. Clause (2) contradicts $x \sim y$ by forcing x and y to have a common feature l_{xy} such that the subtrees of x and y at l_{xy} are incompatible. Clause (3) contradicts $a(x)$ for any label by forcing x to be unlabeled (i.e., compatible with at least two trees with distinct label). $\square$

Definition 11 Saturation. Let φ be an F-closed constraint and $\Gamma_1'(\varphi)$ the F-closure of $\Gamma_1(\varphi)$ which exists according to Lemma 8. The *saturation of φ* is the formula $\text{Sat}(\varphi)$ given by $\text{Sat}(\varphi) = \Gamma_2(\Gamma_1'(\varphi))$.

Lemma 12. *Let φ be an F-closed constraint For all μ such that $V(\mu) \subseteq V(\varphi)$, $\varphi \not\vdash \mu$ implies* $\text{Sat}(\varphi) \models \neg\mu$.

Proof. Let $\Gamma_1'(\varphi)$ the F-closure of $\Gamma_1(\varphi)$ such that $\text{Sat}(\varphi) = \Gamma_2(\Gamma_1'(\varphi))$. If $\varphi \not\vdash \mu$ then $\Gamma_1'(\varphi) \not\vdash \mu$ by Lemma 8.1. If μ is not a selection constraint, then $\Gamma_2(\Gamma_1'(\varphi)) \models \neg\mu$ by Lemma 10. Otherwise, let $\mu = x[a]y$. Hence, $\Gamma_1'(\varphi) \not\vdash v_{xa}{\leq}y$ or $\Gamma_1'(\varphi) \not\vdash y{\leq}v_{xa}$ by Lemma 8.2. By Lemma 10, either $\Gamma_2(\Gamma_1'(\varphi)) \models \neg v_{xa}{\leq}y$ or $\Gamma_2(\Gamma_1'(\varphi)) \models \neg y{\leq}v_{xa}$ holds. In both cases, $\Gamma_2(\Gamma_1'(\varphi)) \models \neg\mu$ follows. $\qquad\square$

Proposition 13. *The notions of entailment and of syntactic containment coincide for basic constraints: If φ is F-closed and μ a basic constraint then $\varphi \models \mu$ iff $\varphi \vdash \mu$.*

Proof. We assume $\varphi \models \mu$ and show $\varphi \vdash \mu$. (The converse is correctness of syntactic containment.) If $V(\mu) \not\subseteq V(\varphi)$ then μ is of the form $x{\leq}x$ or $x{\sim}x$ such that $\varphi \vdash \mu$. Otherwise, $V(\mu) \subseteq V(\varphi)$. If $\varphi \models \mu$, then $\text{Sat}(\varphi) \models \mu$ since $\text{Sat}(\varphi)$ contains φ. Moreover, $\text{Sat}(\varphi)$ is satisfiable (Lemmas 8 and 9) such that $\text{Sat}(\varphi) \not\models \neg\mu$. Hence, $\varphi \vdash \mu$ by Lemma 12. $\qquad\square$

Theorem 14 Entailment. *Entailment problems of the form $\varphi' \models \varphi$ can be tested in cubic time.*

Proof. Let n be the size of $\varphi' \wedge \varphi$. To decide $\varphi' \models \varphi$, first test whether φ' is satisfiable. By Theorem 5 this can be done by computing the F-closure $\tilde{\varphi}'$ of φ' in time $O(n^3)$. If this test fails then the entailment test is trivial. Otherwise, from Lemma 12 we obtain $\tilde{\varphi}' \not\models \mu$ if $\varphi \not\vdash \mu$, and hence that $\tilde{\varphi}' \models \varphi$ iff $\tilde{\varphi}' \vdash \mu$ for all μ in φ. There are $O(n)$ such μ and $\tilde{\varphi}'$ is of size $O(n^2)$, hence, by Lemma 6, this is decidable in time $O(n)$. The overall complexity sums up to $O(n^3)$. $\qquad\square$

Theorem 15 Independence. *The constraint system $FT_{\leq}$ has the independence property; i.e., for every $n \geq 1$ and constraints $\varphi, \varphi_1, \ldots, \varphi_n$:*

$$\text{if } \varphi \models \bigvee_{i=1}^n \varphi_i \text{ then } \varphi \models \varphi_i \text{ for some } i \in \{1, \ldots, n\}.$$

Proof. Assume $\varphi \models \bigvee_{i=1}^n \varphi_i$. If φ is unsatisfiable we are done. Also, if $\varphi \wedge \varphi_j$ is non-satisfiable for some j, then $\varphi \models \bigvee_{i=1}^n \varphi_i$ iff $\varphi \models \bigvee_{i=1, i\neq j}^n \varphi_i$ is. Now let φ and $\varphi \wedge \varphi_i$ be satisfiable for all i and let φ be F-closed (wlog. by Prop. 2). If there exists i with $\varphi \vdash \mu$ for all μ syntactically contained by φ_i, then $\varphi \models \varphi_i$ and we are done. Otherwise, for all i there exists μ_i such that $\varphi \not\vdash \mu_i$. Lemma 12 yields $\text{Sat}(\varphi) \models \bigwedge_{i=1}^n \neg\varphi_i$. Since $\text{Sat}(\varphi)$ is satisfiable (Lemma 8) and entails φ, this contradicts our assumption that $\varphi \models \bigvee_{i=1}^n \varphi_i$. $\square$

Corollary 16 Negation. *The satisfiability of conjunctions of positive and negative $FT_{\leq}$ constraints $\varphi \wedge \neg\varphi_1 \wedge \ldots \wedge \neg\varphi_k$ can be tested in time $O(n^3)$ where n is the size of the given conjunction.*

Proof. If φ is non-satisfiable then $\varphi \wedge (\bigwedge_{i=1}^n \neg\varphi_i)$ is trivially non-satisfiable. By Proposition 5, satisfiability of φ is decidable in time $O(n^3)$. Now assume φ to be satisfiable. By the Independence Theorem 15, $\varphi \wedge (\bigwedge_{i=1}^n \neg\varphi_i)$ is nonsatisfiable if and only if $\varphi \models \varphi_i$ for some i. By Lemma 12 this is equivalent to the existence of i such that for all μ if $\varphi_i \vdash \mu$ then $\varphi \vdash \mu$. Overall, there are $O(n^2)$ candidates μ to be tested for syntactic containment and $O(n)$ possible φ_i. By Lemma 6, $\varphi \vdash \mu$ can be tested in time $O(1)$ such that the total complexity sums up to time $O(n^3)$. $\qquad\square$

6 Weak Subsumption Constraints

We next introduce weak subsumption constraints that are used in computational linguistics [7]. We show that their satisfiability problem is subsumed by the one for $FT_\le$.

Syntax. We assume given a set C of *constants* c and a set $\mathcal{D}$ of features d. We consider the set of labels $L = C \cup \mathcal{D}$. A weak subsumption constraint η is a $FT_\le$ constraint of the following form.

$$\eta ::= c(x) \mid x[d]y \mid x \le y \mid x \sim y \mid \eta \wedge \eta'$$

Note that compatibility constraints do not occur in [7]. We add them here to simplify our comparison.

Semantics. We interpret weak subsumption constraints over the whole class of feature algebras with the induced weak subsumption ordering, which we will define below.

A *feature algebra* $\mathcal{A}$ over C and $\mathcal{D}$ consists of a set $\mathrm{dom}^{\mathcal{A}}$ that is called the *domain* of $\mathcal{A}$, a unary relation $c()^{\mathcal{A}}$ on $\mathrm{dom}^{\mathcal{A}}$ for every constant $c \in C$, and a binary relation $[d]^{\mathcal{A}}$ on $\mathrm{dom}^{\mathcal{A}}$ for every feature $d \in \mathcal{D}$, which satisfy the following properties for all $\alpha, \alpha', \alpha'' \in \mathrm{dom}^{\mathcal{A}}$, constants $c, c_1, c_2 \in C$, and features $d \in \mathcal{D}$:

1. if $\alpha[d]^{\mathcal{A}}\alpha'$ and $\alpha[d]^{\mathcal{A}}\alpha''$ then $\alpha' = \alpha''$
2. if $c_1(\alpha)^{\mathcal{A}}$ and $c_2(\alpha)^{\mathcal{A}}$ then $c_1 = c_2$

In the literature [22, 7] a slightly different notion of *feature algebras with constants* has been considered. We will give a formal comparison between the two notions at the end of the present section.

Proposition 17. *The structure $\mathcal{F}$ over L is a feature algebra over C and $\mathcal{D}$.*

Proof. The above properties follow from the axioms in F and the antisymmetry of the information ordering in $FT_\le$ ($x \le y \wedge y \le x \rightarrow x = y$). □

Given a feature algebra $\mathcal{A}$, we define the weak subsumption ordering $\le^{\mathcal{A}}$ as follows. A *simulation for* $\mathcal{A}$ is a binary relation Δ on the domain of $\mathcal{A}$ that satisfies the following properties for all elements $\alpha_1, \alpha_2, \alpha'_1, \alpha'_2$ of $\mathcal{A}$'s domain:

1. if $\alpha_1 \Delta \alpha_2$, $c_1(\alpha_1)^{\mathcal{A}}$, and $c_2(\alpha_2)^{\mathcal{A}}$ then $c_1 = c_2$
2. if $\alpha_1 \Delta \alpha_2$, $\alpha_1[d]^{\mathcal{A}}\alpha'_1$, and $\alpha_2[d]^{\mathcal{A}}\alpha'_2$ then $\alpha'_1 \Delta \alpha'_2$

The *weak subsumption ordering* $\le^{\mathcal{A}}$ of $\mathcal{A}$ is the greatest simulation relation for $\mathcal{A}$. The weak subsumption relation on $\mathcal{A}$ induces a compatibility relation $\sim^{\mathcal{A}}$:

$$\alpha_1 \sim^{\mathcal{A}} \alpha_2 \text{ iff exists } \alpha \text{ such that } \alpha_1 \le^{\mathcal{A}} \alpha \text{ and } \alpha_2 \le^{\mathcal{A}} \alpha$$

A feature algebra $\mathcal{A}$ induces a structure with the same signature as $\mathcal{F}$, in which $\le$ is interpreted as weak subsumption ordering $\le^{\mathcal{A}}$, $\sim$ as $\sim^{\mathcal{A}}$, $c()$ as $c()^{\mathcal{A}}$, and $[d]$ as $[d]^{\mathcal{A}}$.

Proposition 18 Dörre [8]. *The structure $\mathcal{F}$ coincides with the structure induced by the feature algebra defined by $\mathcal{F}$.*

Proof. It is sufficient to prove that the weak subsumption relation of the feature algebra defined by $\mathcal{F}$ coincides with the information ordering on $\mathcal{F}$. The proof in the case for feature algebras with constants can be found in [8] on page 24 (Satz 6 and Satz 7). There the algebra of feature trees has been called algebra of path functions. A direct proof (additional 5 lines) is omitted for lack of space. □

Theorem 19. *A weak subsumption constraint η is satisfiable (over $\mathcal{F}$) if and only if η is satisfiable over the structure induced by some feature algebra $\mathcal{A}$.*

Proof. If η is satisfiable then it is satisfiable over the structure induced by the feature algebra defined by $\mathcal{F}$. Conversely, every structure induced by a feature algebra is a model of the axioms in F. Thus, if η is satisfiable over one such structure then it is equivalent to an F-closed constraint (and not *false*) and hence satisfiable over $\mathcal{F}$. □

Alternative Notions of Feature Algebras. In the literature [22, 7] a restricted notion of feature algebra has been considered that we call *feature algebra with constants* in the sequel. The focus on feature algebras with constants leads to a restricted satisfiability problem. This shows that the presented results properly extend the results in [7].

A *feature algebra with constants* is a feature algebra with the additional property that

$$\text{if } c(\alpha)^{\mathcal{A}} \text{ then not } \alpha[d]^{\mathcal{A}}\alpha' \tag{1}$$

In order to handle the new property we consider the following mapping of weak subsumption constraints over C and $\mathcal{D}$ to weak subsumption constraints over $C \cup \{\text{label}\}$ and $\mathcal{D}$ where label is a new constant not contained in C.

$$[\![c(x)]\!] = \exists y (x[\text{label}]y \wedge c(y)) \qquad [\![x[d]y]\!] = x[d]y$$
$$[\![x{\le}y]\!] = x{\le}y \qquad [\![x{\sim}y]\!] = x{\sim}y \qquad [\![\eta \wedge \eta']\!] = [\![\eta]\!] \wedge [\![\eta']\!]$$

Proposition 20. *A constraint η is satisfiable in some feature algebra if and only if $[\![\eta]\!]$ is satisfiable in some feature algebra with constants.*

Proof. If $[\![\eta]\!]$ is satisfiable over a feature algebra $\mathcal{A}$ with constants C and features $\mathcal{D} \cup \{\text{label}\}$ then η is satisfiable over the feature algebra $\mathcal{F}$ with labels $C \cup \mathcal{D}$. Given a solution σ' of $[\![\eta]\!]$ over $\mathcal{A}$ a solution σ of η over $\mathcal{F}$ can be defined as follows:

$$D_{\sigma(x)} = \{p \mid \text{exists } \alpha \text{ in domain of } \mathcal{A}: \sigma'(x)[p]^{\mathcal{A}}\alpha \text{ and } p \in \mathcal{D}^*\}$$
$$L_{\sigma(x)} = \{(p, c) \mid \text{exists } \alpha \text{ in domain of } \mathcal{A}: \sigma'(x)[p\text{label}]^{\mathcal{A}}\alpha \text{ and } c(\alpha)^{\mathcal{A}}\}$$

Conversely, let η be satisfiable in a feature algebra $\mathcal{A}$. Then η is satisfiable in $\mathcal{F}$ by Theorem 19. We consider the following feature algebra with constants $\mathcal{F}^*$ and show that $[\![\eta]\!]$ is satisfiable over $\mathcal{F}^*$. The constants and features of $\mathcal{F}^*$ are C and $\mathcal{D} \cup \{\text{label}\}$, respectively. The domain of $\mathcal{F}^*$ contains all feature trees τ without labeled internal nodes where a *labeled internal node* of τ is a path p such that $p \in D_\tau$, exists c with $(p, c) \in L_\tau$, but not exists d with $pd \in D_\tau$. The selection and labeling relations of $\mathcal{F}^*$ are those of $FT_{\le}$ restricted to trees without internal labels. Obviously, $\mathcal{F}^*$ satisfies all three axioms of a feature algebra with constants. Now let σ be an $\mathcal{A}$-solution of η. Then the variable assignment σ' mapping x on $\sigma'(x)$ as given below is an $\mathcal{F}^*$-solution of $[\![\eta]\!]$.

$$D_{\sigma'(x)} = D_{\sigma(x)} \cup \{p\text{label} \mid \text{exists } a \in L: (p, a) \in L_{\sigma(x)}\}$$
$$L_{\sigma'(x)} = \{(p\text{label}, a) \mid (p, a) \in L_{\sigma(x)}\}$$

□

7 Expressiveness

We show that $FT_\leq$ is strictly more expressive than FT but that $FT_\leq$ cannot express an arity constraint. An FT constraint η is of the form $x=y$, $a(x)$, $x[a]y$, or $\eta \wedge \eta'$, and an arity constraint of the form $x\{a_1,\dots,a_n\}$. An arity constraint $x\{a_1,\dots,a_n\}$ holds if x denotes a tree with subtrees at exactly a_1 through a_n.

Proposition 21. *There is no $FT_\leq$ constraint which expresses that a variable x denotes the empty feature tree, i.e., if $a \neq b$ then there is no constraint equivalent to*

$$x\{\} \wedge \exists y \exists z (x \leq y \wedge x \leq z \wedge a(y) \wedge b(z))$$

Proof. If φ were such a $FT_\leq$ constraint, then φ as well as its finite F-closure would entail $x \leq y$ for all variables y. This contradicts Proposition 13 for all those y such that $y \notin \mathcal{V}(\varphi)$ and $x \neq y$ (because if $\varphi \vdash x \leq y$ then $x = y$ or $x,y \in \mathcal{V}(\varphi)$). Such a variable y exists since $V(\varphi)$ is finite. $\square$

Lemma 22. *Let η be an FT constraint. Then $\eta \models x \leq y$ if and only if $\eta \models y \leq x$.*

Proof. The FT constraint η is equivalent to the $FT_\leq$ constraint φ obtained from η by replacing all equalities $x=y$ by inequalities $x \leq y \wedge y \leq x$. Hence, $x \leq y$ in φ iff $y \leq x$ in φ, and since algorithm F preserves this invariant it also holds for the F-closure of φ. The claim follows from Proposition 13. $\square$

Proposition 23. *If $x \neq y$ then there is no FT constraint η equivalent to $x \leq y$.*

Proof. This follows immediately from Lemma 22 and Proposition 13. $\square$

8 Completeness of the Satisfiability Test

Proposition 4. Every F-closed constraint φ is satisfiable over $FT_\leq$.

The proof is based on the notion of path reachability and covers the rest of the section. We proceed as follows. We first define path reachability, then give two Lemmas, and finally compose the proof of Proposition 4 from these Lemmas.

For all paths p and constraint φ, we define a binary relation $\leadsto_p^\varphi$, where $x \leadsto_p^\varphi y$ reads as "y is reachable from x over path p in φ":

$$x \leadsto_\varepsilon^\varphi y \quad \text{if } y \leq x \text{ in } \varphi$$
$$x \leadsto_a^\varphi y \quad \text{if } x[a]y \text{ in } \varphi,$$
$$x \leadsto_{pq}^\varphi y \quad \text{if } x \leadsto_p^\varphi z \text{ and } z \leadsto_q^\varphi y.$$

Define relationships $x \leadsto_p^\varphi a$ meaning that "a can be reached from x over path p in φ":

$$x \leadsto_p^\varphi a \quad \text{if } x \leadsto_p^\varphi y \text{ and } a(y) \text{ in } \varphi,$$

For example, if φ is the constraint $x{\leq}y \wedge a(y) \wedge x[a]u \wedge x[b]z \wedge z[a]x \wedge b(z)$ then the following reachability propositions hold: $y \overset{\varphi}{\leadsto}_\varepsilon x$, $x \overset{\varphi}{\leadsto}_b z$, $x \overset{\varphi}{\leadsto}_{ba} y$, $x \overset{\varphi}{\leadsto}_{ba} x$, etc., as well as $x \overset{\varphi}{\leadsto}_\varepsilon a$, $x \overset{\varphi}{\leadsto}_b b$, $x \overset{\varphi}{\leadsto}_{ba} a$, etc.

Definition 24 Path Consistency. We call a constraint φ *path consistent* if the following two conditions hold for all x, y, p, a, and b.

1. If $x \overset{\varphi}{\leadsto}_p a$, $x{\leq}x$, and $x \overset{\varphi}{\leadsto}_p b$ then $a = b$.
2. If $x \overset{\varphi}{\leadsto}_p a$, $x{\sim}y$, and $y \overset{\varphi}{\leadsto}_p b$ then $a = b$.

Lemma 25. *Every F1-F2-closed and path consistent constraint is satisfiable.*

Proof. Let φ be F1-F2-closed and path consistent. We define the variable assignment $\min_\varphi$ into feature trees as follows:

$$D_{\min_\varphi(x)} = \{p \mid x \overset{\varphi}{\leadsto}_p y\} \qquad \text{and} \qquad L_{\min_\varphi(x)} = \{(p,a) \mid x \overset{\varphi}{\leadsto}_p a\}$$

The path consistency of φ condition 1 implies that $L_{\min_\varphi(x)}$ is a partial function. Thus $\min_\varphi(x)$ is a feature tree. We now verify that $\min_\varphi$ is a solution of φ.

- Let $x{\leq}y$ in φ. For all x', if $y \overset{\varphi}{\leadsto}_p x'$ then $x \overset{\varphi}{\leadsto}_p x'$ by the definition of path reachability. Thus, $D_{\min_\varphi(y)} \subseteq D_{\min_\varphi(x)}$. For all a if $y \overset{\varphi}{\leadsto}_p a$ then $x \overset{\varphi}{\leadsto}_p a$ by the definition of path reachability. Thus, $L_{\min_\varphi(y)} \subseteq L_{\min_\varphi(x)}$, *i.e.*, $\min_\varphi(y){\leq}\min_\varphi(x)$.

- Consider $x[a]y$ in φ. We have to prove for all p, z, and b the equivalences

$$x \overset{\varphi}{\leadsto}_{ap} z \text{ iff } y \overset{\varphi}{\leadsto}_p z \qquad \text{and} \qquad x \overset{\varphi}{\leadsto}_{ap} b \text{ iff } y \overset{\varphi}{\leadsto}_p b$$

The first equivalence is equivalent to $D_{\min_\varphi(y)} = \{p \mid ap \in D_{\min_\varphi(x)}\}$ and the second one to $L_{\min_\varphi(y)} = \{(p,b) \mid (ap,b) \in L_{\min_\varphi(x)}\}$. We start proving the first equivalence. If $y \overset{\varphi}{\leadsto}_p z$ then $x \overset{\varphi}{\leadsto}_{ap} z$ since $x[a]y$ in φ. Suppose $x \overset{\varphi}{\leadsto}_{ap} z$. By definition of path reachability there exists x' and y' such that

$$x \overset{\varphi}{\leadsto}_\varepsilon x', \qquad x'[a]y', \qquad y' \overset{\varphi}{\leadsto}_p z.$$

The F1-closedness of φ and $x \overset{\varphi}{\leadsto}_\varepsilon x'$ imply $x{\leq}x'$ in φ. The F2-closedness ensures $y{\leq}y'$ in φ such that $y \overset{\varphi}{\leadsto}_p z$ holds. We now prove the second equivalence above. If $x \overset{\varphi}{\leadsto}_{ap} b$ then there exists z such that $x \overset{\varphi}{\leadsto}_{ap} z$ and $b(z)$. The first equivalence implies $y \overset{\varphi}{\leadsto}_p z$ and thus $y \overset{\varphi}{\leadsto}_p b$. The converse is simple.

- Let $a(x)$ in φ. Reflexivity (F1.1-closedness) implies $x{\leq}x$ in φ. Thus $x \overset{\varphi}{\leadsto}_\varepsilon a$ such that $(\varepsilon, a) \in L_x$.

- Let $x{\sim}y$ in φ. We have to show that the set $L_{\min_\varphi(x)} \cup L_{\min_\varphi(y)}$ is partial function. If $(p, a) \in L_{\min_\varphi(x)}$ and $(p, b) \in L_{\min_\varphi(y)}$ then $x \overset{\varphi}{\leadsto}_p a$ and $y \overset{\varphi}{\leadsto}_p b$. The path consistency of φ condition 2 implies $a = b$. $\qquad\square$

Lemma 26. *Every* F3, F4, F5-*closed constraint is path consistent.*

Proof. Let φ be F3, F4, F5-closed. Condition 1 of Definition 24 follows from condition 2 of Definition 24 and F3.1-closedness. The proof of condition 2 is by induction on paths p. We assume x, y, a, and b such that $x \overset{\varphi}{\leadsto}_p a$, $x \sim y$ in φ, and $x \overset{\varphi}{\leadsto}_p b$. If $p = \varepsilon$, then there exist $n, m \geq 0$, $x_1, \ldots, x_n, y_1, \ldots y_m$ such that:

$$x \leq x_1 \wedge \ldots \wedge x_{n-1} \leq x_n \wedge a(x_n) \text{ in } \varphi,$$
$$y \leq y_1 \wedge \ldots \wedge y_{m-1} \leq y_m \wedge b(y_m) \text{ in } \varphi.$$

F3-closedness implies that $x_n \sim y_m$ in φ (F3.2 yields $x \sim y_1$ in φ, …, $x \sim y_m$ in φ. Therefore $y_m \sim x$ in φ by F3.3-closedness, and hence $y_m \sim x_1$ in φ, …, $y_m \sim x_n$ in φ by F3.2-closedness.) Hence, F5-closedness implies $a = b$.

In the case $p = a'q$, then there exists there exist x', y', $\tilde{x}$, $\tilde{y}$ with:

$$x \overset{\varphi}{\leadsto}_\varepsilon x', \quad x'[a']\tilde{x} \text{ in } \varphi, \quad \tilde{x} \overset{\varphi}{\leadsto}_p a,$$
$$y \overset{\varphi}{\leadsto}_\varepsilon y', \quad y'[a']\tilde{y} \text{ in } \varphi, \quad \tilde{y} \overset{\varphi}{\leadsto}_p b.$$

Since $x \sim x'$ in φ we have $x' \sim y'$ in φ by F3-closedness (as above). Thus, F4-closedness implies $\tilde{x} \sim \tilde{y}$ in φ such that $a = b$ holds by induction hypothesis. $\square$

Proof of Proposition 4. If φ is F-closed then φ is path consistent by Lemma 26 and thus satisfiable by Lemma 25. $\square$

Corollary 27. *Let* φ *be an* F-*closed constraint. Then* $\varphi \models \exists y (x[a]y)$ *if and only if there are variables* x' *and* y' *such that* $\varphi \vdash x'[a]y'$ *and* $\varphi \vdash x' \leq x$.

Proof. Assume $\varphi \not\vdash x'[a]y' \wedge x' \leq x$. Then it holds for the minimal solution $\min_\varphi$ of an F-closed constraint that $a \notin L_{\min_\varphi(y)}$. Hence $\varphi \not\models \exists y (x[a]y)$. $\square$.

Acknowledgments. We would like to thank Jochen Dörre, Gert Smolka, and Ralf Treinen for discussions on the topic of this paper. We would also like to acknowledge many helpful remarks of the referees. The research reported in this paper has been supported by the the Esprit Working Group CCL II (EP 22457) the SFB 378 at the Universität des Saarlandes.

References

1. H. Aït-Kaci and A. Podelski. Entailment and Disentailment of Order-Sorted Feature Constraints. In A. Voronkov, editor, *4th International Conference on Logic Programming and Automated Reasoning*, LNAI 698, pp. 1–18. Springer, 1993.
2. H. Aït-Kaci and A. Podelski. Towards a Meaning of Life. *The Journal of Logic Programming*, 16(3 and 4):195–234, July, Aug. 1993.
3. H. Aït-Kaci, A. Podelski, and G. Smolka. A feature-based constraint system for logic programming with entailment. *Theoretical Computer Science*, 122(1–2):263–283, Jan. 1994.

4. R. Backofen. A Complete Axiomatization of a Theory with Feature and Arity Constraints. *The Journal of Logic Programming*, 1995. Special Issue on Computational Linguistics and Logic Programming.

5. R. Backofen and G. Smolka. A complete and recursive feature theory. *Theoretical Computer Science*, 146(1–2):243–268, July 1995.

6. A. Colmerauer. Equations and Inequations on Finite and Infinite Trees. In 2nd *Future Generation Computer Systems*, pages 85–99, 1984.

7. J. Dörre. Feature-Logic with Weak Subsumption Constraints. In *Constraints, Languages, and Computation*, chapter 7, pages 187–203. Academic Press, 1994.

8. J. Dörre. Feature-Logik und Semiunifikation. Dissertationen zur Künstlichen Intelligenz, Band 128. Infix-Verlag, St. Augustin, 1996.

9. J. Dörre and W. C. Rounds. On Subsumption and Semiunification in Feature Algebras. In 5th *IEEE Symposium on Logic in Computer Science*, pages 300–310. IEEE Computer Science Press, 1990.

10. R. Helm, K. Marriott, and M. Odersky. Constraint-based Query Optimization for Spatial Databases. In 10th *Annual IEEE Symposium on the Principles of Database Systems*, pages 181–191, May 1991.

11. J. Jaffar and M. J. Maher. Constraint logic programming: A survey. *Journal of Logic Programming*, 19/20:503–582, May-July 1994.

12. R. M. Kaplan and J. Bresnan. Lexical-Functional Grammar: A Formal System for Grammatical Representation. pages 173–381. MIT Press, Cambridge, MA, 1982.

13. M. Kay. Functional Grammar. In C. Chiarello et al., editor, *Proc. of the 5th Annual Meeting of the Berkeley Linguistics Society*, pages 142–158, 1979.

14. J. Lassez and K. McAloon. Applications of a Canonical Form for Generalized Linear Constraints. In 5th *Future Generation Computer Systems*, pages 703–710, Dec. 1988.

15. M. Müller. Ordering Constraints over Feature Trees with Ordered Sorts. In P. Lopez, S. Manandhar, and W. Nutt, eds., *Computational Logic and Natural Language Understanding*, Lecture Notes in Artificial Intelligence, to appear, 1997.

16. M. Müller and J. Niehren. Entailment for Set Constraints is not Feasible. Technical report, Programming Systems Lab, Universität des Saarlandes, 1997. Available at http://www.ps.uni-sb.de/~mmueller/papers/conp97.html.

17. M. Müller, J. Niehren, and A. Podelski. Inclusion Constraints over Non-Empty Sets of Trees. In International Joint Conference on Theory and Practice of Software Development (TAPSOFT), LNCS, Springer, 1997.

18. C. Pollard and I. Sag. *Head-Driven Phrase Structure Grammar*. Studies in Contemporary Linguistics. Cambridge University Press, Cambridge, England, 1994.

19. W. C. Rounds. Feature Logics. In J. v. Benthem and A. ter Meulen, editors, *Handbook of Logic and Language*. Elsevier Science Publishers B.V. (North Holland), 1997.

20. S. Shieber. *An Introduction to Unification-based Approaches to Grammar*. CSLI Lecture Notes No. 4. Center for the Study of Language and Information, 1986.

21. S. Shieber. *Parsing and Type Inference for Natural and Computer Languages*. SRI Internationax[1 Technical Note 460, Stanford University, Mar. 1989.

22. G. Smolka. Feature constraint logics for unification grammars. *Journal of Logic Programming*, 12:51–87, 1992.

23. G. Smolka. The Oz Programming Model. In J. van Leeuwen, editor, *Computer Science Today*, LNCS, vol. 1000, pages 324–343. Springer-Verlag, Berlin, Germany, 1995.

24. G. Smolka and R. Treinen. Records for Logic Programming. *The Journal of Logic Programming*, 18(3):229–258, Apr. 1994.

25. R. Treinen. Feature constraints with first-class features. *Mathematical Foundations of Computer Science*, LNCS, vol. 711, pages 734–743, Springer-Verlag, 1993.

From Restricted Path Consistency to Max-Restricted Path Consistency

Romuald Debruyne and Christian Bessière

LIRMM (UMR 5506 CNRS), 161 rue Ada, 34392 Montpellier Cedex 5 - France
Email: {debruyne, bessiere}@lirmm.fr

Abstract. There is no need to show the importance of the filtering techniques to solve constraint satisfaction problems i.e. to find values for problem variables subject to constraints that specify which combinations of values are consistent. They can be used during a preprocessing step to remove once and for all some local inconsistencies, or during the search to efficiently prune the search tree. Recently, in [5], a comparison of the most practicable filtering techniques concludes that restricted path consistency (RPC) is a promising local consistency that requires little additional cpu time compared to arc consistency while removing most of the path inverse inconsistent values. However, the RPC algorithm used for this comparison (presented in [1] and called RPC1 in the following) has a non optimal worst case time complexity and bad average time and space complexities. Therefore, we propose RPC2, a new RPC algorithm with $O(end^2)$ worst case time complexity and requiring less space than RPC1 in practice. The second aim of this paper is to extend RPC to new local consistencies, k-RPC and Max-RPC, and to compare their pruning efficiency with the other practicable local consistencies. Furthermore, we propose and study a Max-RPC algorithm based on AC-6 that we used for this comparison.

1 Introduction

Finding a solution in a constraint network (CN) involves looking for a set of value assignments, one for each variable, so that all the constraints are simultaneously satisfied. Many exponential search algorithms have been proposed to solve this NP-hard task. To avoid combinatorial explosion, the search tree has to be pruned as much as possible. Thus, filtering techniques are used to remove some local inconsistencies before or during the search.

Arc and path consistencies are the most studied local consistencies. While the latter is seldom used, most of real applications maintain arc consistency (MAC [10]) or a limited version of arc consistency (forward checking [8]) during the search. Indeed, arc consistency (AC) removes some values that cannot belong to any solution, which can strongly reduce the search space. More, AC can be enforced cheaply. On the other hand path consistency (PC) removes some inconsistent pairs of values with a huge complexity. The constraints must be represented in extension, and the structure of the network can be changed. PC is almost never used because of these important drawbacks.

On large and hard CNs, MAC outperforms forward checking. Although maintaining whole arc consistency on easy and very small CNs is useless, it widely speeds up the search on hard CNs. The harder a CN is, the more useful filtering techniques are. It is then necessary to take a careful look at local consistencies stronger than AC that do not fall in the same traps as PC. Recently, some powerful local consistencies have been proposed. A comparison in [5] concludes that restricted path consistency (RPC [1]) is a promising local consistency. It requires little additional cpu time compared to AC while removing most of the path inverse inconsistent values (PIC [7]). Furthermore, it does not delete any pair of values and thus, no constraint is added or modified in the network. In this paper we extend the idea or RPC to new local consistencies, k-RPC and Max-RPC, in order to remove more inconsistent values. The greater k is, the more powerful k-RPC is. Although Max-RPC removes more inconsistent values than PIC and k-RPC for any k, enforcing a high level of k-RPC is often more expensive than achieving Max-RPC. But in order to compare RPC and Max-RPC with the other practicable local consistencies, we need efficient algorithms to achieve them.

The experimental evaluation presented in [5] shows that the non optimal algorithm RPC1 has the same bad behaviour as AC-4 [9] on which it is based. AC-4 has a heavy $O(ed^2)$ data structure and its average time complexity is close to the worst case. In addition to these drawbacks, RPC1 has an $O(end^3)$ worst case time complexity. Therefore, in this paper we propose a new RPC algorithm, called RPC2, which has an $O(end^2)$ worst case time complexity and requires less space than RPC1 in practice. Moreover, we propose and study a Max-RPC algorithm based on AC-6.

After some recalls in section 2, we present the k-RPC and the Max-RPC local consistencies and study their pruning efficiency. Some recalls on RPC1 are given in section 4. We propose a new RPC algorithm called RPC2 in section 5 and a Max-RPC algorithm in section 6. An experimental evaluation is given in section 7 and some remarks conclude this paper.

2   Definitions and notations

A *network of binary constraints* $P = (\mathcal{X}, \mathcal{D}, \mathcal{C})$ is a set $\mathcal{X} = \{ i, j, \ldots \}$ of n *variables*, each taking value in its respective finite *domain* $D_i, D_j, \ldots$ elements of $\mathcal{D}$ and a set $\mathcal{C}$ of e binary constraints. d is the size of the largest domain. A *binary constraint* C_{ij} is a subset of the cartesian product $D_i \times D_j$ that denotes the compatible pairs of values for i and j. We note $C_{ij}(a, b) = true$ to specify that $((i, a), (j, b)) \in C_{ij}$. We then say that (j, b) is a *support* of (i, a) on C_{ij}. With each CN we associate a *constraint graph* in which nodes represent variables and arcs connect pairs of variables which are constrained explicitly. The *neighborhood* of i is the set of variables linked to i in the constraint graph. A domain $\mathcal{D}' = \{D'_i, D'_j, \ldots\}$ is a *sub-domain* of $\mathcal{D} = \{D_i, D_j, \ldots\}$ if $\forall i, D'_i \subseteq D_i$. An *instantiation* of a set of variables S is an indexed set of values $\{I_j\}_{j \in S}$ s.t. $\forall j \in S$ $I_j \in D_j$. An instantiation I of S satisfies a constraint C_{ij} if $\{i, j\} \nsubseteq S$ or $C_{ij}(I_i, I_j)$ is true. An instantiation is *consistent* if it satisfies all the constraints.

A pair of values $((i, a), (j, b))$ is *path consistent* if for all $k \in \mathcal{X}$ s.t. $j \neq k \neq i \neq j$, this pair of values can be extended to a consistent instantiation of $\{i, j, k\}$. (j, b) is a *path consistent support* of (i, a) if $((i, a), (j, b))$ is path consistent. A *solution* of $P = (\mathcal{X}, \mathcal{D}, \mathcal{C})$ is a consistent instantiation of $\mathcal{X}$. A value (i, a) is *consistent* if there is a solution I such that $I_i = a$. A CN is *consistent* if it has at least one solution. In the following we denote by $P \mid_{D_i = \{a\}}$ the CN obtained by restricting D_i to $\{a\}$ in P.

3   Restricted path consistency and its extensions

Restricted path consistency allows to detect more inconsistent values than AC while avoiding the drawbacks of PC. RPC is based on the following remark: If a value (i, a) has an unique support (j, b) on a constraint C_{ij}, the path inconsistency of $((i, a), (j, b))$ leads to the inconsistency of (i, a). So, in addition to the arc inconsistent value deletions, an RPC algorithm checks the path consistency of the pairs of values $((i, a), (j, b))$ if (j, b) is the unique support of (i, a) in D_i. These tests can directly lead to the deletion of (i, a) if $((i, a), (j, b))$ is found to be path inconsistent. RPC does not require to explicitly maintain the list of allowed pairs of values (since it does not remove pairs of values from constraints), and it avoids the prohibitive cost of path consistency, which checks all the pairs of values.

RPC checks the path consistency of a support (j, b) only when it is the unique support of a value (i, a). It can be extended to a more pruningful filtering technique: Instead of checking path consistency of supports only when there is an unique one, we could do that each time (i, a) has at most k supports. This is the principle of k-restricted path consistency (k-RPC), which ensures that the values that have at most k supports on a constraint have at least one path consistent support on this constraint. RPC is 1-RPC and AC corresponds to 0-RPC. The greater k is, the smaller the probability for a value having k supports to have no path consistent support is. But we cannot say that the smaller k is, the smaller the cpu time to number of value deletions ratio of k-RPC is. Indeed, this rely on the constraint network. k-RPC can detect the inconsistency of a CN that has no $(k-1)$-restricted path inconsistent value. A real advantage of k-RPC is that it can be used in an adaptative way, reusing the filtering effort. If k-RPC holds in a CN and we want to enforce $(k+1)$-RPC, we have only to consider the values that have exactly $(k+1)$ supports on a constraint and to propagate their possible deletion. Obviously, we can stop enforcing higher levels of k-RPC as soon as all the values have a path consistent support on each constraint. In this case d-RPC holds (d being the size of the largest domain). If after the deletion of the k'-restricted path inconsistent values no value has more than k' supports on any constraint, k''-RPC holds for all $k'' > k'$. A CN is said Max-restricted path consistent if all the values have a path consistent support on each constraint, whatever is the number of supports they have. Although a Max-restricted path consistent CN is k-restricted path consistent for all k, enforcing Max-RPC can be less expensive than achieving k-RPC. Indeed, as opposed to k-RPC, enforcing Max-RPC does not require to determine the set of values that have no more than k supports on

315

- A binary CN is **(i, j)-consistent** iff $\forall i \in \mathcal{X}$, $D_i \neq \emptyset$ and any consistent instantiation of i variables can be extended to a consistent instantiation including any j additional variables.
- A domain D_i is arc consistent iff, $\forall a \in D_i$, $\forall j \in \mathcal{X}$ s.t. $C_{ij} \in \mathcal{C}$, there exists $b \in D_j$ s.t. $C_{ij}(a, b)$. A CN is **arc consistent** ((1, 1)-consistent) iff $\forall D_i \in D$, $D_i \neq \emptyset$ and D_i is arc consistent.
- A pair of variables (i, j) is path consistent iff $\forall (a, b) \in C_{ij}$, $\forall k \in \mathcal{X}$, there exists $c \in D_k$ s.t. $C_{ik}(a, c)$ and $C_{jk}(b, c)$. A CN is **path consistent** ((2, 1)-consistent) iff $\forall i, j \in \mathcal{X}$, (i, j) is path consistent.
- A binary CN is **strongly path consistent** iff it is node-consistent, arc consistent and path consistent.
- A binary CN is **k-restricted path consistent** iff
  $\forall i \in \mathcal{X}$, D_i is a non empty arc consistent domain and,
  $\forall (i, a) \in D$, for all $j \in \mathcal{X}$ s.t. (i, a) has at most k supports in D_j,
  $\exists b \in D_j$ s.t. $C_{ij}(a, b)$ and for all $k \in \mathcal{X}$ linked to both i and j,
  $\exists c \in D_k$ s.t. $C_{ik}(a, c) \wedge C_{jk}(b, c)$.
- A binary CN is **restricted path consistent** iff it is 1-retricted path consistent.
- A binary CN is **Max-restricted path consistent** iff
  $\forall i \in \mathcal{X}$, D_i is a non empty arc consistent domain and,
  $\forall (i, a) \in D$, for all $j \in \mathcal{X}$ linked to i,
  $\exists b \in D_j$ s.t. $C_{ij}(a, b)$ and for all $k \in \mathcal{X}$ linked to both i and j,
  $\exists c \in D_k$ s.t. $C_{ik}(a, c) \wedge C_{jk}(b, c)$.
- A binary CN is **path inverse consistent** iff it is (1, 2)-consistent i.e. $\forall (i, a) \in D$ $\forall j, k \in \mathcal{X}$ s.t. $j \neq i \neq k \neq j$, $\exists (j, b) \in D$ and $(k, c) \in D$ s.t. $C_{ij}(a, b) \wedge C_{ik}(a, c) \wedge C_{jk}(b, c)$
- A binary CN is **neighborhood inverse consistent** iff $\forall (i, a) \in D$, (i, a) can be extended to a consistent instantiation including the neighborhood of i.
- A binary CN P is **singleton arc consistent** iff $\forall i \in \mathcal{X}$, $D_i \neq \emptyset$ and $\forall (i, a) \in D$, $P\mid_{D_i = \{a\}}$ has an arc consistent sub-domain.
- A binary CN P is **singleton restricted path consistent** iff $\forall i \in \mathcal{X}$, $D_i \neq \emptyset$ and $\forall (i, a) \in D$, $P\mid_{D_i = \{a\}}$ has a restricted path consistent sub-domain.

Fig. 1. The most practicable local consistencies

a constraint (which can be expensive if k is great). The properties corresponding to RPC, k-RPC, Max-RPC and the most usual local consistencies are presented in fig.1.

In order to compare the pruning efficiency of local consistencies, we use the transitive relation "stronger" introduced in [5]. A local consistency LC is *stronger* than another local consistency LC' if in any CN in which LC holds, LC' holds too. For example RPC is stronger than AC since an RPC algorithm removes at least all the arc inconsistent values. A local consistency LC is *strictly stronger* than another local consistency LC' if LC is stronger than LC' and there is at least one CN in which LC' holds and LC does not hold.

Theorem 1. *If $k > k' \geq 0$, k-RPC is strictly stronger than k'-RPC.*

Proof. Trivial. ∎

Theorem 2. *Max-RPC is strictly stronger than k-RPC, $\forall k \geq 0$.*

Proof. Trivial. ∎

Theorem 3. *Singleton arc consistency is stronger than Max-RPC.*

Proof. Suppose that there exists a CN P with a singleton arc consistent value (i, a) that is not max-restricted path consistent. Let $j \in \mathcal{X}$ be a variable such that (i, a) has no path consistent support in D_j. For each support b of (i, a) in D_j, there exists a variable k such that $\not\exists c \in D_k$ / $C_{ik}(a, c) \wedge C_{jk}(b, c)$. Therefore, all the values of D_j are arc inconsistent w.r.t. $P\mid_{D_i = \{a\}}$ and (i, a) is not singleton arc consistent. ∎

Theorem 4. *Neighborhood inverse consistency is stronger than max-restricted path consistency.*

Proof. Let us show that a neighborhood inverse consistent value (i, a) is max-restricted path consistent. If NIC holds for (i, a), there exists a consistent instantiation I including the neighborhood of i. $\forall j \in \mathcal{X}$ linked to i, I_j is a path consistent support of (i, a) since $\forall k \in \mathcal{X}$ linked to i and j, I_k is a support of both (i, a) and (j, I_j). Therefore, Max-RPC holds for (i, a). ∎

Theorem 5. *If $|\mathcal{X}| \geq 3$, max-restricted path consistency is stronger than path inverse consistency.*

Proof. Suppose that there exists a CN P that is max-restricted path consistent but not path inverse consistent. Let (i, a) be a Max-RPC value of P that is not path inverse consistent and j, k two variables such that (i, a) cannot be extended to a consistent instantiation of $\{i, j, k\}$.

- If $\nexists C_{ij} \in \mathcal{C}$ and $\nexists C_{ik} \in \mathcal{C}$: Since PIC does not hold , $\nexists (b, c) \in C_{jk}$ and all the values of D_j are max-restricted path inconsistent. So, Max-RPC does not hold.
- If $\nexists C_{jk} \in \mathcal{C}$: (i, a) is not arc consistent and so (i, a) is max-restricted path inconsistent.
- If $C_{jk} \in \mathcal{C} \wedge \nexists C_{ij} \in \mathcal{C}$ (resp. $C_{jk} \in \mathcal{C} \wedge \nexists C_{ik} \in \mathcal{C}$): If (i, a) has no support in D_k (resp. D_j) it is max-restricted path inconsistent. Otherwise, all the supports of (i, a) in D_k (resp. D_j) have no support in D_j (resp. D_k). So a Max-RPC algorithm will delete all the supports of (i, a) in D_k (resp. D_j) and then (i, a).
- If $C_{ij} \in \mathcal{C}$, $C_{jk} \in \mathcal{C}$ and $C_{ik} \in \mathcal{C}$: Since (i, a) cannot be extended to a consistent instantiation of $\{i, j, k\}$, (i, a) has no path consistent support in D_j and Max-RPC does not hold. ∎

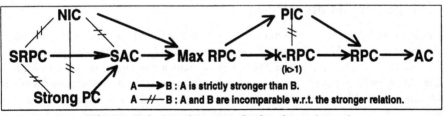

Fig. 2. Relations between the local consistencies

Fig.2 sums up the relations between the most practicable filtering techniques. A continuous arrow from A to B means that the local consistency A is strictly stronger than B. There is a crossed line between A and B if A and B are incomparable w.r.t. the stronger relation. A proof of the relations presented in fig.2 can be found in [6]. Especially, if A is not stronger than B (B is strictly stronger than A or A and B are incomparable), a CN in which A holds and B does not hold can be found in [6] and [4].

Some local consistencies are incomparable with respect to the "strong" relation. Moreover, fig.2 gives some qualitative properties, but no quantitative information. It can be interesting to determine if a local consistency can detect much more inconsistent values than another local consistency.

In order to determine the pruning efficiency of k-RPC, an experimental evaluation has been done. The aim of this evaluation is not to compare the cpu time to number of value deletions ratio. A part of such a comparison can be found in [5]. We only want to show how much a particular local consistency is able to detect inconsistency on some random CNs, with a fixed number of variables and values, when the number of constraints and the constraints tightness are varying. The CN generator involves four parameters: N the number of variables, D the common size of the initial domains, p_1 the proportion of constraints in the network ($p_1=1$ corresponds to the complete graph) and p_2 the proportion of forbidden pairs of values in a constraint (the tightness). For each possible pair (p_1, p_2), 50 random CNs having 100 variables and 20 values in each domain were generated. For each local consistency and each density, fig.3 presents the value of p_2 such that for any tightness greater than this value, the filtering technique has detected the inconsistency of the 50 generated CNs. As an example, for SAC the limit is 0.6 at density 0.15. Therefore, for a smaller tightness, at least one of the 50 random CNs is singleton arc consistent. NIC [7] has an exponential worst case time complexity and becomes really prohibitive when the variables have large neighborhoods. Therefore, this experimental evaluation gives no results on NIC. Path consistency being widely studied, strong path consistency (enforcing both arc and path consistency) is also presented although its huge space and time complexities make it prohibitive on large CNs.

Obviously, Max-RPC removes much more values than AC. But the main result is that 2-RPC is not stronger than PIC because of some very unusual CNs. PIC has only detected the inconsistency of a few 2-restricted path consistent CNs for density between 0.09 and 0.16.

4   Some recalls on RPC1

To enforce RPC we have to achieve arc consistency and to check the path consistency of $((i, a), (j, b))$ pairs of values such that (j, b) is the unique support of (i, a). RPC1 [1] determines the pairs of values that have to be considered using AC-4, which maintains the number of supports that the values have on each constraint. This determination does not require this counting. We have to look for only the arc consistent values that have no more than one support on a constraint. Whatever is the constraint network, RPC1 performs all possible constraint checks to build its lists of supported values and to initialize its counters. RPC1 has a bad average time complexity because most of this costly initialisation phase is useless, especially on networks with loose constraints.

The $O(ed^2)$ worst case space complexity of the lists of supported values is another disadvantage. These lists are often more costly in space than the propagation list $List_{PC}$ used by RPC1 because the average space complexity of $List_{PC}$ is far from its $O(end)$ worst case space complexity.

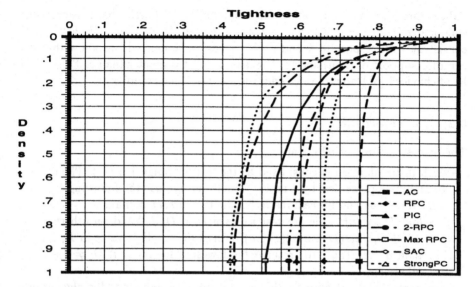

Fig. 3. Evaluation of inconsistency detection on random CNs with N=100 and D=20

But the most important drawback of RPC1 is its worst case time complexity. When a common support (k, c) of (i, a) and (j, b) is found, this information is not stored. Therefore, if a value (k, c') is deleted, RPC1 cannot determine the set of pairs of values that may be no longer path consistent because of (k, c') deletion. It overestimates this set. So, the deletion of a value can lead to some useless path consistency checks. In addition, RPC1 does not store enough information to know the values that have already been considered during some previous path consistency checks. Therefore, to check if a pair of values is still path consistent, RPC1 considers again some already checked values. This leads to an $O(end^3)$ worst case time complexity.

5 RPC2

5.1 Bases of the algorithm

RPC2 enforces AC and determines the pairs of values for which path consistency has to be proved by checking for each arc-value pair $[(i, j), a]$ if (i, a) has zero, one or at least two supports in D_j. If (i, a) has no compatible value in D_j it is an arc inconsistent value, otherwise, if it has an unique support b, the path consistency of $((i, a), (j, b))$ has to be checked. In addition, like AC-7 [2], RPC2 takes advantage of the bidirectionality of constraints to reduce the number of constraint checks performed.

The second idea is that when the path consistency of a pair $((i, a), (j, b))$ has to be checked, for each variable k linked to i and j, RPC2 looks for the smallest common support of (i, a) and (j, b) in D_k. If the pair is path consistent,

RPC2 stores for each smallest common support (k, c) found, that it is currently supporting $((i, a), (j, b))$. So, as long as c is in D_k, $((i, a), (j, b))$ is path consistent with respect to k and if (k, c) has to be deleted, we know that if a common support of (i, a) and (j, b) exists in D_k it is greater than c. This "AC-6 like behavior" [3] leads to an $O(end^2)$ worst case time complexity.

5.2 The algorithm

The data structures of RPC2 are:

- each initial domain is considered as the integer range $1..|D_i|$. The current domain is represented by a table of booleans. We use the following constant time functions and procedures to handle the current domain:
  - $last(D_i)$ returns the greatest value of D_i if $D_i \neq \emptyset$ and nil otherwise.
  - if $a \in D_i \backslash last(D_i)$, $next(D_i, a)$ returns the smallest value in D_i greater than a. $next(D_i, nil)$ returns the lowest value of D_i if $D_i \neq \emptyset$ and nil otherwise.
  - $remove(D_i, a)$ removes the value a from D_i and stops the algorithm if a was the unique value in D_i (the CN is inconsistent).
- a pair of values (b, a') is in S_{ija}^{AC} if (j, b) is currently supported by (i, a). If $a' = nil$ (i, a) is the unique support of (j, b) in D_i, otherwise (i, a) is the second current support of (j, b) and there is a direct access between the pair (b, a') in S_{ija}^{AC} and a pair (b, a) in $S_{ija'}^{AC}$. If $S_{ija}^{AC} \neq \emptyset$, $first(S_{ija}^{AC})$ returns the first pair of values in S_{ija}^{AC} and (nil, nil) otherwise. If (b, a') is in S_{ija}^{AC} and is not the last pair of values of S_{ija}^{AC}, $next(S_{ija}^{AC}, (b, a'))$ returns the successor of (b, a') in S_{ija}^{AC} and (nil, nil) otherwise.
- if we do not consider the constraint checks required to check the path consistency of the pairs of values, RPC2 never performs a constraint check twice. To ensure this property, it uses the array L. $L_{ija} = b$ if $\forall b' \in D_j$ s.t. $b' \leq b$, RPC2 has already checked if (j, b') is a support of (i, a).
- if $((i, a), (j, b)) \in S_{kc}^{PC}$ and $(a \in D_i \wedge b \in D_j)$, (j, b) is the unique support of (i, a) in D_j and (k, c) is currently supporting $((i, a), (j, b))$ i.e. (k, c) is the smallest value in D_k such that $C_{ik}(a, c)$ and $C_{jk}(b, c)$.
- an arc-value pair $[(i, j), a]$ is in $InitList$ if RPC2 has not yet determined if (i, a) has 0, 1 or at least 2 supports in D_j. A value (j, b) is in $DeletionList$ if b has been removed from D_j but this deletion has not been propagated. (i, a, j, b, nil, nil) is in $CheckPCList$ if (j, b) is the unique support of (i, a) in D_j and the path consistency of $((i, a), (j, b))$ has to be checked to determine if (i, a) is restricted path consistent. (i, a, j, b, k, c) with $k \neq nil$ and $c \neq nil$ is in $CheckPCList$ if c has been removed from D_k and a support of $((i, a), (j, b))$ greater than c has to be found in D_k to prove the path consistency of $((i, a), (j, b))$ w.r.t. k.

For each arc-value pair $[(i, j), a]$, RPC2 uses the function $TryToFindTwo-Supports$ to determine if (i, a) has zero, one or at least two supports in D_j. This function tries first to infer two supports looking for undeleted values in

```
procedure RPC2();
1  DeletionList ← ∅; CheckPCList ← ∅; InitList ← ∅;
2  forall (i, a) ∈ D do
3    S^PC_ia ← ∅;
4    forall C_ij ∈ C do
5      S^AC_ija ← ∅; L_ija ← nil; InitList ← InitList ∪ {[(i, j), a)]};
6  while InitList ≠ ∅ or DeletionList ≠ ∅ or CheckPCList ≠ ∅ do
7    if DeletionList ≠ ∅ then
8      choose and delete (i, a) from DeletionList;
9      PropagDeletion(i, a, DeletionList, CheckPCList);
10   else if CheckPCList ≠ ∅ then
11     choose and delete (i, a, j, b, k, c) from CheckPCList;
12     if a ∈ D_i and b ∈ D_j then
13       CheckPC(i, a, j, b, k, c, DeletionList);
14   else choose and delete [(i, j), a] from InitList;
15     b ← nil; NbS ← TryToFindTwoSupports(i, a, j, b);
16     if NbS = 0 then
17       remove(D_i, a); DeletionList ← DeletionList ∪ {(i, a)}
18     else if NbS = 1 then
19       CheckPCList ← CheckPCList ∪ {(i, a, j, b, nil, nil)};
```

Fig. 4. RPC2

S^{AC}_{ija} i.e. the list of the values supported by (i, a) on C_{ij}. If less than two supports have been found, RPC2 goes on with its search looking for the smallest supports in D_j. The array L allows to reduce the number of constraint checks performed. L_{ija} is used to determine the values of D_j that have not already been checked and we check $C_{ij}(a, b)$ only if $L_{jib} < a$. Indeed, if $L_{jib} \geq a$, RPC2 has already checked if (i, a) is a support of (j, b), and if it is a compatible value $TryToFindTwoSupport$ has found b in S^{AC}_{ija}.

If (i, a) has an unique support (j, b) the path consistency of $((i, a), (j, b))$ has to be checked and (i, a, j, b, nil, nil) is put in $CheckPCList$. To check the path consistency of a pair $((i, a), (j, b))$ the procedure $CheckPC$ uses the function $IsPathConsistent$ to find the smallest common support of (i, a) and (j, b) in D_k for all $k \in \mathcal{X}$ linked to both i and j. If path consistency is proved, for each smallest common support (k, c) found, RPC2 stores that it is currently supporting $((i, a), (j, b))$ by updating S^{PC}_{kc}, otherwise (i, a) is not restricted path consistent.

If a value (j, b) is deleted, $PropagDeletion$ checks if the values currently supported by (j, b) (in S^{AC}_{j*b}) are still restricted path consistent and if the pairs of values for which (j, b) is the smallest common support (in S^{PC}_{jb}) are still path consistent.

5.3 Complexity

Since $TryToFindTwoSupports$ removes from S^{AC}_{ija} the values that are no longer in D_j, the test of line 4 is performed at most $O(d)$ times for each arc-value pair.

In addition L_{ija} is bounded above by d and L_{ija} increases at each step of the second loop of $TryToFindTwoSupports$. Thus, the cost of this loop is $O(d)$ for each arc-value pair and the complexity due to the calls to $TryToFindTwo-Supports$ is $O(ed^2)$. The pairs of values $((i, a), (j, b))$ for which the path consistency has to be proved are such that (j, b) is the unique support of (i, a). So, in the worst case path consistency has to be checked for $O(ed)$ pairs of values. Whatever is the pair of values $((i, a), (j, b))$ and $k \in \mathcal{X}$ linked to both i and j,

```
function TryToFindTwoSupports(i, a, j, var b) : integer;
1   if b = nil then NbS ← 0 else NbS ← 1;
2   (b', a') ← first(S^{AC}_{ija});
3   while NbS < 2 and b' ≠ nil do
4       if b' ∉ D_j then
5           delete (b', a') from S^{AC}_{ija}
6       else if b' ≠ b then
7           NbS ← NbS + 1;
8           if NbS = 1 then b ← b';
9       if NbS < 2 then
10          (b', a') ← next(S^{AC}_{ija}, (b', a'));
11  while NbS < 2 and L_{ija} < last(D_j) do
12      b' ← next(D_j, L_{ija}); L_{ija} ← b';
13      if b' ≠ b and (L_{jib'} = nil or L_{jib'} < a) then
14          if C_{ij}(a, b') then
15              NbS ← NbS + 1;
16              if NbS = 1 then b ← b';
17  if NbS = 2 then
18      add (a, b') in S^{AC}_{jib}, (a, b) in S^{AC}_{jib'} and link them
19  else if NbS = 1 then
20      add (a, nil) in S^{AC}_{jib};
21  return NbS;


procedure PropagDeletion(j, b, var DeletionList, var CheckPCList );
1   forall i ∈ X such that C_{ij} ∈ C do
2       while S^{AC}_{jib} ≠ ∅ do
3           choose and delete (a, b') from S^{AC}_{jib};
4           if a ∈ D_i then
5               if b' = nil then
6                   remove(D_i, a); DeletionList ← DeletionList ∪ {(i, a)}
7               else delete (a, b) from S^{AC}_{jib'};    {constant time}
8                   if b' ∉ D_j then b' ← nil;
9                   NbS ← TryToFindTwoSupports(i, a, j, b');
10                  if NbS = 0 then
11                      remove(D_i, a); DeletionList ← DeletionList ∪ {(i, a)}
12                  else if NbS = 1 then
13                      CheckPCList ← CheckPCList ∪ {(i, a, j, b', nil, nil)};
14  while S^{PC}_{jb} ≠ ∅ do
15      choose and delete ((i, a), (k, c)) from S^{PC}_{jb};
16      CheckPCList ← CheckPCList ∪ {(i, a, k, c, j, b)};


procedure CheckPC(i, a, j, b, k, c, var DeletionList);
1   if k = nil then
2       PConsistent ← true; Common ← {k ∈ X | C_{ik} ∈ C and C_{jk} ∈ C};
3       forall k ∈ Common while PConsistent do
4           c' ← nil; PConsistent ← IsPathConsistent(i, a, j, b, k, c'); CS[k] ← c';
5       if PConsistent then
6           forall k ∈ Common do
7               S^{PC}_{k,CS[k]} ← S^{PC}_{k,CS[k]} ∪ {((i, a), (j, b))};
8   else PConsistent ← IsPathConsistent(i, a, j, b, k, c);
9       if PConsistent then
10          S^{PC}_{kc} ← S^{PC}_{kc} ∪ {((i, a), (j, b))};
11  if not PConsistent then
12      remove(D_i, a); DeletionList ← DeletionList ∪ {(i, a)};


function IsPathConsistent(i, a, j, b, k, var c) :boolean;
1   found ← false;
2   while (not found) and c ≠ last(D_k) do
3       c ← next(D_k, c);
4       if C_{ik}(a, c) and C_{jk}(b, c) then found ← true;
5   return found;
```

Fig. 5. The subprocedures used by RPC2

a value of D_k is never checked twice to prove the path consistency of $((i, a), (j, b))$ w.r.t. k. Thus, the complexity due to the calls to $IsPathConsistent$ is $O(end^2)$ and the worst case time complexity of RPC2 is $O(end^2)$.

The worst case space complexity of S_{ija}^{AC} lists is $O(ed)$ because a value (i, a) has at most two current supports on each constraint C_{ij}. The size of $InitList$ is $O(ed)$ since each arc-value pair is put in this list once. A pair of values $((i, a), (j, b))$ such that (j, b) is the unique support of (i, a) has at most one current support in the domain of each variable linked to both i and j. Therefore the worst case space complexity of S_{jb}^{PC} lists is $O(end)$. There is at most $O(ed)$ (i, a, j, b, nil, nil) elements in $CheckPCList$, and whatever is the pair of values $((i, a), (j, b))$ and the variable k linked to both i and j, there is at most one (i, a, j, b, k, c) element in $CheckPCList$. Thus the size of $CheckPCList$ is $O(end)$ and the worst case space complexity of RPC2 is $O(end)$.

6 Max-RPC

6.1 Bases of the algorithm

Max-RPC does not have to determine the set of weakly supported values i.e. those having at most k supports. It only has to ensure that all the values have at least one path consistent support on each constraint. The idea of AC-6 is used twice. First, to prove the Max-restricted path consistency of a value (i, a), Max-RPC looks in the domain of each variable linked to i for the smallest path consistent support this value has. To determine if a value (j, b) compatible with (i, a) is a path consistent support, Max-RPC looks for the smallest common support of (i, a) and (j, b) in the domain of each variable k linked to i and j.

6.2 The algorithm

The data structures of Max-RPC are:

- the same representation of the domains as RPC2.
- the values for which (j, b) is the smallest path consistent support are stored in the list S_{jb}^{AC}.
- the path consistent pairs of values $((i, a), (j, b))$ such that (k, c) is the smallest common support of (i, a) and (j, b) in D_k are stored in the list S_{kc}^{PC}.
- as in RPC2, the deleted values for which the deletion has not been propagated yet are put in $DeletionList$. An arc-value pair $[(i, j), a]$ is in $InitList$ if Max-RPC has not verified if (i, a) has a path consistent support in D_j.

$IsWithoutPCSupport(i, a, j, b)$ is used to determine if (i, a) has a path consistent support greater than b in D_j. It looks for the smallest support (j, b') of (i, a) such that $((i, a), (j, b'))$ is path consistent. If such a support exists, (i, a) is put in $S_{jb'}^{AC}$ in order to store that (j, b') is currently supporting (i, a). In addition, for each $k \in \mathcal{X}$ linked to i and j, $((i, a), (j, b'))$ is put in $_{kc}^{PC}$ where

```
    procedure Max − RPC();
1   DeletionList ← ∅; InitList ← ∅;
2   forall (i, a) ∈ D do
3       S_ia^PC ← ∅; S_ia^AC ← ∅;
4       forall C_ij ∈ C do
5           InitList ← InitList ∪ {[(i, j), a]};
6   while InitList ≠ ∅ or DeletionList ≠ ∅ do
7       if DeletionList ≠ ∅ then
8           choose and delete (i, a) from DeletionList;
9           PropagDeletion(i, a, DeletionList);
10      else choose and delete [(i, j), a] from InitList;
11          if IsWithoutPCSupport(i, a, j, nil) then
12              remove(D_i, a); DeletionList ← DeletionList ∪ {(i, a)};

    function IsWithoutPCSupport(i, a, j, b) : boolean;
1   Common ← {k ∈ X | C_ik ∈ C and C_jk ∈ C};
2   WithoutPCSupport ← true; b' ← b;
3   while b' ≠ last(D_j) and WithoutPCSupport do
4       b' ← next(D_j, b');
5       if C_ij(a, b') then
6           PConsistent ← true;
7           for k ∈ Common while PConsistent do
8               c ← nil;
9               if IsPathConsistent(i, a, j, b', k, c) then
10                  CS[k] ← c;
11              else PConsistent ← false;
12          if PConsistent then
13              forall k ∈ Common do
14                  S_{k,CS[k]}^PC ← S_{k,CS[k]}^PC ∪ {((i, a), (j, b'))};
15              S_{jb'}^AC ← S_{jb'}^AC ∪ {(i, a)};
16              WithoutPCSupport ← false;
17  return WithoutPCSupport;

    procedure PropagDeletion(j, b, var DeletionList);
1   while S_jb^AC ≠ ∅ do
2       choose and delete (i, a) from S_jb^AC;
3       if a ∈ D_i and IsWithoutPCSupport(i, a, j, b) then
4           remove(D_i, a); DeletionList ← DeletionList ∪ {(i, a)};
5   while S_jb^PC ≠ ∅ do
6       choose and delete ((i, a), (k, c)) from S_jb^PC;
7       if a ∈ D_i and c ∈ D_k and (i, a) ∈ S_kc^AC then
8           b' ← b;
9           if IsPathConsistent(i, a, k, c, j, b') then
10              S_{jb'}^PC ← S_{jb'}^PC ∪ {(i, a, k, c)}
11          else remove (i, a) from S_kc^AC;
12              if IsWithoutPCSupport(i, a, k, c) then
13                  remove(D_i, a); DeletionList ← DeletionList ∪ {(i, a)};
```

Fig. 6. Max-RPC

(k, c) is the smallest common support of (i, a) and (j, b') found in D_k. As long as c is in D_k, $((i, a), (j, b'))$ is path consistent w.r.t. k.

If a value (j, b) is deleted, for each value (i, a) currently supported by (j, b) another path consistent support has to be found in D_j to prove that Max-RPC holds for (i, a). If such a support exists it is greater than b since this value was the smallest path consistent support. $PropagDeletion(j, b)$ has also to check for each pair of value $((i, a), (k, c))$ supported by (j, b) if (k, c) is still a path consistent support of (i, a). If $((i, a), (k, c))$ is still path consistent, there is a common support of (i, a) and (k, c) greater than b in D_j. Otherwise, we have to look for another path consistent support greater than c in D_k for (i, a). If there is not any such support, (i, a) is not max-restricted path consistent and must be removed.

6.3 Complexity

If Max-RPC has to look for a path consistent support of a value $(i,\ a)$ in D_j, it considers only the values it has not already checked i.e. those greater than the current support of $(i,\ a)$ on C_{ij}. In the worst case, the path consistency of $O(ed^2)$ pairs of values is checked. In addition, whatever is the pair of values $((i,\ a),\ (j,\ b))$ and $k \in \mathcal{X}$ linked to both i and j, each value of D_k is checked by $IsPathConsistent$ at most once to determine if it is the smallest support of $((i,\ a),\ (j,\ b))$ in D_k. Thus, the worst case time complexity of Max-RPC is $O(end^3)$. Although the worst case time complexity of the best path consistency algorithm (PC-5 [11]) is $O(n^3d^3)$, enforcing Max-RPC is really less expensive than achieving PC. Indeed, the number of constraints e can be far from n^2 on sparse CNs. Furthermore, Max-RPC looks for only one path consistent support for each value on each constraint. So, although in the worst case the path consistency of $O(ed^2)$ pairs of values has to be checked, Max-RPC will check much less than this upper bound in practice.

A value $(i,\ a)$ has at most one current support on each constraint C_{ij} and the size of the S_{jb}^{AC} lists is $O(ed)$. For each value $(j,\ b)$ currently supporting $(i,\ a)$, $((i,\ a),\ (j,\ b))$ is in at most one S_{kc}^{PC} list for each is $k \in \mathcal{X}$ linked to both i and j. Therefore, the size of the S^{PC} data structure is $O(end)$ and the worst case space complexity of Max-RPC is $O(end)$.

7 Experimental evaluation

The generator of the section 3 has been used to evaluate the efficiency of RPC1, RPC2 and Max-RPC. All the generated CNs have 100 variables and 20 values in each initial domain. Fig.7 shows the results for both relatively sparse and dense CNs. For each tightness, 250 instances were generated and fig.7 presents mean values. To give an evaluation of the space required, we sum the number of counters used and the effective maximal size of each list used.

On dense CNs RPC2 outperforms RPC1 in cpu time. On sparse CNs, RPC2 requires less cpu time than RPC1, but when the lists of supported values of RPC1 are very short and when the path consistency of many pairs of values has to be checked, RPC1 can outperform RPC2. Such a situation arise for tightness between 0.63 and 0.87 at density 0.04. But if the path consistency of many pairs of values has to be checked to enforce RPC in a more dense CN, the size of the lists of supported values of RPC1 is more important and RPC2 outperforms RPC1. This can be observed for tightness greater than 0.65 at density 0.25 where the non optimal worst case time complexity of RPC1 is a real drawback. RPC2 always significantly overcomes RPC1 if we consider the number of constraint checks and list checks performed, or the space required.

Obviously in dense CNs, enforcing Max-RPC can be much more expensive than achieving RPC. But Max-RPC is stronger than RPC, and as soon as Max-RPC detects many inconsistent values it becomes less expensive than RPC2. In addition, the seven seconds required for tightness 0.6 at density 0.25 remain very small when compared to the twenty one minutes required to enforce singleton

325

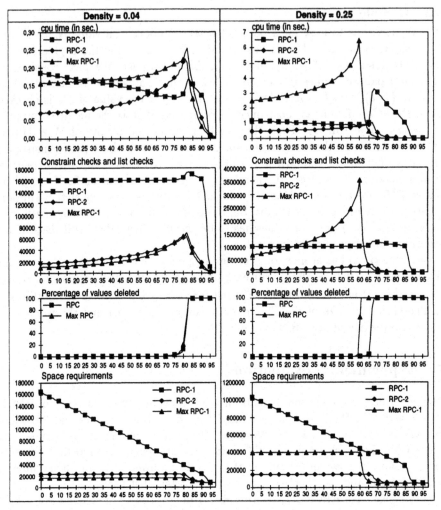

Fig. 7. Comparison of RPC1, RPC2 and Max-RPC on random CNs with n=100 and d=20

arc consistency at tightness 0.53 and the five hours required to achieve path consistency at tightness 0.52. This shows that the average time complexity of Max-RPC is far from its $O(end^3)$ worst case time complexity. Moreover, Max-RPC has the same worst case space complexity as RPC1 or RPC2, and although it requires more space than RPC2, on all the generated CNs RPC1 is more expensive in space than Max-RPC.

8 Conclusion

In this paper we have extended restricted path consistency to k-RPC and Max-RPC. These new local consistencies are more pruningful than RPC while avoiding the drawbacks of path consistency. Two new algorithms have been proposed. A RPC algorithm called RPC2 with an $O(end^2)$ worst case time complexity, and a

Max-RPC algorithm based on AC-6 with an $O(end^3)$ worst case time complexity, both having an $O(end)$ worst case space complexity. An experimental evaluation shows that RPC2 has better cpu time performances and performs less constraint checks than RPC1. Moreover, these experiments highlight that Max-RPC has good average cpu time performances in spite of its $O(end^3)$ worst case time complexity and although it detects much more inconsistent values than RPC.

References

1. Berlandier, P.: Improving Domain Filtering using Restricted Path Consistency. In proceedings of IEEE CAIA-95, Los Angeles CA (1995)
2. Bessière, C., Freuder, E.C., Régin, J.C.: Using inference to reduce arc-consistency computation. In proceedings of IJCAI-95, Montréal, Canada (1995)
3. Bessière, C.: Arc-consistency and arc-consistency again. Artificial Intelligence 65 (1984) 179–190
4. Debruyne, R., Bessière, C.: From Restricted Path Consistency to Max-Restricted Path Consistency. Technical Report 97036, Montpellier, France (1997)
5. Debruyne, R., Bessière, C.: Some Practicable Filtering Techniques for the Constraint Satisfaction Problem. In proceedings of IJCAI-97, Nagoya, Japan (1997) (to appear)
6. Debruyne, R., Bessière, C.: Some Practicable Filtering Techniques for the Constraint Satisfaction Problem. Technical Report 97035, Montpellier, France (1997)
7. Freuder, E., Elfe, D.C.: Neighborood Inverse Consistency Preprocessing. In proceedings of AAAI-96, Portland OR (1996) 202–208
8. Haralick, R., Elliott, G.: Increasing tree search efficiency for constraint satisfaction problems. Artificial Intelligence 14 (1980) 263–313
9. Mohr, R., Henderson, T.C.: Arc and Path Consistency Revisited. Artificial Intelligence 28 (1986) 225–233
10. Sabin, D., Freuder, E.: Contradicting conventional wisdom in constraint satisfaction. In Allan Borning, editor, PPCP'94: second workshop on Principles and Practice of Constraint Programming, Seattle WA (1994)
11. Singh, M.: Path Consistency Revisited. In proceedings of IEEE ICTAI-95, Washington D.C. (1995)

The Constrainedness of Arc Consistency*

Ian P. Gent, Ewan MacIntyre, Patrick Prosser, Paul Shaw, and Toby Walsh

The APES Research Group, Department of Computer Science, University of
Strathclyde, Glasgow G1 1XH, United Kingdom.
Email {ipg,em,pat,ps,tw}@cs.strath.ac.uk

Abstract. We show that the same methodology used to study phase
transition behaviour in NP-complete problems works with a polynomial
problem class: establishing arc consistency. A general measure of the constrainedness of an ensemble of problems, used to locate phase transitions
in random NP-complete problems, predicts the location of a phase transition in establishing arc consistency. A complexity peak for the AC3
algorithm is associated with this transition. Finite size scaling models
both the scaling of this transition and the computational cost. On problems at the phase transition, this model of computational cost agrees
with the theoretical worst case. As with NP-complete problems, constrainedness – and proxies for it which are cheaper to compute – can be
used as a heuristic for reducing the number of checks needed to establish
arc consistency in AC3.

1 Introduction

Following [4] there has been considerable research into phase transition behaviour
in NP-complete problems. Problems from the phase transition are now routinely used to benchmark algorithms for constraint satisfaction, satisfiability and
other NP-complete problems. Phase transition behaviour has even suggested new
heuristics for NP-complete problems [7]. Many interesting questions are raised
by this research. Are phase transitions important in other complexity classes? If
so, do they behave like phase transitions in NP? Does performance at the phase
transition agree with the worst case complexity? Can we use phase transition
behaviour to suggest heuristics for problems in these new complexity classes? In
this paper we show that the same techniques used to study phase transitions in
NP-complete problems can be used to study a phase transition in a polynomial
problem class: establishing arc consistency in constraint satisfaction problems.

2 Constraint satisfaction

A binary constraint satisfaction problem consists of a set of variables V and a
set of constraints C. Each variable $v \in V$ has a domain of values of size m_v.

---

* The authors are supported by EPSRC awards GR/L/24014 and GR/K/65706, and
the EU award EU20603. The authors wish to thank other members of the APES
research group for their help, and Gene Freuder.

Each binary constraint $c \in C$ rules out some proportion p_c of combinations of values for a pair of variables. We call p_c the "tightness" of a constraint. Two variables are adjacent if a constraint acts between them. The constraint satisfaction decision problem is then to determine if there exists an assignment of values to variables such that none of the constraints are violated. Consistency techniques are often applied to simplify such decision problems either before or during search. Arc consistency (or AC) is the simplest and most commonly used such technique. A problem is arc consistent if all values in all variables are *supported*. A value i for variable v is supported if, when i is assigned to v, all variables adjacent to v can be assigned values without violating constraints on v. Any value which is not supported cannot occur in a solution and can be removed. An arc consistency algorithm achieves an arc consistent state by repeatedly removing unsupported values. If it succeeds, we have established AC. If not, a domain wipe out occurs, where one variable has all values in its domain removed and the problem is insoluble. Therefore, the arc consistency decision problem is to determine if there exists a non-empty domain of supported values for each variable. The arc consistency algorithms studied here are AC3 [12] and AC6 [2]. The worst case complexity of AC3 is $O(em^3)$ [13] and of AC6 is $O(em^2)$, where m is the size of the largest domain and e is the number of edges in the constraint graph.

3 Phase transitions in NP

Phase transition behaviour has been studied in many NP-complete problems [4, 14, 9]. To unify such studies, [7] defines the constrainedness, κ of an ensemble of combinatorial problems as,

$$\kappa =_{\text{def}} 1 - \frac{\log_2(\langle Sol \rangle)}{N} \tag{1}$$

where N is the base 2 logarithm of the size of the state space, and $\langle Sol \rangle$ is the expected number of these states that are solutions. Since $0 \leq \langle Sol \rangle \leq 2^N$, κ lies in the range $[0, \infty)$. If $\kappa = 0$ then $\langle Sol \rangle = N$. Problems here are under-constrained since every state is expected to be a solution. If $\kappa = \infty$ then $\langle Sol \rangle = 0$. Problems here are over-constrained since no states are expected to be solutions. If $\kappa \approx 1$ both soluble and insoluble problems can occur. As problems are on the "knife-edge" between solubility and insolubility, it is often difficult to find solutions or prove that none exist.

This definition of constrainedness captures parameters used to study phase transitions in a wide variety of NP-complete problems including constraint satisfaction [6], satisfiability [14], graph colouring [4] and number partitioning [9]. As we vary problem size, the location of the phase transition tends to occur over a small range of κ. Other parameters can be less stable. For example, the expected number of solutions, which is used to predict the location of the phase transition in constraint satisfaction in [20], can grow exponentially with problem size. In random 3-SAT problems, $\langle Sol \rangle$ at the phase transition grows as $2^{0.18N}$ [8].

In this paper, it will be convenient to express κ as,

$$\kappa = -\frac{\log \rho}{N} \tag{2}$$

where $\rho = \langle Sol \rangle / 2^N$ is the *solution density*. That is, the probability that an arbitrarily chosen candidate in the ensemble is a solution.

4 Phase transitions in P

The same methodology developed to study phase transitions in NP-complete problems can be applied to polynomial problems. This yields several immediate results. First, the measure of constrainedness of a particular polynomial problem is the same as that for NP-complete problems. Consequently we are able to observe experimentally scaling of computational cost, and this is consistent with the theoretical worst-case complexity. Finally we use the definition of constrainedness to design new heuristics and explain the performance of existing heuristics.

There is an obvious complexity peak in graphs of the performance for the AC3 and AC6 algorithms in [2]. However, the phase transition in arc consistency was not systematically studied till [10]. For example, in Figure 1 of [10] we see a transition from a region where problems do not benefit from arc consistency, to one which can be proved insoluble by applying arc consistency. In between is a region of problems whose domains get smaller when arc consistency is applied, and which tend to be the hardest to make arc consistent. Graphs in [10] are plotted against κ_{csp}, the constrainedness of the constraint satisfaction decision problem.

Unlike NP-complete problems, the location of the phase transition in establishing arc consistency does not occur around some fixed value of κ_{csp} close to 1. For example, Table 1 of [10] reports the location of the phase transition shifting from $\kappa_{csp} \approx 1.08$ to $\kappa_{csp} \approx 3.68$. This might suggest a different approach is needed to locate phase transitions in polynomial problems compared to NP-complete problems.

In the rest of the paper, we show that the phase transition in establishing arc consistency is in fact very similar to that in NP-complete problems. The problem with the presentation of results in [10] is that κ_{csp} is the constrainedness of the NP-complete decision problem: Is there a consistent assignment of values to variables? But we are merely solving a polynomial problem, establishing arc consistency, and κ_{csp} does not measure the constrainedness of this problem. As soon as we compute the constrainedness of establishing arc consistency, we see very similar phase behaviour in P as in NP.

5 Constrainedness of arc consistency

To compute the constrainedness of establishing arc consistency, κ_{ac}, we need to decide what the state space, S, and a solution within it look like. A solution is a constraint satisfaction problem with arc consistent domains. Each point in the state space represents a constraint satisfaction problem with variables that have domains that are some subset of the original domains. The number of possible subsets of the domain of v is 2^{m_v}. The size of the state space is therefore $\prod_{v \in V} 2^{m_v}$, and hence $N = \sum_{v \in V} m_v$.

We next calculate the probability q that a candidate state is arc consistent. Assume that a constraint c between variables x and y is represented by a conflict matrix of size m'_x by m'_y. The candidate is arc consistent if there is at least one allowable value in each row and each column of every conflict matrix. To simplify the computation of the probability, q we assume independence between the probability that there is an allowable value in each row and the probability that there is an allowable value in each column. Whilst such an assumption is strictly false, similar independence assumptions have proved very successful in predicting the location of phase transitions in NP-complete problems. For example, in number partitioning, assuming independence between the binary digit positions predicts the location of the phase transition to within a 4% accuracy [9].

When we know the tightness of each constraint, it is easy to calculate if there is at least one allowable value. Our ensemble of problems has random independent constraints, of tightness p_c. Note that, on average, all arc consistency candidates for this problem class have constraints that are the same tightness as the corresponding constraints in the original problem. Thus, the values of p_c for each constraint c in the original problem can be used when assessing candidates. It follows that,

$$q = \prod_{c \in C} (1 - p_c^{m'_x})^{m'_y} (1 - p_c^{m'_y})^{m'_x}$$

To derive ρ, we need the mean value of q over the state space: $\rho = 2^{-N} \sum_{s \in S} q_s$. Due to variations in domain sizes over each candidate, this is not a simple calculation. Instead, we estimate ρ using a mean field approximation, and assume that all candidates have an equal value of q, derived from an "average" candidate with domain sizes half that of the original problem. This gives,

$$\rho = \prod_{c \in C} (1 - p_c^{m_x/2})^{m_y/2} (1 - p_c^{m_y/2})^{m_x/2}$$

That is,

$$\kappa_{ac} = \frac{-\sum_{c \in C} m_x \log_2(1 - p_c^{\frac{m_y}{2}}) + m_y \log_2(1 - p_c^{\frac{m_x}{2}})}{2 \sum_{v \in V} m_v} \tag{3}$$

In the remainder of this paper, unless otherwise indicated, we use regular problems with uniform domain size m, exactly $p_1 n(n-1)/2$ constraints between the variables, each of which has the same tightness p_2. These problems are categorised by the tuple of parameters $\langle n, m, p_1, p_2 \rangle$. We can then simplify κ_{ac} to:

$$\kappa_{ac} = -\frac{1}{2} p_1 (n-1) \log_2(1 - p_2^{m/2}) \tag{4}$$

6 Arc consistency phase transition

To test this new parameter we ran experiments on establishing arc consistency with $\langle n, m, p_1, p_2 \rangle$ problems with a domain size $m = 10$ and a varying number of variables n. We fix the average degree of problems at 5 by setting $p_1 = 5/(n-1)$ and at each value of n change p_2 in steps of 0.01. In Figure 1, we test 1000 randomly generated problems at each value of p_2, measuring the probability of establishing AC.

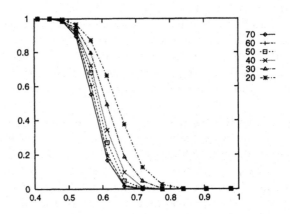

Fig. 1. Probability of establishing AC (y-axis) against κ_{ac} (x-axis) for varying n

As with NP-complete problems, a complexity peak for the cost of establishing arc consistency is associated with this probability phase transition. In Figure 2 we plot the computational cost (in terms of consistency checks) for AC3, establishing arc consistency for the same set of problems as in Figure 1. There is a familiar easy-hard-easy pattern. For $\kappa_{ac} \ll 1$, problems are under-constrained and it is easy to find an arc consistent state. For $\kappa_{ac} \gg 1$, problems are over-constrained and it is easy to observe domain wipe out. The hardest problems tend to occur in the phase transition in between when $\kappa_{ac} \approx 1$.

The complexity peak for AC6 can be observed at similar values of κ_{ac}. Bessière [2] reports experiments on problems $\langle 20, 5, 0.3, p_2 \rangle$, with p_2 varying in steps of 0.05, with 10 problems at each value of p_2. In Figure 4 (in [2]) the complexity peak for AC3 and AC6 occurs at $0.45 < p_2 < 0.5$ corresponding to $0.6 < \kappa_{ac} < 0.8$. And in Figure 5 (again in [2]) the complexity peak for $\langle 12, 16, 0.5, p_2 \rangle$ occurs at $p_2 = 0.8$ corresponding to $\kappa_{ac} = 0.73$.

Schiex *et. al.* established arc consistency with a non-uniform class of problems in which domain size varied randomly between 5 and 25, solving 20 problems at each value of constraint tightness [18]. They observed that "There is no clear "wipe-out" threshold as in the usual [fixed domain size] model" (page 221 of

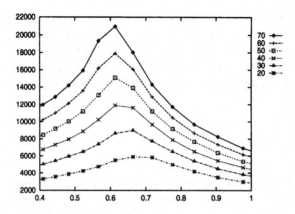

Fig. 2. Median consistency checks used by AC3 (y-axis) against κ_{ac} (x-axis) for varying n.

[18]). We performed experiments to determine if their observation holds true when we classify problems with respect to κ_{ac}.

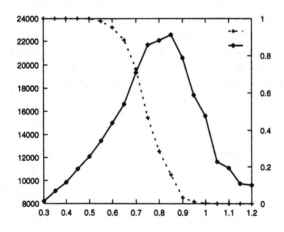

Fig. 3. Problems with non-uniform domain sizes. Y-axis on left and bold contour is computational cost, Y-axis on right and broken contour is probability of establishing AC. X-axis is κ_{ac}.

Problems were generated with $n = 20$ and $p_1 = 0.5$. Half of the variables were randomly chosen to have a domain size of 10, with the rest having a domain size of 20. Constraint tightness, p_2, was then varied from 0.01 to 0.99 in steps of 0.01, with 1000 problems at each point. When a problem was generated its κ_{ac} value was then computed and AC3 was applied. Figure 3 shows a clear phase transition in this non-uniform problem class, again at $\kappa_{ac} \approx 1$. The reason why this was not evident in [18] is due to variation in constrainedness of instances within the ensemble. The contribution to κ_{ac} (in Equation (3)) by a single constraint is sensitive to the tightness of the constraint and size of the domains involved in that constraint.

7 Finite size scaling

In NP-complete problem classes, the technique of finite size scaling has been borrowed from statistical mechanics [1] to model the change in the shape of the phase transition as problem size increases [11]. Around some critical value, κ_c, problems are indistinguishable except for a simple change in scale modelled by a power law. Finite-size scaling also works for this polynomial class. Following [7], we define a rescaled parameter

$$\gamma =_{\text{def}} \frac{\kappa - \kappa_c}{\kappa_c} N^{1/\nu} \tag{5}$$

$(\kappa - \kappa_c)/\kappa_c$ plays the same role as the reduced temperature, $(T - T_c)/T_c$ in a thermodynamic system whilst $N^{1/\nu}$ provides the scaling with problem size. As in [7] we define problem size as the number of bits needed to represent a state. In this case, we have $N = nm$. The values κ_c and ν are found by analysis of the empirical data using the methodology outlined in [6]. This gives $\kappa_c = 0.45$ and $\nu = 3.0$. Figure 4 shows the same data as Figure 1 rescaled by plotting against γ. This graph shows that finite size scaling successfully models the AC phase transition.

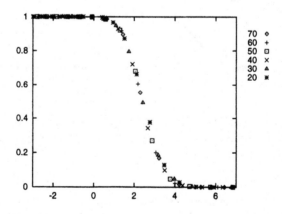

Fig. 4. Probability of establishing AC (y-axis) against γ for varying n with $\kappa_c = 0.45$, $\nu = 3.0$ (x-axis)

The rescaled parameter γ has been used to model growth of search cost as well as changes in probability as size increases in NP-complete problems [19, 6]. Rescaling of the number of checks performed by AC3 also gives a simple and accurate model of computational cost across the phase transition, even though AC3 is a polynomial algorithm. Furthermore this model gives close agreement with previous theoretical results. As the worst case complexity of AC3 is $O(em^3)$, and as the number of edges in the constraint graph, e is proportional to n in this study and m is fixed, computational cost should grow linearly with n. Accordingly we perform linear regression on the median checks performed by AC3 from $\gamma = -3$ to 7 in steps of 0.25, interpolating on observed data where necessary. Figure 5 shows that this linear model fits the data of Figure 2 very well. Note that the lines do *not* join points directly. Instead they join the values

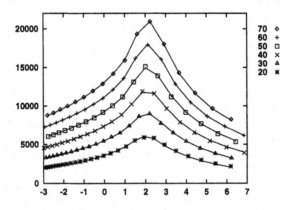

Fig. 5. Median consistency checks used by AC3 (y-axis) against γ (x-axis) for varying n. Points represent observed data while lines join modelled values of the data using linear regression.

modelled by linear regression. For example at $\gamma = 0$ the model is that checks $\approx 189n - 167$ while at $\gamma = 2$ the model is $297n + 87$. The closeness between the lines and points indicate how accurately linear scaling models computational cost. Note that the highest costs occur at $\gamma \approx 2$, very close to the point where 50% of problems could be made arc consistent and 50% could not. This correlation has been noted many times in NP-complete classes.

We also investigate scaling when we fix the number of variables $n = 20$ and vary the domain size. We use a constraint tightness $p_1 = 1$ so that the constraint graphs were cliques, and vary p_2 at each value of m. The probability of establishing AC shows a clear phase transition as κ_{ac} varies. We again rescale this data using finite size scaling with $N = nm$, $\kappa_c = 0.89$ and $\nu = 1.5$. Figure 6 shows that this models the phase transition very well.

We also modelled the growth in computational cost as the domain size varies.

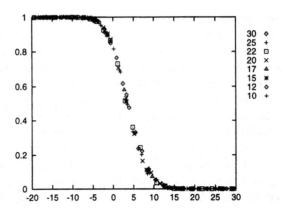

Fig. 6. Probability of establishing AC (y-axis) against γ for varying m with $\kappa_c = 0.89$, $\nu = 1.5$ (x-axis)

We no longer expect linear growth because the theoretical worst case is cubic in m. Since there are always 190 edges in our graphs, we ignored e in our models. We first attempted to model checks used as am^b. This gives a reasonable fit to the data and the peak values of b are close to 3, suggesting cubic growth. To give an explicit comparison between quadratic and cubic growth, we next investigated the model $am^2 + bm^3$ with least square linear fitting using singular value decomposition. This gives a very good fit to the data, as can be seen in Figure 7. Throughout the range of γ shown, our model suggests cubic growth. For example for underconstrained problems at $\gamma = -20$ the model is that checks $\approx 43.1m^2 + 2.26m^3$. For overconstrained problems at $\gamma = 20$ the model is $25.8m^2 + 8.37m^3$, while for critically constrained problems at $\gamma = 5$ the model is $60.0m^2 + 10.8m^3$. Grant and Smith [10] rule out the model em^3 but incorrectly conclude that growth is therefore nearer quadratic than cubic. Our model suggests that, with an appropriate scaling constant, growth is $O(em^3)$ which is the theoretical worst case. The coefficient of the cubic term suggests that problems at the phase boundary are significantly harder to solve than problems away from the boundary.

As the theoretical worst case behaviour seems to be attained, random problems appear to be able to contribute significantly to the study of the performance of polynomial algorithms like AC3. Interestingly, we observe scaling consistent with the theoretical worst case using just the median cost. This would suggest that the worst cases are not confined to rare and pathological examples. Problems at the phase transition may therefore be a valuable testbed for algorithms for AC and other polynomial problems, just as they are for NP-complete problems.

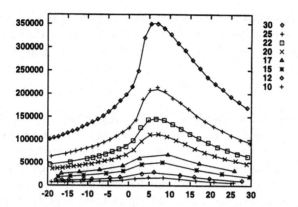

Fig. 7. Median consistency checks used by AC3 (y-axis) against γ (x-axis) for varying m. Points represent observed data while lines join modelled values.

8 Constraint Ordering Heuristics

At the heart of the AC3 algorithm is a set of directed constraints (often called arcs) waiting to be revised. The main loop of AC3 deletes an arc from this set and revises it: depending on the result other arcs may be added to the set if not already in it. This set of arcs is typically presented as a queue [12, 13, 21], such that arcs are removed in the order they were added, and propagation proceeds breadth first. For finite domains, we may use any other method for selecting the next arc to revise, and this opens up the scope for constraint ordering heuristics in AC3.

Wallace and Freuder performed a study on a number of heuristics based upon an intuitive ASAP (as soon as possible) principle where one attempts to prune domain values early [23]. They introduced heuristics based upon choosing (i) the arc with greatest constraint tightness, (ii) the arc for which the variable being checked for support has smallest domain size, (iii) an arc that will update a node which is involved in the most constraints. Heuristics (i) and (ii) worked well, reducing the number of checks by up to a factor of two over random selection or using a queue. Heuristic (iii) did not significantly reduced the number of checks over using a queue or random selection.

For NP-complete problems, the heuristic of making a choice that minimises the constrainedness of the resulting subproblem can reduce search over standard heuristics [7]. The intuition is that we want to branch on the most constrained variable into the least constrained and therefore most soluble subproblem. Similarly, for a polynomial problem like AC, we can use κ_{ac} as a constraint ordering heuristic in AC3. Here, the set of choices is the arcs in the current set maintained by AC3. We consider the remaining subproblem to have the same set of variables as the original problem, but with only those arcs still remaining in the set. We select the arc whose removal minimises the value of κ_{ac} of the remaining subproblem, ignoring the fact that subsequent revision of this arc may lead to new arcs being added to the set. By Equation (3), we choose the directed constraint c from variable x to variable y which has the maximal value of:

$$-m_x \log_2(1 - p_c{}^{m_y/2})$$

Even though this heuristic can significantly reduce the number of constraint checks need to establish arc consistency, it may not reduce runtimes. As with NP-complete problems, there are proxies for the heuristic of minimising constrainedness that are cheap to compute and that offer good performance. For instance, heuristics (i) and (ii) from [23] can be viewed as surrogates of the minimise-κ_{ac} heuristic, and we should expect them to perform well. Heuristic (i) chooses c such that p_c is maximised. Heuristic (ii) chooses c from x to y such that m_y is minimised. Everything else being equal, both these decisions reduce κ_{ac}.

Using the minimise-κ_{ac} heuristic, we performed experiments on the problem class $\langle 20, 10, 0.5\rangle$ with p_2 varied from 0 to 1 in steps of 0.01. Each point in figures 8 and 9 is the median value of 100 samples. For comparison with the minimise-κ_{ac} heuristic, we also implemented five variants of AC3 using a queue, a stack[2], picking a random element of the current set with no heuristic, and heuristics (i) and (ii) of [23]. We also report the number of revisions, *i.e.* the number

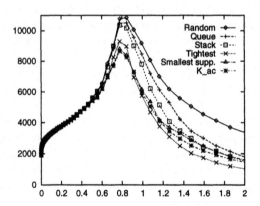

Fig. 8. Median number of checks performed by AC3 (y-axis) using various heuristics, against κ_{ac} (x-axis) for $\langle 20, 10, 0.5\rangle$ problems

of times an arc is taken out of the set. The number of revisions is important, since for problems involving structured (for instance arithmetic) constraints, or

---

[2] The results reported in previous sections used a stack and corresponds to a depth first propagation of constraints.

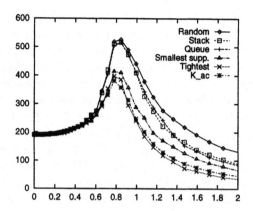

Fig. 9. Median number of revisions performed by AC3 using various heuristics (y-axis) against κ_{ac} (x-axis) for $\langle 20, 10, 0.5 \rangle$ problems

when domains are represented as intervals, arc revisions may take constant time. In this situation, checks is a poor measure of computational effort.

At the phase transition, the κ_{ac} heuristic beats the other heuristics, whilst a random choice is always worst. What is important is that if we ignore the cost of the κ_{ac} heuristic we see that it performs well. If we then have to compromise the heuristic to bring down its cost we might very well have rediscovered Wallace and Freuder's heuristics. Heuristics like these deserve further attention, for example within search algorithms like maintaining arc consistency [17].

9   Related Work

There exist several polynomial problems in which phase transition behaviour has been seen. For example, random 2-SAT problems have a phase transition in satisfiability at a ratio of clauses to variables, L/N of 1 [5], and it has long been known that random graphs display sharp thresholds in properties like graph connectivity at critical values of the average degree [3].

Evidence for a phase transition in establishing arc consistency can be found in [2]. Bessière's graphs show clear peaks in the complexity of AC3 and AC6. Bessière's results suggest that AC4 [15], although of lower complexity, can perform poorly away from the complexity peaks of AC3 and AC6. An empirical study by Wallace reaffirms this; AC3 was nearly always better than AC4 [22].

The phase transition in arc and path consistency was first studied in depth in [10] with problems from the class $\langle 20, 10, p_1, p_2 \rangle$. Using data from Table 1 in [10], we can calculate values for κ_{ac} for this phase transition. Unlike κ_{csp} at the phase transition which varied from 1.08 to 3.68, the phase transition occurs from $\kappa_{ac} \approx 0.6$ to $\kappa_{ac} \approx 1$. In NP-complete problem classes, the phase transition in solubility usually occurs over a similar range of κ [7].

Wallace and Freuder studied a number of constraint ordering heuristics for AC3, two of which we have shown to be proxies for the minimise κ_{ac} heuristic [23]. Nudel derived theoretically 8 constraint ordering heuristics, to maximise the detection of dead ends in forward checking [16]. These heuristics are similar to combinations of those of [23], selecting a constraint with minimum $m_v(1-p_c)$, where v is a future variable and c is incident on the current variable.

There appears to be scope for ordering heuristics within AC6. AC6 maintains a set, the *Waiting-List*, of unsupported values waiting to be propagated. Each element of *Waiting-List* is a pair (j, b), where b is a value removed from the domain of the jth variable. Associated with (j, b) is the set of values S_{jb} that are immediately supported by (j, b) and require new support. One possible heuristic may be to select (j, b) from *Waiting-List* such that $|S_{jb}|$ is maximised. At present we are unsure what decisions within AC6 will tend to minimise constrainedness, but we think this is worth further investigation.

10 Conclusions

We have shown that the same methodology used to study phase transition behaviour in NP-complete problems works with a polynomial problem class, establishing arc consistency in constraint satisfaction problems. The same measure for the constrainedness of an ensemble of problems that locates the phase transitions in random NP-complete problems identifies the location of a phase transition in establishing arc consistency. A complexity peak for the cost of the AC3 and AC6 algorithms is associated with this transition. Finite size scaling of this constrainedness parameter models both the scaling of the probability transition and of the search cost for AC3. This model of search cost agrees with the theoretical cubic worst case for AC3 on problems at the phase transition. This measure of constrainedness and proxies for it can then be used as the basis for constraint ordering heuristics that can reduce the number of checks and revisions performed by AC3.

What general lessons might be learnt from this study? First, we can identify and locate phase transitions in polynomial problem classes using the same constrainedness parameter developed to study NP-complete problems. Second, problems at the phase transition in polynomial problem classes can be more difficult to solve than over- or under-constrained problems away from the phase boundary. Indeed, our empirical model of median search cost for problems at the phase transition agrees with the theoretical worst case. Problems from the phase transition might therefore be useful for suggesting worst case asymptotes or, as in NP-complete domains, for benchmarking competing algorithms. Third, algorithms for polynomial problems can benefit from heuristics to reduce search. As with NP-complete problems, minimising constrainedness (and proxies for it which are cheap to compute) may provide the basis of useful heuristics. Finally, other polynomial problems (for example, path consistency, Horn satisfiability and polynomial approximation procedures for NP-complete problems) as well as other complexity classes might benefit from similar phase transition analysis.

References

1. Michael N. Barber. Finite-size scaling. In *Phase Transitions and Critical Phenomena, Volume 8*, pages 145–266. Academic Press, 1983.
2. C. Bessière. Arc-consistency and arc-consistency again. *Artificial Intelligence*, 65:179–190, 1994.
3. B. Bollobas. *Random Graphs*. Academic Press, 1985.
4. P. Cheeseman, B. Kanefsky, and W.M. Taylor. Where the really hard problems are. In *Proceedings of IJCAI-91*, pages 331–337, 1991.
5. V. Chvatal and B. Reed. Mick gets some (the odds are on his side). In *Proceedings of the 33rd Annual Symposium on Foundations of Computer Science*, pages 620–627. IEEE, 1992.
6. I.P. Gent, E. MacIntyre, P. Prosser, and T. Walsh. Scaling effects in the CSP phase transition. In *Principles and Practice of Constraint Programming (CP-95)*, pages 70–87. Springer, 1995.
7. I.P. Gent, E. MacIntyre, P. Prosser, and T. Walsh. The constrainedness of search. In *Proceedings of AAAI-96*, pages 246–252, 1996.
8. I.P. Gent, E. MacIntyre, P. Prosser, and T. Walsh. The scaling of search cost. In *Proceedings of AAAI-97*, 1997.
9. I.P. Gent and T. Walsh. Phase transitions and annealed theories: Number partitioning as a case study. In *Proceedings of ECAI-96*, pages 170–174, 1996.
10. S.A. Grant and B.M. Smith. The arc and path consistency phase transitions. Report 96.09, Research Report Series, School of Computer Studies, University of Leeds, March 1996.
11. S. Kirkpatrick and B. Selman. Critical behavior in the satisfiability of random boolean expressions. *Science*, 264:1297–1301, May 27 1994.
12. A.K. Mackworth. Consistency in networks of relations. *Artificial Intelligence*, 8:99–118, 1977.
13. A.K. Mackworth and E.C. Freuder. The complexity of some polynomial network consistency algorithms for constraint satisfaction problems. *Artificial Intelligence*, 25:65–74, 1985.
14. D. Mitchell, B. Selman, and H. Levesque. Hard and easy distributions of SAT problems. In *Proceedings of AAAI-92*, pages 459–465. AAAI Press/The MIT Press, 1992.
15. R. Mohr and T.C. Henderson. Arc and path consistency revisited. *Artificial Intelligence*, 28:225–233, 1986.
16. B. Nudel. Consistent-labeling problems and their algorithms: Expected-complexities and theory-based heuristics. *Artificial Intelligence*, 21:135–178, 1983.
17. D. Sabin and E.C. Freuder. Contradicting conventional wisdom in constraint satisfaction. In *Proceedings of ECAI-94*, pages 125–129, 1994.
18. T. Schiex, J-C. Régin, C. Gaspin and G. Verfaille. Lazy Arc Consistency. In *Proceedings of AAAI-96*, pages 216–221, 1996.
19. B. Selman and S. Kirkpatrick. Critical behavior in the computational cost of satisfiability testing. *Artificial Intelligence*, 81:273–295, 1996.
20. B.M. Smith and M.E. Dyer. Locating the phase transition in binary constraint satisfaction problems. *Artificial Intelligence*, 81:155–181, 1996.
21. E.P.K. Tsang. *Foundations of Constraint Satisfaction*. Academic Press, 1993.
22. R.J. Wallace. Why AC-3 is almost always better than AC-4 for establishing arc consistency in CSPs. In *Proceedings of IJCAI-93*, pages 239–245, 1993.
23. R.J. Wallace and E.C. Freuder. Ordering heuristics for arc consistency algorithms. In *Proc. Ninth Canad. Conf. on AI*, pages 163–169, 1992.

Look-Ahead Versus Look-Back for Satisfiability Problems

Chu Min Li and Anbulagan

LaRIA, Université de Picardie Jules Verne
33, Rue St. Leu, 80039 Amiens Cédex 01, France
tel: (33) 3 22 82 78 75, fax: (33) 3 22 82 75 02
e-mail: {cli@laria.u-picardie.fr, Anbulagan@utc.fr}

Abstract. CNF propositional satisfiability (SAT) is a special kind of the more general Constraint Satisfaction Problem (CSP). While look-back techniques appear to be of little use to solve hard random SAT problems, it is supposed that they are necessary to solve hard structured SAT problems. In this paper, we propose a very simple DPL procedure called *Satz* which only employs some look-ahead techniques: a variable ordering heuristic, a forward consistency checking (Unit Propagation) and a limited resolution before the search, where the heuristic is itself based on unit propagation. *Satz* is favorably compared on random 3-SAT problems with three DPL procedures among the best in the literature for these problems. Furthermore on a great number of problems in 4 well-known SAT benchmarks *Satz* reaches or outspeeds the performance of three other DPL procedures among the best in the literature for structured SAT problems. The comparative results suggest that a suitable exploitation of look-ahead techniques, while very simple and efficient for random SAT problems, may allow to do without sophisticated look-back techniques in a DPL procedure.

1 Introduction

Consider a set of Boolean variables $\{x_1, x_2, ..., x_n\}$, a literal l is a variable x or its negated form $\bar{x}$, a clause c is a logical *or* of some literals such as $x_1 \vee \bar{x}_2 \vee x_3$. A propositional formula F in Conjunctive Normal Form (CNF) is a logical *and* of several clauses such as $c_1 \wedge c_2 \wedge ... \wedge c_m$. F is often simply written as a set $\{c_1, c_2, ..., c_m\}$ of clauses.

Given F, the CNF propositional satisfiability (SAT) problem consists in testing whether clauses in F can all be satisfied by some consistent assignment of truth values $\{true, false\}$ to the variables. If it is the case, F is said satisfiable; otherwise, F is said unsatisfiable. SAT is a specific kind of finite-domained Constraint Satisfaction Problem (CSP) in which every variable ranges over the values $\{true, false\}$ and is the first NP-complete problem [4]. When each clause in F exactly contains r literals, the restricted SAT problem is called r-SAT. 3-SAT is the smallest NP-complete subproblem of SAT. We distinguish two types of SAT problems: problems having structures such as regularities, symmetries etc... and random problems without any structure. While real world problems are often structured, random problems represent the "core" of SAT and are independent of any particular domain.

The most effective systematic algorithms are based on the popular Davis-Putnam procedure in Loveland's form (DPL procedure) [6]. DPL procedures such as C-SAT [7], Tableau [5], and POSIT [8] usually employ a variable ordering heuristic and a forward consistency checking (Unit Propagation) known as look-ahead techniques in CSP terms. These algorithms actually have more or less difficulties to solve structured SAT problems. Recently several authors propose to embed (and emphasize) look-back techniques such as backjumping (also known as intelligent backtracking or non-chronological backtracking) and learning (also known as nogood or constraint recording) in a DPL procedure to attack structured SAT problems. GRASP [17] and relsat(4) [2] are such DPL procedures employing both look-ahead and look-back techniques, which are efficient for structured SAT problems but are not effective for random SAT problems.

In this paper we propose a very simple DPL procedure called *Satz* which only employs look-ahead techniques and a simple preprocessing of the input CNF formula to add some resolvents of length ≤ 3 into the clause database. The broad experimental comparative results of *Satz* with several state-of-the-art DPL procedures (C-SAT, Tableau, POSIT, GRASP, relsat(4)) suggest that a suitable exploitation of unit propagation and the preprocessing may be effective for both random SAT problems and a lot of structured ones. Our experience with *Satz* also enforces the belief that if a DPL procedure is efficient for random SAT problems, it should be also efficient for a lot of structured ones.

The paper is organized as follows. Section 2 presents *Satz* by discussing its heuristic and the preprocessing of the CNF formula. Section 3 compares *Satz* on random 3-SAT problems with C-SAT, Tableau, POSIT, the three DPL procedures among the best in the literature for random 3-SAT problems. Section 4 compares *Satz* on 4 well-known SAT benchmarks with GRASP, POSIT, relsat(4), the three DPL procedures among the best in the literature for structured SAT problems. All experiments are made on a SUN Sparc 20 workstation with a 125 MHz CPU. Section 5 discusses the look-ahead and look-back techniques. Section 6 concludes.

2 About *Satz*

We roughly sketch the DPL procedure in Figure 1.

DPL procedure essentially constructs a binary search tree through the space of possible truth assignments until it either finds a satisfying truth assignment or concludes that no such assignment exists, each recursive call constituting a node of the tree. Recall that all leaves (except eventually one for a satisfiable problem) of a search tree represent a dead end where an empty clause is found. Look-ahead techniques such as variable ordering heuristics play a determinant role to reach the dead end early to minimize the length of the current path in the search tree.

```
procedure DPL(F)
Begin
if F is empty, return "satisfiable";
while F contains a pure literal, satisfy the literal and simplify F.
F:=UnitPropagation(F); If F contains an empty clause, return
"unsatisfiable".

/* branching rule */
select a variable x in F according to a heuristic H, if the calling
of DPL(F∪{x}) returns "satisfiable" then return "satisfiable", otherwise
return the result of calling DPL(F∪{x̄}).
End.

procedure UnitPropagation(F)
Begin
While there is no empty clause and a unit clause l exists in F, assign a
truth value to the variable contained in l to satisfy l and simplify F.
Return F.
End.
```

Fig. 1. The DPL Procedure

2.1 Heuristics Based on Unit Propagation: a Simple Look-Ahead Technique

The most popular SAT heuristic actually is Mom's heuristic, which involves branching next on the variable having Maximum Occurrences in clauses of Minimum Size [7, 5, 8, 16, 11, 10]. Intuitively these variables allow to well exploit the power of unit propagation and to augment the chance to reach an empty clause. However Mom's heuristic may not maximize the effectiveness of unit propagation, because it only takes clauses of minimum size into account to weigh a variable, although some extensions try to also take longer clauses into account with exponentially smaller weights (e.g. 5 ternary clauses are counted as 1 binary clause).

Recently another heuristic based on Unit Propagation (UP heuristic) has proven useful and allows to exploit yet more the power of unit propagation [8, 5, 13, 14]. Given a variable x, a UP heuristic examines x by respectively adding the unit clause x and $x̄$ to F and independently makes two unit propagations. A UP heuristic allows then to take all clauses containing a variable and their relations into account in a very effective way to weigh the variable. As a secondary effect, it allows to detect the so-called *failed literals* in F which when satisfied falsify F in a single unit propagation. However since examining a variable by two unit propagations is time consuming, it is natural to try to restrict the variables to be examined.

The success of Mom's heuristic suggests that the larger the number of binary occurrences of a variable is, the higher its probability of being a good branching variable is, implying that one should restrict UP heuristics to those variables having a sufficient number of binary occurrences.

In [14], we have studied the behaviours of different restrictions of UP heuristics on hard random 3-SAT problems. We found that UP heuristic is substantially better than Mom's one even in its pure form where all free variables are examined at all nodes. Furthermore, the more variables are examined, the smaller the search tree is, confirming the advantages of UP heuristic, but too many unit propagations slow the execution. Based on the experimental evaluations of different alternatives we put forward a dynamic restriction of UP heuristic ensuring that at least T variables selected by a Mom's heuristic are examined by unit propagations. The resulted UP heuristic is realized by the unary predicate $PROP_z$:

Definition: Let $PROP$ be a binary predicate such that $PROP(x, i)$ is true iff x occurs both positively and negatively in binary clauses and having at least i binary occurrences in F, T be an integer, then $PROP_z(x)$ is defined to be the first of the three predicates $PROP(x, 4)$, $PROP(x, 3)$, $true$ (in this order) whose denotational semantics contains more than T variables.

$PROP_z$ is optimal for hard random 3-SAT problems. As we will see, it is also very powerful for structured ones.

$Satz$ is a DPL procedure with the UP heuristic $PROP_z$ with T being empirically fixed to 10. Precisely let $diff(F_1, F_2)$ be a function which gives the number of clauses of minimum size in F_1 but not in F_2, $Satz$'s branching rule is sketched in Figure 2, where the equation defining $H(x)$ is suggested by Freeman [8] in POSIT.

```
For each free variable x such that PROP_z(x) is true do
let F' and F" be two copies of F
Begin
    F' := UnitPropagation(F' ∪ {x}); F" := UnitPropagation(F" ∪ {x̄});
    If both F' and F" contain an empty clause then
        return "F is unsatisfiable".
    If F' contains an empty clause then x := 0, F := F"
    else if F" contains an empty clause then x := 1, F := F';
    If neither F' nor F" contains an empty clause then
        let w(x) denote the weight of x
        w(x) := diff(F', F) and w(x̄) := diff(F", F);
End;

For each variable x do H(x) := w(x̄) * w(x) * 1024 + w(x̄) + w(x);

Branching on the free variable x such that H(x) is the greatest.
```

Fig. 2. The Branching Rule of $Satz$

$Satz$ allows a very simple and very natural implementation exactly corresponding to the above algorithm description, except that the backtracking is not recursive and its iterative implementation is originally inspired from U-Log [9], a Prolog language interpreter. There is no other technique in *Satz* apart from the two improvements described in section 2.3. To reproduce the performance of *Satz*, one only uses arrays instead of complex data structures in the program (*Satz* uses linked lists to input the clauses then copies all data into arrays before the searching).

The source code in C of *Satz* is available from the first author.

2.2 Discussion on UP Heuristics

Hooker and Vinay [10] study satisfaction hypothesis and simplification hypothesis which are often used to motivate or explain the branching rule of a DPL procedure. Other things being equal, satisfaction hypothesis assumes that a branching rule performs better when it creates subproblems that are more likely to be satisfiable, while simplification hypothesis assumes that a branching rule works better when it creates subproblems with fewer and shorter clauses. One of their conclusions is that simplification hypothesis is better than satisfaction hypothesis.

Satz uses another hypothesis called *constraint hypothesis* which assumes that a branching rule works better when it creates subproblems with more and stronger constraints so that a contradiction can be found earlier. Since the clauses of minimum size are strongest constraints in a CNF formula, $w(x)$ and $w(\bar{x})$ in Figure 2 represent respectively the new constraints of the two generated subproblems if x is selected as the next branching variable. According to constraint hypothesis a DPL procedure should branch next to x such that $w(x)$ and $w(\bar{x})$ are the greatest. The equation defining $H(x)$ and linking $w(x)$ and $w(\bar{x})$ in Figure 2 to favor x such that $w(x)$ and $w(\bar{x})$ are roughly equal and to balance the two subtrees is experimentally better than the following one:

$$w(x) + w(\bar{x}) + \alpha * min(w(x), w(\bar{x})) \qquad (*)$$

where α is a constant.

It seems that C-SAT uses simplification hypothesis and the equation (*) to define $H(x)$, POSIT tries to combine simplification and constraint hypotheses, Tableau uses constraint hypothesis and the same equation as POSIT to define $H(x)$.

C-SAT [7] examines a variable near the leaves of a search tree by two unit propagations (called local processing) to rapidly detect failed literals. Pretolani also uses a similar approach (called pruning method) based on hypergraphs in H2R [16]. But the local processing and the pruning method as are respectively presented in [7] and [16] do not contribute to the branching variable heuristic. We find the first effective exploitation of UP heuristic in POSIT [8] and Tableau [5]. POSIT and Tableau use similar idea as C-SAT to determine the variables to be examined by unit propagation at a search tree node: x is to be examined by unit propagation iff x is among the k most weighted variables.

The main difference of *Satz* with Tableau and POSIT is that *Satz* does not specify a upper bound k of the number of variables to be examined by unit propagation at a node. Instead, *Satz* specifies a lower bound T. In fact, *Satz* examines many more variables at a node.

Given the depth of a node, Table 1 illustrates the mean number of free variables ($\#free\_vars$) and the mean number of variables examined ($\#examined\_vars$) by *Satz* at the node, with the depth of the root being 0. In order to compare with C-SAT, Tableau and POSIT we also give the theoretical value of k_C (for C-SAT), k_T (for Tableau) and k_P (for POSIT) at the node, respectively according to the definitions of k in [7, 5, 8].

Table 1. Average number of variables examined by *Satz* for 300 variable and 1275 clause random 3-SAT problems (500 problems are solved).

depth	$\#free\_vars$	$\#examined\_vars$	k_C	k_T	k_P
1	298.24	298.24	0	263	265
2	296.52	296.52	0	227	230
3	294.92	293.89	0	193	198
4	292.44	292.21	0	141	149
5	288.60	282.04	0	61	72
6	285.36	252.14	0	0	10 or 3
7	281.68	192.82	0	0	10 or 3
8	277.54	125.13	0	0	10 or 3
9	273.17	71.51	0	0	10 or 3
10	268.76	40.65	0	0	10 or 3
11	264.55	26.81	0	0	10 or 3
12	260.53	21.55	0	0	10 or 3
13	256.79	19.80	0	0	10 or 3
14	253.28	19.24	0	0	10 or 3
15	249.96	19.16	0	0	10 or 3
16	246.77	19.28	0	0	10 or 3
17	243.68	19.57	0	0	10 or 3
18	240.68	19.97	0	0	10 or 3
19	237.73	20.46	0	0	10 or 3
20	234.82	20.97	0	0	10 or 3

It is clear from Table 1 that *Satz* examines many more variables at each node than any of C-SAT, Tableau or POSIT. Near the root, *Satz* examines all free variables. Elsewhere *Satz* examines a sufficient number of variables.

2.3 Resolvents-Driven Improvements to *Satz*

Always under constraint hypothesis, we make two resolvents-driven improvements in *Satz*. The first improvement is the preprocessing of the input formula by adding some resolvents of length ≤ 3, inspired from [3].

For example, if F contains two clauses

$$x_1 \vee x_2 \vee x_3, \bar{x}_1 \vee x_2 \vee \bar{x}_4$$

then we add a clause $x_2 \vee x_3 \vee \bar{x}_4$ to F. The new clauses can in turn be used to produce other resolvents of length ≤ 3. The process is performed until saturation. In practice, we impose two constraints: (1) a resolvent resulted from two binary clauses should be unary to be added into the clause database, (2) a resolvent resulted from a binary clause and a ternary clause should be binary to be added into the clause database. The preprocessing without the two constraints is provided as an option.

Clearly, the added resolvents become explicit constraints in F as other clauses. Moreover a variable constrained both by a literal and its negated form has an occurrence more to be favored by the branching rule, which is the case for x_2 in the above example which is constrained both by x_1 and $\bar{x}_1$.

The standard preprocessing makes *Satz* about 10% faster for hard random 3-SAT problems and allows to instantaneously solve the problems of *aim* class in DIMACS benchmark. It also makes *Satz* 2 times faster when solving the problems of *dubois* class. The preprocessing without the two constraints allows to instantaneously solve all *dubois* problems.

The second improvement consists in weighting more precisely the variables at the nodes where $PROP_z$ is *true* for all variables, because these nodes are often near the root of the search tree and their branching variable has more important effect to reduce the tree size. We define $w(x)$ as the number of resolvents the newly produced binary clauses would result in in F' by a single step of resolution. $w(\bar{x})$ is similarly defined.

Refer to Figure 2, after executing $F' := UnitPropagation(F' \cup \{x\})$, $w(x)$ is defined to be

$$\sum_{l \vee l' \ is \ in \ F' \ but \ not \ in \ F} [f(\bar{l}) + f(\bar{l}')]$$

where $f(\bar{l})$ is the number of weighed occurrences of $\bar{l}$ in F, an occurrence $\bar{l}$ in a binary clause being counted as 5 in ternary clauses, an occurrence $\bar{l}$ in a ternary clause being counted as 5 in clauses of length 4, etc... The exponential factor 5 is empirically fixed and is better in our experimentation than 2, the factor used in Jeroslow-Wang rule [11].

Clearly the refined weight of a variable looks further forward by measuring the impact of the newly produced binary clauses. The improvement allows to accelerate *Satz* by more than 10% for hard random 3-SAT problems.

3 Experimental Comparative Results on Hard Random 3-SAT Problems

We compare *Satz* with C-SAT, Tableau, and POSIT, the three other DPL procedures among the best in the literature for hard random 3-SAT problems. The 3-SAT problems are generated by using the method of Mitchel et al. [15] from 4 sets of n variables and m clauses at the ratio $m/n = 4.25$, n steping from 250 variables to 400 variables by 50. Empirically the random 3-SAT problems generated at the ratio $m/n = 4.25$ are the most difficult to solve.

We use an executable of C-SAT dated July 1996. The version of Tableau used here is called *3tab* and is the same used for the experimentation presented in [5]. POSIT is compiled using the provided *make* commande on the SUN Sparc-20 workstation from the sources named *posit* − 1.0.*tar.gz*[1]. Tables 2, 3 show the performances of the 4 DPL procedures on hard random 3-SAT problems of 250, 300, 350, and 400 variables, where *time* standing for the real mean run time is reported by the unix command /usr/bin/time and *t_size* standing for search tree size is reported or computed from the number of branches reported by the DPL procedures (note that none of C-SAT, POSIT, 3tab, and *Satz* uses backjumping here).

Table 2. Mean run time (in second) and mean search tree size of C-SAT, Tableau, POSIT and *Satz* at the ratio *m/n*=4.25 for satisfiable problems.

| | 250 vars | | 300 vars | | 350 vars | | 400 vars | |
| | 159 problems | | 170 problems | | 144 problems | | 51 problems | |
System	time	t_size	time	t_size	time	t_size	time	t_size
C-SAT	5.3	4610.1	39	23980	240	123198	1813	747478
Tableau	5.3	4013.8	41	22531	272	123106	1836	616693
POSIT	4.9	6393.6	38	40262	270	246715	2362	1814814
Satz	3.8	3846.0	19	18083	106	90071	614	461991

Table 3. Mean run time (in second) and mean search tree size of C-SAT, Tableau, POSIT and *Satz* on ratio *m/n*=4.25 for unsatisfiable problems.

| | 250 vars | | 300 vars | | 350 vars | | 400 vars | |
| | 141 problems | | 130 problems | | 106 problems | | 49 problems | |
System	time	t_size	time	t_size	time	t_size	time	t_size
C-SAT	17.0	16142.0	128	83235	882	481936	5905	2538072
Tableau	16.1	11736.4	128	69862	947	430323	7362	2469466
POSIT	10.8	14455.5	83	89959	665	609623	4872	3726644
Satz	9.6	9864.0	54	51998	335	288812	1825	1389700

Tables 2, 3 show that on hard random 3-SAT problems, *Satz* is faster than the above cited versions of C-SAT, Tableau and POSIT, *Satz*'s search tree size is the smallest, and *Satz*'s run time and search tree size grow more slowly. Table 4 shows the gain of *Satz* compared with the cited version of C-SAT, Tableau and POSIT at the ratio *m/n*=4.25. Each item is computed from Tables 2, 3 (average of all problems at a point) using the following equation:

$$gain = (value(system)/value(Satz) - 1) * 100\%$$

[1] available via anonymous ftp to ftp.cis.upenn.edu in pub/freeman/

where *value* is real mean run time or real mean search tree size and *system* is C-SAT, Tableau or POSIT. From Table 4, it is clear that the gain of *Satz* grows with the size of the input formula.

Table 4. The gain of *Satz* vs. C-SAT, Tableau and POSIT in terms of run time and search tree size on the ratio m/n=4.25 computed from Tables 2 and 3.

	250 vars 300 problems		300 vars 300 problems		350 vars 250 problems		400 vars 100 problems	
System	*time*	*t_size*	*time*	*t_size*	*time*	*t_size*	*time*	*t_size*
C-SAT	66%	50%	126%	51%	152%	58%	216%	77%
Tableau	60%	15%	132%	31%	175%	45%	276%	66%
POSIT	18%	53%	68%	89%	133%	130%	198%	200%

4 Experimental Comparative Results on Structured SAT Problems

We compare *Satz* with three other DPL procedures (POSIT, GRASP and rel-sat(4)) among the best in the literature for structured SAT problems, where GRASP and POSIT are the two best in [17] compared with C-SAT, Tableau, H2R [16], SATO [12], TEGUS [18] on DIMACS and UCSC benchmarks and relsat(4) is the best procedure tested in [2]. We use 4 well-known benchmarks of structured SAT problems: DIMACS[2], UCSC[3], Beijing challenging problems[4] and planning problems proposed by Kautz and Selman[5]. The version of POSIT is the same as in the last section. we use an executable of GRASP system (version May 1996) available from Joao M. Silva[6]. The relsat(4) system v1.00 is received from Roberto J. Bayardo Jr.[7].

Following Hooker & Vinay [10] and Silva & Sakallah [17], we use the cutoff time (two hours) as a surrogate for the real run time and partition the DIMACS and UCSC benchmarks into classes, e.g. class *aim*-100 includes all problems with the name *aim*-100-*. In each class, #*M* denotes the total number of class members, #*S* denotes the number of problems effectively solved by the corresponding DPL procedure in less than two hours. *Time* denotes the total CPU time in seconds taken to process all members of a class (a problem that can not be solved in less than 2 hours contributes 7200 seconds to the total time). We do not include the classes F, G, PAR32 and Hanoi5 that none of *Satz*, GRASP,

---

[2] available from ftp://dimacs.rutgers.edu/pub/challenge/satisfiability
[3] available from ftp://dimacs.rutgers.edu/pub/challenge/sat/contributed/UCSC
[4] available from http://www.cirl.uoregon.edu/crawford/beijing
[5] available from ftp://ftp.research.att.com/dist/ai/logistics.tar.Z
[6] e-mail: jpms@inesc.pt
[7] e-mail: bayardo@cs.utexas.edu

POSIT and relsat(4) solve in less than 2 hours. The Beijing challenging problems and planning problems are individually listed and a problem that can not be solved in less than 2 hours is marked by "> 7200". The obtained results are shown in Tables 5, 6, 7, 8. A first observation is that *Satz*, GRASP, relsat(4) are all significantly better than POSIT on these benchmarks. So in the following we only analyse the performances of *Satz*, GRASP and relsat(4).

We find that *Satz* is comparable with relsat(4) and GRASP on most DIMACS and UCSC problems (a total of 22 classes) except *pret* class where there is no resolvent of length ≤ 3 and most variables are symmetric so that UP heuristics fail to distinguish them. *Satz* is significantly better than both GRASP and relsat(4) in 3 classes (*hole*, *ii16*, *par16*) and for 12 classes *aim-50*, *aim-100*, *aim-200*, *bf*, *dubois*, *ii8*, *jnh*, *par8*, *bf0432*, *ssa0432*, *ssa6288* and *ssa7552*, it has equivalent performance. *Satz* is also very efficient on most *ssa* and *bf* problems except a small number among them (8 *ssa* over 102 and 3 *bf* over 223) which augments the total time for *Satz* to solve the corresponding classes. For example, while most problems in the class *bf1355* can be solved within 3 seconds, the problem *bf1355-243* takes 1395 seconds to be solved. The hardest problem for *Satz* in the *ssa* and *bf* classes is *bf2670-244* which takes 3 hours and 47 minutes to be solved.

In Beijing challenging benchmark, *Satz* solves the same number of problems as relsat(4) and one more than GRASP. On Kautz and Selman's planning problems, *Satz* is also comparable with GRASP and relsat(4) except 4 problems over 31. Note that *Satz* contains a preprocessing of the input CNF formula to delete duplicate clauses, tautologies, and duplicate literals in clauses, which is time consuming for large problems such as some Kautz and Selman's planning problems or some Beijing challenging problems containing more than 100000 clauses and is not negligible especially when the search itself takes little time.

5 Look-Ahead Versus Look-Back

In CSP terms, *Satz* essentially employs some simple look-ahead techniques to reach a dead end as early as possible: a variable ordering heuristic (UP heuristic), a forward consistency checking (Unit Propagation) and a simple preprocessing, the heuristic being itself based on forward consistency checking. However *Satz* does not include look-back techniques such as backjumping and learning, another class of techniques for CSP problems.

The heuristic of GRASP may be explained by the satisfaction hypothesis which intends to directly satisfy the largest number of clauses and that of relsat(4) by simplification hypothesis which intends to value the largest number of variables when branching. Their variable ordering heuristic is simpler than *Satz*. However they exploit sophisticated backjumping and learning to attack structured SAT problems. The experimental results presented in the last section suggests that the good performance of GRASP and relsat(4) on a lot of structured SAT problems can be reached simply by a limited resolution at the top

Table 5. Total run time (in seconds) of DIMACS problems.

Problem Class	#M	Satz		GRASP		POSIT		relsat(4)	
		#S	Time	#S	Time	#S	Time	#S	Time
aim-50	24	24	13.8	24	0.5	24	0.3	24	8.1
aim-100	24	24	3.6	24	1.2	24	352	24	8.4
aim-200	24	24	4.3	24	8.4	13	82792	24	8.2
bf	4	4	25.6	4	5.8	2	14415	4	5.9
dubois	13	13	1.7^a	13	6.0	8	50599	13	4.6
hanoi4	1	1	677	1	3910	1	42.8	1	38.0
hole	5	5	483	4	9838	5	429	5	3671
ii8	14	14	5.6	14	17.1	14	1.0	14	7.5
ii16	10	10	106	9	7515	8	14454	10	331
ii32	17	16	7624	17	6.0	16	7551	17	2158
jnh	50	50	7.0	50	10.8	50	0.3	50	19.4
par8	10	10	0.8	10	0.2	10	0.04	10	3.6
par16	10	10	251	10	11349	10	27.0	10	463
pret	8	4	29612	8	13.0	4	29156	8	5.6
ssa	8	8	1748	8	3.9	8	35.1	8	39.1

^{a} the dubois problems are solved by using an option of *Satz* where all resolvents of length ≤ 3 are added into the clause database. For dubois100.cnf, we add the missing 0 at the end of some clauses.

Table 6. Total run time (in seconds) of UCSC problems.

Problem Class	#M	Satz		GRASP		POSIT		relsat(4)	
		#S	Time	#S	Time	#S	Time	#S	Time
bf0432	21	21	35.7	21	35.3	21	20.6	21	28.0
bf1355	149	149	3576	149	109	68	648849	149	133
bf2670	53	51	26445	53	50.7	53	1149	53	359
ssa0432	7	7	1.7	7	0.6	7	0.1	7	3.6
ssa2670	12	7	40062	12	35.4	12	1139	12	257
ssa6288	3	3	7.2	3	0.2	3	7.7	3	4.4
ssa7552	80	80	60.5	80	15.4	80	1722	76	43.6

of the search tree and an optimal UP heuristic. The latter approach has the advantages of being simpler and much more efficient for random 3-SAT problems.

5.1 Heuristics Versus Backjumping

A better variable ordering heuristic allows to avoid many useless backtracking. In fact, let $x_{i_1}, x_{i_2}, ..., x_{i_b}, ..., x_{i_{d-1}}, x_{i_d}$ be a path from the root to a dead end in a DPL search tree, the standard chronological backtracking backtracks to $x_{i_{d-1}}$ while a backjumping may jump to x_{i_b} in the case where the variables $x_{i_{b+1}}, ..., x_{i_{d-1}}$ do not contribute to the conflict discovered at x_{i_d}, avoiding in this

Table 7. Run time (in seconds) of Beijing challenging problems.

Problem	Type	#vars	#clauses	Satz	GRASP	POSIT	relsat(4)
2bitadd_10	synthesis	590	1422	> 7200	> 7200	> 7200	> 7200
2bitadd_11	synthesis	649	1562	201	6.6	0.3	0.5
2bitadd_12	synthesis	708	1702	0.4	6.0	0.05	0.5
2bitcomp_5	synthesis	125	310	0.03	0.03	0.01	0.5
2bitmax_6	synthesis	252	766	0.07	0.1	0.01	0.4
3bitadd_31	synthesis	8432	31310	> 7200	> 7200	> 7200	> 7200
3bitadd_32	synthesis	8704	32316	4512	> 7200	> 7200	> 7200
3blocks	planning	370	13732	2.0	28.6	1.8	2.9
4blocksb	planning	540	34199	8.2	473	49.3	6.0
4blocks	planning	900	59285	1542	> 7200	> 7200	296
e0ddr2-10-by-5-1	scheduling	19500	108887	215	143	> 7200	299
e0ddr2-10-by-5-4	scheduling	19500	104527	232	88.5	3508	30.8
enddr2-10-by-5-1	scheduling	20700	111567	> 7200	95.3	> 7200	33.2
enddr2-10-by-5-8	scheduling	21000	113729	229	89.6	> 7200	33.7
ewddr2-10-by-5-1	scheduling	21800	118607	339	101	283	33.4
ewddr2-10-by-5-8	scheduling	22500	123329	279	102	> 7200	41.7

way the amount of time exploring a useless region of the search space. However if we look at the case more carefully, we find that if the backjumping allows to avoid the useless exploring, it is because the branching variables $x_{i_{b+1}}, ..., x_{i_{d-1}}$ are not good. If the variable ordering heuristic chose x_{i_d} as the branching variable immediately after x_{i_b}, the backjumping would be simply chronological backtracking.

Clearly the UP heuristic looks further forward and allows $Satz$ to do without backjumping in most cases.

5.2 Learning

$Satz$ does not include any classical learning techniques applied during the search. But $Satz$ does include a standard "statical learning" consisting of a limited resolution before the search to add some resolvents of length ≤ 3 into the clause database. While we believe that the preprocessing is very simple and that these resolvents would be probably learned by a classical learning technique during the search, we think that the "statical learning" in $Satz$ is probably insufficient for some structured problems. For example, a complete search of all resolvents of length ≤ 3 before the search allows to instantaneously solve all problems in dubois class, while the standard "statical learning" only makes $Satz$ two times faster. On the other hand, many problems such as ssa* and ii* would explode the computer memory by a complete search of all resolvents of length ≤ 3.

A careful integration with modest overhead of UP heuristic and a dynamic learning such as the one proposed in relsat(4) seems promising.

Table 8. Run time (in seconds) of Kautz & Selman's planning problems.

Problem	sat	#vars	#clauses	Satz	GRASP	POSIT	relsat(4)
bw_large.a	Y	459	4675	0.4	0.3	0.04	0.6
bw_large.b	Y	1087	13772	1.4	3.1	0.5	1.5
bw_large.c	Y	3016	50457	7.0	225	3.4	95.1
bw_large.d	Y	6325	131973	2980	3915	?	418
f7hh.14	Y	4814	114132	1797	114	> 7200	80.8
f7hh.14.simple	Y	3269	61295	1580	59.8	> 7200	32.1
f7hh.15	Y	5315	140258	28.9	313	> 7200	253
f7hh.15.simple	Y	3759	75030	22.3	153	> 7200	96.7
f8h_10	N	2459	25290	1.6	13.6	0.6	2.6
f8h_10.simple	N	1415	14346	1.1	5.7	0.3	1.2
f8h_11	Y	2883	37388	3.0	23.9	371	3.8
f8h_11.simple	Y	1782	20895	2.2	11.4	26.7	2.9
facts7h.10	N	2218	22539	1.4	12.7	2.0	2.1
facts7h	Y	2595	32952	2.6	19.8	0.9	3.5
facts7hh.12	N	3814	68300	> 7200	784	> 7200	200
facts7hh.12.simple	N	2353	37121	> 7200	165	> 7200	66.6
facts7hh.13-simp	Y	4315	48072	12.1	46.3	> 7200	38.2
facts7hh.13-simp.simple	Y	2514	48072	9.7	36.5	1357	25.0
facts7hh.13	Y	4315	90646	15.1	79.3	> 7200	90.1
facts7hh.13.simple	Y	2809	48920	11.3	45.6	> 7200	19.5
facts7hha.12	N	2990	39618	> 7200	111	> 7200	105
facts7hha.12.simple	N	1729	21943	> 7200	58.3	> 7200	36.4
facts7hha.13	Y	3371	53824	10.0	27.6	2134	7.7
facts7hha.13.simple	Y	2069	29508	7.7	15.2	637	5.9
facts8.13	Y	3727	66735	6.5	49.9	141	14.4
facts8h.12	Y	3303	51223	5.7	27.4	1890	5.0
logistics.a	Y	828	6718	212	31.7	11.8	3.0
logistics.b	Y	843	7301	0.7	34.1	0.3	1.5
logistics.c	Y	1141	10719	6.6	116	> 7200	111
rocket_ext.a	Y	331	4446	0.2	2.6	0.2	0.8
rocket_ext.b	Y	351	2398	0.3	3.8	0.02	0.8

5.3 Random SAT Versus Structured SAT

It seems that the look-back techniques as are described in GRASP and relsat(4) are not suitable for random 3-SAT problems. For example, Table 9 shows the behaviour of GRASP et relsat(4) on hard random 3-SAT problems compared with *Satz*.

On the other hand, look-ahead techniques such as those implemented in *Satz* can be used to attack both random 3-SAT problems and many structured SAT problems. Our experiences enforce the belief: if a technique is powerful for random SAT problems, it is probably powerful for structured SAT problems.

We also believe that the essential strategy to write a DPL procedure is to try to reach a dead end as early as possible and heuristics are probably the most effective method to realize the strategy. However if heuristics fail to work well, e.g. for the problems where most variables are symmetric, one should try other

Table 9. Mean run time (in second) of *Satz*, relsat(4) and GRASP at the ratio m/n=4.25.

System	200 vars 300 problems		250 vars 300 problems	
	161 *sat*	139 *unsat*	159 *sat*	141 *unsat*
Satz	0.8	1.8	3.8	9.6
relsat(4)	10.4	35.3	129.9	571.7
GRASP	280.4	1693.8	—	—

methods such as learning or symmetry detection. In this sense, *Satz* can be still improved in the future.

6 Conclusion

We propose a very simple DPL procedure only employing some look-ahead techniques: a variable ordering heuristic, a forward consistency checking (Unit Propagation) and a limited resolution before the search, where the heuristic is itself based on unit propagation. The comparative experimental results of *Satz* on random 3-SAT problems with three DPL procedures among the best in the literature for these problems show that it is very efficient on random 3-SAT problems. While the best algorithms in the literature to solve structured SAT problems usually employ both look-ahead and look-back techniques and emphasize the latter, *Satz* reaches or outspeeds their performances on a lot of structured SAT problems. The results suggest that a suitable exploitation of look-ahead techniques, while very simple and efficient for random SAT problems, may allow to do without sophisticated look-back techniques in a DPL procedure for many structured SAT problems.

Our experiences with *Satz* also enforce the belief that if a DPL procedure is efficient for random SAT problems, it should be also efficient for many structured ones. For problems in which UP heuristic fails to distinguish the variables, e.g., problems with many symmetries, *Satz* can be still improved by learning techniques.

Acknowledgements: We are very grateful to Bart Selman for fruitful suggestions on the organization of this paper and for informing us the DPL procedures GRASP and relsat(4). We also thank Olivier Dubois, James M. Crawford, Jon W. Freeman, Joao P. Marques Silva, and Roberto J. Bayardo Jr. for providing us their DPL procedures.

References

1. Bayardo Jr. R.J., Schrag R.C., *Using CSP Look-Back Techniques to Solve Exceptionally Hard SAT Instances*, Proceedings of the Second International Conference

355

on Principles and Practice of Constraint Programming (CP96), Cambridge, Massachusetts, USA, August 1996.

2. Bayardo Jr. R.J., Schrag R.C., *Using CSP Look-Back Techniques to Solve Real-World SAT Instances*, to appear in proceedings of AAAI-97, Providence, Rhode Island, July 1997.

3. Billionnet A., Sutter A., *An efficient algorithm for 3-satisfiability problem*, Operations Research Letters, 12:29-36, July 1992.

4. Cook S.A., *The Complexity of Theorem Proving Procedures*, Proceedings of 3rd ACM Symp. on Theory of Computing, Ohio, 1971, pp. 151-158.

5. Crawford J.M., Auton L.D., *Experimental results on the Crossover point in Random 3-SAT*,Artificial Intelligence, No. 81, 1996.

6. Davis M., Logemann G., Loveland D., *A machine program for theorem proving*, Commun. ACM 5, 1962, pp. 394-397.

7. Dubois O., Andre P., Boufkhad Y., Carlier J., *SAT versus UNSAT*. Second DIMACS Implementation Challenge, D. S. Johnson and M. A. Trick (eds.), 1993.

8. Freeman J.W., *Improvements to propositional satisfiability search algorithms*, Ph.D. Thesis, Department of computer and Information science, University of Pennsylvania, Philadelphia, PA, 1995.

9. Gloess P.Y., *U-Log, a Unified Object Logic*, Revue d'intelligence artificielle, Vol. 5, No. 3, 1991, pp. 33-66.

10. Hooker J.N., Vinay V., *Branching rules for satisfiability*, Journal of Automated Reasoning, 15:359-383, 1995.

11. Jeroslow R., Wang J., *Solving propositional satisfiability problems*, Annals of Mathematics and AI 1, 1990, pp. 167-187.

12. Kim S., Zhang H., *ModGen: Theorem proving by model generation*, Proceedings of the 12th National Conference on Artificial Intelligence (AAAI-94), 1994, pp. 162-167.

13. Li C.M., *Exploiting yet more the power of unit clause propagation to solve 3-SAT problem*, Proceedings of the ECAI'96 Workshop on Advances in Propositional Deduction, Budapest, Hungary, August 1996, pp. 11-16.

14. Li C.M., Anbulagan, *Heuristics Based on Unit Propagation for Satisfiability Problems*, to appear in Proceedings of IJCAI'97, Nagoya, Japan, August 1997.

15. Mitchell D., Selman B., Levesque H., *Hard and Easy Distributions of SAT Problems*, Proceedings of the 10th National Conference on Artificial Intelligence (AAAI-92), San Jose, CA, July 1992, pp. 459-465.

16. Pretolani D., *Satisfiability and hypergraphs*, Ph.D. Thesis, Dipartimento di Informatica, Università di Pisa, 1993.

17. Silva J. P. M., Sakallah K. A., *Conflict Analysis in Search Algorithms for Propositional Satisfiability*, Proceedings of the International Conference on Tools with Artificial Intelligence, November 1996.

18. Stephan P. R., Brayton R. K., Sangiovanni-Vincentelli A. L., *Combinational Test Generation Using Satisfiability*, Memorandum No. UCB/ERL M92/112, EECS Department, University of California at Berkeley, October 1992.

Why Adding More Constraints Makes a Problem Easier for Hill-Climbing Algorithms: Analyzing Landscapes of CSPs

Makoto Yokoo

NTT Communication Science Laboratories
2-2 Hikaridai, Seika-cho
Soraku-gun, Kyoto 619-02 Japan
e-mail: yokoo@cslab.kecl.ntt.co.jp

Abstract. It is well known that constraint satisfaction problems (CSPs) in the phase transition region are most difficult for complete search algorithms. On the other hand, for incomplete hill-climbing algorithms, problems in the phase transition region are more difficult than problems beyond the phase transition region, i.e., more constrained problems. This result seems somewhat unnatural since these more constrained problems have fewer solutions than the phase transition problems.

In this paper, we clarify the cause of this paradoxical phenomenon by exhaustively analyzing the state-space landscape of CSPs, which is formed by the evaluation values of states. The analyses show that by adding more constraints, while the number of solutions decreases, the number of local-minima also decreases, thus the number of states that are reachable to solutions increases. Furthermore, the analyses clarify that the decrease in local-minima is caused by a set of interconnected local-minima (*basin*) being divided into smaller regions by adding more constraints.

1 Introduction

Recently, rapid advances have been made in research to clarify what kinds of constraint satisfaction problems (CSPs) are most difficult for complete search algorithms. These works show that the problems in the region where the solvable probability is about 50% (phase transition region) tend to be most difficult [1, 5, 7].

The above results are intuitively natural. If the problem is weakly constrained, a complete algorithm will easily find a solution. Also, if the problem is very strongly constrained, the problem becomes easy since the complete algorithm can prune most of the branches in the search tree. Therefore, the most difficult problems will exist in the middle, i.e., the phase transition region.

On the other hand, what kind of problems are most difficult for incomplete hill-climbing algorithms (such as GSAT [10]) that do not perform an exhaustive search? Since these algorithms cannot discover the fact that a problem is unsolvable, trying to solve unsolvable problems by these algorithms is futile. Therefore, if we choose solvable problem instances and apply the algorithms to these problem instances, what kinds of problems are most difficult?

At first glance, we may think that a problem becomes more difficult for hill-climbing algorithms if we add more constraints, which provides the problem with fewer solutions. However, by actually solving problems using hill-climbing algorithms, the problems in the phase transition region are the most difficult, as with the complete algorithms, although these problems have more solutions that the problems beyond the phase transition region, i.e., more constrained problems. Such paradoxical results have been reported in [2].

In this paper, we clarify the cause of this paradoxical phenomenon by exhaustively analyzing the state-space landscape of CSPs. A state is one possible assignment to all variable values, and the evaluation value of the state is the number of its constraint violations. The landscape of the state-space is formed by the evaluation values of the states. Such analyses are important not only for clarifying the cause of this paradoxical phenomenon, but also for developing more efficient hill-climbing algorithms by utilizing the results of landscape analyses.

For path-planning problems, such landscape analyses have been reported in [6]. On the other hand, as far as the author knows, there has been no research done on analyzing the landscapes of CSPs, with the notable exception of [4]. In this research, the relation between the landscapes of graph-coloring problems and the number of possible colors is analyzed.

In this paper, we first divide the states into two classes: states that are *reachable* to solutions, and states that are unreachable to solutions since they lead to local-minima. Then, we show that the problems beyond the phase transition region actually have more solution-reachable states than the problems in the phase transition region. Next, we show that the number of local-minima decreases by adding more constraints, thus the number of solution-reachable states increases. Furthermore, we examine the number and widths of *basins*, each of which is a set of interconnected local-minima. We show that the number of local-minima decreases because a basin is divided into smaller regions by adding more constraints.

In the following sections of this paper, we first describe CSPs and the algorithm used for the analyses (Section 2), then we show the analyses of the state-spaces of 3-SAT problems (Section 3). Furthermore, we discuss the obtained results in more detail (Section 4).

2 Problem Definition and Algorithm

2.1 Problem Definition

A constraint satisfaction problem can be defined as follows. There exist n variables $x_1, x_2, ..., x_n$, each of which takes its value from a finite, discrete domain $D_1, D_2, ..., D_n$, respectively. There also exists a set of constraints. A constraint among k variables $c(x_{i1}, ..., x_{ik})$ is a subset of a product $D_{i1} \times ... \times D_{ik}$, which represents allowed combinations of variable values. The goal is to find an assignment of all variables that satisfies all constraints.

A satisfiability problem for propositional formulas in conjunctive normal form (SAT) is an important subclass of CSP, and can be defined as follows. A boolean *variable* x_i is a variable that takes the value true or false. We call the value assignment of one variable a *literal*. A *clause* is a disjunction of literals, e.g., $x_1 \vee \overline{x_2} \vee x_4$. Given a set of clauses $C_1, C_2, \ldots, C_m$ and variables $x_1, x_2, \ldots, x_n$, the satisfiability problem is to determine if the formula

$$C_1 \wedge C_2 \wedge \ldots \wedge C_m$$

is satisfiable. That is, is there an assignment of values to the variables that makes the above formula true.

A 3-SAT problem is a SAT problem in which the number of literals in each clause is restricted to 3. The number of clauses divided by the number of variables is called the *clause density*, and the difficulty of a randomly generated 3-SAT problem is mainly determined by this clause density [1, 7].

2.2 Hill-climbing Algorithm

In a hill-climbing algorithm for solving a CSP, each variable has a tentative initial value, and the value of a variable is changed one by one so that the number of constraint violations decreases.

We introduce the following terms for explaining our algorithm and the analyses in the next section.

state: We call one possible assignment of all variables a *state*. In a SAT problem with n variables, the number of states is 2^n.

evaluation value: For a state s, we call the number of constraint violations of the state the *evaluation value* of the state (represented as $eval(s)$).

neighbor: For a state s, we say another state s' is a *neighbor* of s, if s' is obtained by changing one variable value of s. In a SAT problem with n variables, each state has n neighbors.

local-minimum: For a state s that is not a solution, if the evaluation values of all of its neighbors are larger than or equal to s's evaluation value, we say s is a *local-minimum*. Specifically, the following condition is satisfied: $\forall s'$ if s' is a neighbor of s, then $eval(s') \geq eval(s)$.

strict local-minimum: For a state s that is not a solution, if the evaluation values of all of its neighbors are larger than s's evaluation value, we say s is a *strict* local-minimum. Specifically, the following condition is satisfied: $\forall s'$ if s' is a neighbor of s, then $eval(s') > eval(s)$.

non-strict local-minimum: If a state s is a local-minimum, but not a strict local-minimum, we say s is a *non-strict* local-minimum. If s is a non-strict local-minimum, there exists at least one neighbor that has the same evaluation value.

In this paper, we use the algorithm described in Figure 1 for analyses. This algorithm is a greedy, unfair deterministic tie-breaking algorithm [3]. As the basic GSAT, this algorithm moves from the current state to the neighboring state, which has the smallest evaluation value. Also, if the current state is a non-strict local-minimum, this algorithm can move to the neighboring state that has the same evaluation value (sideway move).

On the other hand, unlike GSAT (in which ties are broken randomly), if there exist multiple states that have the best (smallest) evaluation value, ties are broken in a fixed, deterministic, unfair way (e.g., each state has a unique identifier, and a tie is broken by using the alphabetical order of these identifiers). We use this method in order to simplify the analyses in the next section[1].

```
procedure hill_climbing
    restart: set s to a randomly selected initial state;
    for j:=1 to Max-flips
        if eval(s) = 0 then return s;
        else if s is a strict local-minimum then goto restart;
            else s:= a neighbor of s that has the smallest evaluation value;
            (ties are broken deterministically)
            end if;
        end if;
    end;
    goto restart;
```

Fig. 1. Hill-climbing Algorithm

In the following, we mainly use randomly generated 3-SAT problems for analyses. In a randomly generated 3-SAT problem, each clause is generated by randomly selecting three variables, and each of the variables is given the value true or false with a 50% probability. In Figure 2, we show the ratio of solvable problems, in 100 randomly generated 3-SAT problem instances with 24 variables, by varying the clause density (number of clauses/number of variables). We can see that phase transition occurs[2] when the clause density is around 4.67.

Furthermore, we select 50 solvable problem instances from randomly generated problems for each clause density, and solve these instances with the algorithm described in Figure 1. We show the average number of restarts required to solve the problem instances in Figure 3 (for each problem instance, 1000 trials are performed using different initial states). Also, we show the average number of solutions to these solvable problem instances in Figure 4.

From these figures, we can see that the average number of solutions at the clause density 4.67 (where the phase transition occurs) is 11.5, and the average number of solutions at the clause density 5.83 (beyond the phase transition)

---

[1] We discuss the effect of tie-breaking methods on algorithm efficiency in Section 4.2.
[2] Since we use very small-scale problems, the phase transition is not as drastic as with large-scale problems.

is 3.6 (less than 1/3 of the solutions at the phase transition region). However, the required number of restarts at the clause density 5.83 is 6.9 (about 50% fewer than for the phase transition region, i.e., 13.0). Consequently, the problems become easier.

Although we use very small-scale problem instances, we can see the paradoxical phenomenon that the problems with fewer solutions are actually easier than the problems with more solutions.

3 Analyzing State-Space

3.1 Analyzing Solution-Reachability

For each state, the neighboring state that the algorithm can move to is uniquely determined, since ties are broken in a fixed, deterministic method. The state-space of the problem can be described using a graph, in which a state is represented as a node, and a possible transition between states is represented as a directed link (Figure 5). In Figure 5, a symbol near a node represents the identifier of the state, and a value within a node represents the evaluation value of the state. Also, a dotted link connects two neighboring states that do not have a directed link between them. For example, in Figure 5, e and h are neighbors, but there is no directed link between them, since the algorithm moves to f from these states. In this example, we assume that ties are broken in the alphabetical order of identifiers.

Each node has exactly one outgoing link, except for a strict local-minimum (e.g., state g) and a solution (e.g., state f). Also, there can be a cycle that circulates around multiple non-strict local-minima (e.g., links between a and b).

By tracing directed links from a state s, the result will be either to reach a solution or not (i.e., to reach a strict local-minimum, or to go around non-strict local-minima). In the former case, we say s is *reachable* to solutions, and in the latter case, we say s is *unreachable* to solutions. For example, in Figure 5, c, e, f and h are reachable and a, b, d and g are unreachable to solutions.

In Figure 6, we show the average ratio of the states that are solution-reachable. By adding more constrains, the average ratio of solution-reachable states actually increases beyond the phase transition region.

If the probability that a randomly selected state is solution-reachable is given by p, the estimated number of restarts required to find a solution will be $1/p$ (i.e., $p + 2p^2 + 3p^3 \ldots$). In Figure 7, we show the estimated number of restarts[3] derived from Figure 6. The values in Figure 7 are almost identical to the actual measurements in Figure 3.

---

[3] Note that the average ratio at clause density 4.67 is 0.12, but this does not mean the estimated number of restarts will be 8.33=1/0.12. In general, the average of '$1/p$' is not equal to the reciprocal of the average of p. For example, the average of 1/5 and 1/2 is 7/20, while the reciprocal of the average of 5 and 2 is 2/7.

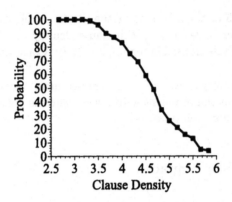

Fig. 2. Probability of satisfiability (3-SAT problems)

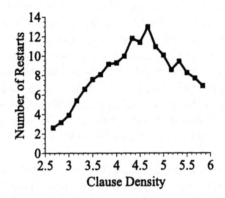

Fig. 3. Average number of restarts (3-SAT problems)

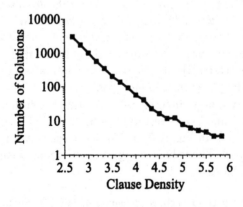

Fig. 4. Average number of solutions (3-SAT problems)

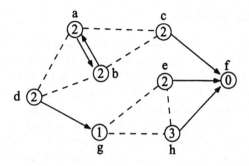

Fig. 5. Example of state-space

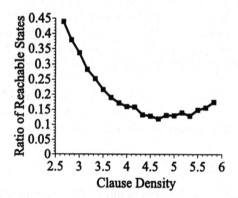

Fig. 6. Average ratio of solution-reachable states (3-SAT problems)

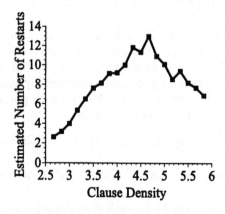

Fig. 7. Average estimated number of restarts (3-SAT problems)

3.2 Analyzing local-minima

In view of the above, why dose adding more constraints increase the number of solution-reachable states beyond the phase transition, although it decreases the number of solutions? As shown in Figure 5, tracing directed links from a state will either result in reaching a solution or reaching a local-minimum (strict or non-strict). Let us examine how the number of local-minima changes by adding constraints. Figure 8 shows the average number of local-minima. We can see that the number of local-minima decreases monotonically by adding constraints.

While adding constraints makes a problem harder for a hill-climbing algorithm by decreasing the number of solutions, it also makes the problem *easier* by decreasing the number of local-minima. As Figure 4 shows, the number of solutions decreases very rapidly around the phase transition region, and then decreases slowly beyond the phase transition region (note that the y-axe of Figure 4 is log-scaled). On the other hand, the number of local minima decreases at a more constant rate (note that the y-axe of Figure 8 is linear). Therefore, we can assume that by adding more constraints, the effect of making the problem easier will exceed the effect of making the problem harder beyond the phase transition region.

Another possible factor is that the evaluation values of local-minima will increase by adding more constraints (while the evaluation values of solutions are always 0), and thus the number of solution-reachable states will increase.

3.3 Analyzing Basins

Considering the above, why does the number of local-minima decrease monotonically by adding more constraints? Adding constraints does not necessarily mean that the number of local-minima must decrease. By adding more constraints and increasing the evaluation values of states, some of these states may change to non local-minima, but some states that are neighbors of the increased states may become local-minima.

This question can be answered by analyzing the landscape of the state-space. By checking each local-minimum, we found that almost all local-minima are non-strict local-minima (there are only a few strict local-minima for each problem) and many non-strict local-minima are interconnected (by neighborhood relation) to create a flat surface in the state-space. We call such parts *basins*.

The formal definition of a basin is as follows.

Definition: A basin is a set of connected[4] states that satisfies the following conditions.
- All states in the basin have the same evaluation value, which is larger than 0.
- For each state s in the basin, each neighboring state s' of s, which is not a member of the basin, has an evaluation value greater than or equal to the evaluation value of s, i.e., $eval(s') \geq eval(s)$.

---

[4] We mean *connected* by neighborhood relation in general, not only by directed links.

We say a basin is *maximal* if the above conditions are violated by adding any neighboring state. Also, we call the number of states in a basin the *width* of the basin. For example, in Figure 5, there are two maximal basins, i.e., $\{a, b\}$ and $\{g\}$. From this definition, any state in a basin is a local-minimum, any local-minimum is a member of some maximal basin, and a state cannot be a member of two different maximal basins. Therefore, the summation of widths of maximal basins is equal to the number of local-minima. Also, a strict local-minimum forms a basin that has only one member.

Figure 9 shows the average width of maximal basins. We can see that the average width of basins decreases monotonically by adding constraints. Figure 10 shows the average number of maximal basins. We can see that the number of basins increases initially, then reaches a peak, and finally slowly decreases. When a problem is very weakly constrained, adding more constraints divides a basin into several regions. When the problem is strongly constrained, each basin is small and the basins tend to be eliminated by adding more constraints. It is obvious that if a basin is divided into several regions, the summation of widths of these parts would be smaller than the original width.

To summarize, most local-minima are interconnected with each other to create basins. By adding constraints, a basin is divided into smaller regions and the summation of widths of maximal basins (the number of local-minima) decreases.

4 Discussion

4.1 3-coloring Problem

The analyses in the previous section give us a clear explanation of the paradoxical phenomenon. However, how general are these results?

To reconfirm the results in other classes of CSPs, we show the evaluation results in another important class of CSPs, i.e., graph-coloring problems. In Figure 11, we show the ratio of solvable problems in 100 randomly generated problem instances having 12 variable and 3 possible colors (3-coloring problems) by varying the link density (number of links/number of variables). We can see that phase transition occurs[5] when the link density is around 1.9.

Furthermore, we select 50 solvable problem instances from randomly generated problems for each link density and solve these instances. We show the average number of restarts required to solve the problem instances in Figure 12, and the average number of solutions of these solvable problem instances in Figure 13. As with the 3-SAT problem, we can see the paradoxical phenomenon in which the problems with fewer solutions are easier than the problems with more solutions.

Figure 14 shows the average ratio of the solution-reachable states. By adding more constrains, the average ratio of solution-reachable states increases beyond the phase transition region. Figure 15 shows the average number of local-minima.

---

[5] As in the case of the 3-SAT problems, the phase transition is not as drastic as with large-scale problems.

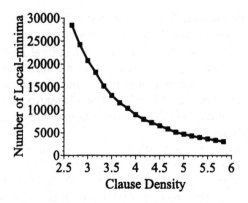

Fig. 8. Average number of local-minima (3-SAT problems)

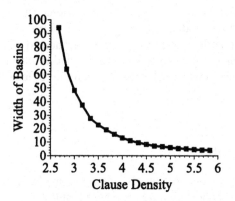

Fig. 9. Average width of basins (3-SAT problems)

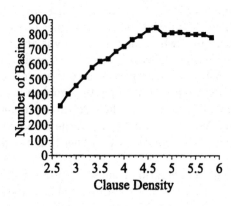

Fig. 10. Average number of basins (3-SAT problems)

As with the 3-SAT problems, the number of local-minima decreases monotonically by adding constraints, except for the part where the link density is very low. Figure 16 shows the average width of maximal basins, and Figure 17 shows the average number of maximal basins. The results are very similar to those obtained for the 3-SAT problems, except that the number of basins increases monotonically.

4.2 Effects of Tie-breaking

We use an algorithm with a unfair deterministic tie-breaking method. As discussed in [3], using an unfair tie-breaking method degrades the performance of the algorithm. In the example problems used in this paper, we can obtain about a two-fold speedup by using a random tie-breaking method.

However, a random tie-breaking method complicates the solution-reachability analyses described in Section 3.1. This is because the same state can be either solution-reachable or unreachable, depending on the tie-breaking. For example, in Figure 5, let us assume that the current state is a. If ties are broken in a fixed way as described in the figure, the algorithm circulates between a and b. On the other hand, if ties are broken randomly, the algorithm may fall into the strict local-minimum g or reach a solution via c.

However, it should be noted that the analyses in Section 3.2 and Section 3.3 are not affected by tie-breaking methods.

4.3 Problem Size

One drawback of our results is that only very small-scale problems were analyzed. In order to perform an analysis of solution-reachability or an analysis of basins within a reasonable amount of time, we need to explicitly construct a state-space within the physical memories of a computer. For example, if the number of variables of a 3-SAT problem is 30, the total number of states becomes 10^9. Even if we could manage to represent each state with 4 bytes, required memory size would be 4GB. Evaluating the number of local-minima could be done without explicitly constructing a state-space. However, we still need to exhaustively check each state. In the case of a 3-SAT problem with 40 variables, the total number of states is 10^{12}. If we could check 10^6 states per second, we would still need more than a week to analyze one problem instance.

However, although the analyses were done only for very small-scale problems, the observed phenomenon is very similar to that of larger-scale problems reported in [2]. Also, very similar results were obtained for two different classes of problems (3-SAT and 3-coloring). Therefore, we can assume that the obtained results would also be valid for large-scale problems.

5 Conclusions

In this paper, we clarified the cause of the paradoxical phenomenon that problems with fewer solutions are easier than problems with more solutions for hill-

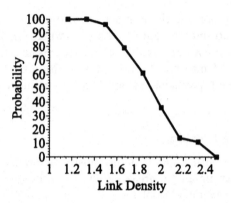

Fig. 11. Probability of satisfiability (3-coloring problems)

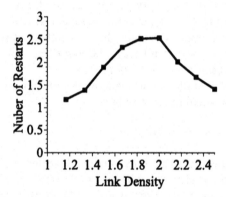

Fig. 12. Average number of restarts (3-coloring problems)

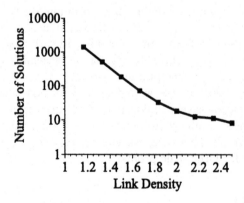

Fig. 13. Average number of solutions (3-coloring problems)

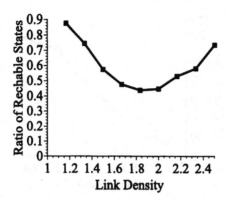

Fig. 14. Average ratio of solution-reachable states (3-coloring problems)

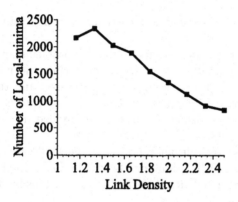

Fig. 15. Average number of local-minima (3-coloring problems)

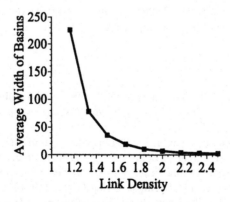

Fig. 16. Average width of basins (3-coloring problems)

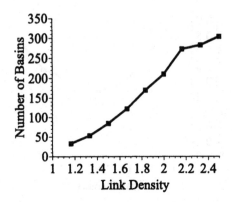

Fig. 17. Average number of basins (3-coloring problems)

climbing algorithms. This was done by exhaustively analyzing the landscape of the state-space.

The analyses of problem instances of 3-SAT problems and 3-coloring problems showed that by adding more constraints, while the number of solutions decreases, the number of local-minima also decreases, and thus the number of solution-reachable states increases. Furthermore, we showed that the number of local-minima decreases since the basins are divided into smaller regions by adding more constraints.

Our future works include analyzing how the landscape of the state-space affects different types of hill-climbing algorithms (e.g., breakout [8], walk-SAT [9]) and developing more efficient hill-climbing algorithms by utilizing the results of landscape analyses.

Acknowledgments

The author wish to thank K. Matsuda and F. Hattori for supporting this research, and K. Ye for helping the analyses.

References

1. Cheeseman, P., Kanefsky, B., and Taylor, W.: Where the really hard problems are, *Proceedings of the Twelfth International Joint Conference on Artificial Intelligence* (1991) 331–337
2. Clark, D. A., Frank, J., Gent, I. P., MacIntyre, E., Tomv, N., and Walsh, T.: Local Search and the Number of Solutions, *Proceedings of the Second International Conference on Principles and Practice of Constraint Programming (Lecture Notes in Computer Science 1118)*, Springer-Verlag (1996) 119–133
3. Gent, I. P. and Walsh, T.: Towards an Understanding of Hill-climbing Procedures for SAT, *Proceedings of the Eleventh National Conference on Artificial Intelligence* (1993) 28–33

4. Hertz, A., Jaumard, B., and de Aragao, M. P.: Local optima topology for the k-coloring problem, *Discrete Applied Mathematics*, Vol. 49, (1994) 257–280
5. Hogg, T., Huberman, B. A., and Williams, C. P.: Phase transitions and the search problem, *Artificial Intelligence*, Vol. 81, No. 1–2, (1996) 1–16
6. Ishida, T.: Real-Time Bidirectional Search: Coordinated Problem Solving in Uncertain Situations, *IEEE Transactions on Pattern Analysis and Machine Intelligence*, Vol. 18, No. 6, (1996) 617–628
7. Mitchell, D., Selman, B., and Levesque, H.: Hard and Easy Distributions of SAT Problem, *Proceedings of the Tenth National Conference on Artificial Intelligence* (1992) 459–465
8. Morris, P.: The Breakout Method for Escaping From Local Minima, *Proceedings of the Eleventh National Conference on Artificial Intelligence* (1993) 40–45
9. Selman, B. and Kautz, H.: Domain-Independent Extensions to GSAT: Solving Large Structured Satisfiability Problems, *Proceedings of the Thirteenth International Joint Conference on Artificial Intelligence* (1993) 290–295
10. Selman, B., Levesque, H., and Mitchell, D.: A New Method for Solving Hard Satisfiability Problems, *Proceedings of the Tenth National Conference on Artificial Intelligence* (1992) 440–446

Interval Methods for Non-linear Constraints

Laurent Michel[1] and Jean-François Puget[2]

[1] Brown University, Box 1910, Providence, RI 02912 (USA)
Email: ldm@cs.brown.edu

[2] ILOG S.A.
9, rue de Verdun, BP 85, 94253 Gentilly Cedex, FRANCE
Email: puget@ilog.fr

Abstract

Many problems in areas as diverse as chemical engineering, economics, logistics, kinematics, statistics or even nuclear engineering are naturally expressed in terms of non-linear equations. Non-linear equations solving, or more generally global optimization, is a difficult problem because of its computational complexity and its numerical pitfalls. Global optimization has been studied for many years. The state of the art offers a wide variety of algorithmic solutions that encompass a number of goals.

The purpose of the tutorial is to introduce the latest techniques used for non-linear constraints. It covers continuation methods from numerical analysis, classical Newton methods and interval methods. It presents each of them and discusses the various strength and weaknesses. These methods are then combined with techniques inspired from artificial intelligence like box-consistency, an approximation of arc-consistency, and bound-consistency. This mix is stirred into a global method, the Interval Newton method. The combination has many advantages to offer. It brings a global component that ensures completeness while the intervals offer soundness. This entails an elegant semantics with strong guarantees on the computation results.

On the other hand, the numerical analysis stronghold plays a major role in the efficiency of the method. Many tools can be adapted and used to improve both the efficiency and the accuracy. The Taylor expansion is a remarkable example. It can be turned into an interval extension just like normal functions are. Moreover, its global nature introduces yet another pruning operator that blends quite nicely with the others. It prunes under different circumstances and helps in establishing the proofs of existence for solutions. Other ideas like the utilization of redundant information has often proved worthy. This track is followed again with the partial Groebner basis that introduces redundant polynomials.

Traditional local techniques can also find their way back under the hood, reinforced by the interval component. This last addition allows better optimization techniques and also gives the power to obtain a single local solution with a well-defined semantics.

Configurable Solvers: Tailoring General Methods to Specific Applications

Steven Minton

USC Information Sciences Institute
4676 Admiralty Way
Marina del Rey, CA 90292
minton@isi.edu

Abstract. Applying constraint-based problem solving methods in a new domain often requires considerable work. In this talk I will examine the state of the art in constraint-based problem solving techniques and the difficulties involved in selecting and tuning an algorithm to solve a problem. Most constraint-based solvers have many algorithmic variations, and it can make a very significant difference exactly which algorithm is used and how the problem is encoded. I will describe promising new approaches in which generic algorithms are automatically configured for specific applications.

Using the "right" heuristic algorithm can make a tremendous difference in the efficiency of solving a constraint-satisfaction problem (CSP). Without a good algorithm, solving even a moderate-sized CSP (or any combinatorial problem) may be extremely time consuming. A great variety of heuristic algorithms have been described in the literature, each purported to perform well on some example problems. Unfortunately, it is rarely clear which method will perform best for a given problem, and the literature provides almost no guidance on this topic.

In the past few years, several research groups have been experimenting with *configurable solvers* that can be automatically, or semi-automatically, configured for new applications. This work capitalizes on the fact that most CSP algorithms can be described as variations of a few basic approaches: backtracking, repair-based local search, branch-and-bound, etc. Rather than focusing on new CSP algorithms, these projects have considered the issues involved in specializing "generic" search methods. Synthesizing problem-specific versions of generic algorithms offers the advantages of both generality and efficiency.

In this talk we will describe and contrast three systems, each of which represents a different approach to creating configurable solvers. The KIDS algorithm synthesis system [5] enables a user to synthesize an algorithm semi-automatically. MULTI-TAC [4] is a system that automatically configures constraint satisfaction algorithms, using a set of sample problem instances to guide the search for the best configuration. Eureka [2] represents a third approach, in which the system learns a classifier that predicts which configuration would be best, based on a set of training instances. The remainder of this paper summarizes my work with MULTI-TAC, outlining some of the basic issues that we have considered.

MULTI-TAC is designed for situations in which a combinatorial search problem must be solved routinely, such as a scheduling application where a set of manufacturing tasks must be assigned each week to a set of workers. In such a situation, the synthesized code will be used repeatedly, and "compile time" is a minor issue. We believe that it is only the relatively rare application where code is used but once. This point is ignored in most research on constraint satisfaction, but it is the central assumption underlying our work.

MULTI-TAC's objective is to synthesize as efficient a program as possible for the instance population. In our previous work [4, 3] we evaluated MULTI-TAC's performance on some NP-hard problems, and the system performed extremely well. Specifically, the system produced code that performed on par with (or better than) hand-coded algorithms written by computer scientists for our test problems. The system also outperformed some general constraint satisfaction algorithms by a very significant margin.

Although MULTI-TAC's learning approach worked well in our experiments, there is an assumption inherent in our design that potentially limits the viability of our approach. MULTI-TAC carries out a hill-climbing search through the space of "algorithm configurations", and evaluating a configuration involves running that configuration on a set of test instances. We have assumed that the time spent learning is not an issue, but in practice, the hill-climbing search can be such a time-consuming process that this is not realistic. The current incarnation of MULTI-TAC can require days of "learning time" if each problem solving run requires more than a minute or two.

To address this problem, we are currently investigating methods for evaluating a configuration on an instance without running the search to completion. For certain families of heuristic algorithms, we have found that we can predict which algorithm will do best after running each of them for a very short time [1]. We do this by identifying "secondary performance characteristics" that tell us whether the heuristic is having a positive effect. If this approach generalizes, we can incorporate similar methods into MULTI-TAC, so that significantly harder problems can be solved. Moreover, it should be possible to use MULTI-TAC in an entirely different way, to create an *instance-specific algorithm*. This would involve trying different configurations on a single instance in order to predict which configuration would be the best to run for a longer time on that instance. This would be useful for very hard, "one-shot" problems, where we could amortize the time spent in configuration search over a relatively long problem-solving run.

References

1. J. Allen and S. Minton. Selecting the right heuristic algorithm: Runtime performance predictors. In *Proceedings of the Canadian AI Conference*, 1996.
2. D.J. Cook and R.Craig Varnell. Maximizing the benefits of parallel search using machine learning. In *Proceedings AAAI-97*, 1997.
3. S. Minton. An analytic learning system for specializing heuristics. In *Proceedings of the Thirteenth International Joint Conference on Artificial Intelligence*, 1993.

4. S. Minton. Automatically configuring constraint satisfaction programs: A case study (in press). *Constraints*, 1(1), 1996.
5. D.R. Smith. KIDS: A knowledge-based software development system. In M.R. Lowry and R.D. McCartney, editors, *Automating Software Design*. AAAI Press, 1991.

Constraint Propagation and Decomposition Techniques for Highly Disjunctive and Highly Cumulative Project Scheduling Problems

Philippe Baptiste[1,2] and Claude Le Pape[1]

[1]Bouygues, Direction Scientifique, 1, av. E. Freyssinet, Saint-Quentin-en-Yvelines, F-78061
[2]UMR CNRS 6599, Université de Technologie de Compiègne

E-mails: baptiste@utc.fr, lepape@dmi.ens.fr

Abstract

In recent years, constraint satisfaction techniques have been successfully applied to "disjunctive" scheduling problems, *i.e.*, scheduling problems where each resource can execute at most one activity at a time. Less significant and less generally applicable results have been obtained in the area of "cumulative" scheduling. Multiple constraint propagation algorithms have been developed for cumulative resources but they tend to be less uniformly effective than their disjunctive counterparts. Different problems in the cumulative scheduling class seem to have different characteristics that make them either easy or hard to solve with a given technique. The aim of this paper is to investigate one particular dimension along which problems differ. Within the cumulative scheduling class, we distinguish between "highly disjunctive" and "highly cumulative" problems: a problem is highly disjunctive when many pairs of activities cannot execute in parallel, *e.g.*, because many activities require more than half of the capacity of a resource; on the contrary, a problem is highly cumulative if many activities can effectively execute in parallel. New constraint propagation and problem decomposition techniques are introduced with this distinction in mind. This includes an $O(n^2)$ "edge-finding" algorithm for cumulative resources, and a problem decomposition scheme which applies well to highly disjunctive project scheduling problems. Experimental results confirm that the impact of these techniques varies from highly disjunctive to highly cumulative problems.

1 Motivations

Many industrial scheduling problems are variants, extensions or restrictions of the "Resource-Constrained Project Scheduling Problem" (RCPSP). Given (1) a set of resources of given capacities, (2) a set of non-interruptible activities of given durations, (3) a network of precedence constraints between the activities, and (4) for each activity and each resource the amount of the resource required by the activity over its execution, the goal of the RCPSP is to find a schedule meeting all the constraints whose makespan (*i.e.*, the time at which all activities are finished) is minimal. The decision variant of the RCPSP, *i.e.*, the problem of determining whether there exists a schedule of makespan smaller than a given deadline, is NP-hard in the strong sense [Garey and Johnson, 1979].

In a constraint programming framework, two integer variables start(A) and end(A), representing the start time and the end time of A, can be associated with each activity A (we assume durations and resource capacities are integers). As usual, the earliest (respectively, latest) start and end times of A, EST_A and EET_A

(LST$_A$ and LET$_A$), are defined as the minimal (maximal) values in the domains of start(A) and end(A). The goal is to minimize max$_A$(end(A)) under the following constraints:

1. $0 \leq$ start(A), for every activity A;
2. start(A) + duration(A) = end(A), for every activity A;
3. end(A) $\leq$ start(B), for every precedence constraint (A $\rightarrow$ B);
4. $\Sigma_{\text{start(A)} \leq t < \text{end(A)}}$(required-capacity(A, R)) $\leq$ capacity(R), for every resource R and time t (cumulative constraint).

Some extensions of the RCPSP include interruptible activities (if all activities are interruptible, the problem is called "preemptive"), resources with capacity that varies over time, consumable resources, and/or "elastic" activities. An activity is "elastic" when tradeoffs can be made between the duration and the amount of resources required by the activity, *e.g.*, when an activity could be performed either by 2 persons in 3 days, or by 3 persons in 2 days. In the most extreme case, the performance of the activity requires a given amount of "energy" (*e.g.*, 6 person-days) to be performed at any regular or irregular rate (*e.g.*, 4 persons on day 1 and 2 persons on day 2).

A common restriction of the RCPSP is encountered when all resources have capacity 1. In this case, any two activities A and B that require a common resource must be ordered: either A will execute before B, or B will execute before A. Such problems are called "disjunctive" scheduling problems. By extension, preemptive problems with resources of capacity 1 are called "disjunctive preemptive problems." A huge amount of work has been carried out on the application of constraint propagation techniques to disjunctive scheduling problems (*e.g.*, [Carlier and Pinson, 1990; Nuijten, 1994; Baptiste and Le Pape, 1995; Caseau and Laburthe, 1995]), with the result that constraint programming is now recognized as a method of choice for these problems.

Constraint programming algorithms have also been developed for "cumulative" scheduling problems, *i.e.*, problems like the RCPSP, such that several activities can use the same resource at the same time (*e.g.*, [Aggoun and Beldiceanu, 1993; Nuijten, 1994; Caseau and Laburthe, 1996a]). However, these algorithms tend to be less uniformly effective than their disjunctive counterparts. Different problems in the cumulative class seem to have different characteristics that make them either easy or hard to solve with a given technique.

The aim of this paper is to investigate one particular dimension along which problems differ. Within the cumulative scheduling class, we distinguish between *highly disjunctive* and *highly cumulative* problems: a scheduling problem is highly disjunctive when many pairs of activities cannot execute in parallel on the same resource; conversely, a scheduling problem is highly cumulative when many activities can execute in parallel on the same resource. To formalize this notion, we introduce the *disjunction ratio, i.e.*, the ratio between a lower bound of the number of pairs of activities which cannot execute in parallel and the overall number of pairs of distinct activities. A simple lower bound of the number of pairs of activities which cannot execute in parallel can be obtained by considering pairs {A, B} such that either there is a chain of precedence constraints between A and B, or there is a resource constraint which is violated if A and B overlap in time. The disjunction ratio can be defined either globally (considering all the activities of a given problem instance) or for each resource R by limiting the pairs of activities to those that require at least one unit of R.

The disjunction ratio of a disjunctive resource is equal to 1. The disjunctive ratio of a cumulative resource varies between 0 and 1, depending on the precedence constraints and on the amounts of capacity that are required to execute the activities. In particular, the ratio is equal to 0 when there is no precedence constraint and no activity requires more than half of the resource capacity.

Needless to say, the disjunction ratio is only one of a variety of indicators that could be associated with scheduling problem instances. For example, the *precedence ratio, i.e.*, the ratio between the number of pairs of activities which are ordered by precedence constraints and the overall number of pairs of distinct activities, is also important (a high precedence ratio makes the problem easier). Although some researchers, *e.g.*, [Kolisch *et al.*, 1995], have worked on such indicators, we believe much more work is necessary to discover which indicators are appropriate for designing, selecting, or adapting constraint programming techniques with respect to the characteristics of a given problem.

In the following, we explore the hypothesis that the disjunction ratio is an important indicator of which techniques shall be applied to a cumulative scheduling problem. Several new constraint propagation and problem decomposition techniques are introduced with this distinction in mind. This includes a simple quadratic "edge-finding" algorithm for cumulative resources, and a problem decomposition scheme dedicated to highly disjunctive project scheduling problems.

The paper is organized as follows: Section 2 presents our general approach to the resolution of the RCPSP; Section 3 presents the constraint propagation techniques we use; Section 4 introduces a heuristic algorithm for the generation of redundant disjunctive resource constraints; Section 5 presents dominance rules, which are used to dynamically decompose an instance of the RCPSP; Section 6 presents experimental results, which confirm that the techniques we use exhibit different behaviors on problems with different disjunction ratios.

2 General Framework

The aim of this section is to present our general approach and establish a list (by no means exhaustive) of possible "ingredients" that can be incorporated in a constraint programming approach to the RCPSP. We limit the discussion to the standard RCPSP. However, some of the techniques we propose also apply to extensions of the RCPSP, such as problems with interruptible activities.

First, the RCPSP is an optimization problem. The goal is to determine a solution with minimal makespan and prove the optimality of the solution. We represent the makespan as an integer variable constrained to be greater than or equal to the end of any activity. Several strategies can be considered to minimize the value of that variable, *e.g.*, iterate on the possible values, either from the lower bound of its domain up to the upper bound (until one solution is found), or from the upper bound down to the lower bound (determining each time whether there still is a solution). In our experiments, a dichotomizing algorithm is used:

1. Compute an initial upper bound UB (the sum of the durations of all activities) and an initial lower bound LB (result of the propagation of the constraints) for the makespan.
2. Set D = (LB + UB) / 2.

3. Constrain the makespan to be lower than or equal to D. Solve the resulting constraint satisfaction problem, *i.e.*, determine a solution with makespan at most D or prove that no such solution exists. If a solution is found, set UB to the makespan of the solution; otherwise, set LB to D + 1.

4. Iterate steps 2 and 3 until UB = LB.

A branching procedure with constraint propagation at each node of the search tree is used to determine whether the problem with makespan at most D accepts a solution. As shown in the literature, there are many possible choices regarding the amount of constraint propagation that can be made at each node. Carlier and Latapie [1991], as well as Demeulemeester and Herroelen [1992], use simple bounding techniques compared to the more complex constraint propagation algorithms proposed by Nuijten [1994] or Caseau and Laburthe [1996a]. Performing more constraint propagation serves two purposes: first, detect that a partial solution at a given node cannot be extended into a complete solution with makespan $\leq$ D; second, reduce the domains of the start and end variables, thereby providing useful information on which variables are the most constrained. However, complex constraint propagation algorithms take time to execute, so the cost of these algorithms may not always be balanced by a subsequent reduction of search. Section 3 introduces a new quadratic edge-finding algorithm (less costly in the worst case than the algorithms of Nuijten [1994] and Caseau and Laburthe [1996a]) for propagating cumulative resource constraints. Experimental results show that it is worth using this algorithm when the disjunction ratio is low.

Artificially adding "redundant" constraints, *i.e.*, constraints that do not change the set of solutions, but propagate in a different way, is another method for improving the effectiveness of constraint propagation. For example, Carlier and Latapie [1991] and Carlier and Néron [1996] present branch-and-bound algorithms for the RCPSP which rely on the generation of redundant resource constraints. If S is a set of activities and m an integer value, and if for any subset s of S such that $|s| > m$, the activities of s cannot all overlap, then the following resource constraint can be added: "Each activity of S requires exactly one unit of a new (artificial) resource of capacity m". Several lower-bounding techniques have been developed for this resource constraint [Perregaard, 1995]. These techniques serve to update the minimal value of the makespan variable, but do not update the domains of the start and end time variables. Section 4 proposes the generation of artificial *disjunctive* resource constraints, for which standard disjunctive resource constraint propagation algorithms can be applied, resulting in a powerful update of earliest and latest start and end times.

Besides constraint propagation, a branching solution search procedure is also characterized by:

- *the types of decisions that are made at each node.* Most search procedures for the RCPSP chronologically build a schedule, from time 0 to time D. At a given time t, Demeulemeester and Herroelen [1992] schedule a subset of the available activities; other subsets are tried upon backtracking. The main interest of this strategy is that some resource can be maximally used at time t, prior to proceed to a time t' > t. However, there may be many subsets to try upon backtracking, especially if the problem is highly cumulative. Caseau and Laburthe [1996a] schedule a single activity and postpone it upon backtracking. The depth of the search tree increases, but each (smaller) decision is propagated prior to the making of the next decision. An example of non-chronological scheduling strategy is given by Carlier and Latapie [1991]. Their strategy is based on dichotomizing the domains of the start variables: at each node, the lower or the upper half of the domain of a chosen variable V is removed and the decision is propagated. This strategy may work well if there are good reasons for selecting the variable V, rather than another variable (*e.g.*, when there is a clear resource bottleneck at a given time).

- *the heuristics that are used to select which possibilities to explore first.* When a chronological strategy is used, one can either try to "fill" the resources at time t (to avoid the insertion of resource idle time in the schedule) or select the most urgent activities among those that are available at time t. When a non-chronological strategy is used, the best is to focus first on identified bottlenecks.
- *the dominance rules that are applied to eliminate unpromising branches.* Several dominance rules have been developed for the RCPSP (see, for example, [Demeulemeester and Herroelen, 1992]). These rules enable the reduction of the search to a limited number of nodes which satisfy the dominance properties. Section 5 proposes a new dominance rule that generalizes the "single incompatibility rule" of Demeulemeester and Herroelen. When it is applied, this rule leads to a decomposition of the remaining problem. As for constraint propagation, dynamically applying complex dominance rules at each node of the search tree may prove more costly than beneficial. Our generalization of the "single incompatibility rule" is worth using when the disjunctive ratio is high.
- *the backtracking strategy that is applied upon failure.* Most constraint programming tools rely on depth-first chronological backtracking. However, "intelligent" backtracking strategies can also be applied to the RCPSP. For example, the cut-set dominance rule of Demeulemeester and Herroelen [1992] can be seen as intelligent backtracking. When backtracking, the unfeasible sub-problem is saved. In the remainder of the search tree, the algorithm checks if the remaining sub-problem is not already proved unfeasible. The advantage of intelligent backtracking is that the identified impossible problem-solving situation is not encountered twice (or is immediately recognized as impossible). However, it requires a large amount of memory to store the unfeasible sub-problems and, in some cases, requires significant time for its application.

Our overall research agenda is to look at all these aspects of the problem-solving strategy and determine (if at all possible) when to apply each technique. As a first step, we designed some of the constraint propagation techniques and dominance rules mentioned above with the intent of applying them either to highly disjunctive or to highly cumulative problems. For this reason, we decided to fix the types of decisions to be made at each node, the heuristics that are used to select which possibilities to explore first, and the backtracking strategy (depth-first chronological backtracking). Our solution search procedure slightly differs from the one proposed by Caseau and Laburthe [1996a]:

1. Select an unscheduled activity A of minimal earliest start time. When several activities have the same earliest start time, select one of the most urgent, *i.e.*, one with minimal latest start time. Create a choice point.

2. <u>Left branch</u>: Schedule A from its earliest start time EST_A to its earliest end time EET_A (in other terms, set start(A) to the smallest value in its domain). Propagate this decision. Apply the dominance rules. Goto step 1.
3. <u>Right branch</u>: If step 2 causes a backtrack, compute the set S of activities that could overlap the interval [EST_A EET_A] (according to current variable domains). Post a delaying constraint: "A executes after at least one activity in S". Propagate this constraint. Apply the dominance rules. Goto step 1.
4. If both branches fail, provoke a backtrack to the preceding choice point (chronological backtracking).

This algorithm stops when all activities are scheduled (in step 1) or all branches have been explored (no more preceding choice point in step 4).

Two points of flexibility remain in this procedure. The first concerns constraint propagation. As shown in Sections 3 and 4, several constraint propagation algorithms can be associated with each resource. One of these algorithms, based on a timetable mechanism, is systematically applied. It guarantees that, at the end of the propagation, the earliest start time of each unscheduled activity is consistent with the start and end times of all the scheduled activities (*i.e.*, activities with bound start and end times). This, in turn, guarantees the correctness of the overall search procedure: adding the constraint "A executes after at least one activity in S" upon backtracking is correct, because if A could start before the end of all activities in S, then A could start at the earliest start time EST_A resulting from previous constraint propagation. The second point of flexibility concerns the dominance rules. Several dominance rules can be applied, which may lead to some decomposition of the problem (cf. Section 5).

3 Constraint Propagation Algorithms

Our implementation is based on CLAIRE SCHEDULE [Le Pape and Baptiste, 1997], a constraint-based library for preemptive and non-preemptive scheduling, itself implemented in CLAIRE [Caseau and Laburthe, 1996b], a high-level functional and object-oriented language. The aim of this section is to review the constraint propagation techniques we use in the context of the RCPSP.

The constraints of the RCPSP and the decisions made in the general framework of Section 2 are of the following types:
1. $0 \leq start(A)$, for every activity A;
2. $start(A) + duration(A) = end(A)$, for every activity A;
3. $end(A) \leq makespan$, for every activity A;
4. $end(A) \leq start(B)$, for every precedence constraint (A $\rightarrow$ B);
5. $\Sigma_{start(A) \leq t < end(A)}(required\text{-}capacity(A, R)) \leq capacity(R)$, for every resource R and time t (cumulative constraint);
6. $makespan \leq D$;
7. $start(A) = s$, where A is an activity and s a value in its domain;
8. "A executes after at least one activity in S" *i.e.*, $min_S(end(S)) \leq start(A)$, where A is an activity and S a set of activities.

Constraints 1, 2, 3, and 6, guarantee that each variable in the problem has a finite domain (since we use integer variables). The initial domain of each variable is set to [0, D]. As often in constraint programming, unary constraints (1, 6, 7) are propagated by reducing the domains of the corresponding variables.

Duration constraints (2) and precedence constraints (3, 4) are propagated using a standard arc-B-consistency algorithm [Lhomme, 1993].[1] In addition, a variant of Ford's algorithm due to Cesta and Oddi [1996] is used to detect any inconsistency between precedence and duration constraints, in time polynomial in the number of constraints (and independent of the domain sizes).

The constraint "A executes after at least one activity in S" (8) is propagated as follows: compute EET_S, the minimal earliest end time of all activities in S, and update EST_A to $\max(EST_A, EET_S)$. Moreover, when there is only one activity B in S that can end before LST_A, then LET_B is set to $\min(LET_B, LST_A)$.

For the resource constraints (5), CLAIRE SCHEDULE includes both a timetable mechanism and an edge-finding algorithm.

The timetable mechanism is an extension of the timetable mechanism of ILOG SCHEDULE [Le Pape, 1994]. This extension supports both non-interruptible and interruptible activities, as well as activities requiring an amount of resource capacity that can vary over time ("elastic" activities). The underlying propagation algorithm is described in [Le Pape and Baptiste, 1997]. It guarantees that, at the end of the propagation, the earliest and the latest start and end times of each unscheduled activity are consistent with the start and end times of all the scheduled activities (i.e., in the non-preemptive case, activities with bound start and end times). This algorithm is systematically applied.

The edge-finding algorithm is an extension of classical *disjunctive* edge-finding bounding techniques [Carlier and Pinson, 1990; Applegate and Cook, 1991; Nuijten, 1994; Baptiste and Le Pape, 1995; Caseau and Laburthe, 1995]. This extension supports both non-interruptible and interruptible activities. It is described in [Le Pape and Baptiste, 1996]. It requires quadratic time and linear space. Compared to the timetable mechanism, it is time-consuming. However, this is usually balanced by a drastic reduction of the search space.

To deal with highly cumulative problems, we developed an extension of this algorithm to the cumulative case. This extension supports both non-interruptible and interruptible activities. It relies on a very simple idea which consists of reducing the cumulative resource to a resource of capacity 1 thanks to the following transformation.

Transformation: Consider a set $\{A_1, ..., A_n\}$ of n activities requiring a resource R of capacity C and let EST_i, LST_i, EET_i, LET_i, p_i, c_i be respectively the earliest start time, latest start time, earliest end time, latest end time, duration, and required capacity (i.e., required amount of resource R) of A_i. Let R' be a resource of capacity 1 and let for each activity A_i, A_i' be an interruptible activity with $EST_i' = C * EST_i$, $LET_i' = C * LET_i$, $p_i' = p_i * c_i$, $c_i' = 1$.

---

[1] Given a constraint c over n variables $v_1 ... v_n$ and a domain D_i for each variable v_i, c is "arc-consistent" if and only if for any variable v_i and any value val_i in the domain of v_i, there exist values $val_1 ... val_{i-1} val_{i+1} ... val_n$ in $D_1 ... D_{i-1} D_{i+1} ... D_n$ such that $c(val_1 ... val_n)$ holds. Arc-B-consistency, where B stands for bounds, guarantees only that $val_1 ... val_{i-1} val_{i+1} ... val_n$ exist for val_i equal to either the smallest or the greatest value in D_i. In CLAIRE SCHEDULE, domains of start and end time variables are represented as intervals, so in general only arc-B-consistency is achieved.

Proposition 1: If there exists a schedule of A_1, ..., A_n on R then there exists a schedule of A_1', ..., A_n' on R'.

Proof : Let $S(A_i, t)$ be the number of units of A_i executed at t on R ($S(A_i, t) = 0$ or $S(A_i, t) = c_i$). A schedule of A_1', ..., A_n' on R' can be built as follows: for each activity A_i (taken in any order) and each time t, schedule $S(A_i, t)$ units of A_i' on R' as early as possible after time $C * t$. For any activity A_i and time t, the number of units of A_i executed at t on R is equal to the number of units of A_i' executed between $C * t$ and $C * (t + 1)$ on R' since this algorithm consists of cutting the schedule of A_1, ..., A_n into slices of one unit and of rescheduling these slices on R'. Consequently, for any activity A_i', exactly $p_i * c_i$ units of A_i' are scheduled between $C * EST_i$ and $C * LET_i$ and thus the release dates as well as the due dates are met. □

The same transformation can be exploited to update time-bounds (earliest and latest start and end times). This leads to a simple edge-finding algorithm for the cumulative case:
1. Apply the transformation
2. Update the earliest end time and the latest start time of A_1', ..., A_n' thanks to the disjunctive edge-finding algorithm;
3. Update the earliest end time and the latest start time of A_1, ..., A_n: EET_i is set to $\lceil EET_i' / C \rceil$ and LST_i is set to $\lfloor LST_i' / C \rfloor$. The earliest start time and the latest end time of A_i can then be updated since $end(A_i) - start(A_i) = p_i$.

This algorithm runs in a quadratic number of steps since the transformation (step 1) is a linear operation, the mixed edge-finding algorithm (step 2) runs in $O(n^2)$, and step 3 is linear. It can compute less precise time-bounds than some other cumulative edge-finding algorithms [Nuijten, 1994; Caseau and Laburthe, 1996a]. However, it has two advantages: it accepts interruptible activities, and its worst case complexity is lower.

As usual in a constraint propagation scheme, it may have to be applied several times during the propagation of the same decisions. For example, let A, B, C be three non-interruptible activities requiring a resource of capacity 2. The tables below provide the temporal characteristics of the cumulative problem and of the corresponding preemptive disjunctive problem.

	EST	LET	p	c
A	0	10	3	1
B	0	1	1	1
C	1	3	2	2

	EST	LET	p
A'	0	20	3
B'	0	2	1
C'	2	6	4

It is easy to see that A' cannot end before time 8. Indeed, we see on the following Gantt chart that if A' ends before 8 then either B' or C' must end after 6; which is impossible.

```
     A'  B'  C'  C'  C'  C'  A'  A'
    |---|---|---|---|---|---|---|---|---|
     0   1   2   3   4   5   6   7   8   9
```

The earliest end time of A can then be set to $\lceil 8 / 2 \rceil = 4$. This wakes up the duration constraint: since p_A is 3, the earliest start time of A is set to 1.

Let us apply again the same algorithm:

	EST	LET	p	c
A	1	10	3	1
B	0	1	1	1
C	1	3	2	2

	EST	LET	p
A'	2	20	3
B'	0	2	1
C'	2	6	4

We can verify on the next chart that activity A' cannot end before time 9; thus, the earliest end time of A can be set to 5, and its earliest start time to 2.

```
         B'        C'   C'   C'   C'   A'   A'   A'
         |---|---|---|---|---|---|---|---|---|
         0   1   2   3   4   5   6   7   8   9
```

4   Redundant Disjunctive Resource Constraints

Since some project scheduling problems are highly disjunctive, we considered the generation of redundant disjunctive resource constraints as a mean to strengthen constraint propagation (see also [Brucker *et al.*, 1997]). The basic idea is simple: if a set S of activities is such that any two activities in S cannot execute in parallel, a new (artificial) resource of capacity 1 can be created, and all the activities in S constrained to require the new resource. The disjunctive edge-finding constraint propagation algorithm can then be applied to the new resource, in order to guarantee a better update of the earliest and latest start and end times of these activities.

To detect the relevant sets S, we use a compatibility graph $G = (X, E)$ where X is a set of vertices corresponding to the activities of the RCPSP and E is a set of edges (A, B), such that $(A, B) \in E$ if and only if A and B are not compatible (*i.e.*, cannot execute in parallel). We distinguish three subsets E_{cap}, E_{prec}, and E_{time} of E. These subsets denote respectively the incompatibilities due to resource constraints, to precedence constraints, and to time-bounds.

- $(A, B) \in E_{cap}$ if and only if there is a resource R such that the sum of the capacities required by A and B on R is greater than the overall capacity of R.
- $(A, B) \in E_{prec}$ if and only if there is a precedence constraint between A and B (the transitive closure[2] of the precedence graph is computed for this purpose).
- $(A, B) \in E_{time}$ if and only if either $LET_A \leq EST_B$ or $LET_B \leq EST_A$.

Any clique[3] of the compatibility graph is a candidate disjunctive resource constraint. However, since the edge-finding constraint propagation algorithm is costly in terms of CPU time, very few redundant disjunctive constraints can be generated. Hence, we have to heuristically select some of these cliques (otherwise, the cost of the disjunctive resource constraint propagation would be too high to be compensated by the subsequent reduction of search). Since the problem of finding a maximal clique (*i.e.*, a clique of maximal size) is NP-hard [Garey and Johnson, 1979], we use a simple heuristic which increases step by step the current clique C: among the activities which are incompatible with all activities of the clique, we select one of maximal duration. Our hope is that the

---

[2] Given a directed graph $G = (X, E)$, $G' = (X, E')$ is the transitive closure of G if and only if $\forall x \in X, \forall y \in X, (x, y) \in E'$ if and only if there exists a directed path from x to y in E.

[3] Given a graph $G = (X, E)$, $C \subseteq X$ is a clique of G if and only if $\forall x \in C, \forall y \in C, (x, y) \in E$.

resulting constraint will be tight since several activities of large processing times will require the same disjunctive resource.

In our first experiments, we built one disjunctive resource per cumulative resource and one more extra disjunctive resource. For each cumulative resource, we arbitrarily put in the clique all the activities requiring more than half of the resource and the clique was completed thanks to the heuristic described above. The extra disjunctive resource was fully generated according to the heuristic rule. A careful examination of the generated problems showed that many activities were added in the cliques because of precedence and time-bound constraints. It is far more interesting to generate disjunctive problems where most of the activities are incompatible because of resources. To achieve this, the generation heuristic has been split in two different procedures: (1) build a maximal clique C_{cap} of (X, E_{cap}); (2) extend C_{cap} to a maximal clique C of G.

Example: Let A, B, C, D, E be five activities requiring respectively 3, 2, 1, 4, 1 units of a resource of capacity 4. These activities last respectively 3, 6, 3, 2 and 5 units of time. Moreover, there are 4 precedence constraints $(A \rightarrow C)$, $(A \rightarrow E)$, $(B \rightarrow C)$, and $(B \rightarrow E)$. Let us build the incompatibility graph of this instance. First, we add the edges corresponding to the precedence constraints (dotted lines). Then we consider each pair of activities and add an edge (solid line) between the corresponding vertices if and only if the sum of the resource requirements of both activities exceed 4. In this example, there are two maximal cliques: {A, B, D, E} and {A, B, D, C}. Our algorithm starts with {A, D} and successively adds B (based on C_{cap}) and E (which is longer than C) to the clique.

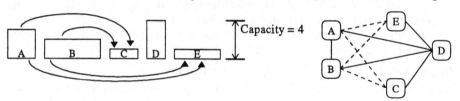

5 Dominance Rules

Our search procedure incorporates several dominance rules. Each of them consists of expressing additional constraints which do not impact the existence of a solution schedule (if there exists a schedule satisfying all constraints posted so far, then at least one such schedule satisfies also the additional constraints).

Immediate scheduling rule

Let A be an unscheduled activity of minimal earliest end time. Let O be the set of activities which can be "partially" scheduled in the interval $[EST_A \, EET_A]$, i.e., $O = \{X \mid LET_X > EST_A \text{ and } EET_A > EST_X\}$.

Proposition 2: If all activities in O can be scheduled in parallel, i.e., on each resource, the amount required to execute all activities in O is lower than or equal to the resource capacity, then A can be scheduled at EST_A.

Proof: Suppose that there is a schedule S that satisfies all the constraints posted so far. Let us examine S. All predecessors of A have been scheduled before EST_A since the earliest end time of A is minimal. Moreover, there is enough space on each resource to schedule A at EST_A since all activities in O can execute in parallel. S can thus be modified by bringing A back to EST_A. □

Single incompatibility rule ([Demeulemeester and Herroelen, 1992])

Let t_{min} be the minimal earliest start time among the earliest start times of unscheduled activities.

Proposition 3: If no activity is in progress at time t_{min} and if there is an activity A such that A cannot be scheduled together with any other unscheduled activity at any time instant without violating precedence or resource constraints, then activity A can be scheduled at time t_{min}.

Proof: see [Demeulemeester and Herroelen, 1992]. □

Incompatible set decomposition rule

We propose an extension of the single incompatibility rule based on a directed compatibility graph. Let t_{min} and t_{max} be respectively the minimal earliest start time and the maximal latest end time among unscheduled activities. Consider the directed graph $\Gamma = (X, U)$, where X is a set of vertices corresponding to the activities A such that $t_{min} < EET_A$ and $LST_A < t_{max}$. U is the set of directed arcs such that $(A, B) \in U$ if and only if either $(A, B) \notin E$ (*i.e.*, A and B are not incompatible as defined in Section 4) or A must precede B in the transitive closure of the precedence network. Let $X_1, X_2, ..., X_m$ be the strongly connected components of Γ, *i.e.*, $\{X_1, X_2, ..., X_m\}$ is a partition of X such that any two activities A and B belong to the same X_i if and only if there is a directed path from A to B and from B to A. Let γ be the quotient graph of Γ (the "strongly connected" relation is an equivalence relation). γ is a directed acyclic graph and thus the strongly connected components can be totally ordered. We suppose without any loss of generality that this total order is $X_1, X_2, ..., X_m$.

Proposition 4: For all i in [1 m], all activities in X_i can be scheduled before all activities in $X_{i,1}$.

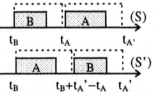

Proof: We only prove that all activities in X_1 can be scheduled before all activities in $X - X_1$. The remaining part of the proof can be achieved by induction.

Suppose that there exists a schedule satisfying all constraints posted so far. Let S be such a schedule, such that the first time point t_A at which an activity A of X_1 is scheduled after an activity of $X - X_1$ is minimal. Let t_A' be the first time after t_A such that no activity of X_1 is scheduled at t_A'. Let t_B be the minimal start time among start times of activities in $X - X_1$ in S. Let us modify S into S' by exchanging the schedule blocks $[t_B \ t_A]$ and $[t_A \ t_A']$ (*cf.* chart). The schedule S' satisfies precedence constraints, otherwise X_1 would not be the first strongly connected component. The resource constraints are also satisfied. Moreover, the activities are not interrupted since at times t_B, t_A and t_A', there is no activity in progress on S (otherwise two activities in different components would be compatible, which is absurd). Thus, schedule S' is a solution and contradicts the hypothesis that t_A exists and is minimal. Absurd. □

Ordering the subsets $X_1, ..., X_m$ is interesting for two reasons. First, additional precedence constraints can be added. Second, the problem can be decomposed into m optimization problems. Indeed, since subsets X_1, ..., X_m are ordered, it is sufficient to find the optimal solutions to the RCPSP restricted to each X_i.

The overall algorithm which implements this incompatible set dominance rule runs in $O(n^2)$ since there are potentially $O(n)$ vertices in X and thus, building the set U requires at most a quadratic number of steps (we assume the transitive closure of the precedence graph has been computed once and for all). Moreover, searching for the strongly connected components of Γ can be done in $O(|U|)$ thanks to the depth first algorithm of Tarjan [Gondran and Minoux, 1984].

Example: Let A, B, C, D, E, F be 6 activities requiring respectively 2, 3, 1, 2, 1 and 2 units of a resource of capacity 4. Let us suppose that the following precedence constraints apply: (A → D), (A → E), (B → E), (C → D), (C → E), and (E → F). To simplify the example, we do not consider the time-bounds of activities and thus, the values of the durations are not necessary for the example.

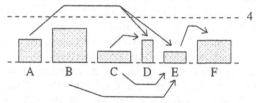

The transitive closure of the precedence network consists of adding arcs (A → F), (B → F) and (C → F). The pairs of activities which are incompatible because of resource constraints are (A, B), (B, D), and (B, F). Consequently, the pairs of activities which are not incompatible are (A, C), (B, C), (D, E), (D, F); which corresponds to the following graph.

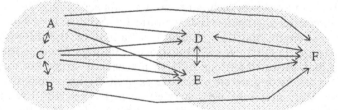

There are two strongly connected components {A, B, C} and {D, E, F}. Our dominance rule states that there exists an optimal solution in which {A, B, C} is scheduled before {D, E, F}.

6 Computational Results

The following tables provide the results obtained on different sets of benchmarks with four different versions of our search procedure: with or without cumulative edge-finding (E.F.), with or without incompatible set decomposition (Dec.). All versions of the algorithm use precedence constraint propagation, resource constraint propagation based on timetables, edge-finding on redundant disjunctive resource constraints, the immediate scheduling rule, the single incompatibility rule, and their symmetric counterparts. In each of the tables, column "Solved" denotes the number of instances solved to optimality (optimality proof included) within a limit of 4000 backtracks. Column "BT" provides the average number of backtracks over those problems that have been solved by all algorithms. Column "CPU" provides the corresponding average CPU time, in seconds on a PC Dell GXL 5133. Table 1 provides the results obtained on the highly disjunctive Patterson problem set (problems with 14 to 51 activities) [Patterson, 1984]. These results compare well to other constraint programming approaches. For example, Caseau and Laburthe [1996a] solve the overall Patterson set in an average of 1000 backtracks and 3.5 seconds. Our algorithm requires approximately the same CPU time, but a much smaller number of backtracks. Using the cumulative edge-finder and the incompatible set decomposition rule on this set decreases the average number of backtracks needed to solve the problem to optimality. However, the cost of these techniques is such that the overall CPU time increases.

We also applied the four algorithms to the 480 instances of Kolisch, Sprecher, and Drexel [1995] (KSD, 30 activities each). These instances are interesting because they are classified according to various indicators, including the "resource strength," *i.e.*, the resource capacity, normalized so that the "strength" is 0 when for each resource R, capacity(R) = $\max_A$(required-capacity(A, R)), and the "strength" is 1 when scheduling each activity at its earliest start time (ignoring resource constraints) results in a schedule that satisfies resource constraints as well. Table 2 provides the results for the 120 instances of resource strength (RS) 0.2, Table 3 provides the results for the 120 instances of resource strength 0.7, and Table 4 provides the overall results. Clearly, the decomposition rule is very useful for the highly disjunctive problems. Considering the overall set, the decomposition rule allows the resolution of 14 additional instances, 13 of which are in the most highly disjunctive set. Unfortunately, the instances of resource strength 0.7 are "easy" (except one of them!), so for this subset the interest of the more complex techniques does not appear.

Table 6 provides the average precedence ratio (cf. Section 1), disjunctive ratio, and resource strength, and their standard deviations on the different problem sets. It clearly appears that even KSD instances with high resource strength have large disjunction ratios (0.53) due to large precedence ratios. For experimental purposes, this led us to generate a new series of 40 highly cumulative problems (the BL set). More precisely, we generated 80 instances with 3 resources, and either 20 or 25 activities, and we kept the 40 most difficult of these instances. Each activity requires the 3 resources, with a required capacity randomly chosen between 0 and 60% of the resource capacity. 15 precedence constraints were randomly generated for problems with 20 activities; 45 precedence constraints were generated for problems with 25 activities. This simple parameter setting allowed us to generate problems with average precedence and disjunctive ratios of 0.33, with a standard deviation of 0.07, smaller than the standard deviation observed on the classical benchmarks from the literature, and a relatively low resource strength (0.34 on average). Table 5 provides the results. It clearly shows that the cumulative edge-finder is a crucial technique for solving these instances. However, one may wonder whether the versions with no cumulative edge-finding could "catch up" if given more CPU time. To evaluate that, we ran the BL instances again with a limit of 20000 backtracks. This led the versions with no cumulative edge-finding to solve only 4 additional instances in an average of 8173 backtracks and 146.7 seconds. With cumulative edge-finding, these 4 instances are solved in an average of 994 backtracks and 23.8 seconds.

388

E.F.	Dec.	Solved	BT	CPU
No	No	110	77	2.68
No	Yes	110	71	3.75
Yes	No	110	63	3.67
Yes	Yes	110	58	4.65

Table 1. Patterson (110 instances
of average disjunctive ratio 0.67)

E.F.	Dec.	Solved	BT	CPU
No	No	51	369	12.52
No	Yes	64	253	11.70
Yes	No	51	366	17.79
Yes	Yes	64	251	14.82

Table 2. KSD RS 0.2 (120 instances
of average disjunctive ratio 0.65)

E.F.	Dec.	Solved	BT	CPU
No	No	119	101	4.85
No	Yes	119	101	7.33
Yes	No	119	100	7.96
Yes	Yes	119	100	10.64

Table 3. KSD RS 0.7 (120 instances
of average disjunctive ratio 0.53)

E.F.	Dec.	Solved	BT	CPU
No	No	388	121	5.19
No	Yes	402	105	7.03
Yes	No	389	119	7.88
Yes	Yes	403	104	9.56

Table 4. KSD ALL (480 instances
of average disjunctive ratio 0.56)

E.F.	Dec.	Solved	BT	CPU
No	No	4	1241	29.5
No	Yes	4	1241	47.0
Yes	No	28	407	13.9
Yes	Yes	28	407	20.1

Table 5. BL (40 instances
of average disjunctive ratio 0.33)

	Precedence ratio		Disjunction ratio		Resource strength	
	Average	Std	Average	Std	Average	Std
Patterson	0.64	0.10	0.67	0.11	0.50	0.21
KSD RS 0.2	0.52	0.09	0.65	0.11	0.20	0.02
KSD RS 0.5	0.52	0.09	0.53	0.09	0.52	0.03
KSD RS 0.7	0.52	0.08	0.53	0.08	0.70	0.03
KSD RS 1.0	0.52	0.09	0.52	0.09	1.00	0.00
BL	0.33	0.07	0.33	0.07	0.34	0.09

Table 6. Average ratios and standard deviations for different problem sets

Globally, these results show that highly disjunctive and highly cumulative problems require different types of constraint propagation and problem decomposition techniques. Yet, even our best results are, in CPU time, not as good as those of Demeulemeester and Herroelen [1992]. As already mentioned, their algorithm relies a lot on the cut-set dominance rule (an intelligent backtracking strategy), which we have deliberately decided not to use in our current study, due to its high memory cost (our current program requires no more than 500K for 51 activities). A limited use of this rule is the subject of a further study.

References

A. Aggoun and N. Beldiceanu [1993], *Extending CHIP in Order to Solve Complex Scheduling and Placement Problems*, Mathematical and Computer Modelling 17:57-73.

D. Applegate and W. Cook [1991], *A Computational Study of the Job-Shop Scheduling Problem*, ORSA Journal on Computing 3(2):149-156.

Ph. Baptiste and C. Le Pape [1995], *A Theoretical and Experimental Comparison of Constraint Propagation Techniques for Disjunctive Scheduling*, Proc. 14th International Joint Conference on Artificial Intelligence.

P. Brucker, S. Knust, A. Schoo, and O. Thiele [1997], *A Branch and Bound Algorithm for the Resource-Constrained Project Scheduling Problem*, Working Paper, University of Osnabrück, 1997.

J. Carlier and B. Latapie [1991], *Une méthode arborescente pour résoudre les problèmes cumulatifs*, RAIRO Recherche opérationnelle / Operations Research 25(3):311-340.

J. Carlier and E. Néron [1996], *A New Branch-and-Bound Method for Solving the Resource-Constrained Project Scheduling Problem*, Proc. International Workshop on Production Planning and Control.

J. Carlier and E. Pinson [1990], *A Practical Use of Jackson's Preemptive Schedule for Solving the Job-Shop Problem*, Annals of Operations Research 26:269-287.

Y. Caseau and F. Laburthe [1995], *Disjunctive Scheduling with Task Intervals*, Technical Report, Ecole Normale Supérieure.

Y. Caseau and F. Laburthe [1996a], *Cumulative Scheduling with Task Intervals*, Proc. Joint International Conference and Symposium on Logic Programming.

Y. Caseau and F. Laburthe [1996b], *CLAIRE: A Parametric Tool to Generate C++ Code for Problem Solving*, Working Paper, Bouygues, Direction Scientifique.

A. Cesta and A. Oddi [1996], *Gaining Efficiency and Flexibility in the Simple Temporal Problem*, Proc. 3rd International Workshop on Temporal Representation and Reasoning.

E. Demeulemeester and W. Herroelen [1992], *A Branch-and-Bound Procedure for the Multiple Resource-Constrained Project Scheduling Problem*, Management Science 38(12):1803-1818.

M. R. Garey and D. S. Johnson [1979], *Computers and Intractability. A Guide to the Theory of NP-Completeness*, W. H. Freeman and Company.

M. Gondran and M. Minoux [1984], *Graphs and Algorithms*, John Wiley and Sons.

R. Kolisch, A. Sprecher, and A. Drexl [1995], *Characterization and Generation of a General Class of Resource-Constrained Project Scheduling Problems*, Management Science 41(10):1693-1703.

C. Le Pape [1994], *Implementation of Resource Constraints in ILOG SCHEDULE: A Library for the Development of Constraint-Based Scheduling Systems*, Intelligent Systems Engineering 3(2):55-66.

C. Le Pape and Ph. Baptiste [1996], *Constraint Propagation Techniques for Disjunctive Scheduling: The Preemptive Case*, Proc. 12th European Conference on Artificial Intelligence.

C. Le Pape and Ph. Baptiste [1997], *A Constraint Programming Library for Preemptive and Non-Preemptive Scheduling*, Proc. 3rd International Conference on the Practical Application of Constraint Technology.

O. Lhomme [1993], *Consistency Techniques for Numeric CSPs*, Proc. 13th International Joint Conference on Artificial Intelligence.

W. P. M. Nuijten [1994], *Time and Resource Constrained Scheduling: A Constraint Satisfaction Approach*, PhD Thesis, Eindhoven University of Technology.

J. H. Patterson [1984], *A Comparison of Exact Approaches for Solving the Multiple Constrained Resource Project Scheduling Problem*, Management Science 30(7):854-867.

M. Perregaard [1995], *Branch and Bound Methods for the Multi-Processor Job Shop and Flow Shop Scheduling Problem*, MSc Thesis, University of Copenhagen.

Five Pitfalls of Empirical Scheduling Research

J. Christopher Beck[*], Andrew J. Davenport[‡], Mark S. Fox[*‡]

Department of Computer Science[*] and Department of Industrial Engineering[‡]
University of Toronto
Toronto, Ontario, CANADA
M5S 3G9

{chris, andrewd, msf}@ie.utoronto.ca

Abstract

A number of pitfalls of empirical scheduling research are illustrated using real experimental data. These pitfalls, in general, serve to slow the progress of scheduling research by obsfucating results, blurring comparisons among scheduling algorithms and algorithm components, and complicating validation of work in the literature. In particular, we look at difficulties brought about by viewing algorithms in a monolithic fashion, by concentrating on CPU time as the only evaluation criteria, by failing to prepare for gathering of a variety of search statistics at the time of experimental design, by concentrating on benchmarks to the exclusion of other sources of experimental problems, and, more broadly, by a preoccupation with optimization of makespan as the sole goal of scheduling algorithms.

Introduction

With the recent burgeoning of interest in empirical approaches to artificial intelligence [AAAI Empirical Workshop, 1994; ECAI Empirical Workshop, 1996], a number of authors have made calls for a more scientifically rigorous basis for such research [Hooker, 1994; Cohen, 1995]. While much of the field of the empirical study of algorithms is relatively immature, empirical scheduling research may be especially so due to the widespread (and currently unmet) demand for scheduling solutions to real problems in industry and elsewhere. This demand has significant positive impact for the research in terms of funding, sources of challenging problems, and opportunities to contribute beyond the academic world. However, the same demand can result in a retardation of the progress of the science through the strong temptation to concentrate on delivering an acceptable solution method for a particular problem rather than on developing an understanding of the relative merits of existing and novel techniques.

We do not claim that developing a novel solution method for a problem is, in itself, anti-productive for the science of scheduling. Indeed, much progress has been produced from such seminal work [Fox, 1983; Zweben et al., 1993]. However, having this mode of progress as the sole or primary motive force is characteristic of an immature field and leads to a balkanization of the research community: each research group has its own problem sets and solution techniques and, though these may both be published and available, there is little cross-fertilization.

A more progressive approach to scheduling research involves not only exploratory forays into new problem areas, but also rigorous adaptation and re-implementation of the work of other researchers, reproduction of results, and hypotheses testing to develop a deeper understanding of the behaviour of scheduling techniques across a wide body of problems. In short, we urge that the calls for a rigorous empirical science of algorithms be heeded particularly well in the scheduling community [Hooker, 1994].

In this paper we present a number of pitfalls that we have observed and experienced in our research. The data used to illustrate each pitfall comes from experiments we have performed over the past few years. The motivation for writing this paper is similar to that of earlier work describing the dangers of empirical testing in the design of algorithms for SAT [Gent et al., 1997]: we hope that by describing our experiences we will further the progress and maturity of the research.

Pitfall I: The Scheduling Monolith

Consider the following experiment, in which two scheduling algorithms, Monolith1 and Monolith2, are compared on a set of problems from the Operations Research library [Beasley, 1990]. Five different CPU time bounds (10 minutes to 50 minutes) are used and the mean relative error[1] from optimal for which each algorithm was able to find a solution is displayed in Figure 1. (See [Beck et al., 1997b] for a full description of this experiment using the 20 minute CPU time bound.) The results are clear-cut: Monolith1 significantly outperforms Monolith2 at each time limit.

Based on this experiment, we can make conclusions concerning the relative abilities of the two algorithms: Monolith1 is better than Monolith2 (at least on the problems tested—see Pitfall IV). There are, however, two major difficulties with the experiment:

1. We are unable to achieve any deeper understanding of the scheduling algorithms because conclusions beyond those comparing the algorithms as a whole are not justified. In particular, this experiment provides no insight as to *why* Monolith1 outperforms Monolith2.

2. If we know the components of Monolith1 (*e.g.*, the heuristic or backtracker that is used), as is common, it is tempting to draw the conclusion that a particular part of the Monolith1 algorithm is responsible for the performance differences.

Algorithms Monolith1 and Monolith2 are actually both of the form shown in Figure 2. Both algorithms use constraint propagators: temporal arc-B-consistency [Lhomme, 1993], constraint-based analysis (CBA) [Erschler et al., 1976; Erschler et al., 1980], and edge-finding [Carlier and Pinson, 1989; Nuijten, 1994]. The differences between the two algorithms are how the heuristic decisions are made (line 7) and how a commitment (search decision) is retracted at a dead-end (line 9).

* Monolith1: uses a heuristic based on the SumHeight contention estimation algorithm [Beck et al., 1997b] and limited discrepancy search (LDS) [Harvey, 1995; Harvey and Ginsberg, 1995] for retraction.

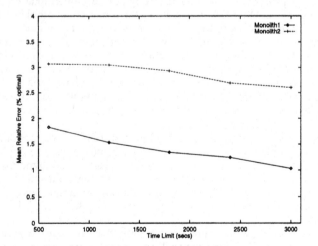

Figure 1. Results from the Monolith Experiment

---

1. Mean relative error (MRE) is the mean smallest amount above the optimal makespan that an algorithm could find a solution expressed as a percentage of the optimal makespan.

- Monolith2: uses the CBASlack heuristic [Smith and Cheng, 1993; Cheng and Smith, 1996] and chronological backtracking.

With this internal information, we see that, due to poor design, the experiment does not provide any insight as to why Monolith1 is better than Monolith2: is it the heuristic or is it the retraction method?

An obvious solution, if we are to examine which heuristic is better, is to use a more rigorous, non-monolithic experimental design. More revealing results are displayed in Figure 3. The results from Figure 1 (Monolith1 is now identified by SumHeight+LDS, Monolith2 is now CBASlack+Chron) are re-displayed together with two other algorithms: CBASlack with LDS (CBASlack+LDS) and SumHeight with chronological backtracking (SumHeight+Chron). These results show an interesting interaction between the heuristic and retraction techniques. With chronological backtracking Sum-Height performs significantly better than CBASlack, however this difference disappears when using LDS.

Our point is not the actual comparison of SumHeight and CBASlack (see [Beck et al., 1997b] for a comparison) but rather that:

```
1:    finished := false
2:    while(finished = false){
3:       edge-finding
4:       if (edge-finding makes no commitments)
5:          CBA
6:       if (no commitments from CBA or from edge-finding)
7:          make heuristic commitment
8:       if (dead-end)
9:          retract some commitment
10:      else
11:         arc-B-consistency temporal propagation
12:      if (all-activities-sequenced OR CPU limit reached)
13:         finished := true
14:   }
```

Figure 2. The Template for Monolith1 and Monolith2

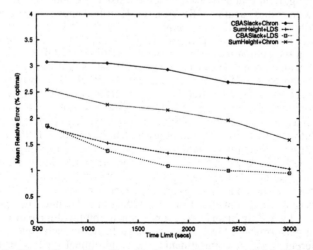

Figure 3. More Revealing Results from a Non-monolithic Experiment

1. Any claim of superiority of the heuristics based on the results of the monolithic experiment is unjustified.

2. The monolithic experiment, even when the components of the algorithms are known, may hide interesting data such as the interactions between heuristics and retraction techniques that we see in Figure 3.

Such experiments do appear in the literature due, partially, to the fact that researchers often work on whole algorithms and test new algorithms against existing ones. For example, [Smith and Cheng, 1993] compare four algorithms:

- PCP – using temporal arc-B-consistency and CBA propagation techniques, the CBASlack heuristic which posts precedence constraints between activities, and no backtracking.
- ORR/FSS [Sadeh, 1991] – using the ORR/FSS heuristic which assigns start-times to activities, temporal arc-B-consistency and resource arc consistency propagation, and chronological backtracking.
- ORR/FSS+ [Xiong et al., 1992] – the same as ORR/FSS using a form of intelligent backtracking instead of chronological backtracking.
- CPS [Muscettola, 1992] – using a heuristic which posts unary temporal constraints, temporal arc-B-consistency, resource arc consistency, and restart backtracking.

Experimental results showed that PCP was competitive (in terms of number of problems solved) with the other algorithms while using significantly less CPU time. In the comparison of scheduling *algorithms*, we agree with these results and the interpretation. However, among the four algorithms there are four different retraction techniques (chronological backtracking, a form of intelligent backtracking, restart, and no backtracking), three different sets of propagation techniques, and four different types of heuristic commitments (*e.g.*, assigning start-times, posting precedence constraints). On that basis, we do not believe the following conclusion is justified: "Evaluation ... has shown that our heuristics provide comparable results at very low computational expense." [Smith and Cheng, 1993, p. 144]. The results may be due to the CBASlack heuristic as claimed, or to the CBA propagation or to the differing types of commitments that each heuristic makes. What happens if we use the CBA propagator with the ORR/FSS heuristic? What happens if we post precedence constraints with CPS?

As a second example, [Nuijten, 1994] compares the SOLVE algorithm (using a randomized heuristic commitment technique to assign start-times, sophisticated propagation (edge-finding, temporal and resource arc consistency), and bounded chronological backtracking with restart) against ORR/FSS (as described above) and against ORR/FSS augmented with the propagation techniques used by SOLVE. The results showed that SOLVE strongly outperforms augmented ORR/FSS which in turn strongly outperforms ORR/FSS. From the comparison of augmented ORR/FSS and ORR/FSS, it is observed that the sophisticated propagation techniques contribute significantly to the scheduling algorithms. In comparing SOLVE and augmented ORR/FSS, however, there are two candidates for the performance difference: the heuristic commitment technique and the retraction technique. Nuijten states that these results do not mean that sophisticated heuristics such as those used in ORR/FSS are not useful, however, despite this statement, the results cast them in a poor light given that they were not directly tested.

In our analysis of existing constraint-directed scheduling techniques [Beck, 1997], we have identified, four key components present in many scheduling algorithms:

- **Commitment Type** We take the general view that a commitment is a set of constraints added to the constraint graph. However, we expect that different types of constraints (*e.g.*, assigning start-times by adding unary equals constraints, sequencing activities by adding binary precedence constraints) will have different effects on scheduling performance. Given that the same heuristic techniques can be used to make different types of commitments, the commitment-type is an important and orthogonal component of a scheduling algorithm.

- **Propagators** A propagator is an algorithm that analyzes the current search state to find new constraints that are logically implied by, but not explicitly present in, the constraint graph. Examples of propagators include the arc-B-consistency, CBA, and edge-finding noted above.

- **Heuristic Commitment Techniques** Heuristic commitment techniques are algorithms that heuristically suggest that a constraint or a set of constraints, though not necessarily implied by the current search state, are likely to lead to a solution. Above we noted the CBASlack heuristic and the heuristic based on the SumHeight contention estimation algorithm.

- **Commitment Retraction Techniques** When a dead-end (*i.e.,* a search state where one or more existing constraints is broken) is reached, the commitment retraction technique identifies a previously made commitment or commitments to be removed from the constraint graph and determines how to handle intervening commitments (*i.e.,* those made between the dead-end state and the state chosen to backtrack to). For example, chronological backtracking and LDS are two retraction techniques.

It is critical that researchers isolate the components of a scheduling algorithm and perform experiments that compare components of the same type. Furthermore, such comparison can not be done simply under one experimental design (*i.e.,* by holding all the other components constant) because, as demonstrated in Figure 3, there is the possibility of interactions among components. Identifying and investigating these interactions is an invaluable addition to understanding at a deep level the behaviour of search on a scheduling problem.

Pitfall II: Measuring CPU Time

Unfortunately, even when taking into account different components of a scheduling algorithm, the basis upon which competing algorithms are evaluated may be a source of errors, confusion, and difficulty. Consider the following experiment designed to test the effectiveness of two heuristic commitment techniques: CBASlack and SumHeight.

The two heuristic commitment techniques are tested with the propagators noted above (CBA, edge-finding, temporal arc-B-consistency) and with the LDS retraction component. The problems are 5 sets of 60 job shop scheduling problems, with sizes of {10×10, 12×12, 15×15, 18×18, 20×20} generated using Taillard's problem generator (Taillard, 1993). A CPU time bound of 20 minutes was allowed for each algorithm on each problem. If the bound was reached, failure on that problem was returned. Results in terms of number of problems solved are shown in Figure 4. The mean CPU time for the problems that both algorithms solved is displayed in Figure 5.

These results indicate that CBASlack and SumHeight perform about equally on these problem sets. However, Figure 6 and Figure 7 show a different perspective on the same experiment. On problems solved by both algorithms, we plot the mean number of implied commitments (those made by a propagator) in Figure 6 and the mean number of heuristic commitments in Figure 7.

Contrary to appearances the only significant difference between the implied commitments is for problems of size 10×10. Figure 6 and Figure 7 demonstrate that by far most of the commitments are implied commitments. Given the shape similarities between Figure 6 and Figure 5, we also might infer that the CPU time is dominated by the propagators.[2] Using CPU time, therefore, when our goal is to compare the heuris-

---

2. Figure 5 and Figure 6 do not directly amount to evidence of the dominance of CPU time by the propagators, however, two additional pieces of information help in the inference. First, we have implemented Nuijten's edge-finding algorithm [Nuijten, 1994] which has a time complexity, in each search state, of $O(mn^2)$ (m is the number of resources, n the number of activities per resource) in both average- and worst-case. This is greater than the worst-case complexity of SumHeight and the average-case complexity of CBASlack. Second, anecdotal evidence indicates that, in our implementation, over 30% of the CPU time is spent in edge-finding alone.

tics does not appear to be helpful. Differences in the heuristic performance are not reflected in the overall CPU time. In particular, CPU time hides the fact that, as shown in Figure 7, SumHeight makes significantly fewer heuristic commitments on each problem set and that SumHeight makes significantly more implied commitments per heuristic commitment on each problem set, as can been seen by comparing Figure 6 and Figure 7.

One view is that if our goal is to solve as many problems as we can in as short a time as we can, the number of heuristic commitments made is not a relevant statistic. We are interested in the bottom line performance and whether that performance is achieved with implied, heuristic, or divine commitments is not important. This view, typical of end-users of scheduling systems, is important especially if we want the systems we are developing to have industrial relevance. However, given that we are developing systems and that experiments must be on some set of problems, differences such as the number of heuristic commitments or the ratio of implied commitments to heuristic commitments are important. We take, for instance, the commitment ratio results to indicate that SumHeight is able to better identify critical, highly constrained areas in the constraint

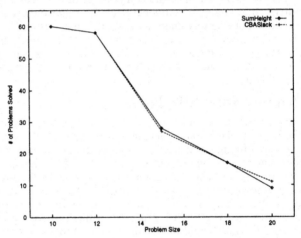

Figure 4. Number of Problems Solved vs. Problem Size

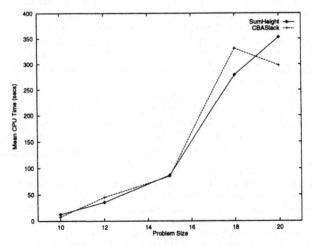

Figure 5. Mean CPU Time for Problems Solved by Both Algorithms

graph than CBASlack and further argue that this ability is important and will be reflected in bottom line performance as we move toward larger, industrial problems [Beck et al., 1997a].

The basis upon which algorithms are compared is an important issue in empirical scheduling research and, indeed, empirical algorithm research more generally. Comparisons based on overall CPU time, though important, lead to a number of issues [Hooker, 1996] such as the need to compare research code against industrial code and therefore to spend time in the software engineering of code optimization rather than on research. As we have shown, an additional difficulty is that overall CPU time may not speak to a comparison of the components of a scheduling algorithm in which the researcher is interested.

Conversely, CPU time can be very relevant in decisions as to the viability of scheduling approaches. For example, we have observed a three order of magnitude improvement in CPU time in algorithms when we have restructured them to optimize average time complexity. This has had significant impact in the research that we have pursued. Results that indicate an average performance of, say 200 CPU seconds, on small job

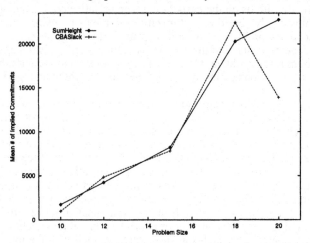

Figure 6. Mean Implied Commitments for Problems Solved by Both Algorithms

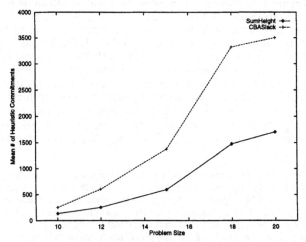

Figure 7. Mean Heuristic Commitments for Problems Solved by Both Algorithms

shop problems, might be taken as evidence that our approach is not going to be able to address larger industrial problems and so we may choose to investigate other options. In contrast, if that performance is 0.2 CPU seconds, our confidence in our methods and their scalability is significantly higher.[3]

We find that both of these arguments have merit and propose a balanced approach. Comparisons should be done both using CPU time and other search statistics (*e.g.*, number of commitments, number of backtracks, the ratio of commitments to backtracks). In the end, gathering and analyzing all these statistics will significantly aid in diagnosing performance and developing a deeper understanding of the algorithm behaviour. Even if CPU time is the main (or only) industrially relevant statistic, in the long term a balanced basis for evaluation will lead to a better understanding and, as a result of the deeper understanding, hopefully, to better CPU performance.

Pitfall III: Measuring Other Search Statistics

One of the problems with gathering multiple search statistics is that the experimental design can effect the validity of the data gathered. In optimization problems, it is common to compare algorithms on the basis of the mean relative error from optimal. Satisfaction algorithms can be tested on optimization problems by using a time bound and attempting to solve the problem at its known optimal. If the algorithm fails, the problem is relaxed (by some percentage of the optimal) and the algorithm is run again. This process is repeated until the problem is solved. The researcher then reports the mean relative error: the mean percentage above the optimal cost at which an algorithm was able to find a solution.

Unfortunately, this method can lead to mistaken assumptions about search statistics other than mean relative error. The difficulty arises because each algorithm (potentially) solves a completely different set of problems. On a single problem in the set, one algorithm may solve it to optimality while another may solve it to 1% of optimality, and a third only to 5%. Each algorithm has solved a different problem. If the problem characteristics change at different percentages of the optimal, this experimental design may have significant impact on results and conclusions. In particular, the interpretation of potentially interesting search statistics other than mean relative error may be suspect.

Table 1 presents a set of results from such a mean relative error experiment designed to test the efficacy of a number of heuristic commitment techniques.[4] A number of potentially interesting search statistics were gathered with the intention of using them subsequently to diagnose search behaviour. Because we are running propagators as well as a heuristic commitment component, an obvious statistic is to identify how many of the commitments are implied, that is, found by propagators. We also calculate the number of commitments for each probe in the search tree (Commitments/Probe), the number of heuristic commitments for each probe (HC/Probe), and the number of implied commitments for each heuristic commitment (IC/HC). A probe is defined to be the sequence of consecutive commitments not interrupted by a dead end.

In examining these statistics we may be able to develop insights into performance differences. Why, for example, was SumHeight able to solve problems significantly closer to optimal than LJRand? We observe that SumHeight has significantly fewer commitments per probe and heuristic commitments per probe. A possible explanation for the performance difference is that the SumHeight heuristic is able to detect dead-

---

3. The argument here is not that because we have good performance on small problems our algorithms will necessarily scale to industrial problems. Rather it is that if we have poor performance on small problems, there is little hope that the algorithms will improve when applied to larger problems. Another pitfall, however, that we do not have space to discuss here, is the common assumption that algorithms that show good results on small problems will scale up. Our experience with large industrial problems suggests that this is not necessarily the case.

4. See [Beck et al., 1997b] for a discussion of each of these heuristic commitment techniques.

ends earlier and therefore backtrack earlier, wasting less time in a sub-tree that will eventually prove fruitless. Unfortunately, an alternative explanation is that SumHeight solved problems with a smaller makespan (*i.e.,* a smaller mean relative error) which correlates highly with how constrained the problem is. Because the problems are more constrained, SumHeight is able to detect dead-ends sooner than LJRand on less constrained problems. The results may not have anything to do with a difference between SumHeight and LJRand but rather between the problems each solved.

To take another example, in Table 1 we see that SumHeight averages almost three times the number of implied commitments per heuristic commitment than CBASlack. It is tempting to conclude that the reason that SumHeight is able to find better solutions is that it is better able to identify and make commitments in highly constrained areas of the graph. This argument is again hampered by the experimental design. CBASlack solved problems with a larger makespan, which therefore are less constrained than those solved by SumHeight. Based on the results in Table 1 it is not justified to attribute the success of SumHeight to the ability to identify highly constrained sub-graphs. The problems solved by SumHeight are more highly constrained and so the IC/HC ratio may simply be an artifact of the problems that were solved.

There do not appear to be easy ways to avoid having experimental design affect the validity of the search statistics. This is especially the case if the gathering of a particular statistic was not planned at design time. While design-for-measurement is important and preferable, unfortunately, it is not always the case that the researchers foresee all the data that might be interesting before the experiment is designed and run. A pragmatic approach suggests care with experimental design to take into account statistics that might be of interest and the less satisfying practice of *a posteriori* vigilance: researchers need to be particularly aware of alternative explanations arising from artifacts of experimental design.

Heuristic	Relative Error	Commitments (HC, IC)[a]	Backtracks	Commitments/ Probe	HC/ Probe	IC/ HC
Sum-Height	2.26	29751 (1426, 28325)	676	87.13	8.93	20.08
CBA-Slack	3.05	10215 (1162,9053)	400	120.74	35.45	6.99
First-Commit	4.49	25650 (1494, 24155)	947	112.79	5.78	19.15
LJRand	10.54	1329 (144, 1184)	9	448.64	50.32	7.86

Table 1: Mean Search Statistics for MRE Experiment with CPU Time Limit of 1200 Seconds

a. HC: Heuristic Commitment, IC: Implied Commitment

Pitfall IV: Dangers of Benchmarking

Until recently, at least within the AI community, there were no widely used scheduling benchmarks. With Sadeh's problem set [Sadeh, 1991] and the adoption of the OR-library benchmark set [Beasley, 1990] this has changed.[5] This is not to say that problem sets were not previously available, but rather than there was little or no effort to cross-

---

5. ORLIB has existed for sometime within the OR community, but it is only in the past few years, due primarily to cross-fertilization from the OR world, that it has been used in the AI community.

validate scheduling strategies on problems generated by other researchers. We view the rise of benchmark sets that are used by a variety of researchers as a positive step in the maturity of the field; however this step is not without its perils. Chief among the perils is a concentration solely on existing benchmarks rather than their use as part of the overall evaluation strategy.

To illustrate a simple interpretation of special case results, we use data from an (unpublished) pilot experiment. The experiment was designed to test the efficacy of a new idea for retraction of commitments that had been developed in our lab, TestBT.[6] We decided to test the new retraction technique against three existing techniques: LDS, chronological backtracking, and random backtracking (RandomBT—randomly select a previously made heuristic commitment, backtrack to it (undoing all intervening commitments) and make an alternative commitment). Each algorithm used the same heuristic commitment technique and propagators.

We had at our disposal the two benchmark sets noted above, Sadeh's problems and the ORLIB set. We first used Sadeh's problems and found that 53 of the 60 problems could be solved with no backtracking. This cut our problem set down to the remaining 7 problems. Table 2 shows the results of running three of the backtracking techniques on the problems (chronological backtracking was not able to solve any of these problems within a bound of 1000 backtracks).

Problem	TestBT		RandomBT		LDS	
	Commitments	BTs	Commitments	BTs	Commitments	BTs
1	291	11	191	3	172	1
2	427	20	203	4	197	2
3	748	48	251	6	203	2
4	288	12	157	1	205	2
5	745	24	179	1	642	7
6	1086	26	1386	42	2593	69
7	237	12	170	2	155	1

Table 2: Number of Commitments and Number of Backtracks (BTs) for 3 Retraction Techniques

Based on these results, TestBT does not look promising—it is even worse than random! Fortunately, we also tested LDS which we had reason to believe would perform better than RandomBT [Harvey, 1995]. The fact that RandomBT is competitive with LDS leads us to believe that the problem set is distorting our results. Possible explanations for these results include the small sample size and/or a floor effect: the problems are just too easy to show any differences among the retraction techniques.

To further investigate the efficacy of TestBT, we used 13 of the ORLIB problems. Using a 600 CPU second time bound, each algorithm attempted to solve each problem at its optimal makespan. If it was unsuccessful, the makespan was expanded by 0.005 times optimal. This continued until 1.1 times optimal, where, if the algorithm could not

---

6. We do not specify the actual retraction technique as it is irrelevant to this discussion and would detract from our main point.

solve the problem, it gave up. Figure 8 shows the results of this experiment (relative error values of 1.11 are used to indicate that the algorithm did not solve the problem at all within the time and makespan bounds).

Results in Figure 8 are very different from Table 2. Now the best algorithm (in terms of finding the closest to optimal makespan) is always either LDS or TestBT while the worst algorithm is always either chronological backtracking or RandomBT. On the basis of these results, we are lead to believe that exploration of TestBT is justified.

Generally, we have one or more of the following goals when running experiments:

- The ability to draw conclusions that are applicable to problems outside the bench-mark set. Our benchmark sets, therefore, need to be representative of some interesting population of scheduling problems.

- The ability to draw conclusions that are applicable (or extendible) to industrial scheduling problems. Industrial problems may be a particular case of an interesting population; however we note them explicitly due to the scope of characteristics that have not been rigorously addressed (see Pitfall V).

- The ability to compare various algorithms.

It is unlikely that one benchmark set can be used toward all these goals. Furthermore, the relative evaluation of algorithms may change depending on the priority of these aims. With these goals in mind, we suggest the following types of problems should make their way into future benchmark sets.

1. **Randomly generated problems** An algorithm independent notion of difficulty (such as the identification of a phase transition [Cheeseman et al., 1991; Gent et al., 1996; Beck and Jackson, 1997]) requires statements about the entire space of problems. Therefore, sets of randomly generated problems of varying sizes are a necessary vehicle of demonstration.

2. **Structured randomly generated problems** Structured problems that are generated with some random component are also necessary. The structure is likely to stem both from the empirical notions of difficulty (*e.g.*, the intuition that bottleneck resources lead to more difficult problems [Sadeh, 1991]), and from structures in and characteristics of real world problems.

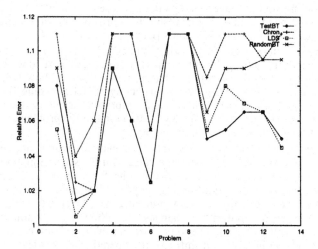

Figure 8. Relative Error on 13 ORLIB Problems

3. **Standard benchmarks** As noted above, standard benchmark problems are becoming widely used in the scheduling community. While these sets are unlikely to be representative of the entire space of problems, their usefulness as data points, given the mass of work that has addressed the problems, is significant.

Pitfall V: Makespan Considered Harmful

A lot of research and CPU cycles have been devoted to the optimization of makespan in job shop problems while, with a few notable exceptions [Saks, 1992; Nuijten, 1994; Le Pape, 1994b; Brucker and Thiele, 1996; Caseau and Laburthe, 1996; Nuijten and Aarts, 1997], little has been done on expanding the scope of constraint-directed scheduling technology much beyond the job shop. This is particularly distressing since, from the inception of constraint-directed approaches to scheduling, it has been recognized that real industrial scheduling is not simply meeting due dates, but rather satisfying many complex (and interacting) constraints from disparate sources within the plant and, indeed, the enterprise as a whole [Fox, 1983; Fox, 1990]. In fact, this was one of the original reasons to believe that scheduling was a prime application of constraint technologies.

It is unclear whether our preoccupation with makespan has allowed us to make many in-roads into the realities of scheduling problems that have existed for decades in industrial settings. Consider the following examples:

- **Varying release dates and due dates** Jobs are released for execution and due to be completed at varying time points over the scheduling horizon. While many advances in makespan optimization (*e.g.*, edge-finding) carry over to these problems, it is not clear if they will have as much of an impact on this class of problems. Furthermore there has been little work of which we are aware that examines techniques (*e.g.*, problem decomposition) that might be especially applicable to such problems. The addition of independent release times and due dates for different jobs is a trivial addition to the job shop model, yet it is unclear what techniques for makespan optimization can be carried over.

- **Advanced temporal constraints** The overwhelmingly most popular temporal relation among activities in scheduling research is the precedence constraint. Given that the 13 Allen relations [Allen, 1983] (*e.g.*, meets, during) have been recognized for many years and have been noted in many scheduling papers, it is surprising how little they have been addressed. Industrially such constraints arise in contexts such as curing, cooling, and spoilage, among others. These constraints have been so ignored that simple-minded techniques can result in surprising gains in scheduling ability in problems that contain such constraints [Davenport et al., 1997].

- **Inventory** Inventory is produced and consumed (often at varying rates) by activities in a manufacturing setting. Inventory must be stored and there may be a host of constraints, both temporal and capacity-based, with respect to how long and where it can be stored. While existing systems (notably ILOG Schedule [Le Pape, 1994b; Le Pape, 1994a] and KBLPS [Saks, 1992]) represent inventory, the only published results appear to be algorithms that are crafted for specific problems rather than generally addressing scheduling with inventory.

- **Time-varying constraints** Constraints, especially resource and inventory constraints in the manufacturing context, change over the scheduling horizon. The simplest example of this is scheduled down-time for a resource. More complicated examples exist, including time varying supply and demand (*e.g.*, in a seasonal business it is desirable to enforce a minimum inventory level that increases as the predicted high-season approaches), changes in staffing (*e.g.*, "learning" time during which new operators are not able to perform at peak speed or the fact that more people call in sick on Friday), and shift-specific operations (*e.g.*, clean-outs can only be done at night or on the weekend).

- **Production choices** There may be many ways to produce any particular finished good or intermediate product. The activity model from raw materials to final product is not, in fact, a simple acyclic temporal network (as it is often modeled) but an acyclic graph with specific choice points. These choices may represent trade-offs in quality, cost of production, or time, and are subject to resource and inventory use. Until we have a partial, evolving schedule, we do not know which choices should be made at these points.

These examples are low-level issues concerning specific scheduling constraints that have received little treatment in the literature. There are also a host of higher-level issues such as the robustness of schedules and the ease of rescheduling at execution time [Ow et al., 1988; Drummond et al., 1994; Hildum, 1994], relaxation of constraints in over-constrained problems [Beck, 1994], and, more generally, what constitutes a good solution. For example, imagine a system that creates schedules with a probabilistic measure of the ability to execute the schedule. Rather than guaranteeing a executable schedule (as is part of the *definition* of a solution in the research world), the system guarantees that the schedule can be executed with a probability of, say, 95%. In the current view of scheduling research, such a scheduler would not solve any problems at all, yet related concepts (*e.g.,* probabilistic customer service levels[7]) are commonly used in the industrial setting.

Constraints can model scheduling problems in a much more flexible, accurate, and representational way than other methods, for example, that rely on mathematical programming techniques. Why then are we spending an inordinate effort in attempting to squeeze the last 0.5% from the makespan of a particular instance of a scheduling problem?

Conclusion

Our purpose in this paper is to raise points for discussion with the eventual goal of facilitating the maturation of the field of empirical scheduling research. We believe that wide awareness of these pitfalls will encourage such maturation and make advances easier to achieve and validate.

In this paper, we have looked at five pitfalls that we have observed in our work in empirical scheduling. In particular, using data from actual experiments, we examined:
- the view of a scheduling algorithm as a monolithic whole,
- the use of CPU time as a performance measure,
- how experimental design can effect search statistics,
- the use of benchmarks, and finally,
- the use of makespan optimization as a primary goal in scheduling research.

The goal of scheduling research is to increase the ability to solve interesting problems. The source of the interest (*e.g.,* industrial need) may be important; however greater and more regular progress will be made if we can form an understanding of the behaviour of scheduling techniques on different problem types. This understanding will arise neither out of a concentration on delivering a solution to a particular type of problem nor out of a wholly abstract approach. A balanced approach suggests two research engines: application of theory to real world problems and generalization of practical advances to theoretical concepts. We believe that an understanding of pitfalls such as we have described here will aid in both of these efforts.

---

7. A probabilistic customer service level of 95% allocates inventory to a warehouse such that all customer orders will be met at least 95% of the time.

Acknowledgments

This research was funded in part by the Natural Science and Engineering Research Council of Canada, Numetrix Limited, the IRIS Research Network, the Manufacturing Research Corporation of Ontario, and Digital Equipment of Canada.

Thanks to Ed Sitarski, Angela Glover, and the anonymous reviewers for comments on and discussion of earlier drafts of this paper.

References

AAAI Empirical Workshop (1994). *Proceedings of the AAAI-94 Workshop on Experimental Evaluation of Reasoning and Search Methods.*

Allen, J. F. (1983). Maintaining knowledge about temporal intervals. *Communications of the ACM*, 26(11):832–843.

Beasley, J. E. (1990). OR-library: distributing test problems by electronic mail. *Journal of the Operational Research Society*, 41(11):1069–1072. Also available by ftp from ftp:// graph.ms.ic.ac.uk/pub/paper.txt.

Beck, J. C. (1994). A schema for constraint relaxation with instantiations for partial constraint satisfaction and schedule optimization. Master's thesis, Department of Computer Science, University of Toronto.

Beck, J. C. (1997). A generic framework for constraint-directed search and scheduling. Technical report, Department of Industrial Engineering, University of Toronto, 4 Taddle Creek Road, Toronto, Ontario M5S 3G9, Canada.

Beck, J. C., Davenport, A. J., Sitarski, E. M., and Fox, M. S. (1997a). Beyond contention: extending texture-based scheduling heuristics. In *Proceedings of AAAI-97*. AAAI Press, Menlo Park, California.

Beck, J. C., Davenport, A. J., Sitarski, E. M., and Fox, M. S. (1997b). Texture-based heuristics for scheduling revisited. In *Proceedings of AAAI-97*. AAAI Press, Menlo Park, California.

Beck, J. C. and Jackson, K. (1997). Constrainedness and the phase transition in job shop scheduling. Technical report, School of Computing Science, Simon Fraser University.

Brucker, P. and Thiele, O. (1996). A branch & bound method for the general-shop problems with sequence dependent set-up times. *OR Spektrum*, 18:145–161.

Carlier, J. and Pinson, E. (1989). An algorithm for solving the job-shop problem. *Management Science*, 35(2):164–176.

Caseau, Y. and Laburthe, F. (1996). Cumulative scheduling with task intervals. In *Proceedings of the Joint International Conference and Symposium on Logic Programming*. MIT Press.

Cheeseman, P., Kanefsky, B., and Taylor, W. (1991). Where the really hard problems are. In *Proceedings of IJCAI-91*, volume 1, pages 331–337.

Cheng, C. C. and Smith, S. F. (1996). Applying constraint satisfaction techniques to job shop scheduling. *Annals of Operations Research, Special Volume on Scheduling: Theory and Practice*, 1. Forthcoming.

Cohen, P. R. (1995). *Empirical Methods for Artificial Intelligence*. The MIT Press, Cambridge, Mass.

Davenport, A. J., Beck, J. C., and Fox, M. S. (1997). Propagation over the meets temporal constraint. Technical report, Department of Industrial Engineering, University of Toronto.

Drummond, M., Bresina, J., and Swanson, K. (1994). Just-in-case scheduling. In *Proceedings of AAAI-94*, pages 1098–1104, Menlo Park, CA. AAAI Press/MIT Press.

ECAI Empirical Workshop (1996). *Proceedings of the ECAI-96 Workshop on Empirical Artificial Intelligence.*

Erschler, J., Roubellat, F., and Vernhes, J. P. (1976). Finding some essential characteristics of the feasible solutions for a scheduling problem. *Operations Research*, 24:772–782.

Erschler, J., Roubellat, F., and Vernhes, J. P. (1980). Characterising the set of feasible sequences for n jobs to be carried out on a single machine. *European Journal of Operational Research*, 4:189–194.

Fox, M. S. (1983). *Constraint-Directed Search: A Case Study of Job-Shop Scheduling*. PhD thesis, Carnegie Mellon University, Intelligent Systems Laboratory, The Robotics Institute, Pittsburgh, PA. CMU-RI-TR-85-7.

Fox, M. S. (1990). Constraint-guided scheduling - a short history of research at CMU. *Computers in Industry*, 14:79–88.

Gent, I. P., Grant, S. A., MacIntyre, E., Prosser, P., Shaw, P., Smith, B. M., and Walsh, T. (1997). How not to do it. Technical Report 97.27, School of Computer Studies, University of Leeds.

Gent, I. P., MacIntyre, E., Prosser, P., and Walsh, T. (1996). The constrainedness of search. In *Proceedings of AAAI-96*, volume 1, pages 246–252.

Harvey, W. D. (1995). *Nonsystematic backtracking search*. PhD thesis, Department of Computer Science, Stanford University.

Harvey, W. D. and Ginsberg, M. L. (1995). Limited discrepancy search. In *Proceedings of IJCAI-95*, pages 607–613.

Hildum, D. W. (1994). *Flexibility in a knowledge-based system for solving dynamic resource-constrained scheduling problems*. PhD thesis, Department of Computer Science, University of Massachusetts, Amherst, MA. 01003-4610. UMass CMPSCI TR 94-77.

Hooker, J. N. (1994). Needed: An empirical science of algorithms. *Operations Research*, 42:201–212.

Hooker, J. N. (1996). Testing heuristics: We have it all wrong. *Journal of Heuristics*, 1:33–42.

Le Pape, C. (1994a). Implementation of resource constraints in ILOG Schedule: A library for the development of constraint-based scheduling systems. *Intelligent Systems Engineering*, 3(2):55–66.

Le Pape, C. (1994b). Using a constraint-based scheduling library to solve a specific scheduling problem. In *Proceedings of the AAAI-SIGMAN Workshop on Artificial Intelligence Approaches to Modelling and Scheduling Manufacturing Processes*.

Lhomme, O. (1993). Consistency techniques for numeric CSPs. In *Proceedings of IJCAI-93*, volume 1, pages 232–238.

Muscettola, N. (1992). Scheduling by iterative partition of bottleneck conflicts. Technical Report CMU-RI-TR-92-05, The Robotics Institute, Carnegie Mellon University.

Nuijten, W. and Aarts, E. (1997). A computational study of constraint satisfaction for multiple capacitated job shop scheduling. *European Journal of Operational Research*. To appear.

Nuijten, W. P. M. (1994). *Time and resource constrained scheduling: a constraint satisfaction approach*. PhD thesis, Department of Mathematics and Computing Science, Eindhoven University of Technology.

Ow, P. S., Smith, S. F., and Thiriez, A. (1988). Reactive plan revision. In *Proceedings of AAAI-88*, pages 77–82. AAAI.

Sadeh, N. (1991). *Lookahead techniques for micro-opportunistic job-shop scheduling*. PhD thesis, Carnegie-Mellon University. CMU-CS-91-102.

Saks, V. (1992). Distribution planner overview. Technical report, Carnegie Group, Inc., Pittsburgh, PA, 1522.

Smith, S. F. and Cheng, C. C. (1993). Slack-based heuristics for constraint satisfaction scheduling. In *Proceedings AAAI-93*, pages 139–144.

Taillard, E. (1993). Benchmarks for basic scheduling problems. *European Journal of Operational Research*, 64:278–285.

Xiong, Y., Sadeh, N., and Sycara, K. (1992). Intelligent backtracking techniques for job-shop scheduling. In *Proceedings of the Third International Conference on Principles of Knowledge Representation and Reasoning, Cambridge, MA*.

Zweben, M., Davis, E., Daun, B., and Deale, M. (1993). Informedness vs. computational cost of heuristics in iterative repair scheduling. In *Proceedings of IJCAI-93*, pages 1416–1422.

Bounding the Optimum
of Constraint Optimization Problems

Simon de Givry[1], Gérard Verfaillie[1], and Thomas Schiex[2]

[1] ONERA-CERT, 2 av. Edouard Belin, BP4025, 31055 Toulouse Cedex 4, France,
{degivry,verfaillie}@cert.fr
[2] INRA, Chemin de Borde Rouge, Auzeville, BP26, 31326 Castanet Tolosan Cedex, France,
tschiex@toulouse.inra.fr

Abstract. Solving constraint optimization problems is computationally so expensive that it is often impossible to provide a guaranteed optimal solution, either when the problem is too large, or when time is bounded. In these cases, local search algorithms usually provide *good* solutions. However, and even if an optimality proof is unreachable, it is often desirable to have some guarantee on the quality of the solution found, in order to decide if it is worthwile to spend more time on the problem.

This paper is dedicated to the production of intervals, that bound as precisely as possible the optimum of *Valued Constraint Satisfaction Problems* (*VCSP*). Such intervals provide an upper bound on the distance of the best available solution to the optimum *i.e.*, on the quality of the optimization performed. Experimental results on random *VCSPs* and real problems are given.

Motivations

The *Constraint Satisfaction Problem* framework is very convenient for representing and solving various problems, related to *Artificial Intelligence* and *Operations Research*: scheduling, assignment, design... But many real overconstrained problems are more faithfully translated to *Constraint Optimization Problems*, and, more precisely, to *Valued Constraint Satisfaction Problems* [16]. The classical objective of constraint satisfaction is replaced by an objective of constraint violation minimization.

Both theoretical and practical observations show that these optimization problems are much more difficult to tackle than satisfaction problems. The construction of a provenly optimal solution is often out of reach. It is the case, either when the problem is too large and difficult, or when time and resources are bounded.

Exact or complete methods, such as *Branch and Bound*, are able to produce both an optimal solution, and a proof of optimality. But, because of their exponential worst-case behavior, they may be extremely time consuming. Moreover, it has been experimentally observed that, due to their systematic way of exploring the search space, the quality of their intermediate solutions is usually very poor [21].

Due to their opportunist way of exploring the search space, approximate or incomplete methods, based on heuristic or stochastic *Local Search* mechanisms, usually provide *good* solutions within a reasonable time. Naturally, the value of the best solution found so far is an upper bound on the optimum. But these algorithms do not provide any information about the distance between this value and the optimum. By themselves, they cannot prove the optimality of a solution and may waste a lot of time trying to improve an already optimal solution: a wasteful behavior if several problems have to be tackled in a time or resource-bounded context.

This situation can be largely improved by computing non trivial lower bounds on the optimum: the distance between, on the one hand, the value of the best solution found so far, and, on the other hand, the best lower bound produced so far, provides an upper bound on the distance to the optimum. This information can be used for deciding, either to stop the optimization process, or to spend more time, in order to get a tighter bounding of the optimum.

This paper is organized as follows: in Section 1, we introduce the *Valued Constraint Satisfaction Problem* framework; in Section 2, we show how problem simplifications can be used for producing lower bounds; we finally present, in Section 3, the results of the experiments which have been performed, both on random *VCSPs* in a time-bounded context, and on large real problems.

1   Valued Constraint Satisfaction Problems

The *Valued Constraint Satisfaction Problem* framework (*VCSP*) [16] is an extension of the *Constraint Satisfaction Problem* framework (*CSP*), which allows overconstrained problems or preferences between solutions to be dealt with. In the *VCSP* framework, a mathematical object, called a *valuation*, is associated with each constraint. The valuation of an assignment is defined as the aggregation of the valuations of the constraints which are violated by this assignment. The goal is to find a complete assignment of minimum valuation.

More formally speaking, whereas a *CSP* is defined as a triple $P = (V, D, C)$, where V is a set of variables, D a set of associated domains, and C a set of constraints between the variables, a *VCSP* can be defined as a *CSP* which is extended with:

- a valuation structure S, which is itself a quintuple $(E, \succ, \top, \bot, \circledast)$, where E is a valuation set, $\succ$ a total order on E, $\top$ and $\bot$ the maximum and the minimum elements in E, and $\circledast$ a binary closed aggregation operator on E which satisfies the following properties: commutativity, associativity, monotonicity according to $\succ$, $\top$ as absorbing element and $\bot$ as identity,
- and a valuation function φ from C to E.

The valuation set E is used for defining a gradual notion of constraint violation and inconsistency. The elements of E can be compared using the total order $\succ$ and aggregated using the operator $\circledast$. The maximum element $\top$ is used for expressing imperative constraint violation and complete inconsistency, the minimum element $\bot$ to express constraint satisfaction and complete consistency. The valuation function φ associates with each constraint a valuation which denotes its importance (the valuation of any imperative constraint equals $\top$).

Let A be an assignment of all the variables and $C_{unsat}(A, P)$ be the set of the problem constraints unsatisfied by A. The valuation $\varphi(A, P)$ of A is the aggregation of the valuations of all the constraints in $C_{unsat}(A, P)$:

$$\varphi(A, P) = \underset{c \in C_{unsat}(A,P)}{\circledast} \varphi(c)$$

The goal is then to find an assignment whose valuation is minimum and lower than $\top$ (all the imperative constraints must be satisfied). The optimal valuation $\varphi(P)$ of a problem P is the valuation of such an assignment.

Note that an equivalent framework can be defined, without any major modification, by assigning a valuation to each tuple of a constraint. Note also that a very close algebraic framework, which only assumes a partial order on E, is defined in [3].

Specific subframeworks can be defined by instantiating the valuation structure S. Table 1 shows the valuation structures which are used by the $\wedge$-VCSP, max-VCSP, lex-VCSP, and Σ-VCSP subframeworks.

- in the $\wedge$-VCSP framework (equivalent to the classical CSP framework), the goal is to find an assignment which satisfies all the constraints;
- in the max-VCSP framework[1] (equivalent to the possibilistic CSP framework), the goal is to find an assignment which minimizes the maximum valuation of the unsatisfied constraints;
- in the lex-VCSP framework[2] (used in the *Hierarchical Constraint Logic Programming* framework [22]), the goal is to find an assignment which minimizes the number of unsatisfied constraints of maximum valuation and then minimizes the number of unsatisfied constraints of lower valuation, and so on, down to the lowest valuation;
- in the Σ-VCSP framework, the goal is to find an assignment which minimizes the sum of the valuations of the unsatisfied constraints.

From an application point of view, many real problems use an additive criterion and can be cast as Σ-VCSPs. In the sequel of this paper, we consequently assume that the target problem is a Σ-VCSP.

2 Bounding the optimum of a VCSP

Let P be a VCSP, $\varphi(P)$ be its optimal valuation, and $P(\alpha)$ be the following *NP-complete* decision problem: does there exist an assignment of the variables in P, whose

---

[1] Traditionally, the set $E = [0, 1]$ is used instead of $\overline{\mathbb{N}}$, the set $\mathbb{N}$ of the natural integers, extended with the element $+\infty$. But obviously any infinite ordered set with a maximum and a minimum element may be used. We have chosen to use $\overline{\mathbb{N}}$, to be homogeneous with the other subframeworks.

[2] To be consistent with our definition of the *max-VCSPs*, *lex-VCSPs* use $E = \overline{\mathbb{N}}^*$, the set of the multi-sets of elements of $\mathbb{N}$, completed with a maximum element. This set is ordered by $>^*$, the lexicographic order induced on $\overline{\mathbb{N}}^*$ by the natural order $>$ on $\overline{\mathbb{N}}$. Let us recall that a multi-set is a set which may contain several times the same element. Let E be a set, totally ordered by $\succ$. Let E^* be the set of the multi-sets of elements of E. The lexicographic order $\succ^*$, which is induced on E^* by the order $\succ$ on E, can be defined as follows: let be $e_1, e_2 \in E^*$, let m be the maximum element of $e_1 \cup e_2$ according to $\succ$, let e_1^m and e_2^m the subsets of e_1 and e_2 whose elements equal m, $e_1 \succ^* e_2 \Leftrightarrow [|e_1^m| > |e_2^m|] \vee [(|e_1^m| = |e_2^m|) \wedge (e_1 - e_1^m \succ^* e_2 - e_2^m)]$.

Subframework	Notation	E	$\succ$	T	$\perp$	$\circledast$
Classical *CSP*	$\wedge$-*VCSP*	$\{t, f\}$	$f \succ t$	f	t	$\wedge$
Possibilistic *VCSP*	*max-VCSP*	$\overline{\mathbb{N}}$	$>$	$+\infty$	0	max
Lexicographic *VCSP*	*lex-VCSP*	$\overline{\mathbb{N}}^*$	$>^*$	T	$\emptyset$	$\cup$
Additive *VCSP*	Σ-*VCSP*	$\overline{\mathbb{N}}$	$>$	$+\infty$	0	$+$

Table 1. Several *VCSP* subframeworks

valuation is strictly lower than α ? Bounding the optimum of P implies solving two different problems:

- to find an upper bound *i.e.*, a valuation *ub* which is as low as possible and such that the answer to $P(ub)$ is *yes*;
- to find a lower bound *i.e.*, a valuation *lb* which is as high as possible and such that the answer to $P(lb)$ is *no*.

It is interesting to observe the behaviour of a standard *Depth First Branch and Bound* algorithm, using *Forward Checking* [8, 16], when solving $P(\alpha)$ with increasing values of α. Figure 1 shows the mean number of nodes in the tree search as a function of α. Each point represents the mean value on 44 different random Σ-*VCSPs*, whose characteristics are the following: they involve 15 variables and 10 values per variable; graph connectivity and constraint tightness equal 70%; all the constraint valuations equal 1; the optimum equals 20.

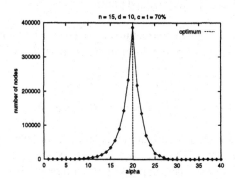

Fig. 1. Number of nodes when looking for an assignment whose valuation is strictly lower than α.

Traditionally, the parameter which appears on the x axis is one of the parameters which have been used for generating the considered instances. Here, it is a parameter of the question. But, the same traditional behavior of the *NP-complete* problems can be observed: a phase transition, which is located round the optimum, separates problems whose answer is *no*, on the left (problems whose solving provides lower bounds on the optimum), from problems whose answer is *yes* on the right (problems whose solving provides upper bounds on the optimum). This curve is enlightning on several points:

- the hardest problem to solve is the problem $P(\varphi(P))$, which consists in proving that there is no assignment whose valuation is strictly lower than the optimum; it is harder than the problem $P(\varphi(P) + 1)$, which consists in producing an optimal assignment;
- a complete algorithm, like a *Branch and Bound*, whose objective is to provide an optimal solution and an optimality proof, has to solve at least both these problems;
- at the same distance from the optimum, producing an upper bound seems easier than producing a lower bound, when using a complete algorithm for both problems; this difference may become more important, when incomplete *Local Search* algorithms are used for producing quickly *good* upper bounds;
- the difficulty of bounding the optimum seems to grow exponentially, when the size of the desired interval decreases.

Incomplete methods seem well suited to the production of upper bounds. On the other hand, complete methods seem well suited to the production of lower bounds. In this paper, we show that optimally solving *simplifications* of an additive target problem can produce both interesting upper and lower bounds. More precisely, we show that simplifications are easier to solve than the target problem, and that solving them allows the optimum of the target problem to be bounded.

2.1 Simplifying a VCSP

The different methods, that will be used for transforming a *VCSP* into a hopefully simpler *VCSP*, are covered by the following definition:

Definition 1. Given two valuation structures $S = (E, \succ, \top, \bot, \circledast)$ and $S' = (E', \succ'$, $\top', \bot', \circledast')$, a simplification function is a function Φ from E to E', such that:

$$\Phi(\bot) = \bot', \Phi(\top) = \top'$$
$$\forall e_1, e_2 \in E, e_1 \succcurlyeq e_2 \Rightarrow \Phi(e_1) \succcurlyeq' \Phi(e_2)$$

In other words, a simplification function is an order morphism. The last condition can be equivalently written $\forall e_1, e_2 \in E, e_1 \succ e_2 \Rightarrow \Phi(e_1) \succcurlyeq' \Phi(e_2)$. This shows that a simplification function may suppress some differences between valuations (two different valuations may map to the same element), but preserves the order, and the maximum and minimum elements. A simplification function between S and S' can be applied to a *VCSP* $P = (X, D, C, S, \varphi)$ and yields the *VCSP* $P' = (X, D, C, S', \Phi \circ \varphi)$, abusively noted $\Phi(P)$. Simplification functions can be composed together and the result is again a simplification function.

The following simplifications will be used in the sequel:

- given any valuation structure S and e any element of E, Φ_e is a simplification from S to S which maps to $\bot$ any valuation strictly lower than e, all the other valuations remaining unchanged; a *VCSP* simplified in this way simply ignores all the constraints whose valuation is strictly lower than e;

- from any valuation structure to $\wedge$-VCSP, $\Phi^\wedge$ is a simplification such that, $\forall e, e \neq \perp, \Phi^\wedge(e) = f$; it maps any VCSP to a classical CSP, where all the soft constraints are made hard;
- from Σ-VCSP to max-VCSP, Φ^{max} is simply the identity; from lex-VCSP to max-VCSP, Φ^{max} is a simplification such that, $\forall e, e \neq \varnothing, e \neq \top, \Phi^{max}(e)$ is the maximum element in the multi-set e;
- from Σ-VCSP to lex-VCSP, Φ^{lex} is a simplification such that $\forall e, e \neq 0, e \neq +\infty, \Phi^{lex}(e) = \{e\}$.

In some cases, when the simplification function is compatible with the aggregation operators which are used in S and S', it is possible to prove that the simplified VCSP is effectively simpler to solve.

Definition 2. A simplification function Φ between S and S' is aggregation-compatible iff $\forall E_1, E_2$, finite subsets of E:

$$\Phi(\underset{e \in E_1}{\circledast} e) \succcurlyeq' \Phi(\underset{e \in E_2}{\circledast} e) \Rightarrow \underset{e \in E_1}{\circledast}' \Phi(e) \succcurlyeq' \underset{e \in E_2}{\circledast}' \Phi(e)$$

Theorem 3. *If Φ is an aggregation-compatible simplification function, then the set of the optimal solutions of $\Phi(P)$ is a superset of the set of the optimal solutions of P. Moreover, the search tree of $\Phi(P)$ is included in the search tree of P, when using a Depth First Branch and Bound algorithm, the same static variable and value orderings, and the same way of computing a lower bound on the global valuation[3] of a partial assignment[4].*

Proof If Φ is an aggregation-compatible simplification function, it follows from Definitions 1 and 2 that, $\forall E_1, E_2$, finite subsets of E:

$$\underset{e \in E_1}{\circledast} e \succcurlyeq \underset{e \in E_2}{\circledast} e \Rightarrow \Phi(\underset{e \in E_1}{\circledast} e) \succcurlyeq' \Phi(\underset{e \in E_2}{\circledast} e) \Rightarrow \underset{e \in E_1}{\circledast}' \Phi(e) \succcurlyeq' \underset{e \in E_2}{\circledast}' \Phi(e) \quad (1)$$

Let $lb(A, P)$ be any lower bound on the global valuation of a partial assignment A in a problem P, which is computed by aggregating constraint valuations, as it is done with *Backward* or *Forward Checking*. From 1, it follows that, $\forall A, A'$, partial assignments:

$$lb(A, P) \succcurlyeq lb(A', P) \Rightarrow lb(A, \Phi(P)) \succcurlyeq' lb(A', \Phi(P)) \quad (2)$$

or equivalently:

$$lb(A', \Phi(P)) \succ' lb(A, \Phi(P)) \Rightarrow lb(A', P) \succ lb(A, P) \quad (3)$$

If A is an optimal complete assignment of P, then $\forall A'$, complete assignment, $\varphi(A', P) \succcurlyeq \varphi(A, P)$. From 2, it follows that, $\forall A'$, complete assignment, $\varphi(A', \Phi(P)) \succcurlyeq' \varphi(A, \Phi(P))$, and that A is an optimal complete assignment of $\Phi(P)$. Thus, the set of the optimal solutions of $\Phi(P)$ is a superset of the set of the optimal solutions of P.

---

[3] The global valuation of a partial assignment is the optimal valuation of all its complete extensions.

[4] Note that, if Φ is an aggregation-compatible simplification function, then P is a *strong refinement* of $\Phi(P)$ [16].

If A is a partial assignment, associated with a node which is expanded, when using on $\Phi(P)$ a *Depth First Branch and Bound* algorithm, static variable and value orderings, and any way of computing a lower bound on the global valuation of a partial assignment, then $\forall A'$, complete assignment, preceding A according to the search order, $\varphi(A', \Phi(P)) \succ' lb(A, \Phi(P))$: if this condition was not satisfied, A would not be expanded. From 3, it follows that, $\forall A'$, complete assignment, preceding A according to the search order, $\varphi(A', P) \succ lb(A, P)$, and that the associated node is expanded, when using on P the same algorithm, the same variable and value orderings, and the same way of computing a lower bound on the global valuation of a partial assignment. Thus, the search tree of $\Phi(P)$ is, under these conditions, included in the search tree of P $\square$

Among the previous simplification functions, it is easy to establish that:

- Φ_e is aggregation-compatible from *max-VCSP* and *lex-VCSP*, but not from Σ-*VCSP*;
- $\Phi^\wedge$ is aggregation-compatible from any valuation structure;
- Φ^{max} is aggregation-compatible from *lex-VCSP*, but not from Σ-*VCSP*;
- Φ^{lex} is not aggregation-compatible from Σ-*VCSP*.

From Σ-*VCSP*, even if Φ_e is not aggregation-compatible, it has been experimentally observed that complexity globally decreases with the number of constraints[5]. In the same way, even if Φ^{max} and Φ^{lex} are not aggregation-compatible, it has been experimentally observed that solving *max-VCSPs* and *lex-VCSPs* is generally simpler than solving Σ-*VCSPs*.

2.2 Building lower bounds from simplifications

Given a problem P and a simplification function Φ, the valuation in P of any optimal solution of $\Phi(P)$ is obviously an upper bound on the optimum of P. Interestingly, the optimum of $\Phi(P)$, or any lower bound on this optimum, can also be used for producing a lower bound on the optimum of P. This is captured by the notion of *transfer function*.

Definition 4. Given a simplification function Φ between S and S', a function Ψ from E' to E is a transfer function for Φ iff:

$$\forall E_1, \text{ finite subset of } E, \forall e' \in E', \underset{e \in E_1}{\circledast}' \Phi(e) \succ' e' \Rightarrow \underset{e \in E_1}{\circledast} e \succ \Psi(e')$$

Theorem 5. *If Ψ is a transfer function for the simplification function Φ between S and S', and if e' is a lower bound on the optimum of $\Phi(P)$, then $\Psi(e')$ is a lower bound on the optimum of P. Particularly:*

$$\varphi(P) \succ \Psi(\varphi(\Phi(P)))$$

---

[5] It remains true with algorithms such as *Russian Doll Search* [19] or *Forward Checking* enhanced with *Directed Arc Consistency* [20, 10], for which what [11] call a phase transition occurs: complexity decreases when constraint tightness increases beyond a point; but, even with these algorithms, complexity continues to increase regularly with graph connectivity.

The proof is straightforward. Note that a trivial transfer function always exists: $\forall e' \in E', \Psi(e') = \bot$. Fortunately, it is possible to define more useful transfer functions. For example, for any valuation structure, identity is a transfer function for the simplification Φ_e.

For any target Σ-VCSP P, let $(e_1, \ldots, e_k)$ be the different valuations which are associated with the constraints in P, from the highest to the lowest, let n_i be the number of constraints in P whose valuation equals e_i, let m_i the number of constraints in P which are violated by an assignment A and whose valuation equals e_i, and let $(e_1^{m_1}, \ldots, e_k^{m_k})$ be the notation we use for representing the lexicographic valuation of A. The following transfer functions can be established[6]:

- $\Psi^{\wedge}(t) = 0, \Psi^{\wedge}(f) = e_k$ is a transfer function for the simplification $\Phi_{\wedge}$;
- $\Psi^{max}(e) = e$ (identity) is a transfer function for the simplification Φ_{max};
- $\Psi^{lex}(e_1^{m_1}, \ldots, e_k^{m_k}) = lex(e_1^{m_1}, \ldots, e_k^{m_k})$ is a transfer function for the simplification Φ^{lex}, where lex is defined as follows:

  $lex() = 0$
  $lex(e_i^{m_i}, \ldots, e_k^{m_k}) =$
  if $m_i = n_i, (n_i.e_i) + lex(e_{i+1}^{m_{i+1}}, \ldots, e_k^{m_k})$
  else $\min[(m_i + 1).e_i, (m_i.e_i) + lex(e_{i+1}^{m_{i+1}}, \ldots, e_k^{m_k})]$

Note that the optimum of a simplified problem is not directly a lower bound on the optimum of the target problem. We need a transfer function to get a lower bound. The notion of simplification is therefore more general than the notion of relaxation widely used in *Operations Research*.

2.3 Other approaches

Other ways of computing lower bounds could be considered:

- we saw that removing some constraints and solving the resulting problem produces a lower bound; it is possible to do that in order to obtain, either a particular constraint graph (for example a tree, which can be polynomially solved), or a problem decomposition; it is also possible to produce a partition of the problem constraints and to use the property that the combination of the optimal valuations of the resulting subproblems is a lower bound;
- it is possible to remove some forbidden tuples from the constraints and to exploit the property that the optimal valuation of the resulting problem is a lower bound; as previously with the constraints, it may be interesting to do that in order to obtain particular constraints; a related approach would consist in merging similar values (values with a similar neighborhood) in a single value and using it as an abstract value as in [18];
- *Iterative Deepening* [9], which solves successive problems with an increasing value for the initial upper bound α, is a natural way of producing lower bounds: when no solution is found, α is a lower bound;

---

[6] Transfer functions can be also established for *lex-VCSP* (from $\wedge$-*VCSP* and *max-VCSP*) and for *max-VCSP* (from $\wedge$-*VCSP*).

- with a *Best First Branch and Bound* algorithm, at any time, the minimum of the lower bounds of the pending nodes is a lower bound, and, in the same way, any *Depth-Bounded Branch and Bound* algorithm produces a lower bound;
- another approach consists in using an ϵ-*Optimal Branch and Bound* algorithm [14], which guarantees to find a solution whose valuation is less than or equal to $\varphi(P)/\epsilon, 0 < \epsilon < 1$: if e is the valuation of the solution found by such an algorithm, e is an upper bound and $\epsilon.e$ a lower bound;
- *Local Consistency* properties can be used; two directions seem possible; one can use the fact the optimum valuation of a problem is also the valuation of an optimal consistent relaxation, as shown in [16]; it is therefore possible to look for an optimal locally consistent relaxation, whose valuation provides a lower bound; another approach consists in using the *Directional Local Consistency* properties which are exploited in [20, 10];
- finally, any Σ-*VCSP* can be translated into the $0/1$ *Integer Linear Programming* framework [13], which offers several ways of computing lower bounds.

Except with a *Tree-structured* simplification and with *Directional Local Consistency*, computing such lower bounds implies solving one or several *NP-hard* problems. The hope is that, even if these problems remain *NP-hard*, they are simpler to solve than the target problem.

Obviously, it is not possible to assess all these approaches in the framework of this paper. In the next section, we show how it is possible to exploit the simplifications which have been presented in Section 2.1: modification of the valuation structure and relaxation of the less important constraints.

2.4 How to use simplifications

In this section, we describe how the simplifications presented in 2.1 and 2.2 can be used to produce tighter and tighter lower bounds.

To schedule the successive simplifications, we follow an order of increasing complexity, which provides us with an increasing lower bound: from the $\wedge$-*VCSP* to the Σ-*VCSP* valuation structure and, for each valuation structure except for the first, from the maximum to the minimum relaxation level. Each time a simplification is solved, existing transfer functions are used for updating the lower bounds on the target problem P and on the next simplifications. Moreover, each time a simplification finds a better solution, the upper bounds on P and on the next simplifications may be updated. Therefore, some simplifications can be short circuited, either if their optimal valuation can be deduced from the previous simplifications, or if it can be established that solving them will not improve the lower bound on P. This process stops as soon as, on P, the upper bound meets the lower bound. Each simplification is solved by a *Depth First Branch and Bound* algorithm, using *Forward Checking*, and dynamic variable and value orderings. The detection of connected components allows us to speed up each solving, especially with the highest relaxations levels.

Figure 2 illustrates this scheduling on a Σ-*VCSP* which involves constraints whose valuation equals $+\infty$, 1000, 100, 10 or 1, and whose optimal valuation equals 835. Each box is associated with a particular simplification, which is a combination of a constraint

414

relaxation and of a modification of the valuation structure (for example, at the step 5, the simplification $\Phi_{100}^{lex}(P)$ is the result of the application to P of the simplifications Φ_{100} and Φ^{lex}). It contains the optimum of the associated simplification which has been obtained, either by a complete solving (denoted by an encircled step number), or by a deduction from a previous simplification (denoted by an arrow).

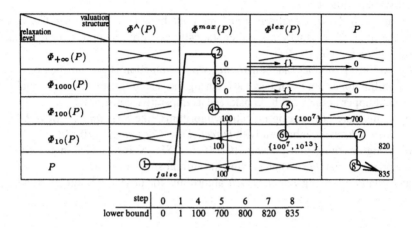

step	0	1	4	5	6	7	8
lower bound	0	1	100	700	800	820	835

Fig. 2. An example of simplification scheduling

The successive simplification steps are:

step 1 the simplification $\Phi^\wedge(P)$ is solved; as it is inconsistent, a first lower bound on the optimum of P, equal to 1, can be deduced, using the transfer function $\Psi^\wedge$;

steps 2-3 the simplifications $\Phi_{+\infty}^{max}(P)$ and $\Phi_{1000}^{max}(P)$ are solved; as they are consistent, we can deduce that the simplifications $\Phi_{+\infty}^{lex}(P)$, $\Phi_{1000}^{lex}(P)$, $\Phi_{+\infty}^{\Sigma}(P)$, and $\Phi_{1000}^{\Sigma}(P)$ are also consistent; they will not be solved;

step 4 the simplification $\Phi_{100}^{max}(P)$ is solved; as it is inconsistent, a second lower bound, equal to 100, can be deduced, using the transfer functions Ψ^{max} and Ψ_{100}; we can also deduce that the simplifications $\Phi_{10}^{max}(P)$ and $\Phi^{max}(P)$ have the same optimal valuation (100); we can avoid solving them;

step 5 the simplification $\Phi_{100}^{lex}(P)$ is solved; as its optimal valuation is $\{100^7\}$ (any optimal solution violates 7 constraints, whose valuation equals 100), a third lower bound, equal to 700, can be deduced, using the transfer functions Ψ^{lex} and Ψ_{100}; we can also deduce that the optimal valuation of the simplification $\Phi_{100}^{\Sigma}(P)$ equals 700; it will not be solved;

step 6 the simplification $\Phi_{10}^{lex}(P)$ is solved; as its optimal valuation is $\{100^7, 10^{13}\}$, a fourth lower bound, equal to 800, can be deduced, using the transfer functions Ψ^{lex} and Ψ_{10}; it is also possible to establish that solving the following lexicographic simplification $\Phi^{lex}(P)$ cannot improve the lower bound on the optimum of P; we can avoid solving it;

step 7 the simplification $\Phi_{10}^{\Sigma}(P)$ is solved; as its optimal valuation equals 820, a fifth lower bound, also equal to 820, can be deduced, using the transfer function Ψ_{10};

step 8 we finally solve the target problem P, whose optimal valuation equals 835.

This scheduling and the resolution of the successive simplifications could be further improved:

- by using a dichotomic order, instead of the sequential order, to process the possibilistic simplifications;
- by applying *Local Consistency Enforcing* methods [12,7], like *Arc Consistency*, to the imperative constraints, either statically as a pre-processing, or dynamically during the search [15,2];
- by exploiting the fact that constraints, whose valuation is greater than or equal to the initial upper bound or becomes, during the search, greater than or equal to the current upper bound, can be considered as imperative constraints;
- by using more efficient optimization algorithms, like *Russian Doll Search* [19] or *Forward Checking* enhanced with *Directed Arc Consistency* [20,10];
- by using *Learning* mechanisms ([6,17] for *CSP*, [5] for *VCSP*), in order to reuse the previous searches, when solving the current simplification;
- and finally, by using *Local Search* algorithms for producing quickly *good* upper bounds.

3 Experiments

3.1 Random VCSPs

The scheduling, which is described above, has been experimented on randomly generated binary Σ-*VCSPs*. Classical parameters were used for generating the problems: number of variables (n), domain size (d), graph connectivity (c) and constraint tightness (t). k different valuations were used for the constraint valuations. Each valuation was associated with the same number of constraints. The constraints which are associated with each valuation were randomly chosen.

We used $n = 15, d = 10, c = 80\%, t$ varying from 10% to 90% in steps of 10%, $k = 4$, with the different valuations in $\{1000, 100, 10, 1\}$, and 100 instances for each value of the parameters.

Figure 3 shows, for a particular problem, the typical evolution of the upper bound which is produced by a classical *Depth First Branch and Bound* algorithm, a *Simulated Annealing* algorithm[7], and of the upper and lower bounds which are produced by solving successive simplifications.

Figure 4 shows the same kind of result for a set of problems: each point corresponds to the mean value, on 100 different problems, of the quality of the bound[8].

Concerning the lower bound which is produced by the successive simplifications, one can observe that it regularly increases and gets very close to the optimum, usually

---

[7] *Simulated Annealing* is not the fastest *Local Search* algorithm we tried, but it is able to get very close to the optimum for a wide range of problems [1].

[8] Let e be the sum of the valuations of the problem constraints. For the upper bound, the measure of the quality is the ratio $(e - ub)/(e - \varphi(P))$. For the lower bound, it is the ratio $lb/\varphi(P)$. These ratios equal 0 at the beginning of the search, and 1 at the end.

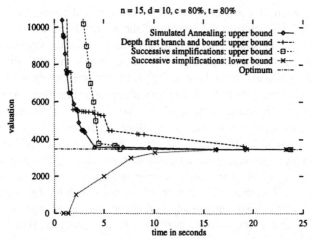

Fig. 3. Upper and lower bound evolutions on a particular problem

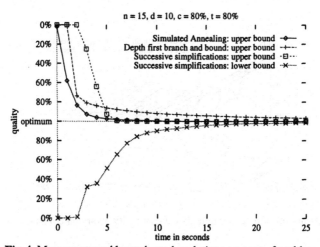

Fig. 4. Mean upper and lower bound evolutions on a set of problems

far before the problem is completely solved by the classical *Depth First Branch and Bound* algorithm. This confirms the interest of the approach: no lower bound is produced by the *Depth First Branch and Bound* algorithm, before it completely solves the problem; within a more limited time, solving the successive simplifications produces very relevant lower bounds. If we look at Fig. 4, we can see that only 10 seconds are needed to be at less than 10% of the optimum with the simplifications, while the mean solving time is about 46 seconds with the *Depth First Branch and Bound* algorithm.

Concerning the upper bounds which are produced, either by the *Depth First Branch and Bound* algorithm, or by the successive simplifications, it is surprising to observe that the latter generally decreases more rapidly than the former. This phenomenon can be explained by the fact that the search trees associated with the successive simplifications are much smaller than the search tree associated with the target problem, and that the search can be consequently much more diversified in the space of the possible assignments. Note that a local search algorithm generally produces even better results, but may be unable to get the optimum.

By varying constraint tightness, Figure 5 shows the mean profiles of the upper and lower bounds which are produced by the successive simplifications on a larger spectrum of problems. This shows that the approach is meaningful on a wide range of problems. However one can observe that the interval which is defined by both the bounds converges more slowly, when constraint tightness increases. This can be explained by the fact that the successive simplifications are more and more difficult to solve.

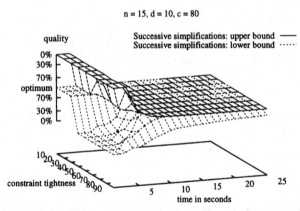

Fig. 5. Mean upper and lower bound evolutions with a varying constraint tigthness

3.2 Real size problems

The French *Centre d'Electronique de l'Armement* (*CELAR*) has made available a set of 11 instances of the *Radio Link Frequency Assignment* problem [4]. These instances have been tackled by several teams, in the framework of the European *EUCLID CALMA* project. Among them, the instances 6,7,8,9 and 10 can be naturally cast as Σ-*VCSPs*.

An *ad hoc* technique was designed during the project, in order to produce lower bounds. It yielded interesting lower bounds on instances 9 and 10, but provided nothing on instances 6, 7 and 8. The instance 6 involves 200 variables, at most 44 values per variable, and 1322 constraints. Like all the *CELAR* instances, it can be preprocessed in order to divide the number of variables by 2. Constraint valuations equal 1000, 100, 10 or 1. It is, with the instance 7, one of the hardest. By now, nobody had been able to produce a guaranteed optimal solution.

Since real problems are usually more structured than random *VCSPs*, an *ad hoc* simplification process, instead of the previously described successive simplifications, has been used, for producing a lower bound on the optimum of this instance: rather than removing constraints whose valuation is lower than a threshold, several strongly inter-connected subproblems[9] have been extracted and solved to optimality. Since all these subproblems involve disjunct subsets of constraints, it is possible to combine their optimal valuations to get a global lower bound of 3389, which is exactly the same as the best known upper bound of 3389.

Conclusion

When a problem is too large and too difficult to be solved to optimality, the traditional approach is to forget optimality and to use *Local Search* algorithms for finding a *good* solution, within a reasonable time. It is however well known, that these algorithms may have a *pathological* behavior on structured instances, that they do not provide any information about the distance to the optimum, and may waste consequently a lot of time trying to improve an optimal solution.

This paper shows that, rather than giving up the idea of getting information about the optimum, one can build lower bounds on this optimum, by solving simplifications of the target problem. We have shown, both on random and real instances, that this approach is effective, even when the optimum is not reachable within the available time.

Finally, we have not considered an important possible use of these lower bounds: at each node, during the search, a high lower bound on the global valuation of the partial associated assignment *i.e.*, on the valuation of the problem restricted by this assignment, is the best means to backtrack early. This may look unreasonnable since nearly all the problems associated with the simplifications we considered are *NP-hard*. However, the *Operations Research* community has shown that such a way may be effective.

References

1. E. Aarts and J. Lenstra, editors. *Local Search in Combinatorial Optimization*. John Wiley & Sons, 1997.
2. C. Bessière and J.C. Régin. MAC and Combined Heuristics: Two Reasons to Forsake FC (and CBJ?). In *Proc. of the 2nd International Conference on Principles and Practice of Constraint Programming (CP-96, LNCS 1118)*, pages 61–75, Cambridge, MA, USA, 1996.

[9] The larger sub-problem involves 22 variables. Globally, about three days were needed to solve all the subproblems, using the *Russian Doll Search* algorithm [19], running on a PVM network of 40 *SPARCstations 4*.

3. S. Bistarelli, U. Montanari, and F. Rossi. Constraint Solving over Semirings. In *Proc. of the 14th International Joint Conference on Artificial Intelligence (IJCAI-95)*, pages 624–630, Montréal, Canada, 1995.
4. CELAR. Radio Link Frequency Assignment Problem Benchmark. URL ftp://ftp.cs.unh.edu/pub/csp/archive/code/benchmarks, 1994. See also http://www-bia.inra.fr/T/schiex or http://www.cert.fr/francais/deri/verfaillie/oc.html.
5. P. Dago and G. Verfaillie. Nogood Recording for Valued Constraint Satisfaction Problems. In *Proc. of the 8th IEEE International Conference on Tools with Artificial Intelligence (ICTAI-96)*, pages 132–139, Toulouse, France, 1996.
6. R. Dechter. Enhancement Schemes for Constraint Processing : Backjumping, Learning and Cutset Decomposition. *Artificial Intelligence*, 41(3):273–312, 1990.
7. E. Freuder. Synthesizing Constraint Expressions. *Communications of the ACM*, 21:958–966, 1978.
8. E. Freuder and R. Wallace. Partial Constraint Satisfaction. *Artificial Intelligence*, 58:21–70, 1992.
9. R. Korf. Depth-First Iterative Deepening: An Optimal Admissible Tree Search. *Artificial Intelligence*, 27:97–109, 1985.
10. J. Larrosa and P. Meseguer. Expoiting the Use of DAC in MAX-CSP. In *Proc. of the 2nd International Conference on Principles and Practice of Constraint Programming (CP-96, LNCS 1118)*, pages 308–322, Cambridge, MA, USA, 1996.
11. J. Larrosa and P. Meseguer. Phase Transition in MAX-CSP. In *Proc. of the 12th European Conference on Artificial Intelligence (ECAI-96)*, pages 190–194, Budapest, Hungary, 1996.
12. A. Mackworth. Consistency in Networks of Relations. *Artificial Intelligence*, 8(1):99–118, 1977.
13. G.L. Nemhauser and L.A. Wolsey. *Integer and Combinatorial Optimization*. John Wiley & Sons, 1988.
14. J. Pearl. *HEURISTICS, Intelligent Search Strategies for Computer Problem Solving*. Addison-Wesley Publishing Company, 1984.
15. D. Sabin and E. Freuder. Contradicting Conventional Wisdom in Constraint Satisfaction. In *Proc. of the 11th European Conference on Artificial Intelligence (ECAI-94)*, pages 125–129, Amsterdam, The Netherlands, 1994.
16. T. Schiex, H. Fargier, and G. Verfaillie. Valued Constraint Satisfaction Problems : Hard and Easy Problems. In *Proc. of the 14th International Joint Conference on Artificial Intelligence (IJCAI-95)*, pages 631–637, Montréal, Canada, 1995.
17. T. Schiex and G. Verfaillie. Nogood Recording for Static and Dynamic Constraint Satisfaction Problems. *International Journal of Artificial Intelligence Tools*, 3(2):187–207, 1994.
18. R. Shrag and D. Miranker. Abstraction and the CSP Phase Transition Boundary. In *Proc. of the 4th International Symposium on Artificial Intelligence and Mathematics*, pages 138–141, Fort Lauderdale, FL, USA, 1996.
19. G. Verfaillie, M. Lemaître, and T. Schiex. Russian Doll Search for Solving Constraint Optimization Problems. In *Proc. of the 13th National Conference on Artificial Intelligence (AAAI-96)*, pages 181–187, Portland, OR, USA, 1996.
20. R. Wallace. Directed Arc Consistency Preprocessing. In *Proc. of the ECAI-94 Workshop on Constraint Processing (LNCS 923)*, pages 121–137. Springer, 1994.
21. R. Wallace. Analysis of Heuristic Methods for Partial Constraint Satisfaction Problems. In *Proc. of the 2nd International Conference on Principles and Practice of Constraint Programming (CP-96, LNCS 1118)*, pages 482–496, Cambridge, MA, USA, 1996.
22. M. Wilson and A. Borning. Hierarchical Constraint Logic Programming. *Journal of Logic Programming*, 16(3):277–318, 1993.

GENIUS-CP:
A Generic Single-Vehicle Routing Algorithm

Gilles Pesant[1], Michel Gendreau[1,2], Jean-Marc Rousseau[1,2,3]

[1] Centre for Research on Transportation,
Université de Montréal,
C.P. 6128, succ. Centre-ville, Montréal, Canada, H3C 3J7
[2] Département d'informatique et de recherche opérationnelle,
Université de Montréal,
C.P. 6128, succ. Centre-ville, Montréal, Canada, H3C 3J7
[3] Les entreprises GIRO inc.,
75, rue de Port-Royal est, bureau 500, Montréal, Canada, H3L 3T1
{pesant,michelg}@crt.umontreal.ca, jeanmarc@giro.ca

Abstract. This paper describes the combination of a well-known TSP heuristic, GENIUS, with a constraint programming model for routing problems. The result, GENIUS-CP, is an efficient heuristic single-vehicle routing algorithm which is generic in the sense that it can solve problems from many different contexts, each with its particular type(s) of constraints. The heuristic quickly constructs high-quality solutions while the constraint model provides great flexibility as to the nature of the problem constraints involved by relieving that heuristic of all constraint satisfaction concerns. We show how those two components are integrated in a clean way with a well-defined, minimal interface. We also describe different routing problems on which this algorithm can be applied and evaluate its performance.

Introduction

Ever since its beginnings in the area of combinatorial optimization, one major advantage of constraint programming (CP) over other methods has been its flexible modeling capabilities. Because of its uniform way of dealing with constraints of all likes, through local propagation, it is able to directly manipulate constraints in the form which most naturally and faithfully models the problem at hand, and quickly adapt to a concrete or new situation featuring *ad hoc* constraints by simply adding them to the model. On the other hand, the natural CP methodology of backtrack search may fail to provide solutions in a reasonable amount of time for some or even most instances of a problem. This lack of robustness can be alleviated somewhat by careful branching decisions but the required insight may not necessarily be available.

The field of operations research has had a long history of heuristic algorithms development in response to difficult combinatorial optimization problems. Heuristic algorithms generally provide near-optimal solutions within a short computing time and tend to scale up well. Their success is usually due to a clever exploitation of the structure of the problem and a good deal of insight. The fact that they are geared toward a particular context also becomes a drawback when faced with an even just slightly different context, such as side constraints: adapting them may demand considerable time, effort, and money.

It is therefore tempting to gain both the flexibility of constraint programming and the efficiency of more conventional heuristic algorithms. The framework for such a combination is a promising area of research, as echoed in a recent survey on applications of constraint programming ([Wal96], p.161). Nevertheless, the efforts outlined in that survey offer more of a juxtaposition than a true combination — some use CP as a preprocessing step for the particular heuristic employed while others use it to "fill in the blanks" once the heuristic has constructed a partial solution (see also the "shuffle" moves of [CL95]). We have proposed in [PG96] a closer interaction of the two in the context of local search methods: as we explore the neighbourhood of some current solution by tree search, constraint propagation is used to both enforce the problem constraints and guide that exploration. This paper promotes the same kind of combination but in the context of a constructive heuristic, GENIUS, in the area of vehicle routing. It also provides numerical results for GENIUS-CP, the implementation of this framework, on different types of routing problems, demonstrating both its efficiency and flexibility.

The rest of the paper is organized as follows. The next section outlines the heuristic algorithm GENIUS. Section 2 is the core of the paper, describing in detail the combination of that heuristic with a constraint model. The resulting algorithm is then applied to several distinct routing problems in section 3. Finally, we conclude with a summary of the contribution and identify perspective research.

1 GENIUS

In this section we describe the routing heuristic used in GENIUS-CP. The traveling salesman problem (TSP) consists of finding a minimum cost tour of a set of cities in which each city is visited exactly once. It is well-known to be NP-complete but because of its practical importance many heuristic algorithms have been developed to rapidly solve instances to near optimality. Among them, GENIUS [GHL92] has been quite successful. It is composed of a tour construction phase and a post-optimization phase.

1.1 GENI: a tour construction heuristic

The heuristic first attempts to build a good initial tour by inserting cities one by one into an originally empty tour. Its novelty lies in the way those insertions are performed. Instead of only considering an insertion between two consecutive cities on the current tour, a generalized insertion (hence the acronym) may take place between any two cities on the current tour. This of course requires repairing the tour, as shown in figure 1. In this sample insertion, let the current

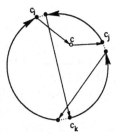

Fig. 1. A generalized insertion

tour be a clockwise walk on the circle. When c is inserted between c_i and c_j, not consecutive, one way the tour may be repaired is by going counterclockwise from c_j to c_i's current successor (thus reversing a segment of the tour), then visiting some c_k and going counterclockwise to c_j's current successor, to finally visit c_k's current successor and then complete the tour. Though more involved, such insertions are much more powerful. In order to cut down on the combinatorics, cities between which an insertion of c is considered are selected among c's closest neighbours. At each step, the current tour is updated with the best generalized insertion.

1.2 US: a post-optimization heuristic

Once an initial tour has been obtained, the heuristic attempts to improve it, again using generalized insertions. Each city is in turn tentatively removed from the tour, using the best reverse generalized insertion, and then inserted back into the tour, using the best generalized insertion. If this leads to an improvement, the move is implemented and the post-optimization phase re-started. The algorithm stops when a complete pass through all cities yields no improvement.

1.3 Adding time windows

The GENIUS heuristic was later adapted to handle time windows at cities: each city must be visited within its own time window (the TSP-TW). These temporal constraints made GENIUS-TW [GHLS95] considerably more specialized and complicated than the original version:

- the need to backtrack appeared as it might prove impossible to insert a city while obeying time windows, due to some bad choice of previous insertions;
- cities with narrow time windows were now inserted first;
- the notion of *closest* neighbour was expanded to represent not only distance but proximity of time windows as well;
- the distinction between neighbour-successor and neighbour-predecessor had to be made, since the orientation of the tour now mattered;
- a *critical departure time* had to be updated at each city to insure feasibility.

2 GENIUS-CP

As we just saw, the introduction of extra constraints (in this case time windows) into the TSP context demanded a restructuring of GENIUS (to provide backtracking capabilities) and the addition of special-purpose code throughout the heuristic in order to ensure feasibility and adjust algorithmic control to the temporal flavour of the problem. Worse yet, the presence of *ad hoc* constraints, often the lot of real-life problems, would complicate further the heuristic, and the problem-specific nature of those constraints may not justify the time and effort required to adapt it. Nevertheless, these real-life problems will not go away on their own and need to be solved.

The idea behind GENIUS-CP is to separate as much as possible the algorithmic part, constructing a good tour, from the declarative part, ensuring the constraints are satisfied. This way the heuristic is kept pure — all additional constraints are dealt with in a uniform manner through constraint propagation.

We show in figure 2 a high-level description of the GENI-CP algorithm — the US-CP algorithm does not contain additional methodological ingredients and so we will concentrate on the former. One city is identified as the *depot* from which the tour starts and ends. Step 1 simply initializes the tour T with two copies of that depot. Step 2 is the main loop which inserts cities. Step 2.1 is where backtracking may occur if the choice of the next city to insert proves unlucky. Step 2.2 declares the constraints for the following subproblem: find a feasible tour on the cities already inserted plus c, the next city to insert. We will come back to it in section 2.1. Step 2.3 attempts each of many types of generalized insertions for that subproblem. Step 2.3.1 is at the heart of the algorithm and we will devote section 2.2 to it. Step 2.4 implements the best insertion and finally step 3 returns the completed tour.

```
1.    T := <origin-depot,destination-depot>;
2.    UNTIL all cities have been inserted
2.1.    choose a city c non-deterministically;
2.2.    create a CP routing model for c and the cities already on T;
2.3.    FOR each insertion type
2.3.1.      perform a branch-and-bound exploration of possible insertions;
2.4.    T := T + the best generalized insertion of c;
3.    Return T;
```

Fig. 2. The GENI-CP algorithm

We now begin to describe how the main components of this algorithm are implemented in a constraint programming framework. Assuming n cities labeled 1 through n are to be inserted, define finite domain variables $\iota_1,\ldots,\iota_n$, each with domain $\{1,\ldots,n\}$, where ι_m is interpreted as the mth city to be inserted. Clearly from that interpretation, $\iota_1,\ldots,\iota_n$ are constrained to take on different values. Let $\mathcal{T}_m$ stand for the partial tour after the mth insertion (with $\mathcal{T}_0$ being the initial tour at step 1); insert($\mathcal{T}_{m-1}, \iota_m, \mathcal{T}_m$) represents the following constraint optimization problem: given a constraint model for $\mathcal{T}_m$, find the least-cost feasible generalized insertion of ι_m into $\mathcal{T}_{m-1}$, yielding $\mathcal{T}_m$. This corresponds to steps 2.2–2.4 in figure 2. A *conditional constraint* $p \Rightarrow q$ enforces the consequent q once the antecedent p is verified. We use the syntax "Var = value" for an antecedent to mean that it is verified when variable Var is instantiated to some value. Our constraint satisfaction problem would then be:

Find a valid assignment of $\iota_1, \ldots, \iota_n$ such that

$$\iota_m \in \{1, \ldots, n\} \qquad \forall\, 1 \le m \le n$$
$$\iota_m \neq \iota_{m'} \qquad \forall\, 1 \le m, m' \le n, \; m < m'$$
$$\iota_m = c \Rightarrow \text{insert}(\mathcal{T}_{m-1}, c, \mathcal{T}_m) \qquad \forall\, 1 \le m \le n,$$

using lexicographic_order as the variable selection rule and fewest_neighbours as the value selection rule. This loosely corresponds to steps 2 and 2.1.

The first rule, lexicographic_order, is self-explanatory and simply spells out the fact that we want to choose the first city to be inserted, then the second one, and so on. The second rule, which expresses how we favour cities for insertion, picks the city that minimizes the total number of possible predecessors and successors for that city.

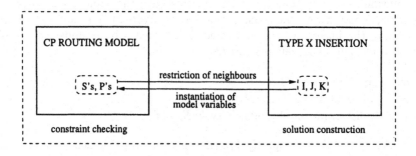

Fig. 3. The interaction between the constraint model and the heuristic

The rest of this section focuses on insert($\mathcal{T}_{m-1}, \iota_m, \mathcal{T}_m$). Figure 3 illustrates the relationship between constraint checking through the model and solution construction through the basic insertion step of the GENIUS heuristic. The next two sections will expand on each component, with the second one particularly stressing their interaction. For now, let us say a few words about the interface. Of the whole routing model, only the successor and predecessor variables (to be introduced shortly) participate directly in the heuristic tour construction. Their constrained domain defines and so restricts the possible neighbours of a city for an insertion; in turn as a tentative insertion materializes, some of the successor and predecessor variables are instantiated.

2.1 The constraint programming routing model

We need to create a separate model for each partial tour, as indicated at step 2.2. To model $\mathcal{T}_m$, we adapted the constraint programming formulation of [PGPR96] for an exact TSP-TW algorithm. We will gradually introduce our model, motivated by the kind of constraints we could wish to express.

Let the origin-depot and destination-depot be identified as 0 and $m+1$, respectively, with cities 1 to m to appear on the tour. Define finite domain variables $S_0, \ldots, S_m$ where S_i represents the immediate successor of i on the tour. Similarly, define variables $P_1, \ldots, P_{m+1}$ for immediate predecessors. Our basic model would be:

$$S_i \in \{1, \ldots, m+1\}, \qquad \forall\, 0 \le i \le m \tag{1}$$

$$P_i \in \{0, \ldots, m\}, \qquad \forall\, 1 \le i \le m+1 \tag{2}$$

$$S_i = j \;\Rightarrow\; P_j = i \qquad \forall\, 0 \le i \le m \tag{3}$$

$$P_j = i \;\Rightarrow\; S_i = j \qquad \forall\, 1 \le j \le m+1 \tag{4}$$

Admittedly, this isn't much and the only potential propagation, in (3)-(4), ensures the consistency of successor/predecessor variables with regard to their interpretation. One would usually expect structural constraints to make sure that the solution is a valid tour (i.e. no two cities have the same successor and no sub-tour is created) but the construction heuristic already guarantees it because of the way the insertions are performed. Even such a bare model nevertheless allows us to express *sequencing constraints*:

- city i must be visited first: $S_0 = i$
- city j must be visited last: $P_{m+1} = j$
- city ℓ must immediately follow city k: $S_k = \ell$

We may also wish to specify *precedence constraints*, which are looser than sequencing constraints: city i must be visited before city j, but not necessarily immediately before. For this purpose, let t_{ij} denote the time it takes to go directly from city i to city j [4] and introduce variables T_i, $i = 1, \ldots, m+1$ representing the time at which we visit city i (T_0 being fixed at 0). Constraint (6) enforces consistency between successor variables and visiting time variables.

$$T_i \in \{0, \ldots, \mathsf{maxTime}\} \qquad \forall\, 1 \le i \le m+1 \tag{5}$$

$$S_i = j \;\Rightarrow\; T_i + t_{ij} \le T_j, \qquad \forall\, 0 \le i \le m \tag{6}$$

Now define set variables $\mathcal{B}_i$ and $\mathcal{A}_i$, $i = 0, \ldots, m+1$, representing the cities which we visit respectively before and after city i. In what follows, the first two

---

[4] In order to simplify the presentation, we will assume that this is the fastest way to get from i to j, though this is not a requirement of the model (see[PGPR96]).

constraints express the fact that each pair $\langle \mathcal{B}_i, \mathcal{A}_i \rangle$ forms a partition while the last one links those set variables to the T_i's:

$$\mathcal{A}_i \cup \mathcal{B}_i = \{0, \ldots, m+1\} \setminus \{i\} \qquad \forall\, 0 \le i \le m+1 \tag{7}$$

$$\mathcal{A}_i \cap \mathcal{B}_i = \emptyset \qquad \forall\, 0 \le i \le m+1 \tag{8}$$

$$T_i + t_{ik} > T_k \;\Rightarrow\; k \in \mathcal{B}_i \wedge i \in \mathcal{A}_k \qquad \forall\, 1 \le i \le m+1,\, 0 \le k \le m,\, i \ne k \tag{9}$$

Stating the earlier precedence constraint now simply amounts to "$i \in \mathcal{B}_j$".

Everything is already in place to express *time window constraints* in the form of lower and upper bounds a_i and b_i on the time we visit city i:

$$a_i \le T_i \le b_i, \qquad \forall\, 1 \le i \le m+1 \tag{10}$$

Using logical connectives, *multiple time windows* can also be handled:

- city i may be visited from 9am to 5pm but not between noon and 1pm: $(9 \le T_i \le 17) \wedge \neg(12 < T_i < 13)$

It is common knowledge that adding redundant constraints to a model often increases the amount of propagation, thus improving inference capabilities, which can make all the difference when tackling combinatorial problems. We reproduce below some powerful redundant constraints for routing/scheduling problems, taken from [PGPR96]. The interested reader may consult that reference for a suitable description of them, as it falls beyond the scope of this paper.

$$T_i + t_{ij} > T_j \;\Rightarrow\; S_i \ne j, \qquad \forall\, 0 \le i,j \le m+1,\, i \ne j \tag{11}$$

$$\mathcal{A}_i \cap \mathcal{B}_j \ne \emptyset \;\Rightarrow\; S_i \ne j, \qquad \forall\, 0 \le i \le m,\, 1 \le j \le m+1, i \ne j \tag{12}$$

$$T_i \ge \min_{k \in \mathrm{dom}(P_i)} (T_k + t_{ki}) \qquad \forall\, 1 \le i \le m+1 \tag{13}$$

$$T_i \le \max_{k \in \mathrm{dom}(S_i)} (T_k - t_{ik}) \qquad \forall\, 0 \le i \le m \tag{14}$$

$$T_i \ge \max_{k \in \mathcal{B}_i}(T_k + t_{ki}) \qquad \forall\, 1 \le i \le m+1 \tag{15}$$

$$T_i \le \min_{k \in \mathcal{A}_i} (T_k - t_{ik}) \qquad \forall\, 0 \le i \le m \tag{16}$$

2.2 The branch-and-bound exploration of insertions

The idea of exploring by depth-first branch-and-bound search a local search space, here the set of tours which can be built using some generalized insertion on the current tour, has already been presented in [PG96]. It is a natural methodology for constraint programming but also for most local search spaces because of their structure. Pruning is achieved when the CP model detects a dead end, discarding an infeasible subset of solutions, or when a lower bound on the cost exceeds that of the best solution so far, discarding an unattractive subset of solutions. We will concentrate here on the interaction between the insertion heuristic and the routing model, using a particular type of insertion as an example.

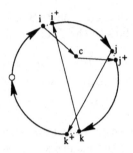

Fig. 4. An insertion which breaks three arcs while preserving orientation

Figure 4 illustrates a generalized insertion which replaces three arcs, (i, i^+), (j, j^+), (k, k^+), by four others, (i, c), (c, j^+), (k, i^+), (j, k^+), thus inserting city c into the tour. The former tour was again the clockwise walk on the circle; the new one is obtained by following the arrows on the tour segments and arcs. Note that this type of insertion preserves the orientation of the tour segments, an asset when confronted with sequencing, precedence or time window constraints.

We will need a bit of notation. Let $\mathcal{T}_{m-1}$ be the current tour (before the mth insertion). i^+ (resp. i^-) stands for the immediate successor (resp. predecessor) of city i on $\mathcal{T}_{m-1}$. We define the following binary constraint on cities of $\mathcal{T}_{m-1}$: $i \prec j$ states that i appears before j on $\mathcal{T}_{m-1}$. The cost associated with arc (i, j) is denoted c_{ij}. Finally, define the unary operator closest_neighbours$(\cdot)$ on successor and predecessor variables which when applied to S_i (resp. P_i) has a behaviour equivalent to sorting the values in its domain, $\{j : j \in \text{dom}(S_i)\}$ (resp. P_i), in non-decreasing order of c_{ij} (resp. c_{ji}) and then removing all but the first ℓ values.

Note that an instance of an insertion of c is totally determined by the value of i, j and k. Examining all insertions therefore amounts to trying all possible combinations of values for i, j, k. In the terminology of [PG96], finite domain variables I, J, K, with domain $\{0, \ldots, m-1\}$ and constraint $I \prec J \prec K$ (since i appears before j which appears before k for this type of insertion), would be our *neighbourhood model*:

$$I, J, K \in \{0, \ldots, m-1\} \tag{17}$$
$$I \prec J \prec K \tag{18}$$

These combinations of values will be implicitly enumerated in a tree search: we first branch on I, then J and finally K. The cost of an insertion is given by

$$(c_{Ic} + c_{cJ^+} + c_{JK^+} + c_{KI^+}) - (c_{II^+} + c_{JJ^+} + c_{KK^+}),$$

the total cost of the arcs we add minus the total cost of the ones we remove. Its smallest possible value will be used as our lower bound and will be refined automatically as the domains of I, J, K shrink (ultimately to a single value).

Recall from section 1.1 that c ends up being inserted between some of its closest neighbours. Consequently even before starting the search, we already know that I and J^+ must be closest neighbours of c (see figure 4):

$$I = \mathsf{closest\_neighbours}(P_c) \tag{19}$$
$$J = \mathsf{closest\_neighbours}(S_c)^- \tag{20}$$

This is principally information traveling from the routing model (the box on the left in figure 3) to the insertion heuristic (the box on the right in the same figure): the successor and predecessor variables, constrained by the model, are used to identify the potential neighbours (instrumental in selecting the arcs to be added and removed) and in so doing restrict the possible values for I and J.

As we try a value for I, say i, lots of information now travels the other way: P_c becomes instantiated as well because of (19); the initial tour segment up to I will remain in the new tour and so the appropriate successor variables can be instantiated. Now that we have a value for I, we may also constrain further K which must be a closest neighbour of i^+.

$$I = i \;\Rightarrow\; \bigwedge_{\ell=0}^{i^-} S_\ell = \ell^+ \tag{21}$$
$$I = i \;\Rightarrow\; K = \mathsf{closest\_neighbours}(P_{i+}) \tag{22}$$

The four conditional constraints below describe the consequences of branching on J and K. As before, information travels to the routing model by instantiating successor variables (constraints (23),(25),(26)) and to the insertion heuristic by restricting the possible values for branching variables (constraint (24)).

$$J = j \;\Rightarrow\; \bigwedge_{\ell=i^+}^{j^-} S_\ell = \ell^+ \tag{23}$$
$$J = j \;\Rightarrow\; K = \mathsf{closest\_neighbours}(S_j)^- \tag{24}$$
$$K = k \;\Rightarrow\; \bigwedge_{\ell=j^+}^{k^-} S_\ell = \ell^+ \tag{25}$$
$$K = k \;\Rightarrow\; \bigwedge_{\ell=k^+}^{n} S_\ell = \ell^+ \tag{26}$$

As we saw, only the S_i's and P_j's in the routing model and the I, J, K variables for the insertion heuristic were involved in the interface.
Our constraint optimization problem $\mathsf{insert}(\mathcal{T}_{m-1}, \iota_m, \mathcal{T}_m)$ finally looks like:

$$\text{Minimize } (c_{I\iota_m} + c_{\iota_m J^+} + c_{JK^+} + c_{KI^+}) - (c_{II^+} + c_{JJ^+} + c_{KK^+})$$

subject to

$$(1) - (16) \qquad \text{(the routing constraints for } \mathcal{T}_m)$$
$$(17) - (26) \qquad \text{(the insertion heuristic constraints)}$$

using lexicographic_order for both the variable and value selection rules on I, J, K.

2.3 On its generic design

In order to make GENIUS-CP generic, we have made the following design choices, which should be compared to the adaptations for GENIUS-TW in section 1.3:

- We provide implicit backtracking when choosing the order of insertions by formulating it as a constraint satisfaction problem, thus allowing the heuristic to recover from unforeseen dead ends.
- Cities to be inserted are selected in non-decreasing number of possible neighbours. This is consistent with the aim found in GENIUS-TW of first dealing with the most difficult cities to insert, and remains a fairly general measure of difficulty since the problem-specific constraints will only *indirectly* affect it by reducing the domain of the appropriate S_i and P_i variables.
- Closest neighbours are determined solely on the basis of the distance (or more generally, cost) involved in reaching them. Since our original pool of neighbours comes from the domain of routing model variables, candidates which would turn out to be incompatible because of problem-specific constraints (such as time windows) should already have been weeded out through propagation.
- The flexibility of distinguishing between neighbour-successor and neighbour-predecessor follows naturally from the use of successor and predecessor variables, respectively, to identify neighbours.
- Several types of insertions are available, both reversing and preserving the orientation of some of the segments of the current tour.

3 Application to routing problems

This section describes three different vehicle routing contexts and reports on the performance of our algorithm on test problems. Emphasis is put on speed and solution quality.

GENIUS-CP was implemented using ILOG Solver 3.2 ([ILO95]) and all tests were performed on a Sun Ultra-1/140. ILOG Solver provided a rich set of primitive constraints (such as set constraints and indexical constraints, which we required) and flexible support for user-defined constraints (another "must" in our case). The fact that it is a C++ library also made the comparison with the existing implementation of GENIUS-TW more fair.

3.1 TSP with (simple) time windows

We considered two sets of symmetric Euclidean problems taken from the literature. The first set considers subproblems of the popular VRPTW benchmark in [Sol87]: the original instances requiring several vehicles, we create our instances by partitioning the cities of each original instance such that every subset can be feasibly visited by a single vehicle. The resulting 27 instances range from 20 to 42 cities. Cities feature a semi-clustered distribution (the rc200 problems) and some instances have a narrow time window on every city while others only have a few cities with a meaningful time window. For the second set, we selected from [DDGS95] 10 instances on 40 cities with time windows of moderate width (the $n = 40; w = 60$ and $n = 40; w = 80$ problems).

The routing constraints used by our algorithm were (1)-(6),(10); in only two instances did the addition of the redundant constraints (11)-(16) and their accompanying constraints (7)-(9) give better results, which we used.

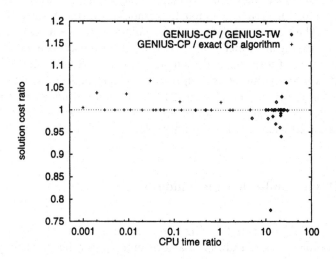

Fig. 5. Comparison of GENIUS-CP with related algorithms on TSP-TW benchmarks

We compared GENIUS-CP with an already existing, efficient implementation of GENIUS-TW and the exact CP algorithm described in [PGPR96] which essentially exhibits the same routing model as our algorithm but adopts a branch-and-bound strategy with a carefully designed variable-ordering heuristic. The graph at figure 5 shows the relative performance of GENIUS-CP with respect to the other two. Each instance is represented by a point whose x-coordinate corresponds to the fraction of the computation time for the exact algorithm (resp. GENIUS-TW) which is spend by GENIUS-CP (note the logarithmic scale) and whose y-coordinate indicates how far from the optimum (resp. GENIUS-TW's solution) our heuristic solution is.

Turning first to the comparison with the specialized heuristic, we note that a bit more than one order of magnitude is lost in speed, the price to pay for a generic heuristic capable of handling much more. The points tend to be clustered in the time axis since the GENIUS heuristic at the basis of both is quite robust in terms of execution time. The solution cost ratio indicates that each algorithm has instances on which it produces a better solution than the other, though GENIUS-CP appears a more regular winner. This may be due to the greater variety of insertion types in our algorithm, particularly the ones which preserve the orientation of route segments.

Moving on to the comparison with the exact algorithm, we observe that our algorithm is generally faster, as expected, and often *much* faster: ratios shown on the graph range from 5 to 0.001. The instances which are solved with comparable or even faster execution times by the exact algorithm correspond to the smaller or heavily constrained ones — the larger and "looser" instances usually require considerably more computation time. In fact, 10 of the 37 instances could not be solved by the exact algorithm within one day of computation and so are not accounted for on the graph, though they should appear at the extreme left if not beyond. The horizontal spread of the points indicates a lack of robustness for the exact algorithm, which makes GENIUS-CP's robustness a clear advantage: in absolute terms, the mean and standard deviation for the execution time of GENIUS-CP over all instances are respectively 89 and 62 seconds whereas for the exact algorithm they are 11 412 and 24 043 seconds. In addition, the heuristic solution is very often optimal and, except in one case, always within 3.8% of the optimum, an indication that high-quality solutions are produced by our heuristic.

3.2 TSP with multiple time windows

Allowing a city to be visited during one of several disjoint time intervals adds sufficient complexity for traditional algorithmic approaches that very little has been published on it yet. Accordingly, no problem set is known to us. We therefore generated our instances, by fragmenting the time windows in the first set of problems of the previous section. Fragmentation takes place in four different ways for each original instance: a few small gaps in the original window, one big gap of about half the window, nine gaps totaling about half the window, and a mix of the above. We therefore generated 108 instances — of these, some may of course have become infeasible. The graph at figure 6 shows the relative performance of our algorithm with respect to the exact algorithm, on the 55 instances which could be solved by both algorithms (comparison with GENIUS-TW is no longer possible since it cannot handle multiple time windows).

The routing constraints were the same as in the previous section and the redundant constraints were added for 12 instances. Here as well we note an important difference in execution time and robustness. Many of the heuristic solutions are optimal or near-optimal; nevertheless in three instances we are between 10% and 16% above the optimum, which is poor performance.

For 4 other instances solved by the exact algorithm, GENIUS-CP could not terminate within a reasonable number of backtracks; for 25 other instances solved by GENIUS-CP, the exact algorithm was interrupted after one day of computation, without having found the optimal solution. This means that 25 more points, about half of the number already on the graph, should appear at the extreme left of that graph, which adds considerable weight to the claim of greater efficiency and robustness.

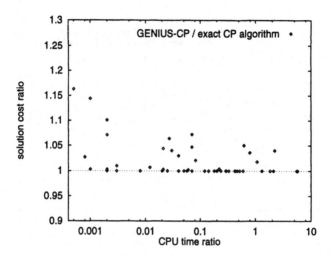

Fig. 6. Comparison of GENIUS-CP with the exact algorithm on TSP-MTW benchmarks

3.3 Pick-up and delivery problems

In this setting, cities come in pairs $\langle c_p, c_d \rangle$ — some goods are picked up at c_p, to be delivered at c_d. Obviously, this imposes a precedence constraint: c_p must be visited before c_d. For a problem of size n we will therefore have $\frac{n}{2}$ precedence constraints, which is quite a few. This serves as a test to see whether the GENIUS heuristic, not designed with this context in mind, can be called upon to provide good-quality solutions, with the routing model handling those additional constraints.

In general, the pick-up and delivery problem with time windows (PDPTW) involves several vehicles and depots as well as time window, precedence and capacity constraints (for a recent survey, see [DDSS95]). We consider the single-vehicle case, 1-PDPTW, without capacity constraints (though such constraints could be easily added to the routing model). To our knowledge there exists no established benchmark for that problem: what one finds in the literature tends to be isolated real-life problems. We therefore generated our problem set using the simulator described in [GGPS97] for a dynamic vehicle dispatching system and made the instances static by knowing all requests ahead of time. We randomly generated 10 instances on 30 cities (15 pick-up/delivery pairs) and 5 instances on 40 cities, each exhibiting fairly wide time windows. The full routing model was used.

Of the 15 instances, one could not be solved by GENIUS-CP within a reasonable number of backtracks. On the other hand, the exact algorithm did not terminate on any of the instances within the fixed limit of one day of computation. Consequently, we present the results in a different way. The graph at figure 7 shows the relative progression over time of the solution cost for the exact al-

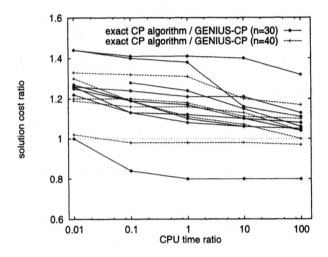

Fig. 7. Comparison of GENIUS-CP with the exact algorithm on pick-up and delivery problems with time windows

gorithm with respect to the cost of the solution found by GENIUS-CP. Note that ratios are taken here as "exact/heuristic". It reveals that in all but two (or *in extremis* three) instances, the quality of the heuristic solution significantly exceeds that of the exact algorithm, even given 100 times more computation time for the latter (the corresponding lines in the graph lie strictly above the dotted line at 1). The average computation time for GENIUS-CP over $n = 30$ and $n = 40$ instances were respectively 152 and 640 seconds.

Conclusion

We have shown in this paper how constraint programming and a conventional heuristic algorithm can be combined to offer the best of both worlds: flexibility, solution quality, efficiency and robustness. Experimental results in three different vehicle routing contexts support our claims. Comparing our algorithm with an exact CP algorithm using the same constraint model but with a branch-and-bound strategy demonstrated the advantage of incorporating a successful solution strategy from operations research.

The investigation of similar combinations of constraint models with other heuristics is clearly an interesting path to follow. In the area of vehicle routing, an appropriate heuristic for problems with multiple vehicles appears the next logical move.

434

Acknowledgments

Financial support for this research was provided by the Natural Sciences and Engineering Research Council of Canada (NSERC).

References

[CL95]   Y. Caseau and F. Laburthe.   Disjunctive Scheduling with Task Intervals.   Technical Report 95-25, Laboratoire d'informatique de l'École Normale Supérieure, Département de mathématiques et d'informatique, 45 rue d'Ulm, 75230 Paris Cedex 05, France, 1995.

[DDGS95] Y. Dumas, J. Desrosiers, É. Gélinas, and M.M. Solomon. An Optimal Algorithm for the Traveling Salesman Problem with Time Windows. *Operations Research*, 43(2):367–371, 1995.

[DDSS95] J. Desrosiers, Y. Dumas, M.M. Solomon, and F. Soumis. Time Constrained Routing and Scheduling. In M.O. Ball, T.L. Magnanti, C.L. Monma, and Nemhauser G.L., editors, *Network Routing*, volume 8 of *Handbooks in Operations Research and Management Science*, pages 35–139. North-Holland, Amsterdam, 1995.

[GGPS97] M. Gendreau, F. Guertin, J.-Y. Potvin, and R. Séguin. A Tabu Search Algorithm for a Vehicle Dispatching Problem. Working paper, 1997.

[GHL92]   M. Gendreau, A. Hertz, and G. Laporte. New Insertion and Postoptimization Procedures for the Traveling Salesman Problem. *Operations Research*, 40:1086–1094, 1992.

[GHLS95] M. Gendreau, A. Hertz, G. Laporte, and M. Stan. A Generalized Insertion Heuristic for the Traveling Salesman Problem with Time Windows. Publication CRT-95-07, Centre de recherche sur les transports, Université de Montréal, Montréal, 1995. To appear in *Operations Research*.

[ILO95]   ILOG S.A., 12, Avenue Raspail, BP7, 94251 Gentilly Cedex, France. *ILOG SOLVER: Object-oriented constraint programming*, 1995.

[PG96]   G. Pesant and M. Gendreau. A View of Local Search in Constraint Programming. In *Principles and Practice of Constraint Programming — CP96: Proceedings of the Second International Conference*, volume 1118 of *Lecture Notes in Computer Science*, pages 353–366. Springer-Verlag, Berlin, 1996.

[PGPR96] G. Pesant, M. Gendreau, J.-Y. Potvin, and J.-M. Rousseau. An Exact Constraint Logic Programming Algorithm for the Traveling Salesman Problem with Time Windows. Publication CRT-96-15, Centre de recherche sur les transports, Université de Montréal, Montréal, 1996. To appear in *Transportation Science*.

[Sol87]   M.M. Solomon. Algorithms for the Vehicle Routing and Scheduling Problem with Time Window Constraints. *Operations Research*, 35:254–265, 1987.

[Wal96]   M. Wallace. Practical Applications of Constraint Programming. *Constraints*, 1:139–168, 1996.

Satisfiability of Quantitative Temporal Constraints with Multiple Granularities*

Claudio Bettini[1], X. Sean Wang[2], Sushil Jajodia[2]

[1] Dept. of Information Science (DSI), Univ. of Milan, Italy. bettini@dsi.unimi.it
[2] Dept. of Information & Software Systems Engineering, George Mason Univ., Fairfax, VA. {xywang,jajodia}@isse.gmu.edu

Abstract. Most work on temporal constraints has ignored the subtleties involved in dealing with multiple time granularities. This paper considers a constraint satisfaction problem (CSP) where binary quantitative constraints in terms of different time granularities can be specified on a set of variables, and unary constraints are allowed to limit the domain of variables. Such a CSP cannot be trivially reduced to one of the known CSP problems. The main result of the paper is a complete algorithm for checking consistency and finding a solution. The complexity of the algorithm is studied in the paper under different assumptions about the granularities involved in the CSP, and a second algorithm is proposed to improve the efficiency of the backtracking process needed to obtain all the solutions of the CSP.

1 Introduction

A *constraint satisfaction problem* (CSP) is defined by (i) a set of variables each with an associated domain of possible values and (ii) a set of constraints on the variables. When variables are used to represent event occurrences and constraints to represent their temporal relations, we are dealing with a *temporal* CSP. Several problems in scheduling, planning, diagnosis, and natural language understanding can be formulated in terms of temporal CSPs. In practical applications, temporal CSPs often involve constraints in terms of multiple granularities. The reason may either be that data are obtained from different sources or that the application has an inherent requirement for multiple granularities. For example, the scheduling problem for an express mail company has to deal with constraints on pick-up and delivery events in terms of hours, particular sets of hours (e.g., nights), business days, etc.

Well-known algorithms for CSPs are so called path- and arc-consistency algorithms [Mon74,Mac77]. Specializations of these algorithms for temporal CSPs have also been proposed (e.g., [All83,vBC90,DMP91,Mei96]). However, most of the work on temporal CSPs has ignored the subtleties involved in the presence of multiple time granularities. The underlying assumption seems to be that the

---

* The work of Wang and Jajodia was partially supported by the National Science Foundation under the grant IRI-9633541.

problem is easily reduced to a single-granularity CSP. This is true if granularities are simply used to describe specific, fixed time intervals or time instants. For example, in [Lad87] different granularities are allowed to describe specific intervals of time instead of using pairs of real numbers, and it is shown that the set of intervals defined through granularities forms a canonical model of Allen's interval calculus [All83]. It follows that the standard polynomial algorithm in [All83] can be applied to reason about these intervals. The constraints considered in this approach are the standard qualitative relations among intervals (e.g., *before*, *overlaps*, ...). Another work considering CSPs involving granularities is [PB91], in which each relation between an interval I and a specific *date* expressed using different granularities (e.g., second business day of first month of 1997-th year) is converted into a constraint between the endpoints of I and the specific instants of the absolute time identified by the date. This conversion is clearly feasible, and, hence, standard algorithms for CSPs without granularities can be applied.

This paper focuses on temporal CSPs supporting relative, quantitative (distance) relationships expressed in terms of multiple granularities. For example, we can represent the constraint enforcing that the event of a package delivery occurs within 2 business days from the occurrence of the pick-up event. Note that in this constraint the granularity is used to define a temporal relation giving the relative distance between events. We limit granularities to those that exhibit a periodic behavior. Hours, days, weeks, business days, business months, fiscal years are common examples. The temporal CSP is defined by binary quantitative constraints, possibly in terms of different periodic granularities, on a set of variables, and by unary constraints on the domain of variables. Unary constraints can be useful, for example, to impose when an event should occur. Referring to the examples given earlier, a unary constraint could impose that the delivery of a package should only occur in business days.

From the results in [BWJ], where temporal constraints with granularities were first defined, it follows that, even if constraints on the domains are excluded, the consistency problem is NP-hard when arbitrary periodic granularities are allowed [BWJ], while the corresponding single-granularity problem is in PTIME [DMP91]. We propose an arc-consistency algorithm that is complete for consistency checking and we show that the algorithm takes polynomial time when the time granularities in the constraints are considered as known by the system on which the algorithm is run (i.e., the description of granularities is not given as part of the CSP). Note that most practical applications can satisfy this condition. We show that the algorithm provides also a solution to the set of constraints. Other properties are investigated and path consistency techniques are proposed to optimize the backtracking process needed to find all solutions. The arc-consistency algorithm is essentially an extension of AC-3 [MFE85] to deal with possibly infinite (but periodic) domains and with constraints in terms of multiple periodic granularities.

As a side contribution, this paper also provides some new results when applied to a CSP with single granularity: arc-consistency is complete and polynomial for consistency checking of STP [DMP91] extended to disjunctive constraints on the domains[1]. The disjunction can be defined using a finite set of intervals, or using the intervals implicitly denoted by a known periodic granularity, so that only the instants within these intervals can instantiate the constrained variable. A similar result (limited to a finite set of intervals) has been recently found independently [SD]. Other researchers [Lad86,MR93] have investigated temporal CSPs involving *non-convex* intervals and periodic intervals, however the considered CSPs are substantially different since their variables must be instantiated with intervals (as opposed to instants in our framework) and only qualitative relations (among intervals) are allowed in the CSP.

In the next section we formalize the concept of periodic granularities. In Section 3 we define our temporal CSP and we provide a complete algorithm for consistency checking. In Section 4, we show that the algorithm also provides a solution, and propose an approximate algorithm to optimize the backtracking process needed to find all solutions. In Section 5 we provide some complexity results. We conclude the paper in Section 6. The Appendix sketches the implementation of the operations on periodic granularities needed for our algorithms, and reports the proofs.

2 Preliminaries

We adopt the notion of *temporal types* ([BWJ]) to formalize time granularities.

Definition 1. A *temporal type* is a mapping μ from the set of the positive integers $\mathcal{N}$ to $2^{\mathcal{R}}$ (the set of absolute time sets) such that for all positive integers i and j with $i < j$, both of the following two conditions are satisfied:
(1) $\mu(i) \neq \emptyset$ and $\mu(j) \neq \emptyset$ imply that each real number in $\mu(i)$ is less than all the real numbers in $\mu(j)$,
(2) $\mu(i) = \emptyset$ implies $\mu(j) = \emptyset$.

Property (1) states that the mapping must be *monotonic*. Property (2) disallows an empty set to be the value of a mapping for a certain time tick $\mu(i)$ unless the empty set will be the value of the mapping for all subsequent time ticks. Intuitive temporal types, such as day, month, week and year, satisfy the above definition. The definition allows *non-standard* temporal types with non-contiguous ticks (e.g., b-day representing business days) and with non-convex sets as ticks (e.g., b-month, where each business month is the union of all b-days in that month).

If μ and ν are temporal types, then μ is said to *group into* ν, denoted $\mu \trianglelefteq \nu$, if for each non-empty tick $\nu(j)$, there exist a (possibly infinite) set S of positive integers such that $\nu(j) = \bigcup_{i \in S}^{k} \mu(i)$. Intuitively, $\mu \trianglelefteq \nu$ means that each tick of ν is a union of some ticks of μ. For example, day$\trianglelefteq$week since a week is composed of 7 days and day$\trianglelefteq$b-day since each business day is a day. The set of all temporal types is a partial order with respect to $\trianglelefteq$, and, for each pair of temporal types μ and ν, there exists a unique greatest lower bound with respect to $\trianglelefteq$, denoted $glb_{\trianglelefteq}(\mu, \nu)$.

---

[1] Note that no disjunction is allowed on binary constraints among variables.

We are particularly interested in periodic temporal types since they have finite representations.

Definition 2. Let μ and ν be temporal types such that $\mu \trianglelefteq \nu$. Then ν is said to be *periodic relative to* μ if there exist (i) a positive integer I (index), (ii) a positive integer N (displacement), and (iii) a non-negative integer P (period) such that for each $i \geq I$, if $\nu(i) = \bigcup_{r=0}^{k} \mu(j_r)$ for some $j_0, \ldots, j_k$, then $\nu(i+N) = \bigcup_{r=0}^{k} \mu(j_r + P)$.

Informally, the ticks of ν before index I are arbitrary sets of ticks of μ (preserving monotonicity of ν). Starting from I, the ticks of ν can be seen as having a repetition of groups, each group having N ticks and all groups behaving similarly, namely, if tick $\nu(i)$ contains certain ticks of μ, then tick $\nu(i + N)$ will contain these ticks of μ shifted by P, where P is the distance, in terms of ticks of μ, between the first ticks of two neighboring groups.

Example 3. The type weekend-day denoting all Saturdays and Sundays is periodic relative to hour, assuming the first hour of a *Sunday* as the first tick in our timeline. Indeed, weekend-day$(1) = \bigcup_{r=0}^{23}$ hour$(r + 1)$, weekend-day$(2) = \bigcup_{r=0}^{23}$ hour$(r + 1 + 6 * 24)$, and weekend-day(i) for $i \geq 3$ is given by the formula in the above definition by using $I = 1$, $N = 2$, and $P = 7 * 24$. For example, weekend-day$(4) = \bigcup_{r=0}^{23}$ hour$(r + 1 + 6 * 24 + 7 * 24)$.

The definition is flexible enough to include all types with a finite number of non-empty ticks.

In order to simplify our discussion, in the rest of the paper we assume that second is a *primitive* temporal type such that each temporal type we consider is periodic relative to second. Furthermore, we shall say that a set of positive integers S is *periodic* if there exists a periodic temporal type μ such that $S = \{i | \text{second}(i) \subseteq \mu(j) \text{ for some } j\}$.

A conversion operation $\lceil z \rceil^\mu$ allows to obtain the tick of μ including the z-th second. $\lceil z \rceil^\mu$ is undefined if second$(z) \not\subseteq \nu(z')$ for all z', as in the case in which μ is b-day and z is a second falling in a Sunday.

3 Constraint networks with multiple granularities

We start with the definition of a temporal constraint with granularity.

Definition 4. Let $m, n \in Z \cup \{-\infty, +\infty\}$ with $m \leq n$ and μ a temporal type. Then $[m, n]\, \mu$, called a *temporal constraint with granularity* (*TCG*), is the binary relation on positive integers defined as follows: For positive integers t_1 and t_2, $(t_1, t_2) \models [m, n]\mu$ ((t_1, t_2) *satisfies* $[m, n]\mu$) iff (1) $\lceil t_1 \rceil^\mu$ and $\lceil t_2 \rceil^\mu$ are both defined, and (2) $m \leq (\lceil t_2 \rceil^\mu - \lceil t_1 \rceil^\mu) \leq n$.

Intuitively, for instants t_1 and t_2 (in terms of seconds), t_1 and t_2 satisfy $[m, n]\, \mu$ if the difference of the integers t_1' and t_2' is between m and n (inclusive), where $\mu(t_1')$ and $\mu(t_2')$ are the ticks of μ (if exist) that cover, respectively, the

t_1-th and t_2-th seconds. That is, the instants t_1 and t_2 are first translated in terms of μ, and then the difference is taken. If the difference is at least m and at most n, then the pair of instants is said to satisfy the constraint. For example, the pair (t_1, t_2) satisfies $[0, 0]$ day if t_1 and t_2 are within the same day. Similarly, (t_1, t_2) satisfies $[-1, 1]$ hour if t_1 and t_2 are at most one hour apart (and the order of them is immaterial). Finally, (t_1, t_2) satisfies $[1, 1]$ month if t_2 is in the next month with respect to t_1.

We now define constraint networks with multiple periodic granularities.

Definition 5. A *constraint network (with granularities)* is a directed graph (W, A, Γ, Dom), where W is a finite set of variables, $A \subseteq W \times W$, Γ is a mapping from A to the finite sets of TCGs, and Dom is a mapping from W to periodic sets.

Intuitively, a constraint network specifies a complex temporal relationship where each variable in W represents a specific instant (for example the occurrence time of an event). Any instant assigned to a variable X must be contained in the periodic set specified by Dom for X. The set of TCGs assigned to an edge is taken as conjunction. That is, for each TCG in the set assigned to the edge (X, Y), the instants assigned to X and Y must satisfy the TCG. Figure 1 shows an example of a constraint network with granularities with no explicit constraint on domains ($Dom(X) = [1, \infty)$ for each variable X).

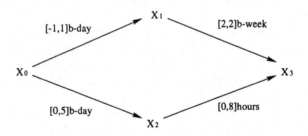

Fig. 1. A constraint network with granularities.

It is important to note that it is not always possible to convert a TCG $[m, n]\,\mu$, with $\mu \neq$ second, into a TCG in seconds (i.e., as $[m', n']$ second for any m' and n'). Indeed, consider $[0, 0]$ day. Two instants satisfy the constraint if they fall within the same day. In terms of second, they could differ from 0 seconds to $24 * 60 * 60 - 1 = 86399$ seconds. However, $[0, 86399]$ second does not reflect the original constraint. For example, if instant t_1 corresponds to 11pm of one day and instant t_2 to 4am in the next day, then t_1 and t_2 do not satisfy $[0, 0]$ day; however, they do satisfy $[0, 86399]$ second. When constraints are in terms of simple granularities, it may be possible to convert a constraint network with multiple granularities into an equivalent one with a single granularity, provided that new nodes and constraints can be added and that domains can be conveniently restricted. However, it is not clear if and how this could be accomplished when constraints involving non-standard granularities (e.g., b-day) are present in the network.[2]

Definition 6. A network $N = (W, A, \Gamma, Dom)$ is consistent if there exists an assignment Σ from each variable X in W into a single value of $Dom(X)$ such that all the TCGs in Γ are satisfied. The assignment Σ is called a *solution* of N.

Definition 7. Two networks are equivalent if they have the same set of solutions.

A subclass of these networks where no constraint is imposed on the domain of the variables and values in TCGs are restricted to be positive and finite has been considered in [BWJ]. It is shown that even for that class of networks the consistency problem is NP-hard and approximate solutions are proposed. Here we show that to obtain a complete consistency algorithm for that class of networks it is necessary to consider implicit constraints on the domains of the variables. Figure 2 shows an example of a constraint network[3] whose inconsistency would not be detected by the algorithms in [BWJ]. To detect the inconsistency, an algorithm has to recognize that the domain of variable X_2 is implicitly constrained to be **February**, and hence recognize that the TCG on (X_2, X_3) is unsatisfiable.

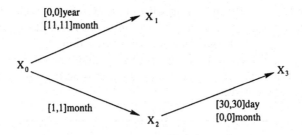

Fig. 2. An inconsistent constraint network.

The following proposition justifies the use of a primitive type as discussed earlier with respect to the solutions of a network. Indeed, the algorithms we are going to present do not rely on the particular choice we made for a primitive type.

---

[2] Consider the constraint $[1,1]$ b-day between variables X and Y and its conversion into an equivalent network with TCGs only in terms of **hour**. Even introducing new variables with domain constrained to beginning/ending of business days, the conversion does not seem to be possible. In this example, whether two event occurrences that are 49 hours apart satisfy the TCG $[1,1]$ b-day or the TCG $[3,3]$ b-day depends on their specific occurrence time.

[3] In this network domains are not explicitly constrained.

Proposition 8. *Let N be a network. If $\mu \unlhd \nu$ for each temporal type ν appearing in N and $(t_1, \ldots, t_n)$ is a solution for N, then any tuple $(t'_1, \ldots, t'_n)$, where $\lceil t'_i \rceil^\nu = \lceil t_i \rceil^\nu$ for each $i = 1, \ldots, n$, is also a solution of N.*

Example 9. Consider the network in Figure 1, where hour groups into all the types appearing in that network. Using an intuitive representation of the index of hour the following is a solution of the network: (X_0=10/7/96:01, X_1=10/4/96:01, X_2=10/14/96:01, X_3=10/14/96:09). This solution represents the set of solutions obtained changing any of the indexes assigned to a variable with any **second** included in the tick of hour identified by that index.

We assume that the set M of types used in the networks is fixed and their definition is given with respect to $\mu = \unlhd\text{-}glb(M)$ (if not, it is easy to transform the definitions to satisfy this condition). In this case a solution is identified by the assignment of the index of a tick of μ to each variable.

Figure 3 shows the algorithm. Without loss of generality, we assume that for each TCG $[m, n]\,\mu$ on arc (X_l, X_k), the TCG $[-n, -m]\,\mu$ exists on arc (X_k, X_l). Basically, the algorithm non-deterministically picks up an arc (X_l, X_k) and uses the domain for X_k to restrict the domain of X_l. This is achieved by the operation $Dom(X_k) \uplus TCGs(X_k X_l)$ that is defined as returning the set $\{t_l \mid \exists t_k \in Dom(X_k)$ and $(t_k, t_l) \models TCGs(X_k X_l)\}$. This ensures that for each value t_l in the domain of X_l, there is a value t_k in the domain of X_k such that (t_k, t_l) satisfies all the TCGs on arc (X_k, X_l). Any other value in the domain of X_l is discarded. Since we are dealing with possibly infinite domains the equality and inequality tests in the algorithms are limited by a finite constant MAX.[4] It is easy to see that if all the temporal types and domains are periodic in the input network, then each step of AC can be carried out effectively. Indeed, we can show that both operations $\uplus$ and $\cap$ are effective and preserve periodicity of the domains (see Appendix).

$Q := \{(X_i, X_j) \mid (X_i, X_j) \in A\}$
while $Q \neq \emptyset$ **do**
  1. select and delete an arc (X_l, X_k) from Q
  2. **if** $Dom(X_l) \neq^{MAX} Dom(X_l) \cap (Dom(X_k) \uplus \Gamma(X_k, X_l))$ **then**
      2.1. $Q := Q \cup \{(X_i, X_l) \mid (X_i, X_l) \in A, i \neq k\}$
      2.2. $Dom(X_l) := Dom(X_l) \cap (Dom(X_k) \uplus \Gamma(X_k, X_l))$
  3. **if** $Dom(X_l) =^{MAX} \emptyset$ **then** $Q := \emptyset$; $Dom(X_l) := \emptyset$
end while

Fig. 3. Arc-consistency (AC) algorithm.

We now show that AC terminates and is complete, i.e. it always discovers if the input network is inconsistent.

---

[4] $S_1 \neq^{MAX} S_2$ ($S_1 =^{MAX} S_2$ resp.) means that S_1 and S_2 are different (equal resp.) if only numbers no greater than MAX are considered.

Proposition 10. *The AC algorithm reaches quiescence in a finite number of steps for each positive integer MAX.*

For a given network N, we look for MAX such that if N has a solution, it must have a solution consisting of positive integers not greater than MAX.

Proposition 11. *Given a constraint network $N = (W, A, \Gamma, Dom)$, let $Lcm_P = lcm(P_1, \ldots, P_k)$ where $P_1, \ldots, P_k$ are the (non-zero) periods of types in Γ, $maxI = max\{i \mid i \in \nu_j(I_j)$ with ν_j among the types in Γ and the periodic sets (viewed as a periodic type) in Dom, and I_j the index of $\nu_j\}$, max-dist the maximum finite distance between any two variables (not necessarily connected by a single arc) as determined using Γ. Then, in the general case (i), $MAX = maxI + Lcm_P * 2 * (max\text{-}dist + 1) * |W|$; if all TCGs have finite ranges (ii), $MAX = maxI + Lcm_P * max\text{-}dist$.*
If a solution of N exists, there exists one such that each value assigned to a variable is not greater than MAX.

Theorem 12. *If AC is applied to network N with MAX fixed as in Proposition 11, N is consistent iff no domain revised by AC becomes empty.*

4   Network Solutions

A solution for a network is easily obtained taking as value for each variable, the minimum value in the domain of that variable as obtained by the AC algorithm.

Theorem 13. *Let (W, A, Γ, Dom') be the network obtained by running AC on network N, and let min_x (max_x, resp.) be the minimum (maximum, resp.) value in $Dom'(X)$ for each variable in W (if they exist and are finite). Then, the assignment of min_x (max_x, resp.) to X for each variable X is a solution of N.*

The problem of finding all solutions turns out to be more difficult with respect to similar networks with single granularity. An interesting negative result is that it is not possible to obtain an equivalent network shrinking TCGs and domains so that, given values t_x and t_y for variables X and Y satisfying the TCGs on (XY), we are guaranteed to find a value for any variable on a path from X to Y satisfying the TCGs on the arcs in the path. This property is usually called path-consistency (see e.g., [DMP91]), and in the case of constraints without granularities it can be achieved by *relaxation* algorithms (also known as *path consistency* algorithms) in cubic time [Mon74,Mac77,MFE85]. The negative result is shown by the following example.

Example 14. Consider a network with variables X, Y and Z with unconstrained domains and the following TCGs: $[0,0]$ week and $[0,2]$ day on (X,Y), $[0,1]$ week and $[0,5]$ day on (Y,Z), $[0,1]$ week and $[0,7]$ day on (X,Z). If we take a Saturday as the value for X and the next Saturday as the value for Z, we satisfy the TCGs on arc (X,Z). However, no value for Y can satisfy the TCGs on the path

$(X, Y), (Y, Z)$ with the above fixed values for X, Z. Hence, the network is not path-consistent and cannot be made path-consistent since any range restriction of a TCG or any domain restriction would exclude a potential solution.

This result implies that constraint networks with multiple granularities are not *decomposable*, a property that allows to find network solutions without back-tracking [DMP91]. Since it is unlikely that backtracking can be avoided, if we are interested in more than one solution it becomes crucial to reduce as much as possible the cardinality of the domains and the ranges of the TCGs without changing the set of solutions. This process is usually known as finding the *minimal network*. In [BWJ] path consistency techniques are used to reduce TCGs ranges obtaining an approximate algorithm for consistency and minimal network. The effectiveness of path consistency as an approximation technique in temporal CSPs has been shown, among other papers, in [vBC90] and [DMP91]. Here we propose to extend those techniques to constraint networks with periodic domains and to integrate them with the complete AC algorithm given above. Figure 4 shows the new algorithm.

1. For each TCG in N derive implicit TCGs in terms of the other types in the network and intersect them with the one possibly present on the same arc.
2. Let N_μ be the network N resulting from Step 2 considering only the TCGs in terms of μ. For each $\mu \in M$, compute the minimal network of N_μ and obtain N as the union of the minimal networks.
3. Apply the AC algorithm to N.
4. For each arc (XY), substitute each TCG $[m, n] \nu$ on (XY) with $Shrink([m, n] \nu, Dom(X), Dom(Y))$
5. Return **inconsistent** if (i) a TCG range is empty, or (ii) a domain is empty; Return N if no new TCGs or domains have been derived in Steps 1–4; Otherwise go to Step 1.

Fig. 4. AC+PC algorithm.

Step 1 is based on granularity conversion; for example, from a TCG $[0, 0]$ day we can easily derive TCGs $[0, 23]$ hour and $[0, 0]$ week on the same arc. The technicalities of these conversions can be found in [BWJ]. Step 2 is based on standard path-consistency algorithms, that for the single-granularity networks N_μ ensure to return a minimal network [DMP91]. The algorithm proposed in [BWJ] is essentially an iteration of these two steps up to a fixpoint. Step 3 is the AC algorithm presented above, and Step 4 is used to further refine the TCGs based on the new domain values obtained in the previous step. Formally, $Shrink([m, n] \nu, Dom(X), Dom(Y))$ returns $[m', n'] \nu$ where $m' = min(D)$, $n' = max(D)$, and $D = \{d \mid m \le d \le n \text{ and } d = \lceil t_y \rceil^\nu - \lceil t_x \rceil^\nu \text{ for some } t_y \in Dom(Y) \text{ and } t_x \in Dom(X)\}$.

Theorem 15. *Algorithm AC+PC terminates. It returns **inconsistent** iff the input network N is inconsistent, and a network equivalent to N otherwise.*

The algorithm does not guarantee to always return the *minimal* TCGs and domains (i.e., the minimal among the equivalent networks), but it usually gives a good approximation.

5 Complexity Results

In [BWJ], it was shown that the consistency problem for a network with arbitrary temporal types associated with TCGs is NP-hard if the representation of the temporal types associated with TCGs is considered to be part of the input. The result holds even with the restriction to periodic types[5], but in this case we can give an upper bound on the computational complexity.

Proposition 16. *When arbitrary periodic temporal types can be used in the input network, consistency can be checked in space polynomial in the number of temporal types and in the maximum range of TCGs.*

This result follows from the observation that if a solution exists, there exists one using only values not greater than the constant MAX, whose value depends on the (representation of) the temporal types appearing in the network.

However, in most practical cases a fixed set of time granularities will be known to the system and available to the user. In such cases we prove that the algorithms proposed in this paper can be considered polynomial.

Proposition 17. *When the set of periodic temporal types that can be used in the input network is fixed, both the AC and AC+PC algorithms take time polynomial in the number of variables and in the maximum range of TCGs.*

Note that these algorithms can be considerably less efficient than their corresponding single granularity versions because of the operations that have to be performed on the representations of periodic sets. The detailed complexity analysis in the proof of Proposition 17 reveals, for example, that the polynomial factor can be high, depending on the number and characteristic of the involved granularities.

Even when the only task is consistency checking or finding a single solution, the use of AC+PC could be a good choice. Indeed, we expect that the AC+PC algorithm will perform better in the average case than AC, since the preliminary steps 1 and 2 help reducing the TCGs ranges on which the quite costly ⋓ operation of AC is applied.

6 Conclusion

In this paper, we studied a temporal CSP with multiple granularities. This class of CSPs is useful in many practical applications in the areas of A.I. and databases

---

[5] The representation of a periodic type μ consists of the values for I, N, and P, as described by Definition 2, and of a set of (sets of) intervals identifying the first $I + N - 1$ ticks of μ. See appendix for more details.

where data are stored and related in terms of different granularities. We are currently investigating the formalization of temporal integrity constraints in databases and knowledge bases as a constraint network with multiple granularities. In this situation, when a new event occurs, one needs to know, based on the past events and their occurrence times, whether the integrity constraints can be satisfied or not by some future events, since if not, some remedial action must be taken.

As future work we also plan to complement the complexity results reported in the previous section with experimental work to understand the variance form the worst case behavior and to evaluate efficiency with respect to the properties of the granularities involved in the CSP.

References

[All83]   James F. Allen. Maintaining knowledge about temporal intervals. *Communications of the ACM*, 26(11):832–843, November 1983.

[BWJ]   C. Bettini, X. Wang, and S. Jajodia. A General Framework for Time Granularity and its Application to Temporal Reasoning. *Annals of Mathematics and Artificial Intelligence*, to appear. A preliminary version of this paper appeared in *Proc. of TIME-96*, IEEE Computer Society Press.

[DMP91]   R. Dechter, I. Meiri, and J. Pearl. Temporal constraint networks. *Artificial Intelligence*, 49:61–95, 1991.

[Lad86]   P. Ladkin. Time representation: a taxonomy of interval relations. In *Proc. of the American National Conference on Artificial Intelligence*, Morgan Kaufmann, Los Altos, CA, pp. 360–366, 1986.

[Lad87]   P. Ladkin. The completeness of a natural system for reasoning with time intervals. In *Proc. of the Intern. Joint Conference on Artificial Intelligence*, Morgan Kaufmann, Los Altos, CA, pp. 462–467, 1987.

[Mac77]   A. K. Mackworth. Consistency in networks of relations. *Artificial Intelligence*, 8:99–118, 1977.

[MFE85]   A. K. Mackworth and E. C. Freuder. The complexity of some polynomial network consistency algorithms for constraint satisfaction problems. *Artificial Intelligence*, 25:65–74, 1985.

[Mei96]   I. Meiri. Combining qualitative and quantitative constraints in temporal reasoning. *Artificial Intelligence*, 87:343–385, 1996.

[Mon74]   U. Montanari. Networks of constraints: Fundamental properties and applications to picture processing. *Information Science*, 7(3):95–132, 1974.

[MR93]   L. Khatib, R.A. Morris, W.D. Shoaff. Path consistency in a network of nonconvex intervals. In *Proc. of the Intern. Joint Conference on Artificial Intelligence*, Morgan Kaufmann, San Mateo, CA, pp. 655–661, 1993.

[PB91]   M. Poesio and R. J. Brachman. Metric constraints for maintaining appointments: Dates and repeated activities. In *Proc. of the American National Conference on Artificial Intelligence*, AAAI Press/MIT Press, Menlo Park, CA, pp. 253–259, 1991.

[SD]   E. Schwalb and R. Dechter. Processing disjunctions in temporal constraint networks. *Artificial Intelligence*. To appear.

[vBC90]   P. van Beek and R. Cohen. Exact and approximate reasoning about temporal relations. *Computational Intelligence*, 6:132–144, 1990.

Appendix: Operations on periodic types

We assumed that all types are periodic relative to the same basic type μ (**second** for simplicity). In general, if ν is periodic relative to μ, we can finitely represent ν based on μ. Indeed, it is sufficient to determine I, N and P, with the properties shown in the paper, and to provide a description of the first $I + N - 1$ ticks of ν in terms of ticks of μ. (Here, a description of tick $\nu(i)$ is the set of positive integers $S = \{i_0, \ldots, i_k\}$, such that $\nu(i) = \bigcup_{r=0}^{k} \mu(i_r)$. This set S is represented as a finite set of intervals for compactness.) In particular, the first $I - 1$ ticks form the non-repeating part of ν, while ticks from I to $I + N - 1$ form the set of repeating ticks. In general, let $k \geq I + N$, $s = (k - I)$ MOD N and S be the representation of $\nu(I + s)$ w.r.t. μ. Then, the representation of $\nu(k)$ w.r.t. μ is $\{i + r * P | i \in S\}$, where $r = (k - I)$ DIV N.

Manipulating periodic types requires some basic operations:

Synchronization. Synchronization of a set of periodic types can be obtained using as a new period length the least common multiple (lcm) of their periods. More precisely, assume ν_1 and ν_2 are originally defined by positive[6] periods P_1 and P_2, index of the first tick in the period I_1 and I_2 and displacement N_1 and N_2 respectively. After synchronization, the same types will be defined by the common period $P = lcm(P_1, P_2)$, index of the first tick (properly contained) in the new period I_1' and I_2', and displacement $N_1 * lcm(P_1, P_2)/P_1$ and $N_2 * lcm(P_1, P_2)/P_2$ respectively. I_k' for $k \in \{1, 2\}$ is obtained as follows: Let $\bar{t} = max(min(\nu_1(I_1)), min(\nu_2(I_2)))$. $I_k' = I_k$ if $\bar{t} = min(\nu_k(I_k))$, otherwise it is the minimum index I_k' such that $\bar{t} < min(\nu_k(I_k'))$. The set of intervals respectively in the non-periodic and periodic part of each synchronized type can be easily computed based on the new period and on the original representation of the types. We use the function $Synchronize()$ to denote this procedure.

Difference and Intersection. Given two finite sets of pairwise disjoint intervals on positive integers $H_1 = \{I_1, \ldots, I_n\}$ and $H_2 = \{J_1, \ldots, J_m\}$,
(1) the difference $H_1 - H_2$ is the set of pairwise disjoint intervals obtained subtracting from each $I_k \in H_1$ all the intervals in H_2 that have a non-empty intersection with I_k.
(2) the intersection $H_1 \sqcap H_2$ is the set of pairwise disjoint intervals obtained as the intersection of each $I_k \in H_1$ with each $J_r \in H_2$.

Operations on periodic sets In the paper we also use several operations on the domains of variables. Given two periodic sets S_1 and S_2 and a set of TCGs on (X, Y) we need to compute intersection $(S_1 \sqcap S_2)$, domain *shifting* $(S_1 \uplus TCGs(XY))$, and constraint *shrinking* $(Shrink([m, n] \mu, S_1, S_2))$. In the following we explain how each operation can be implemented:

• $S_1 \sqcap S_2$. Since a periodic set is equivalent to a particular temporal type taking each interval as a single tick, the $Synchronize()$ procedure can be applied to periodic sets giving as result two 'synchronized' periodic sets. Hence, we apply $Synchronize(S_1, S_2)$ and construct a new periodic expression having as period the period obtained by synchronization, and as non-periodic and periodic sets of intervals, the intersection among the respective sets of intervals. Intersection among sets of intervals was defined above.

• $S \uplus TCGs(X, Y)$. Intuitively, $S \uplus TCGs(X, Y)$ can be obtained as the intersection of the sets obtained considering $S \uplus [m, n] \mu$ for each TCG $[m, n] \mu$ in $TCGs(X, Y)$. The general operation is implemented as follows:

---

[6] The case in which one or both periods are 0 is addressed simply by redefining the end of the non-periodic part in the representation of each type.

(1) For each $[m,n]\,\mu_i$ in $TCGs(X,Y)$, compute $S_i = S \uplus [m,n]\,\mu_i$. This is done first applying $Synchronize(S,\mu_i)$ and then deriving the non-periodic part as the set of intervals corresponding to $\mu_i(\lceil t_X \rceil^{\mu_i} + m) \cup \ldots \cup \mu_i(\lceil t_X \rceil^{\mu_i} + n)$ for each value t_X in the non-periodic part of synchronized S; the periodic part is obtained by the same formula for each value t_X in the periodic part of synchronized S. Values of t_X for which $\lceil t_X \rceil^{\mu_i}$ is not defined are ignored. If $n = +\infty$, then $S_i = \bigcup_{k \geq m} \mu_i(\lceil t_X \rceil^{\mu_i} + k)$, and its periodic representation can be easily obtained. Similarly for $m = -\infty$. Using the first value t_X, after the first period, for which a different tick of μ_i is obtained, we can easily derive the period length and the displacement for S_i. Values of t_X for which $\lceil t_X \rceil^{\mu_i}$ is not defined are ignored. This step can be optimized considering a single t_X for each set of values in S covered by the same tick of μ_i.

(2) $S \uplus TCGs(X,Y) = \bigcap_{i=1}^{k} S_i$.

- $S_1 \neq^{MAX} S_2$. $S_1 =^{MAX} S_2$. These tests can be performed by (1) $Synchronize(S_1, S_2)$, and (2) compare the first intervals of each synchronized set up to the minimum between $S_i(I+N)$ and the interval containing a value greater than MAX, for $i=1,2$ respectively.

- $Shrink([m,n]\,\nu, Dom(X), Dom(Y))$. This operation must derive a TCG $[m',n']\,\nu$ where $m' = min(D)$, $n' = max(D)$, and $D = \{d \mid \exists t_y \in Dom(Y)\, t_x \in Dom(X)\quad m \leq d = \lceil t_y \rceil^{\nu} - \lceil t_x \rceil^{\nu} \leq n\}$.

(1) Let $k = n$. While $(Dom(X) \uplus [k,k]\,\mu) \cap Dom(Y) = \emptyset$ Do $k \leftarrow k-1$. $n' = k$.

(2) Let $k = m$. While $(Dom(X) \uplus [k,k]\,\mu) \cap Dom(Y) = \emptyset$ Do $k \leftarrow k+1$. $m' = k$.

The periodic expression $Dom(X) \uplus [k,k]\,\mu$ can be computed as illustrated above.

Proofs

Proof of Proposition 10.
Termination is based on the fact that domains can only be "refined" by Step 2.2 performing intersection among periodic sets. Let F be the subset of the integers represented by S within $\{0, MAX\}$. By the implementation of intersection, it is easily seen that each time it is performed, if any change occurs, (i) the intervals up to end of first period of the set S are modified dropping some interval or some subinterval, and (ii) some new intervals with values greater than the current ones can also appear due to synchronization. By the condition at Step 2, intersection is performed only if a change occurred in F. By this, (i) and (ii), we can conclude that, for each domain S, at most MAX intersections can be applied to S, since, after that number, F will be empty.

Proof of Proposition 11.
Consider case (i). We show that if a solution exists, there exists one in which all the instants used in the assignments precede MAX as defined in the statement. Suppose that a solution S exists such that t is assigned to $X \in W$ and $t > MAX$. Let λ be the type with only $|W|$ ticks each one covering the span of time $Lcm_P * 2 * (|Max\text{-}dist| + 1)$ starting from the instant $maxI$. Then, if $t > MAX$, there exists a tick i of λ such that no assignment of S falls in $\lambda(i)$. This is trivial since the ticks of λ are as many as the variables and MAX is the last instant of the last tick. We show that a solution S' can be constructed from S as follows: For each t' in an assignment of S such that t' is greater than any instant in $\lambda(i)$, let $t' = t' - Lcm_P * (|Max\text{-}dist| + 1)$. We know that there exists at least one instant (t) satisfying the above condition. Obviously, any constraint in the network between two variables both involved in the new assignments

of S' is satisfied in S', and any constraint in the network involving only variables that maintain the same value in S and S' is still satisfied. Consider constraints between variables X and Y such that in solution S' X maintains the same assignment (t_1) as in S, while Y has the new assignment. We know that $t_2 - t_1 > Lcm_P * 2 * (|Max\text{-}dist| + 1)$. Since the maximum finite distance between X and Y is not greater than $Max\text{-}dist$ we deduce that there is no maximum according to the constraints (i.e., the maximum is $+\infty$). Clearly, this bound is satisfied by the new solution. We conclude that S' is a solution of N. Now we can recursively apply the above construction until a solution is found in which all assignments use instants not greater than MAX.

For case (ii), if any solution exists and one value falls within $maxI + lcm(P_1, \ldots, P_k)$ then any other value must be at most $max\text{-}dist$ seconds from it. Otherwise it is possible to recursively shift all of the values in the solution subtracting $lcm(P_1, \ldots, P_k)$, until the minimal value falls within $maxI + lcm(P_1, \ldots, P_k)$.

Proof of Theorems 12 and 13.

Soundness. The only operation performed on the input network N is the refinement of domains (Step 2.2). By definition of $\uplus$, an element d is deleted from $Dom(X_l)$ if there is a node X_k adjacent to X_l in N such that no element in X_k has a distance from d within the ranges allowed by $\Gamma(X_k, X_l)$. This refinement is clearly sound since d cannot be part of any solution.

Completeness and solution. Let N be the input network and $\bar{N}$ the network returned by AC. If N is consistent, then there exists a solution σ for N. By soundness, $\bar{N}$ is equivalent to N, and, hence, σ is also a solution for $\bar{N}$, implying that its domains are non-empty. In the other direction, if $Dom(X_1), \ldots, Dom(X_r)$ are the domains in $\bar{N}$, we show that $\sigma = d_1^1, \ldots, d_r^1$, where d_i^1 is the minimum number in $Dom(X_i)$ for $i = 1, \ldots, r$, is a solution. Consider an arbitrary arc (X_k, X_l) in $\bar{N}$. Since $\bar{N}$ is the fix-point of AC we know that: (i) $\exists d_l^j$ such that $m_s \leq \lceil d_l^j \rceil^{\mu_s} - \lceil d_k^1 \rceil^{\mu_s} \leq n_s$ for each $[m_s, n_s]\mu_s$ in $\Gamma(X_k, X_l)$; and (ii) $\exists d_k^i$ such that $m_s \leq \lceil d_l^1 \rceil^{\mu_s} - \lceil d_k^i \rceil^{\mu_s} \leq n_s$ for each $[m_s, n_s]\mu_s$ in $\Gamma(X_k, X_l)$. Since $d_l^1 \leq d_l^j$, from (i) we derive $\lceil d_l^1 \rceil^{\mu_s} - \lceil d_k^1 \rceil^{\mu_s} \leq n_s$ for each $[m_s, n_s]\mu_s$ in $\Gamma(X_k, X_l)$. Similarly, since $d_k^1 \leq d_k^i$, from (ii) we derive $m_s \leq \lceil d_l^1 \rceil^{\mu_s} - \lceil d_k^1 \rceil^{\mu_s}$ for each $[m_s, n_s]\mu_s$ in $\Gamma(X_k, X_l)$. Then, (d_k^1, d_l^1) satisfies all the constraints in $\Gamma(X_k, X_l)$. Since the same can be applied to other arcs in $\bar{N}$, σ is a solution. A similar proof can be given considering maximum instead of minimum values to obtain the solution.

Proof of Theorem 15.

Termination. The upper bound on the number of iterations of the 4 steps is $2 * |W|^2 * |M| * MAX$. Indeed, each TCG range can be refined at most MAX times. (If ∞ is refined in a TCG, it must be refined to a value less than MAX.) In the worst case we have a TCG in each granularity for each arc and a single TCG is refined every second iteration. Then, AC+PC always terminates, since AC is known to terminate and steps 1,2, and 4 trivially terminate.

Soundness and equivalent network. Soundness of Steps 1 and 2 follows from results in [BWJ]. Step 3 (AC) guarantees that either a domain is set to the empty set or the revised domain does not exclude any original solution. However, if a domain is empty AC+PC will return **inconsistent**. If it doesn't, then we are guaranteed that we still have an equivalent network after running AC. Finally, Step 4 only exclude values in the range of a TCG if that value is not admitted by the domains. Then, if the algorithm does not return **inconsistent**, it must return an equivalent network.

If AC+PC returns **inconsistent**, then either an empty domain or an empty TCG has been derived. In the first case, the only step that can have changed the domain is AC, and hence, by Theorem 12, the input network to AC is inconsistent. But that network was proved to be equivalent to the input network for AC+PC. In the second case, either step 1,2 or 4 refined the TCG to be empty. Since, these steps are guaranteed to return an equivalent network, the input network must be inconsistent.

Completeness w.r.t. consistency. Since Steps 1,2, and 4 are guaranteed to be sound and AC has been shown to be complete w.r.t. consistency, if the input network is inconsistent, then AC+PC returns **inconsistent**.

Proof of Proposition 16.

By Proposition 11, if there exists a solution for N, then there must be solution in $[1, MAX]$. Consider an algorithm that (non-deterministically) picks (and put on the tape) $|W|$ arbitrary numbers ($|W|$ being the number of variables) within the range $[1, MAX]$ and tests if they satisfy the constraints. The space needed is $|W|*log(MAX)$, that is a polynomial w.r.t. the number of types and the values in the TCGs. This is a NPSPACE algorithm, but NPSPACE = PSPACE.

Proof of Proposition 17.

Complexity of AC. The iterations of the while loop are $MAX * (d_i - 1)$ for each node i, where d_i is the edge degree of node i. Indeed, in each iteration we could get rid of 1 value and add $d_i - 1$ arcs to Q (the maximum number of refinements is MAX). Hence, the total number of iterations is $MAX * (2e - |W|)$ where e is the number of arcs, and $|W|$ is the number of nodes. This quantity is $O(MAX * |W|^2)$.

We now evaluate the complexity of $S \uplus TCGs(X,Y)$. In Step 1, for each type, the synchronization of S with it takes $O(|S| * |\nu|)$, and then $L * R$ operations of $\lceil \rceil$, $+$, and set unions are needed, where L is the maximum number of instants contained in (synchronized) S up to the first period, such that they are all contained in different ticks of ν, and R is the maximum finite range in $TCGs(X,Y)$. $\lceil \rceil^\nu$ takes time linear in the representation of ν, union is linear in its input and $+$ is constant. Hence, Step 1 requires time $O((|S| * |\nu|)^2 * R)$. Step 2 requires time $O(Qlog(Q))$, where $Q = ((|S| * |\nu|)^2 * R)^k$ with k the number of types in $TCGs(X,Y)$. This is also the complexity of $\uplus$.

The complexity of $S_2 \cap (S_1 \uplus TCGs(X_1, X_2))$ is $O(Qlog(Q))$ where $Q = max(|S_2|, ((|S_1| * |\nu|)^2 * R)^k)$. The global complexity is then $O(MAX * |W|^2 * Qlog(Q))$ where $Q = ((|S| * |\nu|)^2 * R)^{|M|})$, $|M|$ is the number of temporal types in the network, $|S|$ is the largest (representation of) a domain obtained during the algorithm, $|\nu|$ is the largest (representation of a) type in the input network, and R is the maximum finite range in the constraints. If we approximate $|S|$ with MAX, the global complexity becomes $O(|W|^2 * Qlog(Q))$ where $Q = ((MAX * |\nu|)^2 * R)^{|M|})$.

Complexity of Steps 1 and 2 of AC+PC. From [BWJ], this is $O((|W|^3 + c|W|^2) * |M|)$ being c the time to convert a single TCG.

Complexity of Step 4 of AC+PC. The upper bound on the number of TCGs on which $Shrink()$ must be applied is $|M|$ times the maximum number of arcs, hence, $|M|*|W|^2$. Each $Shrink()$ operation needs in the worst case $|S|^2 * |\nu|$ for synchronization of the 2 domains and of the TCG type, plus $R \uplus$ operations with a single valued TCG (i.e., a TCG with a single value in its range). Each of these $\uplus$ operations takes $O(Zlog(Z))$ where $Z = (|S| * |\nu|)^2$. Hence, step 4 takes $(|M| * |W|^2 * R * O(Zlog(Z))$.

Complexity of AC+PC. It is easily derived, since the upper bound on the number of iterations of the 4 steps was shown to be $(|W|^2 * |M| * MAX)$ and we also evaluated the complexity of each step.

Since the values $maxI$ and Lcm_P in MAX and the value $|M|$ can be considered constants when the set of temporal types is fixed and domains are constrained to one of these types, both AC and AC+PC take time polynomial in the number of variables and in the maximum range of the TCGs.

Tractable Recursion
over Geometric Data

(Extended Abstract)

Stéphane Grumbach[1*] and Gabriel Kuper[2**]

[1] I.N.R.I.A., Rocquencourt BP 105, 78153 Le Chesnay, France,
stephane.grumbach@inria.fr
[2] U. Libre de Bruxelles Informatique, C.P. 165, 50 Avenue F.D. Roosevelt, 1050
Brussels, Belgium, kuper@cs.ulb.ac.be

Abstract. We study the issue of adding a recursion operator to constraint query languages for linear spatial databases. We introduce a language with a bounded inflationary fixpoint operator which is closed and captures the set of polynomial time computable queries over linear constraint databases. This is the first logical characterization of the class of PTIME queries in this context. To prove the result, we develop original techniques to perform arithmetical and geometric operations with constraints.

1 Introduction

The area of constraint databases is an important area of current research. Since the initial work by Kanellakis, Kuper and Revesz [KKR90], which described the basic methodology for combining constraint solvers and traditional database query languages in a single framework, many related issues concerning expressive power, query languages, potential applications, and other aspects, have been studied.

One area that has received particular attention is that of linear constraints. These are particularly promising for many applications, e.g., for geographical databases [VGV95]. The complexity of the linear relational language (i.e., first-order logic) has been shown to be in NC^1 [GS97]. A lower complexity, AC^0, can be shown for the case of finite, as opposed to finitely representable, databases. There has also been a significant amount of work that studies the expressive power of first-order logic with linear constraints [GST94, PVV95, GS97]. As with the standard relational first-order language, the language of linear constraints with first-order logic turns out to be rather restricted. For example, transitive closure and topological connectivity, the latter a very important query for spatial databases, cannot be expressed in the language.

---

* Work supported in part by TMR Project Chorochronos.
** Work supported by Inria, FNRS and ULB.

As with the relational calculus, it is therefore natural to ask whether the language of first-order logic with linear constraints can be extended to a more powerful language. Such a language should be powerful enough to express connectivity queries, but not too powerful — for example, we would like such a language to have a relatively low complexity. One possibility would be to simply add recursion to the language. Unfortunately, as was pointed out in [KKR90], the resulting language is not closed, i.e., the result of a query is not always finitely expressible using linear constraints. Besides this, it is well-known that in the presence of arithmetic, a fixpoint operator leads in fact to Turing computability. One could solve this problem by allowing recursion only over an order relation, not over the arithmetic predicates, but such a language does not seem to be powerful enough to express connectivity. (A formal proof of this is still an open problem.)

Despite this, it is reasonable to look for a restricted form of recursion that is sufficiently expressive, but has low complexity. If we look at the examples of "bad" recursion, we see that the problem is that they have the ability to create "new" objects (speaking informally) without limit. If we had some formal way to restrict queries to those that do not generate new objects or only in some limited way, we might be able to obtain a reasonable query language with recursion.

This paper describes an attempt to define such a language. We propose a notion of *bounded recursion*: Such a recursion performs, in parallel, two separate recursions, only one of which may involve arithmetic, and terminates as soon as either recursion terminates. Futhermore, the recusion is designed in such a way that only a constant number of new points can be created at each recursive step (non-recursive first-order formulas can still create finite representations of infinite objects, as this does not create any problems). While the language itself is not particularly elegant, it does have nice formal properties. First of all, the language is closed: the result of such a query on a linear constraint database is itself finitely representable by linear constraints. Secondly, the language is quite expressive, for example, natural topological properties such as connectivity can be expressed in this language.

Finally, there is a precise characterization of the expressive power of our language. In the tradition of studying complexity classes over ordered finite structures [Imm86, Var82], we show that our language with bounded recursion over linear constraints expresses precisely the class of linear constraint queries that are computable in polynomial time.

The paper is organized as follows. In the next section, we review two standard formalisms to represent linear geometric data, the linear constraint databases, and the point-based model of computational geometry. In section 3, we introduce the bounded inflationary fixpoint, and give some examples of queries. Finally, in Section 4, we prove the main result of the paper, namely the PTIME characterization.

2 Representation of Geometric Data

Most of the computation on multi-dimensional data is limited to linear varieties, which offer a satisfying approximation of "real-world" data, and can be evaluated efficiently.

There are two alternative ways for representing linear varieties. The most common one, used in particular in computational geometry, relies on a definition of the polygons by their frontier, given as a list of points. More complex polyhedra, are also defined by their frontier, as a set of polygons, and so on. The other way, which is slightly more general, is based on half-planes. A polygon is defined as the intersection of a set of half-planes.

The two representation differ in the sort of objects which can be defined. With lists of points, only compact polygons can be defined. On the other hand, with the half-planes, only convex polygons can be defined. These are not drastic restrictions, since generally collections of spatial objects are considered, and therefore non-convex polygons can be represented as collections of convex ones. Moreover in practice compact polygons are sufficient.

We first present a logical data model, independent of any physical representation, based on linear constraint databases for spatial data [KKR90, GST94, VGV95]. This corresponds to the half-plane approach, and allows the definition of spatial objects in a symbolic and abstract manner, as infinite sets of points.

We consider linear constraints in the first-order language $\mathcal{L} = \{\leq, +\} \cup \mathbb{Q}$ over the structure $\mathcal{Q} = \langle \mathbb{Q}, \leq, +, (q)_{q \in \mathbb{Q}} \rangle$ of the linearly ordered set of the rational numbers with rational constants and addition. Constraints are conjunctions of linear equations and inequalities of the form: $\sum_{i=1}^{p} a_i x_i \Theta a_0$, where Θ is a predicate among $=$ or $\leq$, the x_i's denote variables and the a_i's are integer constants. Note that rational constants can always be avoided in linear equations and inequalities. The multiplication symbol is used as an abbreviation, $a_i x_i$ stands for $x_i + \cdots + x_i$ (a_i times).

Let $\sigma = \{R_1, ..., R_n\}$ be a database schema such that $\mathcal{L} \cap \sigma = \emptyset$, where $R_1, ..., R_n$ are relation symbols. We distinguish between *logical predicates* (e.g., $=, \leq$) in $\mathcal{L}$ and *relations* in σ. Linear constraint relations are defined as follows.

Definition 2.1 Let $S \subseteq \mathbb{Q}^k$ be a k-ary relation. The relation S is a linear constraint relation if there exists a quantifier free formula $\varphi(x_1, ..., x_k)$ in $\mathcal{L}$ with k distinct free variables $x_1, ..., x_k$ (called a *representation* of S) such that:

$$\mathcal{Q} \models \forall x_1 \cdots x_k (S(x_1, ..., x_k) \leftrightarrow \varphi(x_1, ..., x_k))$$

If the formula φ is in disjunctive normal form:

$$\varphi \equiv \bigvee_{i=1}^{k} \bigwedge_{j=1}^{\ell_i} \varphi_{i,j}$$

we will see it as a *generalized relation*, that is a finite set of *generalized tuples*, which are conjunctions of atomic formulae $\varphi_{i,j}$

$$\left\{ t_i \mid 1 \leq i \leq k, \; t_i = \bigwedge_{j=1}^{\ell_i} \varphi_{i,j} \right\}$$

A *(database) instance (of σ)* is a mapping which associates to each k-ary relation symbol R in σ a linear constraint relation of arity k.

Proviso In the sequel, we assume that the relations are *compact*, i.e., that the relation (as a set of points in space) is bounded (as all point-based databases are). This assumption, which holds in pratical systems, ensures an easy translation from one representation to the other, and makes it simpler to define the encoding of a relation, but is not essential.

A *query* is a partial recursive mapping from linear constraint databases over some schema σ to linear constraint relations of a fixed arity k, and the *data complexity* of queries is defined with respect to a standard encoding of the input where integers are encoded in binary.

Most information systems, such as geographic information systems (GIS), have adopted a point-based representation for spatial data [Gue94]. The basic concepts are *points* (pairs of rational numbers), *lines* (sequences of points), and *polygons* (sequences of points). The semantics of these objects are not the same in all models: in some models a line is a consecutive sequence of line segments, but in others it can be a polyline (tree). A polygon is usually defined implicitly to be the inside of a closed line defining its frontier.

In practice, more information is often added in order to overcome the limitations of the point-line-polygon model. Regions with holes, for instance, could not otherwise be represented. Topological relationships between the objects are, in addition, often explicitly represented as well.

There is a very large set of operations on spatial objects: set operations (union, intersection, etc.), geometric operations (scale modification, translation, etc.), metric operations, topological operations, and complex operations (map overlay) on different maps, but there is no satisfying query language per se in such models.

It is now folklore that any compact linear constraint database can be represented in terms of a spatial database in the point-based model, and conversely. The translation nevertheless supposes a sound formalization of the spatial data model, and works at the level of the collection of objects, i.e. linear constraint relation and sets of spatial objects. Indeed, polygons might be non-convex, and need to be mapped to sets of tuples, and conversely, tuples might have holes (e.g. $x \neq 3$), and need to be mapped to sets of spatial atoms.

The translation can be done effectively, using the notion of distinguished points based on [Whi57], and used in [DGVG97]. Intuitively, the distinguished points of a relation R can be thought of as the isolated points and the vertices of the polygons in R. Formally, they correspond to the non-regular points defined in [DGVG97], as follows.

Definition 2.2

1. Let S be a semi-linear set in $\mathbf{R}^n$, and let $\overrightarrow{p}$ be a point of S. $\overrightarrow{p}$ is a *regular point* of S iff there exists a neighborhood V of $\overrightarrow{p}$, and polynomials with real coefficients $P_1, ..., P_k$ in n real variables, such that the following vectors are linearly independent

$$\frac{dP_1}{d\overrightarrow{x}}(\overrightarrow{p}), ..., \frac{dP_n}{d\overrightarrow{x}}(\overrightarrow{p})$$

and $S \cap V = \{\overrightarrow{x} \in V \mid P_1(\overrightarrow{x}) = \cdots = P_k(\overrightarrow{x}) = 0\}$.
2. In such a case, we say that S has dimension $n - k$ in point $\overrightarrow{p}$, and call the maximum of these numbers the overall dimension of S, denoted $\dim(S)$.
3. Let $\text{Reg}(S)$ be the set of regular points of S in which S has dimension $\dim(S)$. The connected components of $\text{Reg}(S)$ are called regular strata. Repeat this with $S - \text{Reg}(S)$, which is semi-linear, and of strictly lower dimension. The points in the strata of dimension 0 are called the *distinguished points* of S.

3 Fixpoint Query Languages

In this section, we introduce a tractable iteration operator. The tractability is ensured by performing a double iteration in parallel, over finite relations. One of these iterations uses no arithmetic, while the other can use arithmetic, but is of a form that limits the number of new objects that can be created. The iteration stops whenever one of the two iterations has reached a fixpoint. We prove that such a fixpoint, under inflationary semantics, captures all PTIME queries over linear constraint databases. In addition, we show that with non-inflationary semantics, it captures all PSPACE queries over linear constraint databases.

The motivation for our choice of fixpoint is as follows. Unrestricted inflationary iteration over linear constraint relations leads to a *complete* language for linear constraint databases, by a combination of fixpoint and successor. Such a language is, however, *not closed*. It is, in general, undecidable whether inflationary iteration over a formula with linear constraints converges in polynomial time. An obvious way to restrict the fixpoint operator would be to limit it to formulae with no arithmetic. This would yield a tractable recursion operator, but one with low expressive power. As we shall see, our choice of a dual fixpoint, results in an operator that is powerful enough to express connectivity (along with many other topological properties), but is still closed.

The recursion is carried on over finite relations only, and can be seen as a computation over the point-based representation of the data, as opposed to the half-plane representation by linear constraints. Other forms of recursion could be envisaged. For example, one could allow for the creation of a limited number of new infinite objects at each step, perhaps by creating a constant number of new cells at each step. However, if such a recursion is in PTIME, it follows from our results that anything expressible in such a language will also be expressible in our language, and therefore that computing only finite points during the recursive steps is expressive enough.

We first recall some definitions. In the sequel, we consider both (linear constraint) instances and finite instances. As defined above, an *instance* over a schema σ is an interpretation of the relation symbols in σ that maps k-ary relation symbols to linear constraint relations in $\mathbb{Q}^k$. A *finite instance* is a mapping to finite relations in $\mathbb{Q}^k$.

We now define the important concept of *active domain* for both linear constraint and (as a special case) finite instances. The definition is based on the notion of distinguished points defined above. The active domain basically consists of the coordinates of the distinguished points, together with an estimate of how large the numbers involved are. Formally, let R be a linear constraint relation in $\mathcal{I}$. The active domain of R consists of the union $A_1 \cup A_2$ of a set of rationals A_1 with a set of natural numbers A_2, where

1. $A_1 = \{k \mid k$ is a coordinate of a distinguished point of $R\}$
2. $A_2 = \{2, 4, ..., 2^{\lceil log_2 r \rceil}\}$, where r is the largest value of all p and q such that $p/q \in A_1$ with p/q in reduced form.

We now introduce two primitive predicates: ν for computing the representation of a rational number, and λ_i^j for reconstructing constraints from points. Note that in this paper, for simplicity of presentation, we shall refer only to λ_i (with $j = 1$) as the predicates for generating lines in an i-dimensional space. The extension to planes ($j = 2$) and higher order objects is straightforward.

We consider the language of first-order logic over $\mathcal{L} \cup \sigma$, augmented with the symbols ν and λ_i ($i \in \mathbb{N}$).

Definition 3.1 Let φ be a formula in $\mathcal{L} \cup \sigma$ with $2i$ free variables that defines a finite relation. Then $\lambda_i(\varphi)$ defines a formula with $3i$ free variables in $\mathcal{L} \cup \sigma$, such that for each tuple $(a_1, ..., a_i, b_1, ..., b_i)$ in the relation defined by φ, $\lambda_i(\varphi)$ contains a generalized tuple, whose projection on the first $2i$ attributes equals $(a_1, ..., a_i, b_1, ..., b_i)$, and, on the remaining i attributes, equals the line passing through the points $(a_1, ..., a_i)$ and $(b_1, ..., b_i)$.

Note that the pre-condition for this definition, that φ defines a finite relation, is expressible in FO+linear. For simplicity, we will often write $\lambda_i(\bar{a})$ for $\lambda_i(\bar{x} = \bar{a})$.

Example 3.1 $\lambda_2(a_1, a_2, b_1, b_2)$ is the formula over the following free variables $x_1, x_2, y_1, y_2, z_1, z_2$:

$$x_1 = a_1 \wedge x_2 = a_2 \wedge y_1 = b_1 \wedge y_2 = b_2 \wedge (a_2 - b_2)z_1 + (b_1 - a_1)z_2 = a_2 b_1 - a_1 b_2$$

We now define the operator ν.

Definition 3.2 Let φ be a formula in $\mathcal{L} \cup \sigma$ with one free variable that defines a unique rational number r. Then $\nu(\varphi)$ defines a formula with 2 free variables in $\mathcal{L} \cup \sigma$, such that $\nu(\varphi)(p,q)$ holds iff p and q are integers, and $\frac{p}{q}$ is a reduced representation of r.

Let $\psi(x_1, ..., x_k) = Q_{k+1}x_{k+1}\cdots Q_{k+\ell}x_{k+\ell}\varphi(x_1, ..., x_{k+\ell})$ be a first-order formula in prenex normal form in $\mathcal{L} \cup \sigma \cup \{\lambda_i, \nu\}$ with k free variables. ψ defines a query over linear constraint instances over σ, that maps instances to k-ary relations. We distinguish between two possible interpretations of such a query.

Under the *natural semantics*, quantifiers in φ range over all rational numbers. The answer to the query, denoted by $\psi^{nat}(\mathcal{I})$, is defined by:

$$\{(a_1, ..., a_k)|a_i \in \mathbb{Q} \wedge \mathcal{Q} \sqcup \mathcal{I} \models (Q_{k+1}x_{k+1} \in \mathbb{Q})\cdots(Q_{k+\ell}x_{k+\ell} \in \mathbb{Q})\varphi(a_1, ..., a_k)\}.$$

Under the *active semantics*, quantifiers in φ range over the active domain. The answer to the query, denoted by $\psi^{act}(\mathcal{I})$, is defined by:

$$\{(a_1, ..., a_k)|a_i \in \mathbb{Q} \wedge \mathcal{Q} \sqcup \mathcal{I} \models (Q_{k+1}x_{k+1} \in adom(\mathcal{I}))$$
$$\cdots(Q_{k+\ell}x_{k+\ell} \in adom(\mathcal{I}))\varphi(a_1, ..., a_k)\}.$$

Let T and S be two new predicate symbols. The *bounded fixpoint* is defined with respect to two formulas $\varphi(T)$, over $\sigma \cup \{T\} \cup \{<\}$ and $\psi(S)$, over $\sigma \cup \{S\} \cup \{<, +\} \cup \{\lambda_i, \nu\}$. $\varphi(T)$ is interpreted over a finite domain under the active semantics, while $\psi(S)$ is interpreted under the natural semantics. In addition, $\psi(S)$ must be *range restricted*, that is, it must be of the form $(\exists! \bar{y})\psi'(\bar{y})$. This ensures that each iteration does not create too many new objects.

In the definition below, the formula $\varphi(T)$ plays the role of a counter which bounds the computation, while $\psi(S)$ is the important formula.

Definition 3.3 Let $\varphi(\bar{x})$ be a formula over the signature $\sigma \cup \{T\} \cup \{<\}$, and $\psi(\bar{y})$ over the signature $\sigma \cup \{S\} \cup \{<, +\} \cup \{\lambda_i, \nu\}$, where $\bar{x}$ and $\bar{y}$ are disjoint vectors of the variables free in φ and ψ respectively, and $\psi(\bar{y})$ is of the form $(\exists! \bar{y})\psi'(\bar{y})$. The pair of formulae $(\varphi(\bar{x}), \psi(\bar{y}))$ defines an operator $\Theta_{(\varphi(\bar{x}), \psi(\bar{y}))}$ with respect to an instance $\mathcal{I}$ of σ, that maps (S, T) instances to (S, T) instances:

$$(I', J') = \Theta_{(\varphi(\bar{x}), \psi(\bar{y}))}(I, J),$$

where $I' = \varphi^{act}(\mathcal{I}, I)$ and $J' = \psi^{nat}(\mathcal{I}, J)$. The *bounded inflationary fixpoint* of the operator $\Theta_{(\varphi(\bar{x}), \psi(\bar{y}))}$ over an instance $\mathcal{I}$ of σ, is defined by

$$\mathbf{I}\Xi_{\varphi(\bar{x})}[\psi(\bar{y})] = J_n,$$

where n is the smallest integer such that

$$(I_1, J_1) = \Theta_{(\varphi(\bar{x}), \psi(\bar{y}))}(\emptyset, \emptyset); \qquad (I_{i+1}, J_{i+1}) = \Theta_{(\varphi(\bar{x}), \psi(\bar{y}))}(I_i, J_i) \cup (I_i, J_i)$$

and either $I_{n+1} = I_n$ or $J_{n+1} = J_n$.

Let $\mathcal{BIFP}$ be the set of queries that are definable with a bounded inflationary fixpoint. Note that fixpoint operators cannot be nested.

We can similarly define the *bounded partial fixpoint* of the operator $\Theta_{(\varphi(\bar{x}),\psi(\bar{y}))}$, with a non-inflationary semantics. The *bounded partial fixpoint* over an instance $\mathcal{I}$ of σ, is defined by

$$\mathbf{P}\underset{\varphi(\bar{x})}{\Xi}[\psi(\bar{y})] = J_n,$$

where n is the smallest integer such that (note the absence of the union with (I_i, J_i))

$$(I_1, J_1) = \Theta_{(\varphi(\bar{x}),\psi(\bar{y}))}(\emptyset, \emptyset); \qquad (I_{i+1}, J_{i+1}) = \Theta_{(\varphi(\bar{x}),\psi(\bar{y}))}(I_i, J_i)$$

and either $I_{n+1} = I_n$ or $J_{n+1} = J_n$.

We denote by $\mathcal{BPFP}$ the set of queries definable with a bounded partial fixpoint.

We illustrate the expressive power of the language $\mathcal{BIFP}$ through several examples. We first consider the expression of non-linear numerical functions.

Example 3.2 The function square over the integers is definable in $\mathcal{BIFP}$. square(x, y) is true whenever $y = x^2$, and x belongs to the active domain.

We first, by repeated addition $(1 + 2 + 4 + 8 + \cdots)$, compute both the smallest number n such that 2^n is greater than all x in the active domain, and all powers of 2 up to 2^n.

Then, using techniques that will be explained in the proof of the main theorem, we compute a predicate $\phi(x, y, z)$ that is true iff x is an integer in the active domain, and z is the yth bit in the binary representation of x.

Finally, we iterate over all x in the active domain, for each such x setting initially $y = 0$, and then, for $i = 1, ..., n$, adding $x \cdot 2^i$ to y iff $\phi(x, i, 1)$ is true.

By appropriate encodings in a relation of higher arity, all this can be expressed by a single application of $\mathbf{I}\Xi$.

We now show that $\mathcal{BIFP}$ can be used to test for topological connectivity of a binary relation. We assume the relation is closed, so that all the distinguished points are actually in the relation, but extending the construction to the open case is not difficult.

We first note that the relation R is connected iff each distinguished point can be connected to each other distinguished point by a sequence of line segments contained entirely in R.

Example 3.3 We select one distinguished point (x_1, y_1). In each iteration we test which other distinguished points are directly connected to a point already reached, and repeat until no changes occur. If all points are reached, the relation is connected.

The key step is testing whether 2 points (x, y) and (x', y') are directly connected. This can be expressed by the formula (assume, w.l.o.g., that $x < x'$ and $y < y'$)

$$(\forall w, z)(\lambda_2(x, y, x', y', w, z) \wedge x \le w \le x' \wedge y \le z \le y' \rightarrow R(w, z))$$

Note that using λ_i as a subformula during the recursion does not cause any problems, but it cannot be part of the output of a recursion step (indeed in such a case the formula would not be range restricted). To ensure that the the iterated formula is range restricted, one must obtain a unique distinguished point at each iteration step (e.g. the closest and furthest north point among those not yet reached).

The *size* of an instance is the size of the encoding of a minimal representation of the instance with integer parameters encoded in binary (see [GST94] for a formal definition). Intuitively an instance of size n can be represented with at most n tuples, n distinct constraints, and integer parameters of value at most 2^n. The size of an instance is related to the size of its active domain.

Proposition 3.1 Let $\mathcal{I}$ be an instance of size n. The size of $adom(\mathcal{I})$, $|adom(\mathcal{I})|$ satisfies $n \leq |adom(\mathcal{I})| \leq 3n^2$.

Proof. (Sketch) Assume the instance $\mathcal{I}$ consists of a single integer p of size $n = \lceil \log_2 p \rceil$. Then $adom(\mathcal{I})$ consists of the set $\{2, 4, ..., 2^{\lceil \log_2 p \rceil}, p\}$, which has cardinality at most $\lceil \log_2 p \rceil + 1$. Now, assume that the instance $\mathcal{I}$ contains n distinct constraints. We sketch the argument in dimension 2. Since by assumption the instance is compact, and the representation is minimal, the n constraints define at least n and at most n^2 distinguished points. Therefore, there are at least n distinct coordinates in $adom(\mathcal{I})$, and at most $2n^2$. If we add the powers of 2 in $adom(\mathcal{I})$, we get a cardinality bounded by $2n^2 + 2$. If the number of tuples is n, the fact that the representation is minimal implies that the number of constraints must be proportional to n. $\square$

4 Expressive power result

The main motivation for the bounded inflationary fixpoint operator is its expressive power. In this section, we show that $\mathcal{BIFP}$ captures all polynomial time queries. We start with the upper bound.

Theorem 4.1

- $\mathcal{BIFP} \subseteq$ PTIME
- $\mathcal{BPFP} \subseteq$ PSPACE

Proof. (sketch) Using the definition of the active domain semantics, we first show that the first recursion (and hence the whole program) will terminate in a polynomial number of steps. In the worst case the bound on the number of recursion steps is that of a recursion using no addition over the active domain, whose size, by Proposition 3.1, is polynomial in the size of the instance.

To complete the proof, we need to show two things: that each iteration of the second recursion takes polynomial time in the size of the relations at that point, and that only a constant number of new values are created at each step.

This guarantees that the size of the fixpoint relation remains polynomial in the size of the input.

The latter follows from the fact that the second recursion only uses safe formulae with quantifiers of the form $(\exists!\bar{y})$, which means that only one new object can be created at each step. To show the former, we need to show that the $\{\lambda_i, \nu\}$ operators can be evalued in PTIME. Evaluation of λ_i is a straightforward matter of computing the parameters of the constraints involved. As for ν, the key point here is that rational numbers are only generated by solving constraints, so that their representation in reduced form can be maintained throughout the evaluation of the formulas. □

Theorem 4.2 $\mathcal{BIFP} = $ PTIME.

Proof (sketch) We have to show PTIME $\subseteq \mathcal{BIFP}$. Let Q be a query on linear constraint databases that is computable in PTIME, i.e., there is a Turing machine M that, given an encoding of a linear constraint database, computes an encoding of the result of Q in polynomial time. We can select any appropriate "reasonable" encoding for the machine we choose to simulate, and shall make use of this fact later on. We must show that there are formulae in $\mathcal{BIFP}$ that: (i) **Encode the input database**; (ii) **Simulate the computation of the Turing Machine**; and (iii) **Decode the output**. The difficult parts are the encoding of the input and the decoding of the output.

Given an instance of a linear constraint database relation, in order to be able to encode it on the Turing tape we need to be able to extract, using $\mathcal{BIFP}$, the representation of the individual constraints. We shall assume that the Turing Machine encodes each equality constraint as a tuple of points that represents the distinguished points satisfying this constraint (recall that we can select a TM that uses any reasonable encoding). Since the database is compact, these points provide enough information to reconstruct the constraint. Inequality constraints are encoded in the same way, along with an indication of the sign of the appropriate inequality.

The fact that the distinguished points can be computed by a $\mathcal{BIFP}$ query follows from work of [DGVG97]:

Lemma 4.3 Let R be a relation. There exists a FO+linear query that computes precisely the set of distinguished points of R.

Given the distinguished points, we use the ν function to compute a pair of integers (p, q) encoding each rational number coordinate. We now have to extract, using $\mathcal{BIFP}$, the binary encoding of each of these integers.

We start by taking $x = 1$, and, by repeatedly multiplying by 2, find the smallest power of 2 (2^n) that is larger than all of the integers under consideration (this is guaranteed to terminate in a linear number of steps, by the definition of the active domain).

We then construct a relation $T(x, y, z)$ such that (x, y, z) is in T whenever the yth bit of x is z, for all integers x as above. This will encode the binary representations we need.

For each x, $T(x, y, z)$ is computed by testing if $2^{n-1} < x$. If so, insert $(x, n - 1, 1)$ into T and repeat with $x - 2^{n-1}$ (and 2^{n-2}), otherwise insert $(x, n - 1, 0)$ into T and repeat with x. The details of the recursion should now be clear.

Note that the algorithm as described above requires a nested use of $\mathcal{BIFP}$: iterate first over all x and then over all powers of 2. Nested use of $\mathcal{BIFP}$ is, however, not allowed, as this could lead to the creation of too many new objects, taking us out of PTIME. We solve this problem by using an application of IΞ over a single relation with additional columns to specify which x is currently being considered.

We now show the main result. Let R be an input relation of arity k (w.l.o.g, assume that there is only one). We first consider the encoding of R on the Turing tape. R is encoded using a model similar to the point-based mode. The distinguished points of $\mathcal{P}oint(R)$ are stored in a relation $D \subseteq \mathbb{Q}^k$. We define $k+1$ relations to store the isolated points, the open line segments, the open triangles, etc., included in R. The simplest way to do this is (for open line segments) to consider each pair of points in $\mathcal{P}oint(R)$, define the line segment between them using λ_1, and test whether it is contained in R. In this way, we obtain relations over rational numbers that encode the contents of the input relation. These rationals are then encoded in terms of pairs of integers, using ν, and the binary representations of these integers are computed as above. The rest of the encoding in a relation that represents the tape of the Turing machine is classical [AHV94].

The simulation of the Turing machine is based on a set of indices for time and space. We consider the active domain and define a successor relation on it. This is generalized to a successor over k-ary tuples to get a sufficient number of indices. The simulation of the transitions of the machine is standard [AHV94].

Finally, given an encoding of the output relation on the machine's output tape, we have to construct a formula in $\mathcal{BIFP}$ that defines the output relation in terms of constraints. Unlike in the classical case [Imm86, Var82], the tape may now contain the encoding of new values, which represent the coordinates of new points. These have to be decoded. Using similar techniques to those used in the encoding step, we decode the binary representation of the numbers on the tape. This gives us pairs of integers, and it would appear that we now need to convert them into rational numbers. This is, however, not neccessary, as constraints with rational coefficients can be converted into constraints with integer coefficients, with only a polynomial increase in space. The constraints themselves are now reconstructed using the λ_i predicates. □

Techniques similar to these can also be used to obtain other characterization results:

Theorem 4.4 $\mathcal{BPFP}$ = PSPACE for linear constraint databases.

The encoding and decoding are done in a similar way. The capture of PSPACE is standard [Var82, AHV94]. □

5 Conclusion

We have exhibited logical query languages which capture precisely the set of polynomial time computable geometric queries on linear constraint databases. These proofs are specific to the case of linear constraints, among other reasons because they encode constraint relations as finite relations by extracting the distinguished points of a relation. The extension of these results to more general constraints such as polynomial constraints would require completely different techniques, and it is not clear to us if there is a logic which characterizes the set of PTIME queries over polynomial constraint databases. This yields a variant of the classical PTIME question [Gur88].

The language we have described is not particularly elegant. More research is needed to come up with nicer languages for handling recursion over linear constraints. One possible approach would be to allow the creation of a new "cell" at each step, rather than just a single point. This would permit simulation of the λ_i predicates in the language, but an elegant formalisation of the notion of adding such a cell is an open problem. Similarly, the need for the ν predicates could perhaps be removed by the use of appropriate number-theoretic techniques.

In another direction, one could look for more elegant approaches to the use of recursion, either simplifying the definition of the active domain, or eliminating the need for a double recursion, perhaps with the goal of capturing all useful queries, even if not all of PTIME.

References

[AHV94] S. Abiteboul, R. Hull, and V. Vianu. *Foundations of Databases*. Addison-Wesley, 1994.

[DGVG97] F. Dumortier, M. Gyssens, L. Vandeurzen, and D. Van Gucht. On the decidability of semi-linearity for semi-algebraic sets and its implications for spatial databases. In *Proc. ACM Symp. on Principles of Database Systems*, 1997.

[GS97] S. Grumbach and J. Su. Queries with arithmetical constraints. *Theoretical Computer Science*, 173(1):151–181, 1997.

[GST94] S. Grumbach, J. Su, and C. Tollu. Linear constraint query languages: Expressive power and complexity. In D. Leivant, editor, *Logic and Computational Complexity*, Indianapolis, 1994. Springer Verlag. LNCS 960.

[Gue94] R. Gueting. An Introduction to Spatial Database Systems. *The VLDB Journal*, 3(4), 1994.

[Gur88] Y. Gurevich. *Current Trends in Theoretical Computer Science, E. Borger Ed.*, chapter Logic and the Challenge of Computer Science, pages 1–57. Computer Science Press, 1988.

[Imm86] N. Immerman. Relational queries computable in polynomial time. *Inf. and Control*, 68:86–104, 1986.

[KKR90] P. Kanellakis, G Kuper, and P. Revesz. Constraint query languages. In *Proc. 9th ACM Symp. on Principles of Database Systems*, pages 299–313, Nashville, 1990.

[PVV95]   J. Paredaens, J. Van den Bussche, and D. Van Gucht. First-order queries on finite structures over the reals. In *Proceedings 10th IEEE Symposium on Logic in Computer Science*. IEEE Computer Society Press, 1995.

[Var82]   M. Vardi. The complexity of relational query languages. In *Proc. 14th ACM Symp. on Theory of Computing*, pages 137–146, 1982.

[VGV95]   L. Vandeurzen, M. Gyssens, and D. Van Gucht. On the desirability and limitations of linear spatial database models. In *Advances in Spatial Databases, 4th Int. Symp., SSD'95*, pages 14–28. Springer, 1995.

[Whi57]   H. Whitney. Elementary structure of real algebraic varieties. *Annals of Mathematics*, 66:545–556, 1957.

Finding Solvable Subsets of Constraint Graphs

Christoph M. Hoffmann[1]   Andrew Lomonosov[2]

Meera Sitharam[23]

Abstract. We present a network flow based, degree of freedom analysis for graphs that arise in geometric constraint systems. For a vertex and edge weighted constraint graph with m edges and n vertices, we give an $O(n(m + n))$ time max-flow based algorithm to isolate a subgraph that can be solved separately. Such a subgraph is called *dense*. If the constraint problem is not overconstrained, the subgraph will be minimal. For certain overconstrained problems, finding minimal dense subgraphs may require up to $O(n^2(m + n))$ steps. Finding a minimum dense subgraph is NP-hard. The algorithm has been implemented and consistently outperforms a simple but fast, greedy algorithm.

Keywords: Extremal subgraph, dense graph, network flow, combinatorial optimization, constraint solving, geometric constraint graph, geometric modeling.

1 Introduction

A geometric constraint problem consists of a finite set of geometric objects and a finite set of constraints between them. Geometric objects include *point, line, plane, circle,* and so on. Constraints between them might be *parallel, perpendicular, distance, tangency,* and so on. Some of these constraints are logical, such as incidence or tangency; others are dimensional such as distance or angle. Geometric constraint systems are the basis for design and manipulation in geometric modeling, and arise in virtual reality, robotics, and computer graphics as well. For applications in CAD, see, e.g., [12, 14, 23]. There is an extensive literature on geometric constraint solving. For recent reviews see, e.g, [7].

Geometric constraint problems can be solved algebraically. Briefly, the geometric objects are coordinatized, and the constraints between them are expressed in the form of polynomial equations. The resulting system of equations is usually nonlinear, and most constraint solvers use techniques for decomposing the

---

[1] Computer Science, Purdue University, West Lafayette, Indiana 47907, USA. Supported in part by NSF Grants CDA 92-23502 and CCR 95-05745, and by ONR Contract N00014-96-1-0635.

[2] Mathematics and Computer Science, Kent State University, Kent, Ohio 44242, USA

[3] Supported in part by NSF Grant CCR 94-09809.

system into small subsystems that can be solved separately where possible; e.g., [2, 8, 13, 17]. Such a decomposition increases solver efficiency and robustness substantially. Direct attempts at processing the entire system include using Gröbner bases [24] or the Wu-Ritt method [3]. They are general but typically do not scale.

Graph Based Constraint Analysis A large class of solvers translates the constraint problem into a graph. Graph vertices represent geometric objects, edges represent constraints. For ternary and higher constraints, the graph is a hypergraph. Analysis and decomposition of the problem is based on isolating subgraphs that correspond to subsystems of the equations that can be solved separately. The graph is *weighted*; both edges and vertices have a positive integer weight. The weight of a vertex is the degree of freedom of the represented geometric entity.[4] The weight of an edge equals the degrees of freedom determined by the represented constraint.

In the case of planar constraint problems, a class widely studied, several solvers decompose the constraint graph recursively into triangles and solve each triangle separately [2, 20, 21]. This decomposition is a special case of a *degree of freedom analysis*. For example, in the solver [2, 7], the geometric objects are points, lines, and rigid clusters of them, with the respective degrees of freedom of 2, 2, and 3. Two specific situations are considered in these graph analyses:

1. An edge of weight 1 is incident to vertices of weight 2. The associated constraint subproblem can be solved: for example, if the vertices are points and the edge a distance constraint, then the solution is a pair of points at fixed distance moving as a rigid body with 3 degrees of freedom.
2. A triangle with vertices of weight 3, and edges weight 2 represents incidences between geometric objects in 3 clusters. By placing the three incident pairs according to the constraints derived from their relative position within each rigid cluster, the three clusters can be placed rigidly with respect to each other and are merged into a bigger cluster.

Many interesting results are known about the properties of this type of constraint analysis, e.g., [9, 10].

Problem Statement and Results A *weighted undirected graph* is a graph where every vertex and every edge has a positive integer weight. We consider the following problem:

$G = (V, E, w)$ is a weighted undirected graph with n vertices V and m edges E; $w(v)$ is the weight of the vertex v and $w(e)$ is the weight of the edge e. Find a vertex-induced subgraph $A \subseteq G$ such that

$$\sum_{e \in A} w(e) - \sum_{v \in A} w(v) > K \qquad (1)$$

---

[4] Roughly speaking, the number of independent variables coordinatizing a geometric object is the number of degrees of freedom.

Such a subgraph A is called *dense*. It's *density* is the quantity on the left handside of (1). Typically, edge and vertex weights have a constant bound. In constraint solving, we seek a *minimal* dense subgraph, that is, a dense subgraph that does not contain a proper dense subgraph.

We design, analyze and implement an algorithm to find dense subgraphs in $O(n(m + n))$ steps. It is essentially a modified version of an incremental, maximum flow algorithm where edge capacities are saturated in certain natural order. This modification is crucial, however, in that it allows one to use existing flows in order to derive useful information about the densities of already examined subgraphs. If the graph arises from a geometric constraint problem that is not overconstrained, then the subgraphs found will be minimal and m will be $O(n)$. For overconstrained problems, additional processing is needed and may require up to $O(n^2(m + n))$ steps. In our experiments, the algorithm has consistently outperformed a simple but fast, greedy algorithm. The related problem of finding the *minimum* dense subgraph A is NP-hard.

Dense Subgraphs and Degrees of Freedom We seek a subgraph of the constraint graph in which the weights of the vertices minus the weights of the edges equals a fixed constant D, exactly the situation expressed by Inequality (1) with $K = -(D+1)$. In the example of planar constraint solvers [2, 7], $D = 3$ because a rigid planar figure has three degrees of freedom (absent symmetries). In 3-space, $D = 6$ in general. If the subproblem is to be fixed with respect to a global coordinate system, then $D = 0$ is required.

When a subgraph of the appropriate density has been found, the corresponding geometric objects can be placed rigidly with respect to each other using only the constraints between them. It is advantageous to find small dense subgraphs so that the associated equation system is as small as possible.

Having processed a dense subgraph, the solver then contracts the the subgraph to a single vertex v_c of weight D, suitably inducing edges between v_c and the other vertices. The full description of this process is beyond the scope of the conference paper, but we note that our algorithm extends to address this iterated dense subgraph problem.

If G is a constraint graph and A a dense subgraph, then density $d(A) = D$ means that the corresponding subproblem is *generically* well-constrained: in general, the geometric problem has a discrete set of solutions. For instance, for six points in space and twelve distance constraints between them, in the topology of the edges of an octahedron, the configuration is rigid, [15, 25]. However, for special distance values we obtain Bricard octahedra and then there would be nonrigid solutions; i.e., the problem would be actually underconstrained [26].

Prior Work on Constraint Graph Analysis Prior attempts at a degree of freedom analysis for constraint graphs often concentrated on recognizing specific dense subgraphs of known shape, such as the triangles of [2, 20, 21] or the patterns of [2, 15, 16]. This approach has limited scope. The scope can always be extended by increasing the repertoire of patterns of dense subgraphs. However, doing so results in greater combinatorial complexity and eventually makes efficient implementation too difficult.

More general attempts reduce the recognition of dense subgraphs in a degree-of-freedom analysis to a maximum weighted matching problem in bipartite graphs using methods from, e.g., [18]. A variation [1] of this approach does not use a degree-of-freedom analysis and directly deals with the algebraic constraints. In this case, a maximum cardinality bipartite matching is used, since no weights are required. The approach can be generalized to a weighted version required for a degree-of-freedom analysis by replicating vertices. We discuss briefly in Section 2 why both approaches are less efficient than the approach presented here. In particular, having found the required matching, finding a dense subgraph requires significant additional work, and it becomes difficult to isolate minimal dense subgraphs. The general approach of [17] appears to be exponential.

A different approach to constraint graph analysis uses rigidity theorems; e.g., [4, 11]. Corresponding decomposition steps may be nondeterministic or require difficult symbolic computations when computing a solution.

2 Finding a Dense Subgraph

We devise a flow-based algorithm for finding dense subgraphs assuming that $K = 0$ in Equation (1). We discuss the case $K \neq 0$ in Section 4.

Definition For $A \subseteq G$ define the **density** function d

$$d(A) = \sum_{e \in A} w(e) - \sum_{v \in A} w(v)$$

Suppose that we want to find a *most* dense subgraph $A \subseteq G$, i.e, one for which $d(A)$ is maximum. We could maximize, over subgraphs A of G, the expression

$$d(A) + \sum_{v \in G} w(v) = \sum_{e \in A} w(e) + \sum_{v \notin A} w(v) \qquad (2)$$

or, in other words, minimize

$$\min_{A \subseteq G} \left(\sum_{e \notin A} w(e) + \sum_{v \in A} w(v) \right) \qquad (3)$$

To do this, consider a bipartite graph $\tilde{G} = (M, N, \tilde{E}, w)$ associated with the given graph $G = (V, E, w)$. The vertices in N are the vertices in V and the vertices in M are the edges in E. Moreover, the edges of $\tilde{G}$ are $\tilde{E} = \{(e, u), (e, v) \mid e = (u, v), e \in E\}$. The weights w now appear on the vertices of $\tilde{G}$. Maximizing the expression (2) reduces to finding a maximum weighted independent set in the bipartite graph $\tilde{G}$, or, equivalently, the minimum weight vertex cover.

There are two ways to try to find the minimum weight vertex cover. The minimum *cardinality* vertex cover in a bipartite graph can be identified with a maximum cardinality matching and can be found using network flow in $O(\sqrt{n}m)$ time [5]. To take advantage of this algorithm, however, we need to replicate edges and vertices corresponding to the weights, find a minimum cardinality vertex cover in this larger graph, and then try to locate a corresponding minimum weight vertex cover in $\tilde{G}$ and the corresponding dense subgraph in the graph G.

The unweighted version of bipartite matching can be used naturally when variables are directly represented as vertices and the algebraic equations are represented as edges (instead of analyzing degrees-of-freedom). This results in a constant factor increase in the size of the graph. Using this approach, the problem of finding a dense subgraph – when $K = -1$ – was solved in [1], however, it is not clear how to extend the algorithm for general K.

A second way is to search for a minimum weighted vertex cover by solving the maximum (vertex) weighted bipartite matching problem. A maximum (edge) weighted bipartite matching problem can be solved in $O(\sqrt{n}m \log n)$ time for bounded weights, [22]. This trivially gives a solution to the maximum (vertex) weighted bipartite matching problem. The catch is that, unlike in the unweighted case, a minimum weighted vertex cover does *not* correspond directly to a maximum weighted matching. Having found a maximum weighted matching, a significant amount of work is needed to obtain the minimum weight vertex cover, and, from it, the corresponding dense subgraph in G.

In general, the maximum matching approach has the following disadvantages. (1) The maximum (weighted) matching in $\tilde{G}$ does not directly correspond to the dense subgraph in G. (2) We need only *some* subgraph of a specific density, not necessarily a *most* dense one. (3) Maximum matching provides no natural way of finding a minimal dense subgraph. We develop a more efficient method analogously based on a different optimization problem (see [19]), but which will be seen to address both drawbacks.

Construction of the Network From the graph G, construct a bipartite *directed* network $G^* = (M, N, s, t, E^*, w)$, where M, N and E^* are as in $\tilde{G}$. The source s is connected by a directed edge to every node in M, and every node in N is connected by a directed edge to the sink t. The capacity of the network edge (s, e), $e \in M$, is the weight $w(e)$ of the edge e in G. The capacity of the network edge (v, t), $v \in N$, is equal to the weight $w(v)$ of the vertex v in G. The capacity of the network edge (e, v), $e \in M$, $v \in N$, is infinite. There are no other network edges. See also Figure 1.

A minimum cut in G^* *directly* defines a subgraph A that minimizes Expression (3). It can be found as the max flow using a netflow algorithm. Now we are only interested in finding a dense subgraph and not necessarily the *most* dense one. So, we are interested in a small enough cut in G^*, not necessarily the smallest one. Thus, to find a dense subgraph, there should be an algorithm that is faster than a general maximum flow (or minimum cut) algorithm.

The algorithm is a modification of the incremental max flow algorithm. The

468

Fig. 1. Constraint graph (left) and associated network (right).

idea of the algorithm (Algorithm Dense below) is to start with the empty subgraph G' of G and add to it one vertex at time. When a vertex v is added, consider the adjacent edges e incident to G'. For each e, try to distribute the weight $w(e)$ to one or both of its endpoints without exceeding their weights; see also Figure 2. As illustrated by Figure 3, we may need to redistribute some of the flow later.

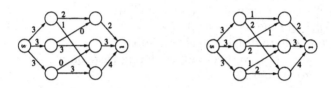

Fig. 2. Two different flows for the constraint graph of Figure 1

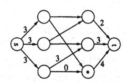

Fig. 3. Initial flow assignment that requires redistribution later

If we are able to distribute all edges, then G' is not dense. If no dense subgraph exists, then the algorithm will terminate in $O(n(m+n))$ steps and announce this fact. If there is a dense subgraph, then there is an edge whose weight cannot be distributed even with redistribution. The last vertex added when this happens can be shown to be in all dense subgraphs $A \subseteq G'$.

Distributing an edge e in G now corresponds to pushing a flow equal to the capacity of (s, e) from s to t in G^*. This is possible either directly by a path of the form $\langle s, e, v, t \rangle$ in G^*, or it might require flow redistribution achieved by a standard search for augmenting paths [6], using network flow techniques, see Figures 4, 5. Note that the search for augmenting paths takes advantage of the fact that the flow through each vertex in M is distributed to exactly 2 vertices in N (lines 4-7) in Algorithm Distribute. While this decreases running time by a constant factor, it doesn't affect complexity.

If there is an augmenting path, then the resulting flows in G^* provide a distribution of the weight of each edge e in the current subgraph G' consisting of the examined vertices and edges of the original graph G as follows: the weight $w(e)$ of each edge e connecting the vertices a and b is split into two parts f_e^a and f_e^b such that $f_e^a + f_e^b = w(e)$ and, for each vertex $v \in G'$, $\sum_{e=(v,*)} f_e^v \leq w(v)$.

If there is no augmenting path for the residual flow on (s, e), i.e, the flow $w(e)$ is undistributable, then a dense subgraph has been found and is identified based on the flows in G^* starting from e.

Algorithm Dense

1. $G' = \emptyset$.
2. **for every** vertex v **do**
3.   **for every** edge e incident to v and to G' **do**
4.   <u>Distribute</u> the weight $w(e)$ of e
5.   **if** not able to distribute all of $w(e)$ **then**
6. A = set of vertices labeled during <u>Distribute</u>
7.   **goto** Step 12
8.   **endif**
9.   **endfor**
10. add vertex v to G'
11. **endfor**
12. **if** $A = \emptyset$ **then** no dense subgraph exists
13. **else** A is a dense subgraph

Algorithm Distribute searches for augmenting paths in G^* to achieve the required flow and the labeling. It repeats a Breadth First Search for augmentation until all of $w(e)$ has been distributed or until there is no augmenting path. The technique is somewhat similar to the one used in max-flow algorithm in [19].

Algorithm Distribute
Input: $(G^*, f, edge)$, where $G^* = (N, M, s, t, E^*, w)$, f is a set of flows f_e^v and $edge$ is the edge that is being distributed.

0. Initialize $scan(v) = 0, label(v) = 0, scan(e) = 0, label(e) = 0$ for all $v \in N, e \in M$
1. $vert = 0$, $capvert = 0$
2. $label(edge) = 1$, $pathcap(edge) = w(edge)$
3. **while** $(w(edge) > \sum_v f_{edge}^v)$ or not all labeled nodes have been scanned
4.   **for** all labeled $e \in M$, with $scan(e) = 0$
5.   label unlabeled neighbors of e (i.e $v \in N$)
6. $scan(e) = 1$, $pred(v) = e$, $pathcap(v) = pathcap(e)$
7.   **endfor**
8.   **for all** labeled $v \in N$ with $scan(v) = 0$
9.   **if** $\min(w(v) - \sum_e f_e^v, pathcap(v)) > capvert$ **then**
10. $vert = v$, $capvert = min(w - \sum_e f_e^v, pathcap(v))$

11.   **else**
12.   label all unlabeled $e' \in M$ s.t $f^v_{e'} > 0$
13.   **endif**
14. $scan(v) = 1$
15.   **endfor**
16.   **if** $vert > 0$ **then**
17.   An augmenting path from s to t has been found: backtrack from $vert$ using $pred()$ and change the values of f^v_e as requirted.
18.   **for all** $e \in M, v \in N$
19.. $label(e) = 0, scan(e) = 0, label(v) = 0, scan(v) = 0$
20.   **endfor**
21. $vert = 0, capvert = 0, label(edge) = 1$
22. $pathcap(edge) = w(edge) - \sum_v f^v_{edge}$
23.   **endif**
24. **endwhile**

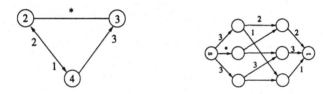

Fig. 4. Current graph G' and corresponding network G^*, the edge marked by asterisk is currently being distributed

Fig. 5. The augmenting path and the distribution of edges in original graph G'

Lemma 1
Let G^* be the bipartite network constructed from G, and $e \in M$. If, after checking all possible augmenting paths originating at e, the flow through (s, e) is less than the capacity of (s, e), and $A = (E_A, V_A)$ is the set of edges and vertices labeled after the search for an augmenting path, then $d(A) > 0$.

Proof: A is a subgraph of G because for every labeled edge $e \in E$ both of its vertices will be labeled. For all $v \in V_A$, the network edges (v, t) are saturated, otherwise there is an augmenting path from e to v and the flow through (s,e) can be increased. Let f be the maximum flow through (E_A, V_A). Since all (v,t) are saturated, $f = \sum_{v \in A} w(v)$, but since at least one edge (s,e) is not distributed $f < \sum_{e \in A} w(e)$; therefore $d(A) = \sum_{e \in A} w(e) - \sum_{v \in A} w(v) > 0$. $\square$

Complexity Analysis In the worst case, constructing an augmenting path labels at most $m + n$ nodes are labeled. Since the algorithm stops when the total edge weight exceeds the total vertex weight, the total edge weight that is distributed is at most the total vertex weight times a constant bound b. Each augmentation increases the flow by least 1 unit. Therefore, the number of augmentations cannot exceed $O(n)$. Hence, Algorithm Dense has complexity $O(n(m+n))$.

3 Finding a Minimal Dense Subgraph

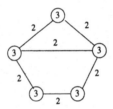

Fig. 6. This graph is dense for $K = -4$, so is upper triangle

Let $G' = (V', E')$ be the subgraph already examined by Algorithm Dense. That is, assume that the vertices V' have been examined and the weight $w(e)$ of all induced edges e has been distributed. Let v be the first vertex that is about to be examined next, such that the weight of one of its incident edges e adjacent to G' cannot be distributed. Let $V_A \subseteq V'$ be the set of vertices labeled while trying to distribute $w(e)$, (which includes the vertex v), and let A be the subgraph induced by V_A. By Lemma 1, A is a dense subgraph.

Lemma 2
Every dense subgraph of A contains v.

Proof: Let A' be a dense subgraph of A not containing v. Then there should be an edge $e \in A'$ such that e was not distributed before v was considered. However, this contradicts our assumption that all edges in G' have been distributed. $\square$

Remark
Similarly, if $(v,v_1), (v,v_2), ..., (v,v_k)$ are undistributed edges of v then every dense subgraph of A contains at least one edge from this list. If $k = 1$ then every dense subgraph of A contains (v,v_1).

Proposition 3

If the amount of undistributable flow, i.e, the density of A is $d(A)$ and A' is a dense proper subgraph of A, then $0 < d(A') < d(A)$ (in general, $K < d(A') < d(A)$).

Proof: Note that the excess flow comes from the edges incident to v. Suppose $A' \subseteq A$ is dense and $d(A') \geq d(A)$. By Lemma 2, A' contains v. Consider the relative complement A^* of A' with respect to A. Then $d(A^*) \leq 0$, which implies that the vertices of A^* could not have been labeled after distributing the flow of the edges of v. Since all vertices in V_A are labeled, we know that $A = A'$. $\square$

Corollary 4

If $d(A) = 1$ then A is minimal. In general, if $d(A) = K + 1$, then A is minimal.

In particular, when $K = 0$, well-constrained or underconstrained problems have $d(A) \leq 1$. Then, by Corollary 4, we know that the subgraph found by Algorithm Dense is minimal. Moreover, if overconstrained problems are rejected, then a first test for overconstrained would be to determine $\sum_{e \in G} w(e) - \sum_{v \in G} w(v) > 1$ in linear time. This test would reject many overconstrained problems. The remaining cases would be found by noting whether $d(A) > 1$ when Algorithm Dense terminates.

We may accept consistently overconstrained problems. In that case, the graph A may have to be analyzed further to extract a minimal dense subgraph. We now develop a method for performing this extraction, once a dense subgraph A has been found by Algorithm Dense and $d(A) > 1$. The algorithm to be developed post-processes only the subgraph A.

Without loss of generality, assume that A contains the vertices $\{v_1, \ldots, v_l, v_{l+1}\}$, and v_{l+1} was the last vertex examined when A was found. The density $d(A)$ is the total undistributed weight of the edges between v_{l+1} and $\{v_1, \ldots, v_l\}$. We begin with the knowledge of a subgraph B of A that is contained in *every* dense subgraph of A. By Lemma 2, B contains initially the vertex v_{l+1}. The algorithm to be developed is to determine either an enlargement of the graph B, or else a reduction of the graph A.

We perform the following step iteratively. Choose a vertex $v_k \notin B$ from A. Determine the quantity $c = d(A) - w(e') + f_{e'}^{v_k} + f_{e'}^{v_{l+1}}$ where e' is the edge (v_k, v_{l+1}). That is, c is the undistributed weight of edges in A without v_k. Remove the vertex v_k from A along with its edges. This would create unutilized capacity in the set of vertices adjacent to v_k (that are in A) through the set E_k of incident edges. The excess vertex capacity is

$$\sum_{e \in E_k} w(e) - w(v_k) - w(e') + f_{e'}^{v_k} + f_{e'}^{v_{l+1}}$$

where e' is the edge between v_k and v_{l+1}. This quantity is the total flow on the edges of v_k, distributed away from v_k. We now attempt to distribute the previously undistributed weight of the edges between v_{l+1} and $\{v_1, \ldots, v_l\} - \{v_k\}$, using redistribution if necessary. We use Algorithm Distribute on the modified network, setting the capacity of (v_k, t) to zero. There are two outcomes possible:

1. If we distribute all of c successfully into the newly created holes, or excess capacity on the vertices adjacent to v_k, then no subgraph of $A - v_k$ is dense, so v_k belongs in every dense subgraph of A, and hence gets restored into A and, moreover, gets added to B.

2. If we were unable to distribute c, then by Lemma 1, we have found a smaller dense subgraph of $A - v_k$. This new subgraph consists only of the vertices labeled by the Algorithm Distribute in the process of distributing one of the undistributed edges adjacent to v_{l+1}. This outcome reduces the size of A. Note that, by Proposition 3, the density (and size) of the new graph A must drop by at least 1.

We repeat this process for the remaining vertices in $A - B$. We stop either when $d(B) > 0$, because then B is minimal dense, or when $d(A) = 1$, because then A is minimal dense.

Complexity Analysis The complexity of each iteration described above is $O(n(m + n))$, since c represents the undistributed weight on at most n edges adjacent to v_{l+1} are distributed at each iteration. We can assume that the sum of capacities of the edges is constant, thus the determination of a minimal dense subgraph takes $O(n^2(m + n))$ steps. Note, however, that by Proposition 3 the actual complexity rarely reaches this upper bound.

The complexity of the iteration is reduced to $O(m+n)$ if the constraint graph has bounded valence or if $d(A)$ has an a-priori constant bound. The latter situation means that the constraint problem has a bound on the "overconstrainedness" of subgraphs, a natural assumption if the constraint problem is specified interactively and we keep track of the density of the full constraint graph. In those cases, the complexity reduces to $O(n(m + n))$ steps.

Algorithm Minimal

Comment: The input is the output of Dense, a dense (sub)graph A of G, and the distribution of edge weights f_e^a and f_e^b for each edge $e = (a, b)$. Note that v_{l+1} is the last vertex added that caused A to be found, and e' is the edge between v_k and v_{l+1}.

1. $B = \{v_{l+1}\}$
2. **while** $d(B) \leq 0$ and $d(A) > 1$ **do**
3.   choose $v_k \in A - B$
4. $c = d(A) - w(e') + f_{e'}^{v_k} + f_{e'}^{v_{l+1}}$
5.   **for** all $v \in N$ (Removing $\{v_k\}$ from A)
6.   Let $e = (v, v_k)$
7.   remove e from M
8.   **endfor**
9.   remove v_k from N
10.   <u>Distribute</u> (in A) excess c from the edges of v
11.   **if** there are some undistributed edges left **then**
12.   set A = new labeled graph

13.   **else**
14.   set $A = A \cup \{v_k\}$ (as well as restoring edges of v_k)
15.   set $B = B \cup \{v_k\}$
16.   **endif**
17. **endwhile**
18. **output** B, **if** $d(B) > 0$, **else output** A.

4 The Case of $K \neq 0$

As presented, our algorithms satisfy Inequality (1) for $K = 0$: keep adding
vertices until we are unable to distribute the edge weight/capacity. The first
undistributable edge signals a dense graph A, for $K = 0$, and $d(A) > d(A - v)$, where v was the last vertex examined. We now explain how to modify the
algorithm to accommodate different values of K.

The modification for $K > 0$ is trivial. Instead of exiting Algorithm Dense
when an edge cannot be distributed, exit when the total undistributable edge
capacity exceeds K. The computation of the total undistributable edge capacity
so far is based only on the weights of the labeled edges and vertices, thus ensuring
that the resulting dense graph is connected. An analogous change is in order for
Algorithm Minimal. Clearly this modification does not affect the performance
complexity of the algorithms.

When $K < 0$ the algorithms can also be modified without increasing the
complexity. Suppose, therefore, that $K < 0$, and consider Step 4 of Algorithm
Dense. If $w(v) + K \geq 0$, simply reduce the capacity of the network edge (v, t)
to $w(v) + K$ and distribute $w(e)$ in the modified network. If the edge cannot be
distributed, then the subgraph found in Step 6 has density exceeding K. If every
incident edge can be distributed, then restore the capacity of the network edge
when adding v to G'.

If the weight $w(v)$ of the added vertex v is too small, that is, if $w(v) + K < 0$,
then a more complex modification is needed. We set the capacity of (v, t) to zero.
Let e be an new edge to be distributed, and do the following.

1. <u>Distribute</u> the edge weight $w(e)$ in the modified network.
2. **if** $w(e)$ cannot be distributed **then**
3.   we have found a dense subgraph for K; exit.
4. **else**
5.   save the existing flow for Step 10.
6.   increase the flow of e by $-(w(v) + K)$
7.   **if** the increased flow cannot be <u>Distributed</u> **then**
8.   we have found a dense subgraph for K; exit.
9.   **else**
10.   restore the old flow. No dense subgraph found
11.   **endif**
12. **endif**

In worst case the algorithm saves and restores the flows for every edge added,
which requires $O(m)$ operations per edge. Distributing the edge flow however

dominates this cost since it may require up to $O(m+n)$ operations per edge; so the modification does not adversely impact asymptotic performance.

5 Implementation

The network flow algorithms were implemented in C. Both Dense and Minimal were run in sequence. We tested the algorithms on low-density graphs G, where $|G| = 40$, $K = -1$, and a typical minimal dense subgraph A' in G would have density 0 or 1. The number of vertices in the initial dense graph A was between 14 and 22. The dense subgraph A is usually also a minimal dense subgraph (the situation $B = A$ in Algorithm Minimal), this being the worst case for the combined algorithm *if* the density of A is > 0. We tested some of the usual (generically well or under constrained) cases where $d(A) = 0 = K+1$, where the Algorithm Minimal is unnecessary by Corollary 4. As a complexity measure, we counted the number of times a vertex or an edge is being labeled.

Heuristically, the selection of the next vertex to be examined and saturated and edges to be distributed can be done in a greedy fashion. That is, at each step choose a vertex with the "heaviest" set of edges connecting it to the set of vertices in G' and start distributing its edges in descending weight order. The distribution and redistribution of the edges is carried out by using flows on the bipartite network G^* described earlier.

In the table, m is the number of edges of the original graph, $(n = 40)$, A is the dense subgraph found, A' is a minimal dense subgraph of A, n_1 is the number of operations required to find A, n_2 is the total number of operations required to find A', p is the number of augmented pathes required to find A'.

m	$|A|$	$|A'|$	$d(A')$	n_1	n_2	p
141	21	20	1	518	1644	162
100	20	20	0	728	728	66
139	18	18	0	680	680	76
191	22	22	0	903	903	91
71	*	*	*	187	187	61
100	23	22	0	624	1232	134
139	20	19	0	623	872	190

Table 1. Performance of the Netflow Algorithms. The case marked * has no dense subgraphs.

Note that since the density of A was small, the minimal part increased a running time by a small constant factor.

We also implemented a simple, but fast greedy algorithm for finding dense subgraphs. In our experiments, the greedy algorithm was consistently and significantly inferior to the network flow algorithms.

6 Conclusions

The algorithms we have developed are general and efficient. Previous degree-of-freedom analyses usually analyze simple loops in the constraint graph, or else are unable to isolate a *minimal* subgraph that is dense. Moreover, by making K a parameter of the algorithm, the method presented here can be applied uniformly to planar or spatial geometry constraint graphs. Extensions to ternary and higher-order constraints can also be made.

When constraint problems are not overconstrained, a typical situation in applications, then the algorithms perform better. This is not uncommon in other constraint graph analyses [10], and is related to the fact that a well-constrained geometric constraint graph has only $O(n)$ edges.

We have implemented an extension of the algorithm that iterates finding dense subgraphs and solves a geometric constraint problem recursively by condensing dense subgraphs to single vertices in the manner first described in [2, 7]. Here, a critical aspect is to account for previously constructed flows and running Algorithm Dense incrementally.

A specific advantage of our flow-based analysis is that we can run the algorithm on-line. That is, the constraint graph and its edges can be input continuously to the algorithm, and for each new vertex or edge the flow can be updated accordingly. Thus, it is a good fit with geometric constraint solving applications.

References

1. S. Ait-Aoudia, R. Jegou, and D. Michelucci. Reduction of constraint systems. In *Compugraphics*, pages 83–92, 1993.
2. W. Bouma, I. Fudos, C. Hoffmann, J. Cai, and R. Paige. A geometric constraint solver. *Computer Aided Design*, 27:487–501, 1995.
3. S. C. Chou, X. S. Gao, and J. Z. Zhang. A method of solving geometric constraints. Technical report, Wichita State University, Dept. of Computer Sci., 1996.
4. G. Crippen and T. Havel. *Distance Geometry and Molecular Conformation*. John Wiley & Sons, 1988.
5. S. Even and R. Tarjan. Network flow and testing graph connectivity. *SIAM journal on computing*, 3:507–518, 1975.
6. L.R. Ford and D.R. Fulkerson. *Flows in Networks*. Princeton Univ. Press, 1962.
7. I. Fudos. *Geometric Constraint Solving*. PhD thesis, Purdue University, Dept of Computer Science, 1995.
8. I. Fudos and C. M. Hoffmann. Constraint-based parametric conics for CAD. *Computer Aided Design*, 28:91–100, 1996.
9. I. Fudos and C. M. Hoffmann. Correctness proof of a geometric constraint solver. *Intl. J. of Computational Geometry and Applications*, 6:405–420, 1996.

10. I. Fudos and C. M. Hoffmann. A graph-constructive approach to solving systems of geometric constraints. *ACM Trans on Graphics*, page in press, 1997.

11. T. Havel. Some examples of the use of distances as coordinates for Euclidean geometry. *J. of Symbolic Computation*, 11:579–594, 1991.

12. C. M. Hoffmann. Solid modeling. In J. E. Goodman and J. O'Rourke, editors, *CRC Handbook on Discrete and Computational Geometry*. CRC Press, Boca Raton, FL, 1997.

13. C. M. Hoffmann and J. Peters. Geometric constraints for CAGD. In M. Daehlen, T. Lyche, and L. Schumaker, editors, *Mathematical Methods fot Curves and Surfaces*, pages 237–254. Vanderbilt University Press, 1995.

14. C. M. Hoffmann and J. Rossignac. A road map to solid modeling. *IEEE Trans. Visualization and Comp. Graphics*, 2:3–10, 1996.

15. Christoph M. Hoffmann and Pamela J. Vermeer. Geometric constraint solving in R^2 and R^3. In D. Z. Du and F. Hwang, editors, *Computing in Euclidean Geometry*. World Scientific Publishing, 1994. second edition.

16. Christoph M. Hoffmann and Pamela J. Vermeer. A spatial constraint problem. In *Workshop on Computational Kinematics*, France, 1995. INRIA Sophia-Antipolis.

17. Ching-Yao Hsu. *Graph-based approach for solving geometric constraint problems*. PhD thesis, University of Utah, Dept. of Comp. Sci., 1996.

18. R. Latham and A. Middleditch. Connectivity analysis: a tool for processing geometric constraints. *Computer Aided Design*, 28:917–928, 1996.

19. E. Lawler. *Combinatorial optimization, networks and Matroids*. Holt, Rinehart and Winston, 1976.

20. J. Owen. Algebraic solution for geometry from dimensional constraints. In *ACM Symp. Found. of Solid Modeling*, pages 397–407, Austin, Tex, 1991.

21. J. Owen. Constraints on simple geometry in two and three dimensions. In *Third SIAM Conference on Geometric Design*. SIAM, November 1993. To appear in Int J of Computational Geometry and Applications.

22. T.L. Magnanti, R.K. Ahuja and J.B. Orlin. *Network Flows*. Prentice-Hall, 1993.

23. Dieter Roller. Dimension-Driven geometry in CAD : a Survey. In *Theory and Practice of Geometric Modeling*, pages 509–523. Springer Verlag, 1989.

24. O. E. Ruiz and P. M. Ferreira. Algebraic geometry and group theory in geometric constraint satisfaction for computer-aided design and assembly planning. *IIE Transactions on Design and Manufacturing*, 28:281–294, 1996.

25. P. Vermeer. Assembling objects through parts correlation. In *Proc. 13th Symp on Comp Geometry*, Nice, France, 1997.

26. W. Wunderlich. Starre, kippende, wackelige und bewegliche Achtflache. *Elemente der Mathematik*, 20:25–48, 1965.

Tractable Disjunctive Constraints

David Cohen[1], Peter Jeavons[1], and Manolis Koubarakis[2]

[1] Department of Computer Science, Royal Holloway, University of London, UK
e-mail: p.jeavons@dcs.rhbnc.ac.uk
[2] Department of Computation, UMIST, Manchester, UK e-mail:
manolis@sna.co.umist.ac.uk

Abstract. Many combinatorial search problems can be expressed as 'constraint satisfaction problems', and this class of problems is known to be NP-complete in general. In this paper we investigate 'disjunctive constraints', that is, constraints which have the form of the disjunction of two constraints of specified types. We show that when the constraint types involved in the disjunction have a certain property, which we call 'independence', and when a certain restricted class of problems is tractable, then the class of all problems involving these disjunctive constraints is tractable. We give examples to show that many known examples of tractable constraint classes arise in this way, and derive new tractable classes which have not previously been identified.

Keywords: Constraint satisfaction problem, complexity, NP-completeness

1 Introduction

The constraint satisfaction problem provides a framework in which it is possible to express, in a natural way, many combinatorial problems encountered in artificial intelligence and elsewhere. The aim in a constraint satisfaction problem is to find an assignment of values to a given set of variables subject to constraints on the values which can be assigned simultaneously to certain specified subsets of variables.

The constraint satisfaction problem is known to be an NP-complete problem in general [19]. However, by imposing restrictions on the constraint interconnections [4, 5, 7, 20, 21], or on the form of the constraints [1, 20, 2, 9, 12, 25, 26], it is possible to obtain restricted versions of the problem which are tractable.

Now that a number of constraint types have been identified which give rise to tractable subproblems of the constraint satisfaction problem, it is of considerable interest to investigate how tractable constraint types may be combined, to yield more general problems which are still tractable.

In this paper we investigate 'disjunctive constraints', that is, constraints which have the form of the disjunction of two constraints of specified types. We show that when the constraint types involved in the disjunction have a certain property, which we call 'independence', and when a certain very restricted subproblem is tractable, then the class of all problems involving these disjunctive constraints is also tractable. This allows new tractable constraint classes to be constructed from existing classes, and so extends the range of known tractable constraint classes.

We give examples to show that many known examples of tractable disjunctive constraints over both finite and infinite domains arise in this way. In particular, we demonstrate that two of the six tractable subproblems of the 'Generalised Satisfiability' problem identified by Schaefer in [23] can be obtained by combining simpler tractable subproblems in this standard way. Furthermore, we show that similar results hold for the 'max-closed' constraints first identified in [2], the ORD-Horn constraints over temporal intervals described in [22], and the disjunctive linear constraints over the real numbers described in [15]. Finally, we describe a new tractable class of constraints over the integers which is derived from the same theorem.

The paper is organised as follows. In Section 2 we give the basic definitions for the constraint satisfaction problem, and define the notion of a tractable set of relations. In Section 3 we introduce the notion of 'independence' of one set of relations with respect to another, and show that this condition, together with the tractability of a certain restricted subproblem, is sufficient to ensure tractability of disjunctive constraints involving two such independent sets. In Section 4 we give examples to illustrate how this property may be used to establish the tractability of a wide variety of tractable constraint classes.

2 Definitions

2.1 The constraint satisfaction problem

Notation 1 *For any set D, and any natural number n, we denote the set of all n-tuples of elements of D by D^n. For any tuple $t \in D^n$, and any i in the range 1 to n, we denote the value in the ith coordinate position of t by $t[i]$. The tuple t may then be written in the form $\langle t[1], t[2], \ldots, t[n] \rangle$.*

A subset of D^n is called an 'n-ary relation' over D.

We now define the 'constraint satisfaction problem' which has been widely studied in the Artificial Intelligence community [19, 20, 16]

Definition 2. An instance of a *constraint satisfaction problem* consists of:

- A finite set of variables, V;
- A domain of values, D;
- A finite set of constraints $C = \{c_1, c_2, \ldots, c_q\}$.
  Each constraint c_i is a pair (S_i, R_i), where S_i is a list of variables of length m_i, called the 'constraint scope', and R_i is an m_i-ary relation over D, called the 'constraint relation'.

The tuples of a constraint relation indicate the allowed combinations of simultaneous values for the variables in the constraint scope. The length of the tuples in the constraint relation will be called the 'arity' of the constraint. In particular, unary constraints specify the allowed values for a single variable, and binary constraints specify the allowed combinations of values for a pair of variables.

To determine the computational complexity of a constraint satisfaction problem we need to specify how each problem instance is encoded in a finite string. In order to simplify this representation, we shall impose the condition that every variable occurs in the scope of some constraint, and hence the set of variables does not need to be specified explicitly, but is given by the union of the constraint scopes. Furthermore, we shall assume that the domain of values is specified implicitly in the definition of the constraint relations. Using these assumptions, we shall specify a constraint satisfaction problem instance by specifying the corresponding set of constraints.

In this specification, each constraint relation R_i is represented by a finite string of symbols $\rho(R_i)$, and we assume that this representation is chosen so that the complexity of determining whether any given tuple is an element of R_i is bounded by a polynomial function of the length of $\rho(R_i)$. A *finite* relation can be represented simply by giving an explicit list of all the tuples it contains, but for infinite relations we need to use a suitable specification language, such as logical formulas, or linear equations.

A *solution* to a constraint satisfaction problem instance is a function from the variables to the domain such that the image of each constraint scope is an element of the corresponding constraint relation. Since we are representing instances by specifying the set of constraints of that instance, we shall talk about solutions to a set of constraints. The set of all solutions to the set of constraints C will be denoted Sol(C).

Deciding whether or not a given set of constraints has a solution is NP-complete in general [19]. In this paper we shall consider how restricting the allowed constraint relations to some fixed subset of all the possible relations affects the complexity of this decision problem. We therefore make the following definition.

Definition 3. For any set of relations, Γ, **CSP**(Γ) is defined to be the decision problem with

INSTANCE: A finite set of constraints C, in which all constraint relations are elements of Γ.
QUESTION: Does C have a solution?

If there is some algorithm which solves every instance in CSP(Γ) in polynomial time, then we shall say that CSP(Γ) is 'tractable', and refer to Γ as a tractable set of relations.

Example 1. The binary inequality relation over a set D is defined as follows.

$$\neq_D = \{\langle d_1, d_2 \rangle \in D^2 \mid d_1 \neq d_2\}$$

CSP($\{\neq_D\}$) corresponds precisely to the GRAPH COLORABILITY problem [6]. This problem is well-known to be tractable when $|D| \leq 2$ and NP-complete when $|D| \geq 3$.

In order to construct new tractable sets of relations, we will make use of the following operation to combine two sets of relations.

Definition 4. For any set of relations Γ, let Γ_i denote the subset of Γ containing all relations in Γ with arity i, together with the empty relation.

For any sets of relations Γ and Δ, define the set of relations $\Gamma \stackrel{\times}{\vee} \Delta$ as follows:

$$\Gamma \stackrel{\times}{\vee} \Delta = \{R \cup R' \mid \exists i, R \in \Gamma_i, R' \in \Delta_i\}$$

Note that the set of relations $\Gamma \stackrel{\times}{\vee} \Delta$ contains all the members of Γ, all the members of Δ, and the union of each possible *pair* of relations from Γ and Δ with the same arity. This set is, in general, much larger than the set $\Gamma \cup \Delta$, and hence able to express many more constraints. The next example shows that when tractable sets of relations are combined using the disjunction operation defined in Definition 4 the resulting set of relations may or may not be tractable.

Example 2. Let Λ be the the set of all Boolean relations which can be specified by a formula of propositional logic consisting of a single literal (where a literal is either a variable or a negated variable).

The subset of relations Λ_1 contains the following two relations (together with the empty relation):

- $\{\langle T\rangle\}$, corresponding to the literal p_1;
- $\{\langle F\rangle\}$, corresponding to the literal $\neg p_1$.

To specify relations of higher arity with a single literal, we associate the literal with one coordinate position in the relation, and allow arbitrary values in the other positions. This means, for example, that the subset Λ_2 contains the following four relations (together with the empty relation):

- $\{\langle T, T\rangle, \langle T, F\rangle\}$, corresponding to the literal p_1;
- $\{\langle F, T\rangle, \langle F, F\rangle\}$, corresponding to the literal $\neg p_1$;
- $\{\langle T, T\rangle, \langle F, T\rangle\}$, corresponding to the literal p_2;
- $\{\langle T, F\rangle, \langle F, F\rangle\}$, corresponding to the literal $\neg p_2$.

The set of relations Λ is clearly tractable, as it is straightforward to verify in linear time whether a collection of literals has a simultaneous solution.

Now consider the set of relations $\Lambda^2 = \Lambda \stackrel{\times}{\vee} \Lambda$. The class of problems $\mathrm{CSP}(\Lambda^2)$ corresponds to the 2-SATISFIABILITY problem, which is well-known to be tractable [6].

Finally, consider the set of relations $\Lambda^3 = \Lambda \stackrel{\times}{\vee} \Lambda^2$. The problem $\mathrm{CSP}(\Lambda^3)$ corresponds to the 3-SATISFIABILITY problem, which is well-known to be NP-complete [6].

When we use the set of relations $\Gamma \overset{\times}{\vee} \Delta$ as constraint relations, we shall assume that the constraint relations in any given problem instance are represented by strings of symbols of the form '$\rho(R) \vee \rho(R')$', for some R in Γ and some R' in Δ. With this convention, we can define two decomposition operations, Π_1 and Π_2 on constraints in $\mathrm{CSP}(\Gamma \overset{\times}{\vee} \Delta)$ which pick out the two components in the disjunction. These operations are defined as follows: for any constraint $c = (S_c, R_c)$, where R_c is represented by the string '$\rho(R) \vee \rho(R')$', we set $\Pi_1(c) = (S_c, R)$ and $\Pi_2(c) = (S_c, R')$. Note that the operations Π_1 and Π_2 can be carried out in linear time.

3 Tractable Disjunctive Constraints

In this section we shall identify certain conditions on sets of relations Γ and Δ which are sufficient to ensure that $\Gamma \overset{\times}{\vee} \Delta$ is tractable. To describe these conditions we will make use of the following definition:

Definition 5. For any sets of relations Γ and Δ, define $\mathrm{CSP}_{\Delta \leq 1}(\Gamma \cup \Delta)$ to be the subproblem of $\mathrm{CSP}(\Gamma \cup \Delta)$ consisting of all instances containing at most one constraint whose constraint relation is a member of Δ.

Using this definition, we now define what it means for one set of relations to be 'independent' with respect to another.

Definition 6. For any sets of relations Γ and Δ, we say that Δ is *independent with respect to* Γ if for any set of constraints C in $\mathrm{CSP}(\Gamma \cup \Delta)$, C has a solution whenever every subset C' of C which belongs to $\mathrm{CSP}_{\Delta \leq 1}(\Gamma \cup \Delta)$ has a solution.

The intuitive meaning of this definition is that the satisfiability of any set of constraints from Δ may be determined by considering those constraints one at a time, even in the presence of arbitrary additional constraints from Γ. In the examples below we shall demonstrate that several important constraint types have this independence property.

A more restrictive notion of independence was described in [18]. This earlier notion of independence was defined for a single set of relations, and has been used to establish the tractability of a number of constraint types. However, we will show below that the more general notion of independence introduced here can be used to prove the tractability of a wide variety of *disjunctive* constraint types for which the earlier notion does not hold.

First, we show that this independence property is preserved over arbitrary disjunctions, in the sense defined by the following lemma.

Lemma 7. *For any set of relations Δ, define the set Δ^* as follows:*

$$\Delta^* = \bigcup_{i=1}^{\infty} \Delta^i$$

where

$$\Delta^1 = \Delta$$
$$\Delta^{i+1} = \Delta^i \overset{\times}{\vee} \Delta \quad for \quad i = 1, 2, 3, \ldots$$

If Δ is independent with respect to Γ, then Δ^* is also independent with respect to Γ.

Proof. Assume that Δ is independent with respect to Γ. In order to show that Δ^* is independent of Γ, let C be any set of constraints in $\text{CSP}(\Gamma \cup \Delta^*)$. We need to show that if every subset of C which belongs to $\text{CSP}_{\Delta^* \leq 1}(\Gamma \cup \Delta^*)$ has a solution, then so does C.

Let C' be a maximal subset of C belonging to $\text{CSP}_{\Delta^* \leq 1}(\Gamma \cup \Delta^*)$ and let s be a solution to C'. Since C' is maximal, it contains the set C_Γ, consisting of all the constraints in C whose constraint relations are elements of $\Gamma \setminus \Delta^*$, so s is a solution to C_Γ. If C' also contains a constraint $d = (S_d, R_d)$ whose constraint relation, R_d, is an element of Δ^*, then there must be at least one relation R'_d in Δ such that s is a solution to the constraint $d' = (S_d, R'_d)$, by the definition of Δ^*. Hence, we may replace d with a (possibly) more restrictive constraint d' whose constraint relation is an element of Δ, without losing the solution s.

If we carry out this replacement for each C', then we have a set of constraints in $\text{CSP}(\Gamma \cup \Delta)$ such that each subset belonging to $\text{CSP}_{\Delta \leq 1}(\Gamma \cup \Delta)$ has a solution. Now, by the fact that Δ is independent with respect to Γ, it follows that this modified set of constraints has a solution, and hence the original set of constraints, C, has a solution.

Now consider the following algorithm for a function **Solvable** which determines whether or not a set of constraints C, with relations chosen from $\Gamma \overset{\times}{\vee} \Delta$, has a solution:

Algorithm 8 *A function to determine if a set of constraints has a solution:*

```
Solvable(C: SET OF CONSTRAINTS IN CSP(Γ ∨ Δ))
    F := ∅
    REPEAT
        X := {c ∈ C | SOL(F ∪ Π₂(c)) = ∅}
        IF X = ∅ THEN
            RETURN TRUE
        ELSE
            C := C \ X
            F := F ∪ {Π₁(x) | x ∈ X}
        ENDIF
    UNTIL SOL(F) = ∅
    RETURN FALSE
```

The next result shows that Algorithm 8 correctly determines whether or not a set of constraints with relations chosen from $\Gamma \overset{\times}{\vee} \Delta$ has a solution in those cases when Δ is independent with respect to Γ.

Theorem 9. *If C is an element of $CSP(\Gamma \overset{\times}{\vee} \Delta)$ and Δ is independent with respect to Γ, then Algorithm 8 correctly determines whether or not C has a solution.*

Proof. Algorithm 8 clearly terminates, because C is finite.

Assume that C is an element of $CSP(\Gamma \overset{\times}{\vee} \Delta)$, for some Γ and Δ such that Δ is independent with respect to Γ. We first prove by induction that after every assignment to F, all of the constraints in F must be satisfied in order to satisfy the original set of constraints, C.

This is vacuously true after the first assignment to F, because F is then equal to the empty set.

At each subsequent assignment, F is augmented with the constraints obtained by applying Π_1 to the constraints in X. Now, the elements of X are constraints c of C such that $\Pi_2(c)$ is incompatible with F. Hence the only way such a c can be satisfied together with the current constraints in F is to satisfy the other disjunct of the constraint relation of c, or in other words, the constraint given by $\Pi_1(c)$. Hence, by the inductive hypothesis, each constraint added to F must be satisfied in order to satisfy the original set of constraints C, and the result follows, by induction.

This result establishes that when **Solvable**(C) returns FALSE, C has no solutions.

Conversely, when **Solvable**(C) returns TRUE, then we know that X is empty. This implies that for each constraint c in C either $\Pi_1(c)$ belongs to F, or else $\Pi_2(c)$ is compatible with the constraints in F. Now, using the fact that Δ is independent with respect to Γ, we conclude that $F \cup \{\Pi_2(c) \mid c \in C,\ \Pi_1(c) \notin F\}$ has a solution, and hence C has a solution.

By analysing the complexity of Algorithm 8 we now establish the following result:

Theorem 10. *For any sets of relations Γ and Δ, if $CSP_{\Delta \leq 1}(\Gamma \cup \Delta)$ is tractable, and Δ is independent with respect to Γ, then $CSP(\Gamma \overset{\times}{\vee} \Delta)$ is tractable.*

Proof. We can bound the time complexity of Algorithm 8 as follows.

First note that $|F|$ increases on each iteration of the repeat loop, but $|F|$ is bounded by $|C|$ since each constraint in F arises from an element of C. Hence there can be at most $|C|$ iterations of this loop.

Now let $l(C)$ be the length of the string specifying C. During each iteration of the loop the algorithm determines whether or not there is a solution to $F \cup \Pi_2(c)$ for each c remaining in C. Since this set of constraints is a member of $CSP_{\Delta \leq 1}(\Gamma \cup \Delta)$, which is assumed to be tractable, these calculations may each be carried out in polynomial time in the size of their input. Note also that the

485

length of this input is less than or equal to $l(C)$. Hence, the time complexity of each of these calculations is $O(l(C)^k)$, for some constant k.

At the end of each iteration of the loop the algorithm determines whether or not there is a solution to F. Since F is also an element of $\text{CSP}_{\Delta \leq 1}(\Gamma \cup \Delta)$, and the length of the specification of F is less than or equal to $l(C)$, this calculation can also be carried out in $O(l(C)^k)$ time.

Hence, the total time required to complete the algorithm is $O(|C|(|C| + 1)l(C)^k)$, which is polynomial in the size of the input.

4 Applications

In this section we will demonstrate that many known tractable sets of relations can be obtained by combining simpler tractable sets of relations using the disjunction operation, as described in the previous section. We will also describe some new tractable sets of relations which have not previously been identified.

Example 3. [**Horn clauses**] One set of disjunctive constraints which are well-known to be tractable is the set of constraints over Boolean variables which ca be expressed using Horn clauses, that is, disjunctions of literals containing at most one positive literal. We will now show that the tractability of Horn clauses is a simple consequence of Theorem 10.

Recall the set of Boolean relations, Λ, defined in Example 2, which may be specified by a propositional formula consisting of a single literal.

Define Λ_+ to be the subset of Λ which may be specified using a single *positive* literal, together with the empty relation, and Λ_- to be the subset of Λ which may be specified using a single *negative* literal, together with the empty relation.

Now set

$$\Lambda_-^1 = \Lambda_-$$

$$\Lambda_-^{i+1} = \Lambda_-^i \overset{\times}{\vee} \Lambda_- \text{ for } i = 1, 2, 3, \ldots$$

and

$$\Lambda_-^* = \bigcup_{i=1}^{\infty} \Lambda_-^i$$

It is clear that Λ_-^* is equal to the set of relations which may be specified by arbitrary finite disjunctions of negative literals.

Finally, it is easily shown that Λ_- is independent with respect to Λ_+, and hence Λ_-^* is independent with respect to Λ_+ by Lemma 7. Furthermore, $\text{CSP}_{\Lambda_+ \leq 1}(\Lambda_+ \cup \Lambda_-^*)$ is tractable, since each instance is specified by a conjunction of single positive literals together with at most one disjunction of negative literals. Hence, $\Theta = \Lambda_+ \overset{\times}{\vee} \Lambda_-^*$ is tractable, by Theorem 10. But Θ is the set of relations which may be specified by a disjunction of literals containing at most one positive literal, so $\text{CSP}(\Theta)$ corresponds to the HORN-CLAUSE SATISFIABILITY problem [23, 6].

By symmetry, it follows that the set of relations which may be specified by a disjunction of literals containing at most one negative literal is also a tractable set of relations.

Example 4. [**Max-closed constraints**]

The class of constraints over finite domains known as 'max-closed' constraints was introduced in [2] and shown to be tractable. These constraints are defined over arbitrary finite domains which are totally ordered.

In this example we will show that this result may be obtained as a simple consequence of Theorem 10. Furthermore, by using Theorem 10 we are able to generalise the result to infinite domains.

The max-closed constraints were originally defined in terms of an algebraic closure property on the constraint relations [2]. However, it is shown in [2] that they can also be characterised as those constraints where the constraint relation can be specified by means of a conjunction of disjunctions of inequalities of the following form:

$$(x_1 < a_1) \vee (x_2 < a_2) \vee \cdots \vee (x_r < a_r) \vee (x_j > a_j)$$

In this expression the x_i are variables and the a_i are constants.

Now let D be any domain which is totally ordered, Proceeding as in the previous example, we define $\Gamma_<$ to be the set of relations over D which may be specified by a single inequality of the form $x_i < a_i$, and $\Gamma_>$ to be the set of relations over D which may be specified by a single inequality of the form $x_i > a_i$. Then we set

$$\Gamma_<^1 = \Gamma_<$$
$$\Gamma_<^{i+1} = \Gamma_<^i \overset{\times}{\vee} \Gamma_< \quad \text{for } i = 1, 2, 3, \ldots$$

and

$$\Gamma_<^* = \bigcup_{i=1}^{\infty} \Gamma_<^i$$

It is clear that $\Gamma_<^*$ is equal to the set of relations which may be specified by arbitrary finite disjunctions of inequalities of the form $x_i < a_i$.

Finally, it is easily shown that $\Gamma_<$ is independent with respect to $\Gamma_>$, so we know that $\Gamma_<^*$ is also independent of $\Gamma_>$, by Lemma 7. Also, $\text{CSP}_{\Gamma_> \leq 1}(\Gamma_> \cup \Gamma_<^*)$ is tractable, since each instance consists of a conjunction of lower bounds for certain variables together with at most one disjunction of upper bounds. Hence, $\Gamma_> \overset{\times}{\vee} \Gamma_<^*$ is a tractable set of relations, by Theorem 10, which establishes that max-closed constraints are tractable, by the result above.

Unlike the arguments used previously to establish that max-closed constraints are tractable [2, 9], all of the techniques used here can still be applied when the domain, D, is infinite.

Example 5. [**Linear Horn constraints**]

The class of constraints over the real numbers known as 'linear Horn' constraints was introduced in [15] (and independently in [10]) and shown to be tractable.

A *linear Horn constraint* is specified by a disjunction of weak linear inequalities and linear disequations where the number of inequalities does not exceed one. The following are examples of linear Horn constraints:

$$3x_1 + x_5 - 3x_4 \leq 10, \quad x_1 + x_3 + x_5 \neq 7,$$
$$3x_1 + x_5 - 4x_3 \leq 7 \vee 2x_1 + 3x_2 - 4x_3 \neq 4 \vee x_2 + x_3 + x_5 \neq 7,$$
$$4x_1 + x_3 \neq 3 \vee 5x_2 - 3x_5 + x_4 \neq 6$$

Linear Horn constraints form an important class of linear constraints with explicit connections to temporal reasoning [10]. In particular, the class of linear Horn constraints properly includes the point algebra of [27], the (quantitative) temporal constraints of [13, 14], and the ORD-Horn constraints of [22]. All these classes of temporal constraints can therefore be shown to be tractable using the framework developed here.

Let the domain D be $\Re$ or $\mathcal{Q}$. Define Γ to be the set of relations defined by a single (weak) linear inequality (e.g., $3x_1 + 2x_2 - x_3 \leq 6$). Define Δ to be the set of relations defined by a single linear disequality (e.g., $x_1 + 4x_2 + x_3 \neq 0$).

Note that Δ^* is the set of relations defined by a disjunction of disequalities, and the problem $\mathrm{CSP}(\Gamma \cup \Delta^*)$ corresponds to deciding whether a convex polyhedron *minus* the union of a finite number of hyperplanes is the empty set. It was shown in [17] that the set $\Gamma \cup \Delta^*$ is independent (using their more restrictive notion of independence referred to above), and hence that this problem is tractable.

However, the set of relations specified by linear Horn constraints corresponds to the much larger set $\Gamma \overset{\times}{\vee} \Delta^*$, and this set is *not* independent in the sense defined in [17] (see [15]). In order to establish that this larger set of constraints is tractable we shall use the more general notion of independence introduced in this paper.

Consider any set of constraints C in $\mathrm{CSP}(\Gamma \cup \Delta)$. Let C' be the subset of C which is specified by weak linear inequalities, and let C'' be the subset of C which is specified by linear disequations. It is clear that C is consistent if and only if C' is consistent, and, for each $c \in C''$, the set $C' \cup \{c\}$ is consistent. Hence, Δ is independent with respect to Γ. By Lemma 7 it follows that Δ^* is also independent with respect to Γ.

Now Theorem 9 implies that Algorithm 8 can be used to determine whether $\mathrm{CSP}(\Gamma \overset{\times}{\vee} \Delta^*)$ has a solution. (In fact, Algorithm 8 can be seen as a simplification of the algorithm CONSISTENCY which was developed specifically for this problem in [15].)

Finally, to establish tractability, we note that whether a set of inequalities, C', is consistent or not can be decided in polynomial time, using Khachian's linear programming algorithm [11]. Furthermore, for any single disjunction of disequalities, d, we can detect in polynomial time whether $C' \cup \{d\}$ is consistent by simply running Khachian's algorithm to determine whether C' implies each equality in the conjunction of equalities corresponding to the negation of d. Hence, $\text{CSP}_{\Delta^* \leq 1}(\Gamma \cup \Delta^*)$ is tractable, so by Theorem 10 we know that $\text{CSP}(\Gamma \overset{\times}{\vee} \Delta^*)$ is tractable.

Having identified the key property of independence, which underlies all of these tractable classes, we are now in a position to identify new tractable classes simply by searching for appropriate sets of tractable relations which have this property.

Example 6. [**Disjunctive congruences**]

One of the fundamental results of elementary number theory is the Chinese Remainder Theorem [8], which states that it is always possible to solve a collection of simultaneous linear congruences with co-prime moduli.

This result can be used to obtain tractable constraint classes in a number of ways. One of the most straightforward is to define, for each integer a, the set of unary relations $\Gamma(a)$, containing all relations of the form $\{\langle x \rangle \mid x \equiv a$ (mod p)$\}$, for some prime $p > |a|$. A problem instance in $\text{CSP}(\Gamma(a))$ may then be specified by a collection of simultaneous congruences. For example, a typical set of constraints in $\text{CSP}(\Gamma(3))$, involving the variables x_1 and x_2, would be:

$$x_1 \equiv 3 \quad (\text{mod } 5),$$
$$x_2 \equiv 3 \quad (\text{mod } 7),$$
$$x_2 \equiv 3 \quad (\text{mod } 11).$$

The Chinese remainder theorem implies that any set of constraints in $\text{CSP}(\Gamma(a))$ has a solution, for any a, so each $\Gamma(a)$ is a tractable set of relations.

Furthermore, any set of constraints in $\text{CSP}(\Gamma(a) \cup \Gamma(b))$ will also have a solution, unless it contains a pair of constraints c_1 and c_2 which are incompatible. (The constraints c_1 and c_2 are incompatible if they both constrain the same variable x with respect to the same prime p, but c_1 requires that $x \equiv a$ (mod p) and c_2 requires that $x \equiv b$ (mod p), and p does not divide $a - b$.) Hence, for any a and b the set $\Gamma(a)$ is independent of the set $\Gamma(b)$, and vice versa.

Finally, the set of problems $\text{CSP}_{\Gamma(b) \leq 1}(\Gamma(a) \cup \Gamma(b))$ is tractable, because we can determine whether or not any given instance has a solution by examining each pair of constraints to see whether they are compatible. If they are all compatible then the instance has a solution, by the Chinese Remainder Theorem, otherwise it does not.

Hence, by Lemma 7 and Theorem 10, we know that $\text{CSP}(\Gamma(a) \overset{\times}{\vee} \Gamma(b)^*)$ is also tractable, for any choice of a and b. This means that there is an efficient way to solve any collection of simultaneous disjunctions of congruences which all have the property that at most one disjunct comes from $\Gamma(a)$ and the remainder from $\Gamma(b)$. For example, when $a = 1$ and $b = 2$ we might have the following collection of congruences:

$$x_1 \equiv 1 \quad (\text{mod } 2) \ \vee \ x_1 \equiv 2 \quad (\text{mod } 3) \ \vee \ x_2 \equiv 2 \quad (\text{mod } 5),$$

$$x_2 \equiv 2 \pmod 3 \lor x_3 \equiv 2 \pmod 5,$$
$$x_3 \equiv 1 \pmod 2,$$
$$x_2 \equiv 1 \pmod 7 \lor x_1 \equiv 2 \pmod{11} \lor x_3 \equiv 2 \pmod 3$$

5 Conclusion

In this paper we have examined the complexity of disjunctive constraints, and established sufficient conditions to ensure tractability. We have shown that these conditions account for a wide variety of known tractable disjunctive classes, and that they aid the search for new tractable constraint classes.

References

1. Cooper, M.C., Cohen, D.A., Jeavons, P.G., "Characterizing tractable constraints", *Artificial Intelligence 65*, (1994), pp. 347–361.
2. Cooper, M.C., & Jeavons, P.G., "Tractable constraints on ordered domains", *Artificial Intelligence 79*, (1995), pp. 327–339.
3. Dechter, R., & Pearl, J., "Structure identification in relational data", *Artificial Intelligence 58* (1992) pp. 237–270.
4. Dechter, R. & Pearl J. "Network-based heuristics for constraint-satisfaction problems", *Artificial Intelligence 34* (1988), pp. 1–38.
5. Freuder, E.C., "A sufficient condition for backtrack-bounded search", *Journal of the ACM 32* (1985) pp. 755–761.
6. Garey, M.R., & Johnson, D.S., *Computers and intractability: a guide to NP-completeness*, Freeman, San Francisco, California, (1979).
7. Gyssens, M., Jeavons, P., Cohen, D., "Decomposing constraint satisfaction problems using database techniques", *Artificial Intelligence 66*, (1994), pp. 57–89.
8. Jackson, T.H., *Number Theory*, Routledge and Kegan Paul, (1975).
9. Jeavons, P., Cohen D., Gyssens, M., "A unifying framework for tractable constraints", In *Proceedings 1st International Conference on Principles and Practice of Constraint Programming—CP '95* (Cassis, France, September 1995), *Lecture Notes in Computer Science*, 976, Springer-Verlag, Berlin/New York, 1995, pp. 276–291.
10. Jonsson, P. and Bäckström, C., "A Linear Programming Approach to Temporal Reasoning", Proceedings of AAAI-96, (1996).
11. Khachian, L.G., "A polynomial time algorithm for linear programming", *Soviet Math. Dokl. 20*, (1979) pp. 191–194.
12. Kirousis, L., "Fast parallel constraint satisfaction", *Artificial Intelligence 64*, (1993), pp. 147–160.
13. Koubarakis, M., "Dense Time and Temporal Constraints with $\neq$", In *Principles of Knowledge Representation and Reasoning: Proceedings of the Third International Conference (KR'92)*, (Ed. B. Nebel, C. Rich and W. Swartout), Morgan Kaufmann, San Mateo, CA, (1992), pp. 24–35.
14. Koubarakis, M., "From Local to Global Consistency in Temporal Constraint Networks", In *Proceedings 1st International Conference on Principles and Practice of Constraint Programming—CP '95* (Cassis, France, September 1995), *Lecture Notes in Computer Science*, 976, Springer-Verlag, Berlin/New York, (1995), pp. 53–69.

15. Koubarakis, M., "Tractable Disjunctions of Linear Constraints", In *Proceedings of the 2nd International Conference on Principles and Practice of Constraint Programming—CP '96* (Boston, MA, August 1996), *Lecture Notes in Computer Science*, 1118, Springer-Verlag, Berlin/New York, (1996), pp. 297–307.

16. Ladkin, P.B., & Maddux, R.D., "On binary constraint problems", *Journal of the ACM 41* (1994), pp. 435–469.

17. Lassez, J-L., and McAloon, K., "A Canonical Form for Generalized Linear Constraints", Technical Report RC15004 (#67009), IBM Research Division, T.J. Watson Research Center, (1989).

18. Lassez, J-L., and McAloon, K., "A Canonical Form for Generalized Linear Constraints", *Lecture Notes in Computer Science*, 351, Springer-Verlag, Berlin/New York, (1989), pp. 19–27.

19. Mackworth, A.K. "Consistency in networks of relations", *Artificial Intelligence 8* (1977) pp. 99–118.

20. Montanari, U., "Networks of constraints: fundamental properties and applications to picture processing", *Information Sciences 7* (1974), pp. 95–132.

21. Montanari, U., & Rossi, F., "Constraint relaxation may be perfect", *Artificial Intelligence 48* (1991), pp. 143–170.

22. Nebel, B. & Burckert, H-J., "Reasoning about temporal relations: a maximal tractable subclass of Allen's interval algebra", *Journal of the ACM 42*, (1995), pp. 43–66.

23. Schaefer, T.J., "The complexity of satisfiability problems", *Proc 10th ACM Symposium on Theory of Computing (STOC)* , (1978) pp. 216–226.

24. Tsang, E., *Foundations of Constraint Satisfaction*, Academic Press, (1993).

25. van Beek, P., "On the Minimality and Decomposability of Row-Convex Constraint Networks", *Proceedings of the Tenth National Conference on Artificial Intelligence, AAAI-92*, MIT Press, (1992) pp. 447–452.

26. Van Hentenryck, P., Deville, Y., Teng, C-M., "A generic arc-consistency algorithm and its specializations", *Artificial Intelligence 57* (1992), pp. 291–321.

27. Vilain, M., Kautz, H., van Beek, P., "Constraint Propagation Algorithms for Temporal Reasoning: A Revised Report", In *Readings in Qualitative Reasoning about Physical Systems*, Ed. Weld, D.S. and de Kleer, J., Morgan Kaufmann, (1989), pp. 373–381.

Compiling Constraint Solving Using Projection

Warwick Harvey[1], Peter J. Stuckey[1], and Alan Borning[1,2]

[1] Department of Computer Science, University of Melbourne, Parkville, Victoria
3052, AUSTRALIA; {warwick,pjs,borning}@cs.mu.oz.au
[2] Permanent address: Dept. of Computer Science & Engineering, University of
Washington, Box 352350, Seattle, Washington 98195, USA;
borning@cs.washington.edu

Abstract. Linear equality and inequality constraints arise naturally in
specifying many aspects of user interfaces, such as requiring that one
window be to the left of another, requiring that a pane occupy the left-
most 1/3 of a window, or preferring that an object be contained within
a rectangle if possible. For interactive use, we need to solve similar constraint satisfaction problems repeatedly for each screen refresh, with each
successive problem differing from the previous one only in the position
of an input device and the previous state of the system. We present an
algorithm for solving such systems of constraints using projection. The
solution is compiled into very efficient, constraint-free code, which is parameterized by the new inputs. Producing straight-line, constraint-free
code of this sort is important in a number of applications: for example,
to provide predictable performance in real-time systems, to allow com-
panies to ship products without including a runtime constraint solver, to
compile Java applets that can be downloaded and run remotely (again
without having to include a runtime solver), or for applications where
runtime efficiency is particularly important. Even for less time-critical
user interface applications, the smooth performance of the resulting code
is more pleasing than that of code produced using other current techniques.

1 Introduction

Constraints are a natural tool for user interface toolkits and other kinds of interactive graphical systems. Some important uses for this application area include
specifying layout and other geometric information, maintaining consistency between application data and a view of that data, and maintaining consistency
among multiple views. It is important to be able to express preferences as well
as requirements in a constraint system. One important use is to express a desire
for stability when moving parts of an image: things should stay where they were
unless there is some reason for them to move. A second use is to process potentially invalid user inputs in a graceful way. For example, if the user tries to move
a figure outside of its bounding window, it is reasonable for the figure just to
bump up against the side of the window and stop, rather than signalling an error.
A third use is to balance conflicting desires, for example in laying out a graph.

The constraints needed to specify and maintain layout information are typically linear equalities and inequalities over the real numbers. Inequality constraints in particular are needed to express relationships such as "inside," "above," "left-of," and "overlaps." For example, we can express the requirement that window1 be to the left of window2 as the constraint window1.rightSide ≤ window2.leftSide. Some of these layout constraints will be requirements, and others preferences.

For interactive systems, a typical requirement is to re-satisfy the constraints repeatedly as the user moves some part of a figure—each time the screen is refreshed the constraints must be re-satisfied. Each of these constraint satisfaction problems differs from the previous ones only in the values of some of the constants in the constraints (for example, the mouse position). One strategy for achieving the required interactive response times is to compile a constraint satisfaction plan: a block of code that can be executed repeatedly to re-solve the constraints with different input parameters. (We can view this as a kind of partial evaluation of the constraint solving algorithm.) This has long been done for local propagation solvers (e.g. [1]), and more recently for simultaneous linear equations [3] and for acyclic sets of inequality constraints [2]. However, there have not been any systems that can compile plans for systems of constraints including both simultaneous equalities and inequalities. That lack is addressed by the research reported here.

In brief, our algorithm works as follows. The original set of constraints is converted into a normal form, *hierarchical normal form*. In this form, the only kind of preferential constraints are ones of the form $v = b$ for a variable v and constant b; all other constraints are required (i.e. we must satisfy them in any solution). It is easy to convert any collection of linear equality and inequality constraints into this form. We then repeatedly perform variable elimination to find the permitted range of values for the variables, given the required constraints. The elimination is performed in such an order that the *last* variable eliminated, say v_n, has the strongest preferential constraint $v_n = b_n$ associated with it. We can then set v_n to that value that best satisfies the preferred constraint (knowing that the value will satisfy the required constraints). Next, we set v_{n-1} to the value that best satisfies *its* preferential constraint $v_{n-1} = b_{n-1}$, and so on. The remaining wrinkle is that we don't do a single computation to find the values for the v_i; rather, we compile code that can repeatedly find such values, given values for the constants b_i as inputs. This allows us to compile efficient, straight-line code to solve the same set of constraints repeatedly for different inputs.

1.1 Applications

The original motivation for this work is constraint solving for user interface toolkits and other kinds of graphical interactive systems. The technique is useful for two reasons: first, it produces code that requires no runtime support for constraint solving; second, the code is very efficient. The technique should also be useful in other applications where either of these considerations is a factor.

The ability to get rid of runtime support is important in many real software tasks. One example of this sort is a constraint-based authoring environment for producing Java applets, where the behavior of the applet is partially specified using constraints. After the applet is written and tested in the authoring environment, the constraint compiler is used to produce straight Java code that can be shipped over the net and run on a remote machine, without requiring a runtime constraint solver on the remote machine. We have done some preliminary work on such an application [5], and have used the constraint compiler to produce Java code for applets for an interactive demonstration of a geometric theorem and for an abacus simulation, which were then included in web documents. As a second example, when building an embedded real-time engine controller, predictable performance is needed: compiled code can provide that, but calls to runtime constraint solvers generally cannot. Finally, in developing a product, a company might use constraints in developing the application and not want to ship a proprietary constraint solving package with that application.[1]

The compiled code is also very efficient—our preliminary measurements show speeds from 5 to 20 times faster than the same test cases performed using a runtime solver based on the simplex algorithm. The runtime solver is reasonably efficient as well, and in many applications the constraint solving time is dominated by the graphics refresh time for either technique. However, in some cases the simplex solver has markedly varying response times—much of the time it is extremely fast, but when a succession of pivots are required it slows down considerably, giving rise overall to a more jerky quality to the interaction. (People prefer uniform response times to varying ones.) The additional speed could be important in other cases as well, for example when the compiled code is to be run on a slower processor.

1.2 Related Work

There is a long history of using constraints in user interfaces and interactive systems, beginning with Ivan Sutherland's pioneering Sketchpad system [15]. Most of the current systems use one-way constraints (e.g. [10, 11]), or local propagation algorithms for acyclic collections of multi-way constraints (e.g. [13, 16]). Indigo [2] handles acyclic collections of inequality constraints, but not cycles. UI systems that handle simultaneous (cyclic) linear equations include DETAIL [9] and Ultraviolet [3]. UI systems that handle simultaneous linear inequalities as well with reasonable efficiency are QOCA [8] and Cassowary [6]. Both of these algorithms are based on the simplex algorithm. We provide timing comparisons between Cassowary and our Fourier compilation algorithm in Section 5.

2 Solving Constraints Using Projection

In this section we briefly illustrate how projection can be used to find solutions to linear equality and inequality constraints. For the moment we will consider only required constraints, and also ignore issues of compilation.

---

[1] Bjorn Freeman-Benson, Object Technology International, Personal Communication.

A *primitive constraint* is a linear inequality or equality. A *constraint* is a set of primitive constraints. We assume every primitive constraint is written in a simplified form so that no variable appears twice in the same primitive constraint. Let $vars(C)$ denote the set of variables appearing in constraint C, and similarly let $vars(c)$ denote the set of variables appearing in equation or inequality c. We denote by $\bar{\exists}_W F$ the formula $\exists v_1 \exists v_2 \cdots \exists v_k \ F$, where W is a set of variables and $\{v_1, \ldots, v_k\} = vars(F) - W$.

For each variable $x \in vars(C)$ we can partition C in the following way. Let C_x^0 be the set of primitive constraints $c \in C$ where $x \notin vars(c)$. Let $C_x^=$ be the set of equations $c \in C$ where $x \in vars(c)$. Let C_x^+ be the set of inequalities $c \in C$ such that c is equivalent to an inequality of the form $x \leq e$, where e is a linear expression not involving x. Finally, let C_x^- be the set of inequalities $c \in C$ such that c is equivalent to an inequality of the form $e \leq x$, again where e is a linear expression not involving x.

The projection algorithm shown below eliminates a variable x from constraint C and returns constraint $D \leftrightarrow \exists x C$ using either Gaussian elimination or Fourier elimination.

```
project(C, x)
    if exists c ∈ C_x^= where c ↔ x = e then
        D := C − {c} with every occurrence of x replaced by e
    else
        D := C_x^0;
        foreach c ∈ C_x^+ where c ↔ x ≤ e^+
            foreach c ∈ C_x^- where c ↔ e^- ≤ x
                D := D ∪ {e^- ≤ e^+};
            endforeach
        endforeach
    endif
    return D;
```

To solve constraints we project out each variable in turn using **project** until no variables remain. The resulting constraint C' is equivalent to $\bar{\exists}_{\emptyset} C$. None of the primitive constraints in C' involve any variables and hence we can straightforwardly determine whether C' is satisfiable or not. This answers the satisfiability question for C. We can then use the intermediate constraints C_i produced after $i-1$ applications of project, as well as the variables $x_1, \ldots, x_n$ in their order of elimination, to build a solution to C. For $1 \leq i \leq n$ it is the case that $vars(C_i) = \{x_i, \ldots, x_n\}$. So C_n only contains variable x_n and hence only contains constraints of the form $x_n = b$, $x_n \leq b$ and $b \leq x_n$. Since C is satisfiable we can find a valuation for x_n which is a solution of C_n.

We can extend a solution $\theta = \{x_{i+1} \mapsto d_{i+1}, \ldots, x_n \mapsto d_n\}$ of C_{i+1} to a solution of C_i as follows. Consider each of the constraints in C_i that involve x_i. If one is an equation equivalent to $x_i = e$, where e is an expression only involving variables $\{x_{i+1}, \ldots, x_n\}$, then we can let $d_i = e\theta$. Otherwise C_i only contains inequalities containing x_i. These can be written in the form $x_i \leq e_j$ or $e_k \leq x_i$, where e_j or e_k is an expression only involving variables $\{x_{i+1}, \ldots, x_n\}$.

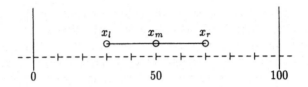

Fig. 1. Simple constrained picture

Using valuation θ we can determine the minimum u of the $e_j\theta$ and maximum l of the $e_k\theta$. Any value for d_i between l and u gives a valid solution of C_i. The new solution is thus $\{x_i \mapsto d_i, x_{i+1} \mapsto d_{i+1}, \ldots, x_n \mapsto d_n\}$.

We now give an example of constraint solving using projection, using the illustration in Figure 1. The constraints are as follows: x_m is constrained to be the midpoint of the line from x_l to x_r, x_l is constrained to be at least 10 to the left of x_r, and all variables must lie in the range 0 to 100.

We can represent this using the constraint C_1 shown below. To solve this constraint using variable elimination, we start with C_1, select a variable and project it out, and continue until no variables remain. Suppose we first select x_l. We can project it out using the equation $2x_m = x_l + x_r$, yielding the constraint C_2, and then project out x_r, yielding the constraint C_3 where we have eliminated some simple redundancy. Finally, eliminating x_r we obtain C_4, which is clearly satisfiable.

C_1	C_2	C_3	C_4
$2x_m = x_l + x_r$ $x_l + 10 \leq x_r$ $x_l, x_m, x_r \leq 100$ $0 \leq x_l, x_m, x_r$	$x_m + 5 \leq x_r$ $2x_m - 100 \leq x_r$ $x_r \leq 2x_m$ $x_m, x_r \leq 100$ $0 \leq x_m, x_r$	$5 \leq x_m$ $x_m \leq 95$	$5 \leq 95$

We now show how to construct a solution from these constraints. By inspecting C_3, we know we can pick any value between 5 and 95 for x_m, say 50. Next we examine the constraints in C_2 involving x_r. These are $\{x_m + 5 \leq x_r, 2x_m - 100 \leq x_r, 0 \leq x_r, x_r \leq 2x_m, x_r \leq 100\}$. Given $x_r = 50$, this becomes $\{55 \leq x_r, 0 \leq x_r, 0 \leq x_r, x_r \leq 100, x_r \leq 100\}$. We can thus pick any value for x_r in the range $[55..100]$, say 70. Finally, examining the constraints in C_1, there is an equation involving x_l, namely $x_l = 2x_m - x_r$, so we can use this equation directly to set x_l to 30.

We now use this information to compile a sequence of statements that constructs a solution to the constraints, and returns it as a triple.

(1) $x_m^l := 5;$

(2) $x_m^u := 95;$

(3)   choose $x_m \in [x_m^l .. x_m^u]$

(4) $x_r^l := \max \{ x_m + 5, \ 2x_m - 100, \ 0 \};$

(5) $x_r^u := \min \{ 2x_m, \ 100 \};$

(6)   choose $x_r \in [x_r^l .. x_r^u]$

(7) $x_l := 2x_m - x_r;$

(8)   return $(x_m, x_r, x_l);$

As it stands this sequence of statements isn't very interesting, since it only solves one problem. However, in the next section we show how to use a similar technique to compile code parameterized by appropriate inputs.

3 Constraint Hierarchies

As described in the introduction, for our intended application domain it is important to be able to express preferences as well as requirements in the constraint system, in particular a desire for minimizing change as a figure is manipulated. We use *constraint hierarchies* [4] for specifying the desired solutions to a collection of required and preferential constraints independent of the particular algorithm involved.

A *labeled primitive constraint* is a primitive constraint labeled with a strength, written sc, where s is a strength and c is a primitive constraint. Strengths are non-negative integers. For clarity, we give symbolic names to the different strengths of primitive constraints. Strength 0, with the symbolic name *required*, is always reserved for required constraints. A *constraint hierarchy* is a multiset of labeled primitive constraints. Given a constraint hierarchy H, H_0 denotes the multiset of required primitive constraints in H, with their labels removed. In the same way, we define the multisets $H_1, H_2, \ldots, H_n$ for levels $1, 2, \ldots, n$. The set S of *solutions* to the hierarchy is defined as follows. S_0 is the set of valuations such that all the H_0 constraints hold; from this we form S by eliminating all potential valuations that are worse than some other potential valuation using the comparator predicate *better*.

$$S_0 = \{\theta \mid \forall c \in H_0 \ c\theta \text{ holds}\}$$
$$S = \{\theta \mid \theta \in S_0 \land \forall \sigma \in S_0 \ \neg better(\sigma, \theta, H)\}$$

In the work described here, we employ *local comparators* for "better," which compare two solutions primitive constraint by primitive constraint. A valuation θ is *locally-better* than another valuation σ if, for each of the primitive constraints through some level $k-1$, the error after applying θ is equal to that after applying σ, and at level k the error is strictly less for at least one primitive constraint and less than or equal for all the rest.

$$locally\text{-}better(\theta, \sigma, H) \equiv \exists k > 0 \text{ such that}$$
$$\forall i \in 1 \ldots k-1 \ \forall p \in H_i \ e(p\theta) = e(p\sigma)$$
$$\land \ \exists q \in H_k \ e(q\theta) < e(q\sigma) \land \ \forall r \in H_k \ e(r\theta) \le e(r\sigma)$$

The definition uses an error function $e(c\theta)$ that returns a non-negative real number indicating how nearly constraint c is satisfied for a valuation θ. In the work described here, the domain is the reals, and the error function returns a value that varies depending on how nearly the constraint is satisfied. For example, the error for $x + y = z$ is $|x + y - z|$, while the error for $x \leq y$ is 0 if $x \leq y$ and $x - y$ otherwise. A locally-better comparator with such an error function is known as *locally-error-better*.

A traditional demonstration of constraint-based graphics is the Quadrilateral Theorem illustrated in Figure 2. The screen snapshots are taken from our Smalltalk implementation, which uses the code produced by the projection algorithm. Each side of the quadrilateral is bisected, and lines are drawn between the midpoints. These inner lines always form a parallelogram. This is expressed as a constraint on each midpoint that it lie halfway between the endpoints of its line. In addition, all points are constrained to be at least 10 pixels from the sides of the window, and the quadrilateral is constrained to have a minimum size of 30 pixels (so that it cannot collapse to a point). Taken together, these constraints are too difficult for most UI constraint solvers, since they involve simultaneous equations and inequalities.

In Figure 2a we have picked up one of the midpoints with the mouse and begun to move it by temporarily adding an *edit constraint* equating the position of the midpoint and the mouse. This constraint is strongly preferred but not required—we will violate it if necessary. The remaining points are weakly constrained to stay where they are by *stay constraints*. In Figure 2b the mouse has been moved to the right, and to keep the midpoint constraint satisfied the right-most vertex has moved as well. We continue moving to the right. In Figure 2c the right-most vertex has run into the imaginary wall resulting from the constraint that it be at least 10 pixels from the window boundary, and can move no further, so the bottom vertex has begun moving as well. Finally, in Figure 2d the mouse has moved beyond the permitted region for the midpoint. The midpoint has moved as close to the mouse as possible, thus causing the two endpoints of its line to be pressed against the boundary as well.

Formally, both stay and edit constraints are simply constraints of the form $v = b$ for variable v and constant b. However, when we come to compile code

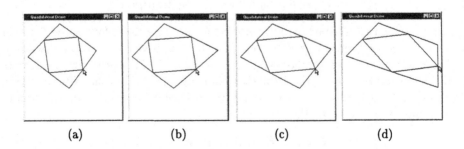

(a)   (b)   (c)   (d)

Fig. 2. Demonstrating a theorem about quadrilaterals

for repeatedly solving a collection of constraints, it will be important to handle these constraints efficiently, since the value of b will change for each solution—for the stay constraints, it will be the value of v on the previous step; for the edit constraints, it will come from some external input. The other constraints will remain unaltered for each step.

4 Compiling Projection for Hierarchies

We can now describe the complete algorithm for compiling code that can repeatedly find a locally-error-better solution to a constraint hierarchy given a series of input values. We assume the constraint hierarchy is in hierarchical normal form. In practice the original problem will usually already be in this form. If not, however, it is easy to transform an arbitrary linear constraint hierarchy into this form by adding error variables. For example, $strong(e = b)$, where e is a linear expression, becomes $required(e = v_e) \land strong(v_e = b)$, where v_e is a new error variable.

Recall that a hierarchical constraint H can be separated into parts H_i, each of which contain the primitive constraints of strength i. If H is in hierarchical normal form, then for $i \geq 1$ H_i will contain only equations of the form $v = b$ where v is a variable and b is a constant. We can use this information to build a strength partitioning of the variables. Let $V_1 = vars(H_1)$. Let $V_{i+1} = vars(H_{i+1}) - (V_1 \cup \cdots \cup V_i)$. Thus V_i contains those variables whose strongest non-required primitive constraint is of strength i. For simplicity, we assume that every variable is involved in a non-required constraint. This will usually be the case in constraint-based graphics applications.

Now we can use the projection algorithm to build code for solving hierarchical normal form constraints, where each problem differs from the others only in the values of the constants b in the non-required primitive constraints. We apply the projection algorithm to eliminate all variables in the set V_j before eliminating any variables in V_i where $j < i$. A total ordering $x_1 \prec x_2 \prec \cdots \prec x_n$ on the variables $x_1, \ldots, x_n$ in a hierarchical normal form constraint H *respects the hierarchy* if

$$\forall i < j \quad v \in V_i \land w \in V_j \rightarrow w \prec v.$$

The full algorithm for generating code takes an ordering of variables $x_1 \prec x_2 \prec \cdots \prec x_n$, and the required constraint C. To solve the constraint C in conjunction with $H_1, H_2, \ldots, H_k$, for each variable $x_i \in V_l$ we select a constraint $x_i = b_i$ from H_l, that is, we arbitrarily choose one of the highest strength non-required constraints on x_i to determine the value b_i. Making such a choice is correct because of the locally-error-better comparator: minimizing the error of one of the strongest non-required constraints will always give a locally-error-better solution. (By choosing a different constraint of the same strength, we would compute a different but still valid locally-error-better solution.)

The code produced by the algorithm shown in Figure 3 will either set x_i to b_i if this is a legitimate choice given the solution determined so far, or set x_i to its lower or upper bound, whichever is closest to the value b_i.

499

```
code_generate({x₁, ..., xₙ}, C)
    C₁ := C;
    for i := 1 to n
        C_{i+1} := project(Cᵢ, xᵢ);
    endfor
    for i := n to 1
        if exists c ∈ Cᵢ where c ↔ xᵢ = e then
            emit( xᵢ := e );
        else
            minset := ∅; maxset := ∅;
            foreach primitive constraint c ∈ Cᵢ where xᵢ ∈ vars(c)
                if c ≡ e ≤ xᵢ then
                    minset := minset ∪ {e};
                elseif c ≡ xᵢ ≤ e then
                    maxset := maxset ∪ {e};
                endif
            endforeach
            emit( xᵢˡ := max { minset } );
            emit( xᵢᵘ := min { maxset } );
            emit( if bᵢ ∈ [xᵢˡ..xᵢᵘ] then );
            emit( xᵢ := bᵢ );
            emit( elseif bᵢ ≤ xᵢˡ then );
            emit( xᵢ := xᵢˡ );
            emit( else xᵢ := xᵢᵘ );
            emit( endif );
        endif
    endfor
    emit( return (x₁, ..., xₙ) );
```

Fig. 3. Code generation algorithm

Theorem 1 (Correctness of code_generate). [2] *Let C be a constraint with variables $\{x_1, \ldots, x_n\}$. Given a variable ordering $x_1 \prec x_2 \prec \cdots \prec x_n$ for variables in constraint C, the solution $(d_1, \ldots, d_n)$ returned by the code produced by code_generate($\{x_1, \ldots, x_n\}, C, V$) will be a locally-error-better solution for the constraint*

$$C \wedge s_1(x_1 = b_1) \wedge \cdots \wedge s_n(x_n = b_n)$$

where for $2 \leq i \leq n$, strength $s_{i-1} \geq s_i > 0$ (i.e. strength s_{i-1} is the same as or weaker than strength s_i). □

As an example imagine that we have augmented the constraints for Figure 1 with $strong(x_m = b_m) \wedge weak(x_r = b_r) \wedge weak(x_l = b_l)$. The resulting code is shown in Figure 4.

Suppose the midpoint of the line is selected by the mouse to move to position 60, and the remaining points are constrained to stay where they are ($x_l = 30$

---
[2] Due to space considerations we omit proofs. See [7].

```
x_m^l := 5;
x_m^u := 95;
if b_m ∈ [x_m^l..x_m^u]
    x_m := b_m;
elseif b_m < x_m^l
    x_m := x_m^l;
else x_m := x_m^u;
x_r^l := max { x_m + 5, 2x_m - 100, 0 };
x_r^u := min { 2x_m, 100 };
if b_r ∈ [x_r^l..x_r^u]
    x_r := b_r;
elseif b_r < x_r^l
    x_r := x_r^l;
else x_r := x_r^u;
x_l := 2x_m - x_r;
return (x_m, x_r, x_l);
```

Fig. 4. Code for the example constraints

and $x_r = 70$). This then imposes constraints $strong(x_m = 60) \wedge weak(x_r = 70) \wedge weak(x_l = 30)$, for which the above code generates the answer $(60, 70, 50)$. If the mouse now moves to position 70, the edit and stay constraints translate as $strong(x_m = 70) \wedge weak(x_r = 70) \wedge weak(x_l = 60)$ and the code generates answer $(70, 75, 65)$. If the mouse now moves to position 0, the code generates the answer $(5, 10, 0)$.

5 Empirical Evaluation

The projection-based compilation algorithm has been implemented and tested. Our prototype implementation is in Mercury [14], and includes a module that is easily adapted to generate code for different target languages. The current implementation produces Smalltalk code, which is stored in a file. Then, in the Smalltalk environment, the code is loaded and incorporated into a graphics application for execution. Advantages of using Smalltalk are that Smalltalk includes an extensive graphics library, making it easy to test interactive graphical programs, and also that we have an implementation in Smalltalk of Cassowary, a simplex-based solver, allowing a head-to-head comparison of the runtimes of the algorithms. We have investigated the performance of the algorithm for several medium-sized examples of constraints for interactive graphics.

The *boxcars* benchmark has a number of boxes in a horizontal row. Each box is constrained to be to the right of the previous one, and all to stay within a specified horizontal range. The *binary tree* benchmark is a complete binary tree of a given height. Each pair of children are constrained to be at the same height, both must be at least some minimum distance below their parent, and they must be separated from each other by some minimum distance. All parent nodes

Problem	size	variables	constraints	compiled constraints	time (secs)
boxcars	50	50	149	100	0.7
	100	100	299	200	1.4
	200	200	599	400	4.5
	400	400	1199	800	15.8
	800	800	2399	1600	62.0
binary tree	5	62	199	111	0.5
	6	126	407	230	1.2
	7	254	823	470	3.7
	8	510	1655	950	12.5
	9	1022	3319	1910	46.2
grid	5 × 5	50	180	60	0.4
	10 × 10	200	760	220	3.3
	20 × 20	800	3120	840	48.1

Fig. 5. Compilation statistics

must be centered over their children, and finally every node must lie within a certain bounding box. This formulation has some redundancy—we could have specified only that the left child be the minimum distance below the parent, rather than both the left and right children, since the children are at the same height. However, this redundancy arises naturally in the specification. The *grid* benchmark is an $n \times n$ grid of points where every point is constrained to be on an imaginary vertical line through the points above and below it, and on a horizontal line through the points to the left and right. No point can be within a given distance of its neighbours, and all points lie within a given box. Again this specification leads to redundancy in the constraints.

The compilation results are shown in Figure 5. For each benchmark we give the following information: the number of variables in the original formulation; the number of constraints in the original formulation; the typical number of constraints in the compiled code (that is, the number of inequalities used for *minset* and *maxset* calculations, and equations used to emit calculation code); and the typical CPU time required for the Mercury program to produce the Smalltalk code. The compilations were done on a DEC AlphaServer 8400 with eight 300 MHz 21164 processors.

The compiled versions did not suffer from an exponential blow-up in the number of constraints, and indeed all contain fewer constraints than were in the input, the reduction being due to the redundancy elimination performed during projection. One important technique for redundancy elimination is the detection and removal of *quasi-syntactic redundancy*. A primitive constraint $c_1 \leftrightarrow a_1 x_1 + \ldots + a_m x_m \leq a_0$ is quasi-syntactic redundant with respect to $c_2 \leftrightarrow a_1 x_1 + \ldots + a_m x_m \leq b_0$, or $c_2 \leftrightarrow a_1 x_1 + \ldots + a_m x_m = b_0$, if $b_0 \leq a_0$; if this is the case c_1 can be dropped without affecting the result. This test is inexpensive, $O(n \log n)$ for testing n primitive constraints, yet allows us to get rid of a significant number

Problem	Time (milliseconds)			Avg. # of pivots (Cassowary only)
	Fourier	Cassowary	Graphics	
50 boxcars (infrequent collisions)	1.0	5.0	38.0	0.11
50 boxcars (frequent collisions)	1.0	16.0	38.0	0.51
depth 5 tree (frequent collisions)	5.3	68.6	46.0	1.55
depth 5 tree (v. frequent collisions)	5.3	124.5	46.0	3.77

Fig. 6. Runtime statistics

of redundant constraints. It is also important to select carefully the variable to be eliminated next. This choice can make a significant difference in the number of redundant constraints produced. Making use of Proposition 4 (Section 6) and more general heuristics, we have had good results with all examples tried. Details about the other redundancy elimination techniques and heuristics we used can be found in [7].

The code produced is extremely efficient, and also has predictable performance irrespective of the input values. Figure 6 gives some measurements of the execution speed of the compiled code as compared with the execution speed of the Cassowary constraint solver [6], which uses an efficient simplex-based algorithm specifically adapted for repeatedly solving constraints arising in interactive graphics applications. All timings were done using OTI Smalltalk Version 4.0, running on an IBM Thinkpad 760EL laptop computer.

The times shown are the average number of milliseconds to perform one update, i.e. to solve the constraint problem with a new value for the mouse position. The Fourier and Cassowary times are both without graphics refresh; the additional refresh time is shown in the "Graphics" column. Finally, for Cassowary, the last column gives the average number of simplex pivots per update. There are two different runs given for the boxcars example, one with the input varying slowly, so that collisions between the boxcars are relatively infrequent, and another with more rapidly varying input, causing more collisions. The time to run the Fourier code is the same for both cases; however, with frequent collisions the Cassowary time per update increases substantially. The reason is that a collision generally requires a pivot in the simplex tableau, which is expensive; when there is no collision, the tableau can be updated very efficiently with no pivoting required. There are also two runs for the tree example. We used a tree with the node displays closely spaced, so that there were many collisions (a moving node bumping into a stationary one) in both cases; the second run involved moving the mouse more quickly to generate even more collisions. (The way in which we coded the tree example has more overhead than the boxcars example, resulting in the times for both algorithms being longer for this test.)

For these examples the Fourier code is approximately 5 to 20 times faster than the runtime simplex solver. For the relatively simple constraints of the boxcars example, however, the graphics refresh time is substantially more than the time required to satisfy the constraints in any of the tests. However, when using the simplex solver for the tree example, the constraint solving time becomes significant as compared to the graphics refresh time. In addition, the simplex solver has variable solving time, which is quite apparent when the mouse is moved very quickly on this example — often the update is extremely fast, but when numerous pivots are needed it slows down, giving a less pleasant jerky quality to the interaction. In fairness to the simplex approach, it should be possible to extrapolate the current direction of the mouse movement and pre-solve some of the pivots; but this has not been done in any of the current systems. In addition, for use with real-time systems the predictable response provided by the compiled Fourier code is essential.

6 Complexity Analysis

Most variable elimination algorithms have bad worst case complexities. Projecting one variable from a system of m linear inequalities produces $O(m^2)$ inequalities in the worst case. Hence eliminating n variables from m primitive constraints can be $O(m^{2^n})$. However, our empirical results so far have shown quite reasonable performance for practical problems. In this section we attempt to analyze the situation and point out reasons for this. This analysis is preliminary. In the long term, we want to develop a set of benchmarks for constraint satisfaction algorithms for user interface applications, measure our projection compilation algorithm against these benchmarks, and characterize which properties of the benchmarks lead to good and to bad performance.

One major factor in the reasonable performance of our algorithm is that in many practical problems each constraint only involves a small number of variables, and hence the worst case does not arise. There are also a number of restricted cases that do have much more reasonable worst case complexities. One such restricted case is when each constraint involves at most 2 variables. The *grid* benchmark above falls into this category.

Theorem 2 (Nelson [12]). *Let C be a set of m inequalities involving n variables where each inequality involves at most 2 variables. Fourier elimination is $O(mn^{\lceil 2\log n\rceil+3}\log n)$.* $\square$

Another example where the worst case phenomena cannot occur is when almost all of the constraints are equations.

Proposition 3. *Let C be a constraint involving n variables, m linearly independent equations, and l inequalities. Then there is a choice of variable elimination order where Fourier elimination is $O(nm(m+l)+l^{2^{n-m}})$.* $\square$

It also appears that, in many practical constraint problems in interactive graphics, the constraints are not tightly connected. As a preliminary analysis of this phenomenon, we examine a class of constraint graph which is not tightly connected. A constraint graph for a constraint C is an undirected graph constructed as follows. There are nodes for each variable in $vars(C)$ and each primitive constraint $c \in C$. There is an edge between variable node v and primitive constraint node c if $v \in vars(c)$. Two nodes x and y in a graph G are *bi-connected* if there exist two node-distinct paths in G from x to y. A bi-connected component of a graph G is a maximal set of nodes N such that each pair $x, y \in N, x \neq y$ is bi-connected in G. A constraint graph G is k *bi-connected* is there are no bi-connected components of G with more than k variable nodes. The *binary tree* benchmark is an example where the constraint graph is 3-bi-connected.

Proposition 4. *Let C be a constraint involving n variables and m primitive constraints whose constraint graph is k-bi-connected. Then there is an choice of variable elimination order where a slightly modified Fourier elimination algorithm with quasi-syntactic redundancy elimination is $O(nm^{2^k})$.*□

7 Conclusions and Future Work

Fourier elimination can be used to generate very fast, constraint-free code to solve problems arising in interactive graphical applications. The approach is useful for applications such as real-time systems that need predictable performance, for smoothing the response time in an interative system, for producing applications that can be run without employing a runtime constraint solver, and when execution speed is very important.

The same approach of compiling constraint solving by projection can be applied to any constraint domain that has a variable elimination function that projects one variable out of a constraint, along with a method for finding solutions of a conjunction of constraints in one variable. Constraint domains that satisfy this property include Boolean constraints, unit two variable per inequality integer linear constraints, and partial order constraints.

Finally, some of our previous work has involved hybrid constraint solving algorithms, which partition a set of constraints into regions that can then be turned over to an appropriate sub-solver for that class of constraint and constraint topology [3]. Compilation based on Fourier elimination is a promising candidate for use in this architecture, to handle collections of simultaneous linear equality and inequality constraints.

Acknowledgments

This project has been funded in part by the National Science Foundation under Grants IRI-9302249 and CCR-9402551 and by Object Technology International. Alan Borning's visit to Monash University and the University of Melbourne was sponsored in part by a Fulbright award.

References

1. A. Borning. The programming language aspects of ThingLab, a constraint-oriented simulation laboratory. *ACM TOPLAS*, 3(4):353–387, 1981.
2. A. Borning, R. Anderson, and B. Freeman-Benson. Indigo: A local propagation algorithm for inequality constraints. In *Procs. ACM Symp. on User Interface Software and Technology*, 129–136, Seattle, 1996.
3. A. Borning and B. Freeman-Benson. The OTI constraint solver: A constraint library for constructing interactive graphical user interfaces. In *Procs. of CP95*, 624–628, Cassis, France, 1995.
4. A. Borning, B. Freeman-Benson, and M. Wilson. Constraint hierarchies. *Lisp and Symbolic Computation*, 5(3):223–270, 1992.
5. A. Borning, R. Lin, and K. Marriott. Constraints for the web. In *Proceedings of ACM MULTIMEDIA '97*, November 1997. To appear.
6. A. Borning, K. Marriott, P. Stuckey, and Y. Xiao. Solving linear arithmetic constraints for user interface applications. In *Proceedings of the 1997 ACM Conference on User Interface Software and Technology*, October 1997. To appear.
7. W. Harvey, P. Stuckey, and A. Borning. Compiling constraint solving using projection. TR 97/6, Dept. of Computer Science, University of Melbourne, 1997.
8. R. Helm, T. Huynh, C. Lassez, and K. Marriott. A linear constraint technology for interactive graphic systems. In *Graphics Interface '92*, 301–309, 1992.
9. H. Hosobe, S. Matsuoka, and A. Yonezawa. Generalized local propagation: A framework for solving constraint hierarchies. In *Procs. of the CP96*, Boston, 1996.
10. S. E. Hudson and I. Smith. SubArctic UI toolkit user's manual. Tech. report, College of Computing, Georgia Institute of Technology, 1996.
11. B. A. Myers. The Amulet user interface development environment. In *CHI'96 Conference Companion: Human Factors in Computing Systems*, Vancouver, B.C., April 1996. ACM SIGCHI.
12. C.G. Nelson. An $n^{\log n}$ algorithm for the two-variable-per-constraint linear programming satisfiability problem. Report STAN-CS-78-689, Stanford, 1978.
13. M. Sannella, J. Maloney, B. Freeman-Benson, and A. Borning. Multi-way versus one-way constraints in user interfaces: Experience with the DeltaBlue algorithm. *Software—Practice and Experience*, 23(5):529–566, 1993.
14. Z. Somogyi, F. Henderson, and T. Conway. Mercury: an efficient purely declarative logic programming language. In *Procs. of the ACSC95*, 499–512, Glenelg, Australia, 1995.
15. I. Sutherland. Sketchpad: A man-machine graphical communication system. In *Proceedings of the Spring Joint Computer Conference*, 329–346. IFIPS, 1963.
16. B. Vander Zanden. An incremental algorithm for satisfying hierarchies of multi-way dataflow constraints. *ACM TOPLAS*, 18(1):30–72, 1996.

Oscillation, Heuristic Ordering and Pruning in Neighborhood Search

Jean-Marc Labat and Laurent Mynard

LIP6,
UPMC, case 169, 4 place Jussieu,
75252 Paris Cedex 05, FRANCE

Abstract. This paper describes a new algorithm for combinatorial optimization problems and presents the results of our experiments. HOLSA -Heuristic Oscillating Local Search Algorithm- is a neighborhood search algorithm using an evaluation function f inspired from A*, a best-first strategy, a pruning of states as in B&B and operators performing variable steps. All these caracteristics lead to an oscillation principle whereby the search alternates between improving the economic function and satisfying the constraints. We specify how to compute the start state, the evaluation function and the variable steps in order to implement the general outline of HOLSA. Its performance is tested on the multidimensional knapsack problem, using randomly generated problems and classical test problems of the litterature. The experiments show that HOLSA is very efficient, according to the quality of the solutions as well as the search speed, at least on the class of problems studied in this paper. Moreover with large problems, and a limited number of generated nodes, we show that it is better than Branch & Bound, simulated annealing, tabu search and GRASP, both for the quality of the solution and the computational time.

1 Introduction

1.1 Overview

In this text, we consider combinatorial optimization problems which are formulated as follows:

> Maximize $g(X)$
> subject to $C_j(X) \le b_j \qquad j = 1, \ldots, p.$

where the state $X = (x_1, \ldots, x_i, \ldots, x_n)$ is an integer vector of decision variables; g and C_j ($j = 1, \ldots, p$) are real valued functions, and $b_j \in \mathbb{R}^+$ ($j = 1, \ldots, p$).

These problems are most of the time NP-hard (see [9, chapter 15] for instance). As the improvement of computers and software does not change the nature of these problems, heuristic searches are necessary to solve large ones in a reasonable amount of time. Among the algorithms which address this large class of problems, many of them deal only with linear functions and/or binary variables. In this work, no such restrictions are necessary. But our algorithm requires some other conditions to be satisfied (see §2.1). In order to compare our results with those of standard algorithms, we study the multidimensional knapsack problem. We use as reference two classes of algorithms. First, we use *Cplex MIP 2.1*, a commercial software using the simplex method coupled with a *Branch-and-Bound* which finds the optimal solution if the number of generated states allowed by resolution is large enough. Secondly, we use our own implementations of simulated annealing (SA), tabu search (TS) and GRASP. Thus, using small problems, we can judge the quality of the solution, as B&B provides the optimal one, and with large ones we can judge the computational time efficiency and more generally the trade-off between quickness and quality of the solution.

In the next paragraph, we briefly recall previous work on this class of problems. In the next section, we give some definitions necessary for understanding our algorithm, called *HOLSA*, for Heuristic Oscillating Local Search Algorithm. Then we present the general outline of HOLSA and we describe its implementation. In section 3, we introduce the multidimensional knapsack problem and we implement HOLSA on this problem. In section 4, we present experimental results comparing HOLSA with other algorithms. We conclude this paper with a short comment about our work and further research.

1.2 Relation to previous work

Four classes of algorithms exist in order to solve combinatorial optimization problems. Firstly, specific algorithms are designed to solve instances of one given type of problem by taking advantage of its structure. We do not consider them in this paper, as we are looking for algorithms able to solve large classes of problems. Secondly, global search algorithms are mainly represented by A* [8], Branch-and-Bound -B&B- and the algorithms derived from them [6]. Nau, Kumar and Kanal [7] proved that A* is a special case of B&B. Pomerol, Labat and Futtersack [11] conversely showed that B&B with best-first strategy can be considered as a special case of A*. If the evaluation function f used in A* or in B&B overestimates the true value (in a maximization problem), they are both admissible [10, page 78]. The third technique is neighborhood search. The most famous algorithms are simulated annealing [5], tabu search [3] and GRASP [2]. Their main advantage is the possible trade-off between quickness and the quality of the solution, often called flexibility. The last class of resolution methods contains the remaining heuristic methods, for example genetic algorithms or neural networks [12].

From A* and B&B, we keep two ideas: a best-first strategy to choose the next state to expand, and an evaluation function f of the states which, in A* and B&B, measures the "promise" of states for ranking the candidates for expansion, to determine which one is the most likely to be on a path to a near-optimal solution [8]. We also keep in mind that, for a maximization problem, this function must overestimate the value of all successors in order to keep the algorithm admissible. But for huge problems, these algorithms are too costly in terms of memory and computational time. The analysis of these weaknesses is well known: finding the optimal solution in every case requires taking a start state without any assignation, and continuously expanding the state with the highest evaluation. This is the reason why we use the ideas issued from neighborhood search, starting with a state which is already a good solution. We can consider HOLSA as a neighborhood search algorithm since all the states are potential solutions and the set of successors obtained by applying the operators can be seen as a neighborhood. The objective function is computed for all the states in the neighborhood and the evaluation function, estimating the promise of successors, is used to escape from local extrema. Therefore, the aim is to limit the search to the subset where near-optimal solutions should be, instead of exploring a large subset of the space, as A* or B&B do or undertaking a partially random exploration of a subset as with Simulated Annealing. Obviously combining such varied ideas makes integration difficult unless the exploration alternates between constructive and destructive phases, which may be translated into alternance between improving the economic function and satisfying the constraints. This mecanism, is called *strategic oscillation* [3].

2 Algorithm

2.1 Preliminary definitions

Feasible and unfeasible states Let define $\Delta C_j(X) = b_j - C_j(X)$, $j \in \{1, \dots, p\}$. The state X is *feasible* if and only if $\Delta C_j(X) \geq 0$ for all $j \in \{1, \dots p\}$. The state X is *unfeasible* if and only if there exists at least one $j \in \{1, \dots, p\}$ such that $\Delta C_j(X) < 0$. The set $\mathcal{F}$ (respectively $\mathcal{U}$) of the feasible (resp. unfeasible) states is called "feasible (resp. unfeasible) set".

Successors The *Operators* make the transition from one given state X to its successors X_k. The oscillating strategy in HOLSA requires that operators satisfy the following condition: $X_k \neq X$ and for all successors X_k of X, for all $j \in \{1, \dots, p\}$, $X \in \mathcal{F} \Rightarrow \Delta C_j(X_k) \leq \Delta C_j(X)$ and $X \in \mathcal{U} \Rightarrow \Delta C_j(X_k) \geq \Delta C_j(X)$. This means that the successors of a state X are "nearer" to the set to which X does not belong (i.e. $\mathcal{F}$ if X is unfeasible, $\mathcal{U}$ is X is feasible) than X itself. Therefore, two types of operators are defined: *inner* operators are applied only to feasible states and *outer* to unfeasible states. The inner operators must increase the value of at least one C_j and also increase the value of g. The outer operators must decrease the value of at least one C_j and decrease the value of g. This hypothesis is necessary to the application of the oscillating principle of HOLSA.

Terminal states The state X is *terminal* if and only if it is feasible and all its successors are unfeasible.

Evaluation function f Our evaluation function f is the sum of g which is the function to maximize, and h which is the heuristic part. Of course it is impossible to precisely define h without a given problem, but we can specify two properties which h must verify: firstly, for every state X, $h(X)$ must be defined in the same terms as $g(X)$; secondly, if the current state belongs to $\mathcal{F}$ (respectively $\mathcal{U}$), $h(X)$ must be positive (resp. negative) and must overestimate the increase (resp. underestimate the decrease) in g between X and Y, for all states Y lying on a path between X and the terminal states obtained from X by iterative application of inner (resp. outer) operators.

2.2 The HOLSA Algorithm

The first versions of HOLSA, based on the ideas presented above, produced better results in term of computational time than A* but are still very costly. Therefore we introduce two new ideas to reduce the size of OPEN (the set of states to expand) and CLOSED (the set of expanded states). The first idea is to prune OPEN and CLOSED. As in B&B, all the states X with an evaluation $f(X)$ lower than the economic value of the current best solution - i.e. X^* in the algorithm - are excluded both from OPEN and CLOSED (steps 12 and 13). Heuristically speaking, these states should not generate a better solution than the current X^* because of the conditions described in §2.1. However, unlike B&B, this pruning does not preserve admissibility because there is no guarantee that we do not cut all paths going to an optimal solution. An additional idea, in order to limit the size of OPEN, is to make large "steps" for generating the successors of the current state when it is heuristically evaluated as being far from the terminal states. Nevertheless, in the algorithm presented below, we only speak of "successors"; the computation of the variable step depends of the concrete problem and will be defined in the next section. With the above definitions, we may formalize HOLSA taking into account all the ideas previouly presented.

1- Let X_0 be the start element.
2- $X^* \leftarrow X_0$; OPEN $\leftarrow \{X_0\}$; CLOSED $\leftarrow \emptyset$.
3- **While** the stop condition is not satisfied **do**
4- Let X be the state in OPEN with the highest evaluation.
5- OPEN $\leftarrow$ OPEN $\setminus \{X\}$; CLOSED $\leftarrow$ CLOSED $\cup \{X\}$.
6- **If** $X \in \mathcal{F}$ **then**
7- Expand X into X_k with all the inner operators.
8- **Else** expand X into X_k with all the outer operators.
9- **For each** successor X_k of X **do**
10- **If** $g(X_k) > g(X^*)$ and $X_k \in \mathcal{F}$ **then**
11- $X^* \leftarrow X_k$.
12- OPEN $\leftarrow$ OPEN $\setminus \{Y; f(Y) < g(X^*)\}$.
13- CLOSED $\leftarrow$ CLOSED $\setminus \{Y; f(Y) < g(X^*)\}$.
14- **If** $f(X_k) \geq g(X^*)$ and $X_k \notin$ CLOSED **then**
15- OPEN $\leftarrow$ OPEN $\cup \{X_k\}$.

Comments: CLOSED and OPEN are pruned each time a new better solution is found. When the increase in the value of the solution is small, only a few states are excluded from CLOSED. Pruning OPEN and CLOSED only when the amelioration of X^* is greater than a given percentage has not been tested yet but could probably reduce the running time.

As such, HOLSA is only an outline. Implementation requires defining: (1) h, the heuristic part of the function f; (2) the construction of X_0; (3) the stop condition; and (4) the successors of a state. The choices for points (2) and (3) are somewhat independent from the concrete problem, therefore in §2.3 we present the different possibilities and the choices we made after numerous experiments. On the other hand, points (1) and (4) narrowly depend on the problem, therefore we present them in section 3, after introducing some complementary definitions concerning the multidimensional knapsack problem.

2.3 Strategic choices

Initial state Any element may be chosen as a start state X_0. However it is better to start with a feasible element such that g is as high as possible, since the basic principle of the algorithm is to restrict as much as possible the search towards such states. There are many methods to obtain such initial states, but the following ones are both easy to implement and not expensive in computational time.

- *One-variable method.* One variable x_{i_0} is chosen as the variable giving the highest value of g and instanciated at its upper bound, while all other variables have zero values, so that the state is feasible.
- *Feasible Hill-Climbing.* All variables have zero values, and a greedy algorithm is applied: the value of one variable is increased at each step so that the value of $g(X)$ increases as much as possible while the values of all the $C_j(X)$ increases as little as possible. The process is repeated until no variable can be changed without breaking at least one constraint. Therefore the greedy process stops on a feasible state.
- *Unfeasible Hill-Climbing.* In the same way, all variables have upper bound values, which give an unfeasible state, and a greedy algorithm is applied: the value of one variable is decreased at each step so that the value of $g(X)$ decreases as little as possible, and the values of all the $C_j(X)$ decrease as much as possible. The process is repeated until a feasible state is found.

Remarks:

1. Unfeasible hill-climbing generally provides better results than the other methods, at least on the multidimensional knapsack problem. This method, rather than the others, is therefore used for the experiments (see §4).
2. The final solution X^* found by HOLSA is dependent on the initial state X_0. The pruning in steps 12 and 13 causes the search to be limited in most cases to a given subset of the search space, determined mainly by the choice of

511

the initial state. This leads to the conclusion that a process of diversification should be added to HOLSA. Further research will be done on the use of parallel computers to spread the search from several initial states on all the processors.

Stop condition There is one obvious condition that must exist whatever the other choices are: if OPEN is empty, the algorithm stops. However, with large problems, the exploration may last for a considerable time even if the best current solution is not improved. Therefore, it is necessary to introduce at least one other stop condition. We did test conditions such as a given time limit or a given limit in the number of generated states. But the stop condition, which is probably the most efficient in terms of flexibility, is "no amelioration of X* over a given number of iterations". However, in order to compare HOLSA with B&B, we impose a limit on the number of generated states because it is the type of limit used by Cplex.

3 Implementation

3.1 The multidimensional knapsack problem

HOLSA has been implemented for the multidimensional knapsack problem.

$$\text{Maximize } \left(\sum_{i=1}^{n} v_i \cdot x_i \right)$$
$$\text{Subject to: } \sum_{i=1}^{n} c_{j,i} \cdot x_i \leq b_j \quad j \in \{1, \ldots, p\}$$

where $v_i \in \mathbb{R}^{+*}$, $c_{j,i} \in \mathbb{R}^{+}$, $b_j \in \mathbb{R}^{+*}$, $X = (x_1, \ldots, x_n) \in \mathbb{N}^n$.

Quality ratio. Let $r_{j,i} \in \overline{\mathbb{R}^+}$ be the *quality ratio* of x_i in the jth constraint.

$$r_{j,i} = \frac{v_i}{c_{j,i}}$$

3.2 Heuristic evaluation h

The heuristic part h of the evaluation function f measures the expected variation of g which can be obtained from the evaluated state. For each constraint j, we determine:

if $X \in \mathcal{F}$: let $r_{j,best}$ be the highest quality ratio of the decision variables whose values can be increased (i.e. lower than its upper bound, and $\Delta C_j(X) \geq c_{j,best}$);

if $X \in \mathcal{U}$: let $r_{j,worst}$ be the lowest quality ratio of the decision variables whose values can be decreased (i.e, $x_{worst} > 0$).

Then, x_{best} and x_{worst} are the "most interesting" variable to modify in the jth constraint. This means that variations of x_{best} imply the highest gain on g compared to the increase in $C_j(X)$ and variations of x_{worst} imply the lowest loss on g compared to the decrease in $C_j(X)$. For each j, the highest possible variation of x_{best} or x_{worst} corresponds to a variation of the value of g, whose minimum over all constraints gives a value to $h(X)$.

if $X \in \mathcal{F}$: $h(X) = \min_j (r_{j,best} \cdot \Delta_j(X))$

if $X \in \mathcal{U}$: $h(X) = \min_j (r_{j,worst} \cdot \Delta_j(X))$

Property of h: The heuristic function h verifies that:

1. for all $X \in \mathcal{F}$, for all Y successors of X by using only inner operators, $g(Y) \leq g(X) + h(X)$;
2. for all $X \in \mathcal{U}$, for all Y successors of X by using only outer operators, $g(Y) \leq g(X) + h(X)$

Sketch of proof: by recurrence on the number of constraints.

3.3 Successors of a state

The most evident way to move from a state X to its successors is to change the value of one variable by one unit, increasing its value if $X \in \mathcal{F}$, decreasing its value if $X \in \mathcal{U}$, generating up to n successors. There may be less than n successors if the value cannot be decreased because it is already zero, or cannot be increased because it would exceed the upper bound of the variable. However, as mentioned in §2.2, the heuristic evaluation $h(X)$ can be used to scale the steps of the operators. That is the reason why we define successors as follows:

$$X = (x_1, \dots, x_i, \dots, x_n) \xrightarrow{i} (x_1, \dots, x_i + p_i(X), \dots, x_n)$$

The integer function p_i $(i = 1, \dots, n)$ is defined by:

$$p_i(X) = \pm \max \left(1, \left\lfloor \frac{|h(X)|}{v_i} \right\rfloor \right)$$

The sign is positive if $X \in \mathcal{F}$, and negative if $X \in \mathcal{U}$.

4 Experimental results

As previously mentioned, we have performed many experiments, generating random problems, with the standard *random* C function under Unix. Values of v_i are in the $]0, 100]$ interval. Values of $c_{j,i}$ are in the $[0, 100]$ interval, with an average 15% of zero values. Values of b_j are in the $]0, 2500]$ interval. With a higher proportion of zero's in the constraint matrix, we obtain too many unsolvable problems since there are unconstrained variables (the optimal value of g being in this case infinite).

Two series of problems are used: series 1 contains one hundred problems with fifty to two hundred variables and ten to twenty constraints; series 2 contains twenty problems with four hundred to five hundred variables and fifty constraints.

4.1 Quality of the solution as a function of the time spent

Local search algorithms are considered as very attractive because of their flexibility which allows the user to choose between quickness and quality of solution. Therefore, before presenting the comparison with the other algorithms, it is interesting to examine the improvement of X^*, the current best solution which is a function of the computational time. With series 1, we obtain the curve in figure 1 where $V = g(X^*_{final})$ and T is the resolution time. It shows that HOLSA keeps the property of flexibility since it rapidly finds an efficient solution.

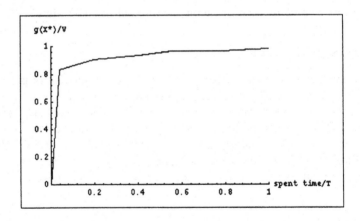

Fig. 1. Quality of the solution as a function of time spent.

4.2 Comparison with B&B

We use the two series. With series 1, B&B always finds the optimum. Although the optimal solution is found by HOLSA in only 25% of cases, the suboptimal solutions found by HOLSA are very good, since the average margin with the solution found by B&B is only 2%. At the same time, these solutions are found rapidly: the resolution time needed by HOLSA is 130 times lower than with B&B (see table 1).

	HOLSA	B&B	TS	SA	GRASP
% of optimal solutions found	25	100	3	0	3
Average margin to the optimal solution (%)	2	0	8	13	7
Average resolution time (s)	0.7	93.4	0.5	1	3.7

Table 1. Comparison of performance on serie 1.

With series 2, this constatation becomes even more obvious. We impose a limit of 20000 generated states to B&B, which represents about 30 minutes of computing time. Within this limit, B&B never finds the optimum, but nevertheless finds good suboptimal solutions. HOLSA finds better solutions than B&B, improving the average value of the solutions by about 23%, with a computational time divided by more than 100 (see table 2).

	B&B	HOLSA
Average resolution time (s)	1376	11.8
Average value of the final solution	1153	1503

Table 2. Comparison of B&B and HOLSA on series 2.

4.3 Comparison with neighborhood search algorithms

Our implementation of tabu search includes the use of aspiration criterion and diversification methods. The tabu tenure is proportional to the size of the problem ($n/5$ provides good results). Our tabu search does not include (for the moment) any strategic oscillation. Therefore the neighborhood contains all feasible states differing from the current state by one unit on one variable. The neighbor chosen is the best non-tabu one, or the best tabu one which satisfies the aspiration criterion (i.e. improves the best solution found).

Our implementation of simulated annealing is classical too. The cooling scheduling is linear, with a constant factor of 0.999. Initial and terminal temperatures are chosen so that the computing time is about the same as the other algorithms. The length of the search chains at each temperature is proportional to the size of the problem. The neighborhood consists in changing randomly the value of a randomly chosen variable.

Our implementation of GRASP uses a randomized unfeasible Hill-Climbing (see §2.3) to determine the initial states. Instead of the chosing the best variable at each step, we chose the kth best, where k is randomly chosen within a range proportional to the size of the problem ($n/5$ provides good results). The number of iterations is chosen so that the computing time is about the same as the other algorithms.

Our implementation of HOLSA provides better results than our implementations of the three classical neighborhood search algorithms on series 1 (see table 1). HOLSA finds better solutions and is at once faster than simulated annealing and GRASP, and almost as fast as tabu search (which finds worse solutions).

With series 2, we impose limits on the number of generated states (HOLSA), on the number of iterations (TS and GRASP) and on the initial temperature and cooling function (SA) so that the four algorithms have approximately the same computing time. These tests confirm that HOLSA provides better average solutions than the three other algorithms with approximately the same resolution time (see table 3).

	HOLSA	TS	SA	GRASP
Average resolution time (s)	11.8	9.5	6.5	10.4
Standard deviation of resolution time (s)	2.8	2.4	0.9	2.5
Average value of the final solution	1503	1420	1274	1458
Standard deviation of the value of the final solution	227	204	233	216

Table 3. Comparison of HOLSA, tabu search, simulated annealing and GRASP on series 2.

4.4 Binary benchmarks

Tests have been made with the 57 $0-1$ benchmark problems provided by Drexl in [1]. No modification have been made in the HOLSA implementation for specifically solving $0-1$ problems: we only added constraints in the problems to specify that variables cannot exceed 1. Results are presented in table 4.

HOLSA finds the optimal solution for 26 problems. The average margin to the optimal solution is only 0.88%. It is difficult to compare computing times with those of other published results, because of the differences between computers used. But for instance Glover and Kochenberger[4] announces 28 minutes on a PC 486 as average computing time, whereas we show 6.2 seconds on a SPARC 5 workstation. And this average time is due mainly to one problems behaving atypically (Petersen 6). Without this instance, the average computing time of HOLSA is only 0.9 second. Another important point is that results in [4] are the best one among 6 runs with various parameters, whereas the results of HOLSA in table 4 are obtained with only one run with fixed parameters. Multiple runs of HOLSA with various starting points and parameters leads to some sort of hybrid of GRASP and HOLSA, and should improve the results.

Problem	N. var.	N.constr.	Opt	HOLSA Value	Average margin (%)	Time (s)
Fréville & Plateau 1	27	646	3090	3073	0.6	0.38
Fréville & Plateau 2	34	4	3186	3079	3.4	3.82
Fréville & Plateau 3	19	2	28642	28642	0.0	0.01
Fréville & Plateau 4	29	2	95168	89209	6.2	0.28
Fréville & Plateau 5	20	10	2139	2022	5.5	0.02
Fréville & Plateau 6	40	30	776	679	12.5	0.12
Fréville & Plateau 7	37	30	1035	992	4.1	0.22
Petersen 1	6	10	3800	3800	0.0	0.01
Petersen 2	10	10	87061	86501	0.6	0.01
Petersen 3	15	10	4015	4015	0.0	0.01
Petersen 4	20	10	6120	6120	0.0	0.04
Petersen 5	28	10	12400	12330	0.6	0.13
Petersen 6	39	5	10618	10601	0.2	301.5
Petersen 7	50	5	16537	16430	0.6	9.75
Hansen & Plateau 1	28	4	3418	3401	0.5	0.49
Hansen & Plateau 2	35	4	3186	3079	3.4	4.71
Weingertner 1	28	2	141278	141278	0.0	0.1
Weingertner 2	28	2	130883	130883	0.0	0.7
Weingertner 3	28	2	95677	95677	0.0	0.3
Weingertner 4	28	2	119337	119317	0.02	0.75
Weingertner 5	28	2	98796	98631	0.2	0.12
Weingertner 6	28	2	130623	130233	0.3	0.11
Weingertner 7	105	2	1095445	1092308	0.3	0.77

continued on next page

continued from previous page						
Problem	N. var.	N.constr.	Opt	HOLSA Value	Average margin (%)	Time (s)
Weingertner 8	105	2	624319	618360	1.0	6.1
Wei Shih 1	30	5	4554	4554	0.0	0.5
Wei Shih 2	30	5	4536	4536	0.0	0.4
Wei Shih 3	30	5	4115	4115	0.0	0.4
Wei Shih 4	30	5	4561	4505	1.2	0.3
Wei Shih 5	30	5	4514	4514	0.0	0.4
Wei Shih 6	40	5	5557	5544	0.2	0.8
Wei Shih 7	40	5	5567	5542	0.4	0.11
Wei Shih 8	40	5	5605	5592	0.2	0.11
Wei Shih 9	40	5	5246	5246	0.0	0.09
Wei Shih 10	50	5	6339	6339	0.0	0.37
Wei Shih 11	50	5	5643	5624	0.3	0.37
Wei Shih 12	50	5	6339	6339	0.0	0.17
Wei Shih 13	50	5	6159	6159	0.0	0.46
Wei Shih 14	60	5	6954	6954	0.0	0.73
Wei Shih 15	60	5	7486	7486	0.0	0.22
Wei Shih 16	60	5	7289	7289	0.0	0.51
Wei Shih 17	60	5	8633	8624	0.1	0.92
Wei Shih 18	70	5	9580	9558	0.2	0.91
Wei Shih 19	70	5	7698	7698	0.0	0.42
Wei Shih 20	70	5	9450	9450	0.0	0.37
Wei Shih 21	70	5	9074	9074	0.0	1.05
Wei Shih 22	80	5	8947	8947	0.0	0.77
Wei Shih 23	80	5	8344	8341	0.01	0.62
Wei Shih 24	80	5	10220	10220	0.0	0.68
Wei Shih 25	80	5	9939	9923	0.2	1.18
Wei Shih 26	90	5	9584	9584	0.0	1.89
Wei Shih 27	90	5	9819	9811	0.08	1.46
Wei Shih 28	90	5	9492	9492	0.0	0.93
Wei Shih 29	90	5	9410	9410	0.0	1.1
Wei Shih 30	90	5	11191	11187	0.04	1.1
Senju & Toyoda 1	60	30	7772	7675	1.2	0.56
Senju & Toyoda 2	60	30	8722	8679	0.5	0.79
Fleisher	20	10	2139	2022	5.5	0.02

Table 4. $0 - 1$ benchmarks tests

5 Conclusion

HOLSA takes advantage of some key points from A*, B&B and neighborhood search algorithms. All these caracteristics lead to an oscillation search between

518

feasible and unfeasible states. The results of the experimental study clearly demonstate the advantage of the approach described in this paper since we obtained, with our experiments on the knapsack problem, better results than Branch & Bound and neighborhood search algorithms, at least in terms of speed and tractability for large problems. However, the choices to make in order to implement concrete problems from the general outline require further research and more experimentation. Another important point is the class of problems which can be addressed by HOLSA. It can address non-linear problems and this is extremely important because few algorithms exist in this area. Of course, in this last case, it is difficult to evaluate the quality of the solution because no exact algorithm exists. For this reason, we have chosen to present our algorithm on the multidimensional knapsack. But oscillation implies that there are two types of operators, some only applied to feasible states and improving the objective function, and some only applied to unfeasible states and decreasing the excess in the constraints. We think that this is the main limitation for using HOLSA.

Acknowledgment

We thank professor Gérard Plateau who provided us with the 0-1 multidimensional knapsack benchmarks.

References

1. Drexl, A.: A Simulated Annealing Approach to the Multiconstraint Zero-One Knapsack Problem. Computing **40** (1987) 1–8.
2. Feo, T. A., Resende, M. G. C.: Greedy Randomized Adaptative Search Procedures. Journal of Global Optimization **6** (1995) 109–133.
3. Glover, F.: Tabu Search - Part I. ORSA Journal on Computing **1**(3) (1989) 190–206.
4. Glover, F., Kochenberger, G. A.: Critical Event Tabu Search For Multidimensional Knapsack Problems. in *Meta-Heuristics: Theory and Applications* (I.H. Osman and J.P. Kelly Eds) Kluwer Academic Publishers (1996) 407–427 .
5. Kirkpatrick, S., Gellat, C. D., Vecchi, M. P.: Optimization by Simulated Annealing. Science **220** (1983) 671–680.
6. Korf, R.: Depth-First Iterative Deepening: an Optimal Admissible Tree Search. Articial Intelligence **27** (1985).
7. Nau, D., Kumar, V., Kanal, L.: General Branch and Bound and its Relation to A* and AO*. Artificial Intelligence **23** (1984) 29–59.
8. Nilsson, N.: Problem-Solving Methods in Artificial Intelligence. MacGraw Hill (1971).
9. Papadimitriou, C. H., Steiglitz, K.: Combinatorial optimization: algorithms and complexity. Prentice-Hall (1982).
10. Pearl, J.: Heuristics: Intelligent Search Strategies for Computer Problem Solving. Addison-Wesley (1984).
11. Pomerol, J.-Ch., Labat, J.-M., Futtersack, M.: Les algorithmes Branch and Bound et A* sont-ils identiques? *in* Premier congrès biennal de l'AFCET **1** (1993) 163–173.
12. Reeves, C. R.: Modern Heuristic Techniques for Combinatorial Problems. Blackwell Scientific Publications (1993).

Programming Constraint Inference Engines

Christian Schulte

Programming Systems Lab, DFKI, Stuhlsatzenhausweg 3, 66123 Saarbrücken, Germany
E-Mail: schulte@dfki.de, Web: www.ps.uni-sb.de/~schulte/

Abstract. Existing constraint programming systems offer a fixed set of inference engines implementing search strategies such as single, all, and best solution search. This is unfortunate, since new engines cannot be integrated by the user. The paper presents first-class computation spaces as abstractions with which the user can program inference engines at a high level. Using computation spaces, the paper covers several inference engines ranging from standard search strategies to techniques new to constraint programming, including limited discrepancy search, visual search, and saturation. Saturation is an inference method for tautology-checking used in industrial practice. Computation spaces have shown their practicability in the constraint programming system Oz.

1 Introduction

Existing constraint programming systems like CHIP [4], clp(FD) [2], ECLiPSe [1], and ILOG Solver [9] offer a fixed set of inference engines for search such as single, all, and best solution search. This is unfortunate, since new engines can only be implemented by the system's designer at a low level and cannot be integrated by the user.

The paper presents first-class computation spaces as abstractions with which the user can program inference engines at a high level. A computation space encapsulates a speculative computation involving constraints. Constraint inference engines are programmed using operations on computation spaces. They are made available as first-class citizens in the programming language to ease their manipulation and control.

We demonstrate that computation spaces cover a broad spectrum of inference engines ranging from standard search strategies to techniques new to constraint programming. The standard strategies discussed include single, all, and branch-and-bound best solution search. Their presentation introduces techniques for programming search engines using computation spaces. It is shown how these techniques carry over to engines like iterative deepening [10] and restart best solution search.

The paper studies limited discrepancy search, visual search, and saturation which are new to constraint programming. Limited discrepancy search (LDS) has been proposed by Harvey and Ginsberg [6] as a strategy to exploit heuristic information. A visual and interactive search engine that supports the development of constraint programs is the Oz Explorer [11]. It is an example where the user directly benefits from the expressiveness of computation spaces. The paper explains recomputation which is related to engines programmed from computation spaces. It allows to solve problems with a large number of variables and constraints that would need too much memory otherwise.

Saturation (also known as Stålmarck's method) is a method for tautology-checking used in industrial practice [5,14]. We show how a generic saturation engine can be built from first-class computation spaces. The engine is generic in that it is not restricted to a particular constraint system, whereas saturation has been originally conceived in the context of tautology-checking of Boolean formulae.

The constraint programming system Oz [8,13] implements computation spaces. While Oz offers computation spaces to the experienced user, it also provides a library of predefined search engines programmed with computation spaces that can be used without requiring detailed knowledge on computation spaces [7]. Search engines programmed from spaces are efficient. For example, solving scheduling problems using these engines is competitive with commercially available systems [16].

This work is based on a previous treatment of the so-called search combinator [12]. It spawns a local computation space and resolves remaining choices by returning them as procedures. First-class computation spaces subsume the search combinator and provide a more natural abstraction for programming inference engines. The paper contributes by introducing first-class computation spaces, but its main contribution is how to employ computation spaces for constraint inference engines that go beyond existing constraint programming systems.

The plan of the paper is as follows. The inference methods studied in the paper are shown in Section 2. Section 3 introduces first-class computation spaces. The rest of the paper is concerned with how the inference methods presented in Section 2 can be programmed with first-class computation spaces. Sections 4 to 10 introduce various search engines, whereas first-class computation spaces are applied to saturation in Section 11. Section 12 gives a brief conclusion.

2 Constraint Inference Methods

This section presents search and saturation as constraint inference methods using computation spaces as their central notion.

A *computation space* consists of propagators connected to a constraint store. The *constraint store* holds information about values of variables expressed by a conjunction of basic constraints. *Basic constraints* are logic formulae interpreted in a fixed first-order structure. In the following we restrict ourselves to finite domain constraints. A basic finite domain constraint has the form $x \in D$ where D is a finite subset of the positive integers. Other relevant basic constraints are $x = y$ and $x = n$, where n is a positive integer.

To keep operations on basic constraints efficient, more expressive constraints, called *nonbasic*, e.g., $x + y = z$, are not written to the constraint store. A nonbasic constraint is imposed by a propagator. A *propagator* is a concurrent computational agent that tries to amplify the store by *constraint propagation*: Suppose a constraint store hosting the constraint C and a propagator imposing the constraint P. The propagator can *tell* a basic constraint B to the store, if $C \wedge P$ entails B and B adds new and consistent information to C. Telling a basic constraint B updates the store to host $C \wedge B$.

A propagator imposing P disappears as soon as it detects that P is entailed by the store's constraints. A propagator imposing P becomes *failed* if it detects that P is inconsistent with the constraints hosted by the store. A space S is *stable*, if no further constraint propagation in S is possible. A stable space that contains a failed propagator is *failed*. A stable space not containing a propagator is *solved*.

Distribution. Typically, constraint propagation is not enough to solve a constraint problem: A space may become stable but neither solved nor failed. Hence, we need distribution. *Distributing* a space S with respect to a constraint D yields two spaces: One is obtained by adding D to S and the other is obtained by adding $\neg D$ to S. The constraint D will be chosen such that adding of D ($\neg D$) enables further constraint propagation.

Search. To solve a constraint problem with search, a space containing basic constraints and propagators of the problem is created. Then constraint propagation takes place until the space becomes stable. If the space is failed or solved, we are done. Otherwise, we select a constraint D with which we distribute the space. A possible distribution strategy for finite domain constraint problems is: Select a variable x which has more than one possible value left and an integer n from these values and then distribute with $x = n$.

Iterating constraint propagation and distribution creates a tree of computation spaces ("search tree") where leaves are failed or solved spaces. In this setup, the search tree is defined entirely by the problem and the distribution strategy. An orthogonal issue is how the search tree is explored by a given search engine.

Saturation. Distributing a space S yields two spaces S_0 and S_1 in which constraint propagation can tell new basic constraints to the stores of S_0 and S_1. The idea of saturation is to add basic constraints to S by *combining* S_0 and S_1: add the basic constraints that are common to both S_0 and S_1 back to the original space S. This might enable further constraint propagation within S. Distribution of S and combination back to S is iterated until a fixed point is reached. In the saturation literature, distribution and combination together is referred to as so-called *dilemma rule*.

Saturation is commonly applied to propositional satisfiability problems involving Boolean variables (finite domain variables restricted to take either 0 (false) or 1 (true) as value). In this context, a possible distribution strategy is: select a variable x from some fixed set of variables X and proceed from a space S by distribution to spaces S_0 by adding $x = 0$ and S_1 by adding $x = 1$. After constraint propagation has finished, S_0 and S_1 are combined as follows: For each variable $y \in X$ where both S_0 and S_1 contain the basic constraint $y = n$ ($n \in \{0, 1\}$), the constraint $y = n$ is added back to S. Distribution and combination is iterated for all variables in X until either S becomes failed or an entire iteration over all variables in X adds no new basic constraints to S. If one of S_0 or S_1 fails, saturation proceeds with the other space. Note that saturation, in contrast to search, is incomplete: after saturation finishes the space might not be solved.

Saturation as sketched above considers only a single variable at a time and thus is called 1-saturation. n-Saturation takes n variables simultaneously into account: it recursively applies $(n-1)$-saturation to the spaces S_0 and S_1 obtained by distribution, where 0-saturation coincides with constraint propagation. In practice only 1-saturation and 2-saturation are used. Harrison reports in [5] that the unsatisfiability of many practical formulae can in fact be proved with 1-saturation.

3 First-Class Computation Spaces

Section 2 demonstrates that computation spaces are a powerful abstraction for constraint inference methods. To control and manipulate computation spaces as needed in inference engines, they should be available as first-class entities. The programming language Oz [8,13] provides computation spaces as first-class citizens. They can be passed as arguments of procedures, can be tested for equality and the like. They can be created, their status can be asked for, they can be copied, their constraints can be accessed, and additional constraints can be injected into them.

Besides constraint store and propagators, a computation space also hosts threads. Like propagators, threads are concurrent computational entities. A *thread* is a stack of statements. It runs by reducing its topmost statement, possibly replacing the reduced statement with new statements. Threads synchronize on their topmost statement: if the topmost statement cannot be reduced, the entire thread cannot be reduced; we say it *suspends*. Statements include procedure application, procedure definition, variable declaration, sequential composition of statements, tell statement, conditional statement, thread creation, propagator creation, and so-called choices. A *choice* is either unary (**choice** S **end**) or binary (**choice** S_1 [] S_2 **end**) where S, S_1, and S_2 are statements called *alternatives*. A thread with a choice as topmost statement suspends.

Reduction of the statement S={NewSpace P} creates a new computation space, where P is a unary procedure and S yields a reference to the newly created space. The newly created space features a single fresh variable, the so-called *root variable*. In S a thread is created that contains as its single statement the application of P to the root variable. Typically, the procedure P represents the problem to be solved, and its single argument gives access to the solution of the problem (see the procedure Money in Section 5). Running the newly created thread typically creates variables, adds basic constraints to the store, spawns further propagators, and creates further threads.

A computation space S is *stable* if no thread and no propagator in S can reduce, and cannot become reducible by means of any other computation (more details on stability can be found in [12]). A computation space S is *failed* if it contains a failed propagator. When a computation space becomes stable and contains a thread with a unary choice as its topmost statement, the unary choice is replaced by its alternative. That is, a unary choice synchronizes on stability (this is used to program distribution strategies, see Section 6). A stable computation space not containing threads with unary choices but with binary choices as their first statements is called *distributable*. When a space becomes distributable one thread containing a binary choice as its topmost statement is selected. A stable space is *succeeded*, if it does not contain threads which suspend on choices.

A computation space S can be asked by A={Ask S} for its status. As soon as S becomes stable, the variable A gets bound. If S is failed then A is bound to failed. If S is distributable, A is bound to alternatives. Otherwise, A is bound to succeeded.

A distributable space S allows to commit to one alternative of the selected choice. By {Commit S I} the space S commits to the I-th alternative of the selected choice. That is, the choice is replaced by its I-th alternative. To explore both alternatives of a selected choice, stable computation spaces can be cloned. Reduction of C={Clone S} creates a new computation space C which is a copy of the stable space S.

The operation {Inject S P} takes a space S and a unary procedure P as arguments. Similar to space creation, it creates a new thread that contains as single statement the application of P to the root variable of S. For example, combination for saturation uses Inject to add constraints to an already existing space.

The constraints of a local computation space S can be accessed by Merge. Reduction of {Merge S X} binds X to the root variable of S and then discards S. The constraints that were referred to by the root variable of S can now be referred to by X.

The presentation here has been simplified in two aspects. Firstly, only binary choices are considered here. Oz in fact provides also for non-binary choices, this requires the operations Ask and Commit to be generalized in a straightforward manner. The second simplification concerns the setup of spaces in Oz. Regular computations in Oz are carried out in the so-called top-level computation space. Computations involving constraint propagation and distribution are speculative in the sense that failure is a regular event. These computations are encapsulated by first-class computation spaces. It is perfectly possible in Oz to create first-class spaces within first-class spaces (think of nested search engines) which leads to a tree of computation spaces (not to be confused with a search tree).

4 Depth-First Search

To familiarize the reader with programming inference engines using spaces, this section introduces simple depth-first search engines.

```
fun {DFE S}
   case {Ask S} of failed then nil
   [] succeeded then [S]
   [] alternatives then C={Clone S} in
      {Commit S 1}
      case {DFE S} of nil then {Commit C 2} {DFE C}
      [] [T] then [T]
      end
   end
end
```

Fig. 1. Depth-first single solution search.

The procedure DFE (see Figure 1) takes a space as argument and tries to solve it following a depth-first strategy. If no solution is found, but search terminates, the empty list nil is returned. Otherwise, the procedure returns the singleton list [T] where T is a succeeded computation space. Depending on the status of S (as determined by Ask), either the empty list nil or a singleton list containing S is returned. Otherwise, after distributing with the first clause (by {Commit S 1}) exploration is carried out recursively. If this does not yield a solution (i.e., nil is returned), a clone C of S is distributed with the second clause and C is solved recursively.

To turn the procedure DFE into a search engine that can be used easily, without any knowledge about spaces, we define the following procedure:

```
fun {SearchOne P}
   case {DFE {NewSpace P}} of nil then nil
   [] [S] then X in {Merge S X} [X]
   end
end
```

SearchOne takes a unary procedure as input, creates a new space in which the procedure P is run, and applies the procedure DFE to the newly created space. In case DFE returns a solved space, its root variable is returned in a list.

The search engine DFE can be adapted easily to accommodate for all solution search, where the entire search tree is explored and a list of all solved spaces is returned. It is sufficient to replace the shaded lines in Figure 1 with:

```
{Commit S 1} {Commit C 2} {Append {DFE S} {DFE C}}
```

Other depth-first search engines can be programmed following the structure of the program in Figure 1. For example, a search engine that puts a depth limit on the explored part of the search tree would just add support for maintaining the exploration depth (incrementing the depth on each recursive application of DFE). Increasing the depth limit until either a solution is found or the entire search tree is explored within the depth limit then yields iterative deepening [10].

5 An Example: Send Most Money

Let us consider a variation of a popular puzzle: Find distinct digits for the variables S, E, N, D, M, O, T, Y such that $S \neq 0$, $M \neq 0$ (no leading zeros) and the equation $SEND + MOST = MONEY$ holds. The program for this puzzle is shown in Figure 2.

```
proc {Money Root}
   money(s:S e:E n:N d:D m:M o:O t:T y:Y) = Root
in
   Root ::: 0#9
   {FD.distinct Root} S\=:0 M\=:0
                  S*1000 + E*100 + N*10 + D
                + M*1000 + O*100 + S*10 + T
   =: M*10000 + O*1000 + N*100 + E*10 + Y
   {FD.distribute ff Root}
end
```

Fig. 2. A program for the $SEND + MOST = MONEY$ puzzle.

The problem is defined as unary procedure, where its single argument Root is constrained to the solution of the problem. Here, the solution is a record that maps letters to variables for the digits. Execution of Root ::: 0#9 tells the basic constraints that each field of Root is an integer between 0 and 9. The propagator FD.distinct enforces all fields of the record to be distinct, whereas the propagators S\=:0 and M\=:0 enforce the variables S and M to be distinct from zero. The gray-shaded lines display the propagator that enforces *SEND + MOST = MONEY*. The variables for the letters are distributed (by FD.distribute) according to a strategy as sketched in Section 2, where variable selection follows the first-fail heuristic: the variable with the smallest number of possible values is distributed first.

Applying the search engine (i.e., SearchOne) to the problem (i.e., Money) by {SearchOne Money} returns the following first solution:

[money(d:2 e:3 m:1 n:4 o:0 s:9 t:5 y:7)]

Search engines usually are not built from scratch. Oz comes with a library of predefined search engines [7] programmed from computation spaces. The interface between search engine and problem is well defined by the choices as created by the distribution strategy. The next section shows how to program distribution strategies with choices.

6 Programming Distribution Strategies

Figure 3 shows a distribution strategy similar to that mentioned in Section 2. The procedure Distribute takes a list of finite domain variables to be distributed. A unary choice is employed to synchronize the execution of the gray-shaded statement on stability of the executing space. Since a distribution strategy typically inspects the constraint store's current state, it is important that variable and value selection for choice creation takes place only after constraint propagation has finished.

```
proc {Distribute Xs}
    choice  case {SelectVar Xs} of nil then skip
            [] [X] then N={SelectVal X} in
                choice X=N [] X\=:N end {Distribute Xs}
            end
    end
end
```

Fig. 3. Programming a distribution strategy with choices.

After synchronizing on stability, SelectVar selects a variable X that has more than one possible value left, whereas SelectVal selects one possible value N for X. The binary choice states that either X is equal or not equal to N. The first-fail strategy as used in Section 5, for example, would implement SelectVar as to return the variable with the smallest number of possible values and SelectVal as to return its minimal value.

7 Best Solution Search

Best solution search determines a best solution with respect to a problem-dependent ordering among the solutions of a problem. It is important to not explore the entire search tree of a problem but to use solutions as they are found to prune the rest of the search space as much as possible.

An Example: Send Most Money. Let us reconsider the example of Section 5. Suppose that we want to find the solution of the puzzle *SEND + MOST = MONEY* where we can get the most money: *MONEY* should be as large as possible. For this, we define the binary procedure More that takes two root variables O and N and imposes the constraint that N is better than O (O.m returns the variable at field m in record O):

```
proc {More O N}
    O.m*10000 + O.o*1000 + O.n*100 + O.e*10 + O.y <:
    N.m*10000 + N.o*1000 + N.n*100 + N.e*10 + N.y
end
```

We can search for the best solution by {SearchBest Money More} (SearchBest will be explained later), which returns a singleton list with the best solution as follows:

```
[money(d:2 e:7 m:1 n:8 o:0 s:9 t:4 y:6)]
```

Essential for best solution search is to inject to a space an additional constraint that the solution must be better than a previously found solution. The procedure

```
proc {Constrain S SolS O}
    {Inject S proc {$ NR}
                OR in {Merge {Clone SolS} OR} {O OR NR}
            end}
end
```

takes a space S, a solved space SolS (the so far best solution) and a binary procedure implementing the order (e.g., More in the above example). It injects into S the constraint that S must yield a better solution than SolS which is implemented by an order O on the constraints accessible from the root variables of the solution and the space S itself. Note that the solution's constraints are made accessible by merging a clone of SolS rather than merging SolS itself. This allows to use SolS again with Constrain and to possibly return it as best solution.

The procedure BAB (shown in Figure 4) implements branch-and-bound search. It takes the space S to be explored, the space SolS as the so far best solution, and the order O as arguments. It returns the space for the best solution or nil if no solution exists. Initially, SolS is nil. The procedure maintains the invariant that S can only lead to a solution that is better than SolS. In case that S is failed the so far best solution is returned. In case S is solved, it is returned as a new and better solution (which is guaranteed by the invariant). The central part is shaded gray: if following the first alternative returns a better solution (the invariant ensures that a different space is also a better one), the space for the second alternative is constrained to yield an even better solution than SolS. Note that here the unique identity of spaces is exploited and that nil is different from any space. The latter ensures that Constrain never gets applied to nil. A procedure SearchBest as used in the above example can be obtained easily. Like the search engines presented so far, it creates a space running the procedure to be solved, applies BAB, and possibly returns the best solution.

A different technique for best solution search is restart. After a solution is found, search restarts from the original problem together with the constraint to yield a better

```
fun {BAB S SolS O}
   case {Ask S} of failed then SolS
   [] succeeded then S
   [] alternatives then
      C={Clone S} {Commit S 1} {Commit C 2}
      NewS={BAB S SolS O}
   in
      case NewS==SolS then skip else {Constrain C NewS O} end
      {BAB C NewS O}
   end
end
```

Fig. 4. Branch-and-bound best solution search engine.

solution. Suppose S is a space for the problem to be solved. A best solution can be computed by iterating application of a search engine to a clone of S and application of Constrain until no further solution is found. Then, the last solution found is best. Restart can be beneficial if it is easier to find a first solution rather than exploring large parts of the search tree to proceed from one solution to a better one by branch-and-bound. Any single solution search engine can be used together with the restart technique. For example, limited discrepancy search (see Section 8) together with restart can compute a solution that is an upper bound for a best solution. Then branch-and-bound search can be used to find a solution better than this upper bound.

8 Limited Discrepancy Search

Usually distribution strategies follow a heuristic that has been carefully designed to suggest most often "good" alternatives, where good alternatives are those leading to a solution. This is taken into account by limited discrepancy search (LDS), which has been introduced by Harvey and Ginsberg [6]. LDS has been successfully applied to scheduling problems [3]. Experimental results on frequency assignment problems [15] provide evidence for the potential of LDS in constraint programming.

Central to LDS is to *probe* the search tree with a fixed number of discrepancies. A *discrepancy* is a decision made during exploration of the search tree against the 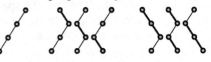 heuristic. In our setting a discrepancy thus amounts to committing to the second alternative of a choice first, rather than to its first alternative. *Probing* means to explore the search tree with a fixed number of discrepancies d. Probing for $d = 0, 1$, and 2 is sketched to the right, where discrepancies are shown as thick vertices (the illustration is adapted from [6]).

Since only little information is available at the root of the search tree, it is more likely for a heuristic to make a wrong suggestion there. Probing takes this into account by making discrepancies at the root of the search tree first. If this does not lead to a solution discrepancies are made further down in the tree (as sketched by the order in the illustration above).

```
fun {Probe S N}
  case {Ask S} of failed then nil
  [] succeeded then [S]
  [] alternatives then
    case N>0 then C={Clone S} in
      {Commit S 2}
      case {Probe S N-1} of nil then {Commit C 1} {Probe C N}
      [] [T] then [T]
      end
    else {Commit S 1} {Probe S 0}
    end
  end
end
```

Fig. 5. Probing for limited discrepancy search.

LDS now iterates probing with 0, 1, 2, ... discrepancies until a solution is found or a given limit for the discrepancies is reached.

Figure 5 shows Probe that implements probing. It takes a space S and the number of discrepancies N as input, and returns either the empty list in case no solution is found or a singleton list containing a solved space. The case where the space is failed or solved is as usual. If S is distributable and N is greater than zero, a discrepancy is made (by {Commit S 2}). If the recursive application of probing with one discrepancy less does not yield a solution, probing continues by making the discrepancy further down in the search tree. Otherwise (that is, N is zero) probing continues without any discrepancy.

It is interesting that the program shown in Figure 5 is close both in length and structure to the pseudo-code for probing in [6]. This demonstrates that spaces provide an adequate level of abstraction for search engines of this kind.

A complete implementation of LDS that takes a procedure P and a maximal limit M for the discrepancies as input can be obtained straightforwardly from Probe. Similar to SearchOne in Section 4 a space S running P is created. Then application of Probe to a clone of S and the number of allowed discrepancies is iterated until either a solution is found or the discrepancy limit M is reached.

9 The Oz Explorer: A Visual Search Engine

The Oz Explorer [11] is a visual search engine that supports the development of constraint programs. It uses the search tree as its central metaphor. The user can interactively explore the search tree which is visualized as it is explored. Visible nodes carry as information the corresponding computation space that can be accessed interactively by predefined or user-defined procedures. The Explorer also supports best solution search.

The Explorer is implemented using first-class computation spaces. Its main data structure is the search tree implemented as a tree of objects. Each node is an object that stores a computation space. The object's class depends on the status of its stored space (that is, whether the space is failed, solved, or distributable) and provides methods for exploration and visual appearance. Invoking an operation at the interface sends a message to the object and triggers execution of the corresponding method.

The Explorer demonstrates nicely that new and interesting search engines can be designed and programmed easily with computation spaces (as is reported in [11]). Interactive exploration presupposes that search is not limited to a depth-first strategy. User access to the computation state of a search tree's node requires that computation spaces are first-class. Hence, the user of the Explorer directly profits from the expressiveness of first-class computation spaces.

10 Recomputation: Trading Space for Time

When solving complex real-world problems, computation spaces might contain a large number of variables and constraints. Since Clone creates a copy of a space to be held in memory, search engines that create many clones might use too much memory. A drastic example is the Explorer: It needs to store all spaces in the already explored part of a search tree to provide user access to them. That leads to space requirements similar to breadth-first search. A solution to this problem is recomputation, where spaces are recomputed on demand rather than being cloned in advance.

```
fun {Recompute S Is}
   case Is of nil then
      {Clone S}
   [] I|Ir then
      C={Recompute S Ir}
   in
      {Commit C I} C
   end
end
```

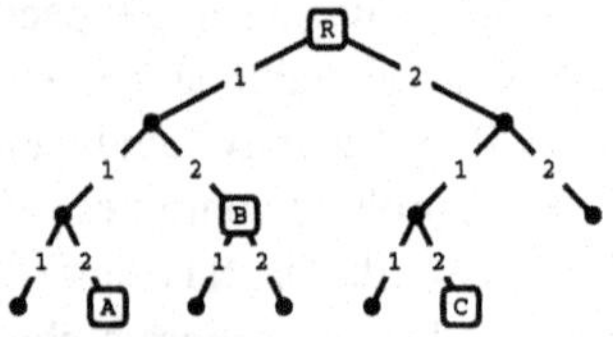

A={Recompute R [2 1 1]}
B={Recompute R [2 1]}
C={Recompute R [2 1 2]}

Fig. 6. Recomputing spaces.

The procedure Recompute (see Figure 6) recomputes a space from a space S higher up in the search tree and a list of integers Is describing the path between the two spaces. The path is represented bottom-up, since it can be constructed easily that way by adding the alternative's number to the path's head during top-down exploration.

The most extreme version of recomputation is to always recompute from the search tree's root space. The procedure DFE as shown in Figure 1 can be extended by two additional arguments: R for the root space and Is for the path of the current space S to the root. Cloning is replaced by recomputation. Recursive applications of DFE additionally maintain the path to the root of the search tree. For example, the part of the search engine that explores the second alternative of a space looks as follows:

··· C={Recompute R Is} **in** {Commit C 2} {DFE C R 2|Is}

A more practical strategy for recomputation is the idea of a maximal recomputation distance n: Clone a space once in a while such that recomputation never must recompute more than n applications of Commit. For example, the Explorer uses this strategy.

11 A Generic Saturation Engine

This section shows how to build a generic saturation (for saturation see Section 2) engine from computation spaces. The engine is generic in the sense that it is not limited to Boolean problems.

An Example. As an example we apply saturation to check whether the Boolean formula $A \wedge (B \vee (A \wedge B))$ is unsatisfiable: Does $A \wedge (B \vee (A \wedge B)) \Leftrightarrow 0$ hold, where $\Leftrightarrow$ reads as equivalence and 0 as false. The first step is a translation into so-called triplets by introducing new Boolean variables C and D: $A \wedge B \Leftrightarrow C$ $\ulcorner \vee C \Leftrightarrow D$, and $A \wedge D \Leftrightarrow 0$. What is called triplets in the saturation literature we implement as Boolean propagators:

```
proc {P Xs} [A B C D]=Xs in
    Xs ::: 0#1
    {FD.conj A B C} {FD.disj B C D} {FD.conj A D 0}
    {SatDist Xs}
end
```

Here Xs:::0#1 constrains the variables A, B, C, and D to take Boolean values and FD.conj (FD.disj) spawns a propagator for equivalence to a conjunction (disjunction). The details of SatDist are explained below. It is important to also take into account variables introduced for subformulas (C and D in our example) [5]. For example, distribution and combination on C can add information on both A and B.

During saturation the following happens. First, constraint propagation takes place but cannot add new constraints. Suppose that SatDist distributes first on A. Constraint propagation in the space for A=0 adds C=0 (by {FD.conj A B C}), in the space for A=1 it first adds D=0 (by {FD.conj A D 0}), and in turn B=0 and C=0 (by {FD.disj B C D}). Combination then adds the common constraint C=0 back to the original space, without triggering further constraint propagation. Distribution on the remaining variables do not exhibit further information. Hence, saturation could neither prove nor disprove the formula unsatisfiable.

Distribution. The distribution strategy SatDist for 1-saturation as used in the above example takes as arguments a list of Boolean variables Xs to be distributed. For a single variable X three alternatives are needed. Two alternatives state that X takes either 0 or 1. The third alternative allows to proceed without assigning a value to X. These three alternatives are programmed from two nested choices as sketched in Figure 7.

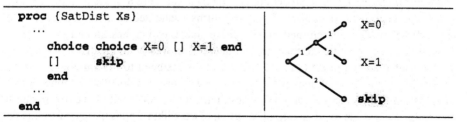

Fig. 7. Distribution for saturation.

To commit to the alternative for X=0 (X=1), first the outer choice must be committed to its first clause, and then the inner choice must be committed to its first (second) clause. To proceed without assigning a value to X, the outer choice must be committed to its second clause. This protocol of committing choices will be implemented by the saturation engine.

Choice creation is iterated for all variables X in Xs not yet assigned a value until a fixed point is reached. The fixed point is reached when the number of variables not yet assigned a value has not changed after an entire iteration over all variables.

Combination. As distribution, combination is specific to the underlying constraint system. To parameterize the saturation engine with respect to combination, the engine takes a procedure for combination as input. The combination procedure for the Boolean case takes three lists X0s, X1s, and Xs of Boolean variables, of which X0s and X1s have been computed by the spaces obtained by distribution. Xs are the variables of the original space. A simple strategy is: If a variable has assigned the same value $n \in \{0, 1\}$ in both X0s and X1s, the variable at that position in Xs is assigned to n.

```
fun {Sat S CB}
   case {Ask S}==alternatives then
      S0={Clone S} {Commit S0 1} {Commit S0 1}
      S1={Clone S} {Commit S1 1} {Commit S1 2}
   in
      case     {Ask S0}==failed then {Sat S1 CB}
      elsecase {Ask S1}==failed then {Sat S0 CB}
      else R0 R1 in
         {Merge S0 R0} {Merge S1 R1}
         {Inject S proc {$ R} {CB R0 R1 R} end}
         {Commit S 2} {Sat S CB}
      end
   else S
   end
end
```

Fig. 8. A generic saturation engine.

The Saturation Engine. The procedure Sat (shown in Figure 8) takes as input a space S and a procedure CB for combination. Sat returns a saturated computation space. If S is not distributable, it is returned. If S is distributable, two clones S0 and S1 of S are created and are committed to their appropriate alternatives (with the distribution strategy presented above, in S0 (S1) the value 0 (1) is assigned to the variable X). If S0 (S1) fails, saturation continues with S1 (S0). Otherwise, combination is done as follows. Merging the spaces S0 and S1 makes their root variables with the corresponding constraints accessible by R0 and R1. Execution of CB within S adds basic constraints on variables accessible from R and might trigger further constraint propagation in S.

532

The saturation engine is parametrized by the problem and how combination is done. Similar to search, the choices created by the distribution strategy comprise the interface between problem and saturation engine. The saturation engine as presented above can also be applied to non Boolean finite domain problems. The distribution strategy can still follow the same structure as presented above. However, it must employ constraints that fit the context of finite domain variables as alternatives. Combination in this context must also be generalized. Combination of the basic constraints $x \in D_0$ and $x \in D_1$ leads to the basic constraint $x \in (D_0 \cup D_1)$.

The engine only supports 1-saturation. To implement n-saturation for $n > 1$, the distribution strategy must be extended to recursively create additional choices. This also requires the saturation engine to handle these additional choices.

Since search engines as well as the saturation engine compute with spaces, it is straightforward to combine them. One possible approach is to first use saturation to infer as many additional basic constraints as possible, and then use search to actually solve the problem. A different approach is to interleave search and saturation.

12 Conclusion

We have presented first-class computation spaces as an abstraction to develop and program constraint inference engines at a high level. Computation spaces have been demonstrated to cover single, all, and best solution search, which are the inference engines found in existing constraint programming systems. Using computation spaces, we have developed inference engines for limited discrepancy search, visual search, and saturation. This has demonstrated that computation spaces can be applied to inference engines that go beyond existing constraint programming systems.

We are confident that computation spaces as high-level abstractions make it possible to adapt (like saturation) and invent (like visual search) further constraint inference methods. We expect that by this, computation spaces can contribute to the power of constraint programming.

Acknowledgements

I am grateful to Martin Henz and Joachim Walser for frequent and fruitful discussions, especially on saturation. Martin Henz had the initial idea to use computation spaces for saturation. The search engine for LDS has been developed together with Joachim Walser. I would like to thank Martin Henz, Tobias Müller, Ralf Treinen, Joachim Walser, Jörg Würtz, and the anonymous referees for providing comments on this paper.

The research reported in this paper has been supported by the Bundesminister für Bildung, Wissenschaft, Forschung und Technologie (FKZ ITW 9601) and the Esprit Working Group CCL-II (EP 22457).

References

1. Abderrahamane Aggoun, David Chan, Pierre Dufresne, Eamon Falvey, Hugh Grant, Alexander Herold, Geoffrey Macartney, Micha Meier, David Miller, Shyam Mudambi, Bruno

533

Perez, Emmanuel Van Rossum, Joachim Schimpf, Periklis Andreas Tsahageas, and Dominique Henry de Villeneuve. ECL^{i}PS^e 3.5. User manual, European Computer Industry Research Centre (ECRC), Munich, Germany, December 1995.

2. Philippe Codognet and Daniel Diaz. Compiling constraints in clp(FD). *The Journal of Logic Programming*, 27(3):185–226, June 1996.

3. James M. Crawford. An approach to resource constrained project scheduling. In George F. Luger, editor, *Proceedings of the 1995 Artificial Intelligence and Manufacturing Research Planning Workshop*, Albuquerque, NM, USA, 1996. The AAAI Press.

4. Mehmet Dincbas, Pascal Van Hentenryck, Helmut Simonis, Abderrahamane Aggoun, Thomas Graf, and F. Berthier. The constraint logic programming language CHIP. In *Proceedings of the International Conference on Fifth Generation Computer Systems FGCS-88*, pages 693–702, Tokyo, Japan, December 1988.

5. John Harrison. Stålmarck's algorithm as a HOL derived rule. In Joakim von Wright, Jim Grundy, and John Harrison, editors, *Theorem Proving in Higher Order Logics: 9th International Conference, TPHOLs'96*, volume 1125 of *Lecture Notes in Computer Science*, pages 221–234, Turku, Finland, August 1996. Springer-Verlag.

6. William D. Harvey and Matthew L. Ginsberg. Limited discrepancy search. In Chris S. Mellish, editor, *Proceedings of the Fourteenth International Joint Conference on Artificial Intelligence*, pages 607–615, Montreal, Canada, August 1995. Morgan Kaufmann Publishers.

7. Martin Henz, Martin Müller, Christian Schulte, and Jörg Würtz. The Oz standard modules. DFKI Oz documentation series, German Research Center for Artificial Intelligence (DFKI), Stuhlsatzenhausweg 3, D-66123 Saarbrücken, Germany, 1997.

8. Martin Henz, Gert Smolka, and Jörg Würtz. Object-oriented concurrent constraint programming in Oz. In Vijay Saraswat and Pascal Van Hentenryck, editors, *Principles and Practice of Constraint Programming*, pages 29–48. The MIT Press, Cambridge, MA, USA, 1995.

9. ILOG. ILOG Solver: User manual, July 1996. Version 3.2.

10. Richard E. Korf. Depth-first iterative deepening: An optimal admissible tree search. *Artificial Intelligence*, 27(1):97–109, 1985.

11. Christian Schulte. Oz Explorer: A visual constraint programming tool. In Lee Naish, editor, *Proceedings of the Fourteenth International Conference on Logic Programming*, pages 286–300, Leuven, Belgium, July 1997. The MIT Press.

12. Christian Schulte and Gert Smolka. Encapsulated search in higher-order concurrent constraint programming. In Maurice Bruynooghe, editor, *Logic Programming: Proceedings of the 1994 International Symposium*, pages 505–520, Ithaca, NY, USA, November 1994. The MIT Press.

13. Gert Smolka. The Oz programming model. In Jan van Leeuwen, editor, *Computer Science Today*, volume 1000 of *Lecture Notes in Computer Science*, pages 324–343. Springer-Verlag, Berlin, 1995.

14. Gunnar Stålmarck. A system for determining propositional logic theorems by applying values and rules to triplets that are generated from a formula. U.S. patent 5 276 897, 1994. Also as Swedish patent 467 076, 1991.

15. Joachim Paul Walser. Feasible cellular frequency assignment using constraint programming abstractions. In *Proceedings of the Workshop on Constraint Programming Applications, in conjunction with the Second International Conference on Principles and Practice of Constraint Programming (CP96)*, Cambridge, MA, USA, August 1996.

16. Jörg Würtz. Oz Scheduler: A workbench for scheduling problems. In *Proceedings of the 8th IEEE International Conference on Tools with Artificial Intelligence*, pages 132–139, Toulouse, France, November 1996. IEEE Computer Society Press.

NeMo+: Object-Oriented Constraint Programming Environment Based on Subdefinite Models

Igor Shvetsov, Vitaly Telerman, Dmitry Ushakov

Institute of Informatics Systems,
Russian Academy of Sciences, Siberian Division &
Russian Research Institute of Artificial Intelligence
email: {shvetsov,telerman,ushakov}@iis.nsk.su

Abstract. In this paper we examine a constraint programming environment *NeMo+*, which embraces a "C++ – based" technique. It includes a high-level object-oriented declarative language for specification of data types and constraints. To solve systems of constraints, *NeMo+* uses the method of so-called subdefinite models, which we briefly review in the first part of the paper. The architecture of *NeMo+* and its main capabilities are presented in the paper.

1 Introduction

Modern constraint programming is based on two groups of techniques which could be called "Prolog-based" and "C++ – based". The techniques in the first, larger group are developed in the context of CLP and are represented, for example, by systems like Prolog III [1], CLP(R) [2], CLP(BNR) [3], CHIP [4], clp(FD) [5], etc. The most remarkable representative of the second group is ILOG [6]. An important advantage of the CLP techniques is a sold theoretical foundation, which enables one to define classes of problems to be solved and to evaluate formally the quality of the resulting solutions. At the same time, constraint technologies embedded in C++ are more flexible, allow one to use the entire power of the object-oriented approach and are often more efficient in the solution of realistic problems.

In this paper we examine a constraint programming environment *NeMo+*, which embraces a "C++ – based" technique. It differs from other techniques in this class in the following properties:

1. An extended set of predefined data types which may have finite as well as infinite domains of values.
2. Availability of high-level facilities for specification of problem-oriented constraints and data types.
3. Use of the method of subdefinite models to satisfy systems of constraints.

The first property means that *NeMo+* includes an extensive library of basic (i.e. implemented in C++) constraints for such data types as set, Boolean, intervals of integer and real numbers, multi-intervals, etc. The user may extend the library by adding new constraints and data types for the subject domain.

NeMo+ is not just a comprehensive and extensive C++ library which supports solution of systems of constraints. It also includes a high-level language for specification of systems of constraints. This language is a purely declarative one and allows one to describe a system of constraints (model of a problem) as a collection of formulas. Object-oriented properties of the *NeMo+* language are used to define the structure of a model and to define problem-oriented data types and constraints from the base ones. In addition, the language includes sophisticated means for controlling the constraint propagation process.

To solve a system of constraints, *NeMo+* uses the method of subdefinite models (or SD-models) based on ideas proposed by A. S. Narin'yani in the early 80s [7,8]. A current description of the method can be found, for example, in [9]. One of the most successful applications based on SD-models is the *UniCalc* interval solver of mathematical problems [10] and the constraint project manager *Time-Ex* [11]. The main feature of the method of SD-models is that it uses a single algorithm of constraint propagation to process data of different types. This allows one to solve mixed of constraints including simultaneously, e.g., set, Boolean, integer and real variables.

The first part of the paper briefly reviews the method of SD-models. The second part describes the architecture of *NeMo+* and the main capabilities of the model specification language. The third part presents some tables illustrating efficiency of *NeMo+* in some benchmarks. In the fourth part we compare *NeMo+* with some related works.

2 Method of subdefinite models

2.1 Subdefinite Extensions of Values

Suppose we have an object v with an associated set X of admissible values, which will be called its *universe*. The elements of X will be denoted by x.

Definition 1. The *subdefinite extension* (SD-extension) $^*X$ of the universe X is any finite set of subsets of X with the following properties:

1. $\emptyset \in {}^*X$;
2. $X \in {}^*X$;
3. $\forall {}^*x, {}^*y \in {}^*X \quad {}^*x \cap {}^*y \in {}^*X$.

The class of all possible SD-extensions of X will be denoted by SD(X). Let X_0 be a finite subset of X.

1) The simplest SD-extension of a universe X is the SD-extension *Single*, which has the following form:

$$X^{Single} = \{\emptyset\} \cup \{X\} \cup \{\{x\} \mid x \in X_0\},$$

It is clear that X^{Single} is obtained by adding to the set X_0 two special elements, UNDEFINE ($\{X\}$) and CONTRADICTION ($\{\emptyset\}$).

2) The maximal SD-extension of X, which we denote by X^{Enum}, is the set of all subsets of X_0 plus X, that is,

$$X^{Enum} = 2^{X_0} \cup \{X\}.$$

In the case when X is a lattice (a set with two associative and commutative operations $\vee$ and $\wedge$ obeying the absorption law and the idempotent law) it is possible to define such types of SD-extensions of X as *intervals* [12, 13] and *multi-intervals* [14]. Let $-\infty$ be the minimal, and $+\infty$ be the maximal element of X (if they do not exists we add them to X with $-\infty \wedge x = -\infty$, $+\infty \vee x = +\infty$ for any $x \in X$). Let now X_0 be a finite sublattice of X which includes $-\infty$ and $+\infty$.

3) SD-extension by intervals

$$X^{Interval} = \{[x^{Lo}, x^{Up}] \mid x^{Lo}, x^{Up} \in X_0\}.$$

Here $[x^{Lo}, x^{Up}] = \{x \in X \mid x^{Lo} \wedge x = x^{Lo}$ and $x \vee x^{Up} = x^{Up}\}$, x^{Lo} is called the lower bound of the interval, and x^{Up} is the upper one. It is obvious that
$$[x^{Lo}, x^{Up}] \cap [y^{Lo}, y^{Up}] = [x^{Lo} \vee y^{Lo}, x^{Up} \wedge y^{Up}].$$
Here the empty set is represented by any interval $[x^{Lo}, x^{Up}]$, where $x^{Lo} \vee x^{Up} \neq x^{Up}$. The entire universe X is represented by the interval $[inf X, sup X]$, and a single element by $\{x\} = [x, x]$.

4) SD-extension by multi-intervals

$$X^{Multiinterval} = \{\alpha \mid \alpha = \cup \alpha_k, \alpha_k \in X^{Interval}, k = 1, 2, \ldots\}.$$

It is obvious that $\emptyset$, X, and $\{x\}$ are represented exactly as in the case of intervals, and $\alpha \cap \beta = \{\alpha_i \cap \beta_i \mid i = 1, 2, \ldots; j = 1, 2, \ldots\}$.

Interval and multi-interval SD-extensions can be applied to continuous universes. For example, the interval extension of the set $\mathbf{R}$ of real numbers may look as follows:

$$\mathbf{R}^{Interval} = \{[x^{Lo}, x^{Up}] \mid x^{Lo}, x^{Up} \in R_0\} \cup$$
$$\cup \{[x^{Lo}, +\infty) \mid x^{Lo} \in R_0\} \cup \{(-\infty, x^{Up}] \mid x^{Up} \in R_0\} \cup \{(-\infty, +\infty)\},$$

where R_0 is a finite subset of $\mathbf{R}$, for example the set of floating-point numbers.

Intervals are of interest not only for lineary ordered universes, like real numbers, but also for such universes as sets. Indeed, let us consider $X = 2^U$ for some set U and two elements $x, y \in X$. Let us define $x \wedge y \equiv x \cap y$, $x \vee y \equiv x \cup y$. (that is, we define the natural order on the sets). What is then the semantics of the interval $[x^{Lo}, x^{Up}]$? Obviously $x^{Lo} \subseteq U$ includes those elements of U about which we have already learned that they belong to the set modeled by the interval. Elements of $x^{Up} \subseteq U$ can potentially belong to the set. If we prove that some element cannot belong, then we must delete it from x^{Up}, that is, decrease the upper boundary of the interval. The cardinality of the set is modeled by the integer interval $[\#x^{Lo}, \#x^{Up}]$. Such sets were first proposed by A.S.Narin'yani in [7].

5) *Structural SD-extension.* Consider now the universe defined as a Cartesian product of sets: $X = X_1 \times \cdots \times X_n$. Just as to any other sets, we can apply to it the SD-extensions X^{Single} and X^{Enum}. Moreover, if each of X_i is a lattice, then X is a lattice also (as a Cartesian product of lattices), and so we can apply to X the SD-extensions $X^{Interval}$ and $X^{Multiinterval}$ as well. However, one more SD-extension of X can be proposed.

Let $^*X_i \in SD(X_i), i = 1, \ldots, n$. Then the system $^*X_1 \times \cdots \times {}^*X_n$ will satisfy the definition 1 too, that is, $^*X_1 \times \cdots \times {}^*X_n \in SD(X_1 \times \cdots \times X_n)$. The following question is of interest: if the form of an SD-extension applicable to X_i as well as to X is fixed, then what will be the relationship between the set systems $^*(X_1 \times \cdots \times X_n)$ and $^*X_1 \times \cdots \times {}^*X_n$? It is easy to show that only for intervals the choice of the SD-extension in the form $^*(X_1 \times \cdots \times X_n)$ or $^*X_1 \times \cdots \times {}^*X_n$ is unimportant. In other case, this choice is essential.

Definition 2. The *subdefinite representation* $^*[\xi]$ of any set $\xi \subseteq X$ in the SD-extension $^*X$ is the minimal subset from $^*X$ which contains ξ, namely,

$$^*[\xi] = \bigcap_{\xi \subseteq {}^*\psi \in {}^*X} {}^*\psi.$$

Property 3 from the definition of an SD-extension guarantees that for any set $\xi \subseteq X$ its SD-representation is *unique*.

For instance, an integer SD-object I with the universe $\{1, 2, 7, 3\}$, can be associated with one of the following representations:

$$I^{Single} = \mathbf{Z} \text{ (fully indefinite);} \quad I^{Interval} = [1, 7];$$
$$I^{Enum} = \{1, 2, 7, 3\}; \quad I^{Multiinterval} = \{[1, 3], [7, 7]\}.$$

2.2 Subdefinite Extensions of Constraints

To define dependences between objects in SD-models, we construct SD-extensions of functions over them. Suppose we have a function

$$f : X_1 \times \cdots \times X_m \to X_{m+1},$$

and some SD-extensions $^*X_i \in SD(X_i), (i = 1, \ldots, m + 1)$.

Definition 3. The SD-extension of f is a function

$$^*f : {}^*X_1 \times \cdots \times {}^*X_m \to {}^*X_{m+1},$$

such that

$$^*f(^*x_1, {}^*x_2, \ldots, {}^*x_m) = {}^*[f(^*x_1, {}^*x_2, \ldots, {}^*x_m)].$$

Here $f(^*x_1, {}^*x_2, \ldots, {}^*x_m)$ is the image of the function f on the set $^*x_1 \times \ldots \times {}^*x_m$.

For instance, in the case of enumerations (Enum) the computation of an SD-extended operation may amount to examining possible values of its arguments; for intervals and multi-intervals one can use the well-known rules of interval arithmetic [12].

This definition implies that $^*f$ is a total simple function even if f did not have these properties.

Suppose that there is a relation $r(x_1, \ldots, x_n)$ defined in the subject domain, which determines a subset of values in the Cartesian product $X_1 \times \cdots \times X_n$.

Definition 4. The function f_i $(i = 1, \ldots, n)$ is called the interpretation function for the relation r if $x_i = f_i(x_1, \ldots, x_{i-1}, x_{i+1}, \ldots, x_n)$, on the set $r(x_1, \ldots, x_n)$.

For example, the equation $x + y = z$; may be interpreted by the following three functions: $z := x + y$; $x := z - y$; $y := z - x$;

In what follows, such functionally interpretable relations will be called constraints.

The problem of constraint satisfaction in SD-models is described as a set of objects in the subject domain and a set of constraints on these objects. To each object we assign a universe and a kind of an SD-extension.

All functions of constraint interpretation, if we regard them as operators on the set of SD-values of the objects of the model, are monotone with respect to inclusion and nonexpanding. These two properties and the finiteness of the set of all SD-values imply that there exists the largest (with respect to inclusion) fixed point for an arbitrary system of such operators, and the point may be reached in finitely many steps via the method of successive approximations. A version of this method is the data-driven computation algorithm used in SD-models, to be treated below.

2.3 Subdefinite Models

A *subdefinite model* M consists of the four sets $(V, C, W, CORR)$, where

- V is the set of SD-objects from a given subject domain,
- C is the set of constraints defined on SD-objects from V,
- W is the set of assignment functions, and
- $CORR$ is the set of correctness check functions.

With each SD-object $v \in V$ we associate a subdefinite type T_v, thus defining its set of admissible values and its set of operations, the initial value $*a_v$, the assignment function $w_v \in W$, and the correctness check function $Corr_v \in CORR$.

The *assignment function* is a function of two arguments which is computed for each attempt of assignment of a new value to the SD-object and determines its new value depending on the current and the assigned values. For example, suppose that the current value of a numerical SD-object v is the set $\{1, 3, 6, 9\}$, and we assign to it a new value $\{1, 2, 3, 4, 5\}$. Suppose that the assignment function operates by intersecting the two sets. In this case, the new current value of the SD-object v will be the set $\{1, 3\}$.

The *correctness check function* is a unary predicate which verifies that the value of an SD-object v is admissible. In the preceding example, the correctness check function must verify that the current value of the SD-object v does not become empty.

The algorithm of computations implemented in SD-models is a highly parallel data-driven process. Modification of the values of some variables in the common memory automatically results in calling and executing those constraints for which these variables are arguments. The process halts when the network stabilizes, i.e., execution of constraints does not change the objects of the model.

A constraint satisfaction algorithm in a SD-model M is defined as follows ('$\leftarrow$' is the assignment operation):

algorithm $SD\_CONSTRAINT\_SATISFACTION$

var $u_i \in V_s,, i = 1, \ldots, k$ are auxiliary variables,

   Q is the set of active constraints.

begin $\forall v_i \in X : \quad v_i \leftarrow \alpha_i$

     $Q \leftarrow R$

     while $Q \neq \emptyset$

        Choose $c \in Q$

        $Q \leftarrow Q \setminus \{c\}$

     (* Let $c = <f, In = \{v_1, \ldots, v_m\}, Out = \{v_{m+1}, \ldots, v_{m+n}\} >$ *)

        $\forall v_{m+i} \in Out$

        $u_{m+i} \leftarrow v_{m+i}$ (* save the old value *)

        $v_{m+i} \leftarrow w_{v_{m+i}}(v_{m+i}, f^i(v_1, \ldots, v_m))$

        if $u_{m+i} \neq v_{m+i}$ **then**

        begin

           if $Corr_{v_{m+i}}(v_{m+i})$ **then** $\quad Q \leftarrow Q \cup \{c' | v_{m+i} \in In_{c'}\}$

           else return $FAILURE$

        end

     end while

     return $SUCCESS$

end algorithm.

The result of the algorithm is either SUCCESS, in which case the current values of the variables will point to possible values of objects of the model, or FAILURE, which signals that during the execution of the algorithm the value of one of the variables became invalid. The operator $Choose$ assumes a certain strategy of choosing the next constraint from the set Q of active constraints.

Suppose that the assignment functions and the correctness check functions satisfy the following requirements:

$$w(^{\bullet}x, ^{\bullet}y) = {}^{\bullet}x \cap {}^{\bullet}y; \quad Corr(^{\bullet}x) = \text{ if } {}^{\bullet}x \neq \emptyset \text{ then } true \text{ else } false \text{ fi.}$$

In this case, the following assertions are valid [9]:

- The algorithm of constraint satisfaction in SD-models converges.
- Establishing inconsistency of an SD-model is independent of the strategy of choosing the next constraint for interpretation.
- In a consistent SD-model, the output values of SD-objects for the same input values do not depend on the strategy.
- Every solution of the constraint satisfaction problem (if there exists) lies in the domain of output values of the corresponding objects of the SD-model.

Independently of our approach the similar results in the case of the interval representation of real, integer and boolean variables have been proved in [15].

3 Constraint Programming Environment NeMo+

3.1 Architecture of NeMo+

SD-models in fact determine a certain common technique for representation and solution of constraint satisfaction problems in any subject domains and in any classes of problems. In the most advance manner this technique was implemented in the constraint programming environment *NeMo+*.

The principal feature of *NeMo+* is its two-level architecture. The first (basic) level consists of a C++ library which has a rich set of predefined data types and constraints, as well as a universal (i.e. applicable to any data types) constraint propagation algorithm. The second level contains the language for specification of CSPs, which makes it possible to give high-level descriptions of user problems in terms of the subject domain.

In the most general form the architecture of *NeMo+* is shown in Fig. 1.

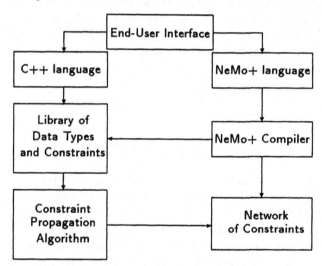

Fig. 1. The architecture of NeMo+.

The object-oriented approach was used in the implementation of all components of *NeMo+*. The *NeMo+* language is used to structure the statement of the problem and to define problem-oriented data types and constraints. A new data type is described as a class of objects whose slots are linked by a certain set of constraints. The user may define his own constraints over these; these new constraints are in fact parameterized sets of simpler, and eventually of basic constraints.

The compiler transforms the high-level specification of the problem into a network containing just the basic data types and constraints. This network preserves the structure of the original object-oriented description of the problem. This makes it possible to control the constraint propagation process more flexibly and efficiently. For instance, one can simultaneously activate or block groups of semantically related (referring to one object) constraints.

The library of basic data types and constraints is implemented as a system of C++ classes. This library can be extended in two ways. Firstly, the user can define a new notion described in the *NeMo+* language which is then compiled and placed in the library. If the means provided by the language are insufficient, or if the user wants to implement a problem-oriented constraint more efficiently, C++ entry points may be used.

At present *NeMo+* uses one algorithm of constraint propagation which has two peculiarities. Firstly, it is applied to an object-structured network of constraints. Secondly, this network may contain variables of different types.

The ability to specify problems in terms of their subject domains increases significantly efficiency of application of any software technology. In the *NeMo+* environment this ability is provided within the language of specification of SD-models. The knowledge representation language of *NeMo+* represents a combination of the object-oriented approach and the paradigm of constraint programming. In the *NeMo+* language both internal semantics of the objects and all aspects of interaction between them are described by relations and constraints. Only those properties of the object-oriented approach are used which support knowledge structuring, including construction of an hierarchy of notions, inheritance and incapsulation.

3.2 NeMo+ language

The main features of the *NeMo+* language are the following:

1. The language has a rather broad set of built-in basic types: integer, real, character, boolean, string, and their subdefinite extensions (Single, Enum, Interval, Multiinterval).

2. Abstract data types are supported (for example, *number* is integer or real). An abstract data type is refined when the computational network is generated (*number* is transformed into integer or real depending on the environment of the variable of this type).

3. There are two kind of generic data types in the language: *set*, and *array*.

4. It allows the user to define new data types, functions, and constraints.

5. The language allows one to specify extensional constraints as a tabular relation.

6. The language is object-oriented, i.e., it is possible to describe for each data type its own constraints (its own submodel), or to describe a submodel for each variable; there is also a mechanism of inheritance for constraints and the structure of data types (classes).

7. The language provides the means for controlling the process of computations, such as **if** and **alternate**. Both are not operators, but rather special constructions allowing one to change the network during computations.

8. The language supports modular program development (creation and use of libraries).

The data types in the *NeMo+* language. Due to object-oriented nature of the knowledge representation language of *NeMo+*, we can define new data types (classes) from existing ones, with possible inheritance of properties. Each data type has a certain structure (a set of slots) and a so-called "active part." The active part of a type is some submodel reflecting interdependencies between the slots of this type. For instance, in the data type *Triangle* the active part of the type may contain constraints reflecting the sine theorem, the cosine theorem, and various formulas computing area, perimeter of a triangle, etc. Thus, the main functional semantics of the type is described via constraints linking its slots rather than by means of methods.

There are two important facilities which significantly enhance the type construction system: abstraction-concretisation and inheritance. Abstraction means that when we define a type we can omit a specific kind of subdefiniteness for objects of this type. Such an abstract type may be concretised when it is used, by defining one of the SD-extensions defined in Section 1.

Fig. 2 presents the inheritance lattice for abstract data types of the *NeMo+* language. Abstract types define their interface as operations applicable to some abstract entity (for instance, = and ! = for *any*, *min* and *max* for *scalar*, +, −, * and / for *number*, *mod* and *f act* for *int*, etc.).

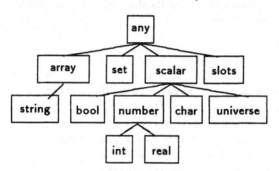

Fig. 2. Inheritance lattice for abstract classes

Thus, the types *int*, *real*, *bool* and others in the *NeMo+* language are abstract data types as well as *any*, or *numbers*. Each of these types has several possible SD-extensions: Single and Interval (for all types), Enum (only for discrete types) and Multiinterval (only for numerical types). Examples of such types are *Interval int*, *Multiinterval real*, *set of Enum int*. Abstract types enable us to have, for example, just one addition constraint instead of manipulating a large set of such constraints, in which we consider various combinations of reals and integers.

An *universe* is an abstract type defined by enumeration of possible values. For instance, the universe *fruits* may be given in the following form:

```
class fruits = universe {apple, orange, lemon, ...}.
```

The *NeMo+* language allows us to have data aggregates. To this end, the language has two built-in generic types: *set* and *array*.

All of *NeMo+* arrays are one-dimensional. A two-dimensional array may be represented as a one-dimensional array in which each element is a one-dimensional array as well.

There is a binary relation for arrays: "take element." Like any other binary relation, it is interpreted in three directions: to the array, to the index and to the result.

Suppose, for example, that an SD-model has a constraint $x = m[i]$, where x is a real interval equal to $[-2.5, 5.5]$, m has the type *array* [5] *of interval int*, and the index i is declared as an integer interval equal to $[2, 5]$. If the elements of the array m have the values

$$m[1] = [-10, 10], m[2] = [15, 20], m[3] = [-5, 5], m[4] = [7, 8], m[5] = [-3, 10],$$

then after interpretation of this constraint the index i will equal the interval $[3, 5]$. This happens because the variable x cannot be equal to the element $m[2]$. An even stronger refinement of i occurs if it is represented by an enumeration rather than an interval. In this case the new value will be the set $\{3, 5\}$.

In the description of a new user-defined type we can define its ancestors, slots and the active part as an internal model. The derived type inherits all the properties of its ancestors (slots and active part) and the set of operations defined over them, but redefinition of the inherited information is not allowed.

For instance, a triangle defined by its sides (a, b, c) and angles $(alpha, beta, gamma)$ is declared as follows:

```
class Triangle;
    slots (a, b, c, alpha, beta, gamma : real);
    a > 0; b > 0; c > 0; a < b + c; b < c + a; c < a + b;
    alpha = [0.0, Pi]; beta = [0.0, Pi]; gamma = [0.0, Pi];
    alpha + beta + gamma = PI;
    a^2 = b^2 + c^2 - 2 * b * c * cos( alpha );
    b^2 = c^2 + a^2 - 2 * b * c * cos( beta );
    c^2 = a^2 + b^2 - 2 * b * c * cos( gamma );
    a * sin( beta )  = b * sin( alpha );
    b * sin( gamma ) = c * sin( beta );
    c * sin( alpha ) = a * sin( gamma );
end;
```

Suppose now that we have a data type *Point*:

```
class Point; slots (X, Y : real ); end;
```

In this case the triangle type in Cartesian coordinates may be declared as a successor of the type *Triangle* with three new slots (planar coordinates of the vertices):

```
class DecartTriangle : Triangle;
    slots (A, B, C: Point);
    Distance(A,B) = c; Distance(B,C) = a; Distance(C,A) = b;
end;
```

It is assumed here that *Distance* is a real function defined earlier which calculates the distance between two points.

Constraints in the NeMo+ language. The *NeMo+* language makes it possible to raise the level of problem specification via introducing problem-oriented dependencies between objects. These dependencies are given as constraints.

Constraints in *NeMo+* constitute an hierarchical system whose lowest level consists of basic constraints, i.e. constraints written in C++.

NeMo+ constraints are subdivided into three syntactic groups: functions, infix and prefix constraints.

Functions are parameterized sets of constraints with a distinguished result. For instance, a function computing the distance between two points can be declared as follows:

```
function Distance (a, b : Point) : real;
    (a.x - b.x)^2 + (a.y - b.y)^2 = Result^2;
end;
```

Here *Result* is a distinguished name denoting a real variable in which the result returned by the function is stored.

Infix constraints can be either binary or n-ary. The use of n-ary infix relations makes it possible to reduce significantly the size of internal representation of the model in the form of a network of constraints.

Let us consider, for example, the equation $y = x1 + x2 + x3 + x4$. Using the n-ary operator "+", we obtain: "+"(y,x1,x2,x3,x4), but in the case of the infix "+" the result is the following

```
"+"(Tmp1, x1, x2); "+"(Tmp2, Tmp1,x3); "+"(Tmp3, Tmp2, x4);
```

Each infix constraint has a priority in accordance with which the corresponding expressions are parsed.

Here is an example of an infix constraint defining the relation of similarity of two objects of type *Triangle*:

```
inf priority = 10 "~" (t1, t2 : Triangle) : bool;
    coef : real with This > 0.0; end;
    t1.a = t2.a * coef;  t1.b = t2.b * coef;  t1.c = t2.c * coef;
    t1.alpha = t2.alpha;  t1.beta = t2.beta;  t1.gamma = t2.gamma;
end;
```

Here *coef* is a local variable which takes positive values and is the coefficient of similarity of the sides of the triangles.

In real problems we often have to deal with constraints defined extensionally (by enumerating all tuples, or the sets of values satisfying this constraint). Each extensional constraint is most conveniently represented by a table in which the number of columns coincides with the number of arguments of the constraint, and each row has one possible set of the values of its arguments. There are many examples of such constraints: timetables (transport or classes), technical tables, interest rates, etc.

The specification of a tabular constraint in the *NeMo+* language looks as follows:

```
table Name (arg1:type1, arg2:type2, ...) from File; end;
```

Here *File* defines the name of the file describing the table. The description of the table has a natural form: in which row we enumerate the values whose types correspond to the types of arguments of the constraint *Name*. The number of values in each row of the file (the number of columns) corresponds to the number of arguments of the tabular constraint. The number of rows of the table is not limited. Declarative semantics of a tabular constraint is as follows. Each table defines a relation on the Cartesian product of the universes of its arguments. Each relation is defined by an explicit enumeration of all tuples of values which satisfy it. The operational semantics of satisfying the tabular constraint is defined as the intersection of the Cartesian product of subdefinite values of the arguments with this relation.

The language provides special constructions allowing run-time modification of the network of constraints: **if**, and **alternate**.

A conditional constraint is different from the traditional conditional operators of conventional programming languages. Since the tested condition may have three values (*true, false,* and *undefined*), a conditional constraint may contain three parts: **then**, **else**, and **undef**. Initially the computational network will contain the condition and the **undef**-part (if it is not omitted). If the condition becomes *true* during interpretation of the network, the **then**-part is added to the network, and if the condition becomes *false*, the **else**-part is added. In both cases, the **undef**-part is deleted.

The specifier of alternatives makes it possible to organize an automated case analysis during the interpretation of a computational network. Each case is a subset of constraints defined over the objects of the SD-model. The specifier offers the interpreter to test all the alternatives in turn, one by one. The specifier of alternatives has the lowest priority among all constraints of the SD-model.

4 Benchmarks

In this section we discuss how some benchmarks are solved with the *NeMo+* environment.

Integer Benchmarks. Let us consider the following well known problems.

Zebra. The problem, proposed by Lewis Carroll.

Cryptarithmetic puzzles. We consider two problems: $SEND + MORE = MONEY$ (Send) and $DONALD + GERALD = ROBERT$ (Donald).

Queens. Place N queens on a $N \times N$ chessboard so that there is no pair of queens threatening each other.

Square. Place the numbers $\{1, 2, \ldots, n^2\}$ into the $n \times n$ board so that the sums of numbers in each row, column and main diagonal are equal. To exclude symmetrical solutions we assume that $M(1,1) < M(1,n) < M(n,1), M(1,1) < M(n,n)$, where M is a mapping from $\{1, \ldots, n^2\}$ to $\{1, \ldots, n\} \times \{1, \ldots, n\}$.

The following three problems are taken from [15].

$\sum \prod$. Find integer $x_1, x_2, \ldots, x_N$ such that $\sum_{i=1}^{N} x_i = \sum_{i=1}^{N} i$, and $\prod_{i=1}^{N} x_i = \prod_{i=1}^{N} i$. To exclude symmetrical solutions we assume that $x_1 \le x_2 \le \cdots \le x_N$.

Equations. Find integer values from $\{1, 2, \ldots, 100\}$ such that the corresponding equation is true. To exclude symmetrical solutions we assume that $x \leq y$ in the first case, and $x \leq y \leq w$ in the second.

The table below summarizes the results. The first column gives the problem name and its size if needed. The ff word indicates the use of the first fail principle heuristic. The last column gives the running time for *NeMo+*. These time were measured on a PC Pentium 133 MHz with 16 MB of RAM.

Problem	Variables	Constraints	Solutions	Fails	Time (sec.)
Zebra ff	28	22	1	5	0.01
Send ff	20	18	1	1	less than 0.01
Donald ff	29	19	1	6	0.03
Queens 8 ff	22	33	92	375	1.53
Queens 10 ff	28	64	724	5285	29.48
Queens 12 ff	34	89	first sol.	1	0.06
Queens 16 ff	46	151	first sol.	14	0.28
Square 3 ff	9	9	1	6	0.01
Square 4 ff	16	11	880	21871	127.75
$\Sigma \Pi$ 9	9	11	2	445	0.75
$\Sigma \Pi$ 12	12	14	22	7355	17.71
$x^2 + y^2 = z^2$	6	6	52	86	0.83
$x^2 + y^2 + w^2 = z^2$	8	8	573	2331	18.58

Boolean Benchmarks. Now we consider a set of traditional Boolean benchmarks [5]. Instead of Boolean variables we use integer ones with domain $[0, 1]$.

Schur: Put the integers $\{1, 2, \ldots, N\}$ in three boxes so that for any $x, y \in \{1, 2, \ldots, N\}$ x and $2x$ are placed in different boxes and if x and y are placed in the same box than $x + y$ is placed in a different box.

Pigeon: Put N pigeons in M holes with at most 1 pigeon per hole.

Queens: Boolean version of the $N-$Queens problem described above.

All results are summarized in the following table.

Problem	Variables	Constraints	Solutions	Fails	Time (sec.)
Schur 13	39	135	18	179	0.44
Schur 14	42	156	0	179	0.49
Pigeon 6/6	36	13	720	719	0.74
Pigeon 8/7	56	16	0	5039	5.41
Queens 8	64	43	92	391	0.81
Queens 10	100	55	724	5904	15.90
Queens 12	144	67	first sol.	37	0.17
Queens 16	256	91	first sol.	1208	6.54

5 Related works

Among the CP methods the authors are aware of, the *tolerance propagation (TP)* proposed by E.Hyvonen [13], the approaches proposed in *CLP(BNR)* [15], and the *Newton* system [3]. Very similar theoretical frameworks had been introduced in [16] and in [17]. All these approaches use the similar constraint satisfaction algorithms. Nevertheless, differences between them exist.

The key idea behind subdefiniteness is that SD-models approach is open for new SD-extensions and constraints over them. In the SD-models with each traditional class of objects we can associate several SD-extensions, which differ in their expressive power. Some of them were considered in section 1. The mechanism of SD-models has served as a base for high-technology software products capable of a relatively simple tuning to diverse subject domains.

Like constraints from SD-models each constraint from the *TP* is considered as a special case of the interaction of a group of interpretation functions, that implement the recalculation of its parameters. But the *TP* works only with the interval and, recently, multi-interval representations of real variables. The *Newton* system works with the interval representation of real variables too. In both *TP* and *Newton* several interval methods have been implemented for improving the accuracy of the results. In the *NeMo+* system methods like these are lacking at that time, but this environment allows one to put in them.

The approach proposed in *CLP(BNR)* works with the intervals representation of real, integer and boolean variables. It seems van Emden's *VC* approach to be the closest to SD-models because it works with variables of arbitrary types, which are associated sets of admissible values.

The main difference between SD-models and the other approaches is that SD-models are not implemented into Logic Programming paradigm. Hence, the resolution method or terms unification are lacking in the *NeMo+* environment. One can consider the SD-models apparatus as a purely constraint satisfaction technique that can be used for solving a wide class of problems.

6 Conclusion

The paper examines an object-oriented constraint programming environment *NeMo+*. This system allows one to describe at a high level and to solve CSPs which may include at the same time different data types related to finite and continuous domains. In addition, it provides well-developed means for definition of problem-oriented data types and constraints, as well as for structuring the description of the problem.

The *NeMo+* environment is intended, first of all, to solve problems described by large and heterogeneous systems of constraints. These problems arise, for instance, in the area of CAD/CAM applications. *NeMo+* makes it possible to design complex technical devices by representing them in the form of an hierarchy of objects (in the sense of the relationship "part-whole") with semantics expressed by systems of constraints. In this class of applications constraints are often defined by tables of values. *NeMo+* provides advanced means to define tabular constraints which are the most natural way of linking parameters of different types. At present we are working (jointly with DASSAULT) on applying *NeMo+* technology to solve a number of applied problems in the design of automobiles and airplanes.

548

The current implementation of *NeMo+* uses one common algorithm of constraint satisfaction for heterogeneous systems. In the future we plan to incorporate in the system a number of specialized techniques which can be used to solve efficiently some particular kinds of CSP. For example, the interval constraint solver *Unicalc*, which is intended to solve purely numerical problems, contains a number of algorithms which combine methods of classical and interval mathematics, as well as the methods of computer algebra with constraint propagation. We plan to integrate some of these algorithms in the *NeMo+* technology.

One more direction of development of *NeMo+* is concerned with a transition from the constraint satisfaction paradigm to concurrent constraint programming.

References

[1] Colmerauer A. *An introduction to Prolog III*, Comm.ACM, 33(7),(1990), 69-90.
[2] Jaffar J., et al. *The CLP(R) language and system*, ACM Transactions on Programming Languages and Systems, 14(3), (1992), 339 – 395.
[3] Benhamou F., McAllester D., Van Hentenryck P. *CLP(Intervals) Revisited*, Proceedings of ILPS–94, Ithaca, NY, (1994), (124 – 138).
[4] Van Hentenryck P. *Constraint Satisfaction in Logic Programming*, Logic Programming Series, The MIT Press, Cambridge, MA, 1989.
[5] Codognet P., Diaz D. Boolean Constraint Solving Using clp(FD). Proc. of the International Logic Programming Symposium, (1993), 525 – 539.
[6] Puget J.-F. *A C++ Implementation of CLP*, Tech. Report, Ilog, January 1994.
[7] Narin'yani A.S. *Subdefinite Set – a Formal Model of Uncompletely Specified Aggregate*, Proc. of the Symp. on Fuzzy Sets and Possibility Theory, Acapulco, (1980).
[8] Narin'yani A.S. *Subdefiniteness and Basic Means of Knowledge Representation*, Computers and Artificial Intelligence, Bratislawa, 2, No.5, (1983), 443 – 452.
[9] Telerman V., Ushakov D. *Subdefinite Models as a Variety of Constraint Programming*, Proc. of the Intern. Conf. Tools of Artificial Intelligence, Toulouse, 1996.
[10] Shvetsov I., Semenov A., Telerman V. *Application of Subdefinite Models in Engineering*, Artificial Intelligence in Engineenring 11 (1997), 15 – 24.
[11] Narin'yani A.S., Borde S.B., Ivanov D.A. *Subdefinite Mathematics and Novel Scheduling Technology*, Artificial Intelligence in Engineenring 11 (1997).
[12] Alefeld G., Herzberger Ju.: *Introduction in Interval Computations*, Academic Press, New York, 1983.
[13] Hyvonen E. *Constraint Reasoning Based on interval Arithmetic: the tolerance propagation approach*, Artificial Intelligence, V.58, (1992), 71 – 112.
[14] Telerman V., et al. *Interval and Multiinterval Extensions in Subdefinite Models*, International Conf. on Interval Methods and Computer Aided Proofs in Science and Engineering (INTERVAL'96), Wurzburg, (1996), 131 – 132.
[15] Benhamou F., Older W.J. *Applying Interval Arithmetic to Real, Integer and Boolean Constraints*, Journal of Logic Programming, 1996.
[16] van Emden M.H. *Value constraints in the CLP scheme*, Proc. of the ILPS-95, Workshop on Interval Constraints, Portland, Oregon, 1995.
[17] Benhamou F. *Heterogeneous Constraint Solving*, Proc. of the 5th Intern. Conf. on Algebraic and Logic Programming, LNCS 1139, Springer, (1996), 62 – 76.

Set Constraints: A Pearl in Research on Constraints

Leszek Pacholski[1] and Andreas Podelski[2]

[1] Institute of Computer Science, University of Wrocław
Przesmyckiego 20, PL-51-151 Wrocław, Poland
www.tcs.uni.wroc.pl/~pacholsk
pacholsk@tcs.uni.wroc.pl
[2] Max-Planck-Institut für Informatik
Im Stadtwald, D-66123 Saarbrücken, Germany
www.mpi-sb.mpg.de/~podelski
podelski@mpi-sb.mpg.de

Abstract. The topic of set constraints is a pearl among the research topics on constraints. It combines theoretical investigations (ranging from logical expressiveness, decidability, algorithms and complexity analysis to program semantics and domain theory) with practical experiments in building systems for program analysis, addressing questions like implementation issues and scalability. The research has its direct applications in type inference, optimization and verification of imperative, functional, logic and reactive programs.

1 Introduction

Set constraints are first-order logic formulas interpreted over the domain of sets of trees. These sets of trees are possibly recursively defined. The first-order theory that they form is interesting on its own right. Essentially, we study it because the problem of computationally reasoning about sets (of trees) is fundamentally important. Thus, research on set constraints can be fundamental research.

Research on set constraints can also be applied research. This is because set constraints form the algorithmic basis for a certain kind of program analysis that is called set-based. Here, the problem of reasoning about runtime properties of a programs is transferred to the problem of solving set constraints. Several systems have been built, each addressing a particular program analysis problem (obtained, for example, by the restriction to a particular class of programs). The latter means to single out a subclass of set constraints that fits with the analysis problem and to build a system solving set constraints in this subclass (efficiently).

In the next two sections, we will survey results that cover both these aspects of resesearch on set constraints.

2 Constraint solving

The history of set constraints and set-based program analysis goes back to Reynolds [82] in 1969. He was the first to derive recursively defined sets as approximations of runtime values from programs, here first-order functional programs. Jones and Muchnick [60] had a similar idea in 1979 and applied it to imperative programs with data constructors like cons and nil (and data destructors like car and cdr). The set constraints used in these approaches were rather inexpressive. It was only in the nineties when people crystallized the problem of solving set constraints and studied it systematically.

Heintze and Jaffar [52] coined the term of set constraints in 1990 and formulated the general problem (schema) which has occupied a number of people since then: is the satisfiability of inclusions between set expressions decidable, when these set expressions are built up by

- variables (interpreted over sets of trees),
- tree constructors (interpreted as functions over sets of trees),
- a specific choice of set operators, Boolean and possibly others.

Assume given a signature Σ fixing the arity of the function symbols f, g, a, b ... and defining the set T_Σ of trees. The symbol f denotes a function over trees, $f : (T_\Sigma)^n \to T_\Sigma$, $\bar{t} \mapsto f(\bar{t})$ (where $\bar{t} = (t_1, \ldots, t_n)$ is a tuple of length $n \geq 0$ according to the arity of f). By the canonical extension of this function to sets $M_1, \ldots, M_n \in 2^{T_\Sigma}$,

$$f(M_1, \ldots, M_n) = \{f(t_1, \ldots, t_n) \in T_\Sigma \mid t_1 \in M_1, \ldots, t_n \in M_n\},$$

the symbol f denotes also an operator over *sets* of trees, $f : (2^{T_\Sigma})^n \to 2^{T_\Sigma}$, $\bar{M} \mapsto f(\bar{M})$. The "inverse" of this operator is the *projection* of f to the k-th argument,

$$f_{(k)}^{-1}(M) = \{t \in T_\Sigma \mid \exists t_1, \ldots, t_n \ t_k = t, \ f(t_1, \ldots, t_n) \in M\}.$$

A *general* set expression e is built up by: variables (that range over 2^{T_Σ}), function symbols, the Boolean set operators and the projection operator [52]. If e does not contain the complement operator, then e is called a *positive* set expression. A *general* set constraint φ is a conjunction of inclusions of the form $e \subseteq e'$. The full class of general set constraints is not motivated by a program analysis problem. Note that, generally, φ does not have a least or greatest solution.

Heintze and Jaffar [52] also gave the first decidability result for a class of set constraints that they called *definite*, for the reason that all satisfiable constraints in the class have a least solution (the class seems to be the largest one having this property). A definite set constraint is a conjunction of inclusions $e_l \subseteq e_r$ between positive set expressions, where the set expressions e_r on the right-hand side of $\subseteq$ are furthermore restricted to contain only variables, constants and function symbols and the intersection operator (that is, no projection or union). This class is used for the set-based analysis of logic programs [53].

Two years later, in 1992, Aiken and Wimmers [8] proved the decidability for the class of *positive* set constraints (in NEXPTIME). Their definition is so natural (the choice of set operators are exactly the Boolean ones) that the term set constraints is often used to refer to this class. Ganzinger assisted Aiken's presentation at LICS'92 and, during the talk, he recognized that this class is equivalent to a certain first-order theory called the *monadic class*. One can test the satisfiability of a set constraint φ by transforming φ into a so-called flat clause, which is a skolemized form of a formula of the monadic class and for which a decision procedure based on *ordered resolution* exists [61]. Thus, the history of set constraints goes in fact back to 1915 when Löwenheim [68] gave the first decision procedure for the monadic class. The proof by Ackermann [1] of the same result gives an algorithm that appears to be usable in practice. The equivalence between set constraints and the monadic class lead Bachmair, Ganzinger and Waldmann [11] to give a lower bound and thus characterize the complexity of the satisfiability problem, namely by NEXPTIME. Aiken, Kozen, Vardi and Wimmers [3] gave the detailed analysis of the complexity of the set-constraint solving problem depending on the given signature of function symbols. Later, the decidability, and with it that same complexity result, was extended to richer classes of set constraints with negation [44,4,87,19] and then with projection by Charatonik and Pacholski [20] (which settled the open problem for the general class formulated by Heintze and Jaffar [52]). Set constraints were also studied from the logical and topological point of view [62,25,64,22] and also in domains different from the Herbrand universe [49,17,70]. Kozen [63] explores the use of set constraints in constraint logic programming. Uribe [91] uses set constraints in order-sorted languages. Seynhave, Tommasi and Treinen [84] showed that the $\exists^*\forall^*$-fragment of the theory of set constraints is undecidable.

Charatonik [17,18] studied set constraints in the presence of additional equational axioms like associativity or commutativity. It turns out that in the most interesting cases (associativity, associativity together with commutativity) the satisfiability problem becomes undecidable. McAllester, Givan, Witty and Kozen [70] liberalized the notions of set constraints to so-called Tarskian set constraints over arbitrary first-order domain, with a link to modal-logics. Recently, Charatonik and Podelski [24] singled out *set constraints with intersection* (the choice of set operators includes only the intersection), shown that they are equivalent to definite set constraints, and gave the first DEXPTIME characterization for set constraints. They have also defined *co-definite* set constraints (which have a greatest solution, if satisfiable) and shown the same complexity for this class [23,80]. A co-definite set constraint is a conjunction of inclusions $e_l \subseteq e_r$ between positive set expressions, where the set expressions e_l on the left-hand side of $\subseteq$ are furthermore restricted to contain only variables, constants, unary function symbols and the union operator (that is, no projection, intersection or function symbol of arity greater than one). Recently, Devienne, Talbot and Tison [29] have improved the algorithms for the two classes of definite and co-definite set constraints (essentially, by adding strategies); although the theoretical complexity does not change, an exponential gain can be obtained in some cases.

The DEXPTIME lower bound can be expected for any class of of set constraints that can express regular sets of trees, since conjunction corresponds to intersection (and since the emptiness of intersection of n tree automata is DEXPTIME-hard [35,83]). Note that there is a close relation between (certain classes of) set constraints and two-way alternating tree automata [35,24,80,16,85,93,92,39,77] (cf., however, also the formalization of a connection with 2NPDA's by Heintze and McAllester [58]).

To give some intuition, we will translate the tree automaton with the transitions below (over the alphabet with the constant symbol 0 and the unary symbol s; note that a string automaton is the special case of a tree automaton over unary function symbols and a constant symbol)

$$\text{init} \xrightarrow{\ 0\ } x$$
$$x \xrightarrow{\ s\ } y$$
$$y \xrightarrow{\ s\ } x$$

first into the regular tree grammar [39]

$$x \to 0$$
$$x \to s(y)$$
$$y \to s(x)$$

and from there into the regular systems of equations [10,39]

$$x = s(y) \cup 0$$
$$y = s(x).$$

We observe that regular systems of equations have:

- variables interpreted as sets of trees,
- tree constructors applied on sets of trees, and
- the Boolean set operator "union".

We generalize regular systems of equations to set constraints by

- replacing equality "=" with inclusion "$\subseteq$",
- allowing composed terms on both sides of "$\subseteq$" (which introduces the "two-way" direction of the automata),
- adding more set operators, Boolean and others (roughly, alternation accounts for intersection on the right hand side of "$\subseteq$").

Many set constraints algorithm have to deal with the special role played by the empty set. Namely, when testing the satisfiability of, for example, the set constraint

$$\varphi \wedge f(a,y) \subseteq f(b,y'),$$

we can derive $a \subseteq b$ (and, thus, *false*, showing that the set constraint is not satisfiable) only after we have derived "y is nonempty" from the rest constraint φ. Otherwise, if the value of y in a solution α of φ can be $\emptyset$, then $f(\{a\}, \alpha(y)) = \{f(a, t_2) \mid t_2 \in \emptyset\} = \emptyset$ and the inclusion $f(a, y) \subseteq f(b, y')$ is satisfied. It thus seems natural to investigate the satisfiability problem when the empty set is excluded from the domain [75,22,24]. It turns out that *nonempty-set constraints* have interesting algorithmic properties [74] and logic properties, such as the fundamental property of independence for set constraints with intersection [22,24].

3 Set-based analysis

Before we survey results, we will give some intuition. We obtain the *set-based abstract semantics* of a program by executing the program with *set* environments. A set environment at program point [1] assigns each variable x a set $x_{[1]}$ of values. That is, for the abstract semantics, we replace the pointwise environments <program point> $\mapsto$ <runtime value> of the concrete semantics by set environments: <program point> $\mapsto$ <set of runtime values>. A set constraint expresses the relation between these sets $x_{[k]}$.

We take, for example, the set-based analysis of an imperative programming language with data constructors (e.g., cons for lists) [48,63]. If [1] and [2] are the two program points before and after the instruction

[1]
$$x := \text{cons}(y, x)$$
[2]

then the derived set constraint is

$$x_{[2]} = \text{cons}(y_{[1]}, x_{[1]}) \wedge y_{[2]} = y_{[1]},$$

which expresses naturally the relation between the sets of possible values of x and y at the two program points.

The following example program illustrates that the set-based analysis ignores dependencies between variables in the pointwise environments. If the set $x_{[1]}$ contains two elements, then the set $x_{[2]}$ will contain four.

[1]
$$y := \text{car}(x)$$
$$z := \text{cdr}(x)$$
$$x := \text{cons}(y, z)$$
[2]

In summary, in set-based analysis, one expresses the abstract semantics of a program P by a set constraint φ_P (which is obtained by a syntactical transformation

of the program text) and then computes the abstract semantics of P by solving
φ_P; the latter means to compute effective representations of the values for $x_{[k]}$
under a distinguished (the least, or the greatest) solution of φ_P. The values are
approximations of the sets of runtime values at $_{[k]}$. The two steps correspond to
the specification of the analysis and to its implementation, respectively.

We next analyse a small example program.

```
while x =/= nil do
  i := i+1
  x := cdr(x)
```

The derived set constraint is

$$nil \subseteq x \land x \subseteq cons_{(2)}^{-1}(x)$$

whose solved form is

$$nil \cup [\top | x] \subseteq x$$

with the set of all lists as the value for x under the least solution.

To give an example of a set-based analysis of a reactive program, we take the
following definition of a procedure in Oz [86].

```
proc {P X I}
  local Y in
    X=I|Y
    {P Y (I+1)}
  end
end
```

The derived set constraint is

$$x \subseteq cons(\top, y) \land y \subseteq x$$

with the solved form

$$x \subseteq [\top | x]$$

whose *greatest* solution assigns x the set of all infinite lists.

The analysis of logic programs is one area of application of set constraints where
systems were and are being built. The area was developed mainly due to the
work of Heintze and Jaffar [53,55,48,56]. Other research groups, for example in
Bristol [37,36] and also in Saarbrücken, are now building systems too. Heintze
and Jaffar started by observing the lack of a formal definition of *set-based approximation* in the earlier work of Mishra [71] and Yardeni and Shapiro [96,97].
They gave such a definition for logic programs in terms of the $\mathcal{T}_P$ operator, which
is obtained from the T_P operator by replacing substitutions with set-valued substitutions (later, McAllester and Heintze [69] gave such a definition for functional
languages). The $\mathcal{T}_P$ operator formalizes the intuition of set environments given

above. They gave an equivalent characterization of the set-based approximation of the logic program P via a transformation of P to another logic program P'. They were probably the first to look at decidability issues (most of the previous works just had various ad hoc algorithms). Namely, is the least fixpoint of the $\mathcal{T}_P$ operator, or, equivalently, the least model of P', effectively representable (such that, for example, emptiness is decidable)? The effective representation is, as mentioned above, by tree automata, whose emptiness test is linear. Frühwirth, Shapiro, Vardi and Yardeni [35] present a set-based analysis with (a restricted class of) logic programs and showed the DEXPTIME-completeness of the problem of membership (i.e., of a ground atom in the set-based approximation). Logic programs are also set constraints in the sense that they express a relation between sets of trees (namely, the denotations of the predicates in models of the program). There is also recent work on the set-based analysis of reactive infinite-state systems that are specified by logic programs [80]; here, definite and co-definite set constraints are derived from logic programs with oracles in order to approximate temporal logic properties of possibly infinite program executions. That work also yields that the analysis of Mishra [71] is so weak that it approximates even the greatest model of a logic program.

The standard Hindley-Milner type system is extended by type inference systems based on set constraints (soft typing) and it can be weakened even further to provide a family of set based safety analysis. Early work in this domain was done by Mishra and Reddy [72] and Thatte [89] and was extended by many researchers including Aiken, Wimmers and Lakshman [5-7,2,9], Palsberg and O'Keefe [78], Palsberg and Schwartzbach [79]. McAllester and Heintze [69] systematized the notion of set-based analyses of functional languages and gave a thorough study of its complexity. Heintze and McAllester [57,58] address the complexity of control-flow analysis, which is at the heart of set-based analyses for ML. Cousot and Cousot [27] showed that set-based analysis can be seen as an instance of an abstract interpretation in the sense that the process of solving a set constraint is isomorphic to the iteration of an appropriate fixpoint operator (defining an abstract program semantics).

The work on Tarskian set constraints [70] employs different constraint solving techniques and has applications different from program analysis; this area has much in common with the areas of artifical intelligence, model checking and the μ-calculus.

Several set-based analysis systems have been built. The origins of inefficiency and other insufficiencies in early systems have by now been recognized. The language and system CLP(SC) of Kozen [63] and Foster [32] allows one to easily prototype a set-based analysis system. The systems built by Aiken and Fähndrich [32] at Berkeley and by Heintze [51] at Bell Labs perform the analysis of functional programs of several thousand lines of code in acceptable time. The concentrated effort on the set constraint solving problem was the precondition for the existence of such systems.

Acknowledgements. We thank Witold Charatonik for helpful comments.

References

1. W. Ackermann. *Solvable Cases of the Decision Problem*. North-Holland, Amsterdam, 1954.
2. A. Aiken. Set constraints: Results, applications and future directions. In *Proceedings of the Workshop on Principles and Practice of Constraint Programming*, LNCS 874, pages 326–335. Springer-Verlag, 1994.
3. A. Aiken, D. Kozen, M. Y. Vardi, and E. L. Wimmers. The complexity of set constraints. In *1993 Conference on Computer Science Logic*, LNCS 832, pages 1–17. Springer-Verlag, Sept. 1993.
4. A. Aiken, D. Kozen, and E. L. Wimmers. Decidability of systems of set constraints with negative constraints. *Information and Computation*, 122(1):30–44, Oct. 1995.
5. A. Aiken and B. Murphy. Implementing regular tree expressions. In *ACM Conference on Functional Programming Languages and Computer Architecture*, pages 427–447, August 1991.
6. A. Aiken and B. Murphy. Static type inference in a dynamically typed language. In *Eighteenth Annual ACM Symposium on Principles of Programming Languages*, pages 279–290, January 1991.
7. A. Aiken and E. Wimmers. Type inclusion constraints and type inference. In *Proceedings of the 1993 Conference on Functional Programming Languages and Computer Architecture*, pages 31–41, Copenhagen, Denmark, June 1993.
8. A. Aiken and E. L. Wimmers. Solving systems of set constraints (extended abstract). In *Seventh Annual IEEE Symposium on Logic in Computer Science*, pages 329–340, 1992.
9. A. Aiken, E. L. Wimmers, and T. Lakshman. Soft typing with conditional types. In *Twenty-First Annual ACM Symposium on Principles of Programming Languages*, Portland, Oregon, Jan. 1994.
10. D. Arden. Delayed logic and finite state machines. In *Proceedings of the 2nd Annual Symposium on Switching Circuit Theory and Logical Design*, pages 133–151, 1961.
11. L. Bachmair, H. Ganzinger, and U. Waldmann. Set constraints are the monadic class. In *Eighth Annual IEEE Symposium on Logic in Computer Science*, pages 75–83, 1993.
12. C. Beeri, S. Nagvi, O. Schmueli, and S. Tsur. Set constructors in a logic database language. *The Journal of Logic Programming*, pages 181–232, 1991.
13. S. K. Biswas. A demand-driven set-based analysis. In *The 24th ACM Symposium on Principles of Programming Languages POPL '97*, pages 372–385, Paris, France, January 1997.
14. B. Bogaert and S. Tison. Automata with equality tests. Technical Report IT 207, Laboratoire d'Informatique Fondamentale de Lille, 1991.
15. P. Bruscoli, A. Dovier, E. Pontelli, and G. Rossi. Compiling intensional sets in CLP. In *Proceedings of the International Conference on Logic Programming*, pages 647–661. The MIT Press, 1994.
16. J. Brzozowski and E. Leiss. On equations for regular languages, finite automata, and sequential networks. *Theorical Computer Science*, 10:19–35, 1980.
17. W. Charatonik. Set constraints in some equational theories. In *1st International Conference Constraints in Computational Logics*, LNCS 845, pages 304–319. Springer-Verlag, 1994. Also to appear in *Information and Computation*.
18. W. Charatonik. Set constraints in some equational theories. PhD thesis, Polish Academy of Sciences, 1995.

19. W. Charatonik and L. Pacholski. Negative set constraints with equality. In *Ninth Annual IEEE Symposium on Logic in Computer Science*, pages 128–136, 1994.

20. W. Charatonik and L. Pacholski. Set constraints with projections are in NEXP-TIME. In *Proceedings of the 35th Symposium on Foundations of Computer Science*, pages 642–653, 1994.

21. W. Charatonik and L. Pacholski. Negative set constraints: an easy proof of decidability. Technical Report MPI-I-93-265, Max-Planck Institute für Informatik, December 1993.

22. W. Charatonik and A. Podelski. The independence property of a class of set constraints. In *Conference on Principles and Practice of Constraint Programming*, LNCS 1118, pages 76–90. Springer-Verlag, 1996.

23. W. Charatonik and A. Podelski. Set constraints for greatest models. Technical Report MPI-I-97-2-004, Max-Planck-Institut für Informatik, April 1997. http://www.mpi-sb.mpg.de/~podelski/papers/greatest.html.

24. W. Charatonik and A. Podelski. Set constraints with intersection. In G. Winskel, editor, *Twelfth Annual IEEE Symposium on Logic in Computer Science (LICS)*, pages 362–372. IEEE, June 1997.

25. A. Cheng and D. Kozen. A complete Gentzen-style axiomatization for set constraints. In *ICALP: Annual International Colloquium on Automata, Languages and Programming*, LNCS 1099, 1996.

26. P. Cousot and R. Cousot. Inductive definitions, semantics and abstract interpretation. In *Proc. POPL '92*, pages 83–94. ACM Press, 1992.

27. P. Cousot and R. Cousot. Formal language, grammar and set-constraint-based program analysis by abstract interpretation. In *Record of FPCA '95 - Conference on Functional Programming and Computer Architecture*, pages 170–181, La Jolla, California, USA, 25-28 June 1995. SIGPLAN/SIGARCH/WG2.8, ACM Press, New York, USA.

28. P. W. Dart and J. Zobel. *A regular type language for logic programs*, chapter 5, pages 157–188. MIT Press, 1992.

29. P. Devienne, J.-M. Talbot, and S. Tison. Solving classes of set constraints with tree automata. In G. Smolka, editor, *Proceedings of the Third International Conference on Principles and Practice of Constraint Programming - CP97*, LNCS, Berlin, Germany, October 1997. Springer-Verlag. To appear.

30. A. Dovier. *Computable Set Theory and Logic Programming*. PhD thesis, Dipartimento di Informatica, Università di Pisa, 1996.

31. A. Dovier and G. Rossi. Embedding Extensional Finite Sets in CLP. In *International Logic Programming Symposium*, 1993.

32. M. Fähndrich and A. Aiken. Making set-constraint based program analyses scale. Computer Science Division Tech Report 96-917, Computer Science Division, University of California at Berkeley, September 1996. Also presented at the Workshop on Set Constraints, Cambridge MA, August 1996.

33. J. S. Foster. CLP(SC): Implementation and efficiency considerations. workshop on set constraints. Available at http://http.cs.berkeley.edu/~jfoster/. Presented at the Workshop on Set Constraints, Cambridge MA, August 1996, August 1996.

34. J. S. Foster, M. Fähndrich, and A. Aiken. Flow-insensitive points-to analysis with term and set constraints. Computer Science Division Tech Report 97-964, , University of California at Berkeley, September 1997. Also presented at the Workshop on Set Constraints, Cambridge MA, August 1996.

558

35. T. Frühwirth, E. Shapiro, M. Y. Vardi, and E. Yardeni. Logic programs as types for logic programs. In *Sixth Annual IEEE Symposium on Logic in Computer Science*, pages 300–309, July 1991.

36. J. P. Gallagher, D. Boulanger, and H. Saglam. Practical model-based static analysis for definite logic programs. In *Proceedings of the 1995 International Symposium on Logic Programming*, pages 351–368.

37. J. P. Gallagher and L. Lafave. Regular approximation of computation paths in logic and functional languages. In *Proceedings of the Dagstuhl Workshop on Partial Evaluation*, pages 1–16. Springer-Verlag, February 1996.

38. K. L. S. Gasser, F. Nielson, and H. R. Nielson. Systematic realisation of control flow analyses for CML. In *Proceedings of ICFP'97*, pages 38–51. ACM Press, 1997.

39. F. Gécseg and M. Steinby. *Tree Automata*. Akademiai Kiado, Budapest, 1984.

40. C. Gervet. Conjuto: Constraint logic programming with finite set domains. In M. Bruynooghe, editor, *Proceedings of the International Logic Programming Symposium*, pages 339–358, 1994.

41. C. Gervet. *Set Intervals in Constraint-Logic Programming: Definition and Implementation of a Language*. PhD thesis, Université de Franche-Compté, 1995. European Thesis.

42. C. Gervet. Interval Propagation to Reason about Sets: Definition and Implementation of a Practical Language. *Constraints*, 1(2), 1997.

43. R. Gilleron, S. Tison, and M. Tommasi. Solving systems of set constraints using tree automata. In *10th Annual Symposium on Theoretical Aspects of Computer Science*, LNCS 665, pages 505–514. Springer-Verlag, 1993.

44. R. Gilleron, S. Tison, and M. Tommasi. Solving systems of set constraints with negated subset relationships. In *Proceedings of the 34th Symp. on Foundations of Computer Science*, pages 372–380, 1993. Full version in [45].

45. R. Gilleron, S. Tison, and M. Tommasi. Solving systems of set constraints with negated subset relationships. Technical Report IT 247, Laboratoire d'Informatique Fondamentale de Lille, 1993.

46. R. Gilleron, S. Tison, and M. Tommasi. Set constraints and automata. Technical Report IT 292, Laboratoire d'Informatique Fondamentale de Lille, 1996.

47. R. Gilleron, S. Tison, and M. Tommassi. Some new decidability results on positive and negative set constraints. In *1st International Conference Constraints in Computational Logics*, LNCS 845, pages 336–351. Springer-Verlag, 1994.

48. N. Heintze. Set based program analysis. PhD thesis, School of Computer Science, Carnegie Mellon University, 1992.

49. N. Heintze. Set based analysis of arithmetic. Draft manuscript, July 1993.

50. N. Heintze. Set based analysis of ML programs. Technical Report CMU–CS–93–193, School of Computer Science, Carnegie Mellon University, July 1993.

51. N. Heintze. Set based analysis of ML programs. In *Conference on Lisp and Functional Programming*, pages 306–317. ACM, 1994. Preliminary version in [50].

52. N. Heintze and J. Jaffar. A decision procedure for a class of set constraints (extended abstract). In *Fifth Annual IEEE Symposium on Logic in Computer Science*, pages 42–51, 1990.

53. N. Heintze and J. Jaffar. A finite presentation theorem for approximating logic programs. In *Seventeenth Annual ACM Symposium on Principles of Programming Languages*, pages 197–209, January 1990.

54. N. Heintze and J. Jaffar. A finite presentation theorem for approximating logic programs. Technical report, School of Computer Science, Carnegie Mellon University, Aug. 1990. 66 pages.

55. N. Heintze and J. Jaffar. An engine for logic program analysis. In *Proceedings, Seventh Annual IEEE Symposium on Logic in Computer Science*, pages 318–328, 1992.

56. N. Heintze and J. Jaffar. *Semantic Types for Logic Programs*, chapter 4, pages 141–156. MIT Press, 1992.

57. N. Heintze and D. McAllester. Linear-time subtransitive control-flow analysis. In *ACM Conference on Programming Language Design and Implementation*, 1997. To appear.

58. N. Heintze and D. McAllester. On the cubic bottleneck in subtyping and flow analysis. In G. Winskel, editor, *Twelfth Annual IEEE Symposium on Logic in Computer Science (LICS)*, pages 342–351. IEEE, June 1997.

59. ILOG. ILOG SOLVER 3.2 user manual. www.ilog.com.

60. N. D. Jones and S. S. Muchnick. Flow analysis and optimization of lisp-like structures. In *Sixth Annual ACM Symposium on Principles of Programming Languages*, pages 244–256, January 1979.

61. W. Joyner. Resolution strategies as decision procedures. *Journal of the Association for Computing Machinery*, 23(3):398–417, 1979.

62. D. Kozen. Logical aspects of set constraints. In *1993 Conference on Computer Science Logic*, LNCS 832, pages 175–188. Springer-Verlag, Sept. 1993.

63. D. Kozen. Set constraints and logic programming (abstract). In *1st International Conference Constraints in Computational Logics*, LNCS 845. Springer-Verlag, 1994. Also to appear in *Information and Computation*.

64. D. Kozen. Rational spaces and set constraints. In *TAPSOFT: 6th International Joint Conference on Theory and Practice of Software Development*, LNCS 915, pages 42–61. Springer-Verlag, 1995.

65. D. Kozen. Rational spaces and set constraints. *Theoretical Computer Science*, 167(1–2):73–94, October 1996.

66. G. Kuper. Logic programming with sets. New York, NY, 1990. Academic Press.

67. B. Legeard and E. Legros. Short Overview of the CLPS System. 1991.

68. L. Löwenheim. Über Möglichkeiten im Relativkalkül. *Mathematische Annalen*, 76:228–251, 1915.

69. D. McAllester and N. Heintze. On the complexity of set-based analysis. www.ai.mit.edu/people/dam/setbased.ps.

70. D. A. McAllester, R. Givan, C. Witty, and D. Kozen. Tarskian set constraints. In *Proceedings, 11th Annual IEEE Symposium on Logic in Computer Science*, pages 138–147, New Brunswick, New Jersey, July 1996. IEEE Computer Society Press.

71. P. Mishra. Towards a theory of types in Prolog. In *IEEE International Symposium on Logic Programming*, pages 289–298, 1984.

72. P. Mishra and U. Reddy. Declaration-free type checking. In *Twelfth Annual ACM Symposium on the Principles of Programming Languages*, pages 7–21, 1985.

73. M. Müller. *Type Analysis for a Higher-Order Concurrent Constraint Language*. PhD thesis, Universität des Saarlandes, Technische Fakultät, 66041 Saarbrücken, Germany, expected 1997.

74. M. Müller, J. Niehren, and A. Podelski. Inclusion constraints over non-empty sets of trees. In M. Bidoit and M. Dauchet, editors, *Proceedings of the 9th International Joint Conference on Theory and Practice of Software Development (TAPSOFT)*, volume 1214 of *LNCS*, pages 345–356, Berlin, April 1997. Springer-Verlag.

75. M. Müller, J. Niehren, and A. Podelski. Ordering constraints over feature trees. In G. Smolka, editor, *Proceedings of the Third International Conference on Principles and Practice of Constraint Programming - CP97*, LNCS, Berlin, Germany, October 1997. Springer-Verlag. To appear.

76. T. Müller and M. Müller. Finite set constraints in Oz. In *13. Workshop Logische Programmierung*, Technische Universität München, September 1997. to appear.
77. M. Nivat and A. Podelski. *Tree Automata and Languages*. North-Holland, Amsterdam, 1992.
78. J. Palsberg and O'Keefe. A type system equivalent to flow analysis. In *Symposium of Principles of Programming Languages*, pages 367–378. ACM, 1995.
79. J. Palsberg and M. Schwartzbach. Safety analysis versus type inference. *Information and Computation*, 118(1):128–141, April 1995.
80. A. Podelski, W. Charatonik, and M. Müller. Set-based analysis of reactive infinite-state systems. Submitted for publication, 1997.
81. J. F. Puget. Finite Set Intervals. In *Proceedings of the Second International Workshop on Set Constraints*, Cambridge, Massachusetts, 1996.
82. J. C. Reynolds. Automatic computation of data set definitions. *Information Processing*, 68:456–461, 1969.
83. H. Seidl. Haskell overloading is DEXPTIME-complete. *Information Processing Letters*, 52:57–60, 1994.
84. F. Seynhave, M. Tommasi, and R. Treinen. Grid structures and undecidable constraint theories. In M. Bidoit and M. Dauchet, editors, *Proceedings of the 9th International Joint Conference on Theory and Practice of Software Development (TAPSOFT)*, volume 1214 of *LNCS*, pages 357–368, Berlin, April 1997. Springer-Verlag.
85. G. Slutzki. Alternating tree automata. *Theoretical Computer Science*, 41:305–318, 1985.
86. G. Smolka. The Oz programming model. In *Volume 1000 of Lecture Notes in Computer Science*, 1995.
87. K. Stefansson. Systems of set constraints with negative constraints are *NEXPTIME*-complete. In *Ninth Annual IEEE Symposium on Logic in Computer Science*, pages 137–141, 1994.
88. F. Stolzenburg. Membership-constraints and complexity in logic programming with sets. In F. Baader and K. U. Schulz, editors, *Frontiers in Combining Systems*, pages 285–302. Kluwer Academic, Dordrecht, The Netherlands, 1996.
89. S. Thatte. Type inference with partial types. In *15th International Colloquium on Automata, Languages and Programming*, volume 317 of *LNCS*, pages 615–629. Springer-Verlag, 1988.
90. W. Thomas. *Handbook of Theoretical Computer Science*, volume B, chapter Automata on Infinite Objects, pages 134–191. Elsevier, 1990.
91. T. E. Uribe. Sorted unification using set constraints. In *11th International Conference on Automated Deduction*, LNAI 607, pages 163–177. Springer-Verlag, 1992.
92. M. Y. Vardi. An automata-theoretic approach to linear-temporal logic. *In Logics for Concurrency: Structure versus Automata. LNCS*, 1043:238–266, 1996.
93. M. Y. Vardi and P. Wolper. Automata-theoretic techniques for modal logics of programs. *J. Comput. Syst. Sci.*, 32, 1986.
94. C. Walinsky. CLP(Σ^*): Constraint Logic Programming with Regular Sets. In *Proceedings of the International Conference on Logic Programming*, pages 181–190, 1989.
95. E. Yardeni, , T. Frühwirth, and E. Shapiro. *Polymorphically typed logic programs*, chapter 2, pages 157–188. MIT Press, 1992.
96. E. Yardeni. A type system for logic programs. Master's thesis, Weizmann Institute of Science, 1987.
97. E. Yardeni and E. Shapiro. *A type system for logic programs*, volume 2, chapter 28, pages 211–244. The MIT Press, 1987.

98. E. Yardeni and E. Shapiro. A type system for logic programs. *Journal of Logic Programming*, 10:125–153, 1991. Preliminary version in [97].

99. J. Young and P. O'Keefe. Experience with a type evaluator. In D. Bjørner, A. P. Ershov, and N. D. Jones, editors, *Partial Evaluation and Mixed Computation*, pages 573–581. North-Holland, 1988.

Author Index

Springer
and the
environment

At Springer we firmly believe that an international science publisher has a special obligation to the environment, and our corporate policies consistently reflect this conviction.
We also expect our business partners – paper mills, printers, packaging manufacturers, etc. – to commit themselves to using materials and production processes that do not harm the environment. The paper in this book is made from low- or no-chlorine pulp and is acid free, in conformance with international standards for paper permanency.

Lecture Notes in Computer Science

For information about Vols. 1–1253

please contact your bookseller or Springer-Verlag

Vol. 1292: H. Glaser, P. Hartel, H. Kuchen (Eds.), Programming Languages: Implementations, Logigs, and Programs. Proceedings, 1997. XI, 425 pages. 1997.

Vol. 1293: C. Nicholas, D. Wood (Eds.), Principles of Document Processing. Proceedings, 1996. XI, 195 pages. 1997.

Vol. 1294: B.S. Kaliski Jr. (Ed.), Advances in Cryptology — CRYPTO '97. Proceedings, 1997. XII, 539 pages. 1997.

Vol. 1295: I. Prívara, P. Ružička (Eds.), Mathematical Foundations of Computer Science 1997. Proceedings, 1997. X, 519 pages. 1997.

Vol. 1296: G. Sommer, K. Daniilidis, J. Pauli (Eds.), Computer Analysis of Images and Patterns. Proceedings, 1997. XIII, 737 pages. 1997.

Vol. 1297: N. Lavrač, S. Džeroski (Eds.), Inductive Logic Programming. Proceedings, 1997. VIII, 309 pages. 1997. (Subseries LNAI).

Vol. 1298: M. Hanus, J. Heering, K. Meinke (Eds.), Algebraic and Logic Programming. Proceedings, 1997. X, 286 pages. 1997.

Vol. 1299: M.T. Pazienza (Ed.), Information Extraction. Proceedings, 1997. IX, 213 pages. 1997. (Subseries LNAI).

Vol. 1300: C. Lengauer, M. Griebl, S. Gorlatch (Eds.), Euro-Par'97 Parallel Processing. Proceedings, 1997. XXX, 1379 pages. 1997.

Vol. 1301: M. Jazayeri, H. Schauer (Eds.), Software Engineering - ESEC/FSE'97. Proceedings, 1997. XIII, 532 pages. 1997.

Vol. 1302: P. Van Hentenryck (Ed.), Static Analysis. Proceedings, 1997. X, 413 pages. 1997.

Vol. 1303: G. Brewka, C. Habel, B. Nebel (Eds.), KI-97: Advances in Artificial Intelligence. Proceedings, 1997. XI, 413 pages. 1997. (Subseries LNAI).

Vol. 1304: W. Luk, P.Y.K. Cheung, M. Glesner (Eds.), Field-Programmable Logic and Applications. Proceedings, 1997. XI, 503 pages. 1997.

Vol. 1305: D. Corne, J.L. Shapiro (Eds.), Evolutionary Computing. Proceedings, 1997. X, 307 pages. 1997.

Vol. 1306: C. Leung (Ed.), Visual Information Systems. X, 274 pages. 1997.

Vol. 1307: R. Kompe, Prosody in Speech Understanding Systems. XIX, 357 pages. 1997. (Subseries LNAI).

Vol. 1308: A. Hameurlain, A M. Tjoa (Eds.), Database and Expert Systems Applications. Proceedings, 1997. XVII, 688 pages. 1997.

Vol. 1309: R. Steinmetz, L.C. Wolf (Eds.), Interactive Distributed Multimedia Systems and Telecommunication Services. Proceedings, 1997. XIII, 466 pages. 1997.

Vol. 1310: A. Del Bimbo (Ed.), Image Analysis and Processing. Proceedings, 1997. Volume I. XXII, 722 pages. 1997.

Vol. 1311: A. Del Bimbo (Ed.), Image Analysis and Processing. Proceedings, 1997. Volume II. XXII, 794 pages. 1997.

Vol. 1312: A. Geppert, M. Berndtsson (Eds.), Rules in Database Systems. Proceedings, 1997. VII, 214 pages. 1997.

Vol. 1313: J. Fitzgerald, C.B. Jones, P. Lucas (Eds.), FME '97: Industrial Applications and Strengthened Foundations of Formal Methods. Proceedings, 1997. XIII, 685 pages. 1997.

Vol. 1314: S. Muggleton (Ed.), Inductive Logic Programming. Proceedings, 1996. VIII, 397 pages. 1997. (Subseries LNAI).

Vol. 1315: G. Sommer, J.J. Koenderink (Eds.), Algebraic Frames for the Perception-Action Cycle. Proceedings, 1997. VIII, 395 pages. 1997.

Vol. 1316: M. Li, A. Maruoka (Eds.), Algorithmic Learning Theory. Proceedings, 1997. XI, 461 pages. 1997. (Subseries LNAI).

Vol. 1317: M. Leman (Ed.), Music, Gestalt, and Computing. IX, 524 pages. 1997. (Subseries LNAI).

Vol. 1318: R. Hirschfeld (Ed.), Financial Cryptography. Proceedings, 1997. XI, 409 pages. 1997.

Vol. 1319: E. Plaza, R. Benjamins (Eds.), Knowledge Acquisition, Modeling and Management. Proceedings, 1997. XI, 389 pages. 1997. (Subseries LNAI).

Vol. 1320: M. Mavronicolas, P. Tsigas (Eds.), Distributed Algorithms. Proceedings, 1997. X, 333 pages. 1997.

Vol. 1321: M. Lenzerini (Ed.), AI*IA 97: Advances in Artificial Intelligence. Proceedings, 1997. XII, 459 pages. 1997. (Subseries LNAI).

Vol. 1322: H. Hußmann, Formal Foundations for Software Engineering Methods. X, 286 pages. 1997.

Vol. 1323: E. Costa, A. Cardoso (Eds.), Progress in Artificial Intelligence. Proceedings, 1997. XIV, 393 pages. 1997. (Subseries LNAI).

Vol. 1324: C. Peters, C. Thanos (Eds.), Research and Advanced Technology for Digital Libraries. Proceedings, 1997. X, 423 pages. 1997.

Vol. 1325: Z.W. Raś, A. Skowron (Eds.), Foundations of Intelligent Systems. Proceedings, 1997. XI, 630 pages. 1997. (Subseries LNAI).

Vol. 1326: C. Nicholas, J. Mayfield (Eds.), Intelligent Hypertext. XIV, 182 pages. 1997.

Vol. 1327: W. Gerstner, A. Germond, M. Hasler, J.-D. Nicoud (Eds.), Artificial Neural Networks – ICANN '97. Proceedings, 1997. XIX, 1274 pages. 1997.

Vol. 1328: C. Retoré (Ed.), Logical Aspects of Computational Linguistics. Proceedings, 1996. VIII, 435 pages. 1997. (Subseries LNAI).

Vol. 1329: S.C. Hirtle, A.U. Frank (Eds.), Spatial Information Theory. Proceedings, 1997. XIV, 511 pages. 1997.

Vol. 1330: G. Smolka (Ed.), Principles and Practice of Constraint Programming – CP 97. Proceedings, 1997. XII, 563 pages. 1997.

Vol. 1331: D. Embley, R. Goldstein (Eds.), Conceptual Modeling – ER '97. Proceedings, 1997. XV, 479 pages. 1997.

Vol. 1332: M. Bubak, J. Dongarra, J. Waśniewski (Eds.), Recent Advances in Parallel Virtual Machine and Message Passing Interface. Proceedings, 1997. XV, 518 pages. 1997.

Vol. 1334: Y. Han, T. Okamoto, S. Qing (Eds.), Information and Communications Security. Proceedings, 1997. X, 484 pages. 1997.